NEIL GAIMAN

ETERNALS

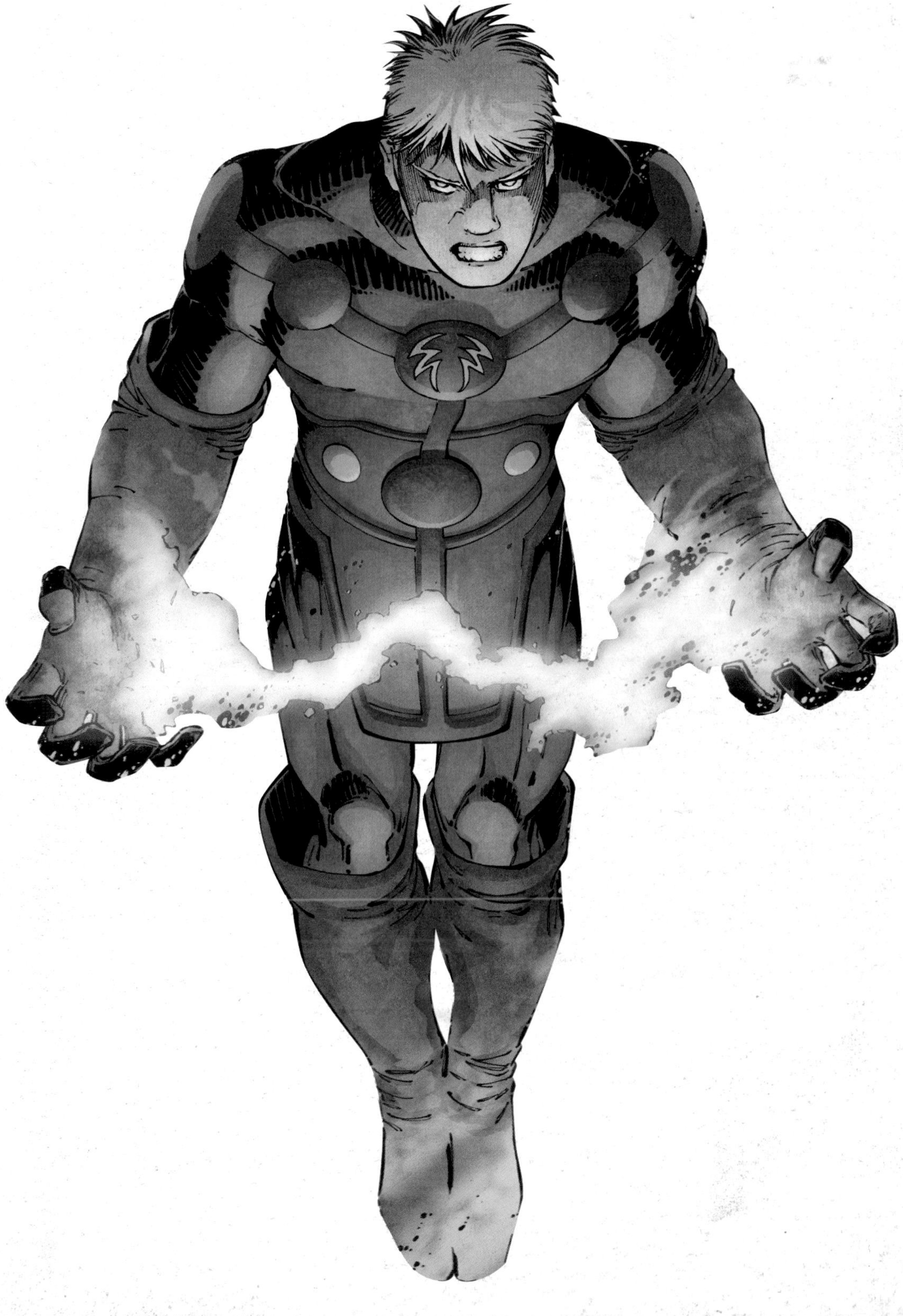

NEIL GAIMAN'S ETERNALS

WRITER: NEIL GAIMAN
ARTIST: JOHN ROMITA JR
INKS: DANNY MIKI, TOM PALMER, JESSE DELPERDANG & KLAUS JANSON

COLOUR: MATT HOLLINGSWORTH & PAUL MOUNTS
LETTERS: TODD KLEIN
COVER ART: MIKE BERRY
PRODUCTION: RICH GINTER, KATE LEVIN & BRAD JOHANSEN
ASSISTANT EDITOR: SEAN RYAN
CONSULTING EDITOR: MIKE MARTS
EDITOR: NICK LOWE

ETERNALS SKETCHBOOK
ARTIST: JOHN ROMITA JR
EDITOR: MICHAEL SHORT
SENIOR EDITOR, SPECIAL PROJECTS: JEFF YOUNGQUIST
VICE PRESIDENT OF SALES: DAVID GABRIEL
DESIGNER: PATRICK McGRATH
VICE PRESIDENT OF CREATIVE: TOM MARVELLI

MARVEL SPOTLIGHT: NEIL GAIMAN
WRITER/COORDINATOR: JOHN RHETT THOMAS
EDITOR: JEFF YOUNGQUIST
WRITERS: MATT ADLER & BOB GREENBERGER
ASSISTANT EDITOR: MICHAEL SHORT
ASSOCIATE EDITORS: JENNIFER GRUNWALD & MARK D BEAZLEY
VICE PRESIDENT OF SALES: DAVID GABRIEL
DESIGNER: PATRICK McGRATH
LAYOUT: BLAMMO! CONTENT & DESIGN, JERRY FARMER &
JERRY KALINOWSKI
VICE PRESIDENT OF CREATIVE: TOM MARVELLI
PHOTOS OF TORI AMOS COURTESY OF THE BRIDGE ENTERTAINMENT GROUP.

EDITOR IN CHIEF: JOE QUESADA
PUBLISHER: DAN BUCKLEY

ETERNALS CREATED BY JACK KIRBY

 presents: **NEIL GAIMAN'S ETERNALS**

NEIL GAIMAN'S ETERNALS. Contains material originally published in magazine form as ETERNALS #1-7, ETERNALS SKETCHBOOK AND MARVEL SPOTLIGHT: NEIL GAIMAN AND SLAVADOR LAROCCA. Published by Panini Publishing, a division of Panini UK Limited. Mike Riddell, Managing Director. Alan O'Keefe, Managing Editor. Mark Irvine, Production Manager. Marco M. Lupoi, Publishing Director Europe. Brady Webb, Reprint Editor. Melanie Wilson, Designer. Office of publication: Panini House, Coach & Horses Passage, The Pantiles, Tunbridge Wells, Kent TN2 5UJ. Tel: 01892 500 100. Third impression 2008; First impression 2007 Copyright © 2006, 2007 by Marvel Characters, Inc. All rights reserved. No similarity between any of the names, characters, persons and/or institutions in this magazine with any living or dead person or institution is intended, and any similarity which may exist is purely coincidental. This publication may not be sold except by authorised dealers and is sold subject to the conditions that it shall not be sold or distributed with any part of its cover or markings removed, nor in a mutilated condition. SPIDER-MAN (including all prominent characters featured in this issue and the distinctive likeness thereof) is a trademark of MARVEL CHARACTERS, INC. and this publication is under license from Marvel Characters, Inc. through Panini S.p.A. Printed in Italy. ISBN:978-1-905239-57-3

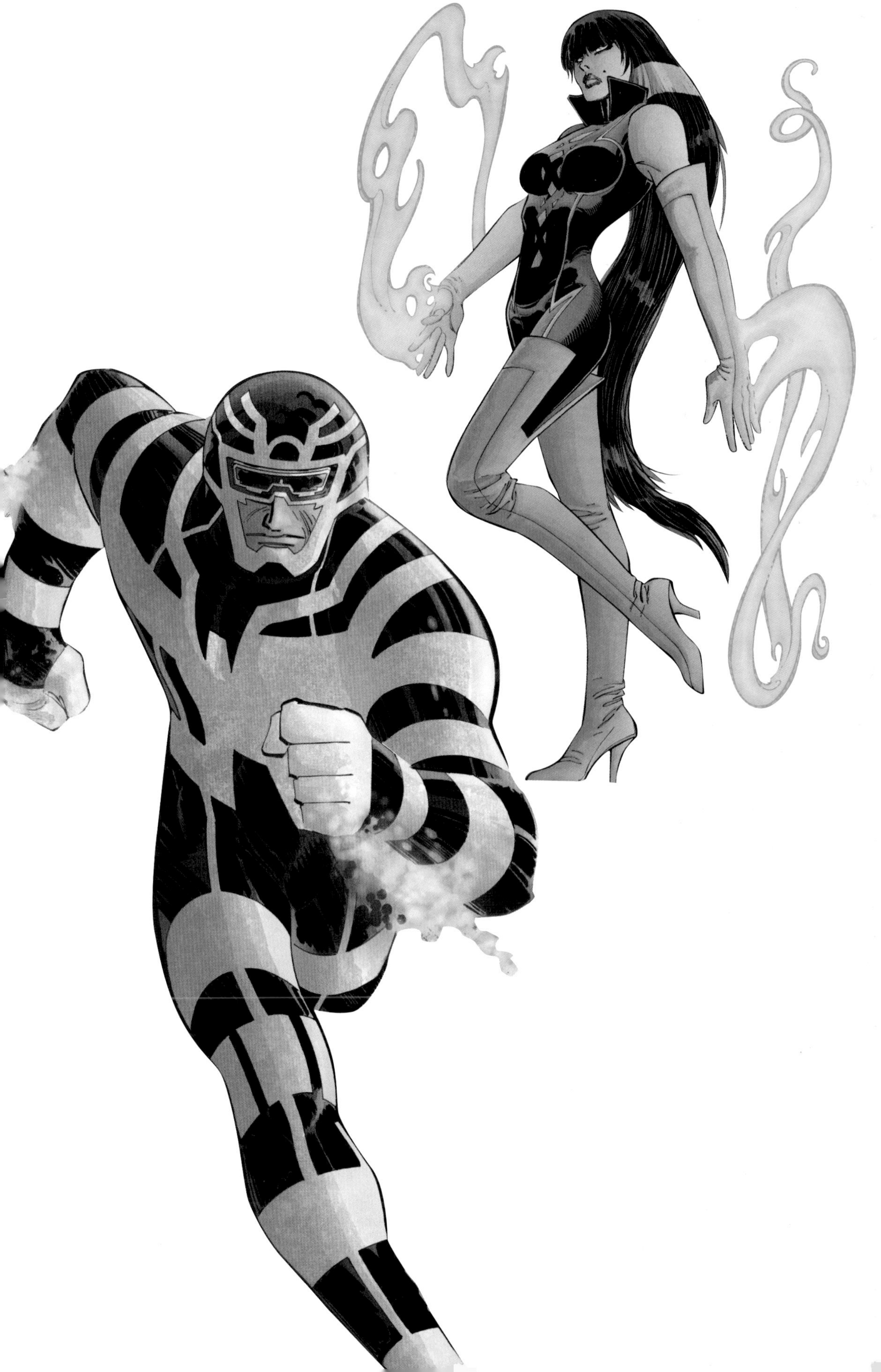

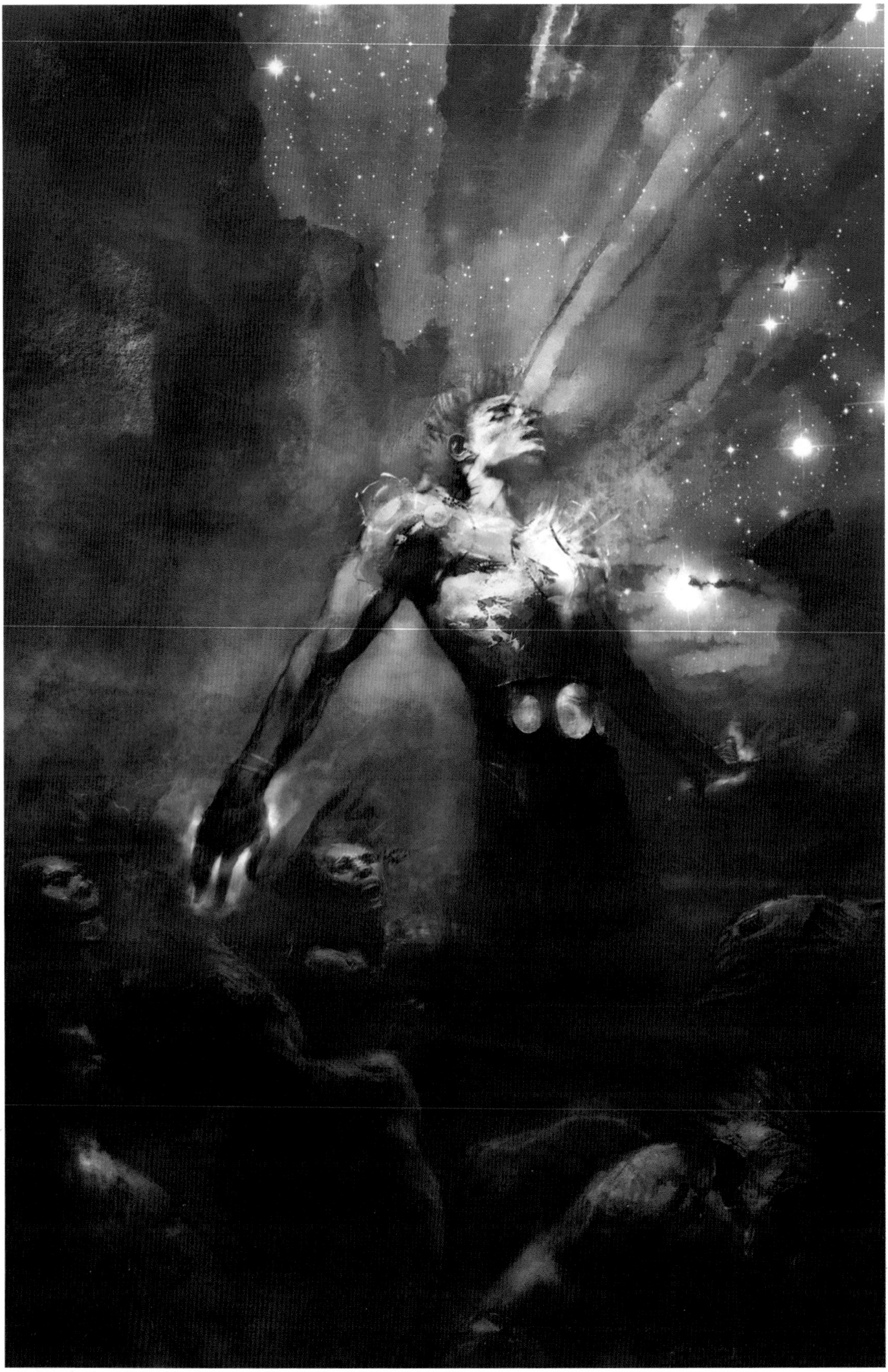

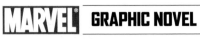

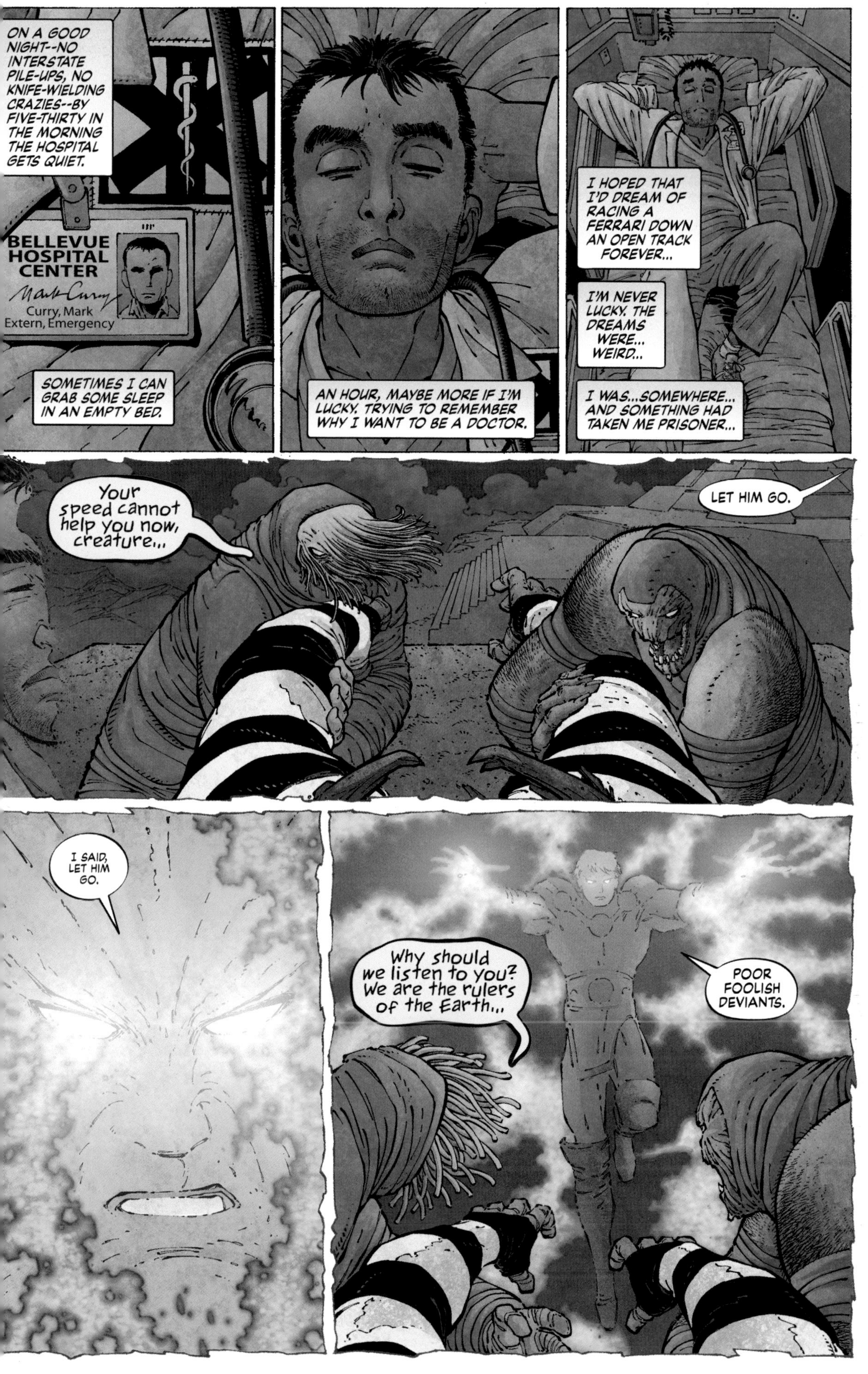
ON A GOOD NIGHT--NO INTERSTATE PILE-UPS, NO KNIFE-WIELDING CRAZIES--BY FIVE-THIRTY IN THE MORNING THE HOSPITAL GETS QUIET.
BELLEVUE HOSPITAL CENTER
Curry, Mark
Extern, Emergency
SOMETIMES I CAN GRAB SOME SLEEP IN AN EMPTY BED.
AN HOUR, MAYBE MORE IF I'M LUCKY. TRYING TO REMEMBER WHY I WANT TO BE A DOCTOR.
I HOPED THAT I'D DREAM OF RACING A FERRARI DOWN AN OPEN TRACK FOREVER...
I'M NEVER LUCKY. THE DREAMS WERE... WEIRD...
I WAS...SOMEWHERE... AND SOMETHING HAD TAKEN ME PRISONER...
Your speed cannot help you now, creature...
LET HIM GO.
I SAID, LET HIM GO.
Why should we listen to you? We are the rulers of the Earth...
POOR FOOLISH DEVIANTS.

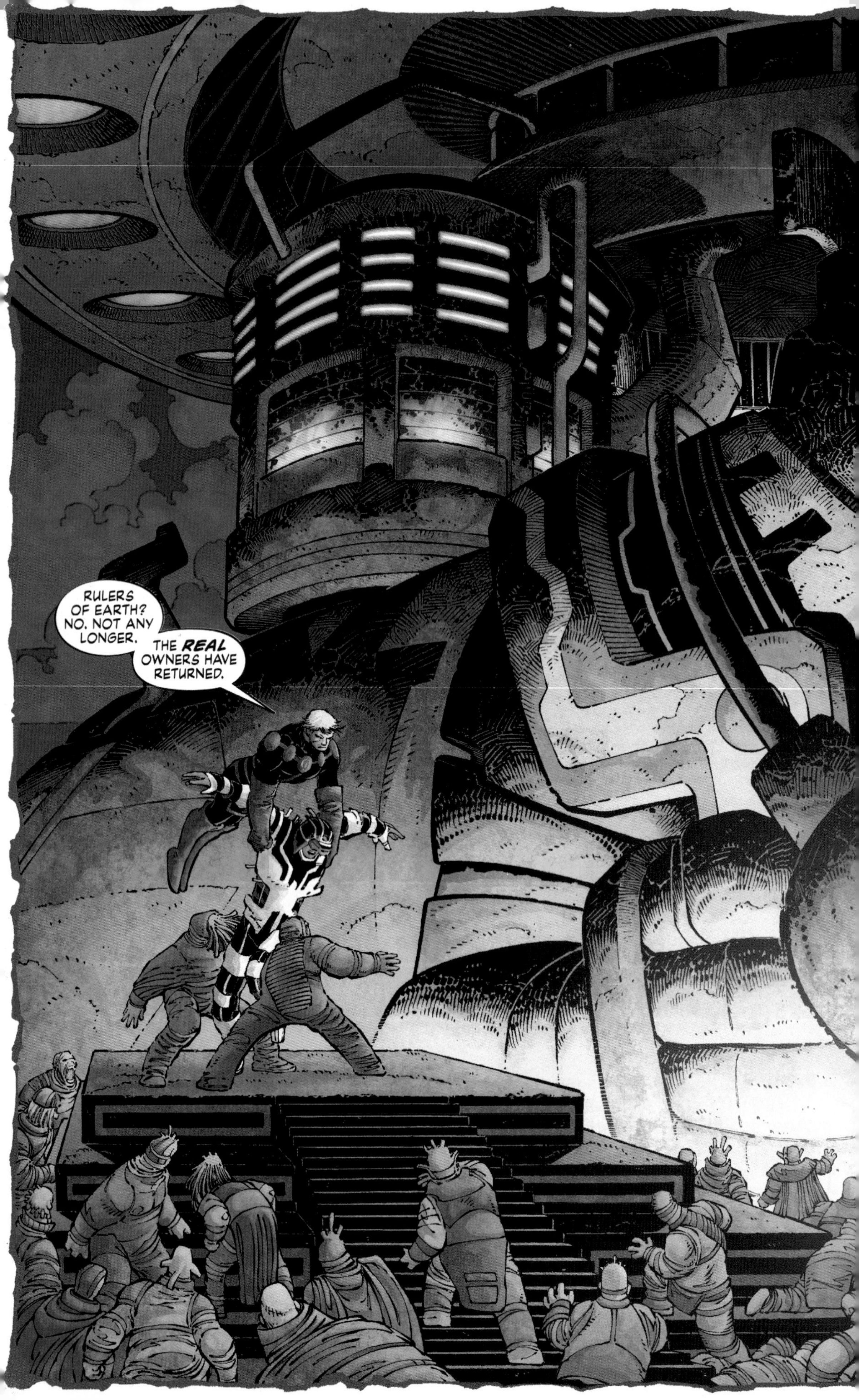
RULERS OF EARTH? NO. NOT ANY LONGER.
THE REAL OWNERS HAVE RETURNED.

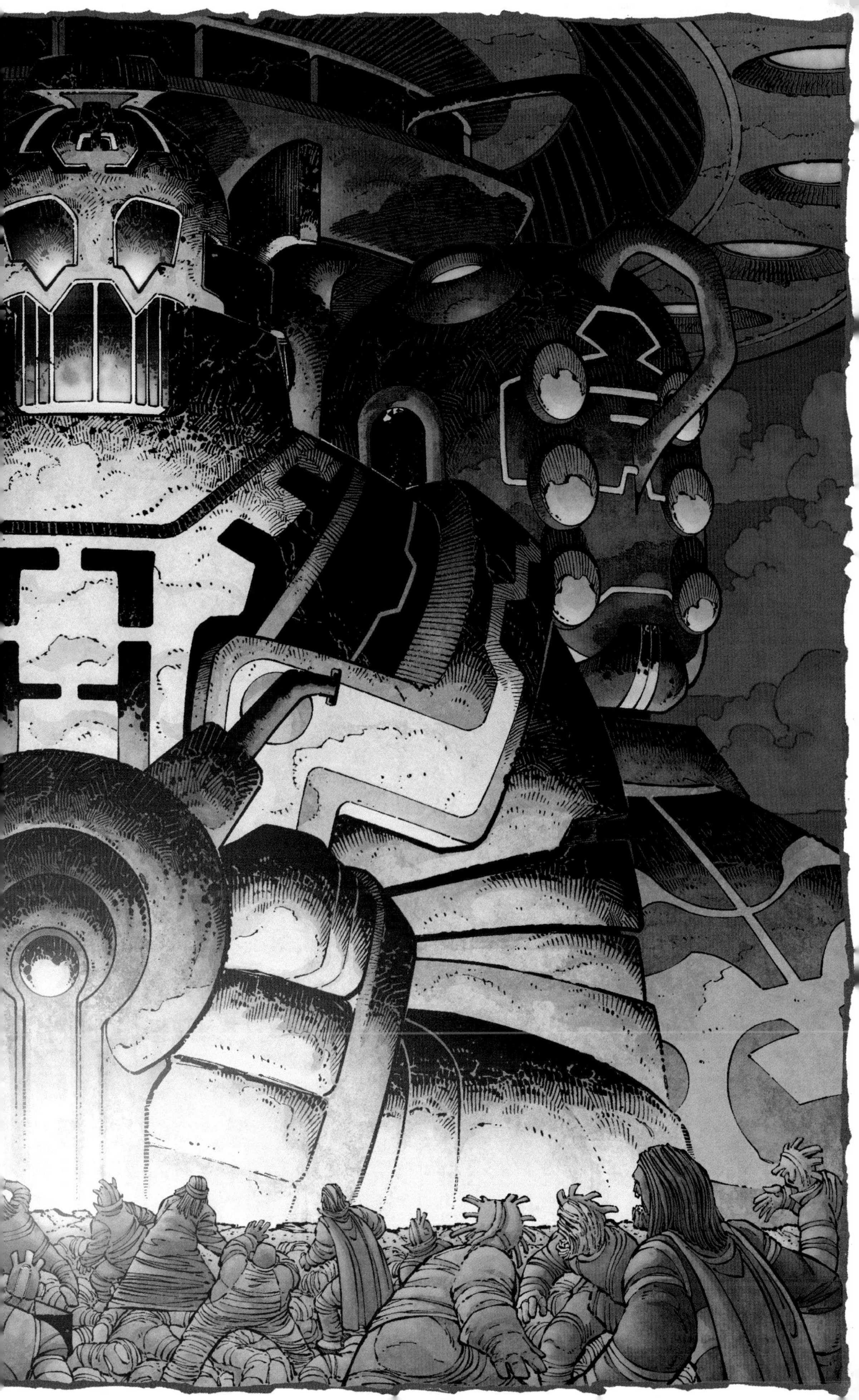

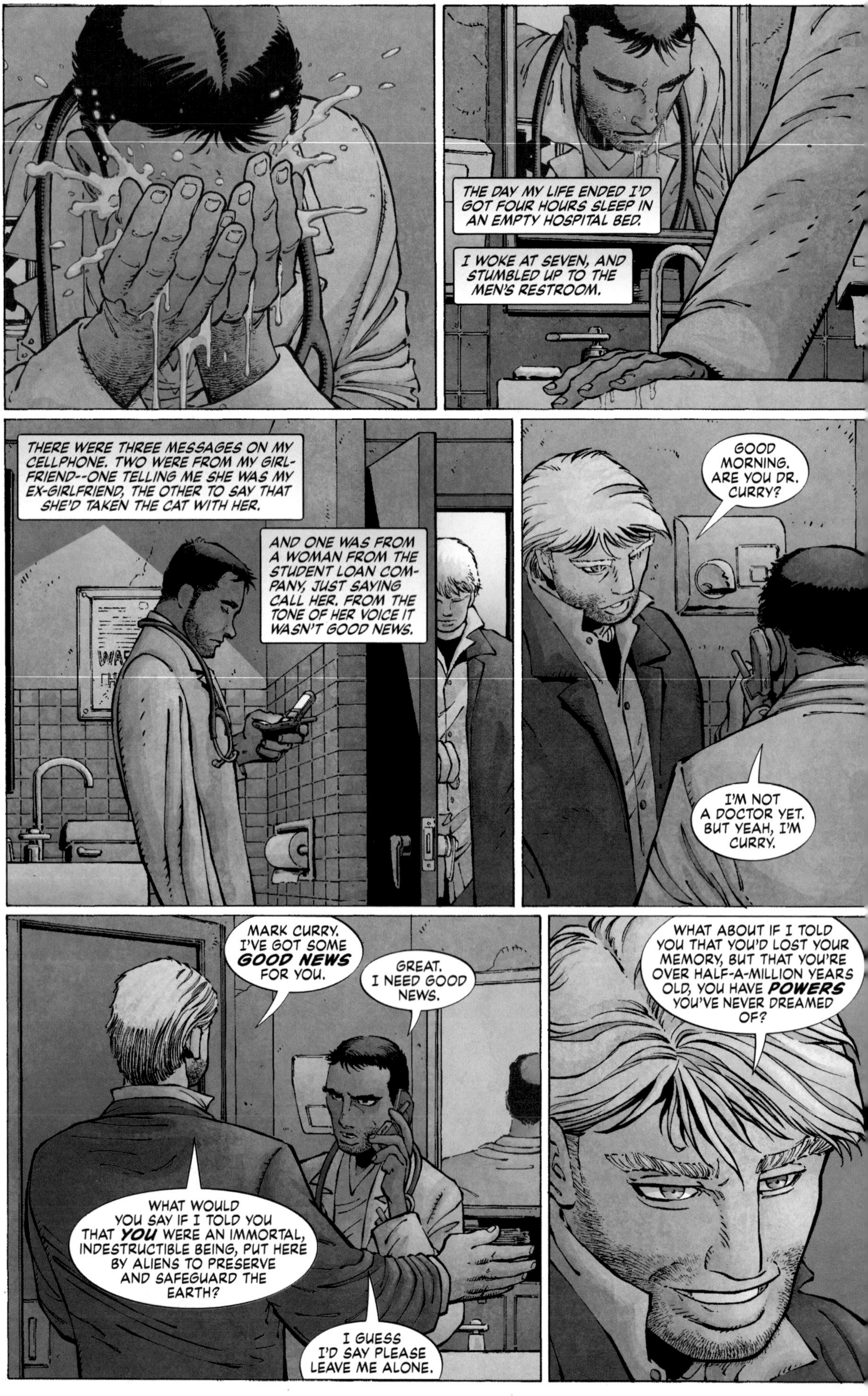
THE DAY MY LIFE ENDED I'D GOT FOUR HOURS SLEEP IN AN EMPTY HOSPITAL BED.
I WOKE AT SEVEN, AND STUMBLED UP TO THE MEN'S RESTROOM.
THERE WERE THREE MESSAGES ON MY CELLPHONE. TWO WERE FROM MY GIRLFRIEND--ONE TELLING ME SHE WAS MY EX-GIRLFRIEND, THE OTHER TO SAY THAT SHE'D TAKEN THE CAT WITH HER.
AND ONE WAS FROM A WOMAN FROM THE STUDENT LOAN COMPANY, JUST SAYING CALL HER. FROM THE TONE OF HER VOICE IT WASN'T GOOD NEWS.
GOOD MORNING. ARE YOU DR. CURRY?
I'M NOT A DOCTOR YET. BUT YEAH, I'M CURRY.
MARK CURRY. I'VE GOT SOME GOOD NEWS FOR YOU.
GREAT. I NEED GOOD NEWS.
WHAT WOULD YOU SAY IF I TOLD YOU THAT YOU WERE AN IMMORTAL, INDESTRUCTIBLE BEING, PUT HERE BY ALIENS TO PRESERVE AND SAFEGUARD THE EARTH?
I GUESS I'D SAY PLEASE LEAVE ME ALONE.
WHAT ABOUT IF I TOLD YOU THAT YOU'D LOST YOUR MEMORY, BUT THAT YOU'RE OVER HALF-A-MILLION YEARS OLD, YOU HAVE POWERS YOU'VE NEVER DREAMED OF?

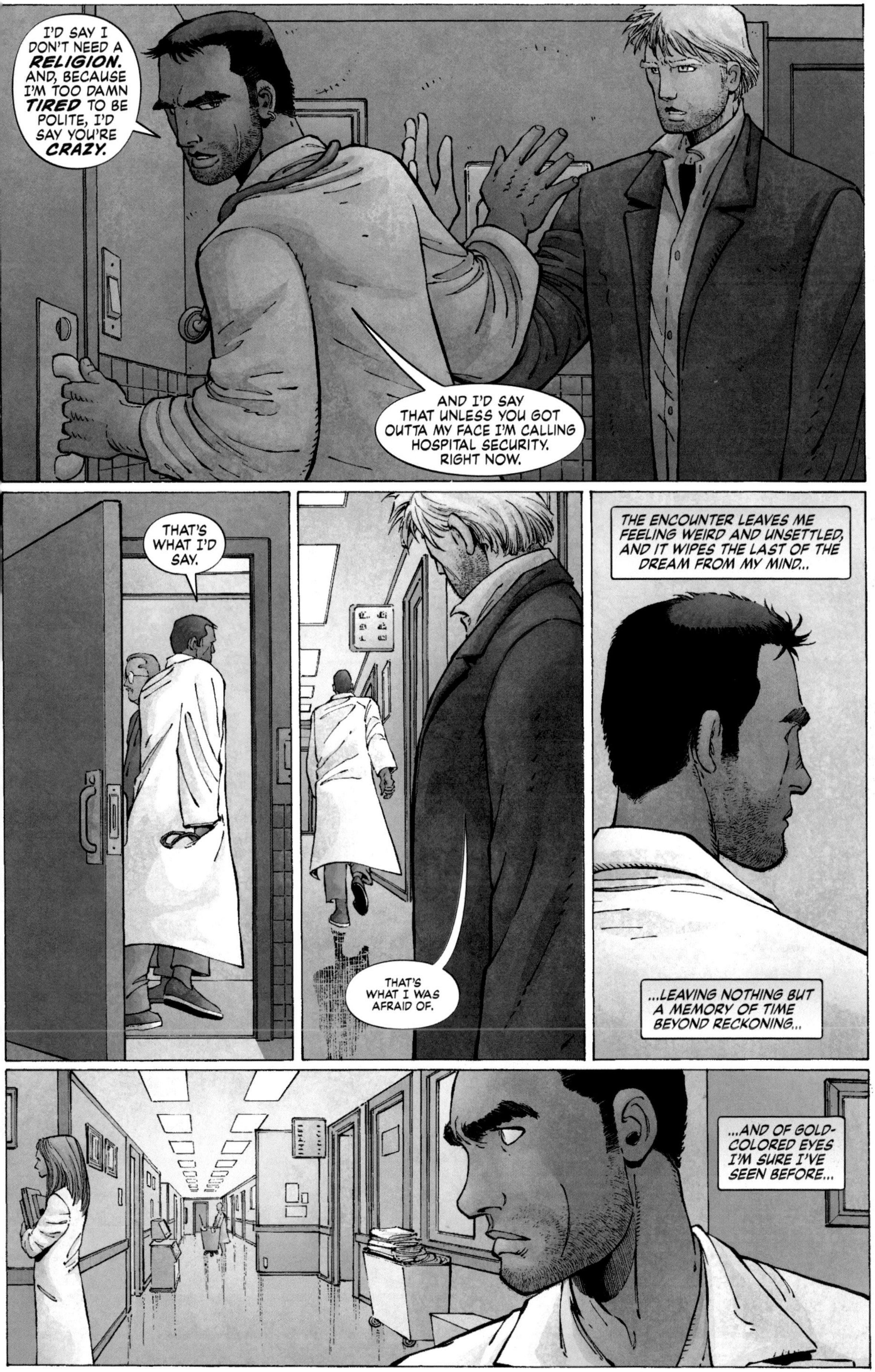

I'D SAY I DON'T NEED A **RELIGION.** AND, BECAUSE I'M TOO DAMN **TIRED** TO BE POLITE, I'D SAY YOU'RE **CRAZY.**
AND I'D SAY THAT UNLESS YOU GOT OUTTA MY FACE I'M CALLING HOSPITAL SECURITY. RIGHT NOW.
THAT'S WHAT I'D SAY.
THAT'S WHAT I WAS AFRAID OF.
THE ENCOUNTER LEAVES ME FEELING WEIRD AND UNSETTLED, AND IT WIPES THE LAST OF THE DREAM FROM MY MIND...
...LEAVING NOTHING BUT A MEMORY OF TIME BEYOND RECKONING...
...AND OF GOLD-COLORED EYES I'M SURE I'VE SEEN BEFORE...

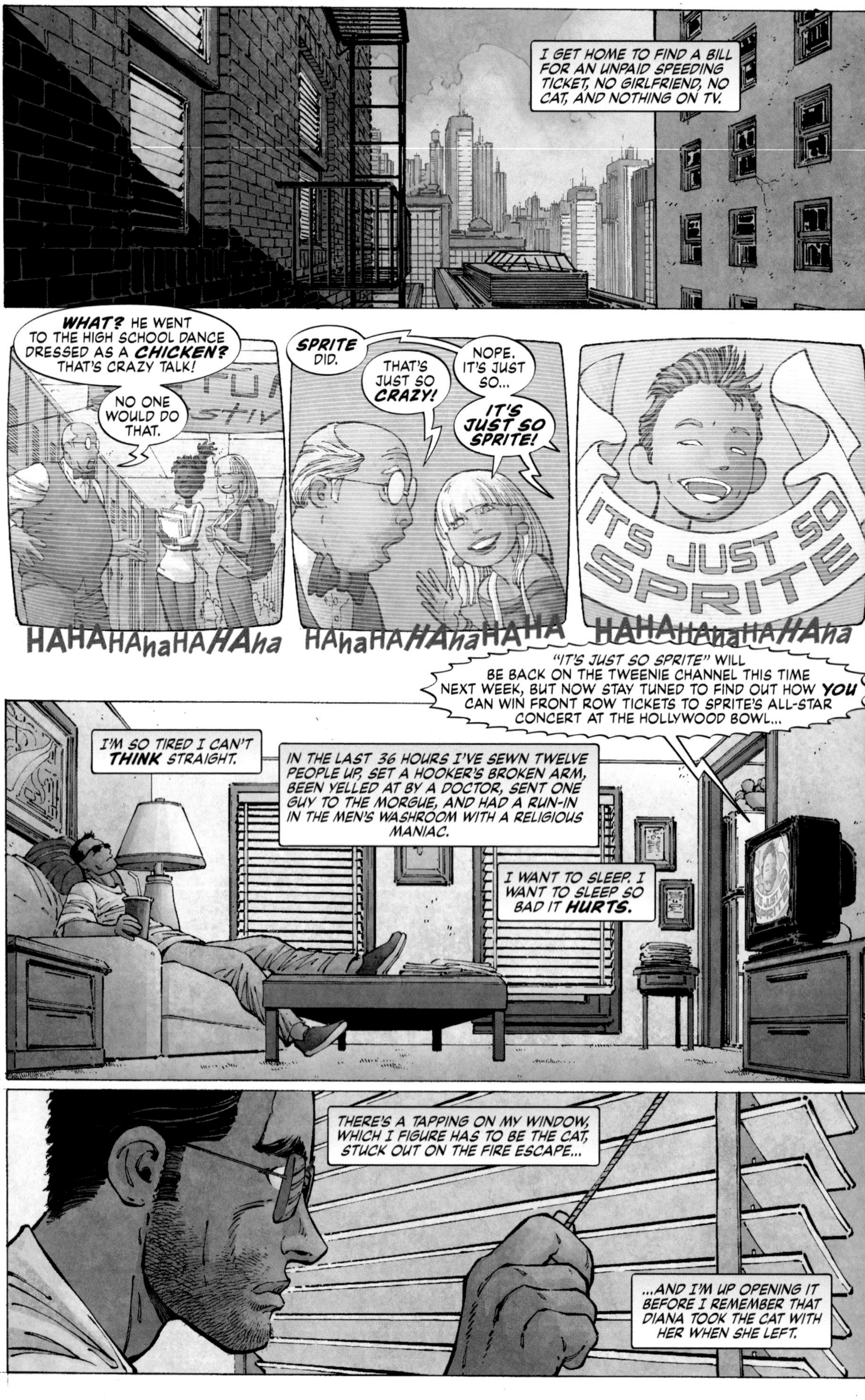

I GET HOME TO FIND A BILL FOR AN UNPAID SPEEDING TICKET, NO GIRLFRIEND, NO CAT, AND NOTHING ON TV.
WHAT? HE WENT TO THE HIGH SCHOOL DANCE DRESSED AS A CHICKEN? THAT'S CRAZY TALK!
NO ONE WOULD DO THAT.
SPRITE DID.
THAT'S JUST SO CRAZY!
NOPE. IT'S JUST SO...
IT'S JUST SO SPRITE!
ITS JUST SO SPRITE
HAHAHAhaHAHAha
HAhaHAHAhaHAHA
HAHAHAhaHAHAha
"IT'S JUST SO SPRITE" WILL BE BACK ON THE TWEENIE CHANNEL THIS TIME NEXT WEEK, BUT NOW STAY TUNED TO FIND OUT HOW YOU CAN WIN FRONT ROW TICKETS TO SPRITE'S ALL-STAR CONCERT AT THE HOLLYWOOD BOWL...
I'M SO TIRED I CAN'T THINK STRAIGHT.
IN THE LAST 36 HOURS I'VE SEWN TWELVE PEOPLE UP, SET A HOOKER'S BROKEN ARM, BEEN YELLED AT BY A DOCTOR, SENT ONE GUY TO THE MORGUE, AND HAD A RUN-IN IN THE MEN'S WASHROOM WITH A RELIGIOUS MANIAC.
I WANT TO SLEEP. I WANT TO SLEEP SO BAD IT HURTS.
THERE'S A TAPPING ON MY WINDOW, WHICH I FIGURE HAS TO BE THE CAT, STUCK OUT ON THE FIRE ESCAPE...
...AND I'M UP OPENING IT BEFORE I REMEMBER THAT DIANA TOOK THE CAT WITH HER WHEN SHE LEFT.

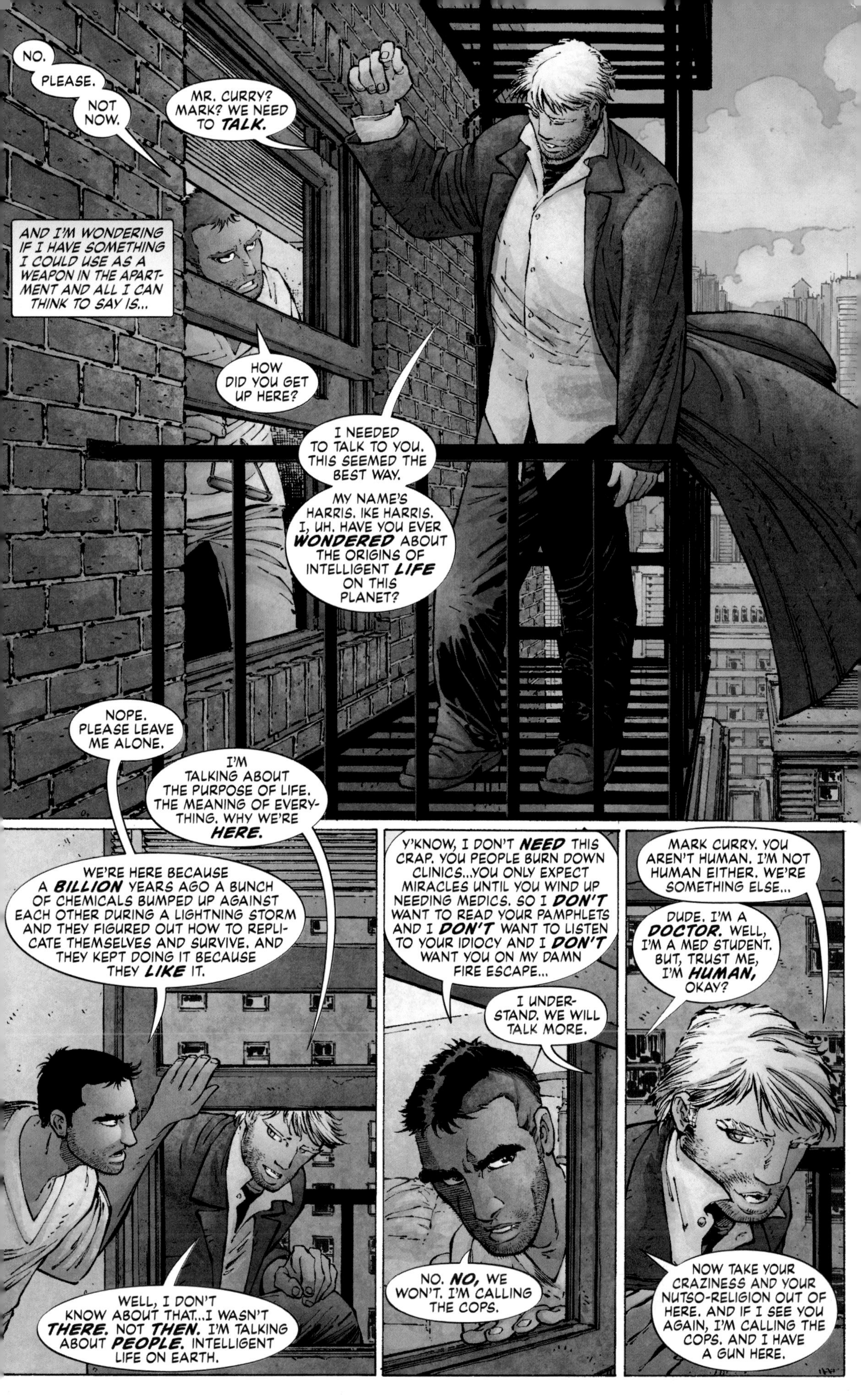
NO.
PLEASE.
NOT NOW.
MR. CURRY? MARK? WE NEED TO TALK.
AND I'M WONDERING IF I HAVE SOMETHING I COULD USE AS A WEAPON IN THE APARTMENT AND ALL I CAN THINK TO SAY IS...
HOW DID YOU GET UP HERE?
I NEEDED TO TALK TO YOU. THIS SEEMED THE BEST WAY.
MY NAME'S HARRIS. IKE HARRIS. I, UH. HAVE YOU EVER WONDERED ABOUT THE ORIGINS OF INTELLIGENT LIFE ON THIS PLANET?
NOPE. PLEASE LEAVE ME ALONE.
I'M TALKING ABOUT THE PURPOSE OF LIFE. THE MEANING OF EVERYTHING. WHY WE'RE HERE.
WE'RE HERE BECAUSE A BILLION YEARS AGO A BUNCH OF CHEMICALS BUMPED UP AGAINST EACH OTHER DURING A LIGHTNING STORM AND THEY FIGURED OUT HOW TO REPLICATE THEMSELVES AND SURVIVE. AND THEY KEPT DOING IT BECAUSE THEY LIKE IT.
WELL, I DON'T KNOW ABOUT THAT...I WASN'T THERE. NOT THEN. I'M TALKING ABOUT PEOPLE. INTELLIGENT LIFE ON EARTH.
Y'KNOW, I DON'T NEED THIS CRAP. YOU PEOPLE BURN DOWN CLINICS...YOU ONLY EXPECT MIRACLES UNTIL YOU WIND UP NEEDING MEDICS. SO I DON'T WANT TO READ YOUR PAMPHLETS AND I DON'T WANT TO LISTEN TO YOUR IDIOCY AND I DON'T WANT YOU ON MY DAMN FIRE ESCAPE...
I UNDERSTAND. WE WILL TALK MORE.
NO. NO, WE WON'T. I'M CALLING THE COPS.
MARK CURRY. YOU AREN'T HUMAN. I'M NOT HUMAN EITHER. WE'RE SOMETHING ELSE...
DUDE. I'M A DOCTOR. WELL, I'M A MED STUDENT. BUT, TRUST ME, I'M HUMAN, OKAY?
NOW TAKE YOUR CRAZINESS AND YOUR NUTSO-RELIGION OUT OF HERE. AND IF I SEE YOU AGAIN, I'M CALLING THE COPS. AND I HAVE A GUN HERE.

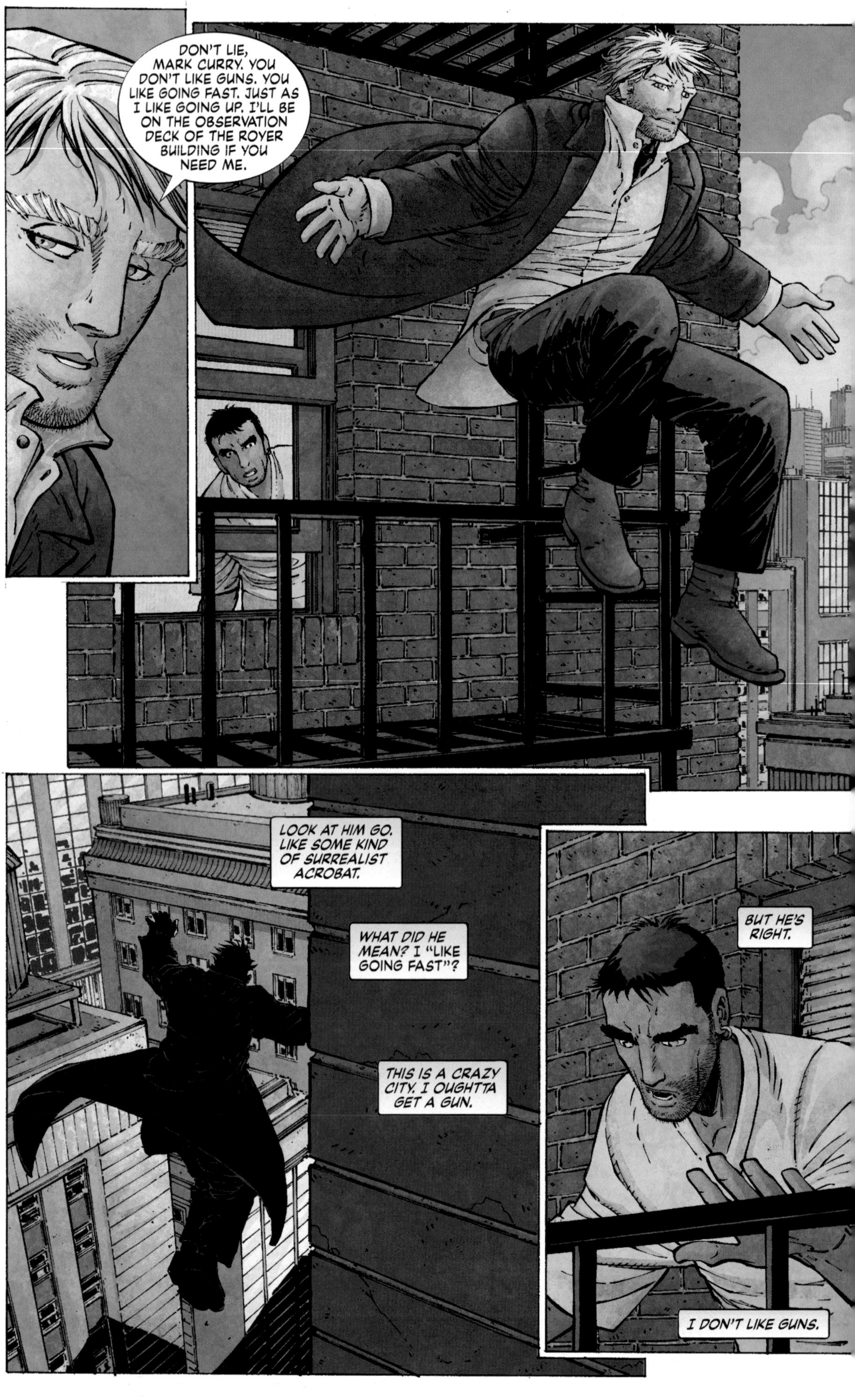
DON'T LIE, MARK CURRY. YOU DON'T LIKE GUNS. YOU LIKE GOING FAST. JUST AS I LIKE GOING UP. I'LL BE ON THE OBSERVATION DECK OF THE ROYER BUILDING IF YOU NEED ME.
LOOK AT HIM GO. LIKE SOME KIND OF SURREALIST ACROBAT.
WHAT DID HE MEAN? I "LIKE GOING FAST"?
THIS IS A CRAZY CITY. I OUGHTTA GET A GUN.
BUT HE'S RIGHT.
I DON'T LIKE GUNS.

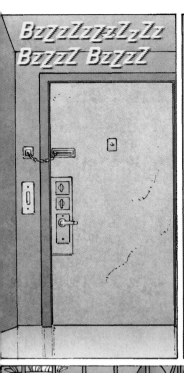

BzzZzzzZzZz
BzzzZ BzzzZ

BzzzZzzzZzZzZz

MORNING, ABI.

SERSI?

I BROUGHT YOU A CUP OF CAFFEINATED MORNING HAPPINESS.

HEY, ABIGAIL. SINCE I'M HERE, CAN I ASK A FAVOR?

WHAT?

UH. CAN I BORROW NINE HUNDRED BUCKS?

WHAT?

NINE HUNDRED BUCKS. C'MON. IT'S NOT THAT MUCH. WELL, IT IS TO ME. NOT TO YOU.

WHY?

RENT. C'MON, ABI. MY LANDLORD'S STARTED LURKING ON THE STAIRWELL. NEXT THING HE'S GOING TO CHANGE THE LOCKS. HE HATES THAT I'M IN A RENT-CONTROLLED APARTMENT ANYWAY...

GET A JOB.

I'VE *GOT* A JOB.

HON, INSTIGATING FLASH CROWDS IS NOT A JOB. GOING TO PARTIES IS NOT A JOB.

NO. BUT *PLANNING* PARTIES IS A JOB.

WHO THE HELL'S GOING TO PAY *YOU* FOR *THAT?*

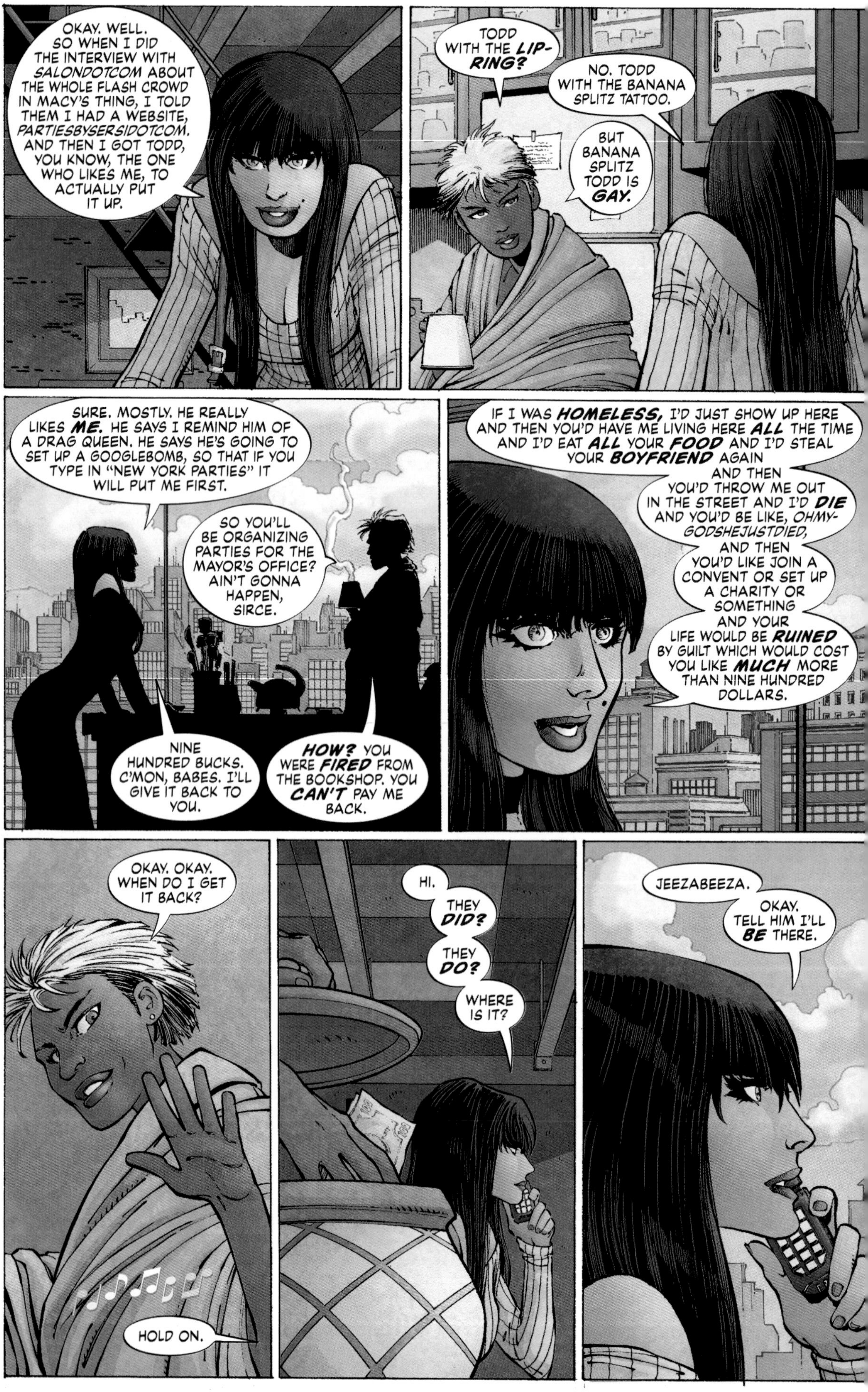
OKAY. WELL. SO WHEN I DID THE INTERVIEW WITH SALONDOTCOM ABOUT THE WHOLE FLASH CROWD IN MACY'S THING, I TOLD THEM I HAD A WEBSITE, PARTIESBYSERSIDOTCOM. AND THEN I GOT TODD, YOU KNOW, THE ONE WHO LIKES ME, TO ACTUALLY PUT IT UP.
TODD WITH THE LIP-RING?
NO. TODD WITH THE BANANA SPLITZ TATTOO.
BUT BANANA SPLITZ TODD IS GAY.
SURE. MOSTLY. HE REALLY LIKES ME. HE SAYS I REMIND HIM OF A DRAG QUEEN. HE SAYS HE'S GOING TO SET UP A GOOGLEBOMB, SO THAT IF YOU TYPE IN "NEW YORK PARTIES" IT WILL PUT ME FIRST.
SO YOU'LL BE ORGANIZING PARTIES FOR THE MAYOR'S OFFICE? AIN'T GONNA HAPPEN, SIRCE.
NINE HUNDRED BUCKS. C'MON, BABES. I'LL GIVE IT BACK TO YOU.
HOW? YOU WERE FIRED FROM THE BOOKSHOP. YOU CAN'T PAY ME BACK.
IF I WAS HOMELESS, I'D JUST SHOW UP HERE AND THEN YOU'D HAVE ME LIVING HERE ALL THE TIME AND I'D EAT ALL YOUR FOOD AND I'D STEAL YOUR BOYFRIEND AGAIN AND THEN YOU'D THROW ME OUT IN THE STREET AND I'D DIE AND YOU'D BE LIKE, OHMY-GODSHEJUSTDIED, AND THEN YOU'D LIKE JOIN A CONVENT OR SET UP A CHARITY OR SOMETHING AND YOUR LIFE WOULD BE RUINED BY GUILT WHICH WOULD COST YOU LIKE MUCH MORE THAN NINE HUNDRED DOLLARS.
OKAY. OKAY. WHEN DO I GET IT BACK?
HOLD ON.
HI.
THEY DID?
THEY DO?
WHERE IS IT?
JEEZABEEZA.
OKAY. TELL HIM I'LL BE THERE.

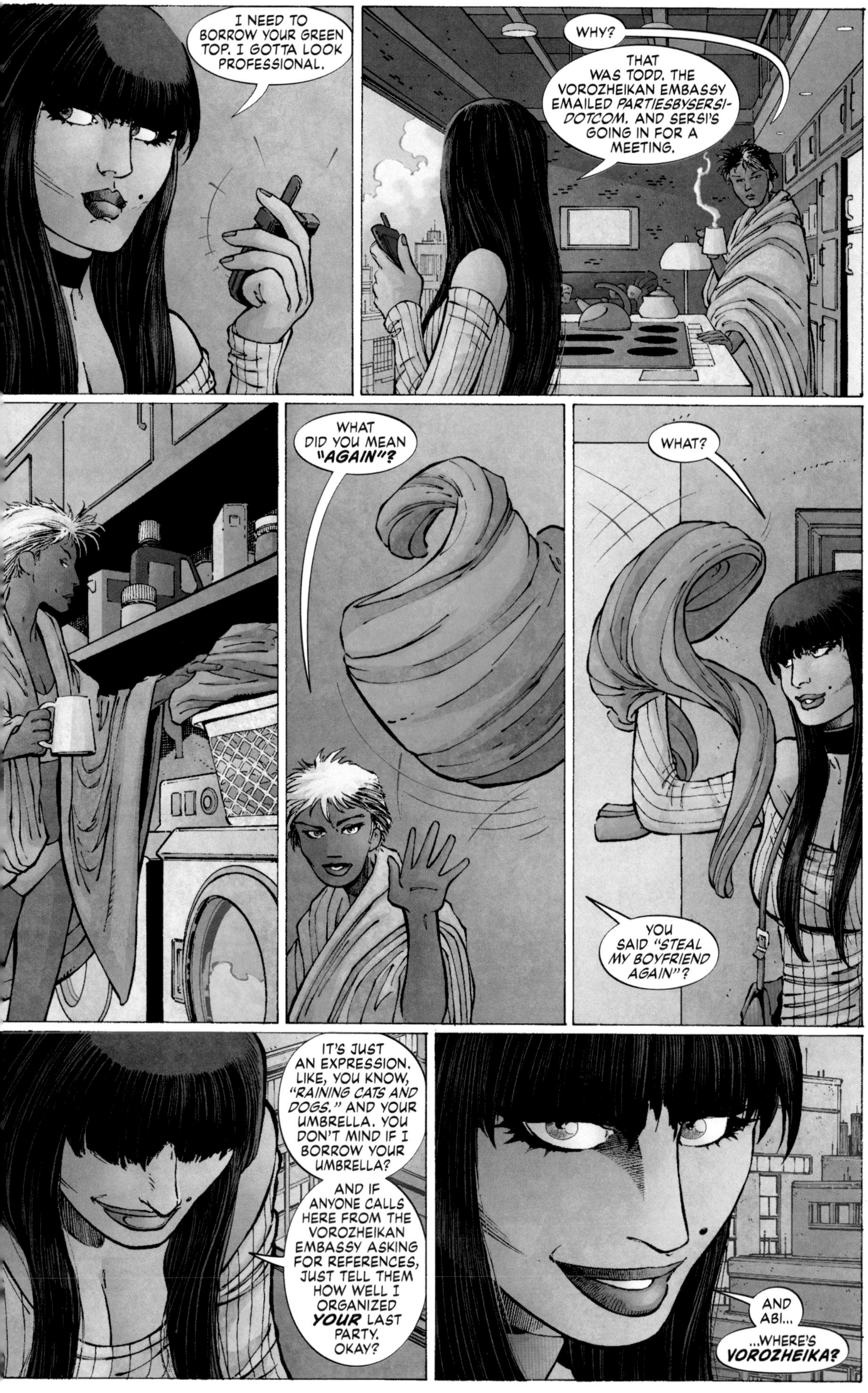

I NEED TO BORROW YOUR GREEN TOP. I GOTTA LOOK PROFESSIONAL.
WHY?
THAT WAS TODD. THE VOROZHEIKAN EMBASSY EMAILED *PARTIESBYSERSI-DOTCOM*. AND SERSI'S GOING IN FOR A MEETING.
WHAT DID YOU MEAN **"AGAIN"?**
WHAT?
YOU SAID *"STEAL MY BOYFRIEND AGAIN"*?
IT'S JUST AN EXPRESSION. LIKE, YOU KNOW, *"RAINING CATS AND DOGS."* AND YOUR UMBRELLA. YOU DON'T MIND IF I BORROW YOUR UMBRELLA?
AND IF ANYONE CALLS HERE FROM THE VOROZHEIKAN EMBASSY ASKING FOR REFERENCES, JUST TELL THEM HOW WELL I ORGANIZED **YOUR** LAST PARTY. OKAY?
AND ABI...
...WHERE'S **VOROZHEIKA?**

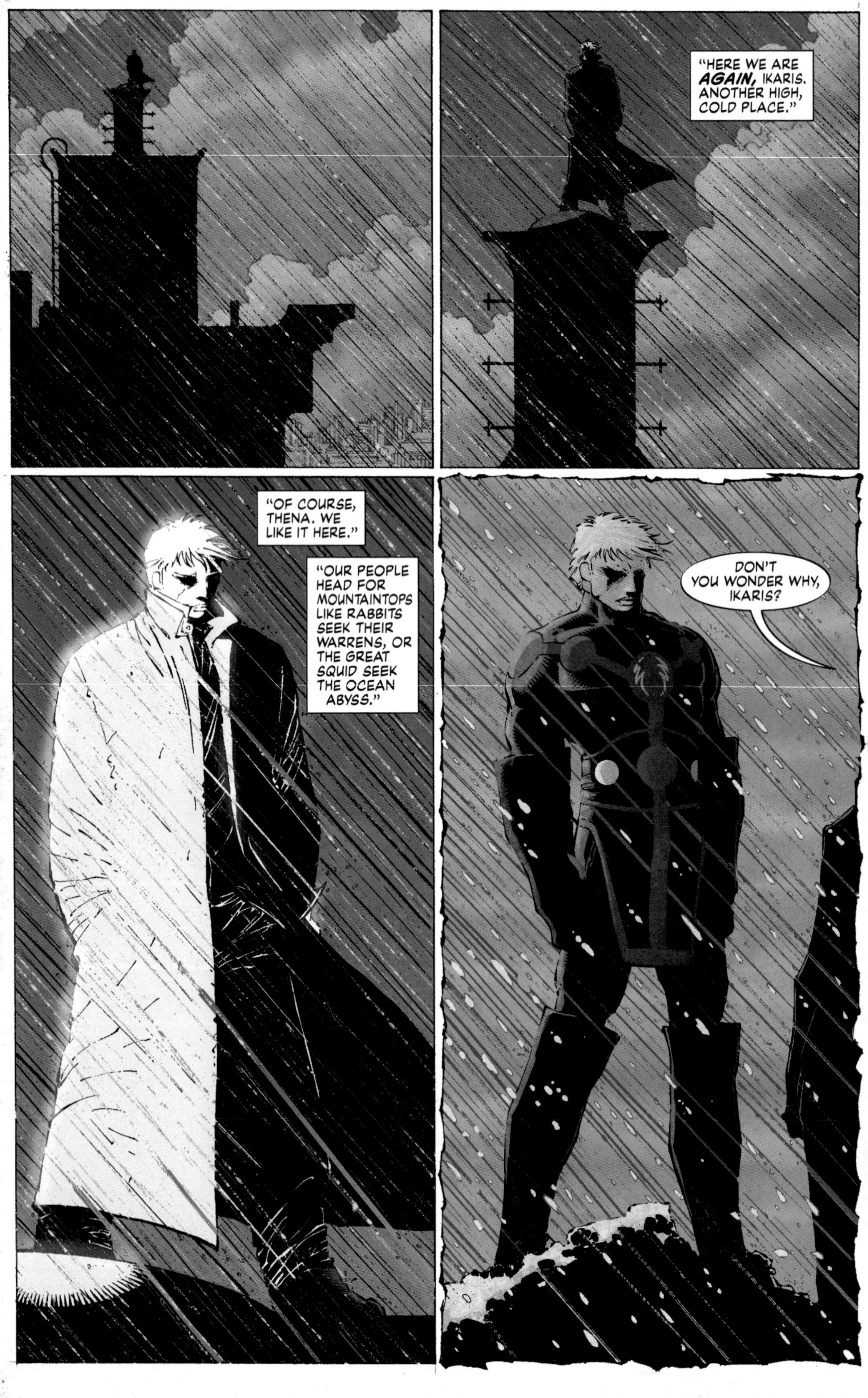
"HERE WE ARE AGAIN, IKARIS. ANOTHER HIGH, COLD PLACE."
"OF COURSE, THENA. WE LIKE IT HERE."
"OUR PEOPLE HEAD FOR MOUNTAINTOPS LIKE RABBITS SEEK THEIR WARRENS, OR THE GREAT SQUID SEEK THE OCEAN ABYSS."
DON'T YOU WONDER WHY, IKARIS?

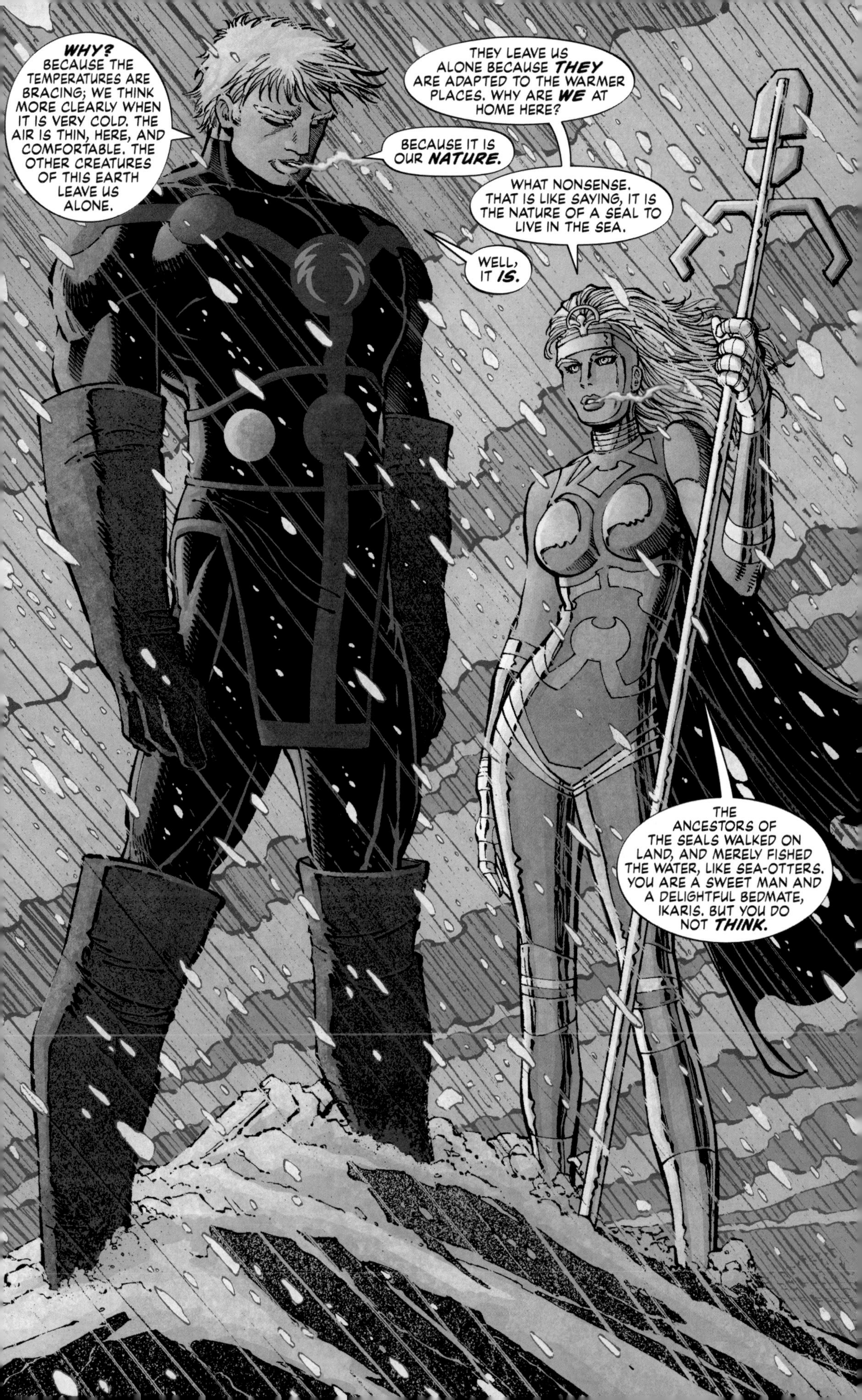
WHY? BECAUSE THE TEMPERATURES ARE BRACING; WE THINK MORE CLEARLY WHEN IT IS VERY COLD. THE AIR IS THIN, HERE, AND COMFORTABLE. THE OTHER CREATURES OF THIS EARTH LEAVE US ALONE.
THEY LEAVE US ALONE BECAUSE THEY ARE ADAPTED TO THE WARMER PLACES. WHY ARE WE AT HOME HERE?
BECAUSE IT IS OUR NATURE.
WHAT NONSENSE. THAT IS LIKE SAYING, IT IS THE NATURE OF A SEAL TO LIVE IN THE SEA.
WELL, IT IS.
THE ANCESTORS OF THE SEALS WALKED ON LAND, AND MERELY FISHED THE WATER, LIKE SEA-OTTERS. YOU ARE A SWEET MAN AND A DELIGHTFUL BEDMATE, IKARIS. BUT YOU DO NOT THINK.

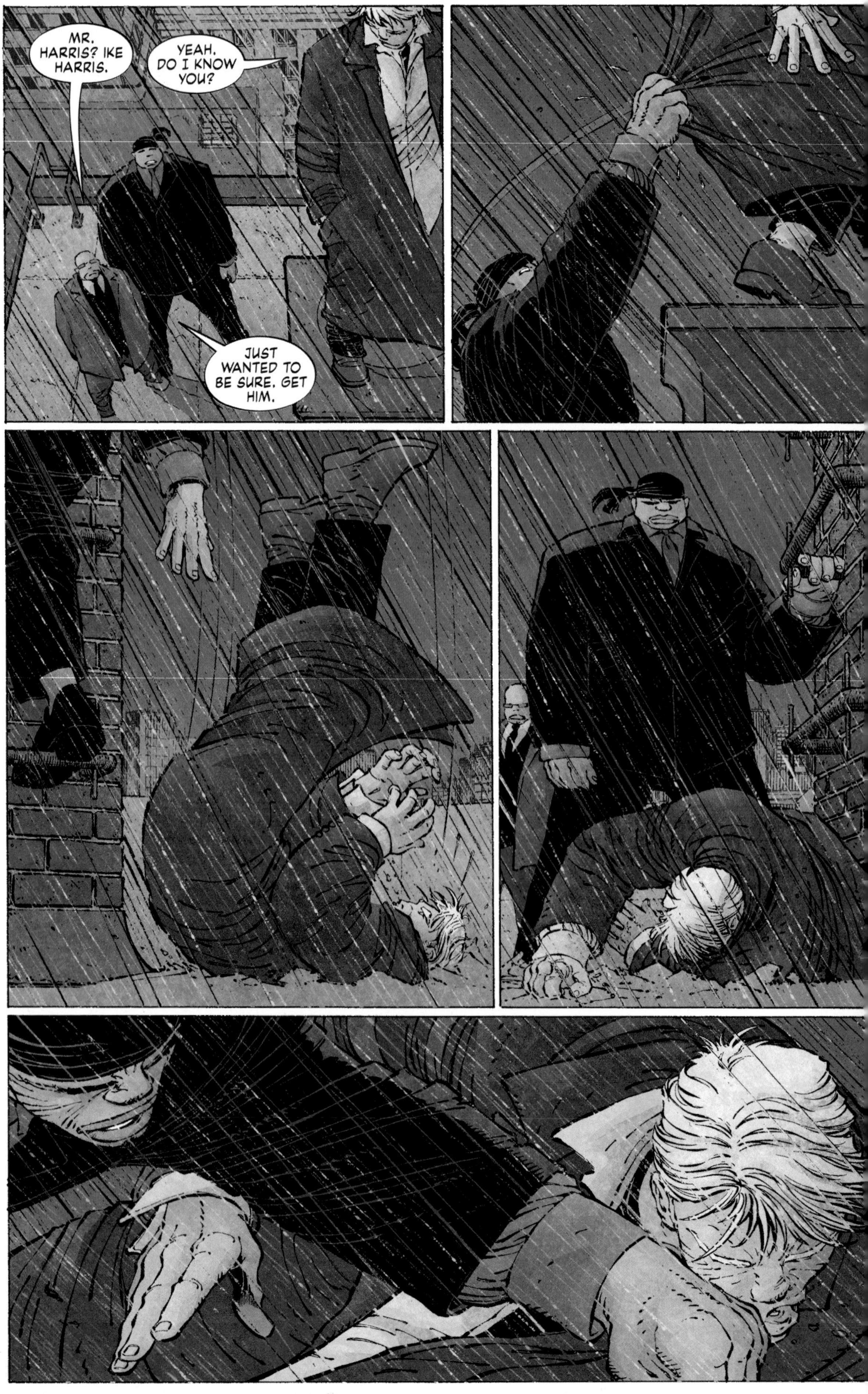
MR. HARRIS? IKE HARRIS.
YEAH. DO I KNOW YOU?
JUST WANTED TO BE SURE. GET HIM.

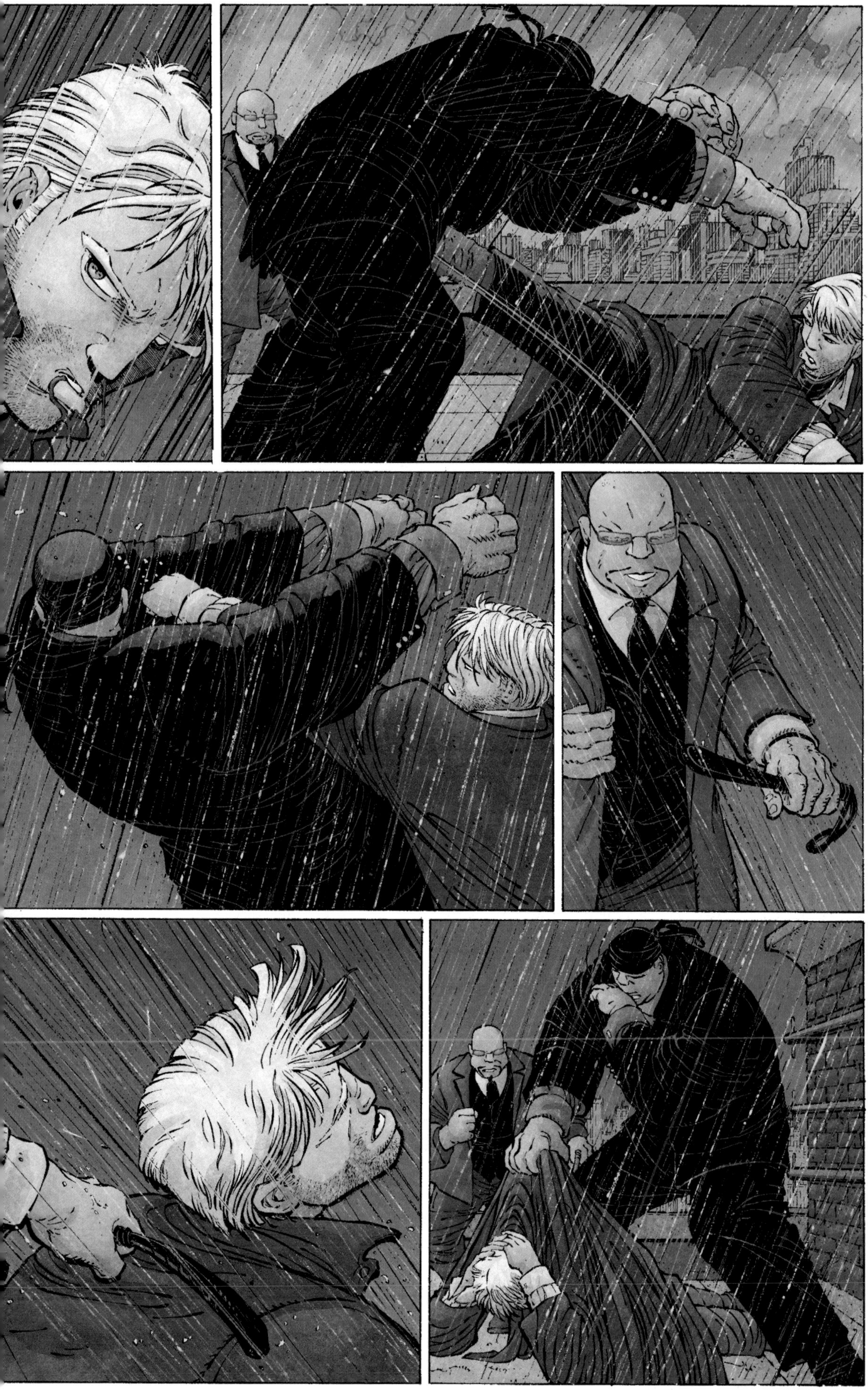

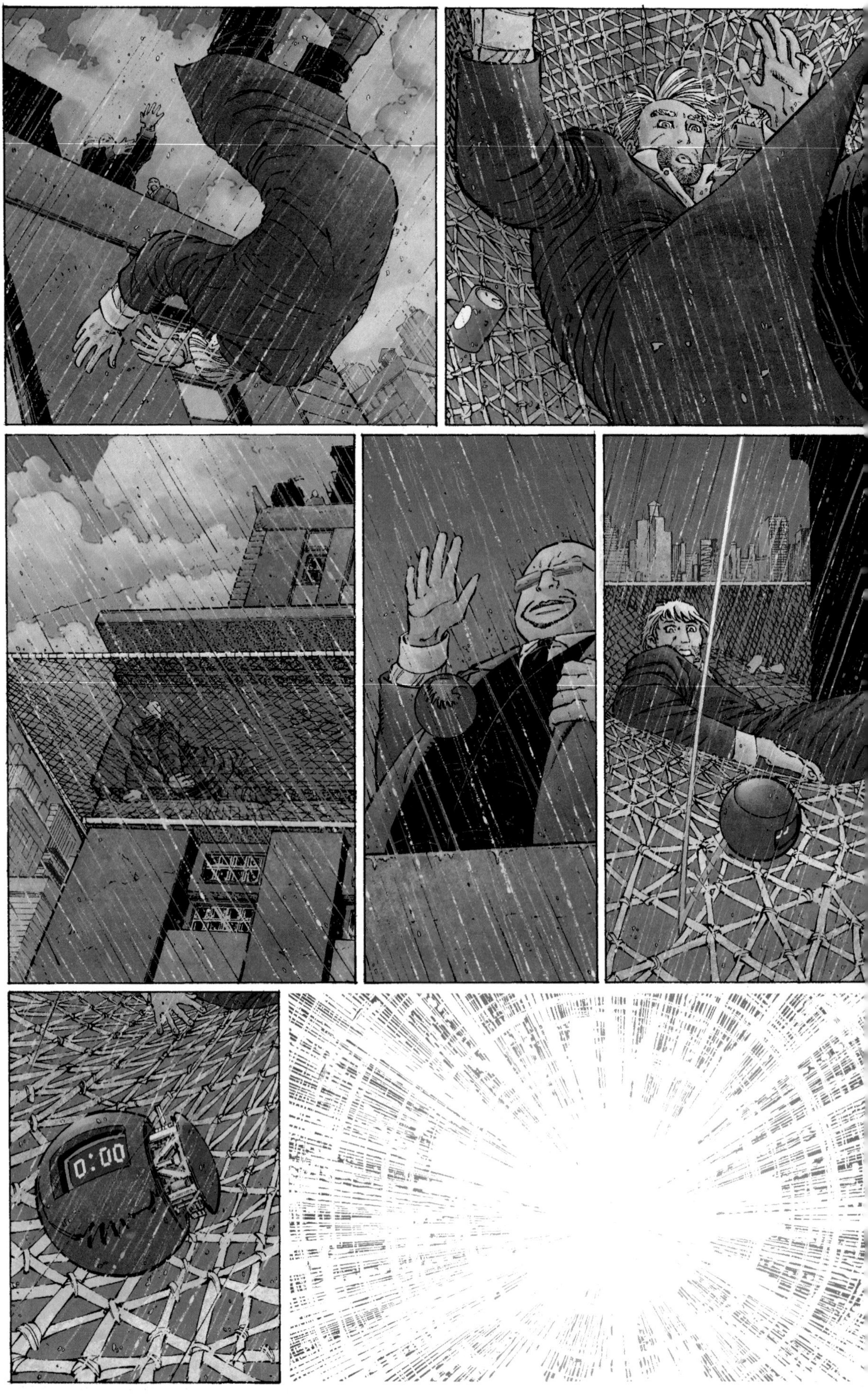
0:00

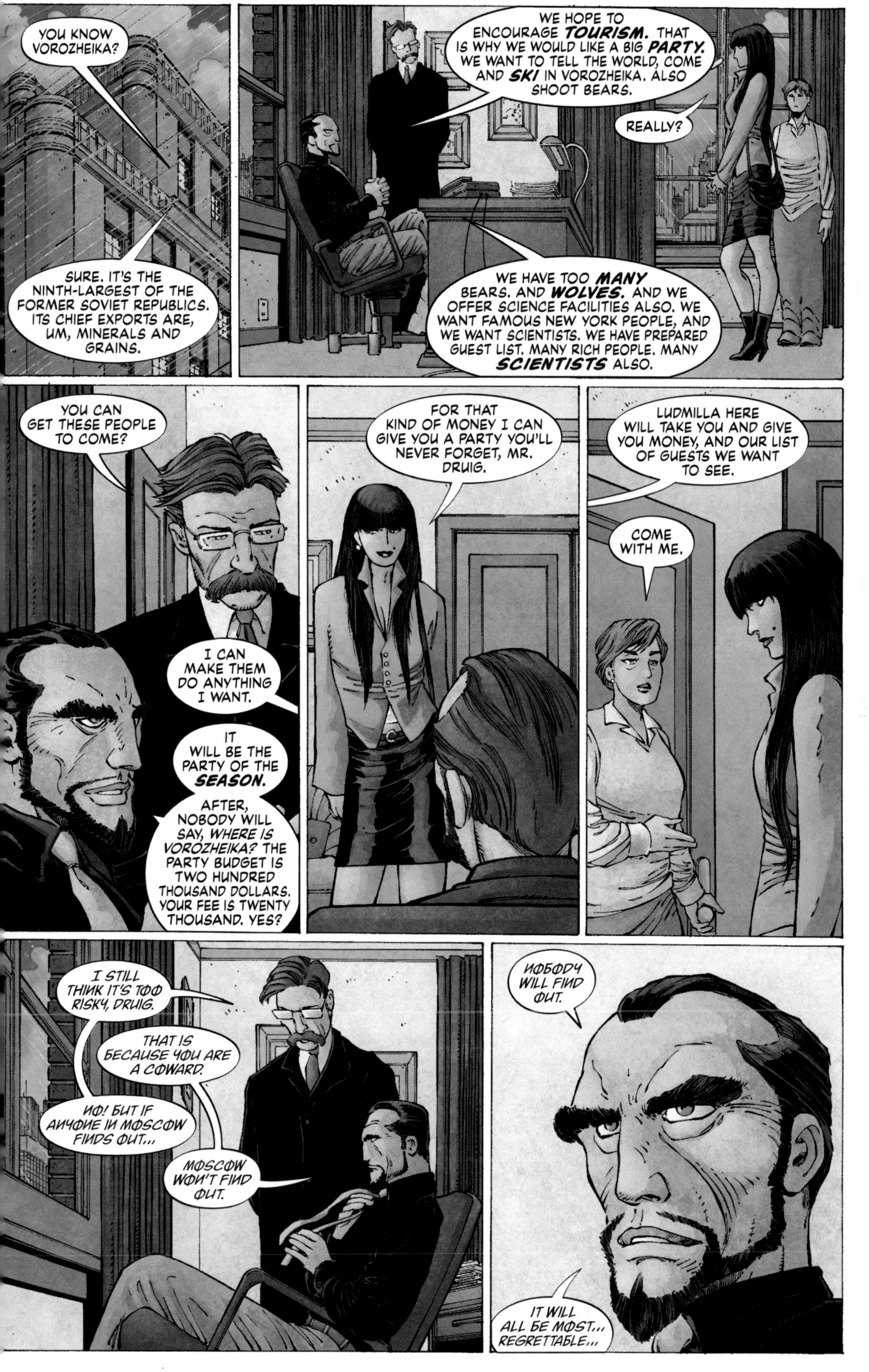
YOU KNOW VOROZHEIKA?
SURE. IT'S THE NINTH-LARGEST OF THE FORMER SOVIET REPUBLICS. ITS CHIEF EXPORTS ARE, UM, MINERALS AND GRAINS.
WE HOPE TO ENCOURAGE TOURISM. THAT IS WHY WE WOULD LIKE A BIG PARTY. WE WANT TO TELL THE WORLD, COME AND SKI IN VOROZHEIKA. ALSO SHOOT BEARS.
REALLY?
WE HAVE TOO MANY BEARS. AND WOLVES. AND WE OFFER SCIENCE FACILITIES ALSO. WE WANT FAMOUS NEW YORK PEOPLE, AND WE WANT SCIENTISTS. WE HAVE PREPARED GUEST LIST. MANY RICH PEOPLE. MANY SCIENTISTS ALSO.
YOU CAN GET THESE PEOPLE TO COME?
I CAN MAKE THEM DO ANYTHING I WANT.
IT WILL BE THE PARTY OF THE SEASON.
AFTER, NOBODY WILL SAY, WHERE IS VOROZHEIKA? THE PARTY BUDGET IS TWO HUNDRED THOUSAND DOLLARS. YOUR FEE IS TWENTY THOUSAND. YES?
FOR THAT KIND OF MONEY I CAN GIVE YOU A PARTY YOU'LL NEVER FORGET, MR. DRUIG.
LUDMILLA HERE WILL TAKE YOU AND GIVE YOU MONEY, AND OUR LIST OF GUESTS WE WANT TO SEE.
COME WITH ME.
I STILL THINK IT'S TOO RISKY, DRUIG.
THAT IS BECAUSE YOU ARE A COWARD.
NO! BUT IF ANYONE IN MOSCOW FINDS OUT...
MOSCOW WON'T FIND OUT.
NOBODY WILL FIND OUT.
IT WILL ALL BE MOST... REGRETTABLE...

PLEASE LET ME THROUGH. I *WORK* HERE...

BELLEVUE HOSPITAL CENTER
EMERGENCY

WHAT THE HELL'S WITH ALL THE *CAMERAS* OUTSIDE?

BOMBING AT THE ROYER TOWER. SOME KIND OF TERRORIST ATTACK. THEY BROUGHT THE WOUNDED HERE, ALONG WITH ONE MIRACLE SURVIVOR.

HE'S UNDER SEDATION IN INTENSIVE CARE, WITH BURNS AND MULTIPLE FRACTURES.

HE OUGHT TO BE *DEAD.*

BIG GUY? LOOKS LIKE A NORDIC BRICK WALL?

HOW'D YOU KNOW?

LUCKY GUESS.

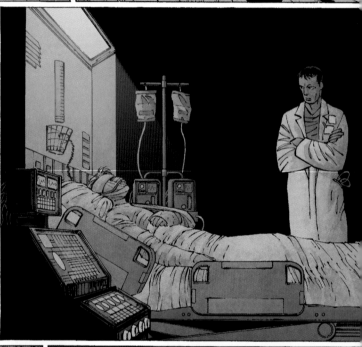

HI, MARK.

HOW DID YOU KNOW IT WAS ME?

I'VE KNOWN YOUR BREATHING PATTERNS FOR A VERY LONG TIME.

ARE YOU READY TO LISTEN?

I GUESS.

THEN COME BACK TOMORROW NIGHT. I NEED TIME TO HEAL.

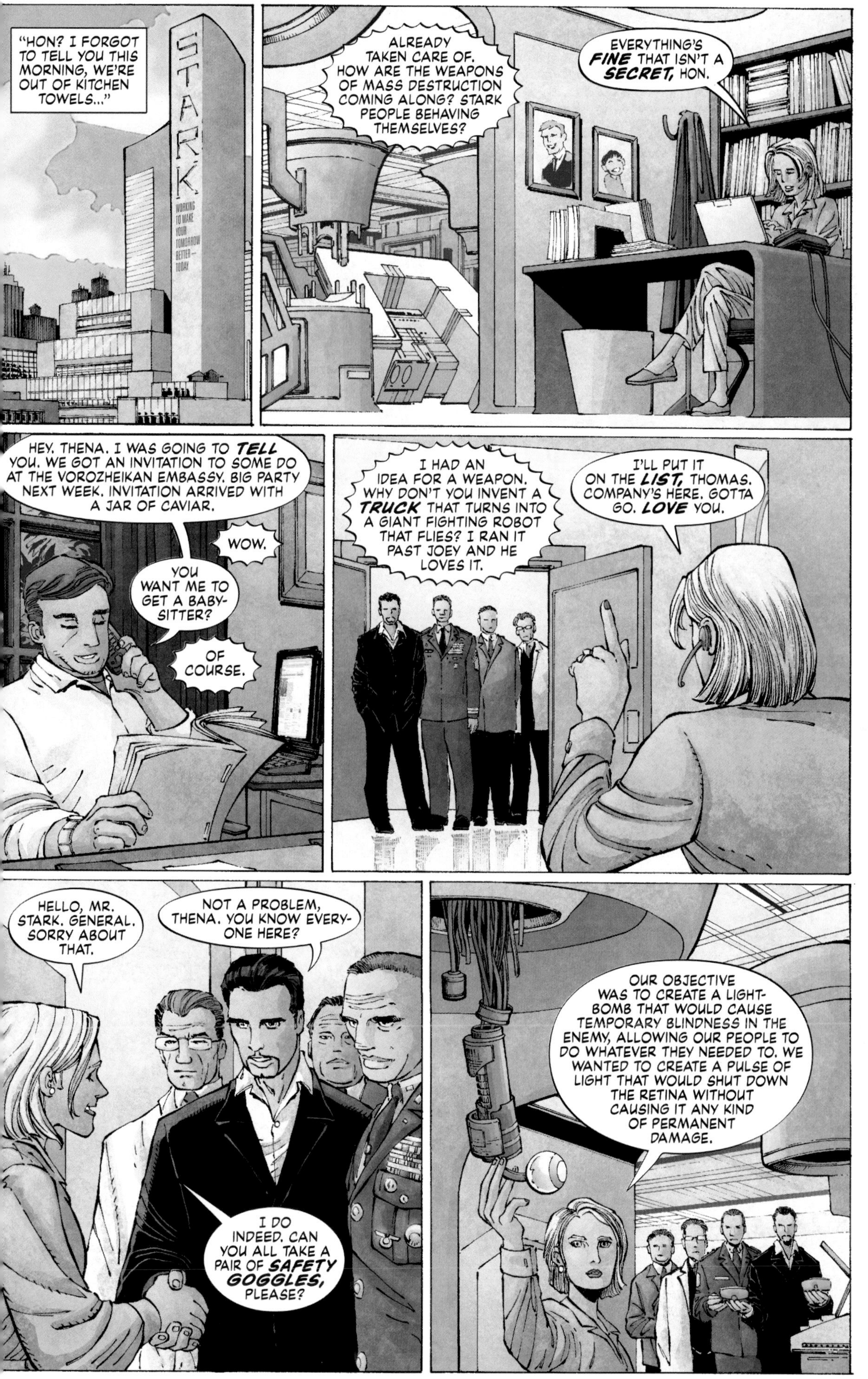
"HON? I FORGOT TO TELL YOU THIS MORNING, WE'RE OUT OF KITCHEN TOWELS..."
STARK
WORKING TO MAKE YOUR TOMORROW BETTER—TODAY
ALREADY TAKEN CARE OF. HOW ARE THE WEAPONS OF MASS DESTRUCTION COMING ALONG? STARK PEOPLE BEHAVING THEMSELVES?
EVERYTHING'S *FINE* THAT ISN'T A *SECRET,* HON.
HEY. THENA. I WAS GOING TO *TELL* YOU. WE GOT AN INVITATION TO SOME DO AT THE VOROZHEIKAN EMBASSY. BIG PARTY NEXT WEEK. INVITATION ARRIVED WITH A JAR OF CAVIAR.
WOW.
YOU WANT ME TO GET A BABY-SITTER?
OF COURSE.
I HAD AN IDEA FOR A WEAPON. WHY DON'T YOU INVENT A *TRUCK* THAT TURNS INTO A GIANT FIGHTING ROBOT THAT FLIES? I RAN IT PAST JOEY AND HE LOVES IT.
I'LL PUT IT ON THE *LIST,* THOMAS. COMPANY'S HERE. GOTTA GO. *LOVE* YOU.
HELLO, MR. STARK. GENERAL. SORRY ABOUT THAT.
NOT A PROBLEM, THENA. YOU KNOW EVERY-ONE HERE?
I DO INDEED. CAN YOU ALL TAKE A PAIR OF *SAFETY GOGGLES,* PLEASE?
OUR OBJECTIVE WAS TO CREATE A LIGHT-BOMB THAT WOULD CAUSE TEMPORARY BLINDNESS IN THE ENEMY, ALLOWING OUR PEOPLE TO DO WHATEVER THEY NEEDED TO. WE WANTED TO CREATE A PULSE OF LIGHT THAT WOULD SHUT DOWN THE RETINA WITHOUT CAUSING IT ANY KIND OF PERMANENT DAMAGE.

THE LAST THING WE WANT IS A NATION OF BLIND FORMER ENEMY COMBATANTS SUING THE UNITED STATES.

MR. STARK, YOU NEED GOGGLES TOO.

DR. ELIOT? SHOULDN'T YOU?

NOT FOR THIS DEMONSTRATION, NO, GENERAL.

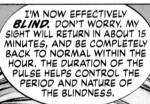

I'M NOW EFFECTIVELY **BLIND.** DON'T WORRY. MY SIGHT WILL RETURN IN ABOUT 15 MINUTES, AND BE COMPLETELY BACK TO NORMAL WITHIN THE HOUR. THE DURATION OF THE PULSE HELPS CONTROL THE PERIOD AND NATURE OF THE BLINDNESS.

THERE IS **NO** DAMAGE TO THE RETINA. THE PULSE SIMPLY TELLS THE BRAIN TO IGNORE ANY SIGNALS COMING FROM THE EYE.

STARK LABORATORIES HAVE BEEN WORKING ON THE PULSE PROJECT FOR FIVE YEARS. THE ARMY LOANS YOU TO US, AND YOU CRACK IT IN TWO MONTHS. YOU'RE A WONDER, THENA.

JUST DOING MY JOB. ANYWAY, IT WAS **EASY.**

LIKE **REMEMBER-ING.**

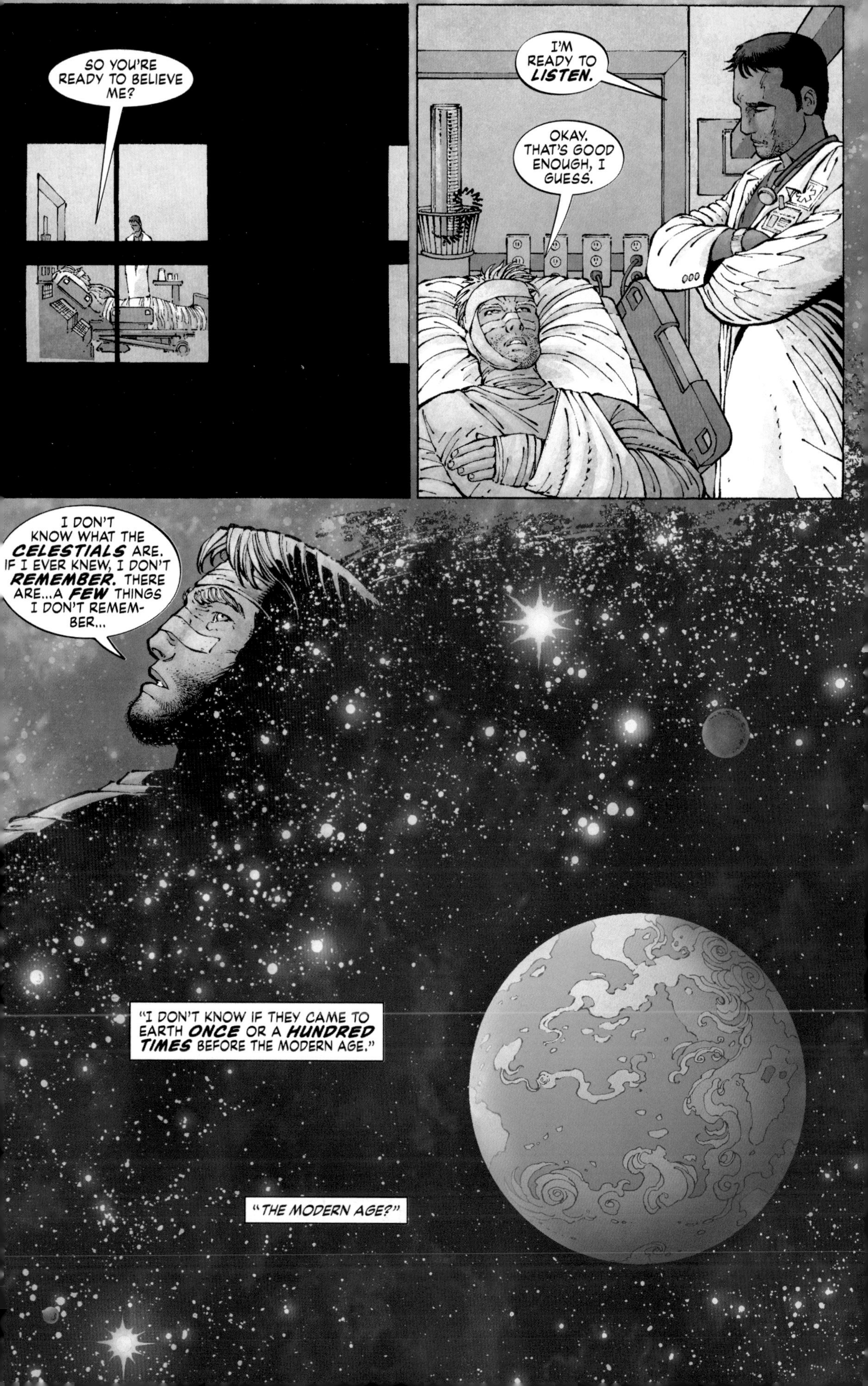
SO YOU'RE READY TO BELIEVE ME?
I'M READY TO LISTEN.
OKAY. THAT'S GOOD ENOUGH, I GUESS.
I DON'T KNOW WHAT THE CELESTIALS ARE. IF I EVER KNEW, I DON'T REMEMBER. THERE ARE...A FEW THINGS I DON'T REMEMBER...
"I DON'T KNOW IF THEY CAME TO EARTH ONCE OR A HUNDRED TIMES BEFORE THE MODERN AGE."
"THE MODERN AGE?"

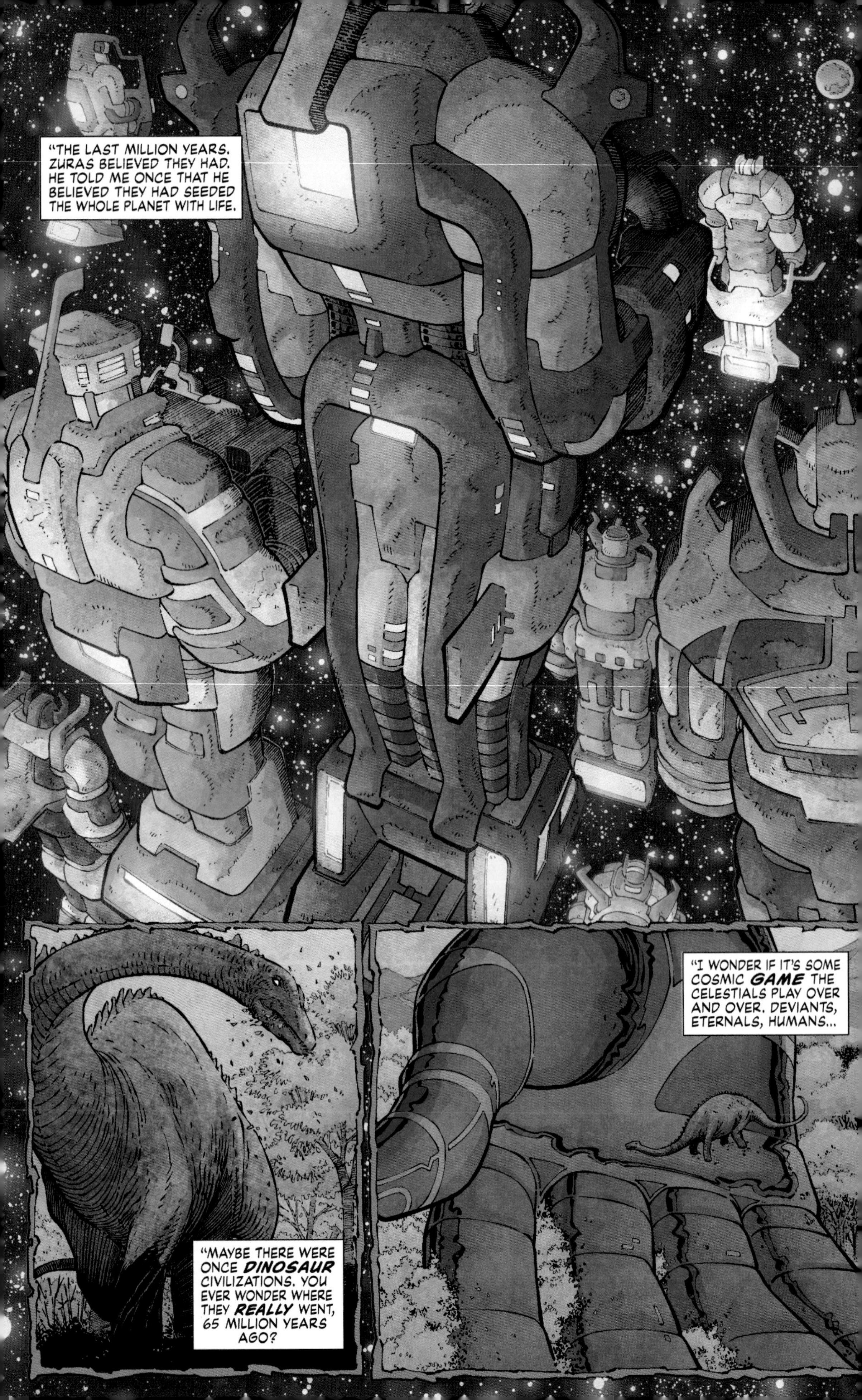
"THE LAST MILLION YEARS. ZURAS BELIEVED THEY HAD. HE TOLD ME ONCE THAT HE BELIEVED THEY HAD SEEDED THE WHOLE PLANET WITH LIFE.
"MAYBE THERE WERE ONCE ***DINOSAUR*** CIVILIZATIONS. YOU EVER WONDER WHERE THEY ***REALLY*** WENT, 65 MILLION YEARS AGO?
"I WONDER IF IT'S SOME COSMIC ***GAME*** THE CELESTIALS PLAY OVER AND OVER. DEVIANTS, ETERNALS, HUMANS...

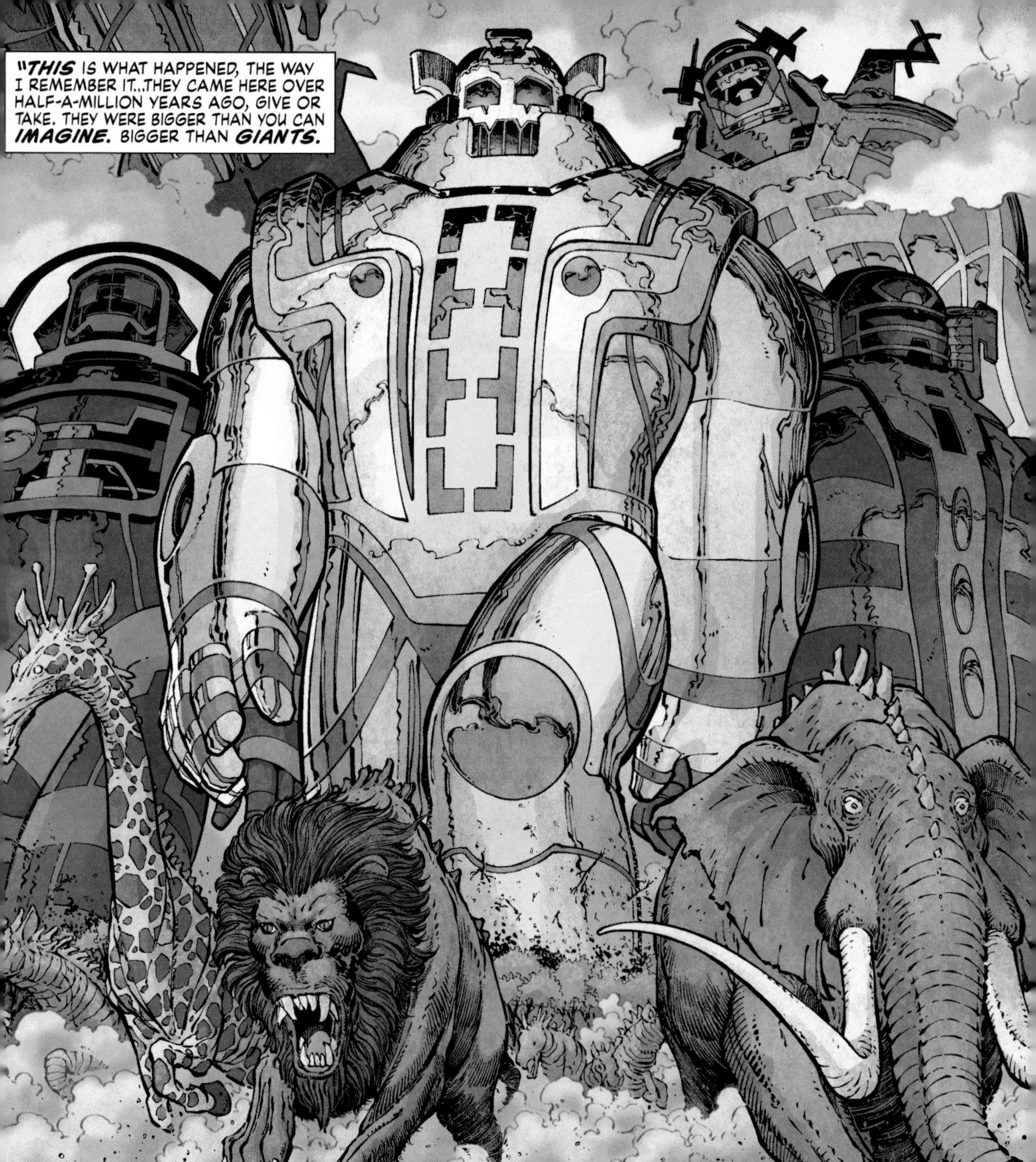
"THIS IS WHAT HAPPENED, THE WAY I REMEMBER IT...THEY CAME HERE OVER HALF-A-MILLION YEARS AGO, GIVE OR TAKE. THEY WERE BIGGER THAN YOU CAN IMAGINE. BIGGER THAN GIANTS.

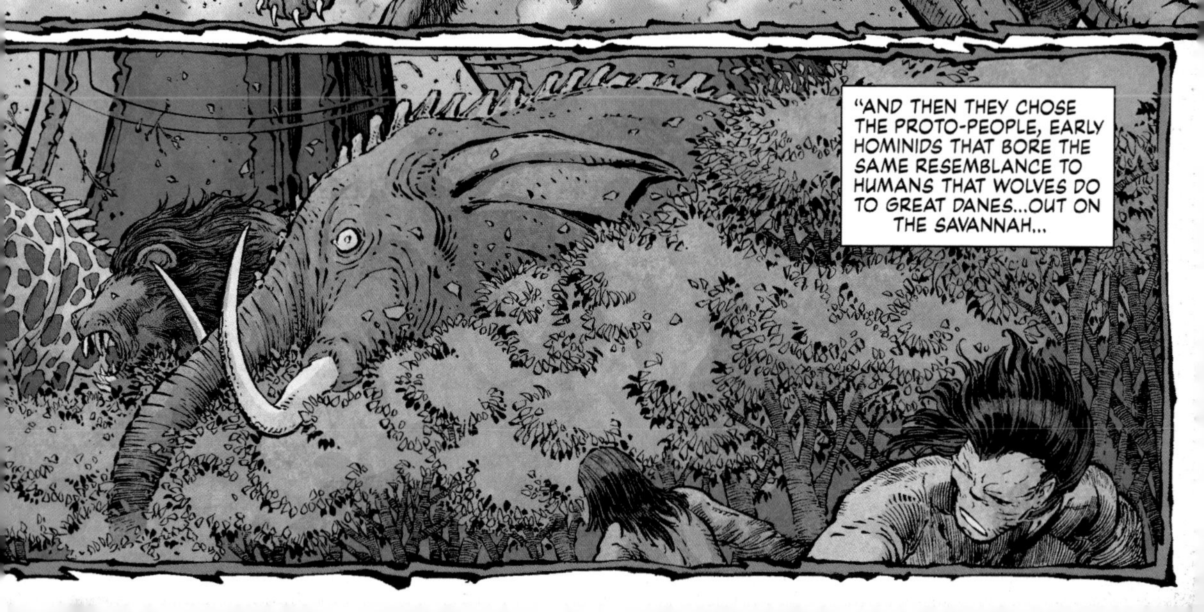
"AND THEN THEY CHOSE THE PROTO-PEOPLE, EARLY HOMINIDS THAT BORE THE SAME RESEMBLANCE TO HUMANS THAT WOLVES DO TO GREAT DANES...OUT ON THE SAVANNAH...

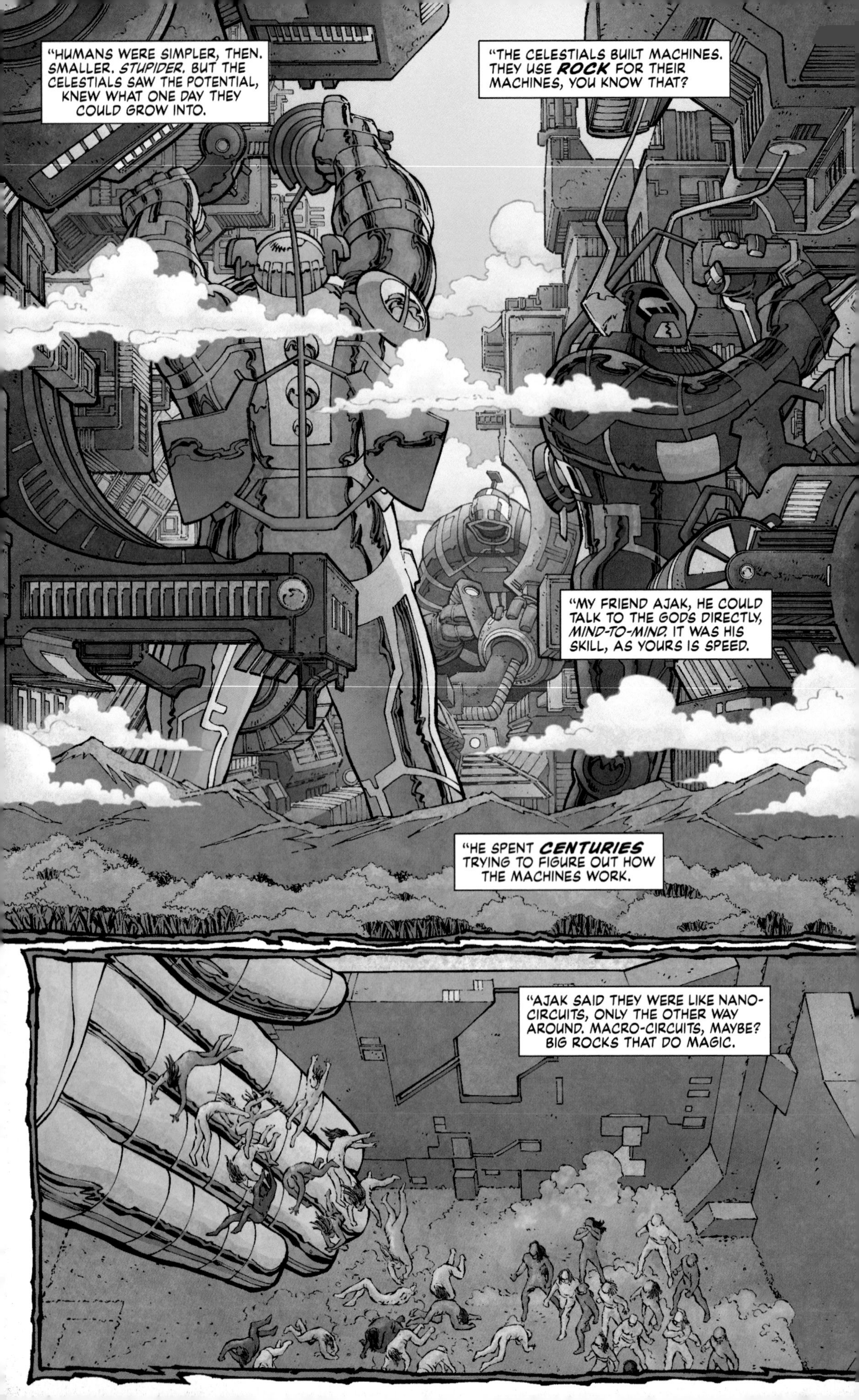
"HUMANS WERE SIMPLER, THEN. SMALLER. STUPIDER. BUT THE CELESTIALS SAW THE POTENTIAL, KNEW WHAT ONE DAY THEY COULD GROW INTO.
"THE CELESTIALS BUILT MACHINES. THEY USE ROCK FOR THEIR MACHINES, YOU KNOW THAT?
"MY FRIEND AJAK, HE COULD TALK TO THE GODS DIRECTLY, MIND-TO-MIND. IT WAS HIS SKILL, AS YOURS IS SPEED.
"HE SPENT CENTURIES TRYING TO FIGURE OUT HOW THE MACHINES WORK.
"AJAK SAID THEY WERE LIKE NANO-CIRCUITS, ONLY THE OTHER WAY AROUND. MACRO-CIRCUITS, MAYBE? BIG ROCKS THAT DO MAGIC.

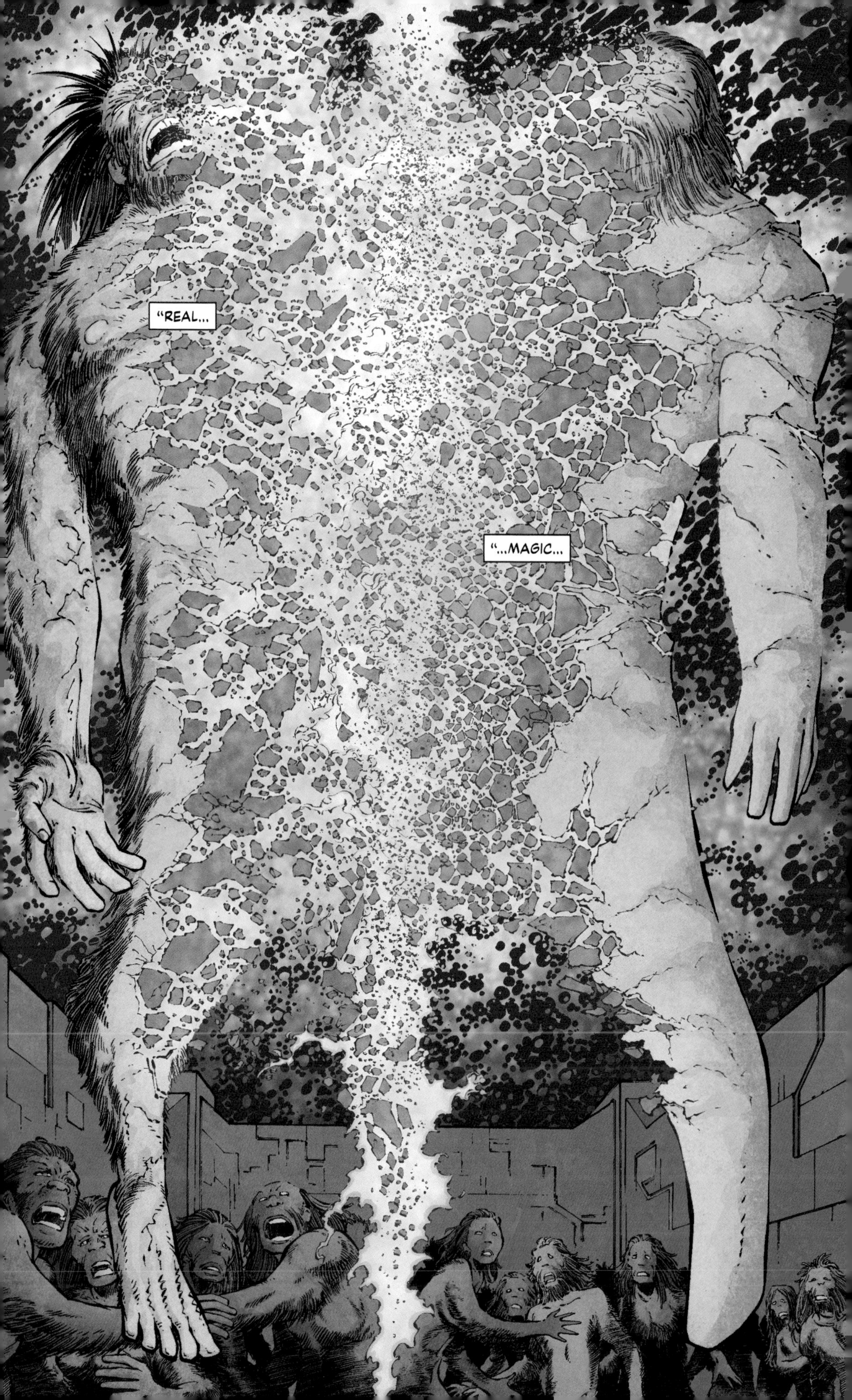
"REAL...
"...MAGIC...

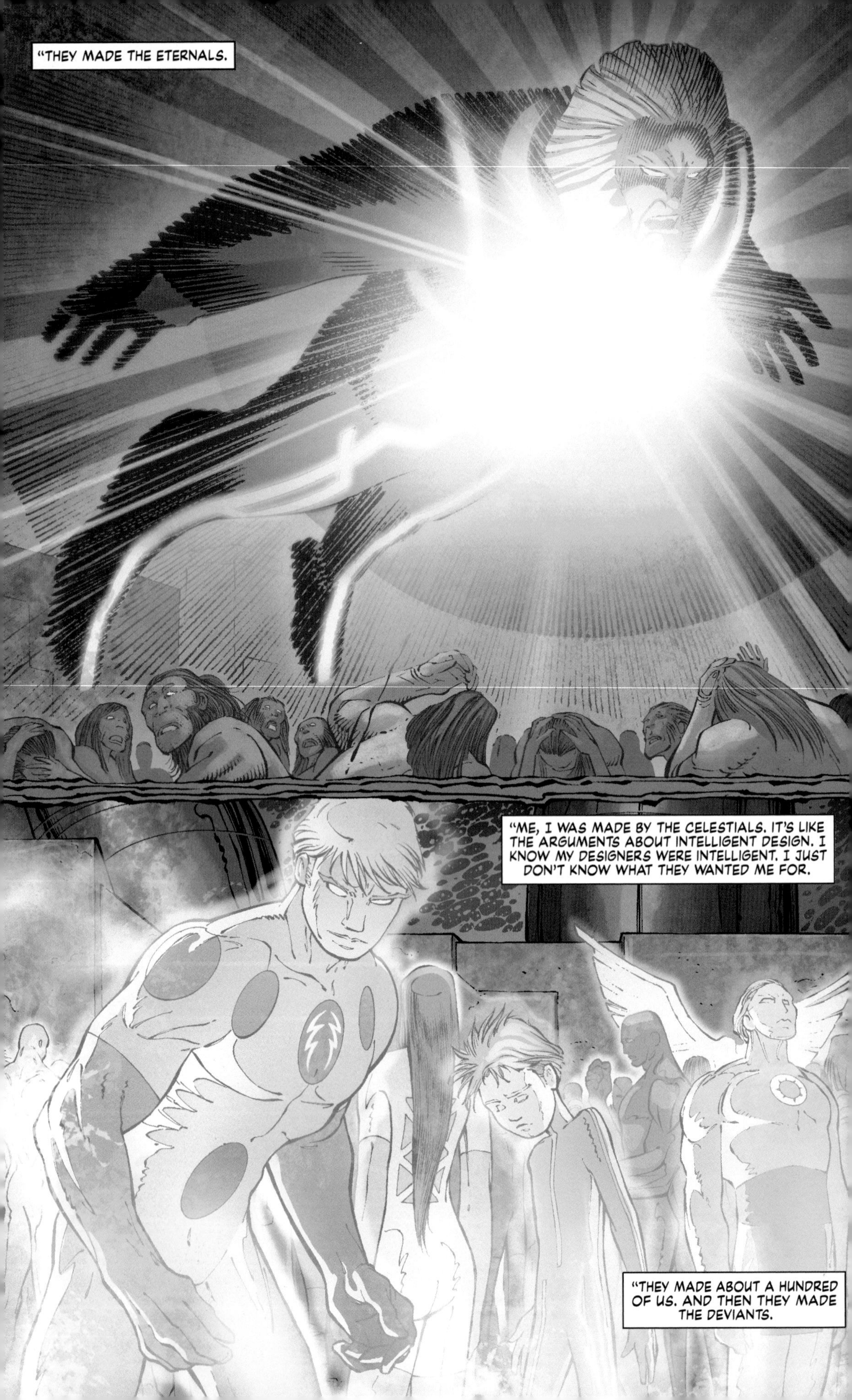
"THEY MADE THE ETERNALS.
"ME, I WAS MADE BY THE CELESTIALS. IT'S LIKE THE ARGUMENTS ABOUT INTELLIGENT DESIGN. I KNOW MY DESIGNERS WERE INTELLIGENT. I JUST DON'T KNOW WHAT THEY WANTED ME FOR.
"THEY MADE ABOUT A HUNDRED OF US. AND THEN THEY MADE THE DEVIANTS.

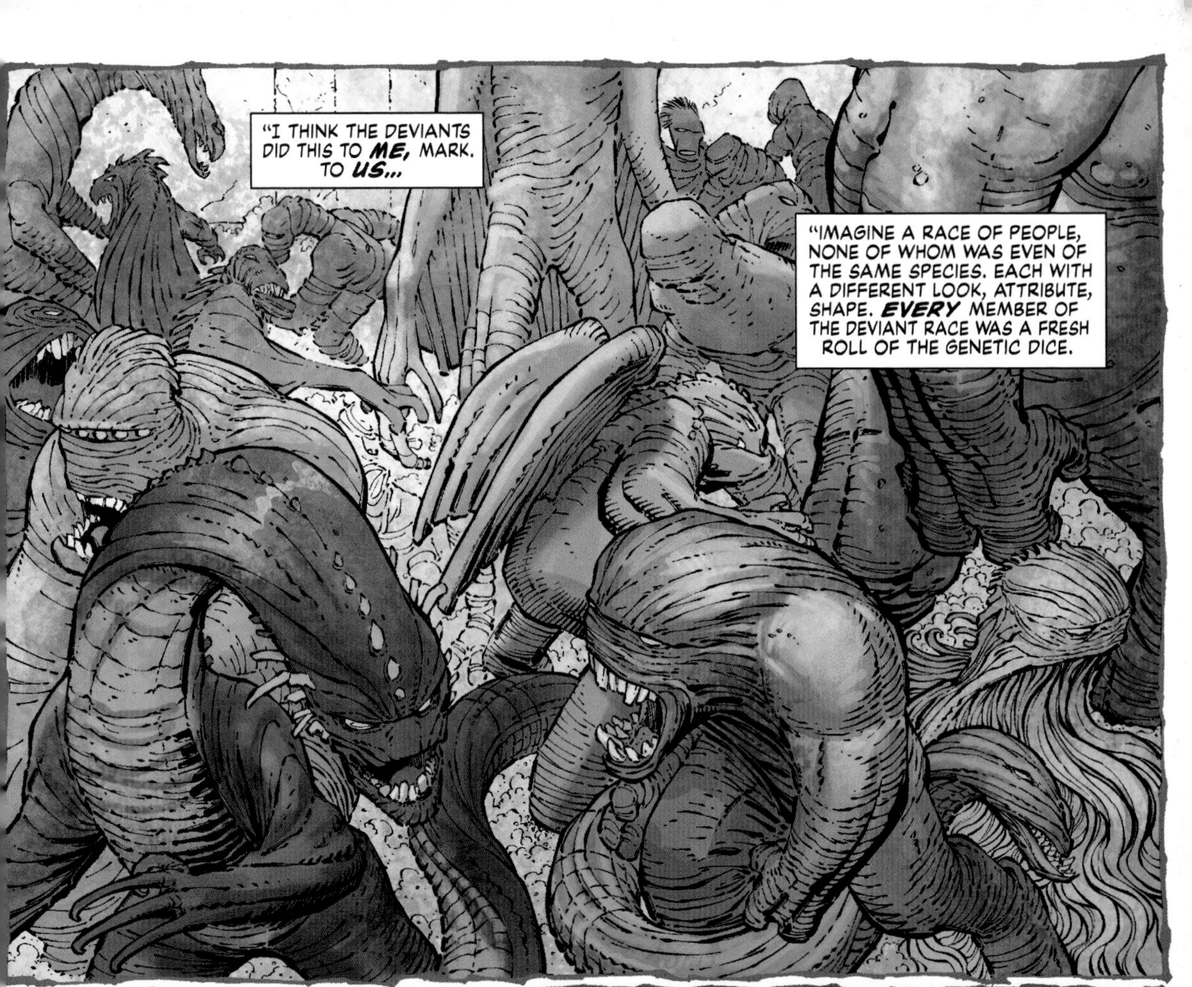
"I THINK THE DEVIANTS DID THIS TO ME, MARK. TO US...
"IMAGINE A RACE OF PEOPLE, NONE OF WHOM WAS EVEN OF THE SAME SPECIES. EACH WITH A DIFFERENT LOOK, ATTRIBUTE, SHAPE. EVERY MEMBER OF THE DEVIANT RACE WAS A FRESH ROLL OF THE GENETIC DICE.

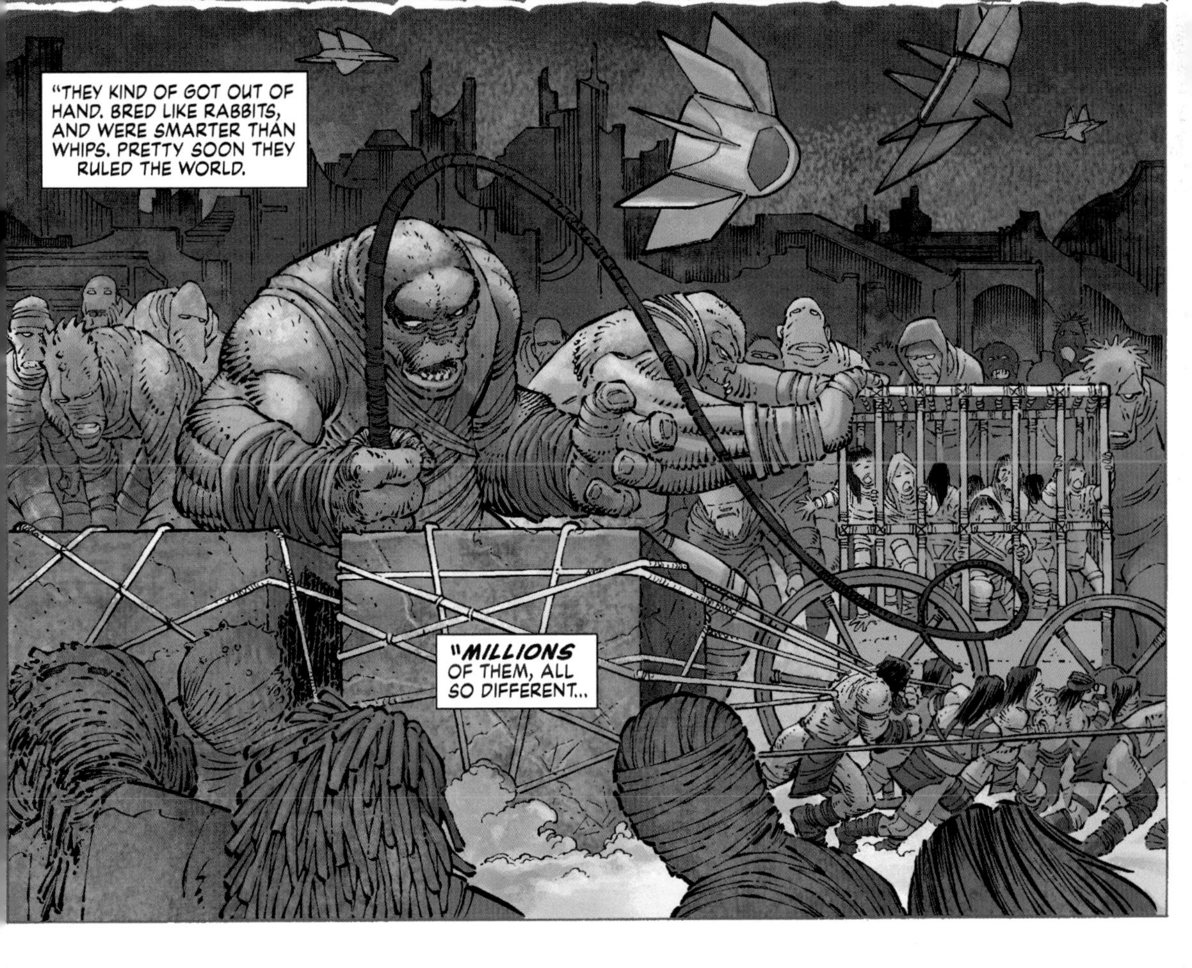
"THEY KIND OF GOT OUT OF HAND. BRED LIKE RABBITS, AND WERE SMARTER THAN WHIPS. PRETTY SOON THEY RULED THE WORLD.
"MILLIONS OF THEM, ALL SO DIFFERENT...

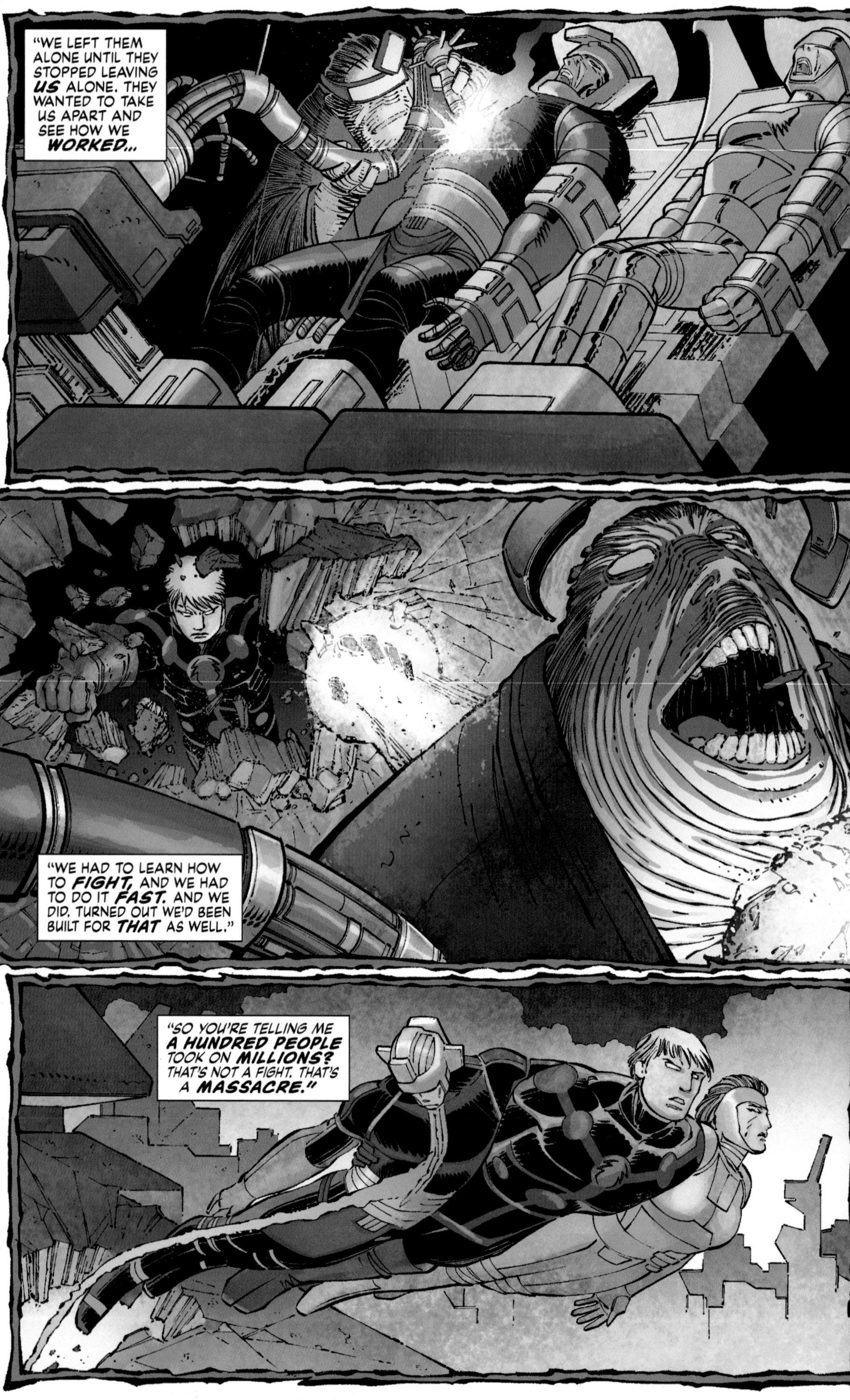
"WE LEFT THEM ALONE UNTIL THEY STOPPED LEAVING US ALONE. THEY WANTED TO TAKE US APART AND SEE HOW WE WORKED...
"WE HAD TO LEARN HOW TO FIGHT, AND WE HAD TO DO IT FAST. AND WE DID. TURNED OUT WE'D BEEN BUILT FOR THAT AS WELL."
"SO YOU'RE TELLING ME A HUNDRED PEOPLE TOOK ON MILLIONS? THAT'S NOT A FIGHT. THAT'S A MASSACRE."

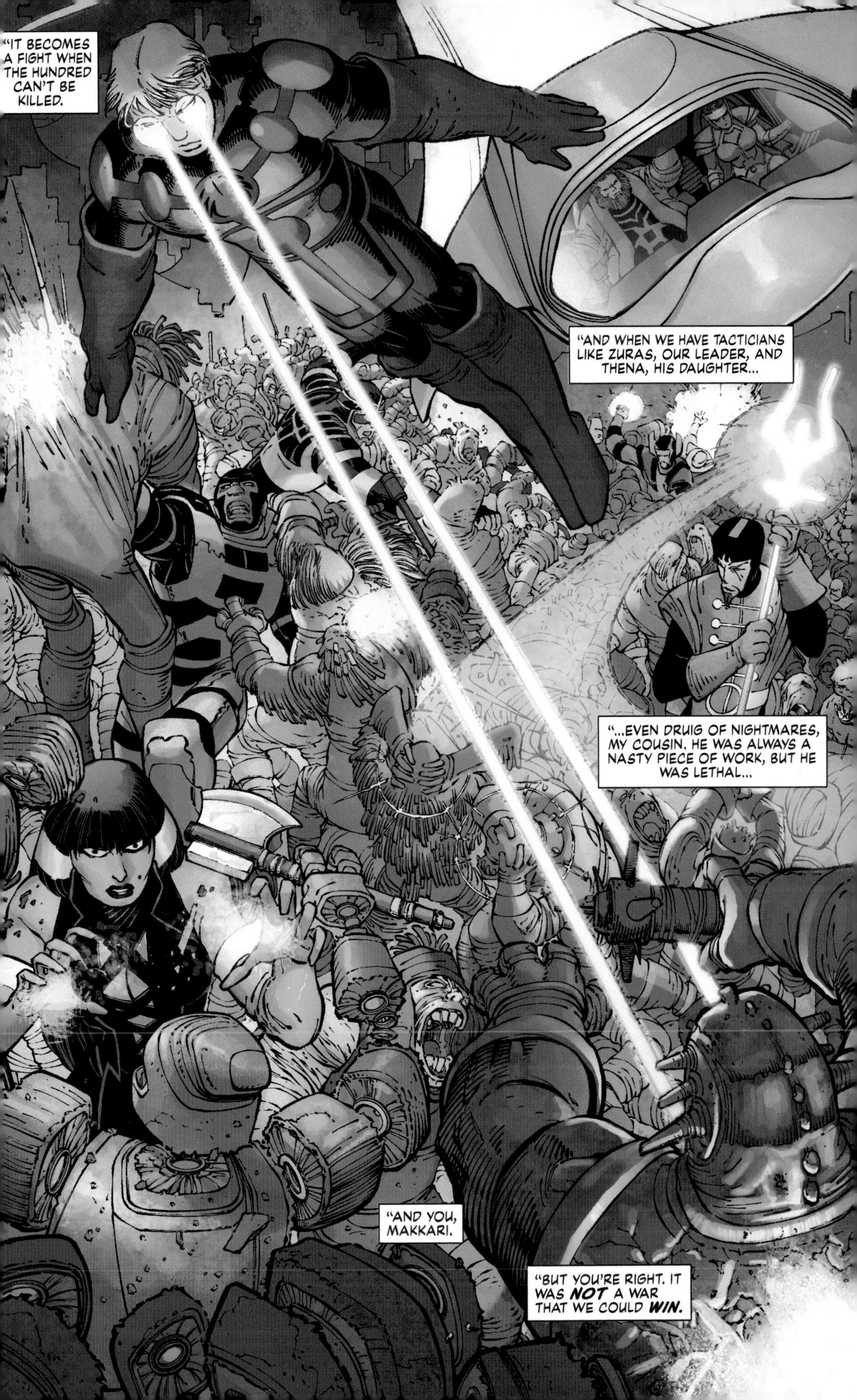
"IT BECOMES A FIGHT WHEN THE HUNDRED CAN'T BE KILLED.
"AND WHEN WE HAVE TACTICIANS LIKE ZURAS, OUR LEADER, AND THENA, HIS DAUGHTER...
"...EVEN DRUIG OF NIGHTMARES, MY COUSIN. HE WAS ALWAYS A NASTY PIECE OF WORK, BUT HE WAS LETHAL...
"AND YOU, MAKKARI.
"BUT YOU'RE RIGHT. IT WAS NOT A WAR THAT WE COULD WIN.

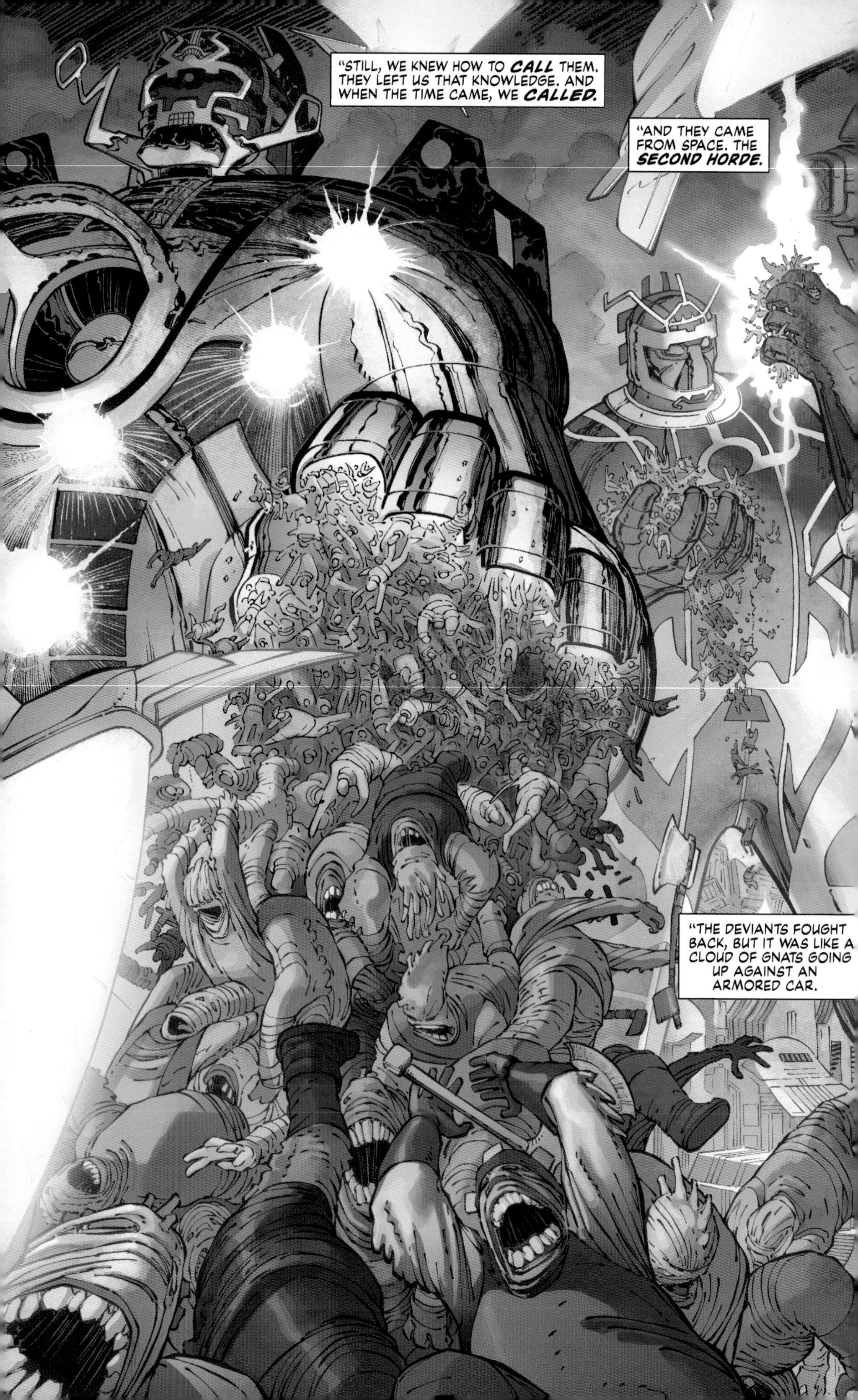
"STILL, WE KNEW HOW TO CALL THEM. THEY LEFT US THAT KNOWLEDGE. AND WHEN THE TIME CAME, WE CALLED.
"AND THEY CAME FROM SPACE. THE SECOND HORDE.
"THE DEVIANTS FOUGHT BACK, BUT IT WAS LIKE A CLOUD OF GNATS GOING UP AGAINST AN ARMORED CAR.

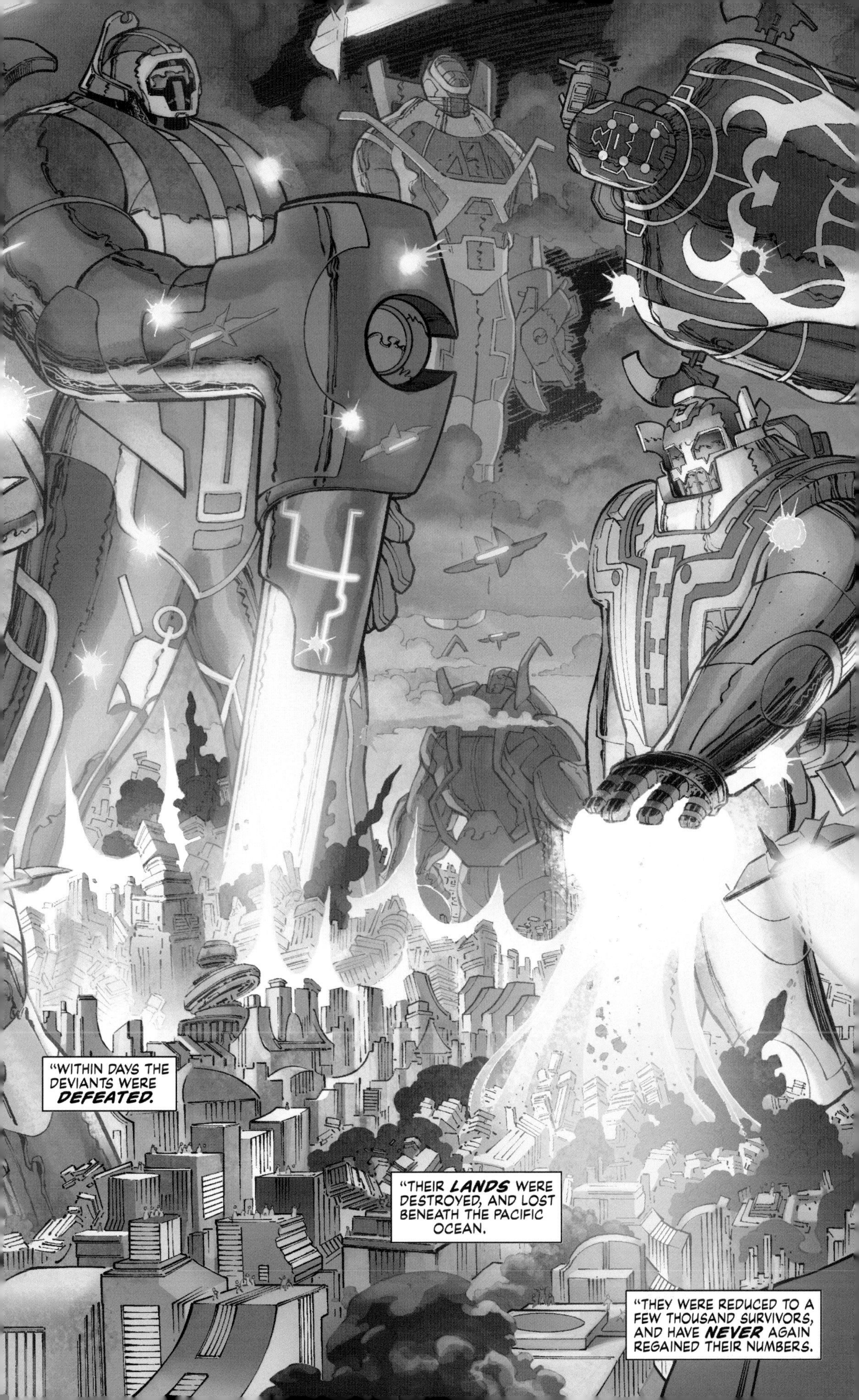
"WITHIN DAYS THE DEVIANTS WERE **DEFEATED.**
"THEIR **LANDS** WERE DESTROYED, AND LOST BENEATH THE PACIFIC OCEAN.
"THEY WERE REDUCED TO A FEW THOUSAND SURVIVORS, AND HAVE **NEVER** AGAIN REGAINED THEIR NUMBERS.

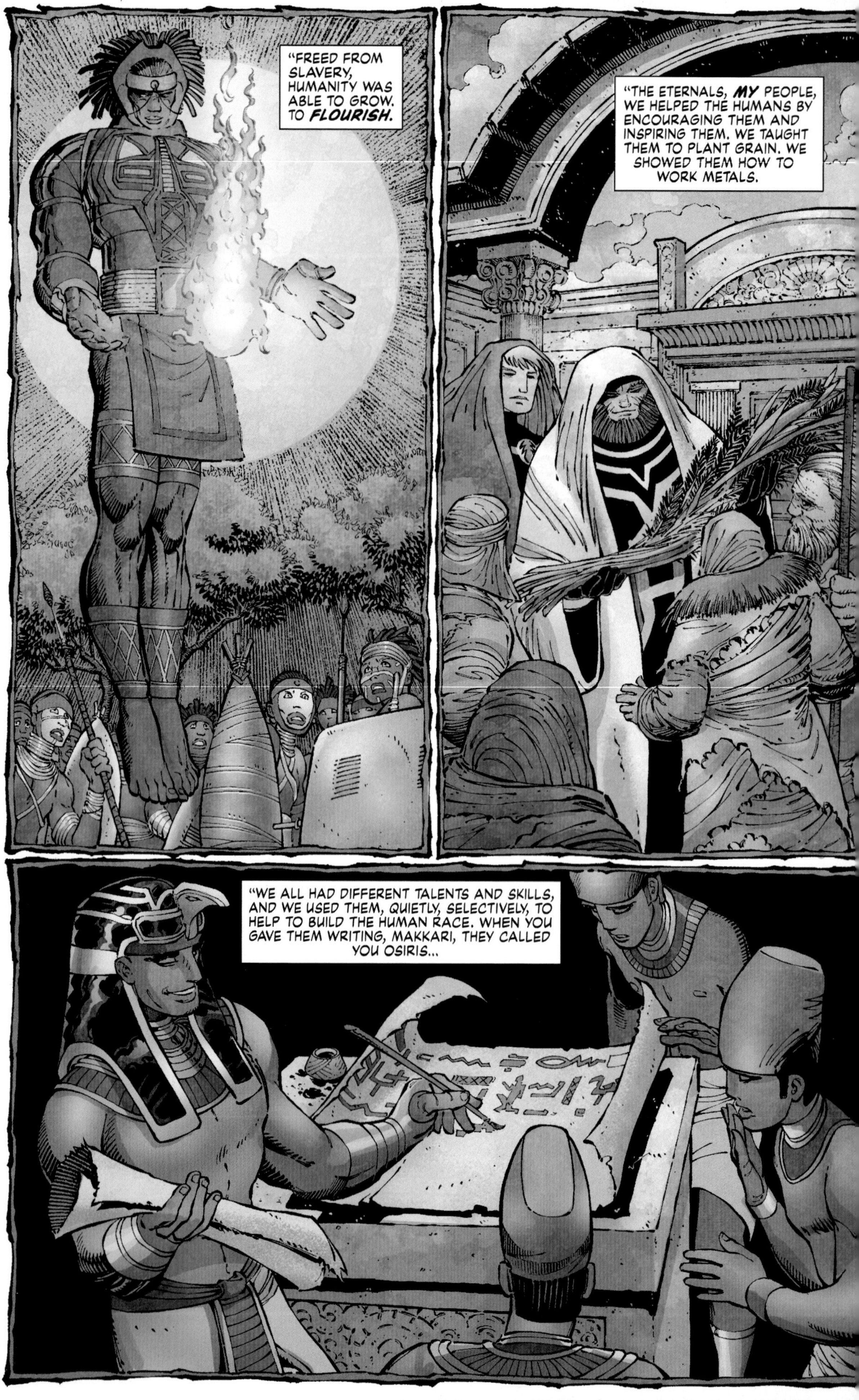
"FREED FROM SLAVERY, HUMANITY WAS ABLE TO GROW. TO *FLOURISH*.
"THE ETERNALS, *MY* PEOPLE, WE HELPED THE HUMANS BY ENCOURAGING THEM AND INSPIRING THEM. WE TAUGHT THEM TO PLANT GRAIN. WE SHOWED THEM HOW TO WORK METALS.
"WE ALL HAD DIFFERENT TALENTS AND SKILLS, AND WE USED THEM, QUIETLY, SELECTIVELY, TO HELP TO BUILD THE HUMAN RACE. WHEN YOU GAVE THEM WRITING, MAKKARI, THEY CALLED YOU OSIRIS...

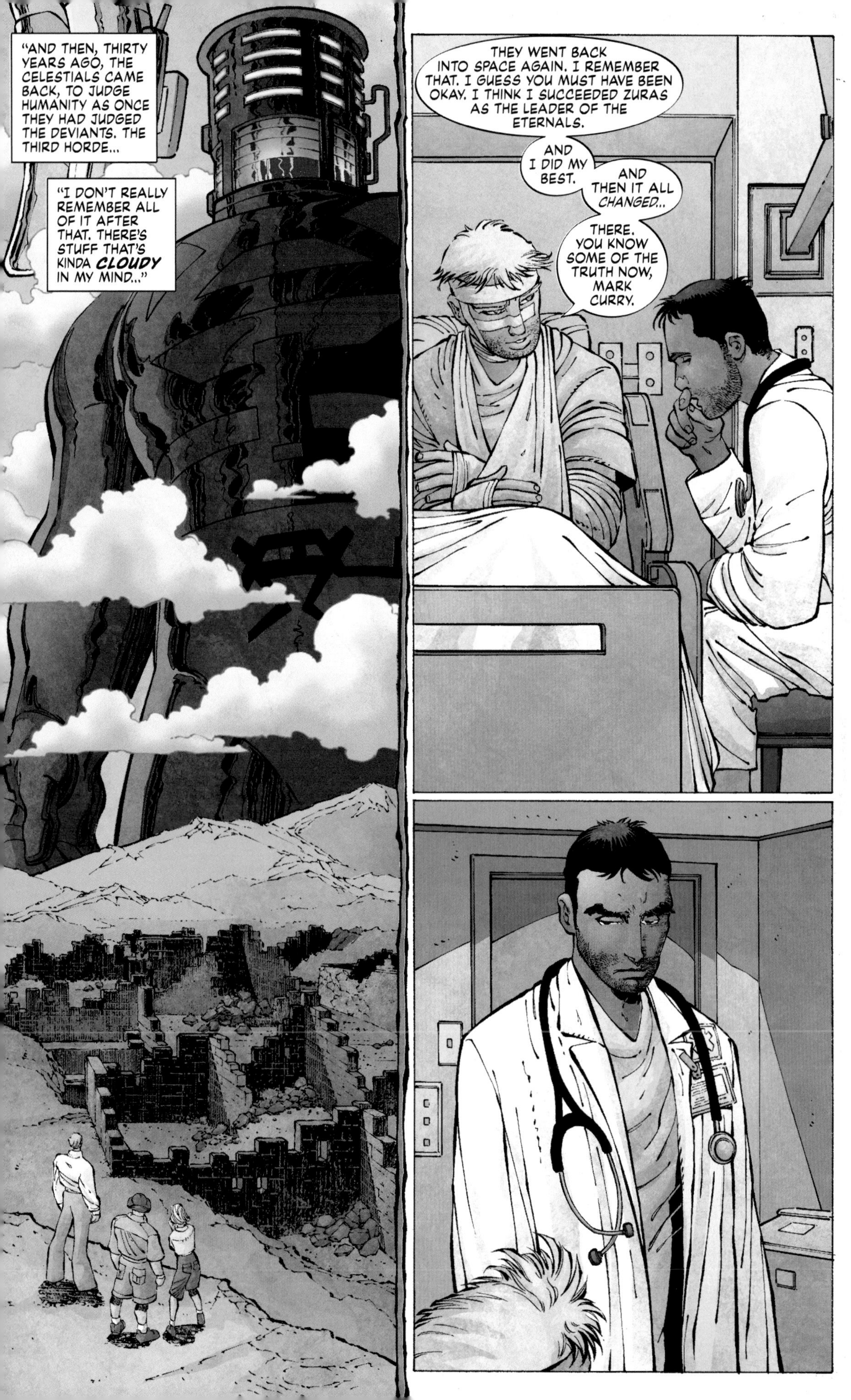
"AND THEN, THIRTY YEARS AGO, THE CELESTIALS CAME BACK, TO JUDGE HUMANITY AS ONCE THEY HAD JUDGED THE DEVIANTS. THE THIRD HORDE...
"I DON'T REALLY REMEMBER ALL OF IT AFTER THAT. THERE'S STUFF THAT'S KINDA CLOUDY IN MY MIND..."
THEY WENT BACK INTO SPACE AGAIN. I REMEMBER THAT. I GUESS YOU MUST HAVE BEEN OKAY. I THINK I SUCCEEDED ZURAS AS THE LEADER OF THE ETERNALS.
AND I DID MY BEST.
AND THEN IT ALL CHANGED...
THERE. YOU KNOW SOME OF THE TRUTH NOW, MARK CURRY.

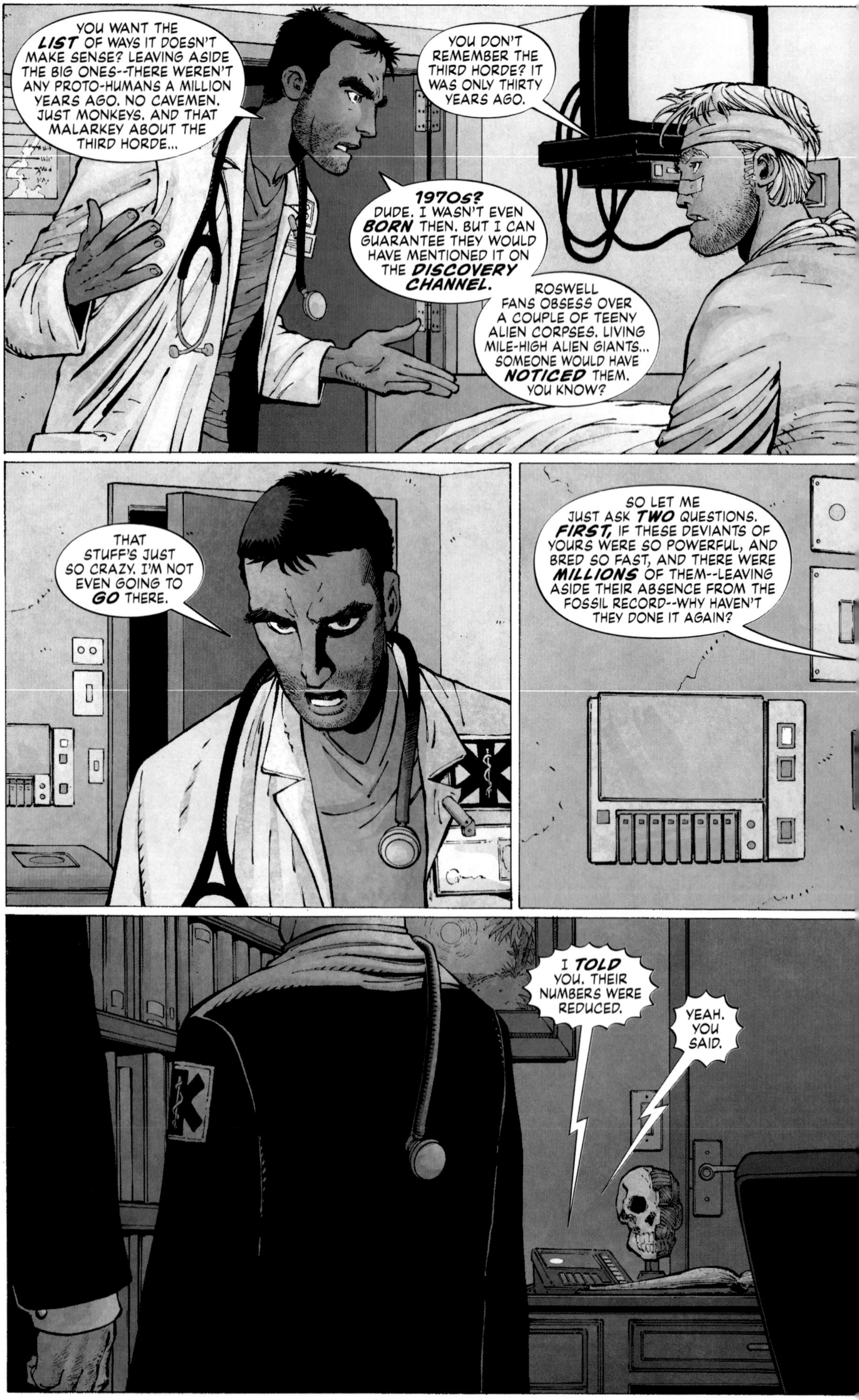
YOU WANT THE LIST OF WAYS IT DOESN'T MAKE SENSE? LEAVING ASIDE THE BIG ONES--THERE WEREN'T ANY PROTO-HUMANS A MILLION YEARS AGO. NO CAVEMEN. JUST MONKEYS. AND THAT MALARKEY ABOUT THE THIRD HORDE...
YOU DON'T REMEMBER THE THIRD HORDE? IT WAS ONLY THIRTY YEARS AGO.
1970s? DUDE. I WASN'T EVEN BORN THEN. BUT I CAN GUARANTEE THEY WOULD HAVE MENTIONED IT ON THE DISCOVERY CHANNEL.
ROSWELL FANS OBSESS OVER A COUPLE OF TEENY ALIEN CORPSES. LIVING MILE-HIGH ALIEN GIANTS... SOMEONE WOULD HAVE NOTICED THEM. YOU KNOW?
THAT STUFF'S JUST SO CRAZY. I'M NOT EVEN GOING TO GO THERE.
SO LET ME JUST ASK TWO QUESTIONS. FIRST, IF THESE DEVIANTS OF YOURS WERE SO POWERFUL, AND BRED SO FAST, AND THERE WERE MILLIONS OF THEM--LEAVING ASIDE THEIR ABSENCE FROM THE FOSSIL RECORD--WHY HAVEN'T THEY DONE IT AGAIN?
I TOLD YOU. THEIR NUMBERS WERE REDUCED.
YEAH. YOU SAID.

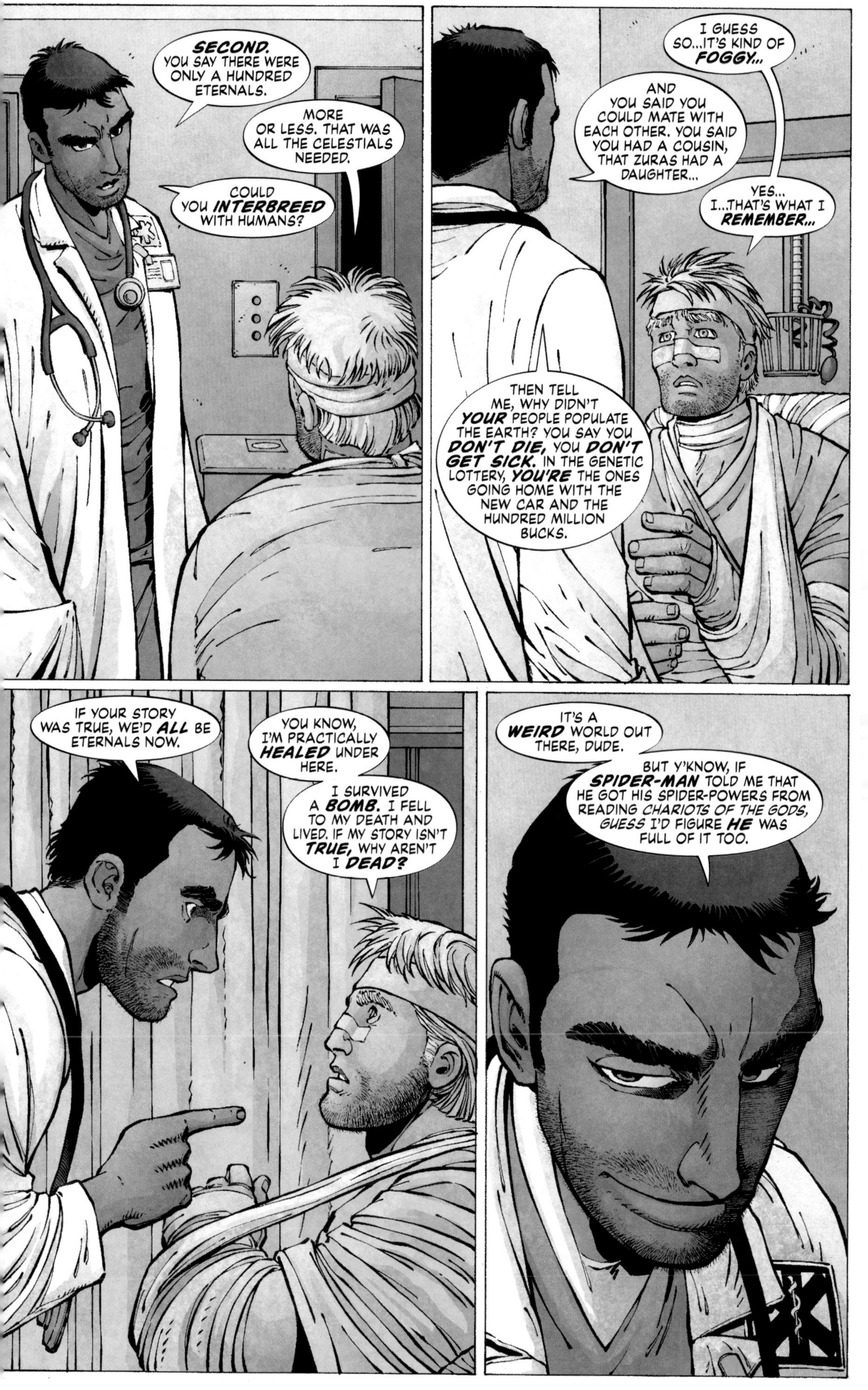

SECOND. YOU SAY THERE WERE ONLY A HUNDRED ETERNALS.
MORE OR LESS. THAT WAS ALL THE CELESTIALS NEEDED.
COULD YOU INTERBREED WITH HUMANS?
I GUESS SO...IT'S KIND OF FOGGY...
AND YOU SAID YOU COULD MATE WITH EACH OTHER. YOU SAID YOU HAD A COUSIN, THAT ZURAS HAD A DAUGHTER...
YES... I...THAT'S WHAT I REMEMBER...
THEN TELL ME, WHY DIDN'T YOUR PEOPLE POPULATE THE EARTH? YOU SAY YOU DON'T DIE, YOU DON'T GET SICK. IN THE GENETIC LOTTERY, YOU'RE THE ONES GOING HOME WITH THE NEW CAR AND THE HUNDRED MILLION BUCKS.
IF YOUR STORY WAS TRUE, WE'D ALL BE ETERNALS NOW.
YOU KNOW, I'M PRACTICALLY HEALED UNDER HERE.
I SURVIVED A BOMB. I FELL TO MY DEATH AND LIVED. IF MY STORY ISN'T TRUE, WHY AREN'T I DEAD?
IT'S A WEIRD WORLD OUT THERE, DUDE.
BUT Y'KNOW, IF SPIDER-MAN TOLD ME THAT HE GOT HIS SPIDER-POWERS FROM READING CHARIOTS OF THE GODS, GUESS I'D FIGURE HE WAS FULL OF IT TOO.

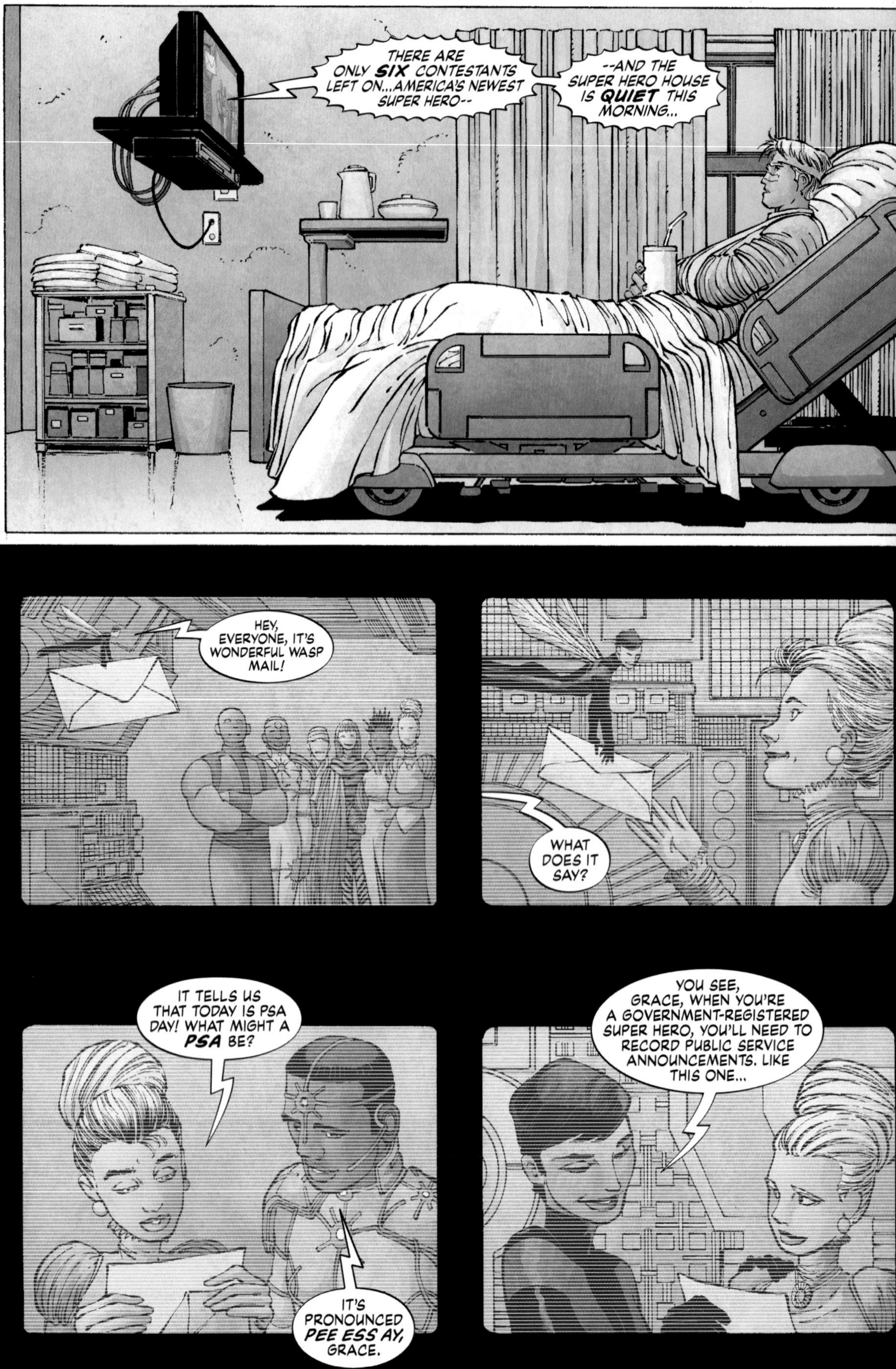
THERE ARE ONLY SIX CONTESTANTS LEFT ON...AMERICA'S NEWEST SUPER HERO--
--AND THE SUPER HERO HOUSE IS QUIET THIS MORNING...
HEY, EVERYONE, IT'S WONDERFUL WASP MAIL!
WHAT DOES IT SAY?
IT TELLS US THAT TODAY IS PSA DAY! WHAT MIGHT A PSA BE?
IT'S PRONOUNCED PEE ESS AY, GRACE.
YOU SEE, GRACE, WHEN YOU'RE A GOVERNMENT-REGISTERED SUPER HERO, YOU'LL NEED TO RECORD PUBLIC SERVICE ANNOUNCEMENTS. LIKE THIS ONE...

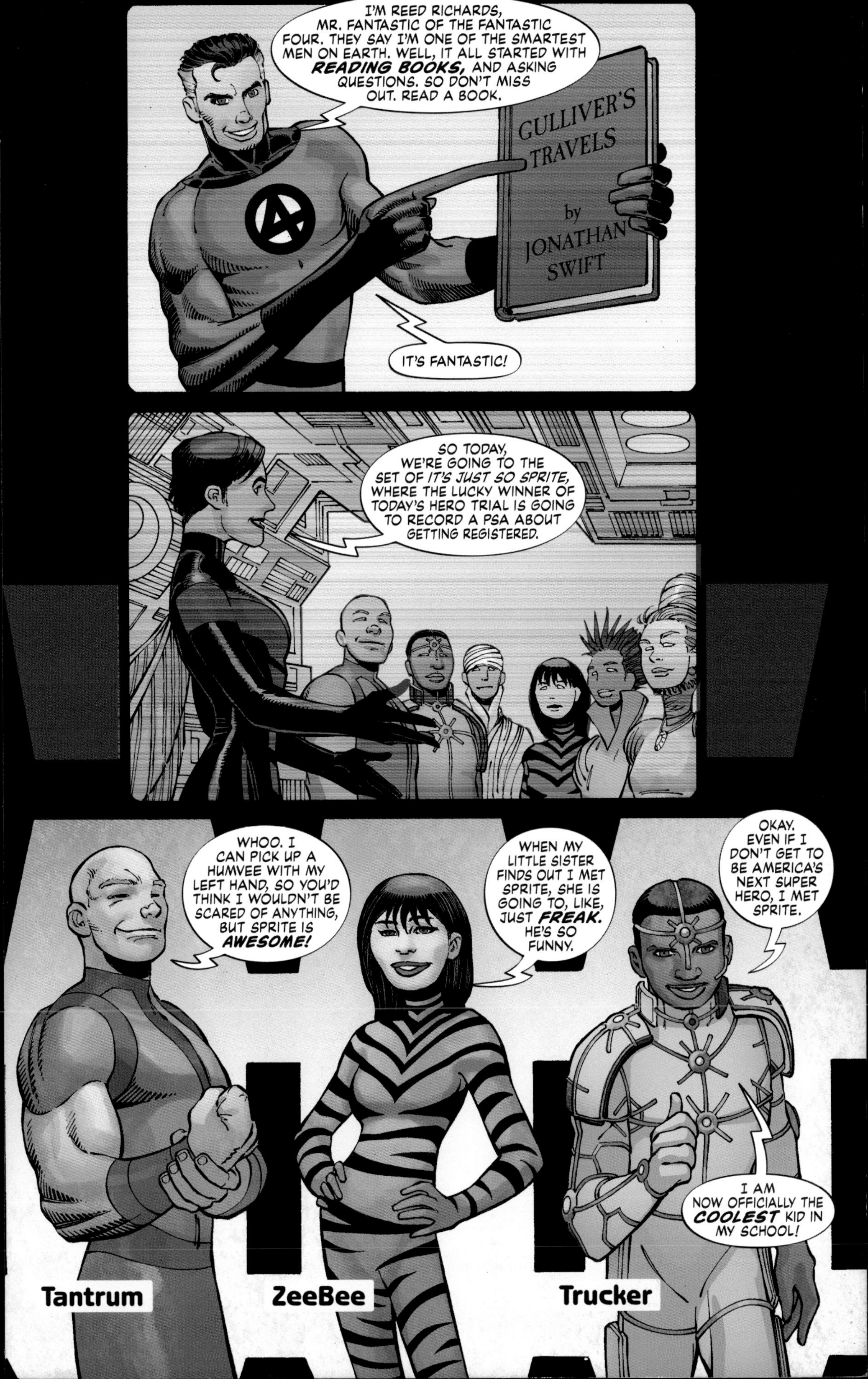

I'M REED RICHARDS, MR. FANTASTIC OF THE FANTASTIC FOUR. THEY SAY I'M ONE OF THE SMARTEST MEN ON EARTH. WELL, IT ALL STARTED WITH READING BOOKS, AND ASKING QUESTIONS. SO DON'T MISS OUT. READ A BOOK.
GULLIVER'S TRAVELS by JONATHAN SWIFT
IT'S FANTASTIC!
SO TODAY, WE'RE GOING TO THE SET OF IT'S JUST SO SPRITE, WHERE THE LUCKY WINNER OF TODAY'S HERO TRIAL IS GOING TO RECORD A PSA ABOUT GETTING REGISTERED.
WHOO. I CAN PICK UP A HUMVEE WITH MY LEFT HAND, SO YOU'D THINK I WOULDN'T BE SCARED OF ANYTHING, BUT SPRITE IS AWESOME!
WHEN MY LITTLE SISTER FINDS OUT I MET SPRITE, SHE IS GOING TO, LIKE, JUST FREAK. HE'S SO FUNNY.
OKAY. EVEN IF I DON'T GET TO BE AMERICA'S NEXT SUPER HERO, I MET SPRITE.
I AM NOW OFFICIALLY THE COOLEST KID IN MY SCHOOL!
Tantrum
ZeeBee
Trucker

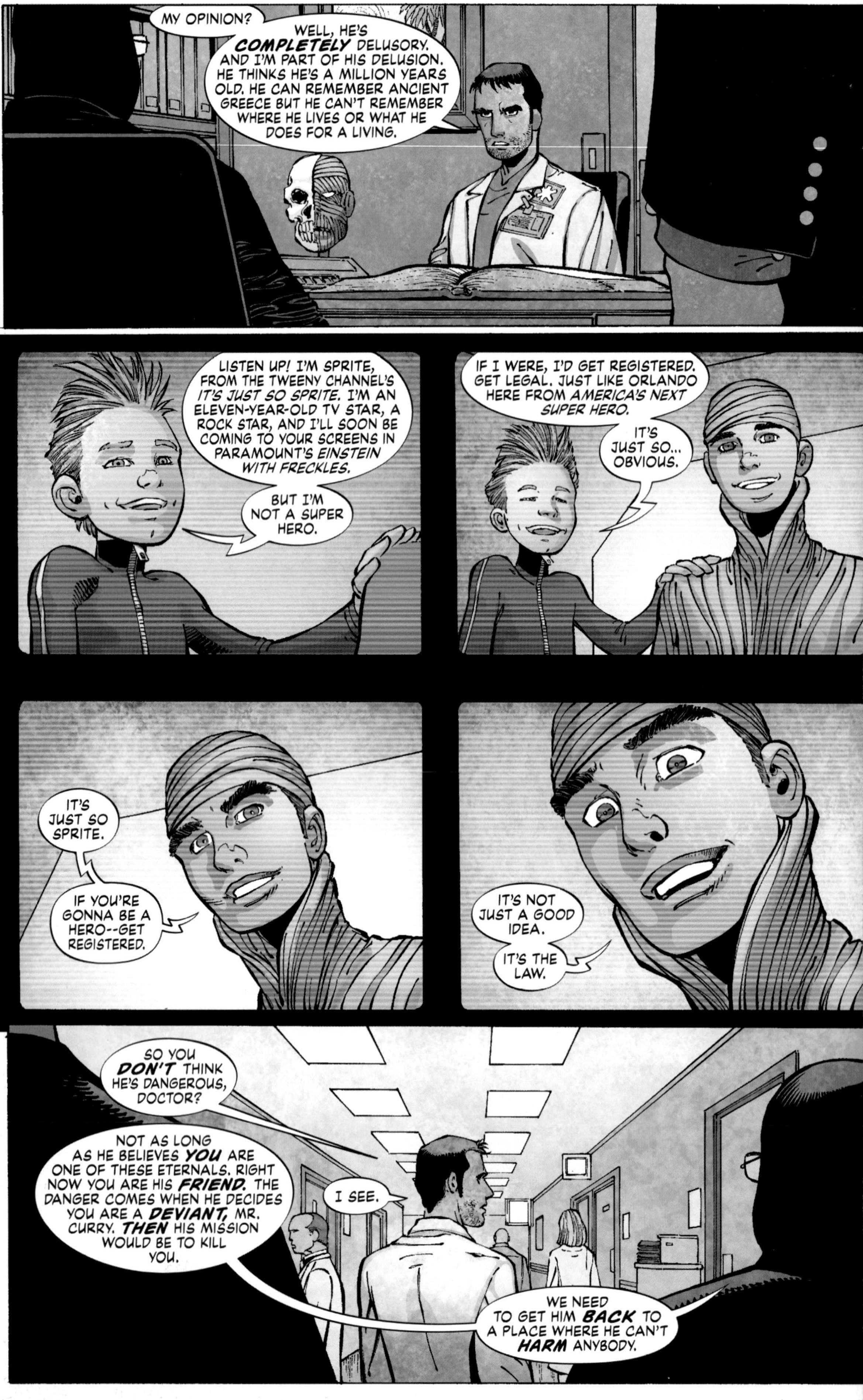
MY OPINION?
WELL, HE'S COMPLETELY DELUSORY. AND I'M PART OF HIS DELUSION. HE THINKS HE'S A MILLION YEARS OLD. HE CAN REMEMBER ANCIENT GREECE BUT HE CAN'T REMEMBER WHERE HE LIVES OR WHAT HE DOES FOR A LIVING.
LISTEN UP! I'M SPRITE, FROM THE TWEENY CHANNEL'S IT'S JUST SO SPRITE. I'M AN ELEVEN-YEAR-OLD TV STAR, A ROCK STAR, AND I'LL SOON BE COMING TO YOUR SCREENS IN PARAMOUNT'S EINSTEIN WITH FRECKLES.
BUT I'M NOT A SUPER HERO.
IF I WERE, I'D GET REGISTERED. GET LEGAL. JUST LIKE ORLANDO HERE FROM AMERICA'S NEXT SUPER HERO.
IT'S JUST SO... OBVIOUS.
IT'S JUST SO SPRITE.
IF YOU'RE GONNA BE A HERO--GET REGISTERED.
IT'S NOT JUST A GOOD IDEA.
IT'S THE LAW.
SO YOU DON'T THINK HE'S DANGEROUS, DOCTOR?
NOT AS LONG AS HE BELIEVES YOU ARE ONE OF THESE ETERNALS. RIGHT NOW YOU ARE HIS FRIEND. THE DANGER COMES WHEN HE DECIDES YOU ARE A DEVIANT, MR. CURRY. THEN HIS MISSION WOULD BE TO KILL YOU.
I SEE.
WE NEED TO GET HIM BACK TO A PLACE WHERE HE CAN'T HARM ANYBODY.

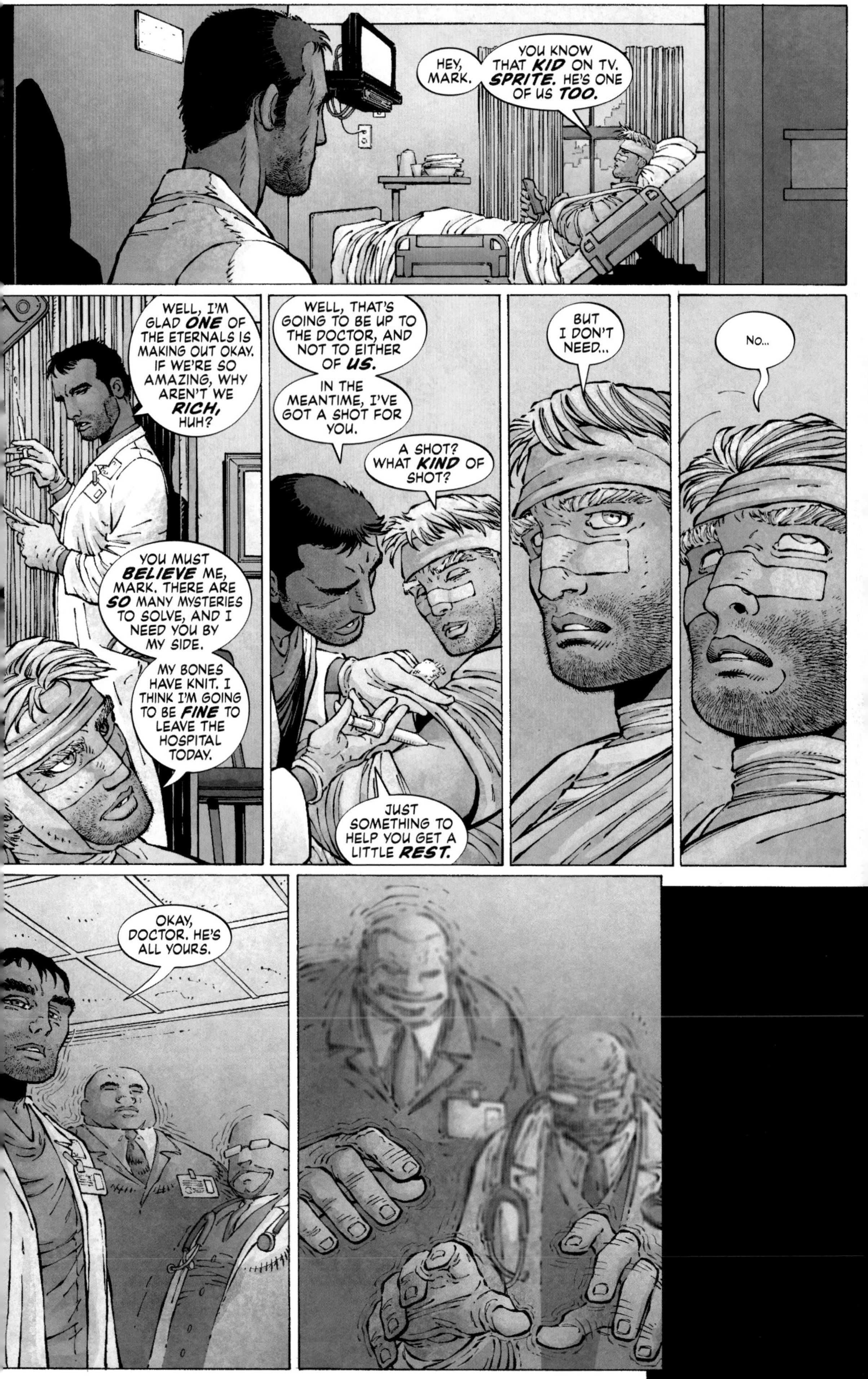
HEY, MARK.
YOU KNOW THAT KID ON TV. SPRITE. HE'S ONE OF US TOO.
WELL, I'M GLAD ONE OF THE ETERNALS IS MAKING OUT OKAY. IF WE'RE SO AMAZING, WHY AREN'T WE RICH, HUH?
YOU MUST BELIEVE ME, MARK. THERE ARE SO MANY MYSTERIES TO SOLVE, AND I NEED YOU BY MY SIDE.
MY BONES HAVE KNIT. I THINK I'M GOING TO BE FINE TO LEAVE THE HOSPITAL TODAY.
WELL, THAT'S GOING TO BE UP TO THE DOCTOR, AND NOT TO EITHER OF US.
IN THE MEANTIME, I'VE GOT A SHOT FOR YOU.
A SHOT? WHAT KIND OF SHOT?
JUST SOMETHING TO HELP YOU GET A LITTLE REST.
BUT I DON'T NEED...
No...
OKAY, DOCTOR. HE'S ALL YOURS.

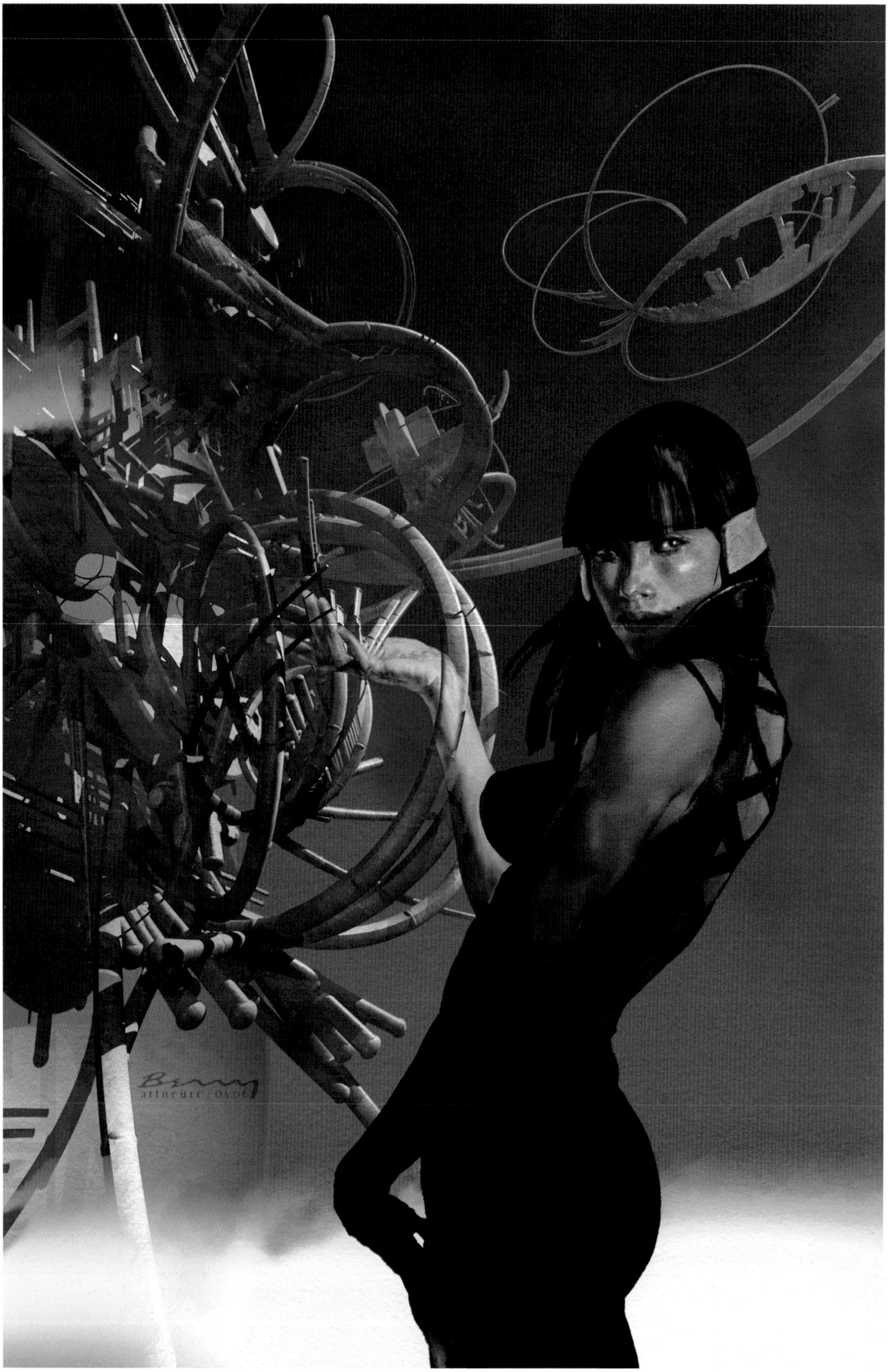

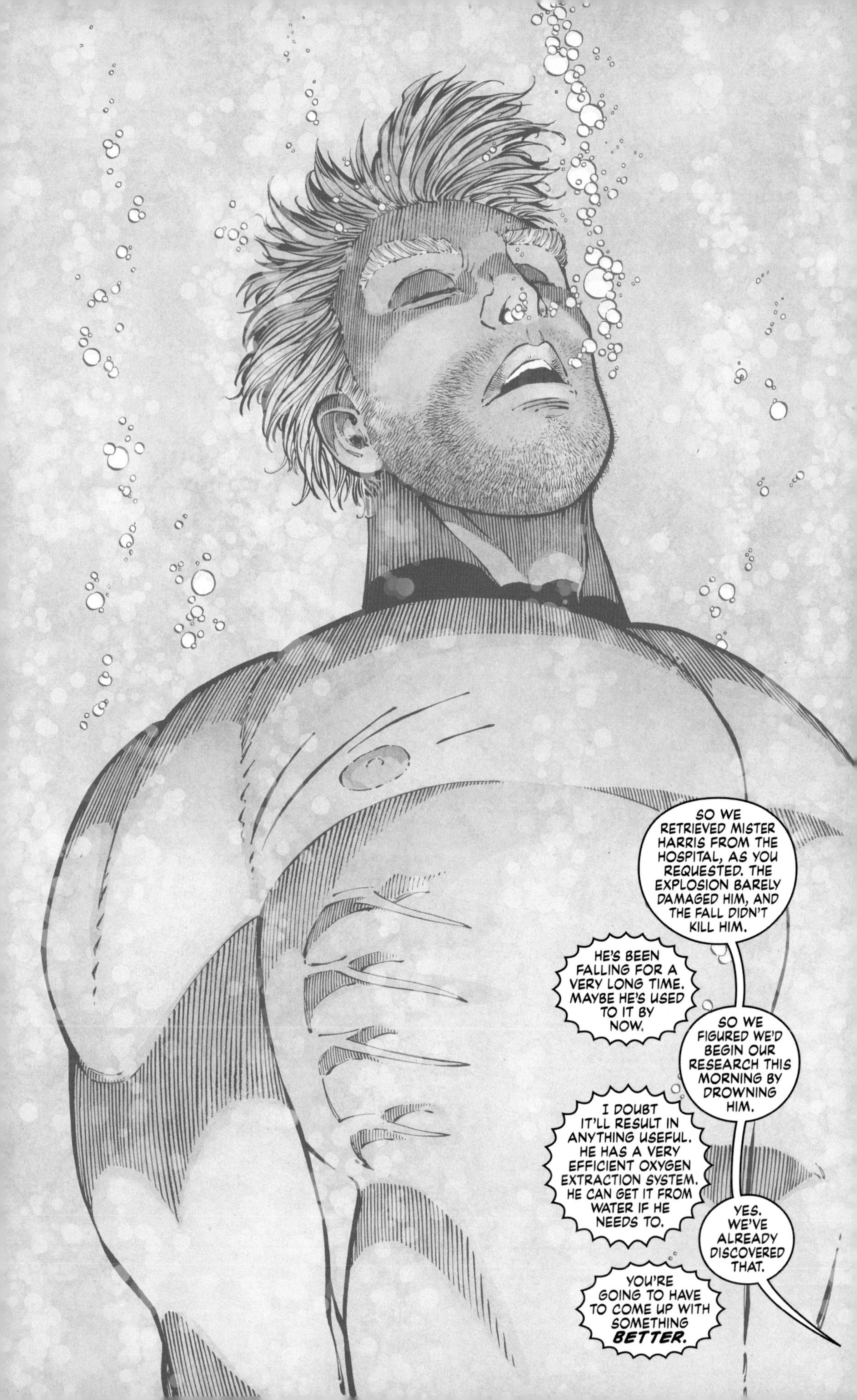
SO WE RETRIEVED MISTER HARRIS FROM THE HOSPITAL, AS YOU REQUESTED. THE EXPLOSION BARELY DAMAGED HIM, AND THE FALL DIDN'T KILL HIM.
HE'S BEEN FALLING FOR A VERY LONG TIME. MAYBE HE'S USED TO IT BY NOW.
SO WE FIGURED WE'D BEGIN OUR RESEARCH THIS MORNING BY DROWNING HIM.
I DOUBT IT'LL RESULT IN ANYTHING USEFUL. HE HAS A VERY EFFICIENT OXYGEN EXTRACTION SYSTEM. HE CAN GET IT FROM WATER IF HE NEEDS TO.
YES. WE'VE ALREADY DISCOVERED THAT.
YOU'RE GOING TO HAVE TO COME UP WITH SOMETHING **BETTER**.

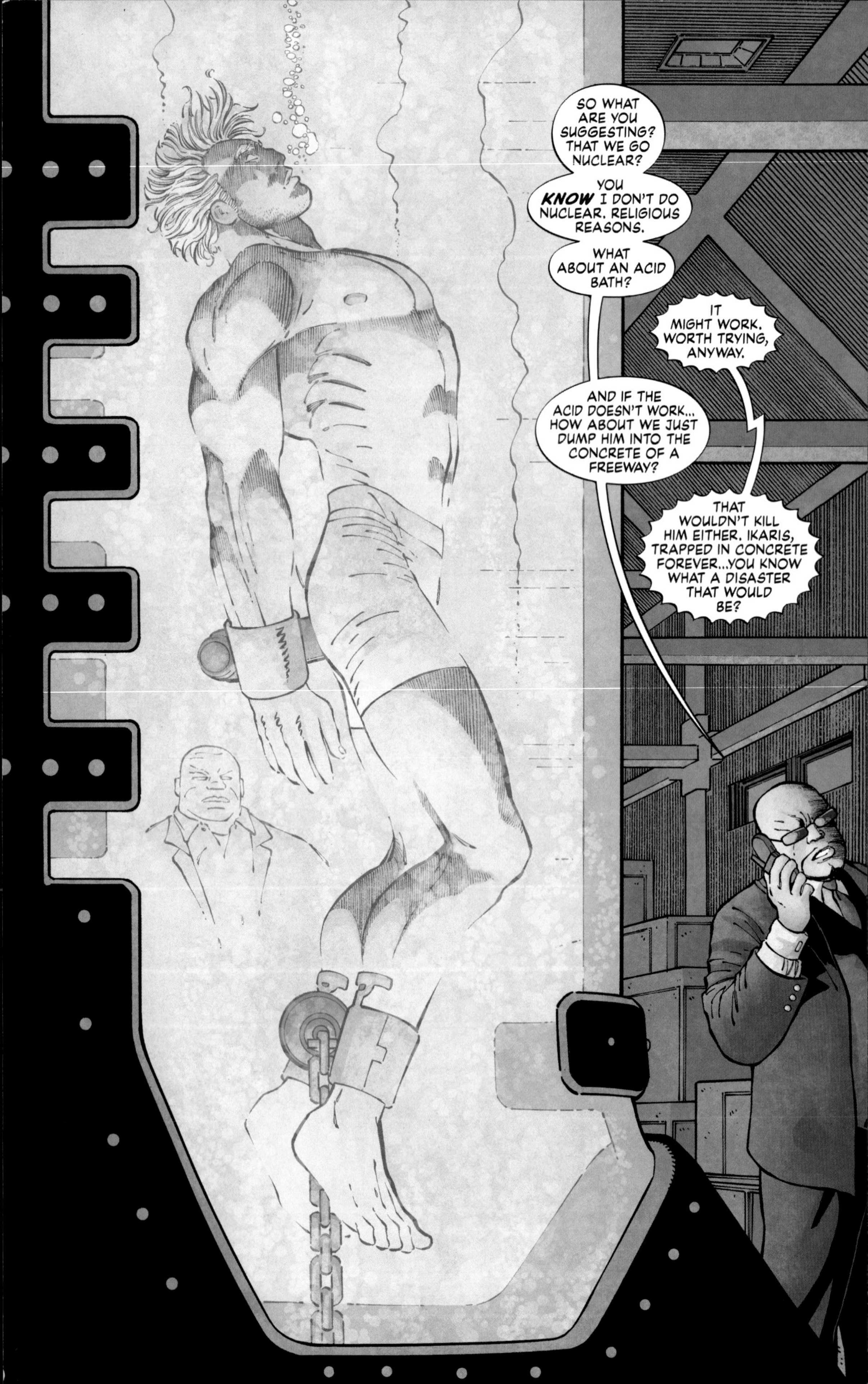
SO WHAT ARE YOU SUGGESTING? THAT WE GO NUCLEAR?
YOU **KNOW** I DON'T DO NUCLEAR. RELIGIOUS REASONS.
WHAT ABOUT AN ACID BATH?
IT MIGHT WORK. WORTH TRYING, ANYWAY.
AND IF THE ACID DOESN'T WORK... HOW ABOUT WE JUST DUMP HIM INTO THE CONCRETE OF A FREEWAY?
THAT WOULDN'T KILL HIM EITHER. IKARIS, TRAPPED IN CONCRETE FOREVER...YOU KNOW WHAT A DISASTER THAT WOULD BE?

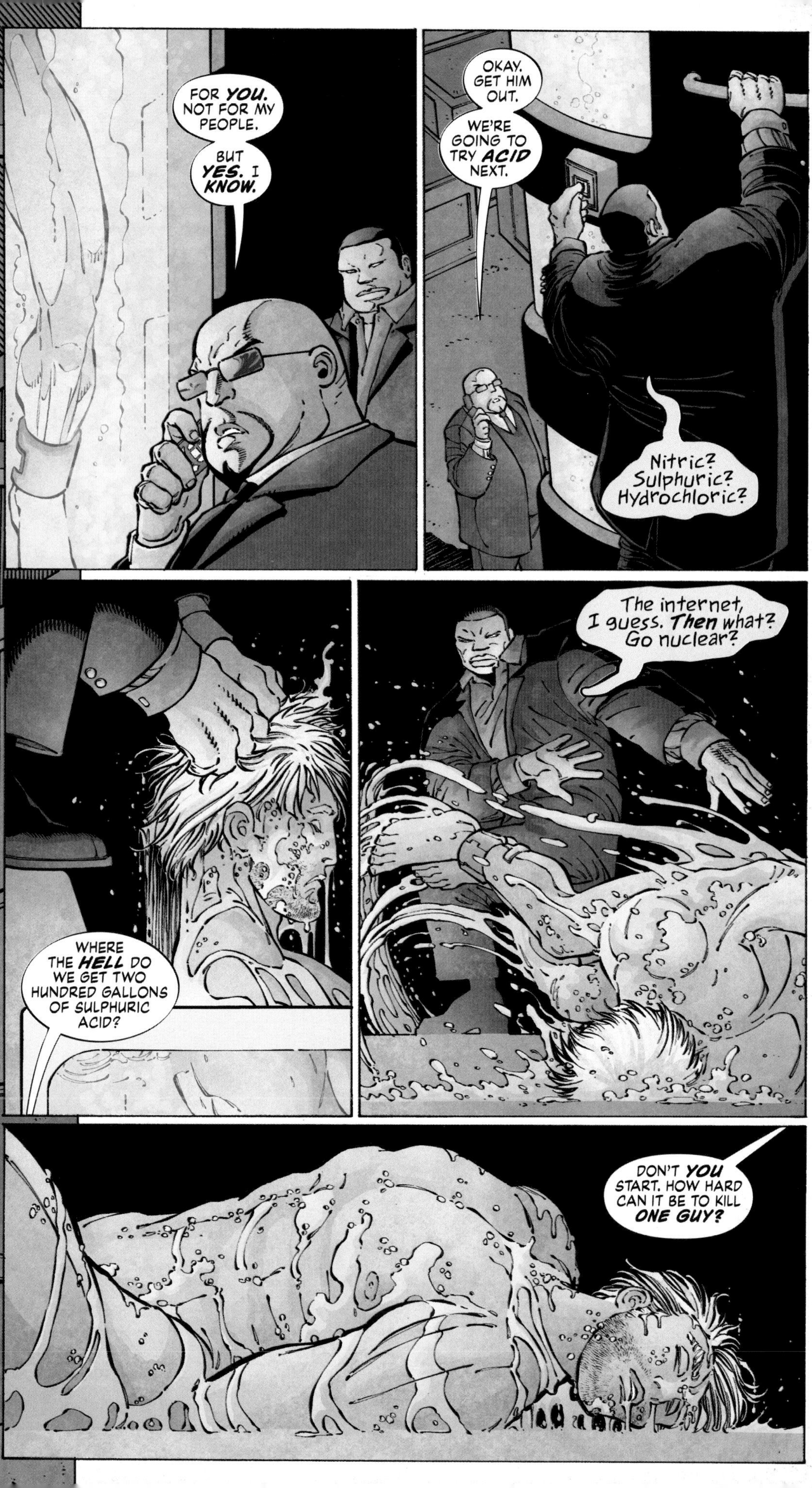
FOR **YOU.** NOT FOR MY PEOPLE.
BUT **YES.** I **KNOW.**
OKAY. GET HIM OUT.
WE'RE GOING TO TRY **ACID** NEXT.
Nitric? Sulphuric? Hydrochloric?
WHERE THE **HELL** DO WE GET TWO HUNDRED GALLONS OF SULPHURIC ACID?
The internet, I guess. **Then** what? Go nuclear?
DON'T **YOU** START. HOW HARD CAN IT BE TO KILL **ONE GUY?**

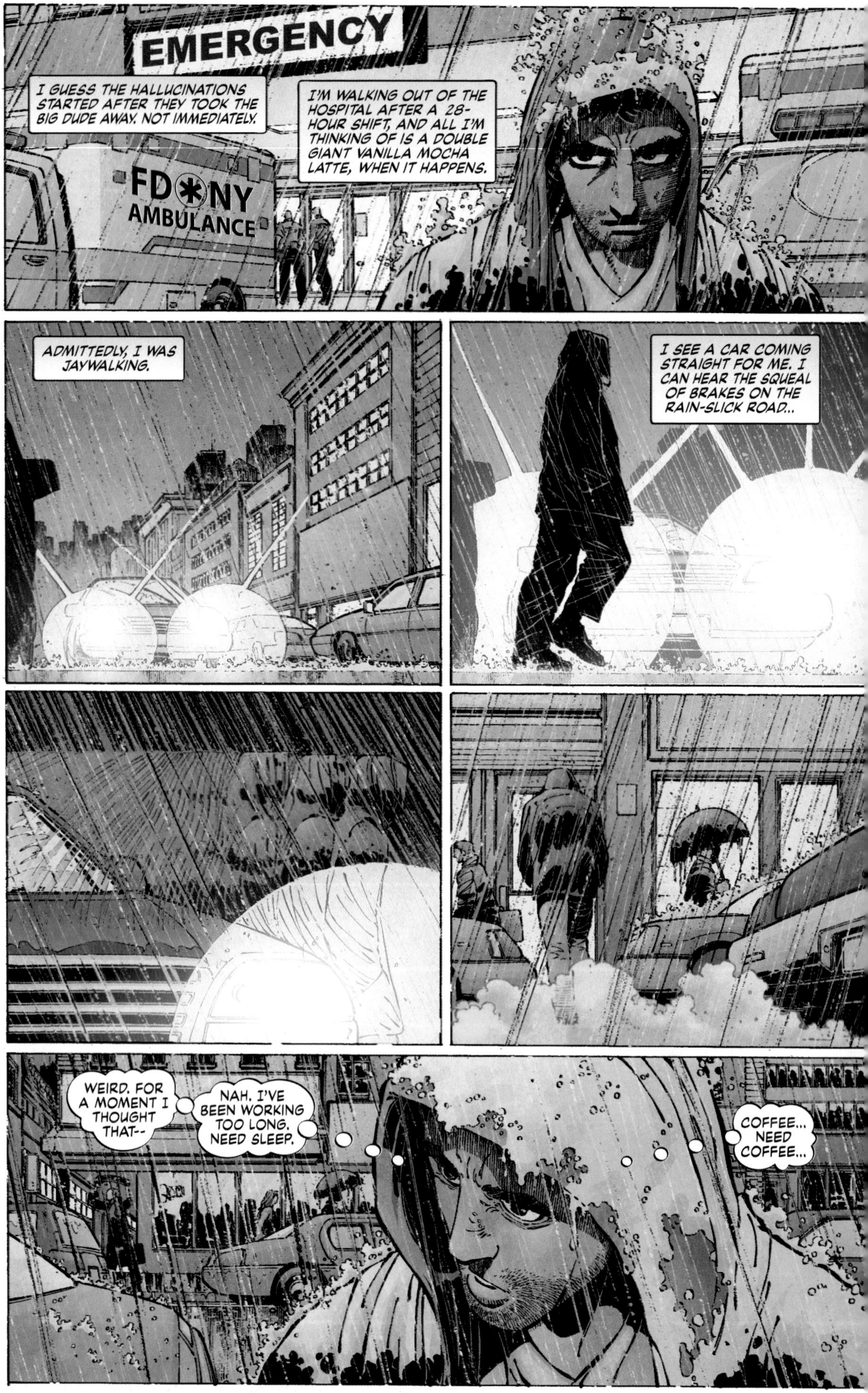
EMERGENCY
I GUESS THE HALLUCINATIONS STARTED AFTER THEY TOOK THE BIG DUDE AWAY. NOT IMMEDIATELY.
I'M WALKING OUT OF THE HOSPITAL AFTER A 28-HOUR SHIFT, AND ALL I'M THINKING OF IS A DOUBLE GIANT VANILLA MOCHA LATTE, WHEN IT HAPPENS.
FD*NY
AMBULANCE
ADMITTEDLY, I WAS JAYWALKING.
I SEE A CAR COMING STRAIGHT FOR ME. I CAN HEAR THE SQUEAL OF BRAKES ON THE RAIN-SLICK ROAD...
WEIRD. FOR A MOMENT I THOUGHT THAT--
NAH. I'VE BEEN WORKING TOO LONG. NEED SLEEP.
COFFEE... NEED COFFEE...

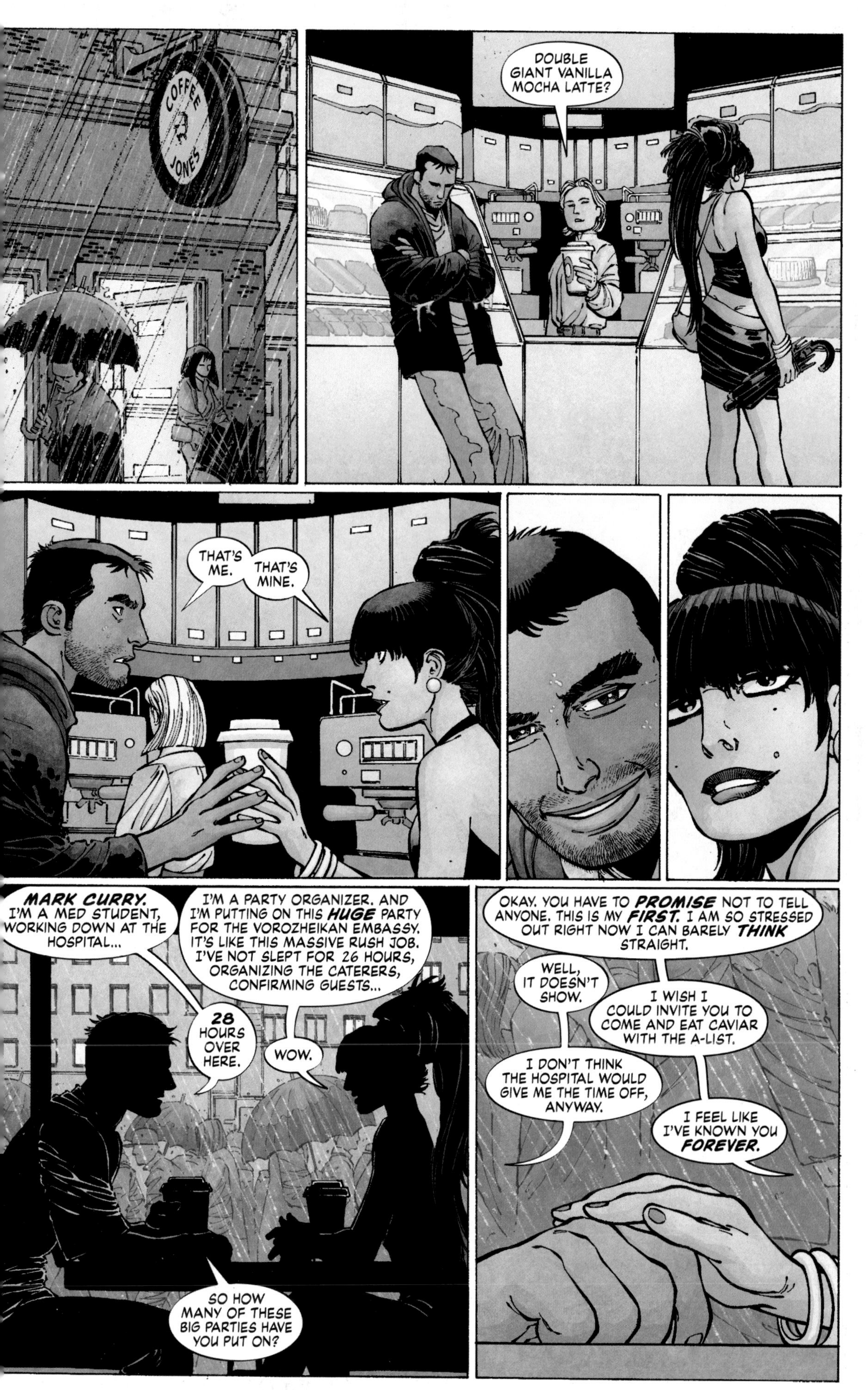
COFFEE JONES
DOUBLE GIANT VANILLA MOCHA LATTE?
THAT'S ME.
THAT'S MINE.
MARK CURRY. I'M A MED STUDENT, WORKING DOWN AT THE HOSPITAL...
I'M A PARTY ORGANIZER. AND I'M PUTTING ON THIS HUGE PARTY FOR THE VOROZHEIKAN EMBASSY. IT'S LIKE THIS MASSIVE RUSH JOB. I'VE NOT SLEPT FOR 26 HOURS, ORGANIZING THE CATERERS, CONFIRMING GUESTS...
28 HOURS OVER HERE.
WOW.
SO HOW MANY OF THESE BIG PARTIES HAVE YOU PUT ON?
OKAY. YOU HAVE TO PROMISE NOT TO TELL ANYONE. THIS IS MY FIRST. I AM SO STRESSED OUT RIGHT NOW I CAN BARELY THINK STRAIGHT.
WELL, IT DOESN'T SHOW.
I WISH I COULD INVITE YOU TO COME AND EAT CAVIAR WITH THE A-LIST.
I DON'T THINK THE HOSPITAL WOULD GIVE ME THE TIME OFF, ANYWAY.
I FEEL LIKE I'VE KNOWN YOU FOREVER.

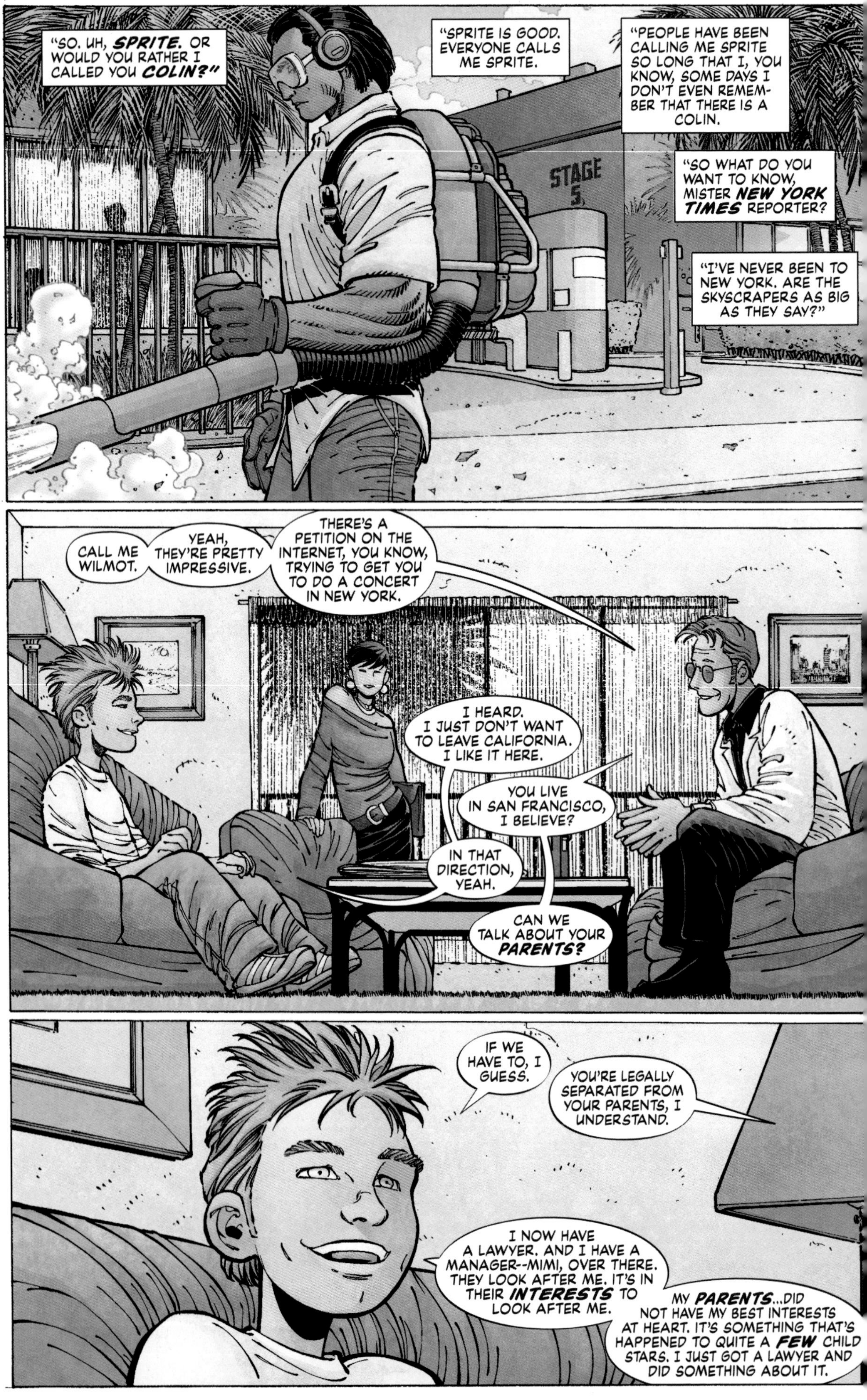
"SO. UH, SPRITE. OR WOULD YOU RATHER I CALLED YOU COLIN?"
"SPRITE IS GOOD. EVERYONE CALLS ME SPRITE.
"PEOPLE HAVE BEEN CALLING ME SPRITE SO LONG THAT I, YOU KNOW, SOME DAYS I DON'T EVEN REMEMBER THAT THERE IS A COLIN.
STAGE 5
"SO WHAT DO YOU WANT TO KNOW, MISTER NEW YORK TIMES REPORTER?
"I'VE NEVER BEEN TO NEW YORK. ARE THE SKYSCRAPERS AS BIG AS THEY SAY?"
CALL ME WILMOT.
YEAH, THEY'RE PRETTY IMPRESSIVE.
THERE'S A PETITION ON THE INTERNET, YOU KNOW, TRYING TO GET YOU TO DO A CONCERT IN NEW YORK.
I HEARD. I JUST DON'T WANT TO LEAVE CALIFORNIA. I LIKE IT HERE.
YOU LIVE IN SAN FRANCISCO, I BELIEVE?
IN THAT DIRECTION, YEAH.
CAN WE TALK ABOUT YOUR PARENTS?
IF WE HAVE TO, I GUESS.
YOU'RE LEGALLY SEPARATED FROM YOUR PARENTS, I UNDERSTAND.
I NOW HAVE A LAWYER. AND I HAVE A MANAGER--MIMI, OVER THERE. THEY LOOK AFTER ME. IT'S IN THEIR INTERESTS TO LOOK AFTER ME.
MY PARENTS...DID NOT HAVE MY BEST INTERESTS AT HEART. IT'S SOMETHING THAT'S HAPPENED TO QUITE A FEW CHILD STARS. I JUST GOT A LAWYER AND DID SOMETHING ABOUT IT.

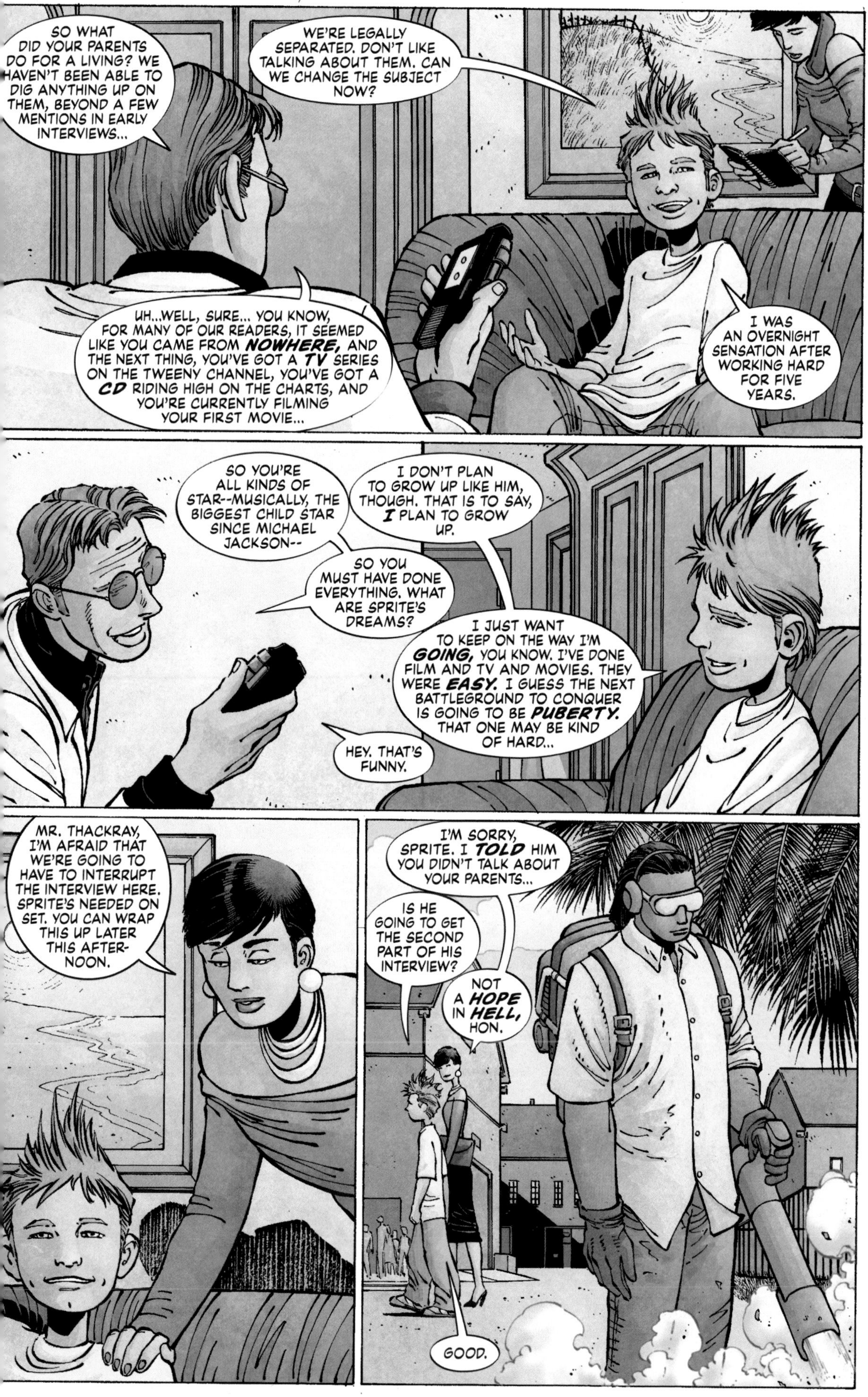
SO WHAT DID YOUR PARENTS DO FOR A LIVING? WE HAVEN'T BEEN ABLE TO DIG ANYTHING UP ON THEM, BEYOND A FEW MENTIONS IN EARLY INTERVIEWS...
WE'RE LEGALLY SEPARATED. DON'T LIKE TALKING ABOUT THEM. CAN WE CHANGE THE SUBJECT NOW?
UH...WELL, SURE... YOU KNOW, FOR MANY OF OUR READERS, IT SEEMED LIKE YOU CAME FROM NOWHERE, AND THE NEXT THING, YOU'VE GOT A TV SERIES ON THE TWEENY CHANNEL, YOU'VE GOT A CD RIDING HIGH ON THE CHARTS, AND YOU'RE CURRENTLY FILMING YOUR FIRST MOVIE...
I WAS AN OVERNIGHT SENSATION AFTER WORKING HARD FOR FIVE YEARS.
SO YOU'RE ALL KINDS OF STAR--MUSICALLY, THE BIGGEST CHILD STAR SINCE MICHAEL JACKSON--
I DON'T PLAN TO GROW UP LIKE HIM, THOUGH. THAT IS TO SAY, I PLAN TO GROW UP.
SO YOU MUST HAVE DONE EVERYTHING. WHAT ARE SPRITE'S DREAMS?
I JUST WANT TO KEEP ON THE WAY I'M GOING, YOU KNOW. I'VE DONE FILM AND TV AND MOVIES. THEY WERE EASY. I GUESS THE NEXT BATTLEGROUND TO CONQUER IS GOING TO BE PUBERTY. THAT ONE MAY BE KIND OF HARD...
HEY. THAT'S FUNNY.
MR. THACKRAY, I'M AFRAID THAT WE'RE GOING TO HAVE TO INTERRUPT THE INTERVIEW HERE. SPRITE'S NEEDED ON SET. YOU CAN WRAP THIS UP LATER THIS AFTER-NOON.
I'M SORRY, SPRITE. I TOLD HIM YOU DIDN'T TALK ABOUT YOUR PARENTS...
IS HE GOING TO GET THE SECOND PART OF HIS INTERVIEW?
NOT A HOPE IN HELL, HON.
GOOD.

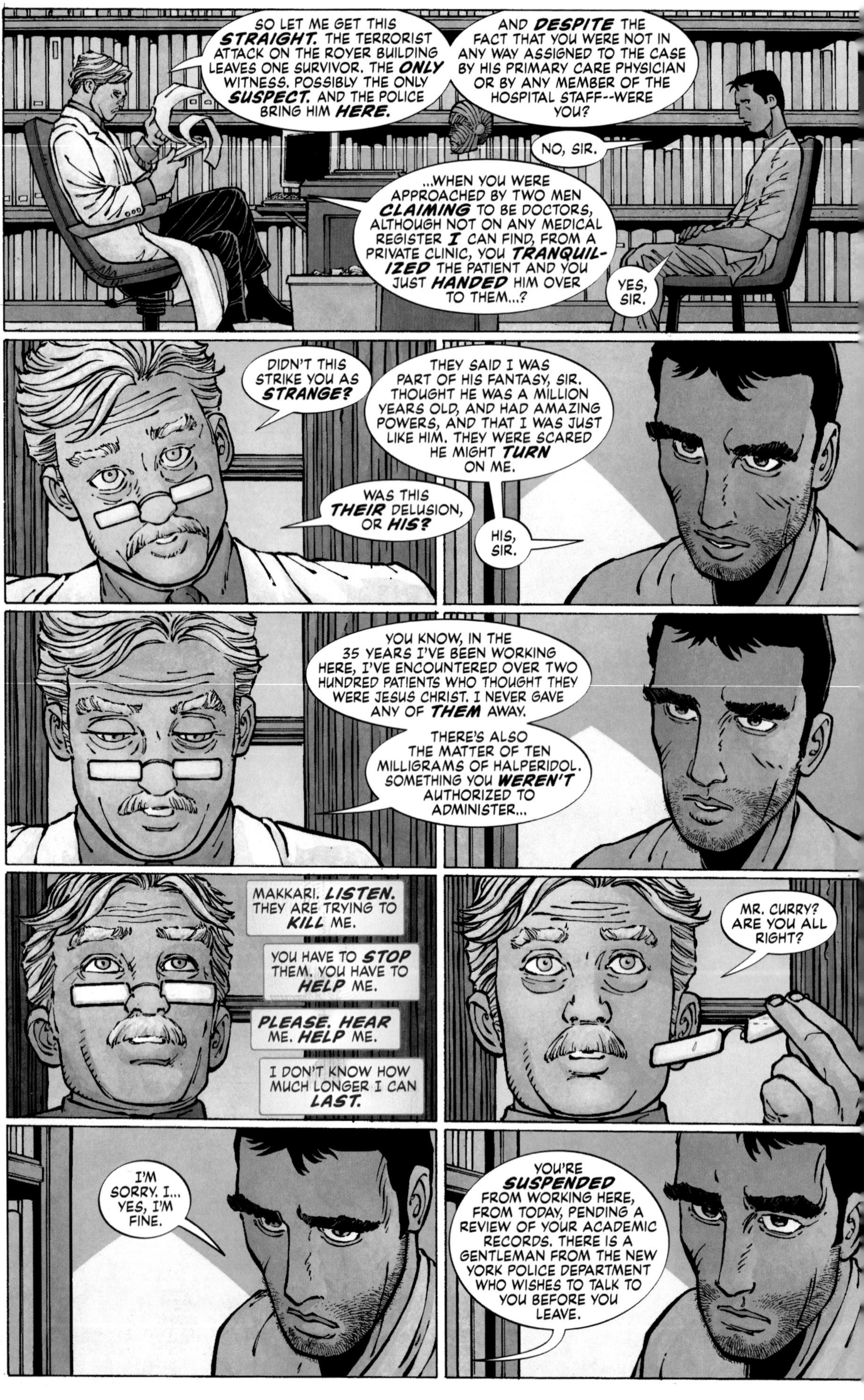
SO LET ME GET THIS STRAIGHT. THE TERRORIST ATTACK ON THE ROYER BUILDING LEAVES ONE SURVIVOR. THE ONLY WITNESS. POSSIBLY THE ONLY SUSPECT. AND THE POLICE BRING HIM HERE.
AND DESPITE THE FACT THAT YOU WERE NOT IN ANY WAY ASSIGNED TO THE CASE BY HIS PRIMARY CARE PHYSICIAN OR BY ANY MEMBER OF THE HOSPITAL STAFF--WERE YOU?
NO, SIR.
...WHEN YOU WERE APPROACHED BY TWO MEN CLAIMING TO BE DOCTORS, ALTHOUGH NOT ON ANY MEDICAL REGISTER I CAN FIND, FROM A PRIVATE CLINIC, YOU TRANQUIL-IZED THE PATIENT AND YOU JUST HANDED HIM OVER TO THEM...?
YES, SIR.
DIDN'T THIS STRIKE YOU AS STRANGE?
THEY SAID I WAS PART OF HIS FANTASY, SIR. THOUGHT HE WAS A MILLION YEARS OLD, AND HAD AMAZING POWERS, AND THAT I WAS JUST LIKE HIM. THEY WERE SCARED HE MIGHT TURN ON ME.
WAS THIS THEIR DELUSION, OR HIS?
HIS, SIR.
YOU KNOW, IN THE 35 YEARS I'VE BEEN WORKING HERE, I'VE ENCOUNTERED OVER TWO HUNDRED PATIENTS WHO THOUGHT THEY WERE JESUS CHRIST. I NEVER GAVE ANY OF THEM AWAY.
THERE'S ALSO THE MATTER OF TEN MILLIGRAMS OF HALPERIDOL. SOMETHING YOU WEREN'T AUTHORIZED TO ADMINISTER...
MAKKARI. LISTEN. THEY ARE TRYING TO KILL ME.
YOU HAVE TO STOP THEM. YOU HAVE TO HELP ME.
PLEASE. HEAR ME. HELP ME.
I DON'T KNOW HOW MUCH LONGER I CAN LAST.
MR. CURRY? ARE YOU ALL RIGHT?
I'M SORRY. I... YES, I'M FINE.
YOU'RE SUSPENDED FROM WORKING HERE, FROM TODAY, PENDING A REVIEW OF YOUR ACADEMIC RECORDS. THERE IS A GENTLEMAN FROM THE NEW YORK POLICE DEPARTMENT WHO WISHES TO TALK TO YOU BEFORE YOU LEAVE.

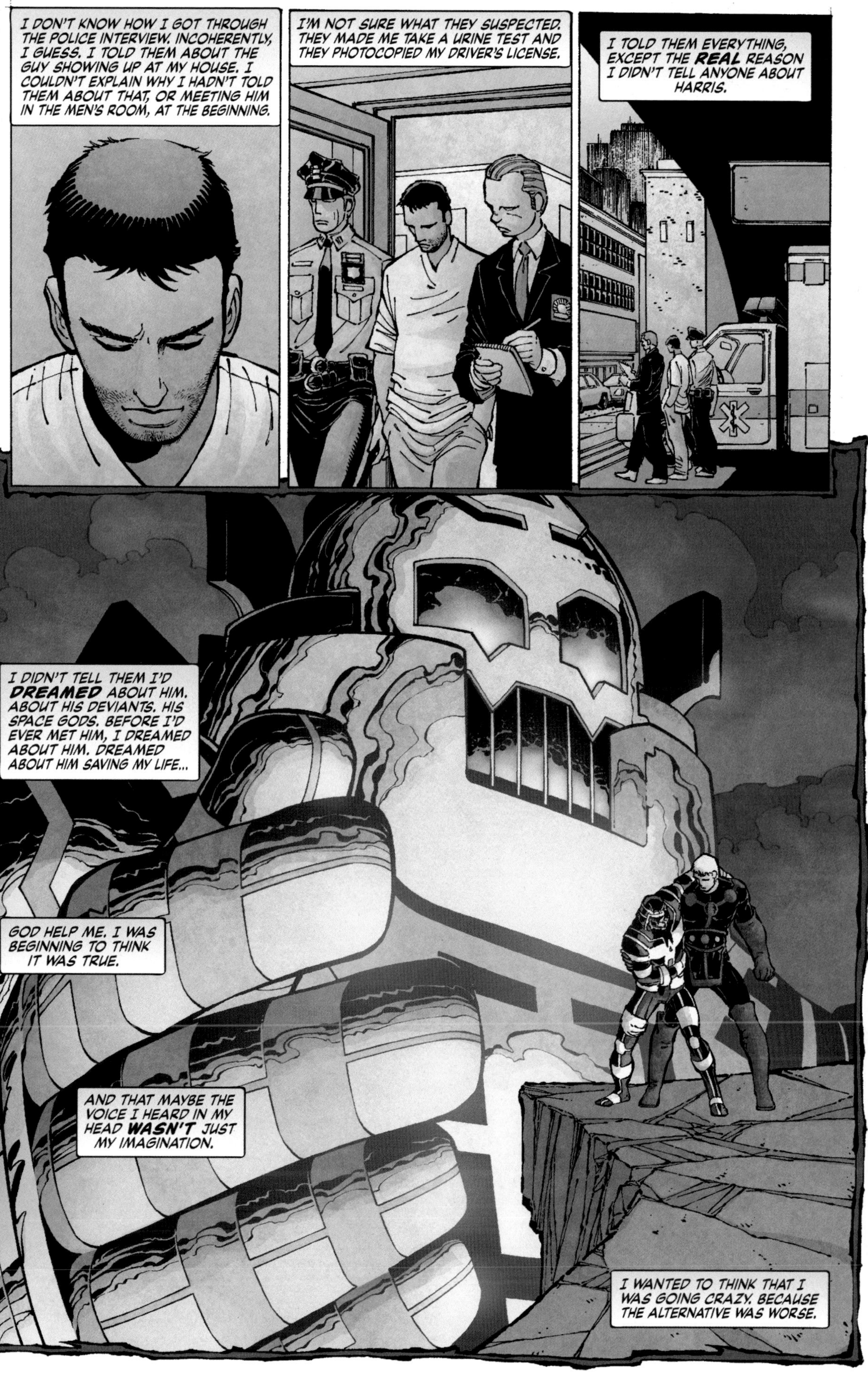
I DON'T KNOW HOW I GOT THROUGH THE POLICE INTERVIEW. INCOHERENTLY, I GUESS. I TOLD THEM ABOUT THE GUY SHOWING UP AT MY HOUSE. I COULDN'T EXPLAIN WHY I HADN'T TOLD THEM ABOUT THAT, OR MEETING HIM IN THE MEN'S ROOM, AT THE BEGINNING.
I'M NOT SURE WHAT THEY SUSPECTED. THEY MADE ME TAKE A URINE TEST AND THEY PHOTOCOPIED MY DRIVER'S LICENSE.
I TOLD THEM EVERYTHING, EXCEPT THE REAL REASON I DIDN'T TELL ANYONE ABOUT HARRIS.
I DIDN'T TELL THEM I'D DREAMED ABOUT HIM. ABOUT HIS DEVIANTS. HIS SPACE GODS. BEFORE I'D EVER MET HIM, I DREAMED ABOUT HIM. DREAMED ABOUT HIM SAVING MY LIFE...
GOD HELP ME. I WAS BEGINNING TO THINK IT WAS TRUE.
AND THAT MAYBE THE VOICE I HEARD IN MY HEAD WASN'T JUST MY IMAGINATION.
I WANTED TO THINK THAT I WAS GOING CRAZY. BECAUSE THE ALTERNATIVE WAS WORSE.

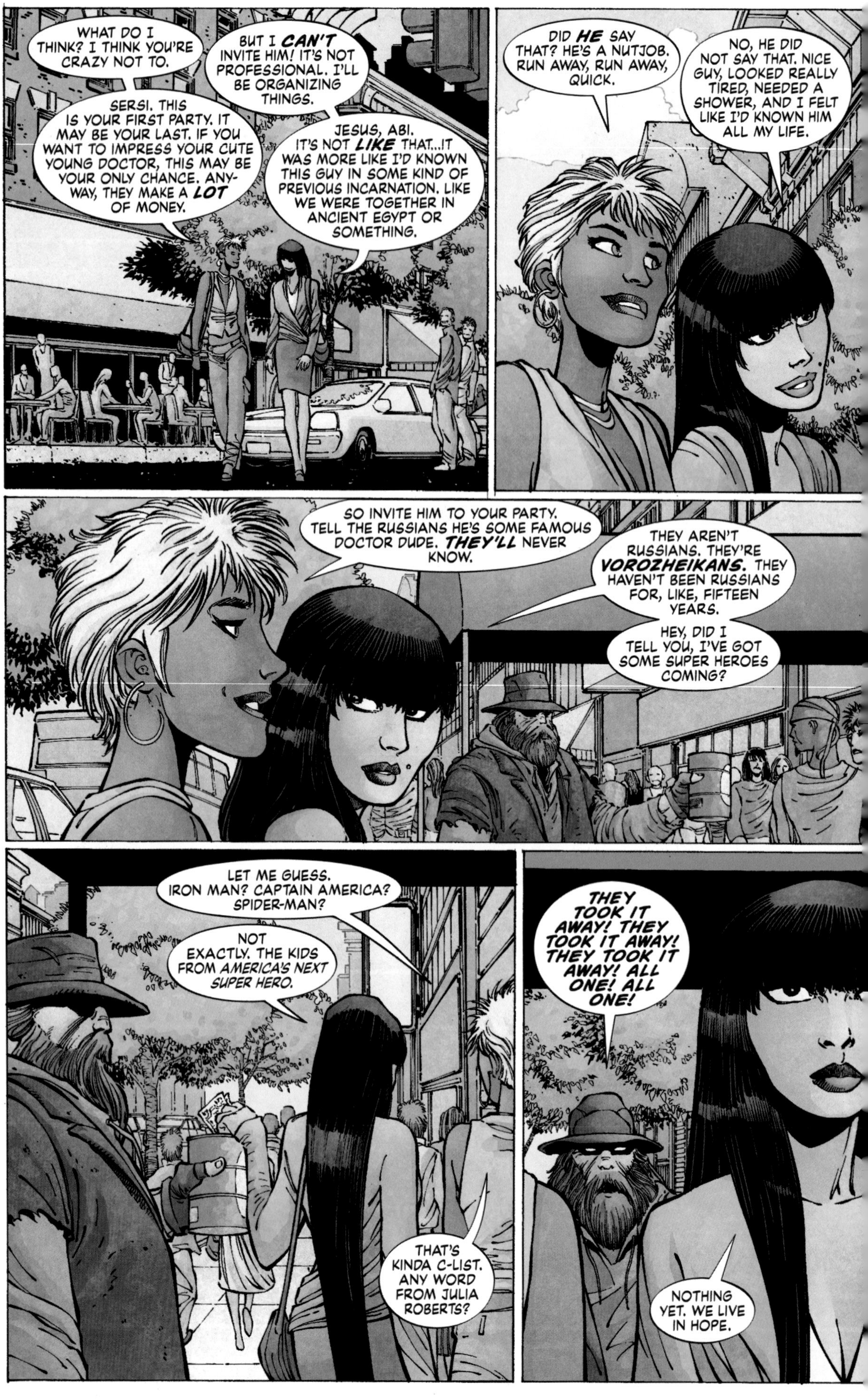
WHAT DO I THINK? I THINK YOU'RE CRAZY NOT TO.
BUT I *CAN'T* INVITE HIM! IT'S NOT PROFESSIONAL. I'LL BE ORGANIZING THINGS.
SERSI. THIS IS YOUR FIRST PARTY. IT MAY BE YOUR LAST. IF YOU WANT TO IMPRESS YOUR CUTE YOUNG DOCTOR, THIS MAY BE YOUR ONLY CHANCE. ANYWAY, THEY MAKE A *LOT* OF MONEY.
JESUS, ABI. IT'S NOT *LIKE* THAT...IT WAS MORE LIKE I'D KNOWN THIS GUY IN SOME KIND OF PREVIOUS INCARNATION. LIKE WE WERE TOGETHER IN ANCIENT EGYPT OR SOMETHING.
DID *HE* SAY THAT? HE'S A NUTJOB. RUN AWAY, RUN AWAY, QUICK.
NO, HE DID NOT SAY THAT. NICE GUY, LOOKED REALLY TIRED, NEEDED A SHOWER, AND I FELT LIKE I'D KNOWN HIM ALL MY LIFE.
SO INVITE HIM TO YOUR PARTY. TELL THE RUSSIANS HE'S SOME FAMOUS DOCTOR DUDE. *THEY'LL* NEVER KNOW.
THEY AREN'T RUSSIANS. THEY'RE *VOROZHEIKANS.* THEY HAVEN'T BEEN RUSSIANS FOR, LIKE, FIFTEEN YEARS.
HEY, DID I TELL YOU, I'VE GOT SOME SUPER HEROES COMING?
LET ME GUESS. IRON MAN? CAPTAIN AMERICA? SPIDER-MAN?
NOT EXACTLY. THE KIDS FROM *AMERICA'S NEXT SUPER HERO.*
THAT'S KINDA C-LIST. ANY WORD FROM JULIA ROBERTS?
THEY TOOK IT AWAY! THEY TOOK IT AWAY! THEY TOOK IT AWAY! ALL ONE! ALL ONE!
NOTHING YET. WE LIVE IN HOPE.

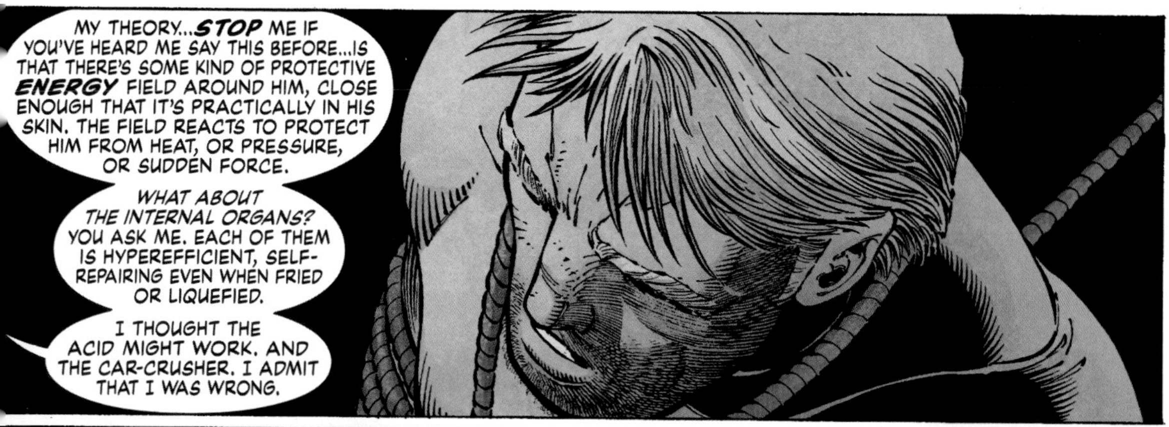
MY THEORY...STOP ME IF YOU'VE HEARD ME SAY THIS BEFORE...IS THAT THERE'S SOME KIND OF PROTECTIVE ENERGY FIELD AROUND HIM, CLOSE ENOUGH THAT IT'S PRACTICALLY IN HIS SKIN. THE FIELD REACTS TO PROTECT HIM FROM HEAT, OR PRESSURE, OR SUDDEN FORCE.
WHAT ABOUT THE INTERNAL ORGANS? YOU ASK ME. EACH OF THEM IS HYPEREFFICIENT, SELF-REPAIRING EVEN WHEN FRIED OR LIQUEFIED.
I THOUGHT THE ACID MIGHT WORK. AND THE CAR-CRUSHER. I ADMIT THAT I WAS WRONG.

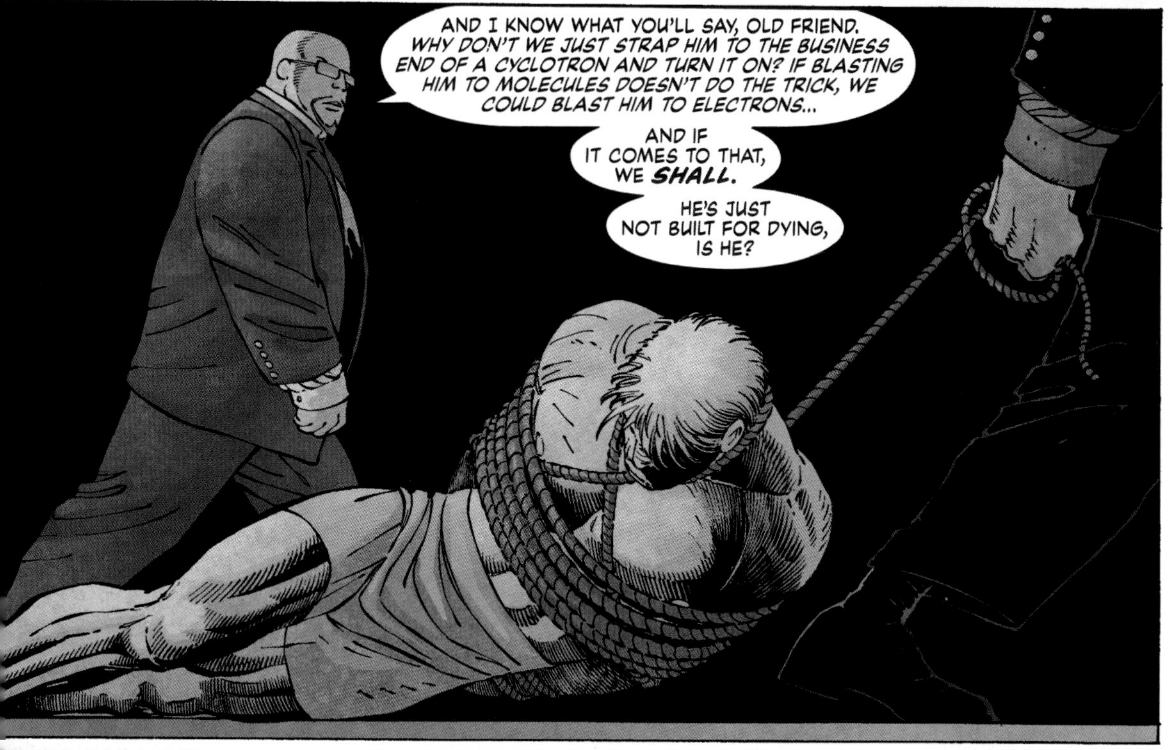
AND I KNOW WHAT YOU'LL SAY, OLD FRIEND. WHY DON'T WE JUST STRAP HIM TO THE BUSINESS END OF A CYCLOTRON AND TURN IT ON? IF BLASTING HIM TO MOLECULES DOESN'T DO THE TRICK, WE COULD BLAST HIM TO ELECTRONS...
AND IF IT COMES TO THAT, WE SHALL.
HE'S JUST NOT BUILT FOR DYING, IS HE?

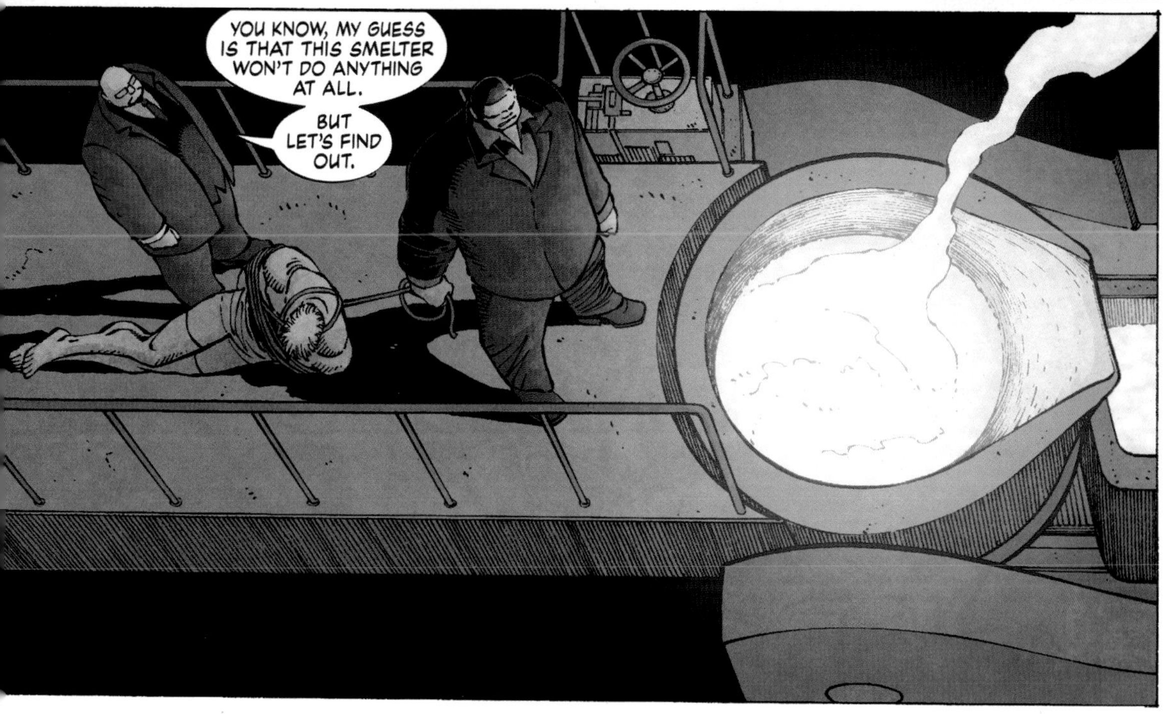
YOU KNOW, MY GUESS IS THAT THIS SMELTER WON'T DO ANYTHING AT ALL.
BUT LET'S FIND OUT.

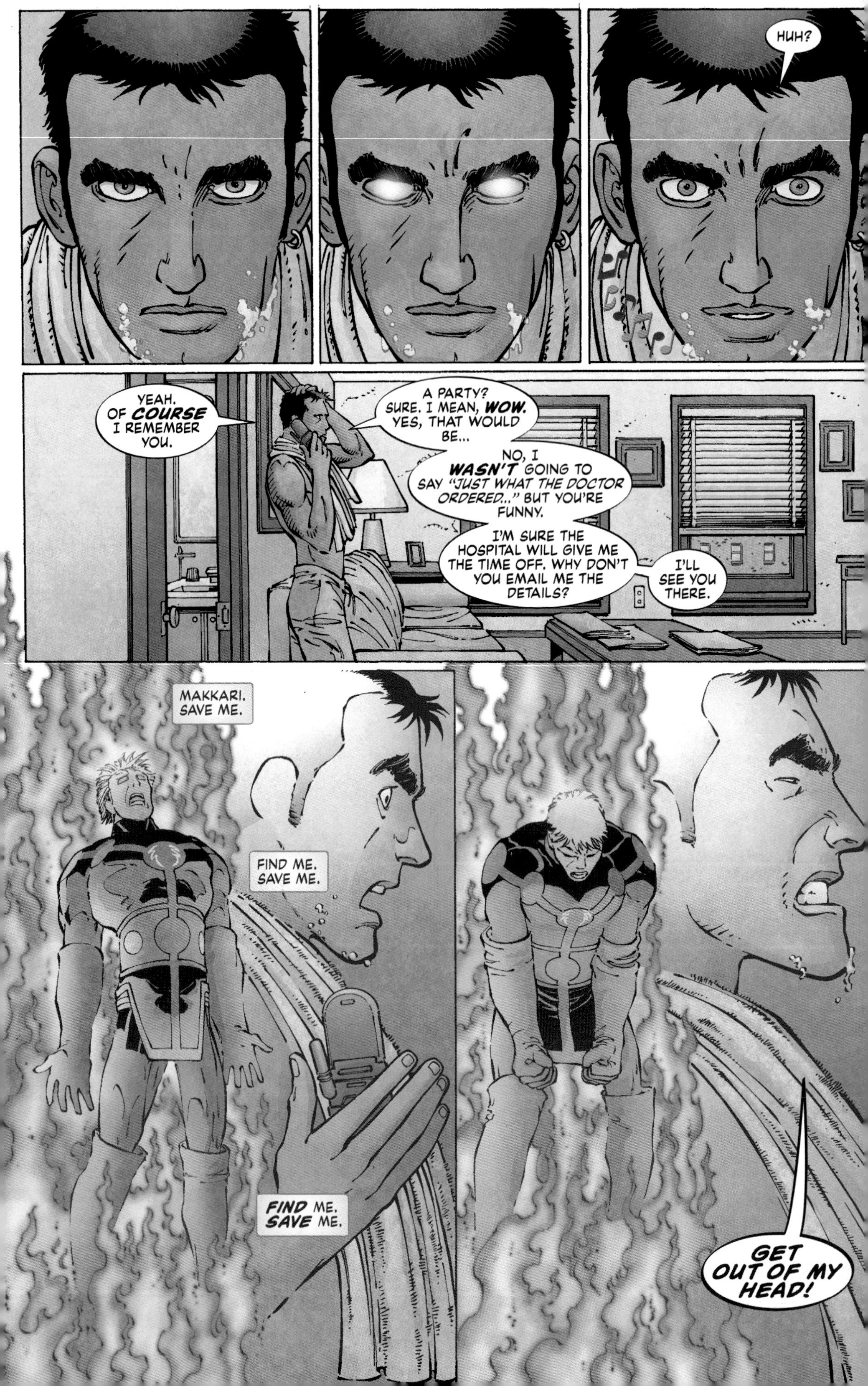
HUH?
YEAH. OF COURSE I REMEMBER YOU.
A PARTY? SURE. I MEAN, WOW. YES, THAT WOULD BE...
NO, I WASN'T GOING TO SAY "JUST WHAT THE DOCTOR ORDERED..." BUT YOU'RE FUNNY.
I'M SURE THE HOSPITAL WILL GIVE ME THE TIME OFF. WHY DON'T YOU EMAIL ME THE DETAILS?
I'LL SEE YOU THERE.
MAKKARI. SAVE ME.
FIND ME. SAVE ME.
FIND ME. SAVE ME.
GET OUT OF MY HEAD!

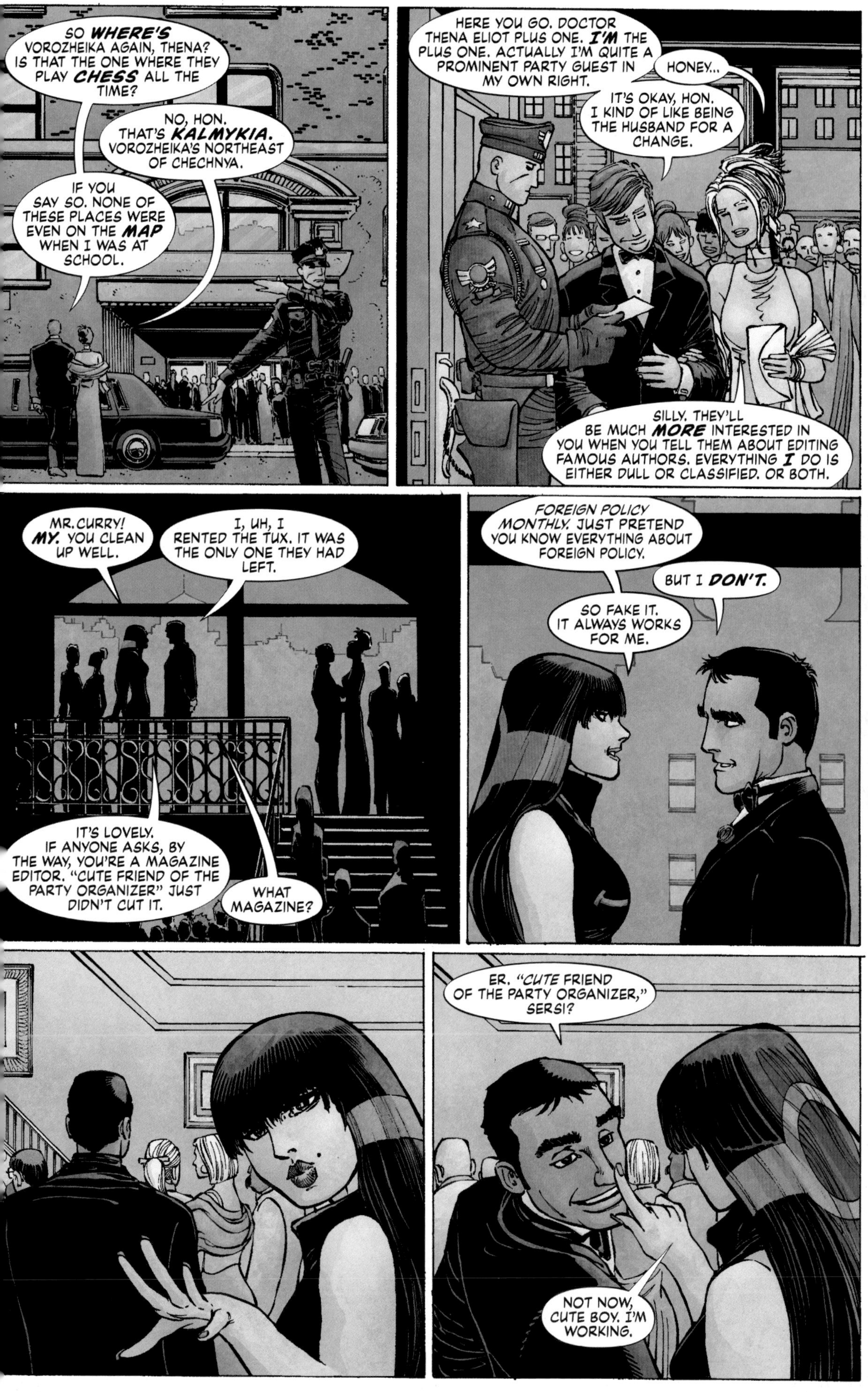
SO WHERE'S VOROZHEIKA AGAIN, THENA? IS THAT THE ONE WHERE THEY PLAY CHESS ALL THE TIME?
NO, HON. THAT'S KALMYKIA. VOROZHEIKA'S NORTHEAST OF CHECHNYA.
IF YOU SAY SO. NONE OF THESE PLACES WERE EVEN ON THE MAP WHEN I WAS AT SCHOOL.
HERE YOU GO. DOCTOR THENA ELIOT PLUS ONE. I'M THE PLUS ONE. ACTUALLY I'M QUITE A PROMINENT PARTY GUEST IN MY OWN RIGHT.
HONEY...
IT'S OKAY, HON. I KIND OF LIKE BEING THE HUSBAND FOR A CHANGE.
SILLY. THEY'LL BE MUCH MORE INTERESTED IN YOU WHEN YOU TELL THEM ABOUT EDITING FAMOUS AUTHORS. EVERYTHING I DO IS EITHER DULL OR CLASSIFIED. OR BOTH.
MR. CURRY! MY. YOU CLEAN UP WELL.
I, UH, I RENTED THE TUX. IT WAS THE ONLY ONE THEY HAD LEFT.
IT'S LOVELY. IF ANYONE ASKS, BY THE WAY, YOU'RE A MAGAZINE EDITOR. "CUTE FRIEND OF THE PARTY ORGANIZER" JUST DIDN'T CUT IT.
WHAT MAGAZINE?
FOREIGN POLICY MONTHLY. JUST PRETEND YOU KNOW EVERYTHING ABOUT FOREIGN POLICY.
BUT I DON'T.
SO FAKE IT. IT ALWAYS WORKS FOR ME.
ER. "CUTE FRIEND OF THE PARTY ORGANIZER," SERSI?
NOT NOW, CUTE BOY. I'M WORKING.

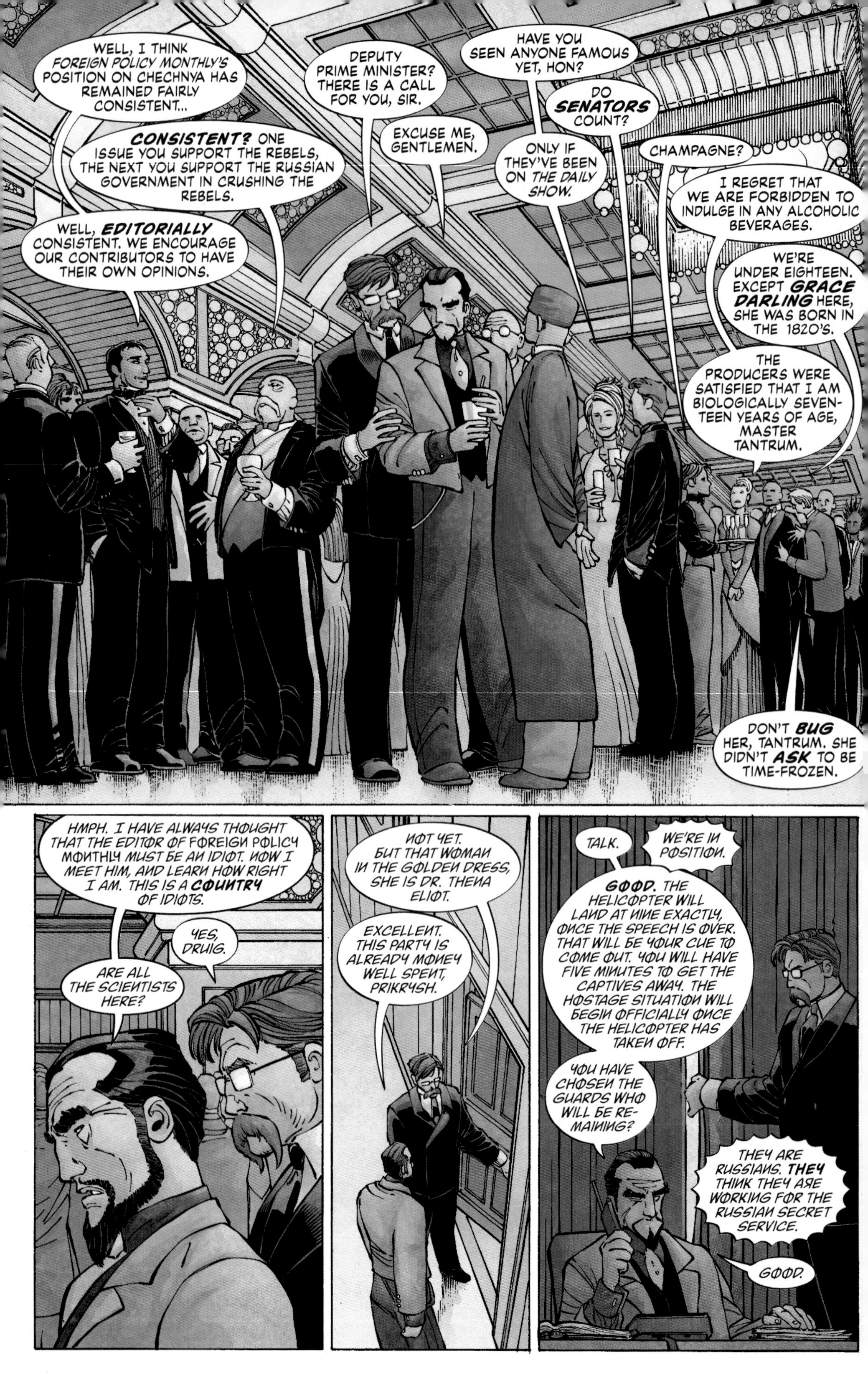
WELL, I THINK FOREIGN POLICY MONTHLY'S POSITION ON CHECHNYA HAS REMAINED FAIRLY CONSISTENT...
CONSISTENT? ONE ISSUE YOU SUPPORT THE REBELS, THE NEXT YOU SUPPORT THE RUSSIAN GOVERNMENT IN CRUSHING THE REBELS.
WELL, EDITORIALLY CONSISTENT. WE ENCOURAGE OUR CONTRIBUTORS TO HAVE THEIR OWN OPINIONS.
DEPUTY PRIME MINISTER? THERE IS A CALL FOR YOU, SIR.
EXCUSE ME, GENTLEMEN.
HAVE YOU SEEN ANYONE FAMOUS YET, HON?
DO SENATORS COUNT?
ONLY IF THEY'VE BEEN ON THE DAILY SHOW.
CHAMPAGNE?
I REGRET THAT WE ARE FORBIDDEN TO INDULGE IN ANY ALCOHOLIC BEVERAGES.
WE'RE UNDER EIGHTEEN. EXCEPT GRACE DARLING HERE, SHE WAS BORN IN THE 1820'S.
THE PRODUCERS WERE SATISFIED THAT I AM BIOLOGICALLY SEVEN-TEEN YEARS OF AGE, MASTER TANTRUM.
DON'T BUG HER, TANTRUM. SHE DIDN'T ASK TO BE TIME-FROZEN.
HMPH. I HAVE ALWAYS THOUGHT THAT THE EDITOR OF FOREIGN POLICY MONTHLY MUST BE AN IDIOT. NOW I MEET HIM, AND LEARN HOW RIGHT I AM. THIS IS A COUNTRY OF IDIOTS.
YES, DRUIG.
ARE ALL THE SCIENTISTS HERE?
NOT YET. BUT THAT WOMAN IN THE GOLDEN DRESS, SHE IS DR. THENA ELIOT.
EXCELLENT. THIS PARTY IS ALREADY MONEY WELL SPENT, PRIKRYSH.
TALK.
WE'RE IN POSITION.
GOOD. THE HELICOPTER WILL LAND AT NINE EXACTLY, ONCE THE SPEECH IS OVER. THAT WILL BE YOUR CUE TO COME OUT. YOU WILL HAVE FIVE MINUTES TO GET THE CAPTIVES AWAY. THE HOSTAGE SITUATION WILL BEGIN OFFICIALLY ONCE THE HELICOPTER HAS TAKEN OFF.
YOU HAVE CHOSEN THE GUARDS WHO WILL BE RE-MAINING?
THEY ARE RUSSIANS. THEY THINK THEY ARE WORKING FOR THE RUSSIAN SECRET SERVICE.
GOOD.

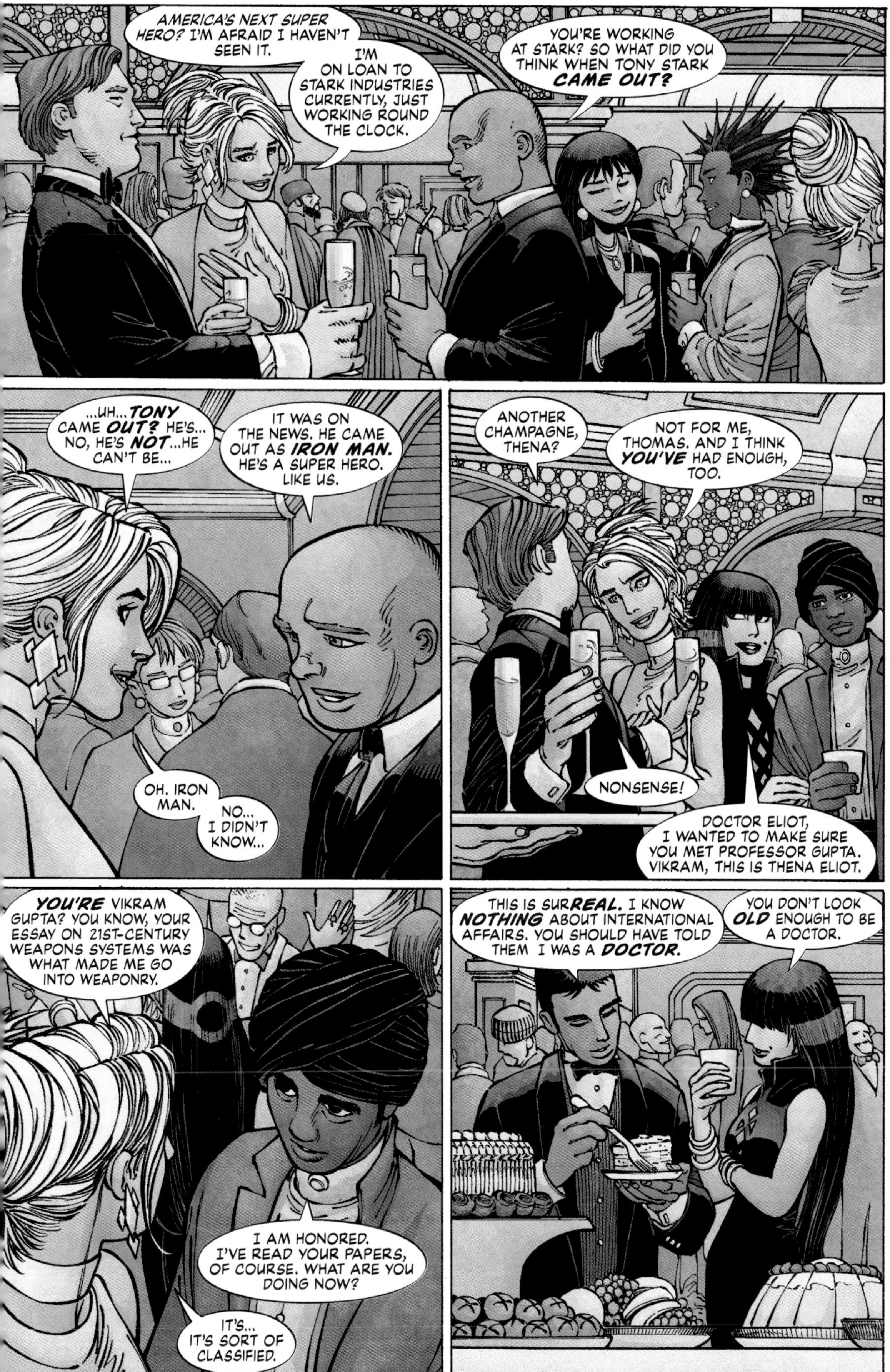
AMERICA'S NEXT SUPER HERO? I'M AFRAID I HAVEN'T SEEN IT.
I'M ON LOAN TO STARK INDUSTRIES CURRENTLY, JUST WORKING ROUND THE CLOCK.
YOU'RE WORKING AT STARK? SO WHAT DID YOU THINK WHEN TONY STARK CAME OUT?
...UH...TONY CAME OUT? HE'S... NO, HE'S NOT...HE CAN'T BE...
IT WAS ON THE NEWS. HE CAME OUT AS IRON MAN. HE'S A SUPER HERO. LIKE US.
OH. IRON MAN.
NO... I DIDN'T KNOW...
ANOTHER CHAMPAGNE, THENA?
NOT FOR ME, THOMAS. AND I THINK YOU'VE HAD ENOUGH, TOO.
NONSENSE!
DOCTOR ELIOT, I WANTED TO MAKE SURE YOU MET PROFESSOR GUPTA. VIKRAM, THIS IS THENA ELIOT.
YOU'RE VIKRAM GUPTA? YOU KNOW, YOUR ESSAY ON 21ST-CENTURY WEAPONS SYSTEMS WAS WHAT MADE ME GO INTO WEAPONRY.
I AM HONORED. I'VE READ YOUR PAPERS, OF COURSE. WHAT ARE YOU DOING NOW?
IT'S... IT'S SORT OF CLASSIFIED.
THIS IS SURREAL. I KNOW NOTHING ABOUT INTERNATIONAL AFFAIRS. YOU SHOULD HAVE TOLD THEM I WAS A DOCTOR.
YOU DON'T LOOK OLD ENOUGH TO BE A DOCTOR.

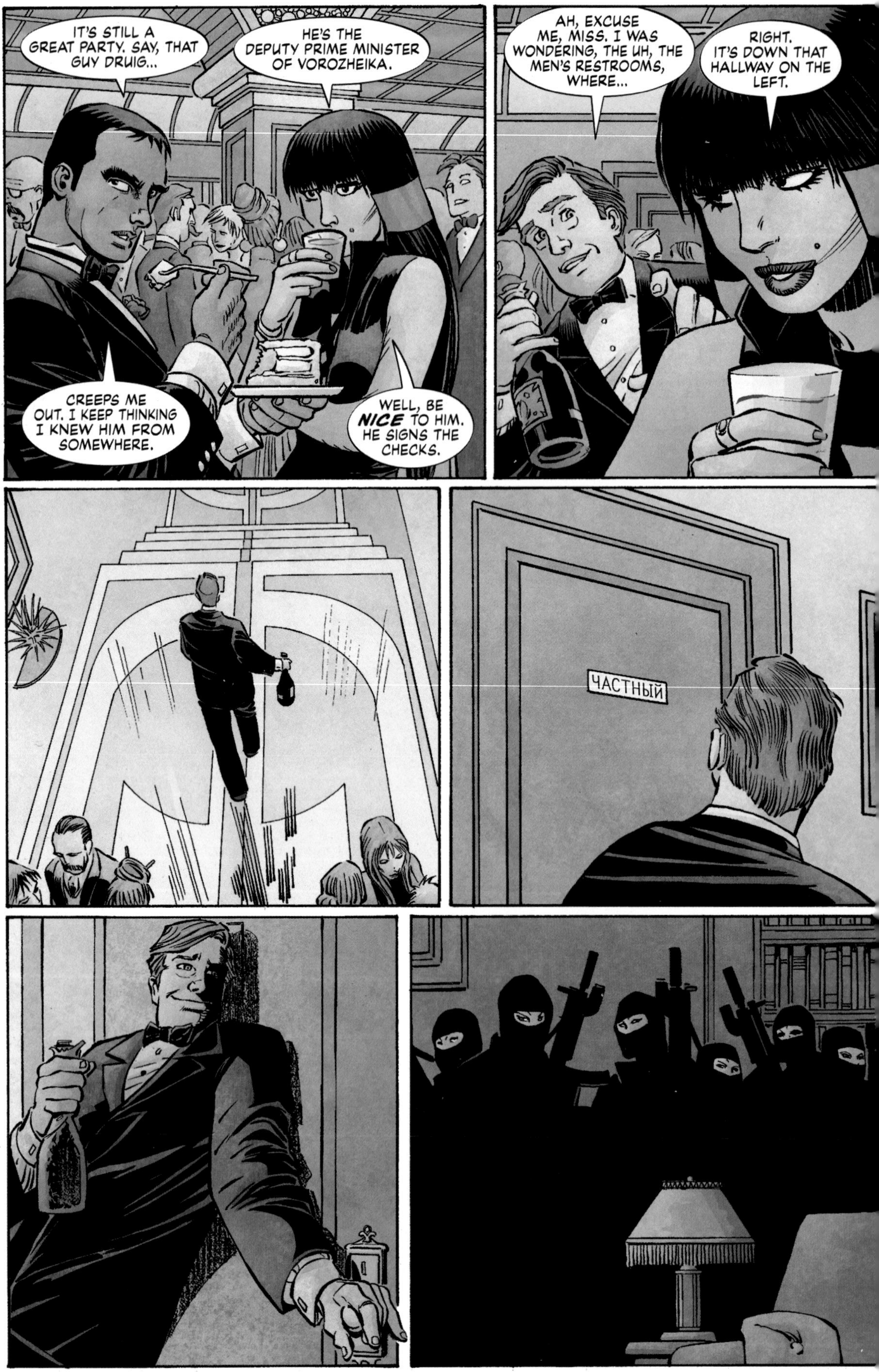
IT'S STILL A GREAT PARTY. SAY, THAT GUY DRUIG...
HE'S THE DEPUTY PRIME MINISTER OF VOROZHEIKA.
CREEPS ME OUT. I KEEP THINKING I KNEW HIM FROM SOMEWHERE.
WELL, BE NICE TO HIM. HE SIGNS THE CHECKS.
AH, EXCUSE ME, MISS. I WAS WONDERING, THE UH, THE MEN'S RESTROOMS, WHERE...
RIGHT. IT'S DOWN THAT HALLWAY ON THE LEFT.
ЧАСТНЫЙ

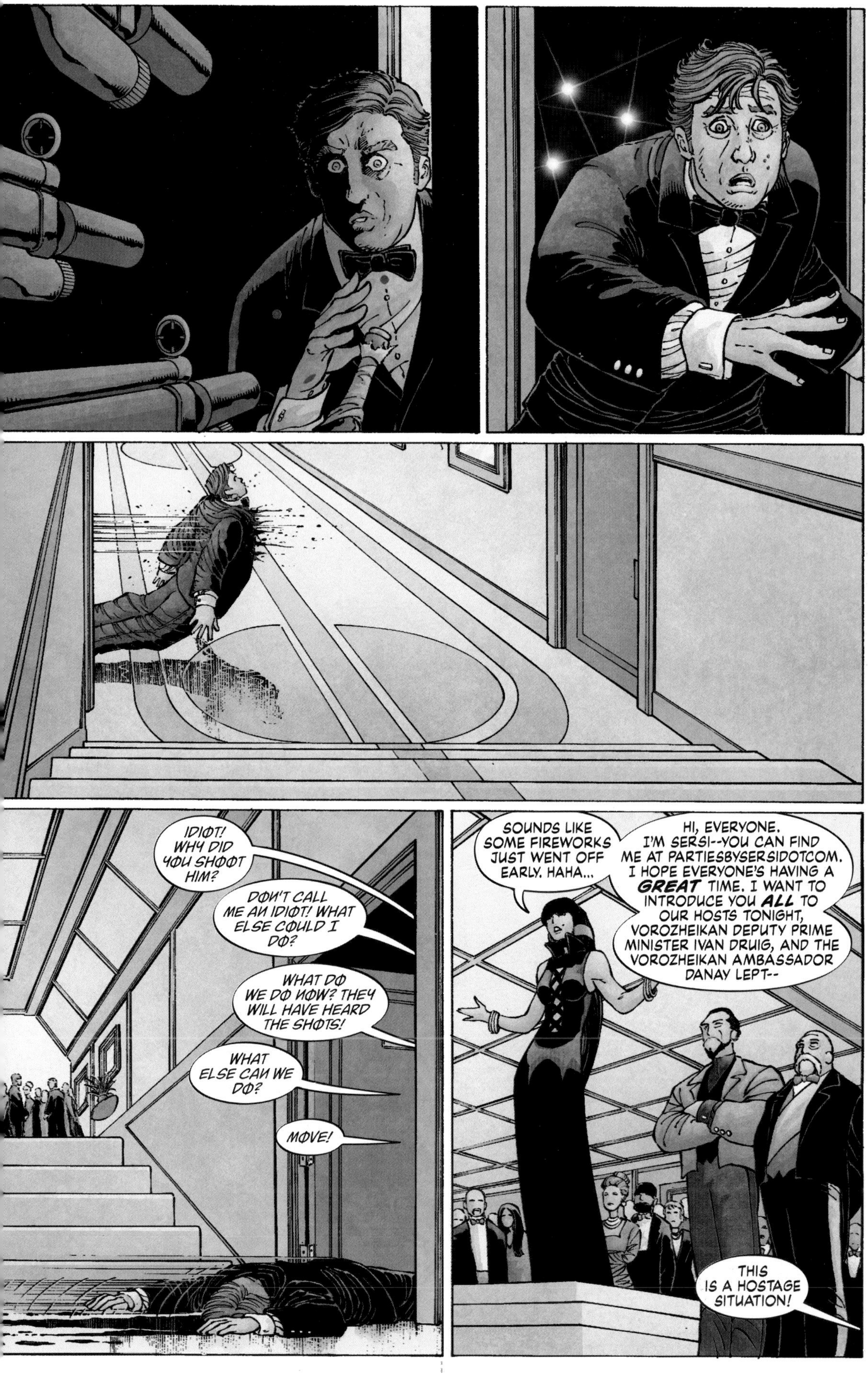
IDIOT! WHY DID YOU SHOOT HIM?
DON'T CALL ME AN IDIOT! WHAT ELSE COULD I DO?
WHAT DO WE DO NOW? THEY WILL HAVE HEARD THE SHOTS!
WHAT ELSE CAN WE DO?
MOVE!
SOUNDS LIKE SOME FIREWORKS JUST WENT OFF EARLY. HAHA...
HI, EVERYONE. I'M SERSI--YOU CAN FIND ME AT PARTIESBYSERSIDOTCOM. I HOPE EVERYONE'S HAVING A GREAT TIME. I WANT TO INTRODUCE YOU ALL TO OUR HOSTS TONIGHT, VOROZHEIKAN DEPUTY PRIME MINISTER IVAN DRUIG, AND THE VOROZHEIKAN AMBASSADOR DANAY LEPT--
THIS IS A HOSTAGE SITUATION!

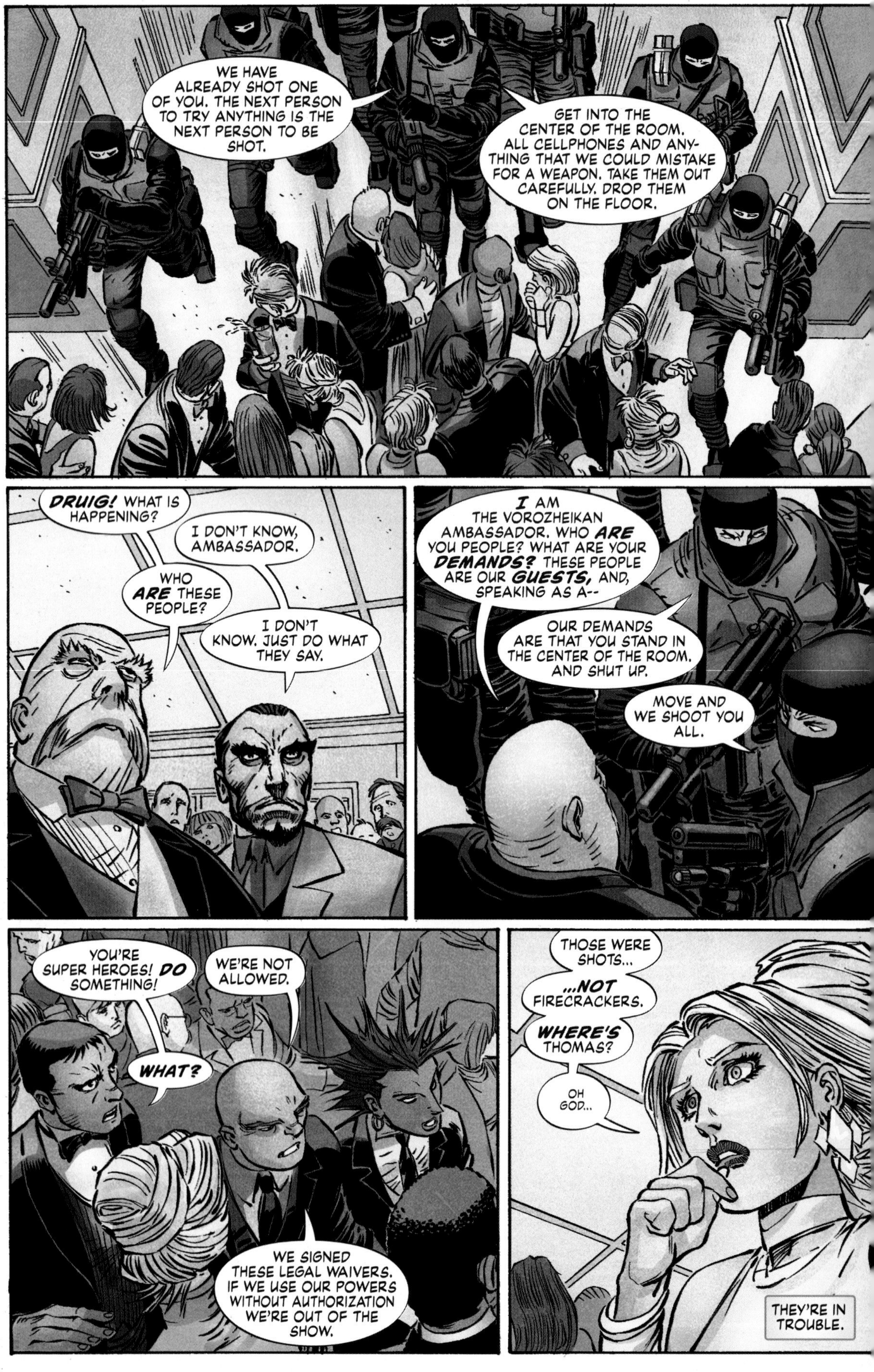
WE HAVE ALREADY SHOT ONE OF YOU. THE NEXT PERSON TO TRY ANYTHING IS THE NEXT PERSON TO BE SHOT.
GET INTO THE CENTER OF THE ROOM. ALL CELLPHONES AND ANY-THING THAT WE COULD MISTAKE FOR A WEAPON. TAKE THEM OUT CAREFULLY. DROP THEM ON THE FLOOR.
DRUIG! WHAT IS HAPPENING?
I DON'T KNOW, AMBASSADOR.
WHO ARE THESE PEOPLE?
I DON'T KNOW. JUST DO WHAT THEY SAY.
I AM THE VOROZHEIKAN AMBASSADOR. WHO ARE YOU PEOPLE? WHAT ARE YOUR DEMANDS? THESE PEOPLE ARE OUR GUESTS, AND, SPEAKING AS A--
OUR DEMANDS ARE THAT YOU STAND IN THE CENTER OF THE ROOM. AND SHUT UP.
MOVE AND WE SHOOT YOU ALL.
YOU'RE SUPER HEROES! DO SOMETHING!
WE'RE NOT ALLOWED.
WHAT?
WE SIGNED THESE LEGAL WAIVERS. IF WE USE OUR POWERS WITHOUT AUTHORIZATION WE'RE OUT OF THE SHOW.
THOSE WERE SHOTS...
...NOT FIRECRACKERS.
WHERE'S THOMAS?
OH GOD...
THEY'RE IN TROUBLE.

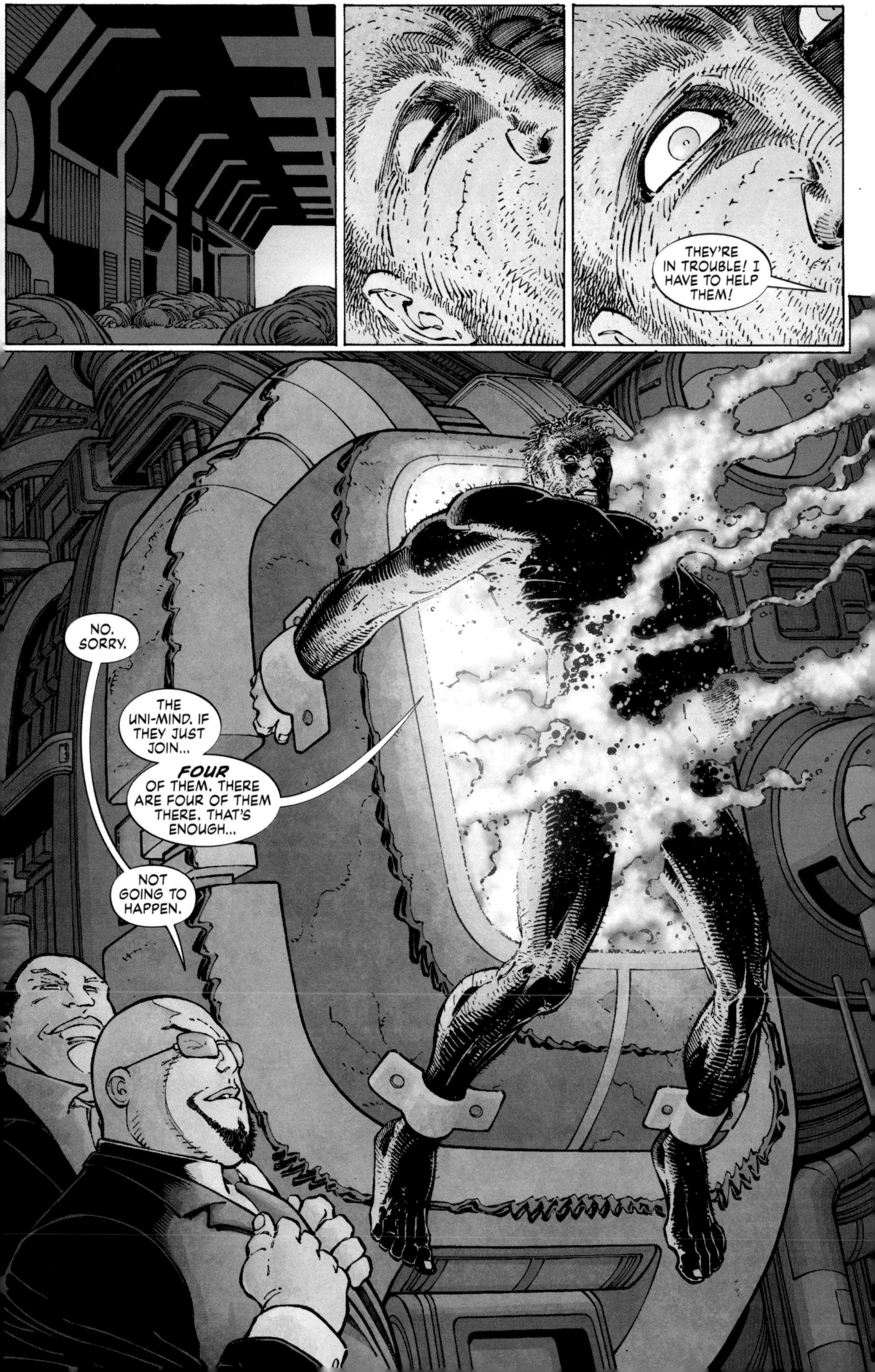
THEY'RE IN TROUBLE! I HAVE TO HELP THEM!
NO. SORRY.
THE UNI-MIND. IF THEY JUST JOIN...
FOUR OF THEM. THERE ARE FOUR OF THEM THERE. THAT'S ENOUGH...
NOT GOING TO HAPPEN.

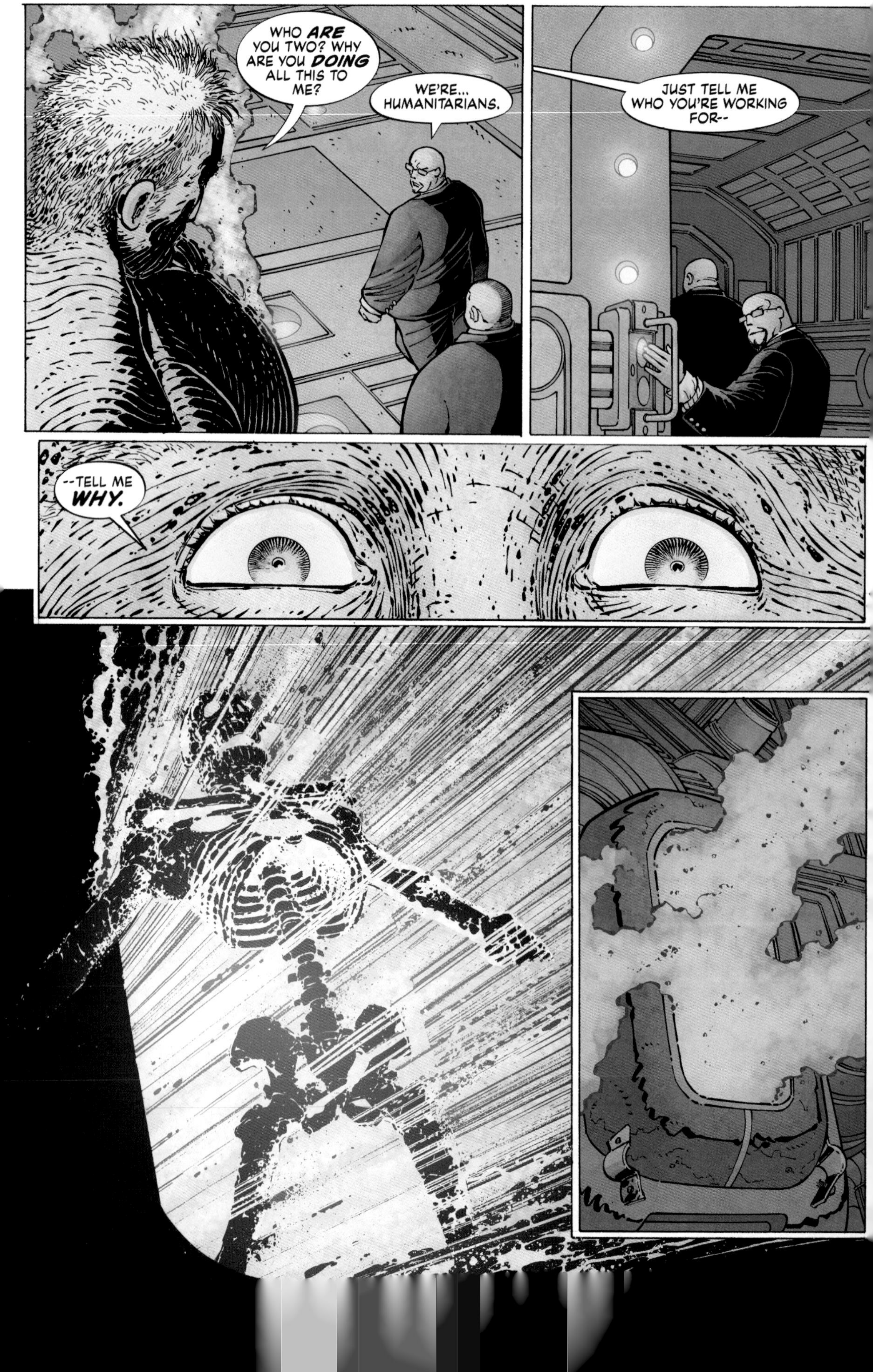
WHO ARE YOU TWO? WHY ARE YOU DOING ALL THIS TO ME?
WE'RE... HUMANITARIANS.
JUST TELL ME WHO YOU'RE WORKING FOR--
--TELL ME WHY.

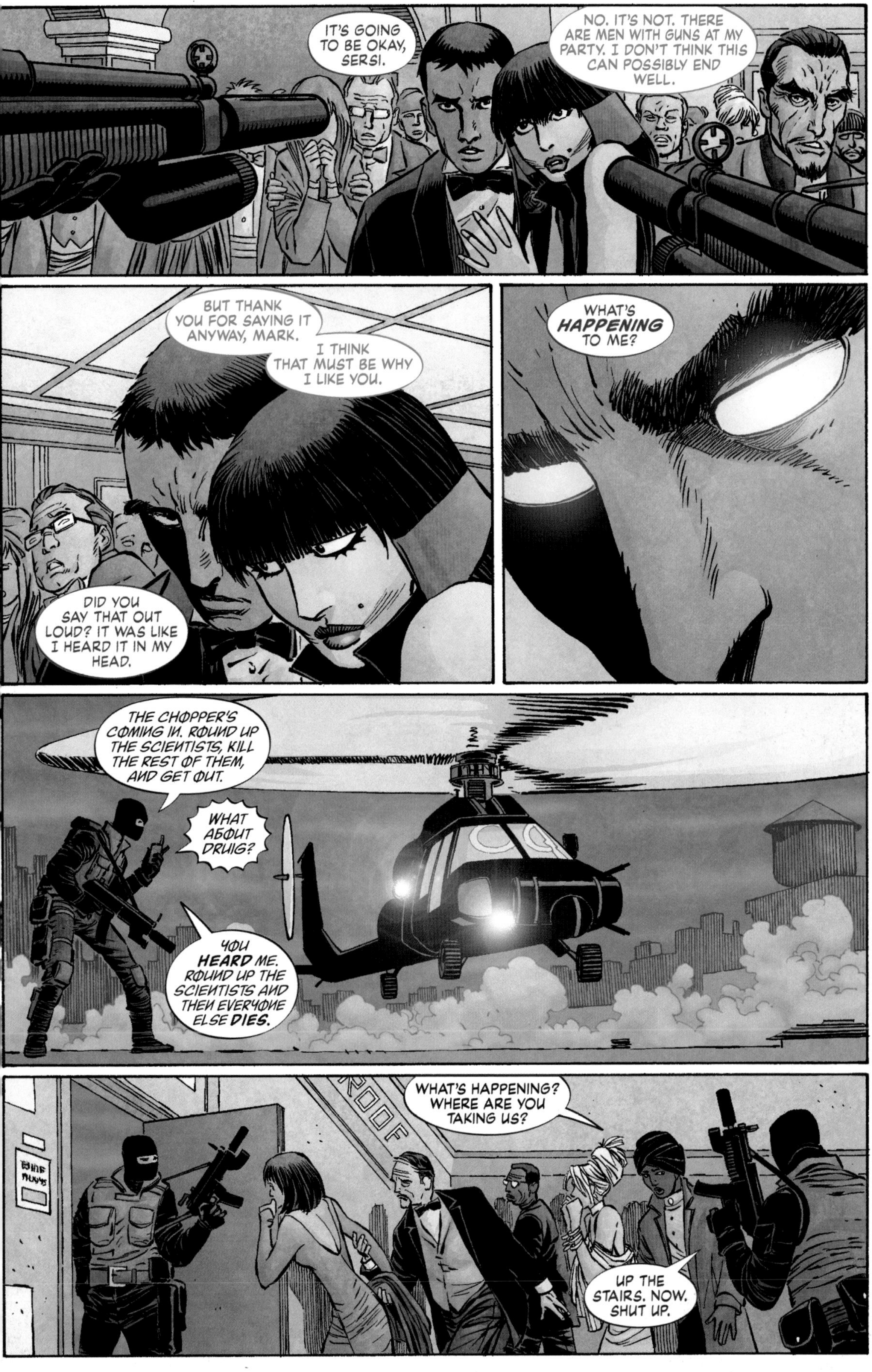
IT'S GOING TO BE OKAY, SERSI.
NO. IT'S NOT. THERE ARE MEN WITH GUNS AT MY PARTY. I DON'T THINK THIS CAN POSSIBLY END WELL.
BUT THANK YOU FOR SAYING IT ANYWAY, MARK.
I THINK THAT MUST BE WHY I LIKE YOU.
DID YOU SAY THAT OUT LOUD? IT WAS LIKE I HEARD IT IN MY HEAD.
WHAT'S HAPPENING TO ME?
THE CHOPPER'S COMING IN. ROUND UP THE SCIENTISTS, KILL THE REST OF THEM, AND GET OUT.
WHAT ABOUT DRUIG?
YOU HEARD ME. ROUND UP THE SCIENTISTS AND THEN EVERYONE ELSE DIES.
ROOF
WHAT'S HAPPENING? WHERE ARE YOU TAKING US?
UP THE STAIRS. NOW. SHUT UP.

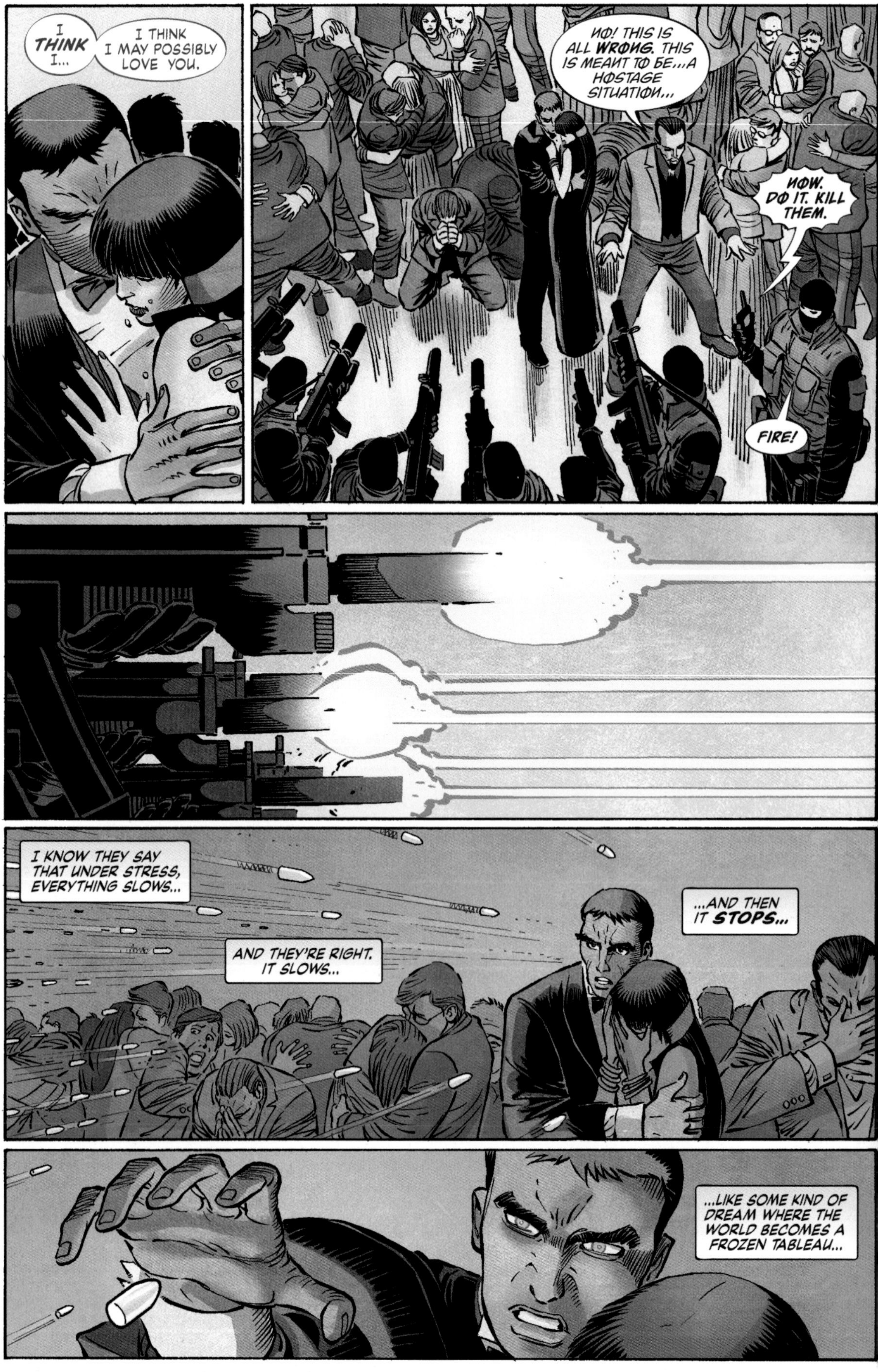
I THINK I...
I THINK I MAY POSSIBLY LOVE YOU.
ИФ! THIS IS ALL WRФNG. THIS IS MEAИT TФ БE...A HФSTAGE SITUATIФИ...
ИФW. DФ IT. KILL THEM.
FIRE!
I KNOW THEY SAY THAT UNDER STRESS, EVERYTHING SLOWS...
AND THEY'RE RIGHT. IT SLOWS...
...AND THEN IT STOPS...
...LIKE SOME KIND OF DREAM WHERE THE WORLD BECOMES A FROZEN TABLEAU...

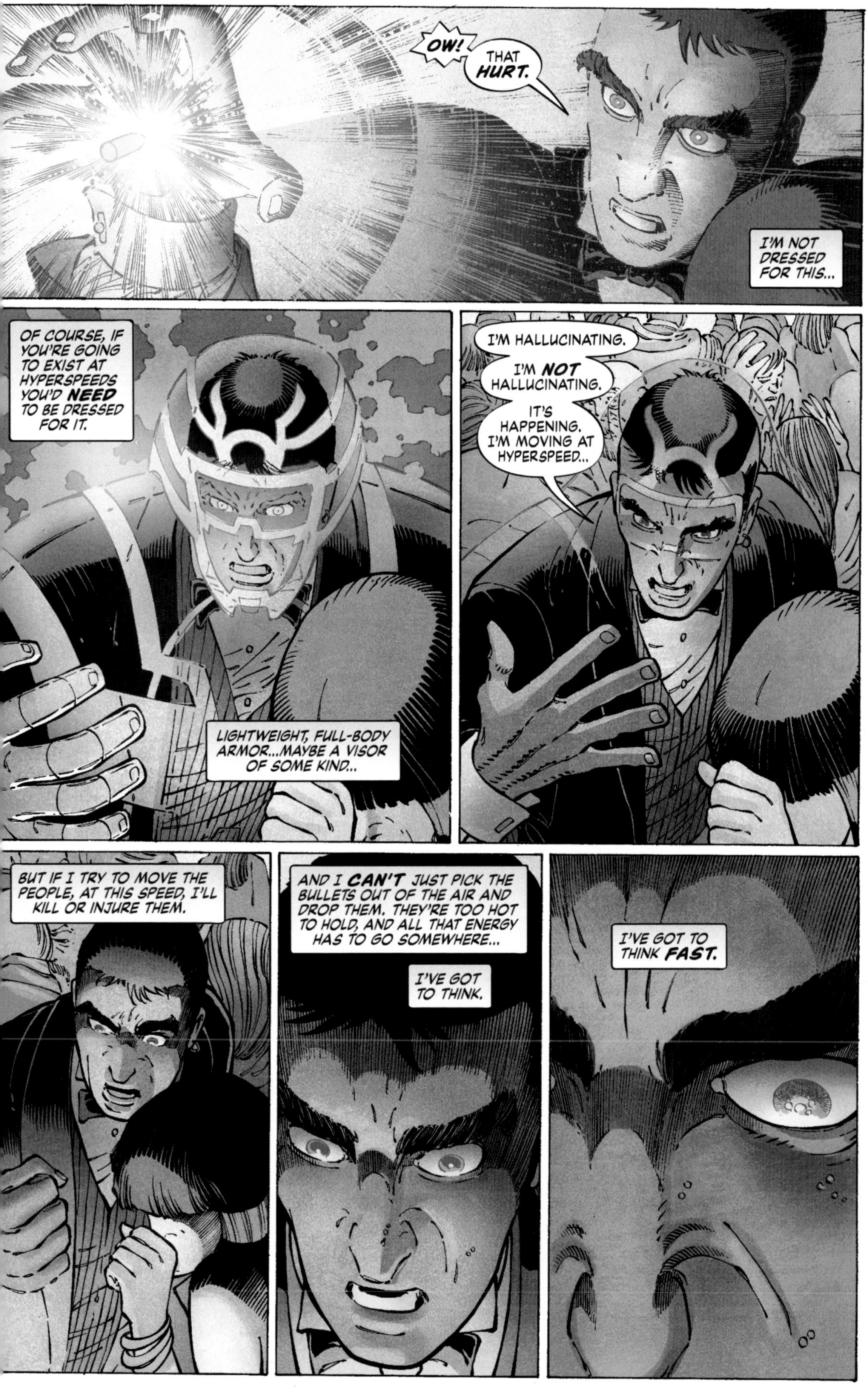

OW!
THAT HURT.
I'M NOT DRESSED FOR THIS...
OF COURSE, IF YOU'RE GOING TO EXIST AT HYPERSPEEDS YOU'D NEED TO BE DRESSED FOR IT.
LIGHTWEIGHT, FULL-BODY ARMOR...MAYBE A VISOR OF SOME KIND...
I'M HALLUCINATING.
I'M NOT HALLUCINATING.
IT'S HAPPENING. I'M MOVING AT HYPERSPEED...
BUT IF I TRY TO MOVE THE PEOPLE, AT THIS SPEED, I'LL KILL OR INJURE THEM.
AND I CAN'T JUST PICK THE BULLETS OUT OF THE AIR AND DROP THEM. THEY'RE TOO HOT TO HOLD, AND ALL THAT ENERGY HAS TO GO SOMEWHERE...
I'VE GOT TO THINK.
I'VE GOT TO THINK FAST.

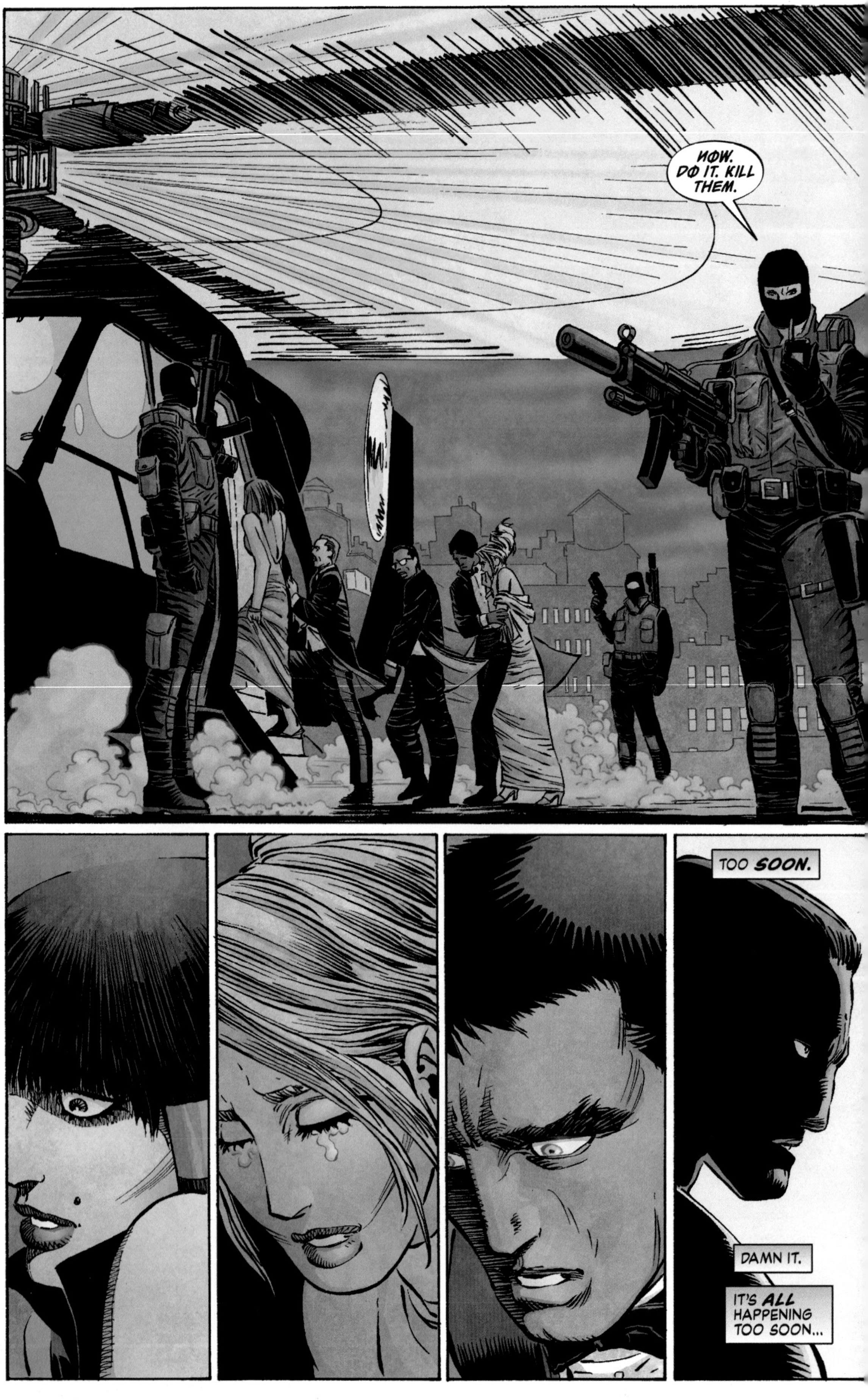
NOW. DO IT. KILL THEM.
TOO SOON.
DAMN IT.
IT'S ALL HAPPENING TOO SOON...

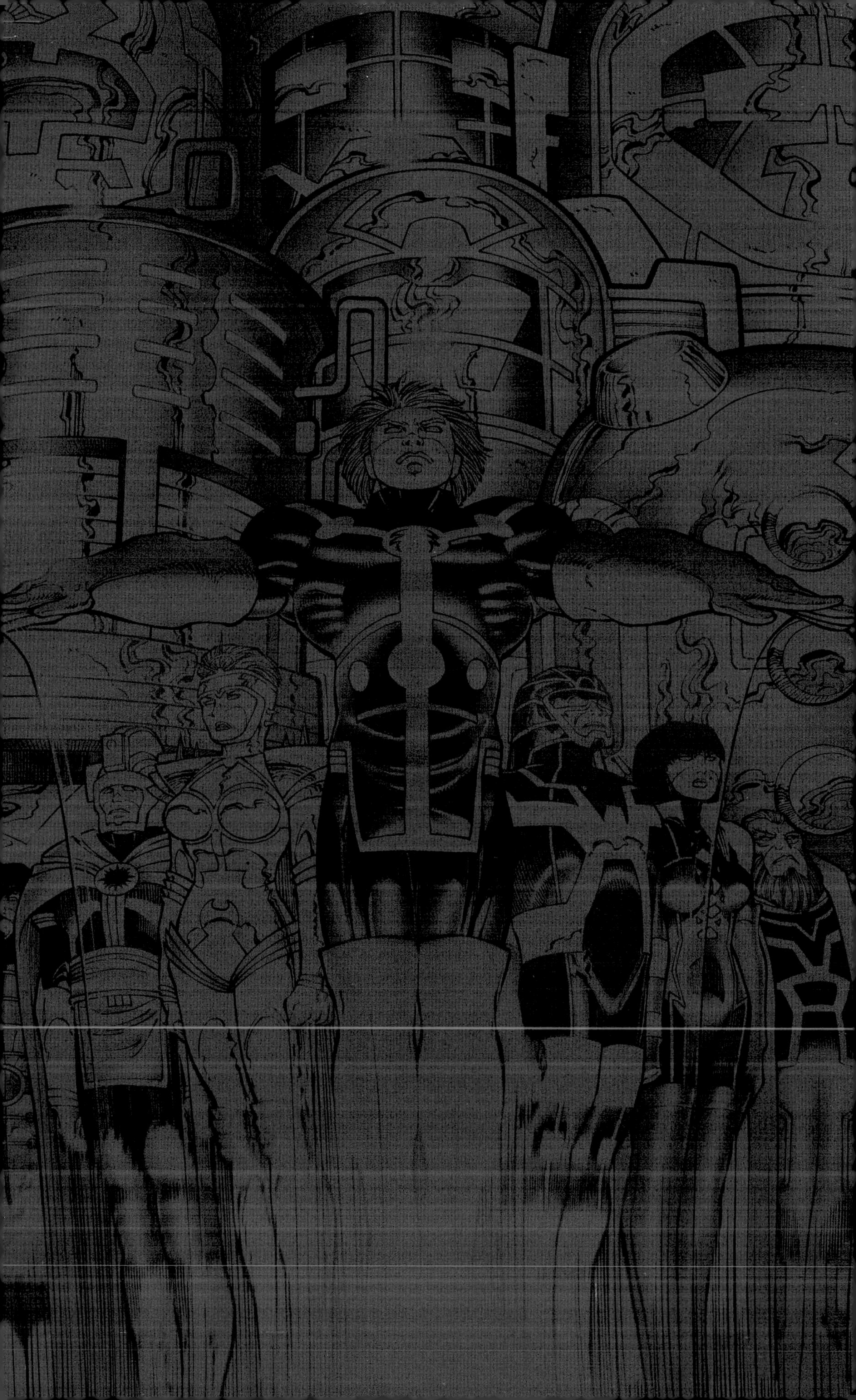

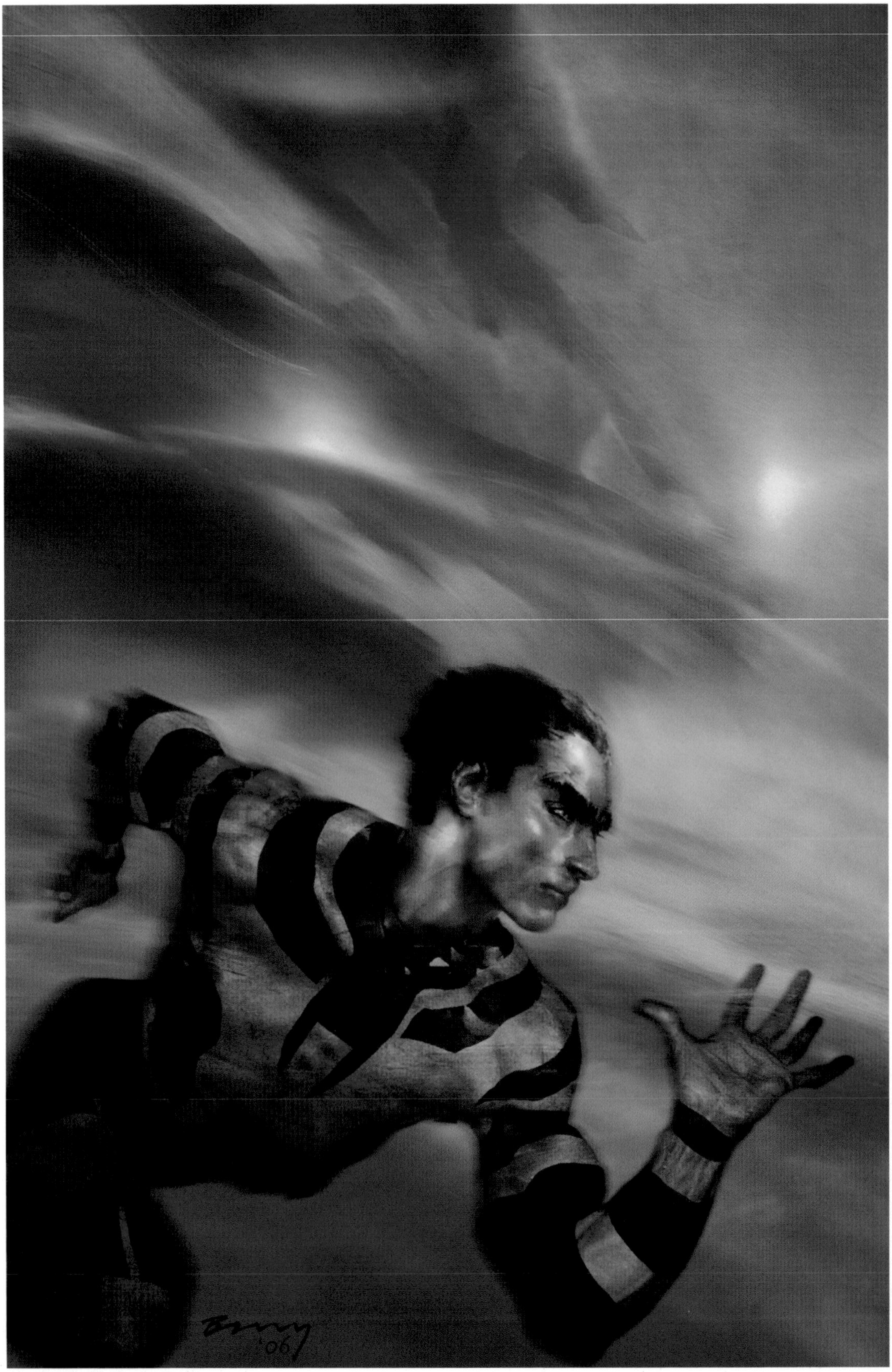

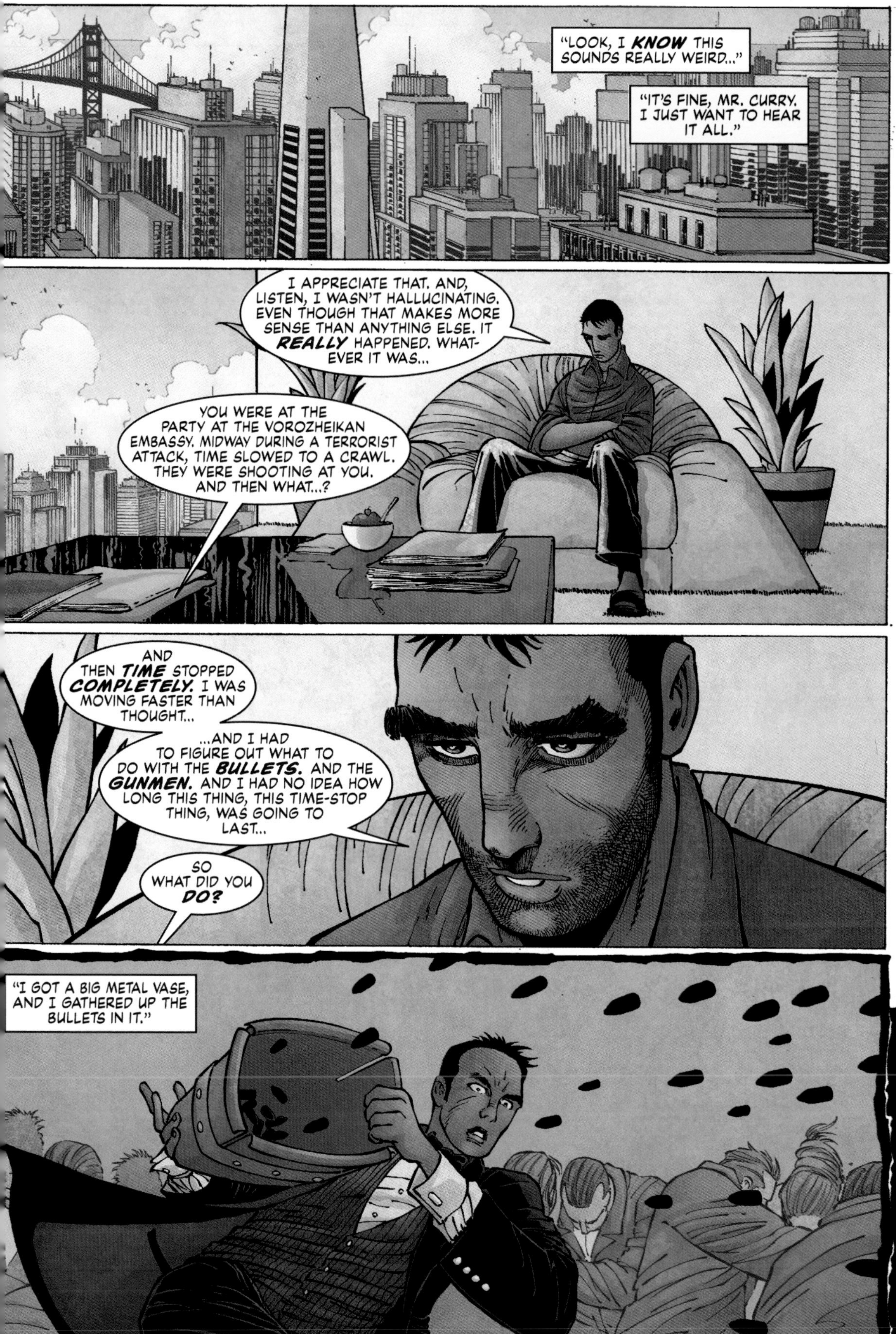
"LOOK, I KNOW THIS SOUNDS REALLY WEIRD..."
"IT'S FINE, MR. CURRY. I JUST WANT TO HEAR IT ALL."
I APPRECIATE THAT. AND, LISTEN, I WASN'T HALLUCINATING. EVEN THOUGH THAT MAKES MORE SENSE THAN ANYTHING ELSE. IT REALLY HAPPENED. WHAT-EVER IT WAS...
YOU WERE AT THE PARTY AT THE VOROZHEIKAN EMBASSY. MIDWAY DURING A TERRORIST ATTACK, TIME SLOWED TO A CRAWL. THEY WERE SHOOTING AT YOU. AND THEN WHAT...?
AND THEN TIME STOPPED COMPLETELY. I WAS MOVING FASTER THAN THOUGHT...
...AND I HAD TO FIGURE OUT WHAT TO DO WITH THE BULLETS. AND THE GUNMEN. AND I HAD NO IDEA HOW LONG THIS THING, THIS TIME-STOP THING, WAS GOING TO LAST...
SO WHAT DID YOU DO?
"I GOT A BIG METAL VASE, AND I GATHERED UP THE BULLETS IN IT."

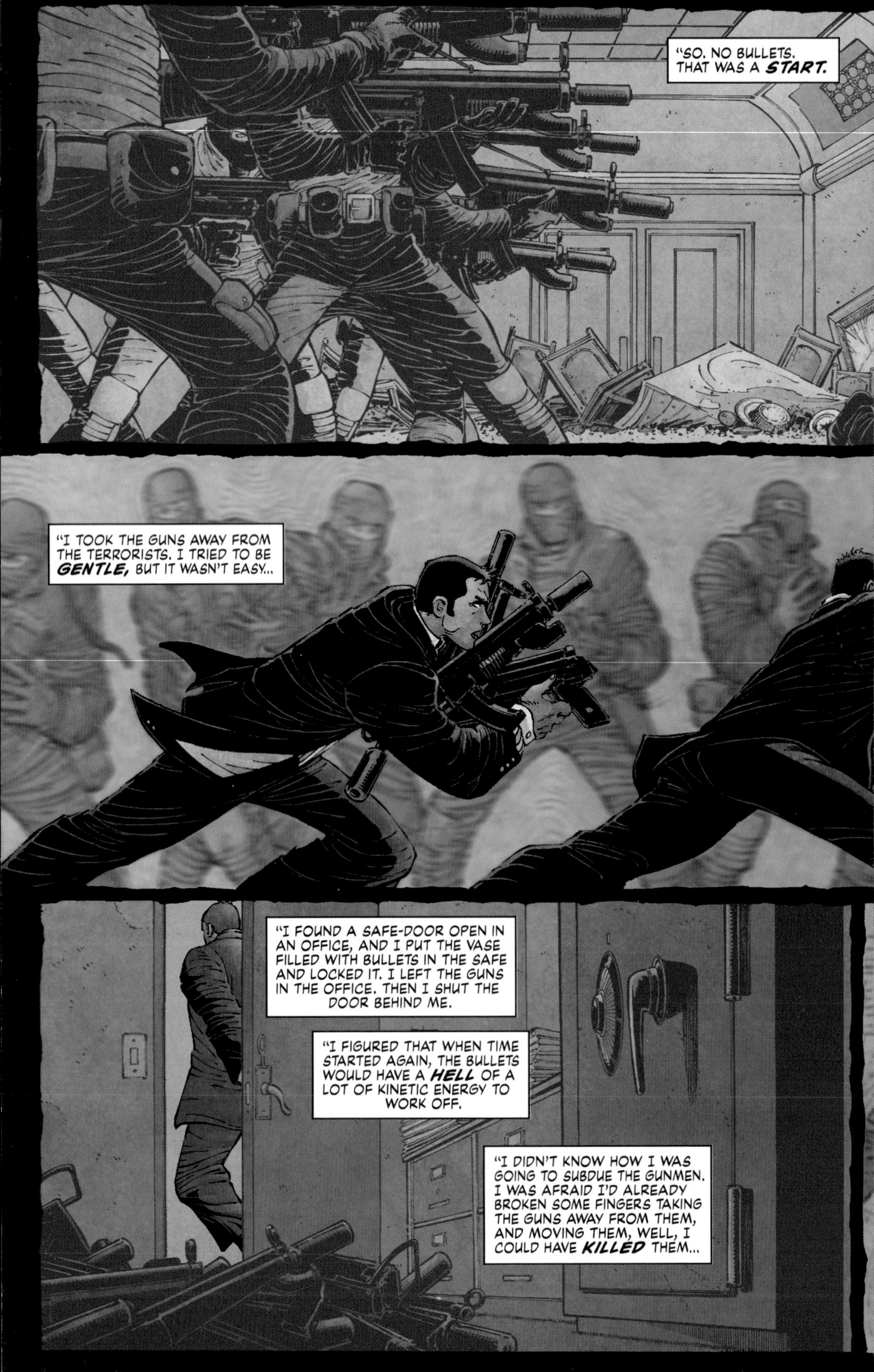
"SO. NO BULLETS. THAT WAS A START.
"I TOOK THE GUNS AWAY FROM THE TERRORISTS. I TRIED TO BE GENTLE, BUT IT WASN'T EASY...
"I FOUND A SAFE-DOOR OPEN IN AN OFFICE, AND I PUT THE VASE FILLED WITH BULLETS IN THE SAFE AND LOCKED IT. I LEFT THE GUNS IN THE OFFICE. THEN I SHUT THE DOOR BEHIND ME.
"I FIGURED THAT WHEN TIME STARTED AGAIN, THE BULLETS WOULD HAVE A HELL OF A LOT OF KINETIC ENERGY TO WORK OFF.
"I DIDN'T KNOW HOW I WAS GOING TO SUBDUE THE GUNMEN. I WAS AFRAID I'D ALREADY BROKEN SOME FINGERS TAKING THE GUNS AWAY FROM THEM, AND MOVING THEM, WELL, I COULD HAVE KILLED THEM...

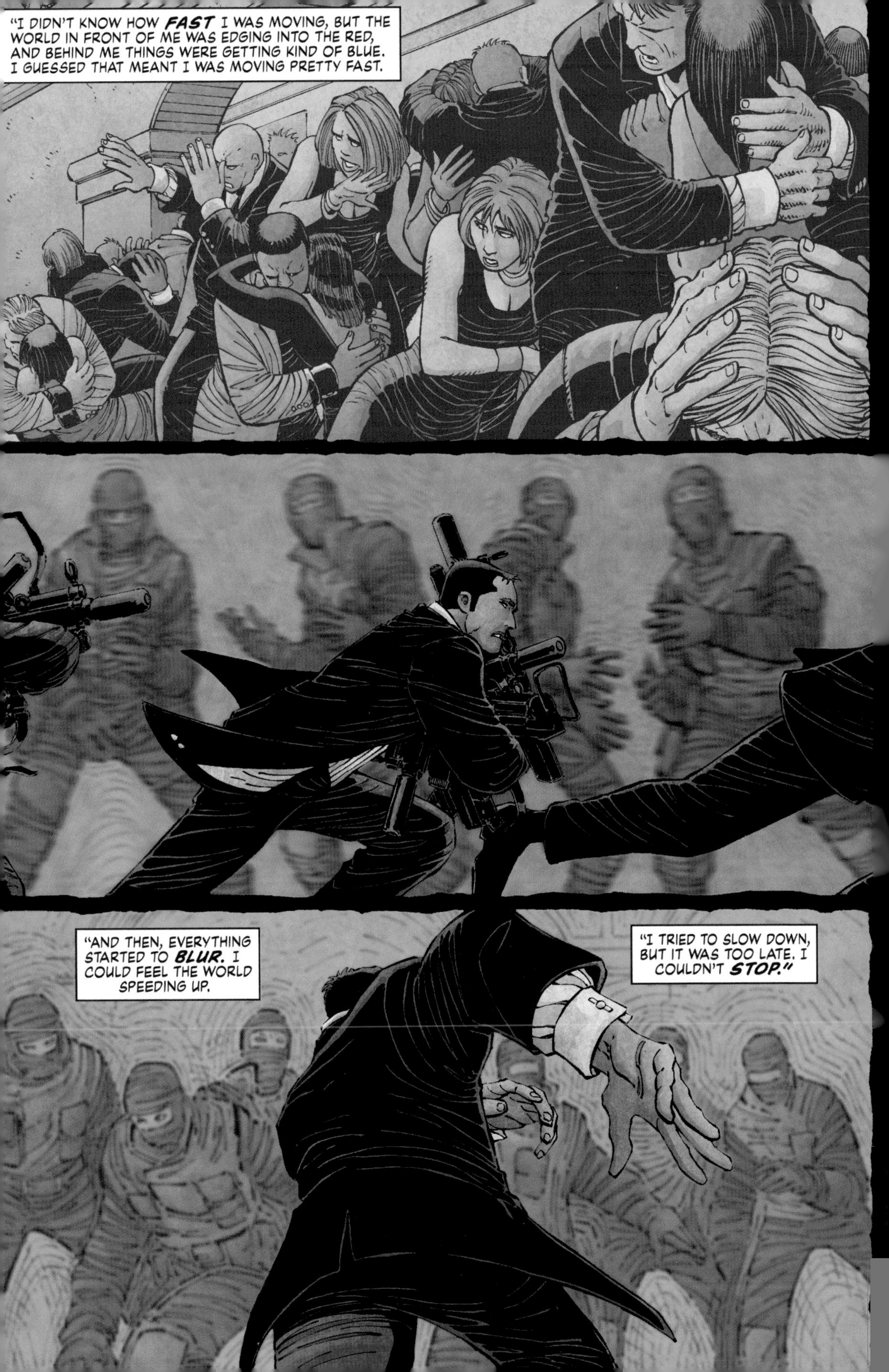
"I DIDN'T KNOW HOW FAST I WAS MOVING, BUT THE WORLD IN FRONT OF ME WAS EDGING INTO THE RED, AND BEHIND ME THINGS WERE GETTING KIND OF BLUE. I GUESSED THAT MEANT I WAS MOVING PRETTY FAST.
"AND THEN, EVERYTHING STARTED TO BLUR. I COULD FEEL THE WORLD SPEEDING UP.
"I TRIED TO SLOW DOWN, BUT IT WAS TOO LATE. I COULDN'T STOP."

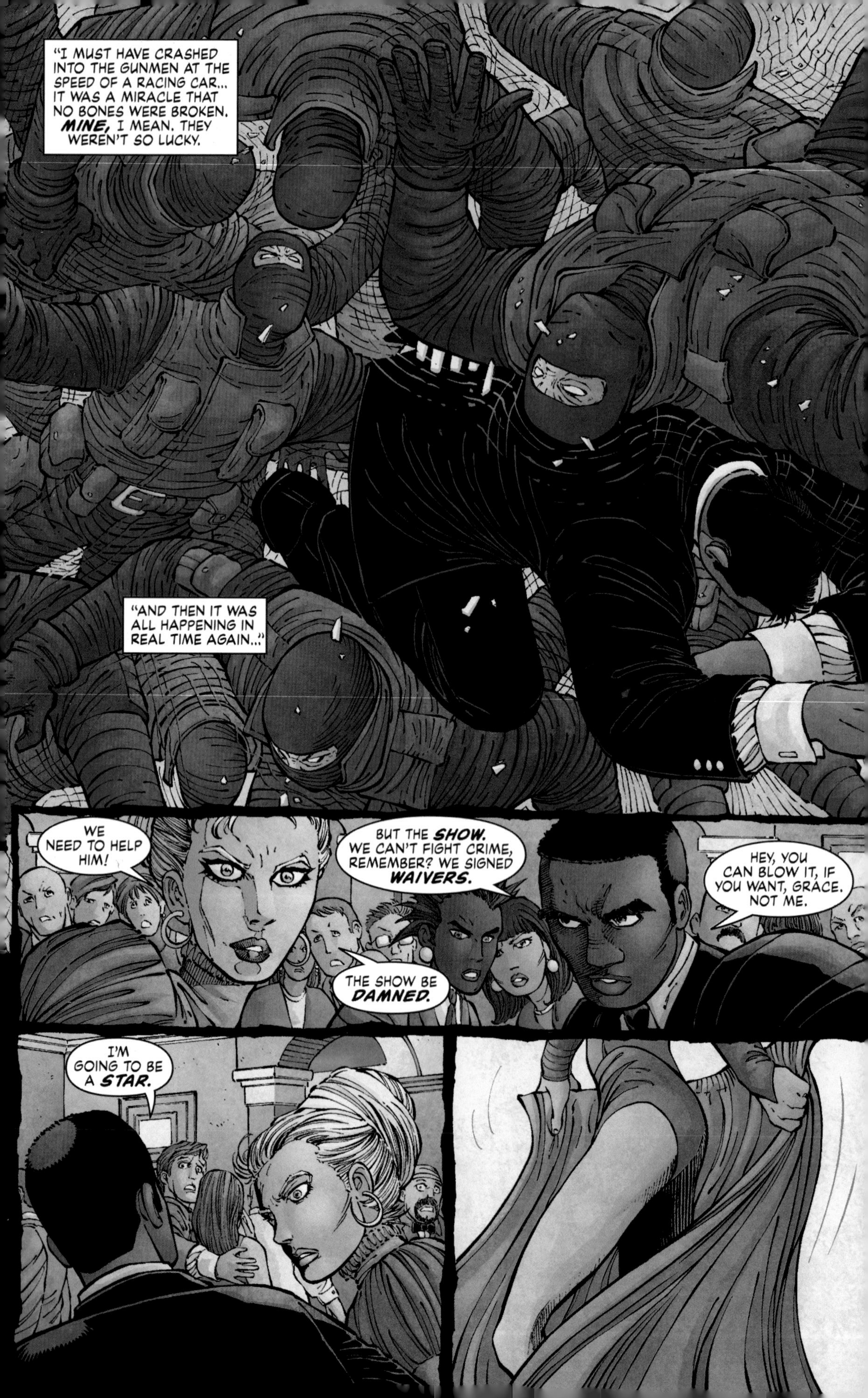
"I MUST HAVE CRASHED INTO THE GUNMEN AT THE SPEED OF A RACING CAR... IT WAS A MIRACLE THAT NO BONES WERE BROKEN. MINE, I MEAN. THEY WEREN'T SO LUCKY.
"AND THEN IT WAS ALL HAPPENING IN REAL TIME AGAIN..."
WE NEED TO HELP HIM!
BUT THE SHOW. WE CAN'T FIGHT CRIME, REMEMBER? WE SIGNED WAIVERS.
HEY, YOU CAN BLOW IT, IF YOU WANT, GRACE. NOT ME.
THE SHOW BE DAMNED.
I'M GOING TO BE A STAR.

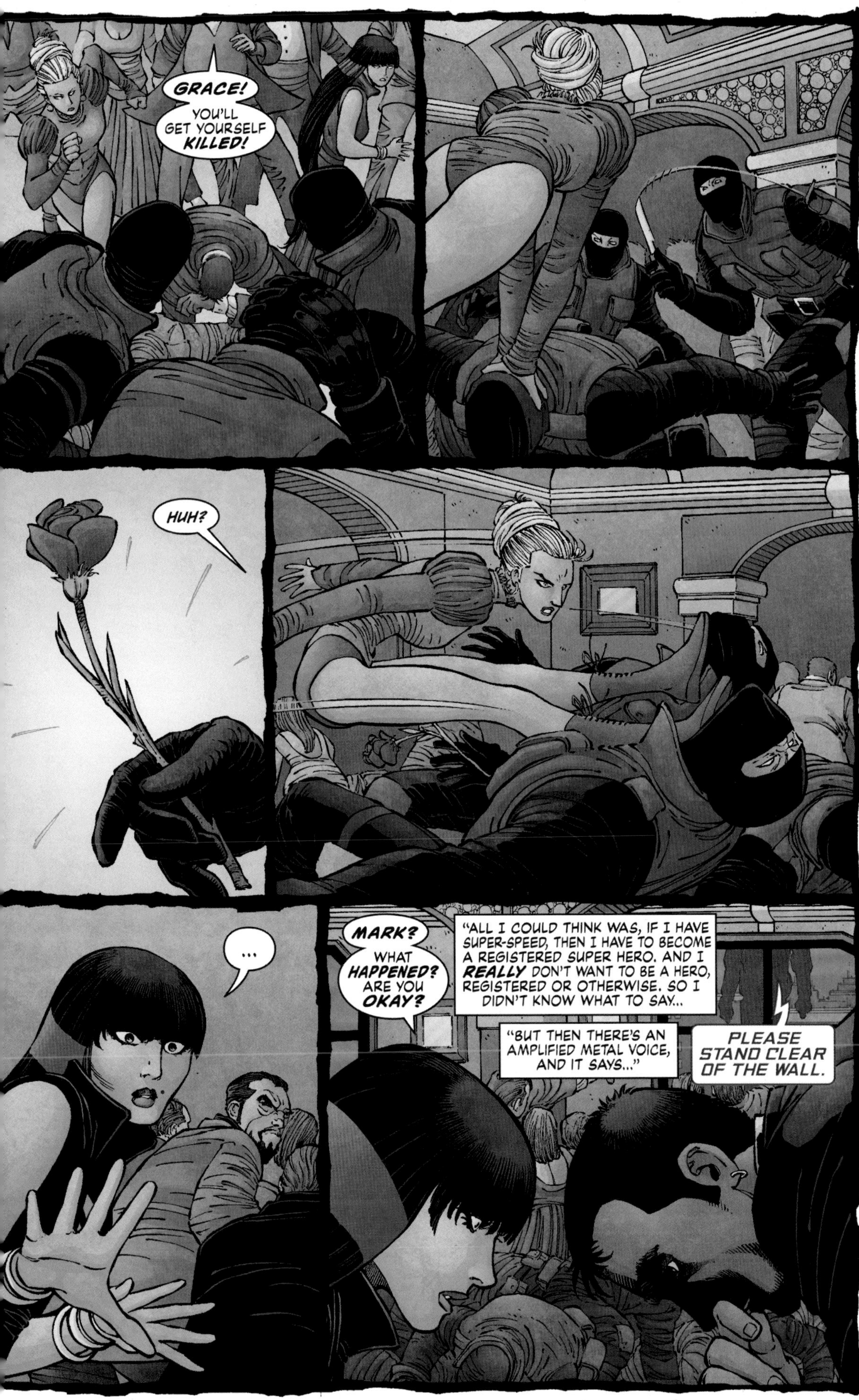
GRACE! YOU'LL GET YOURSELF KILLED!
HUH?
...
MARK? WHAT HAPPENED? ARE YOU OKAY?
"ALL I COULD THINK WAS, IF I HAVE SUPER-SPEED, THEN I HAVE TO BECOME A REGISTERED SUPER HERO. AND I REALLY DON'T WANT TO BE A HERO, REGISTERED OR OTHERWISE. SO I DIDN'T KNOW WHAT TO SAY...
"BUT THEN THERE'S AN AMPLIFIED METAL VOICE, AND IT SAYS..."
PLEASE STAND CLEAR OF THE WALL.

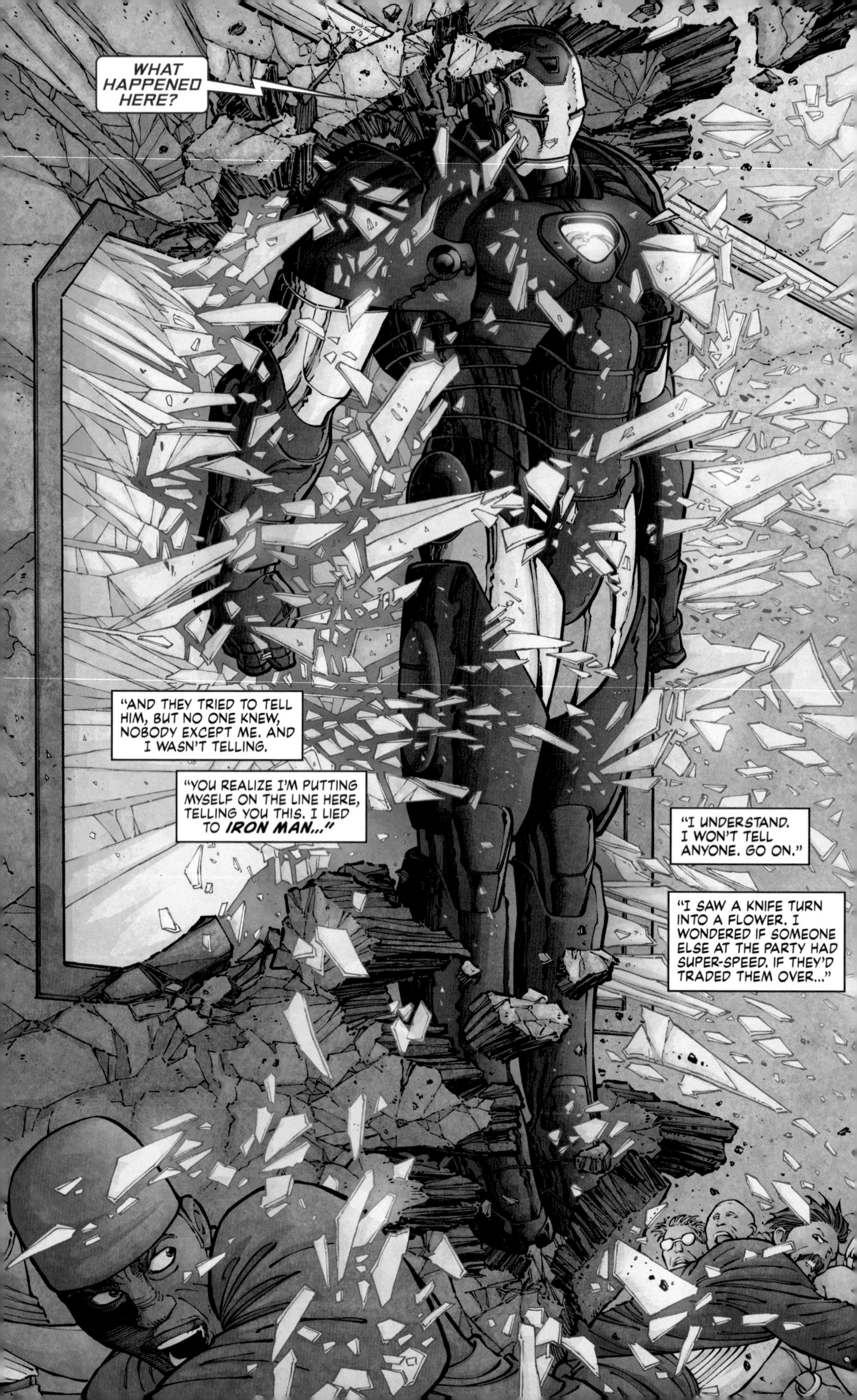
WHAT HAPPENED HERE?
"AND THEY TRIED TO TELL HIM, BUT NO ONE KNEW, NOBODY EXCEPT ME. AND I WASN'T TELLING.
"YOU REALIZE I'M PUTTING MYSELF ON THE LINE HERE, TELLING YOU THIS. I LIED TO IRON MAN..."
"I UNDERSTAND. I WON'T TELL ANYONE. GO ON."
"I SAW A KNIFE TURN INTO A FLOWER. I WONDERED IF SOMEONE ELSE AT THE PARTY HAD SUPER-SPEED. IF THEY'D TRADED THEM OVER..."

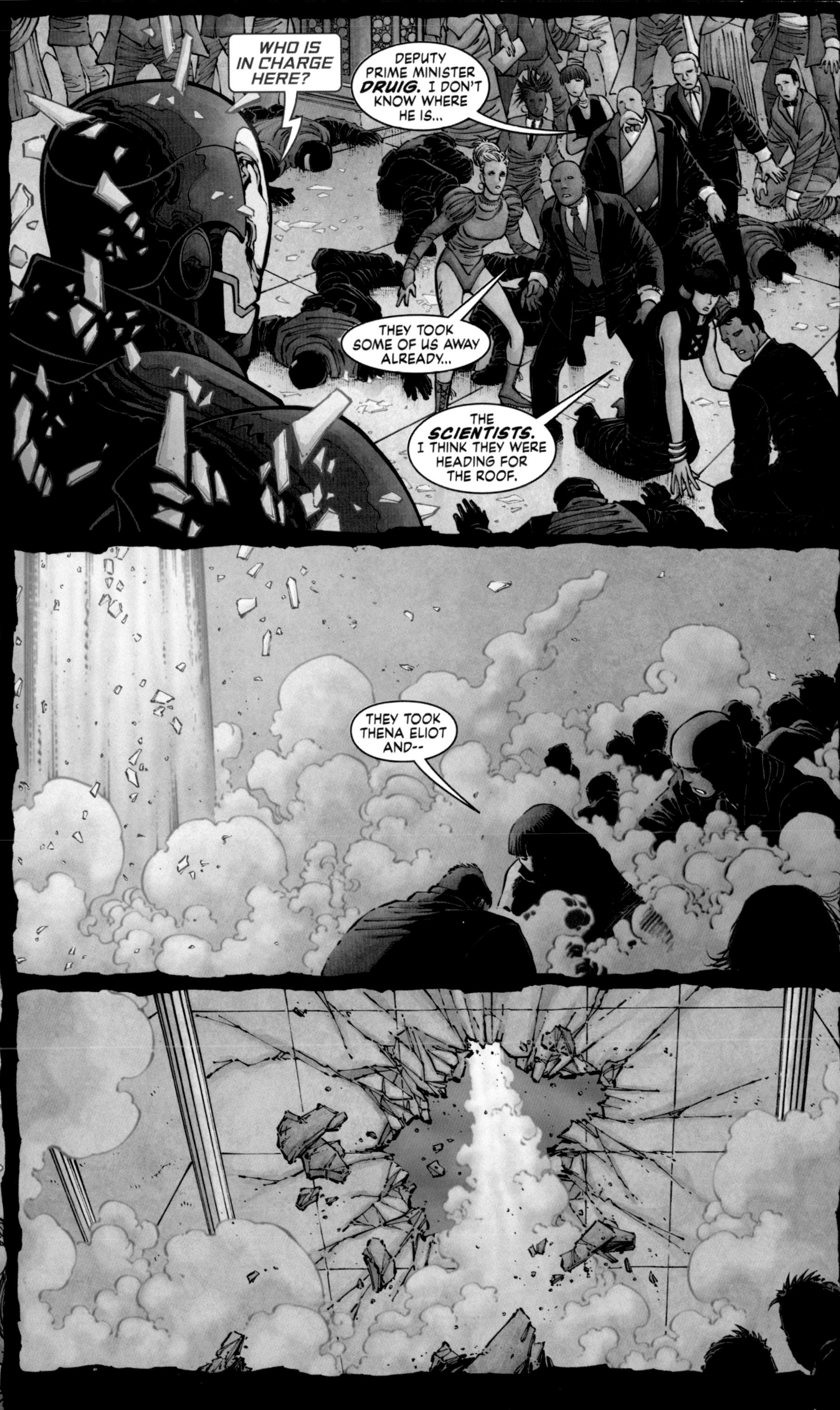
WHO IS IN CHARGE HERE?
DEPUTY PRIME MINISTER DRUIG. I DON'T KNOW WHERE HE IS...
THEY TOOK SOME OF US AWAY ALREADY...
THE SCIENTISTS. I THINK THEY WERE HEADING FOR THE ROOF.
THEY TOOK THENA ELIOT AND--

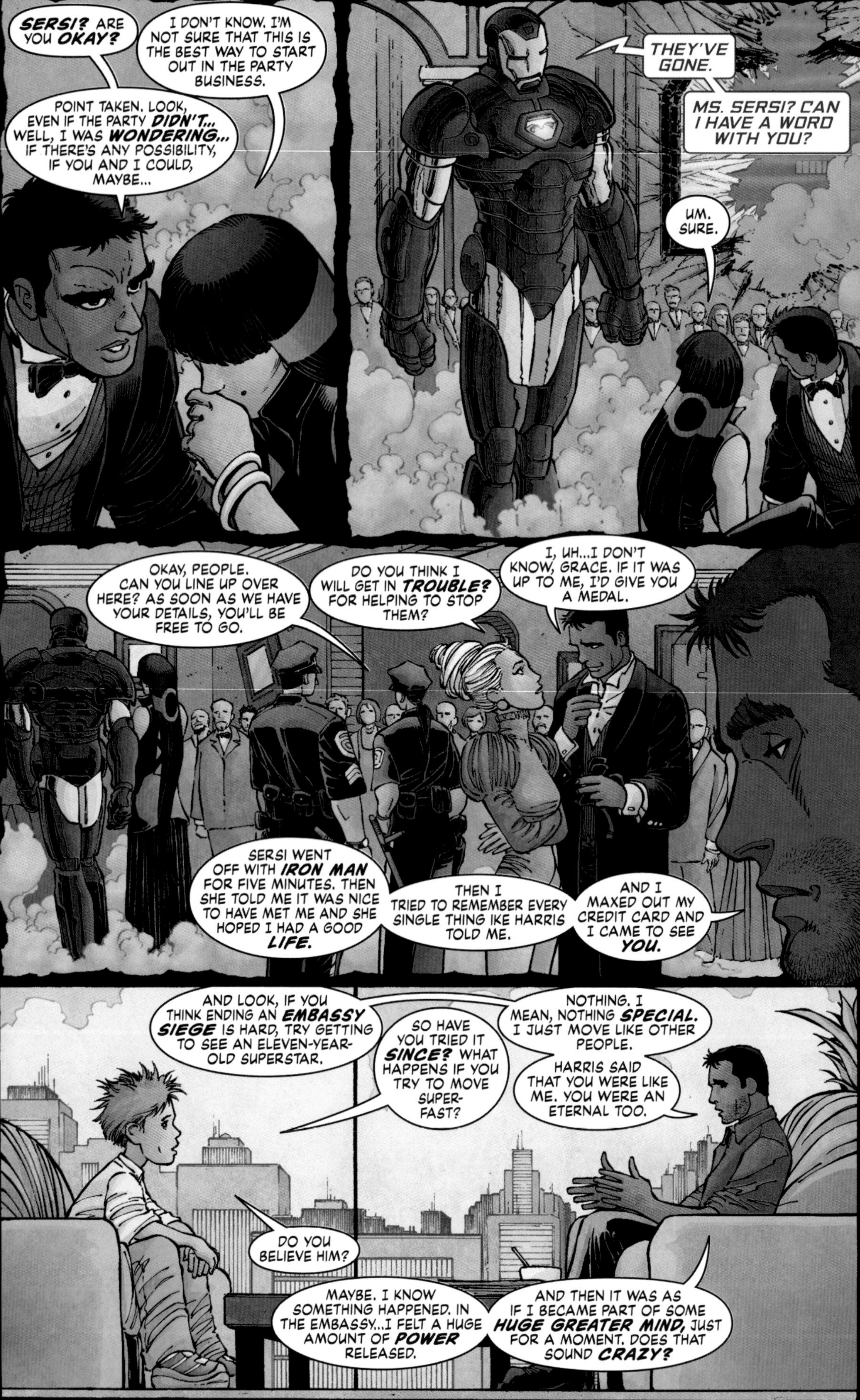
SERSI? ARE YOU OKAY?
I DON'T KNOW. I'M NOT SURE THAT THIS IS THE BEST WAY TO START OUT IN THE PARTY BUSINESS.
POINT TAKEN. LOOK, EVEN IF THE PARTY DIDN'T... WELL, I WAS WONDERING... IF THERE'S ANY POSSIBILITY, IF YOU AND I COULD, MAYBE...
THEY'VE GONE.
MS. SERSI? CAN I HAVE A WORD WITH YOU?
UM. SURE.
OKAY, PEOPLE. CAN YOU LINE UP OVER HERE? AS SOON AS WE HAVE YOUR DETAILS, YOU'LL BE FREE TO GO.
DO YOU THINK I WILL GET IN TROUBLE? FOR HELPING TO STOP THEM?
I, UH...I DON'T KNOW, GRACE. IF IT WAS UP TO ME, I'D GIVE YOU A MEDAL.
SERSI WENT OFF WITH IRON MAN FOR FIVE MINUTES. THEN SHE TOLD ME IT WAS NICE TO HAVE MET ME AND SHE HOPED I HAD A GOOD LIFE.
THEN I TRIED TO REMEMBER EVERY SINGLE THING IKE HARRIS TOLD ME.
AND I MAXED OUT MY CREDIT CARD AND I CAME TO SEE YOU.
AND LOOK, IF YOU THINK ENDING AN EMBASSY SIEGE IS HARD, TRY GETTING TO SEE AN ELEVEN-YEAR-OLD SUPERSTAR.
SO HAVE YOU TRIED IT SINCE? WHAT HAPPENS IF YOU TRY TO MOVE SUPER-FAST?
NOTHING. I MEAN, NOTHING SPECIAL. I JUST MOVE LIKE OTHER PEOPLE.
HARRIS SAID THAT YOU WERE LIKE ME. YOU WERE AN ETERNAL TOO.
DO YOU BELIEVE HIM?
MAYBE. I KNOW SOMETHING HAPPENED. IN THE EMBASSY...I FELT A HUGE AMOUNT OF POWER RELEASED.
AND THEN IT WAS AS IF I BECAME PART OF SOME HUGE GREATER MIND, JUST FOR A MOMENT. DOES THAT SOUND CRAZY?

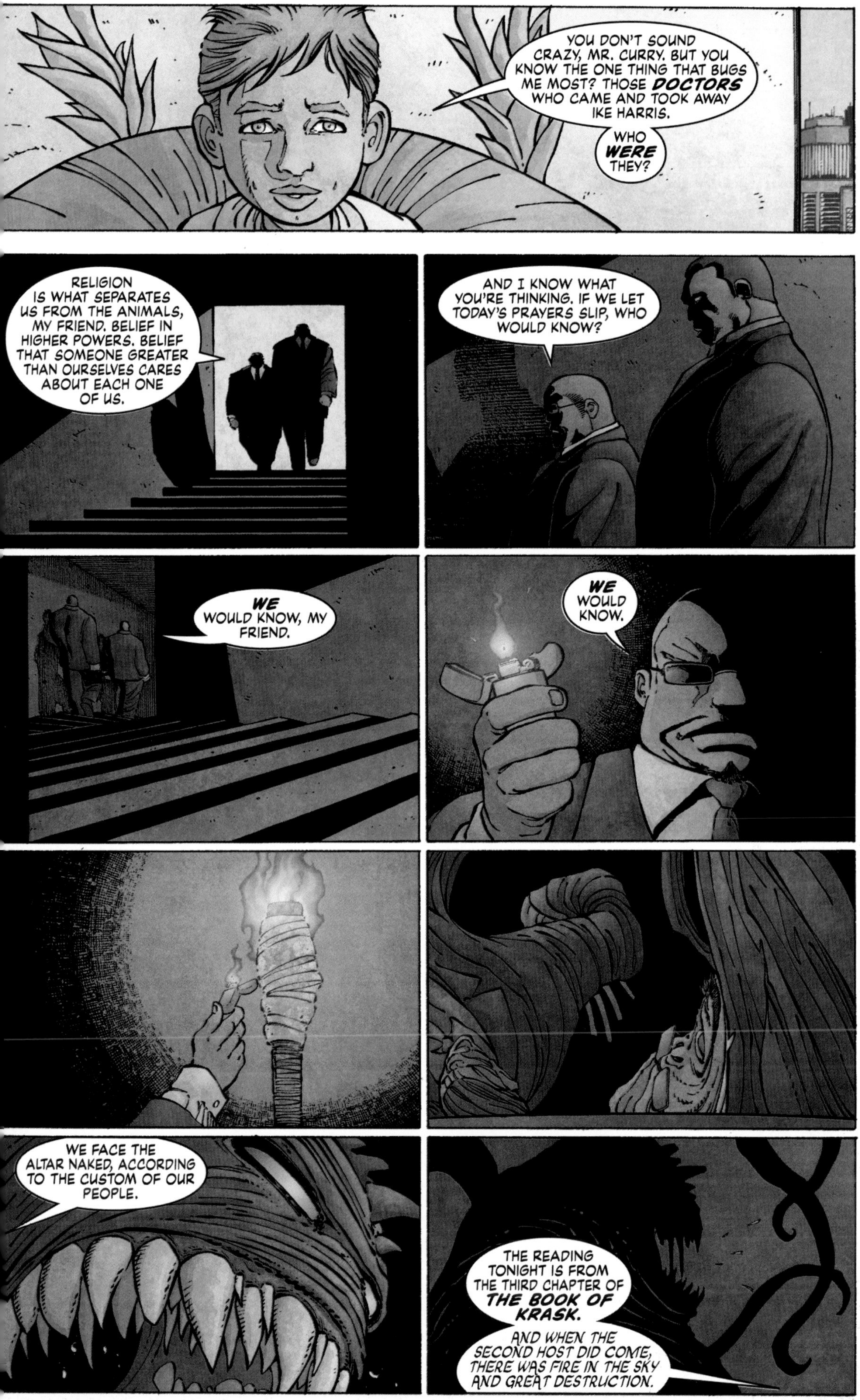
YOU DON'T SOUND CRAZY, MR. CURRY. BUT YOU KNOW THE ONE THING THAT BUGS ME MOST? THOSE DOCTORS WHO CAME AND TOOK AWAY IKE HARRIS.
WHO WERE THEY?
RELIGION IS WHAT SEPARATES US FROM THE ANIMALS, MY FRIEND. BELIEF IN HIGHER POWERS. BELIEF THAT SOMEONE GREATER THAN OURSELVES CARES ABOUT EACH ONE OF US.
AND I KNOW WHAT YOU'RE THINKING. IF WE LET TODAY'S PRAYERS SLIP, WHO WOULD KNOW?
WE WOULD KNOW, MY FRIEND.
WE WOULD KNOW.
WE FACE THE ALTAR NAKED, ACCORDING TO THE CUSTOM OF OUR PEOPLE.
THE READING TONIGHT IS FROM THE THIRD CHAPTER OF THE BOOK OF KRASK.
AND WHEN THE SECOND HOST DID COME, THERE WAS FIRE IN THE SKY AND GREAT DESTRUCTION.

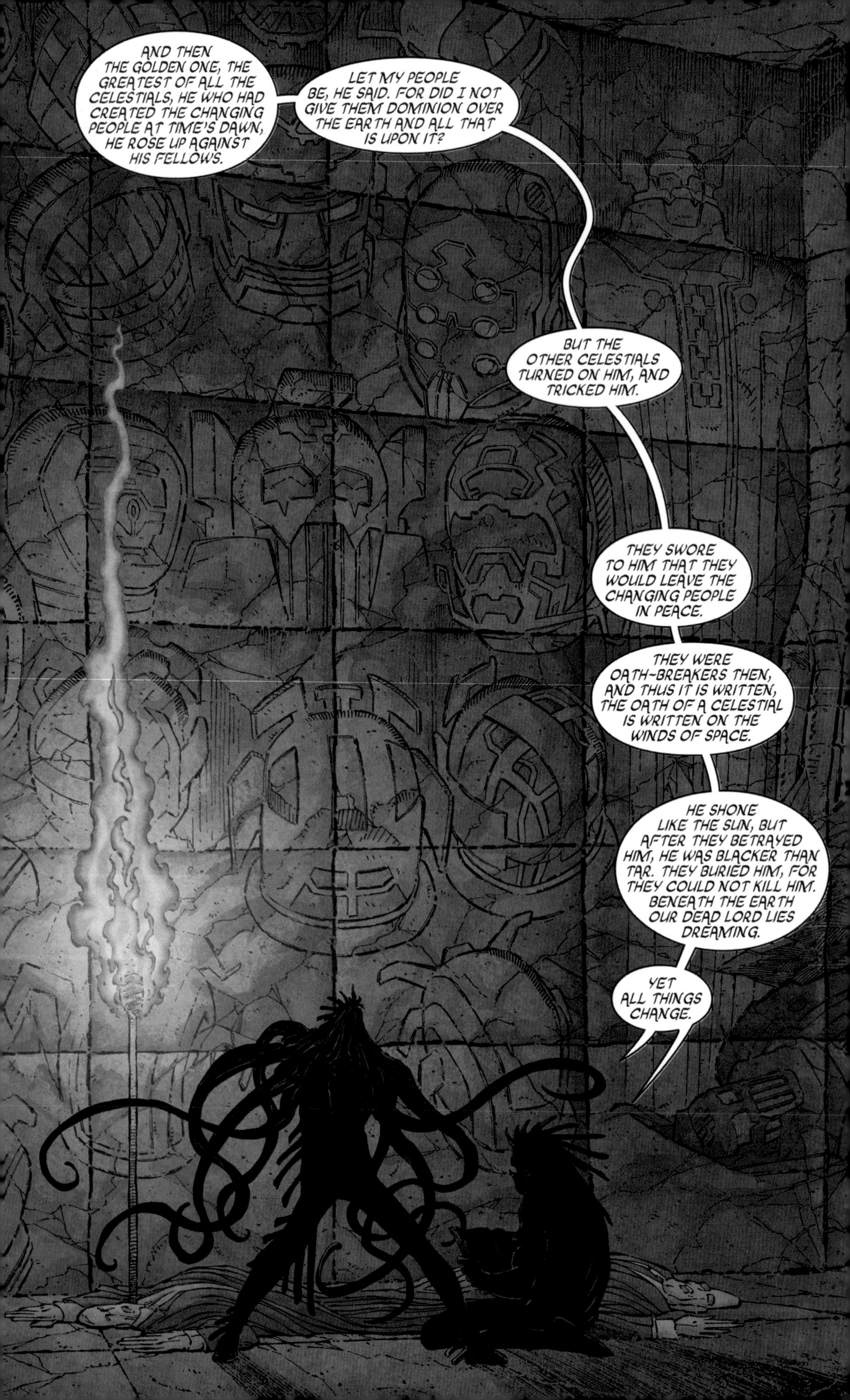
AND THEN THE GOLDEN ONE, THE GREATEST OF ALL THE CELESTIALS, HE WHO HAD CREATED THE CHANGING PEOPLE AT TIME'S DAWN, HE ROSE UP AGAINST HIS FELLOWS.
LET MY PEOPLE BE, HE SAID. FOR DID I NOT GIVE THEM DOMINION OVER THE EARTH AND ALL THAT IS UPON IT?
BUT THE OTHER CELESTIALS TURNED ON HIM, AND TRICKED HIM.
THEY SWORE TO HIM THAT THEY WOULD LEAVE THE CHANGING PEOPLE IN PEACE.
THEY WERE OATH-BREAKERS THEN, AND THUS IT IS WRITTEN, THE OATH OF A CELESTIAL IS WRITTEN ON THE WINDS OF SPACE.
HE SHONE LIKE THE SUN, BUT AFTER THEY BETRAYED HIM, HE WAS BLACKER THAN TAR. THEY BURIED HIM, FOR THEY COULD NOT KILL HIM. BENEATH THE EARTH OUR DEAD LORD LIES DREAMING.
YET ALL THINGS CHANGE.

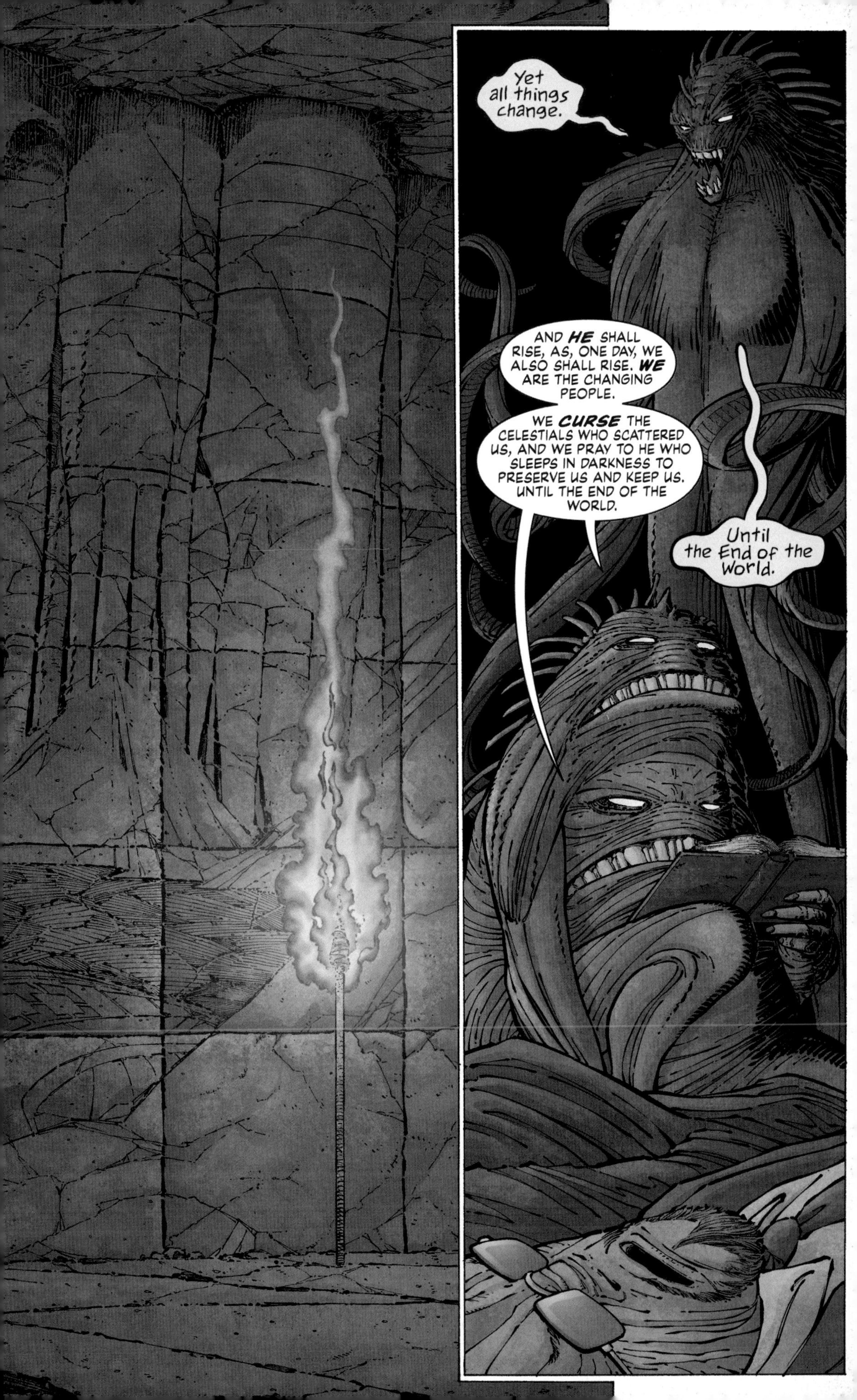
Yet all things change.
AND ***HE*** SHALL RISE, AS, ONE DAY, WE ALSO SHALL RISE. ***WE*** ARE THE CHANGING PEOPLE.
WE ***CURSE*** THE CELESTIALS WHO SCATTERED US, AND WE PRAY TO HE WHO SLEEPS IN DARKNESS TO PRESERVE US AND KEEP US. UNTIL THE END OF THE WORLD.
Until the End of the World.

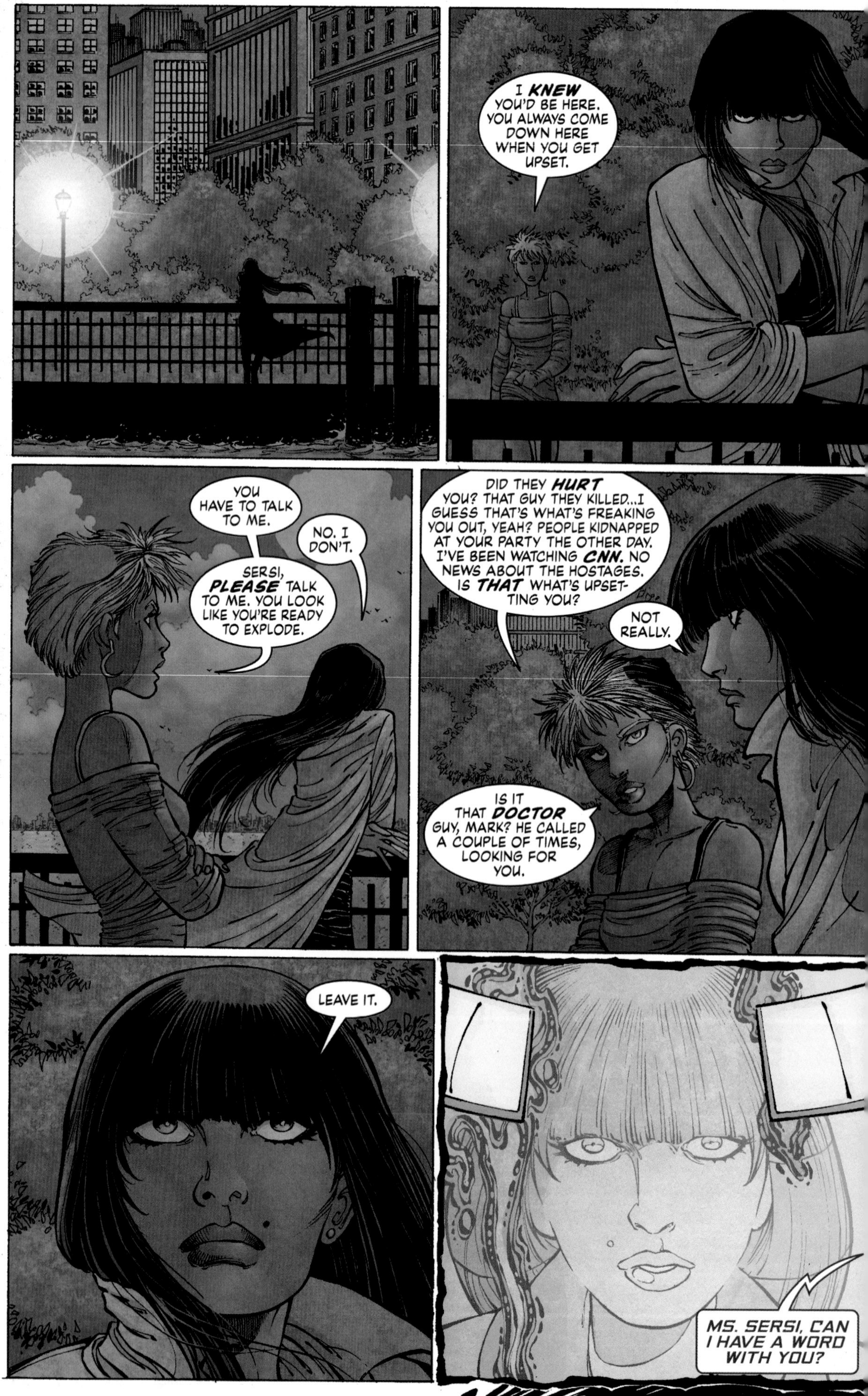
I KNEW YOU'D BE HERE. YOU ALWAYS COME DOWN HERE WHEN YOU GET UPSET.
YOU HAVE TO TALK TO ME.
NO. I DON'T.
SERSI, PLEASE TALK TO ME. YOU LOOK LIKE YOU'RE READY TO EXPLODE.
DID THEY HURT YOU? THAT GUY THEY KILLED...I GUESS THAT'S WHAT'S FREAKING YOU OUT, YEAH? PEOPLE KIDNAPPED AT YOUR PARTY THE OTHER DAY. I'VE BEEN WATCHING CNN. NO NEWS ABOUT THE HOSTAGES. IS THAT WHAT'S UPSETTING YOU?
NOT REALLY.
IS IT THAT DOCTOR GUY, MARK? HE CALLED A COUPLE OF TIMES, LOOKING FOR YOU.
LEAVE IT.
MS. SERSI, CAN I HAVE A WORD WITH YOU?

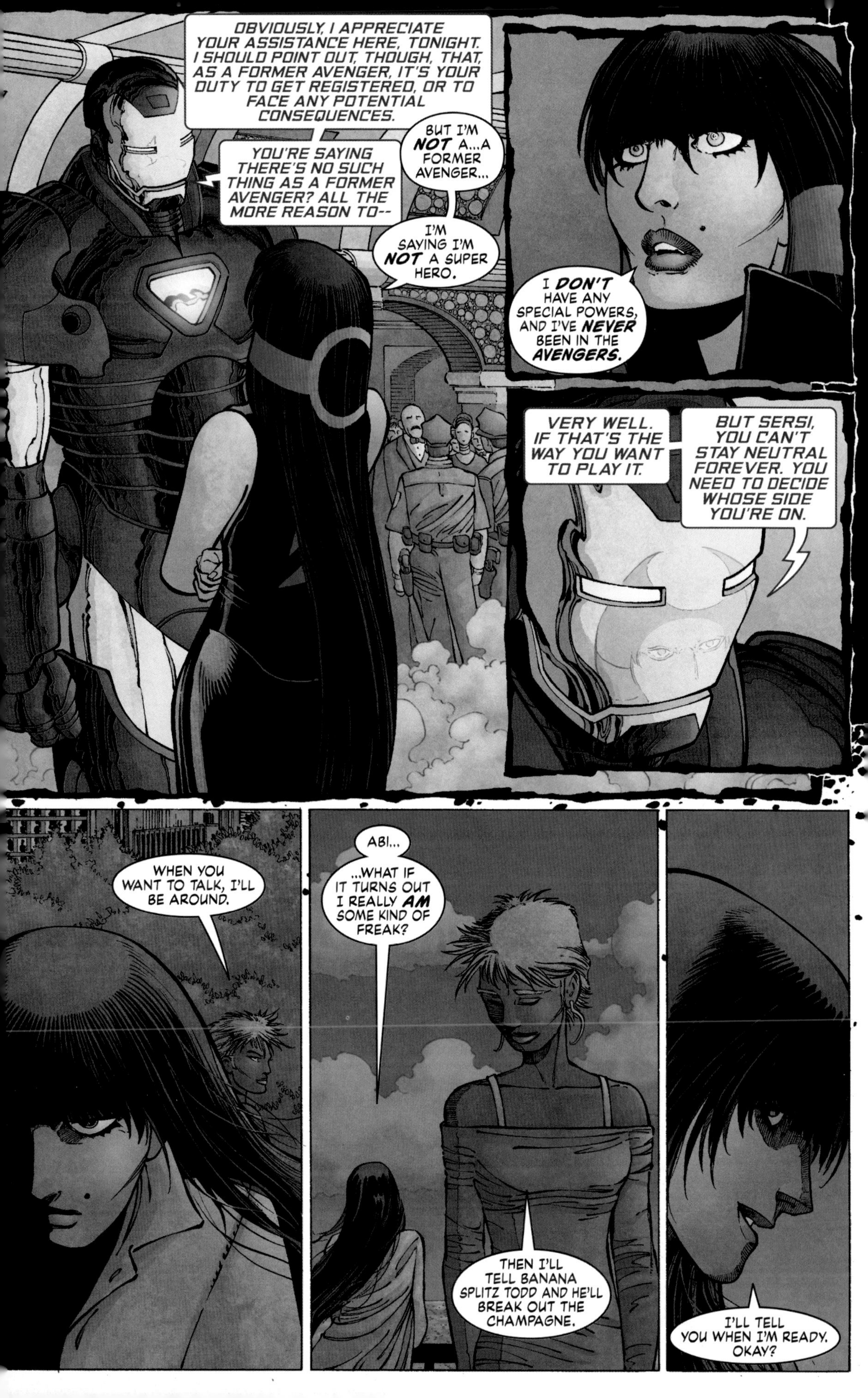
OBVIOUSLY, I APPRECIATE YOUR ASSISTANCE HERE, TONIGHT. I SHOULD POINT OUT, THOUGH, THAT, AS A FORMER AVENGER, IT'S YOUR DUTY TO GET REGISTERED, OR TO FACE ANY POTENTIAL CONSEQUENCES.
BUT I'M NOT A...A FORMER AVENGER...
YOU'RE SAYING THERE'S NO SUCH THING AS A FORMER AVENGER? ALL THE MORE REASON TO--
I'M SAYING I'M NOT A SUPER HERO.
I DON'T HAVE ANY SPECIAL POWERS, AND I'VE NEVER BEEN IN THE AVENGERS.
VERY WELL. IF THAT'S THE WAY YOU WANT TO PLAY IT.
BUT SERSI, YOU CAN'T STAY NEUTRAL FOREVER. YOU NEED TO DECIDE WHOSE SIDE YOU'RE ON.
WHEN YOU WANT TO TALK, I'LL BE AROUND.
ABI...
...WHAT IF IT TURNS OUT I REALLY AM SOME KIND OF FREAK?
THEN I'LL TELL BANANA SPLITZ TODD AND HE'LL BREAK OUT THE CHAMPAGNE.
I'LL TELL YOU WHEN I'M READY. OKAY?

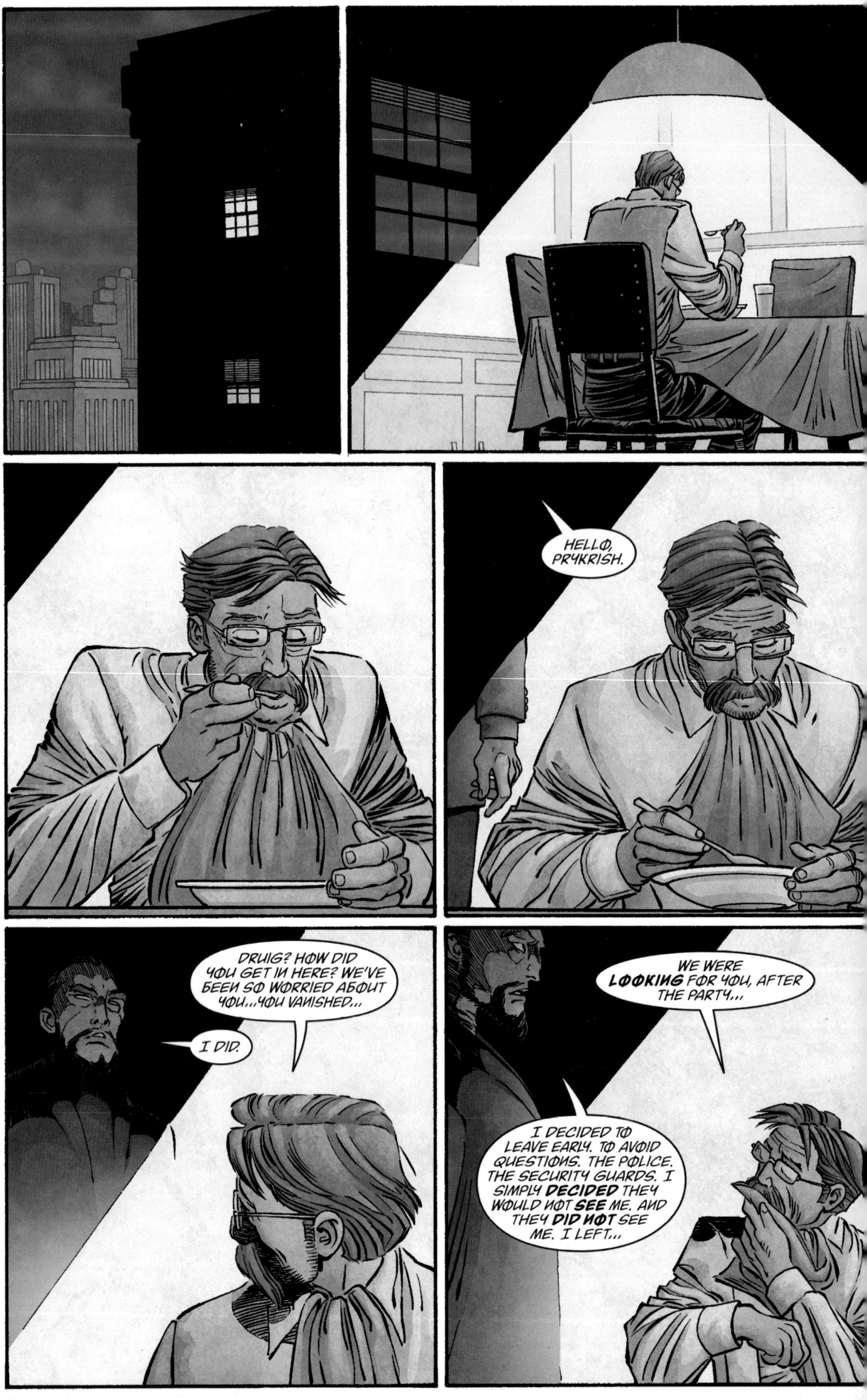
HELLO, PRYKRISH.
DRUIG? HOW DID YOU GET IN HERE? WE'VE BEEN SO WORRIED ABOUT YOU...YOU VANISHED...
I DID.
WE WERE LOOKING FOR YOU, AFTER THE PARTY...
I DECIDED TO LEAVE EARLY. TO AVOID QUESTIONS. THE POLICE. THE SECURITY GUARDS. I SIMPLY DECIDED THEY WOULD NOT SEE ME. AND THEY DID NOT SEE ME. I LEFT...

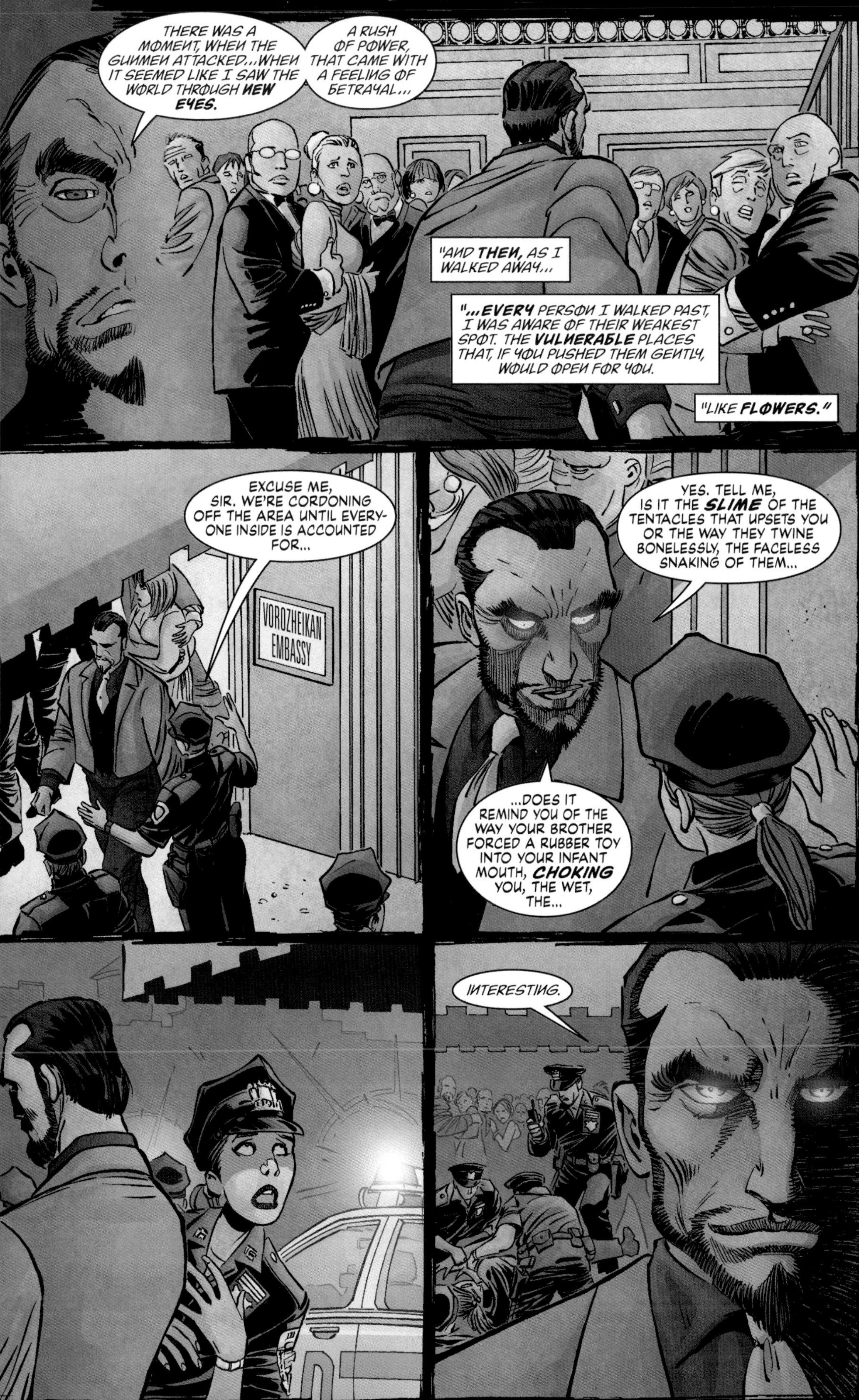
THERE WAS A MOMENT, WHEN THE GUNMEN ATTACKED... WHEN IT SEEMED LIKE I SAW THE WORLD THROUGH NEW EYES.
A RUSH OF POWER, THAT CAME WITH A FEELING OF BETRAYAL...
"AND THEN, AS I WALKED AWAY...
"...EVERY PERSON I WALKED PAST, I WAS AWARE OF THEIR WEAKEST SPOT. THE VULNERABLE PLACES THAT, IF YOU PUSHED THEM GENTLY, WOULD OPEN FOR YOU.
"LIKE FLOWERS."
EXCUSE ME, SIR. WE'RE CORDONING OFF THE AREA UNTIL EVERY-ONE INSIDE IS ACCOUNTED FOR...
VOROZHEIKAN EMBASSY
YES. TELL ME, IS IT THE SLIME OF THE TENTACLES THAT UPSETS YOU OR THE WAY THEY TWINE BONELESSLY, THE FACELESS SNAKING OF THEM...
...DOES IT REMIND YOU OF THE WAY YOUR BROTHER FORCED A RUBBER TOY INTO YOUR INFANT MOUTH, CHOKING YOU, THE WET, THE...
INTERESTING.

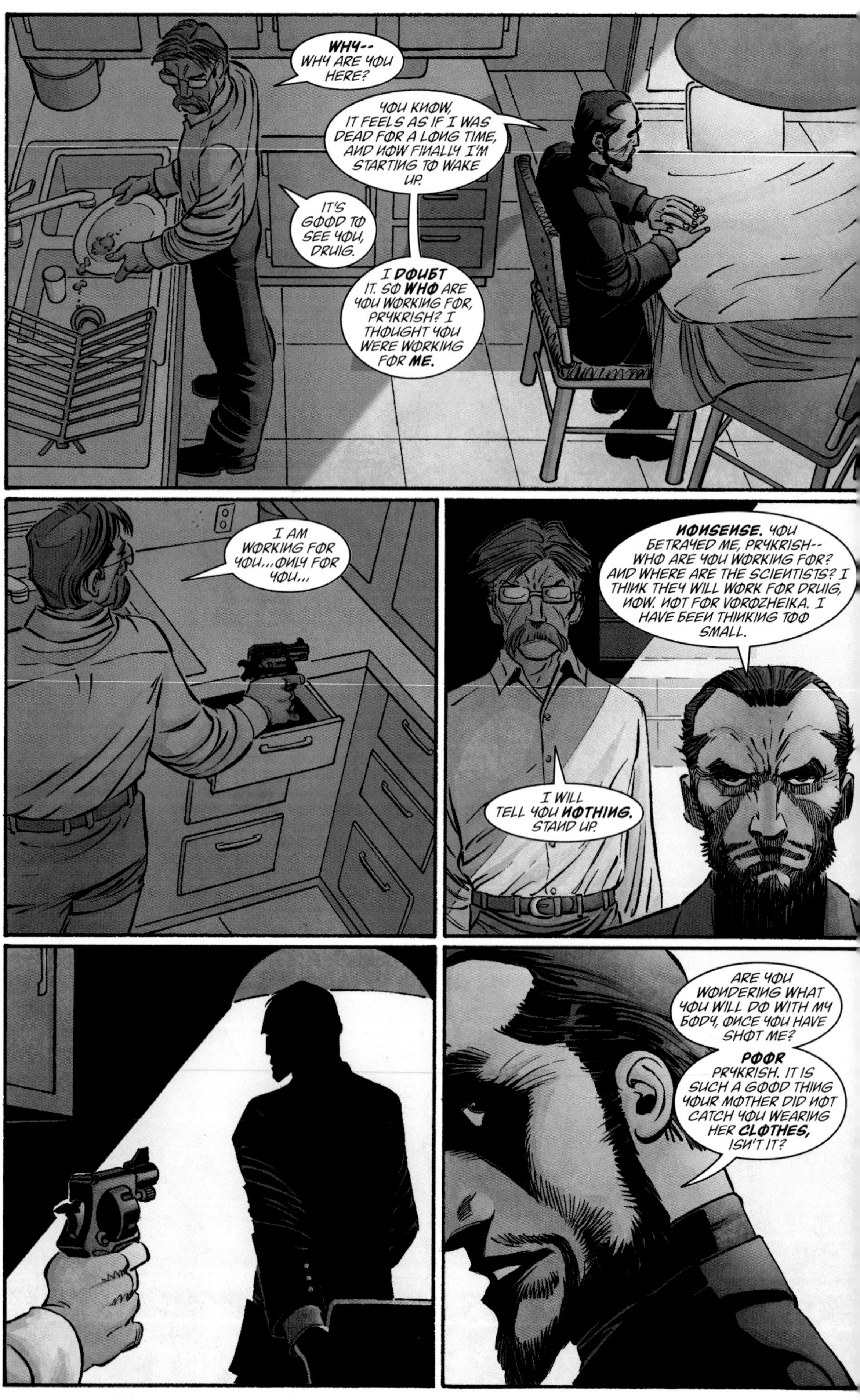
WHY--
WHY ARE YOU HERE?
YOU KNOW, IT FEELS AS IF I WAS DEAD FOR A LONG TIME, AND NOW FINALLY I'M STARTING TO WAKE UP.
IT'S GOOD TO SEE YOU, DRUIG.
I DOUBT IT. SO WHO ARE YOU WORKING FOR, PRYKRISH? I THOUGHT YOU WERE WORKING FOR ME.
I AM WORKING FOR YOU...ONLY FOR YOU...
NONSENSE. YOU BETRAYED ME, PRYKRISH-- WHO ARE YOU WORKING FOR? AND WHERE ARE THE SCIENTISTS? I THINK THEY WILL WORK FOR DRUIG, NOW. NOT FOR VOROZHEIKA. I HAVE BEEN THINKING TOO SMALL.
I WILL TELL YOU NOTHING. STAND UP.
ARE YOU WONDERING WHAT YOU WILL DO WITH MY BODY, ONCE YOU HAVE SHOT ME?
POOR PRYKRISH. IT IS SUCH A GOOD THING YOUR MOTHER DID NOT CATCH YOU WEARING HER CLOTHES, ISN'T IT?

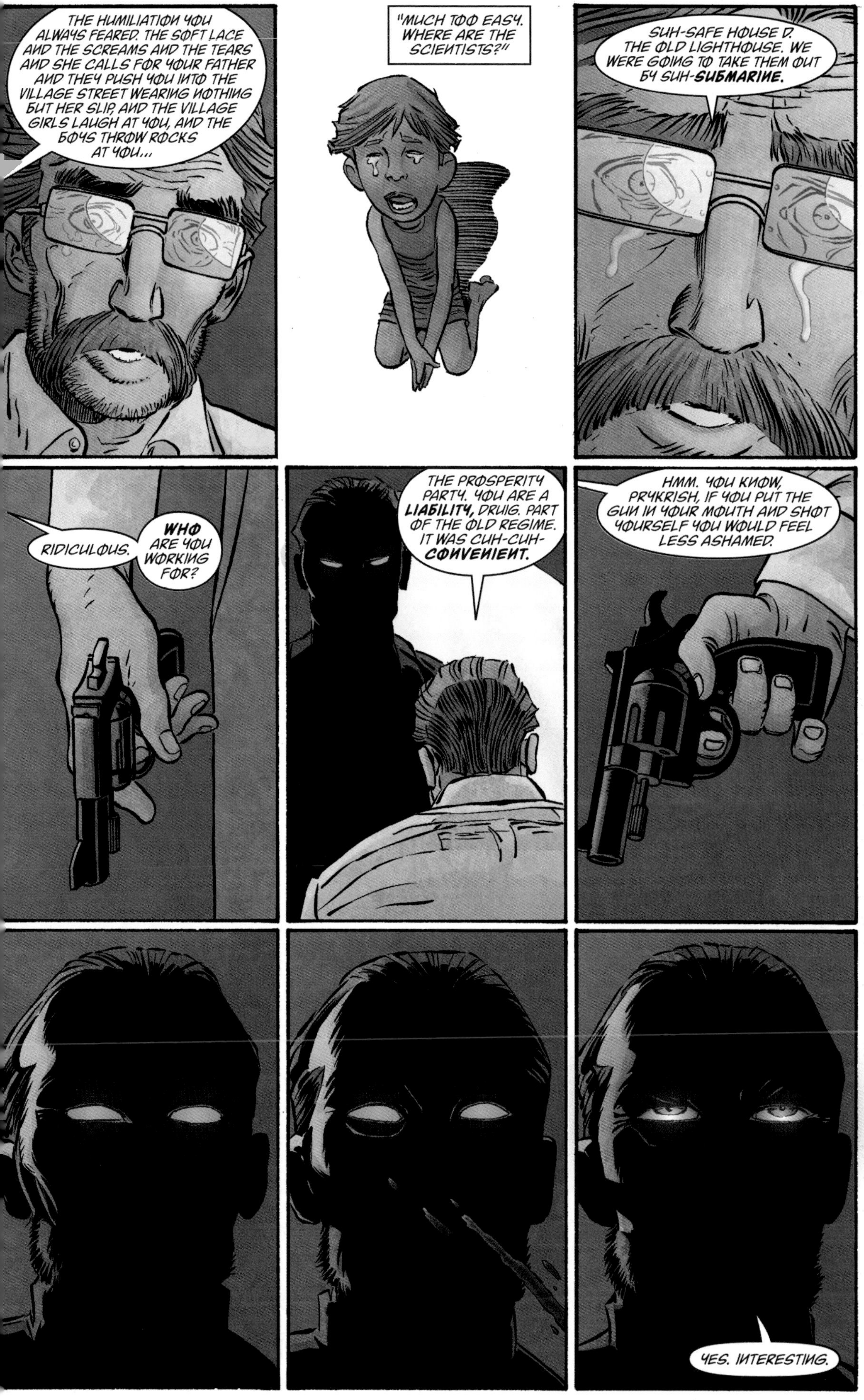
THE HUMILIATION YOU ALWAYS FEARED. THE SOFT LACE AND THE SCREAMS AND THE TEARS AND SHE CALLS FOR YOUR FATHER AND THEY PUSH YOU INTO THE VILLAGE STREET WEARING NOTHING BUT HER SLIP, AND THE VILLAGE GIRLS LAUGH AT YOU, AND THE BOYS THROW ROCKS AT YOU...
"MUCH TOO EASY. WHERE ARE THE SCIENTISTS?"
SUH-SAFE HOUSE D. THE OLD LIGHTHOUSE. WE WERE GOING TO TAKE THEM OUT BY SUH-**SUBMARINE.**
RIDICULOUS.
WHO ARE YOU WORKING FOR?
THE PROSPERITY PARTY. YOU ARE A **LIABILITY,** DRUIG. PART OF THE OLD REGIME. IT WAS CUH-CUH-**CONVENIENT.**
HMM. YOU KNOW, PRYKRISH, IF YOU PUT THE GUN IN YOUR MOUTH AND SHOT YOURSELF YOU WOULD FEEL LESS ASHAMED.
YES. INTERESTING.

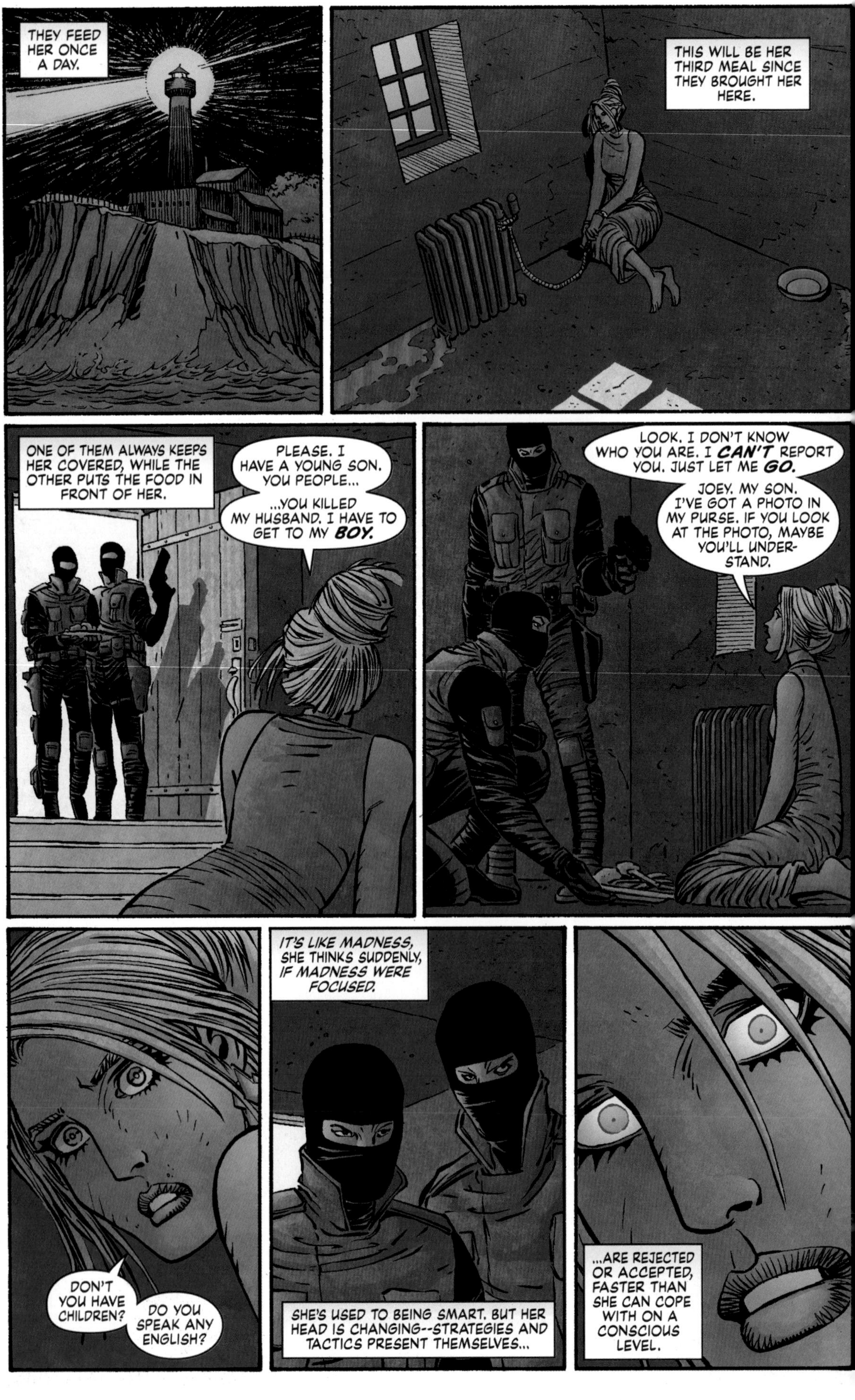
THEY FEED HER ONCE A DAY.
THIS WILL BE HER THIRD MEAL SINCE THEY BROUGHT HER HERE.
ONE OF THEM ALWAYS KEEPS HER COVERED, WHILE THE OTHER PUTS THE FOOD IN FRONT OF HER.
PLEASE. I HAVE A YOUNG SON. YOU PEOPLE...
...YOU KILLED MY HUSBAND. I HAVE TO GET TO MY BOY.
LOOK. I DON'T KNOW WHO YOU ARE. I CAN'T REPORT YOU. JUST LET ME GO.
JOEY. MY SON. I'VE GOT A PHOTO IN MY PURSE. IF YOU LOOK AT THE PHOTO, MAYBE YOU'LL UNDER-STAND.
DON'T YOU HAVE CHILDREN?
DO YOU SPEAK ANY ENGLISH?
IT'S LIKE MADNESS, SHE THINKS SUDDENLY, IF MADNESS WERE FOCUSED.
SHE'S USED TO BEING SMART. BUT HER HEAD IS CHANGING--STRATEGIES AND TACTICS PRESENT THEMSELVES...
...ARE REJECTED OR ACCEPTED, FASTER THAN SHE CAN COPE WITH ON A CONSCIOUS LEVEL.

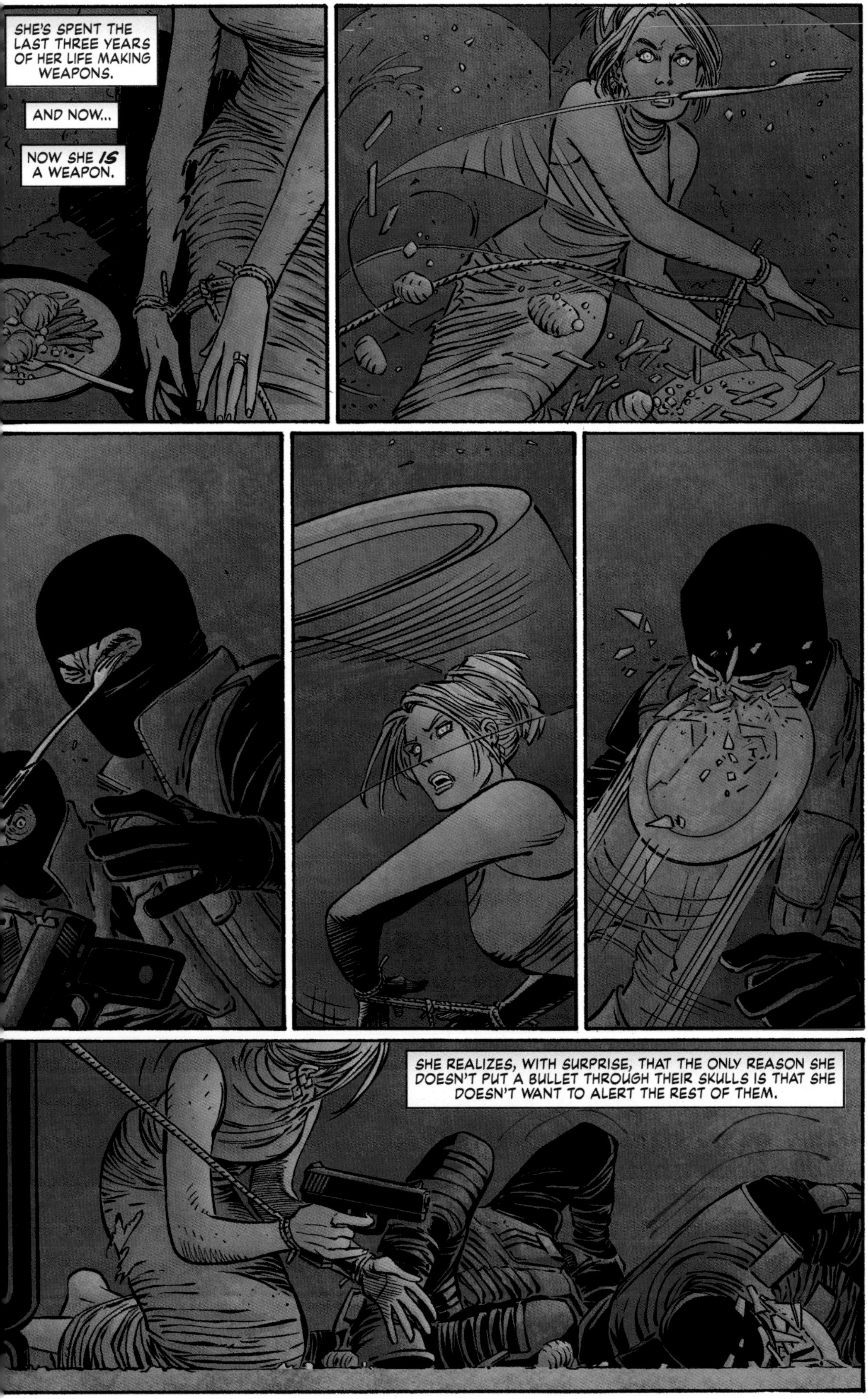
SHE'S SPENT THE LAST THREE YEARS OF HER LIFE MAKING WEAPONS.
AND NOW...
NOW SHE *IS* A WEAPON.
SHE REALIZES, WITH SURPRISE, THAT THE ONLY REASON SHE DOESN'T PUT A BULLET THROUGH THEIR SKULLS IS THAT SHE DOESN'T WANT TO ALERT THE REST OF THEM.

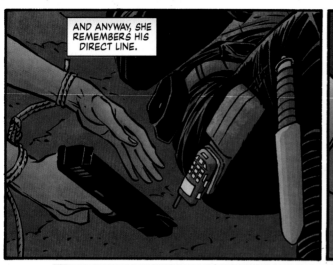

AND ANYWAY, SHE REMEMBERS HIS DIRECT LINE.

AVENGERS HEADQUARTERS, STARK TOWER...

GIVE ME ALL RECORDS ON FORMER AVENGER SERSI.

CLEARANCE LEVEL?

ULTIMATE.

NO RECORDS FOUND.

HUH?

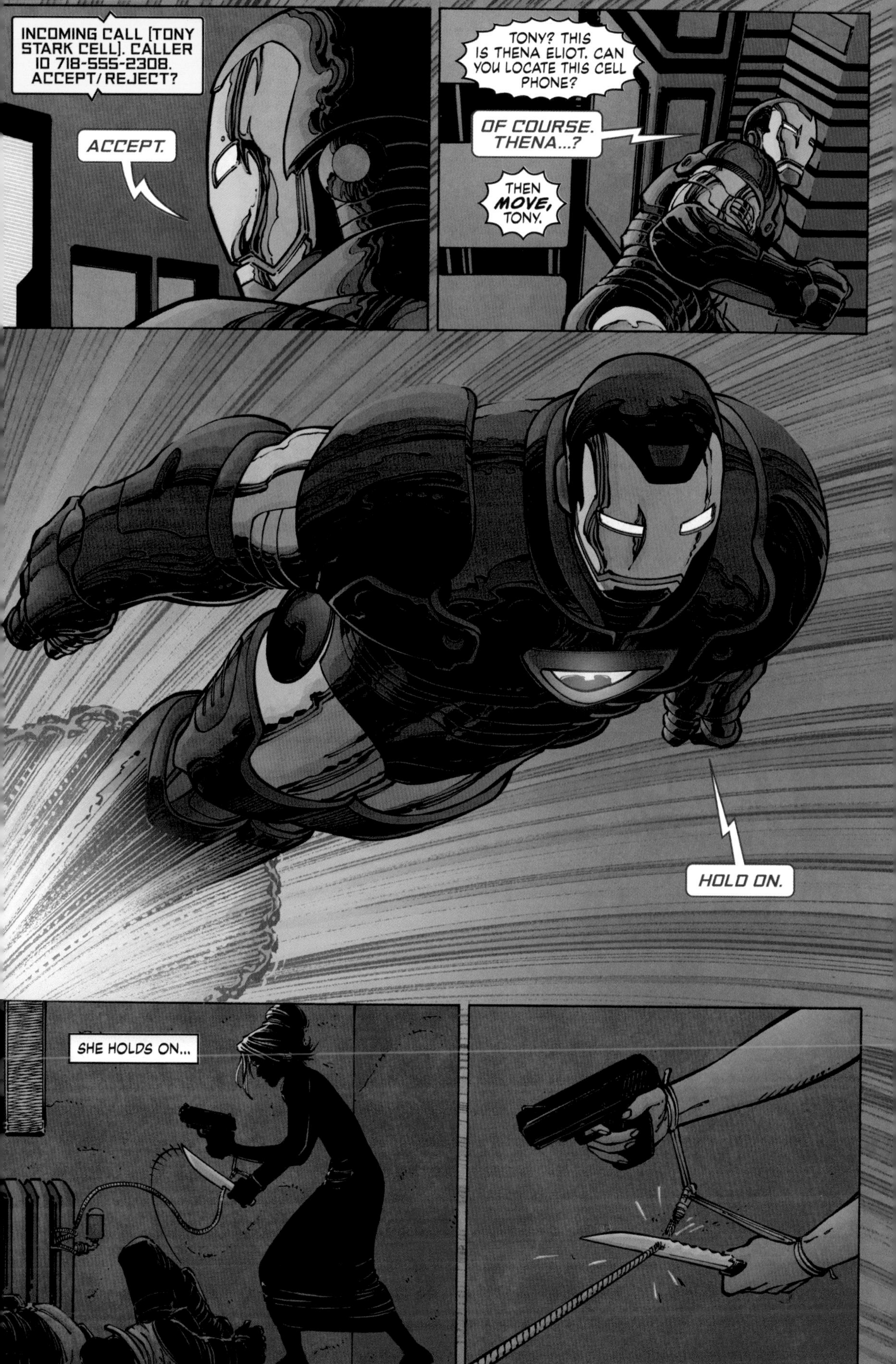
INCOMING CALL [TONY STARK CELL]. CALLER ID 718-555-2308. ACCEPT/REJECT?
ACCEPT.
TONY? THIS IS THENA ELIOT. CAN YOU LOCATE THIS CELL PHONE?
OF COURSE. THENA...?
THEN MOVE, TONY.
HOLD ON.
SHE HOLDS ON...

...UNTIL SHE HEARS THE SONIC BOOM.

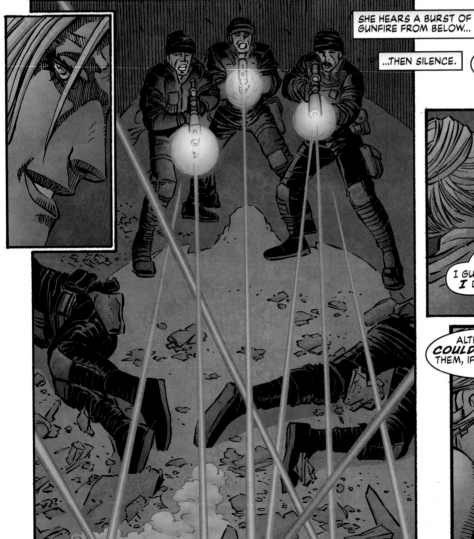

SHE HEARS A BURST OF GUNFIRE FROM BELOW...

...THEN SILENCE.

HELLO, TONY. THAT WAS FAST.

WHAT HAPPENED TO THOSE TWO MEN?

I GUESS *I* DID.

I DON'T THINK THEY'RE DEAD.

ALTHOUGH I *COULD* HAVE KILLED THEM, IF I'D WANTED TO.

THEY MURDERED MY HUSBAND, DID YOU KNOW THAT?

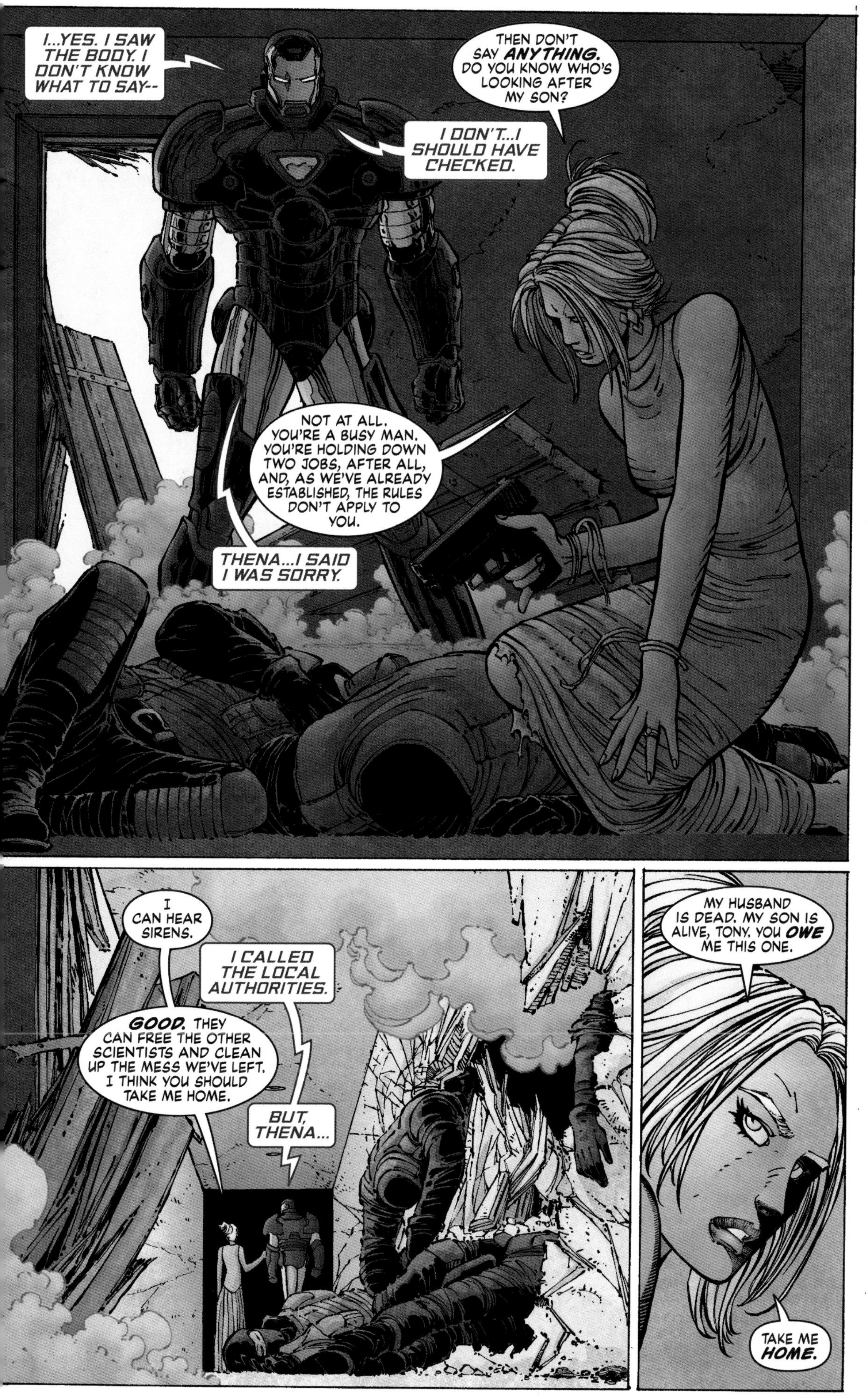
I...YES. I SAW THE BODY. I DON'T KNOW WHAT TO SAY--
THEN DON'T SAY **ANYTHING.** DO YOU KNOW WHO'S LOOKING AFTER MY SON?
I DON'T...I SHOULD HAVE CHECKED.
NOT AT ALL. YOU'RE A BUSY MAN. YOU'RE HOLDING DOWN TWO JOBS, AFTER ALL, AND, AS WE'VE ALREADY ESTABLISHED, THE RULES DON'T APPLY TO YOU.
THENA...I SAID I WAS SORRY.
I CAN HEAR SIRENS.
I CALLED THE LOCAL AUTHORITIES.
GOOD. THEY CAN FREE THE OTHER SCIENTISTS AND CLEAN UP THE MESS WE'VE LEFT. I THINK YOU SHOULD TAKE ME HOME.
BUT, THENA...
MY HUSBAND IS DEAD. MY SON IS ALIVE, TONY. YOU **OWE** ME THIS ONE.
TAKE ME **HOME.**

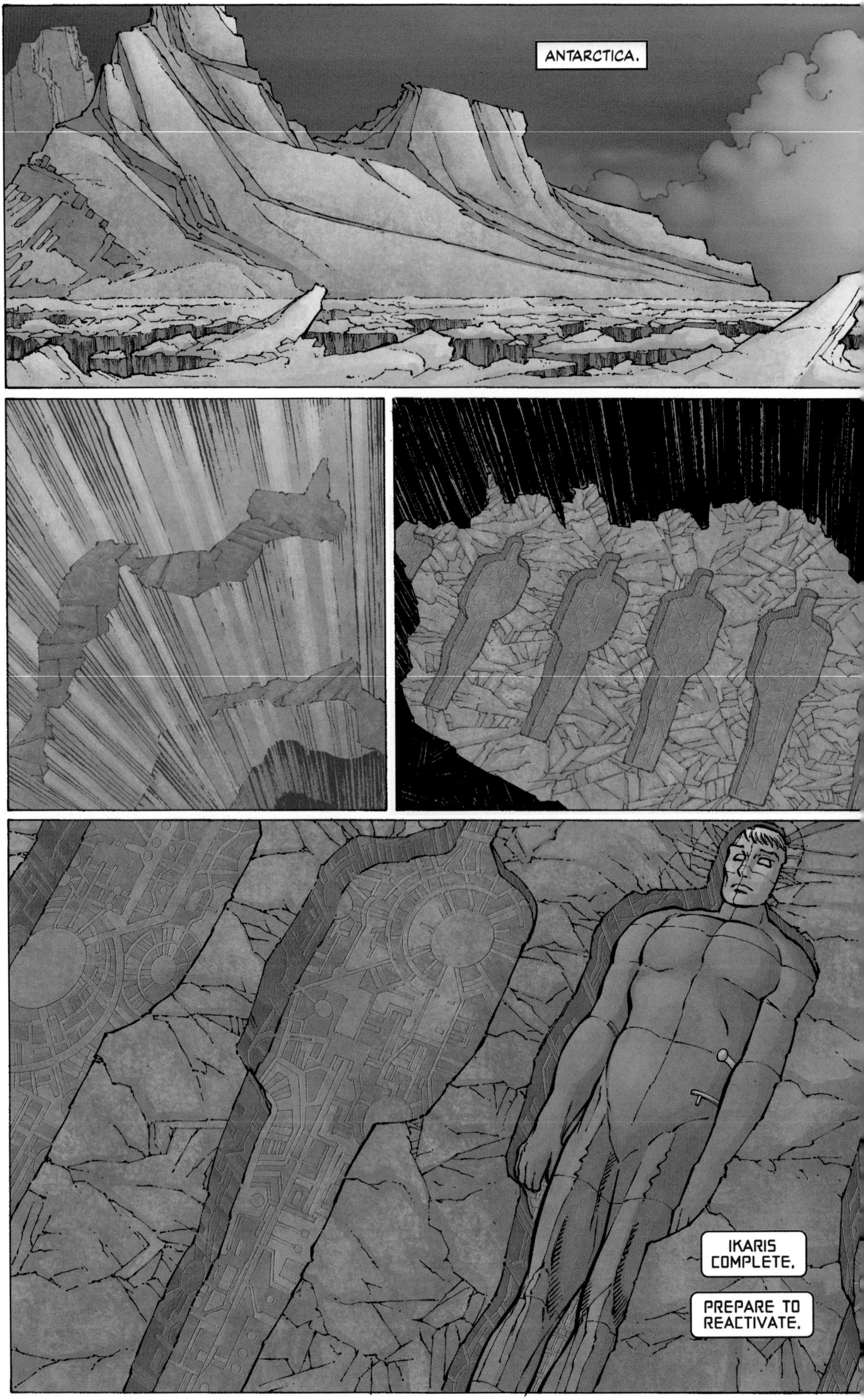
ANTARCTICA.
IKARIS COMPLETE.
PREPARE TO REACTIVATE.

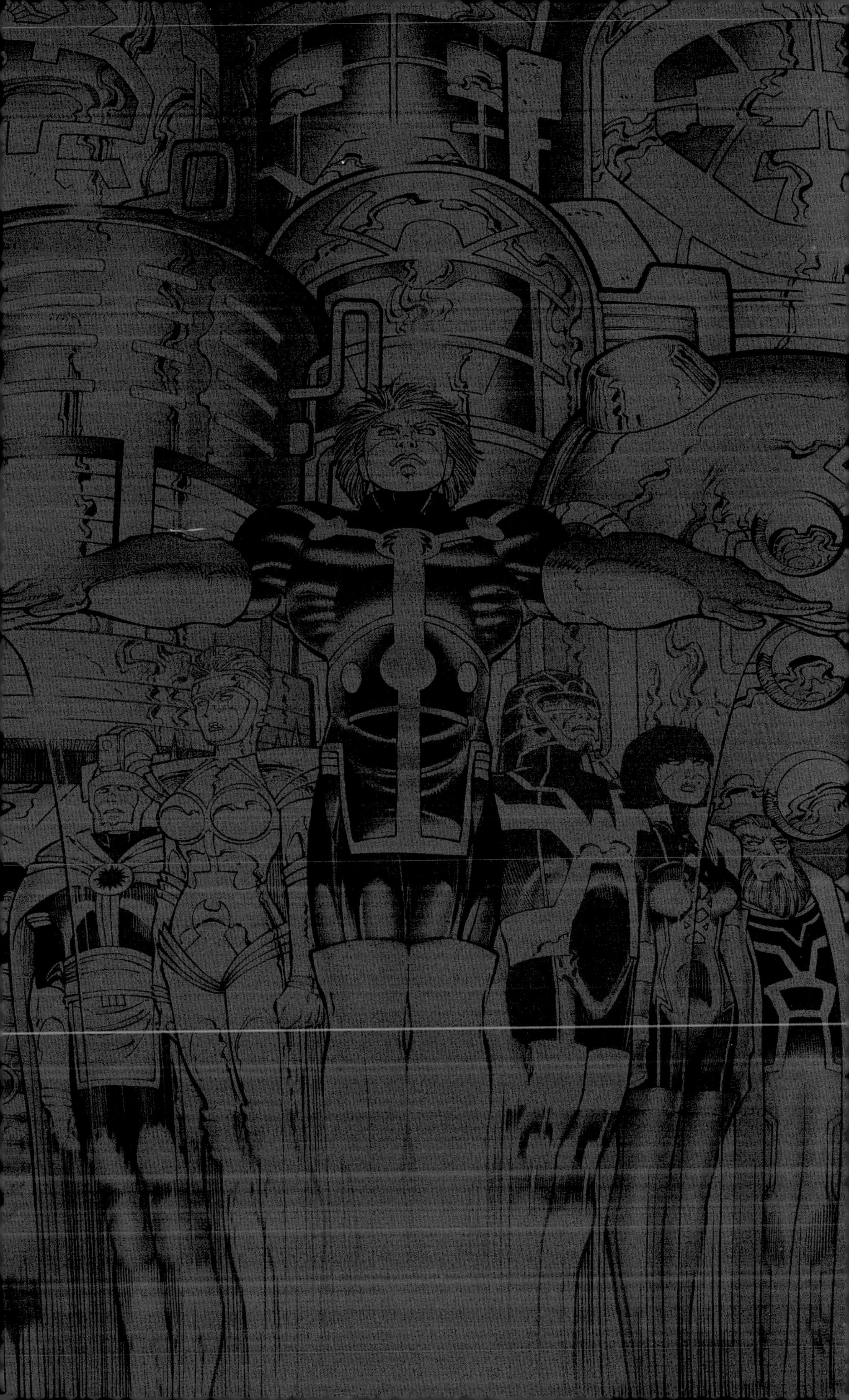

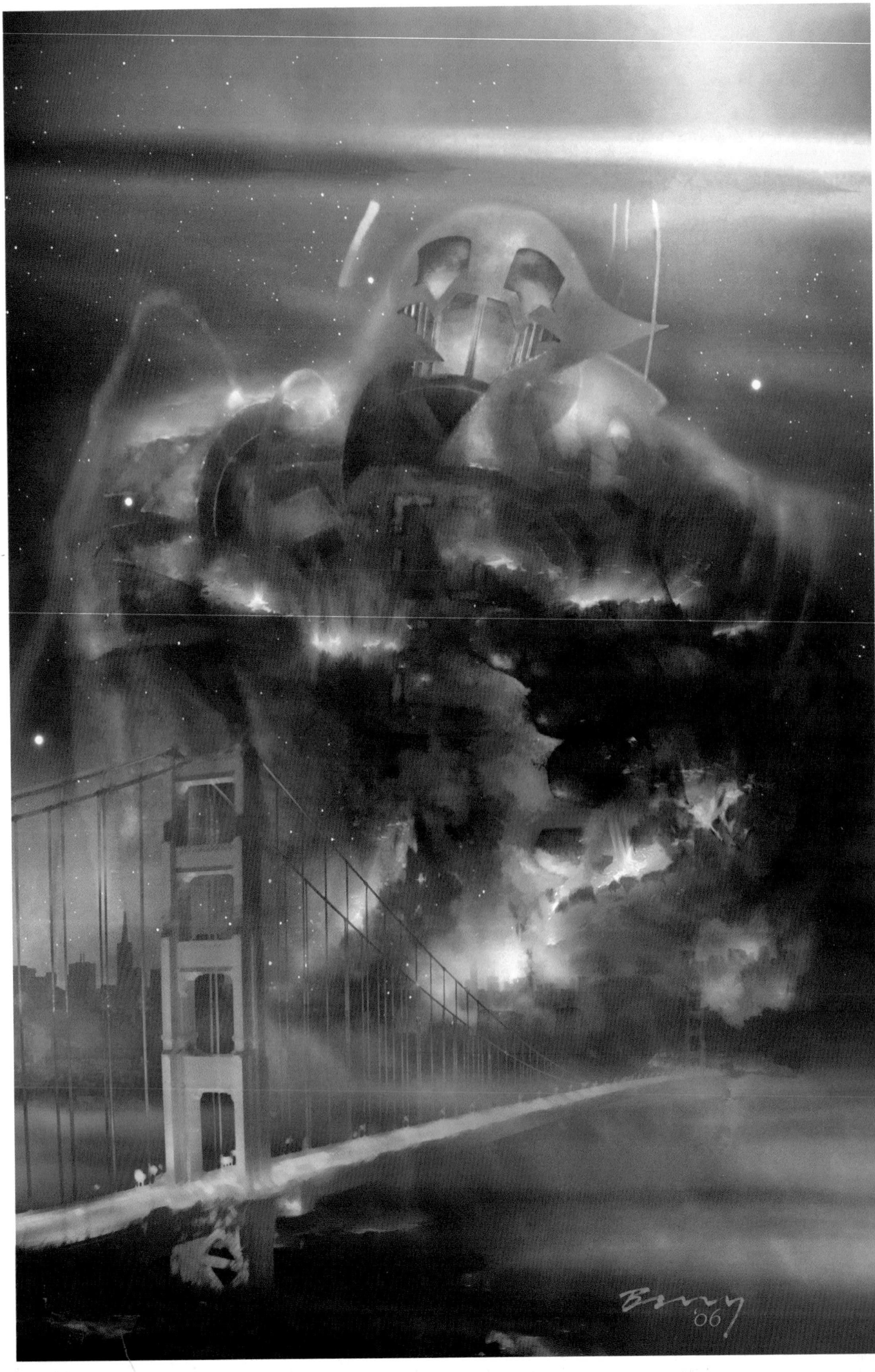

ANTARCTICA.

...TO AWAKE, PLEASE GET UP AND GO THROUGH THE DOORS.

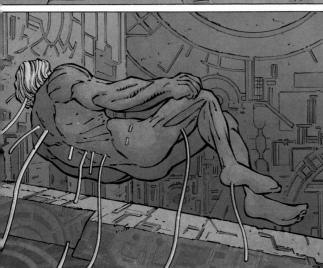

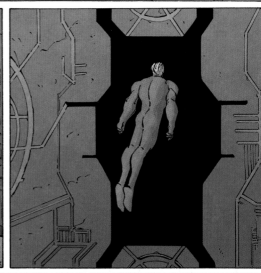

ETERNAL. IKARIS, IDENTIFIED,

ETERNAL IKARIS, REACTIVATION COMPLETE.

YOU ARE NOW LEAVING THE REACTIVATION CHAMBER.

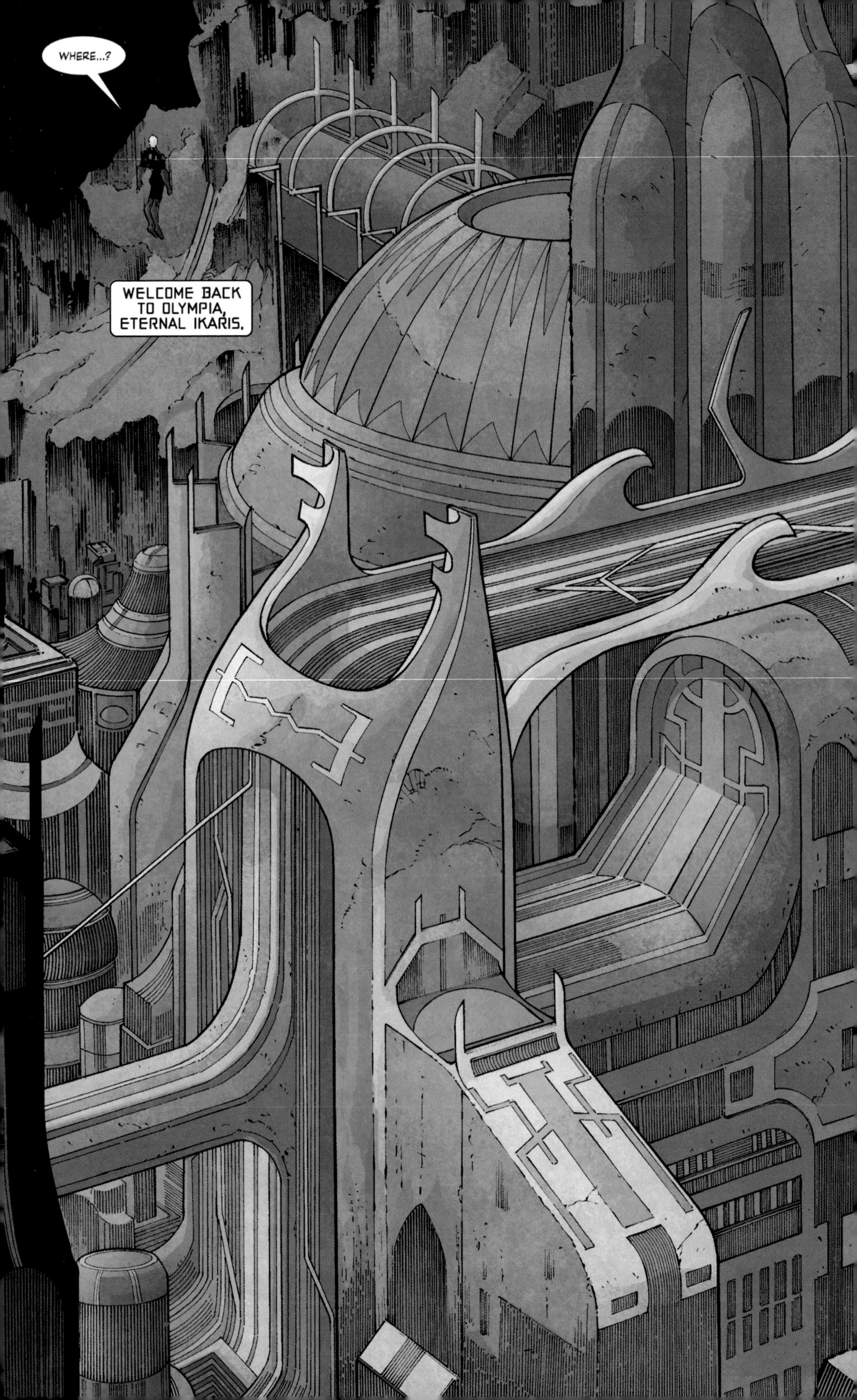
WHERE...?
WELCOME BACK TO OLYMPIA, ETERNAL IKARIS.

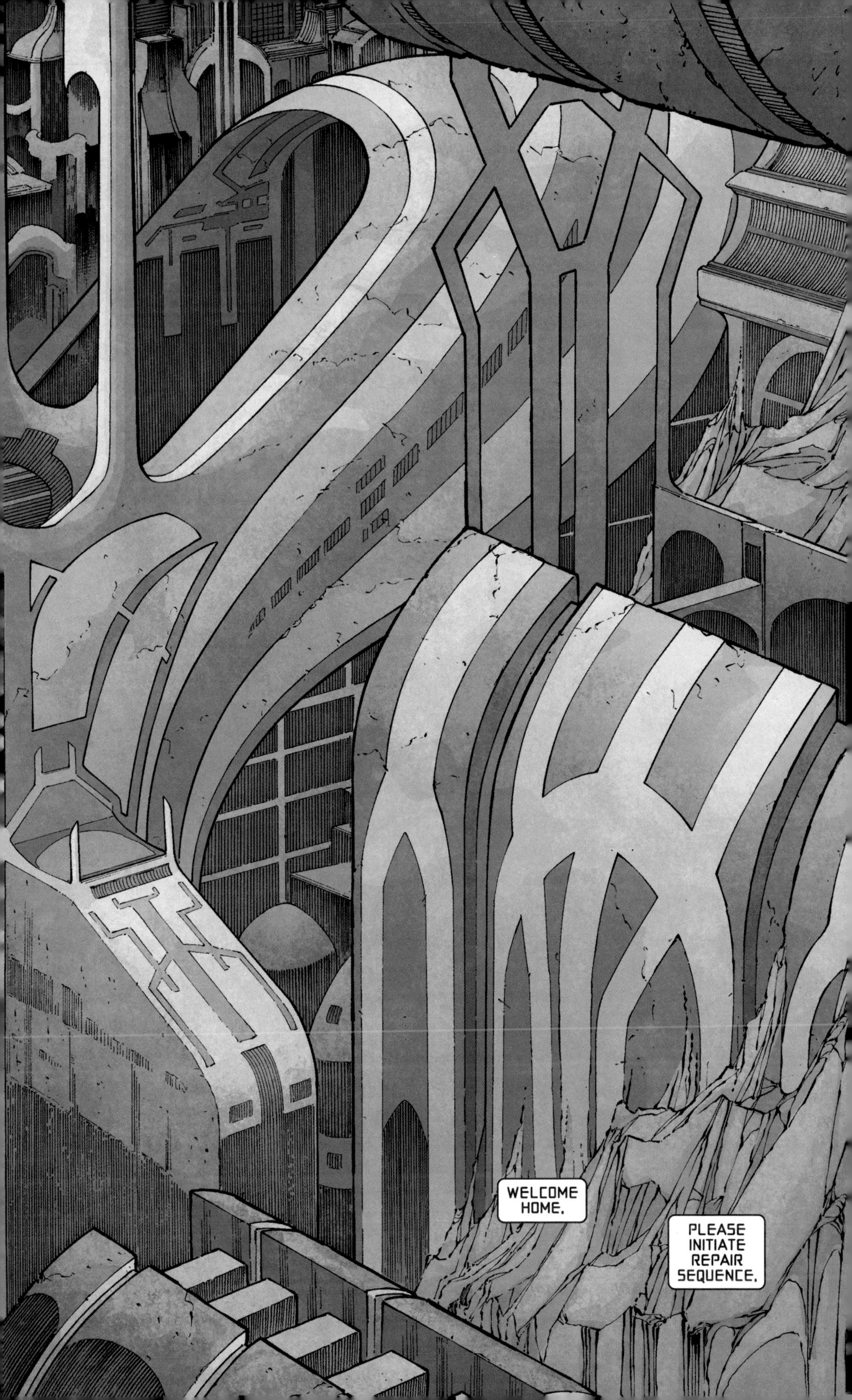
WELCOME HOME.
PLEASE INITIATE REPAIR SEQUENCE.

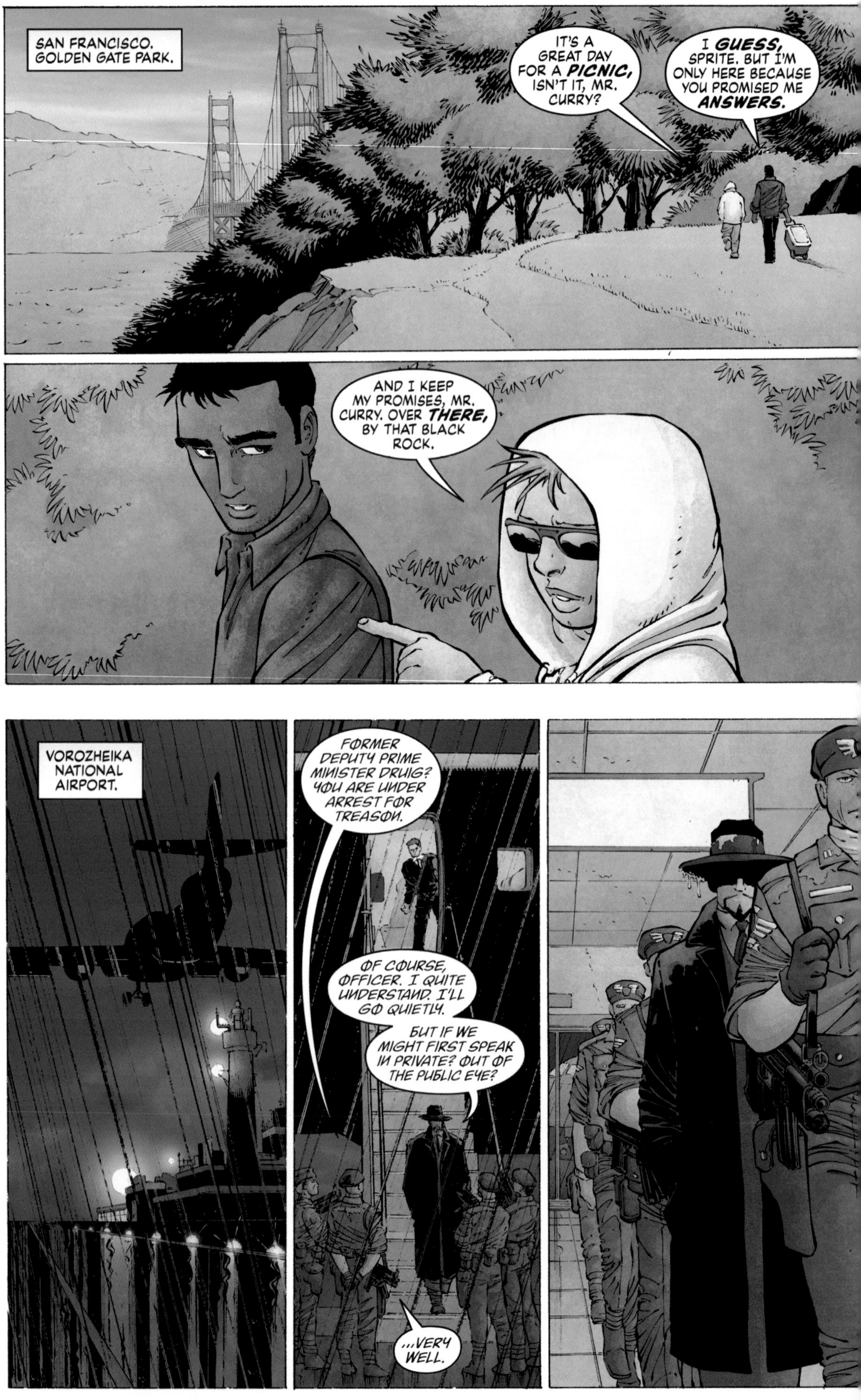
SAN FRANCISCO. GOLDEN GATE PARK.
IT'S A GREAT DAY FOR A PICNIC, ISN'T IT, MR. CURRY?
I GUESS, SPRITE. BUT I'M ONLY HERE BECAUSE YOU PROMISED ME ANSWERS.
AND I KEEP MY PROMISES, MR. CURRY. OVER THERE, BY THAT BLACK ROCK.
VOROZHEIKA NATIONAL AIRPORT.
FORMER DEPUTY PRIME MINISTER DRUIG? YOU ARE UNDER ARREST FOR TREASON.
OF COURSE, OFFICER. I QUITE UNDERSTAND. I'LL GO QUIETLY.
BUT IF WE MIGHT FIRST SPEAK IN PRIVATE? OUT OF THE PUBLIC EYE?
...VERY WELL.

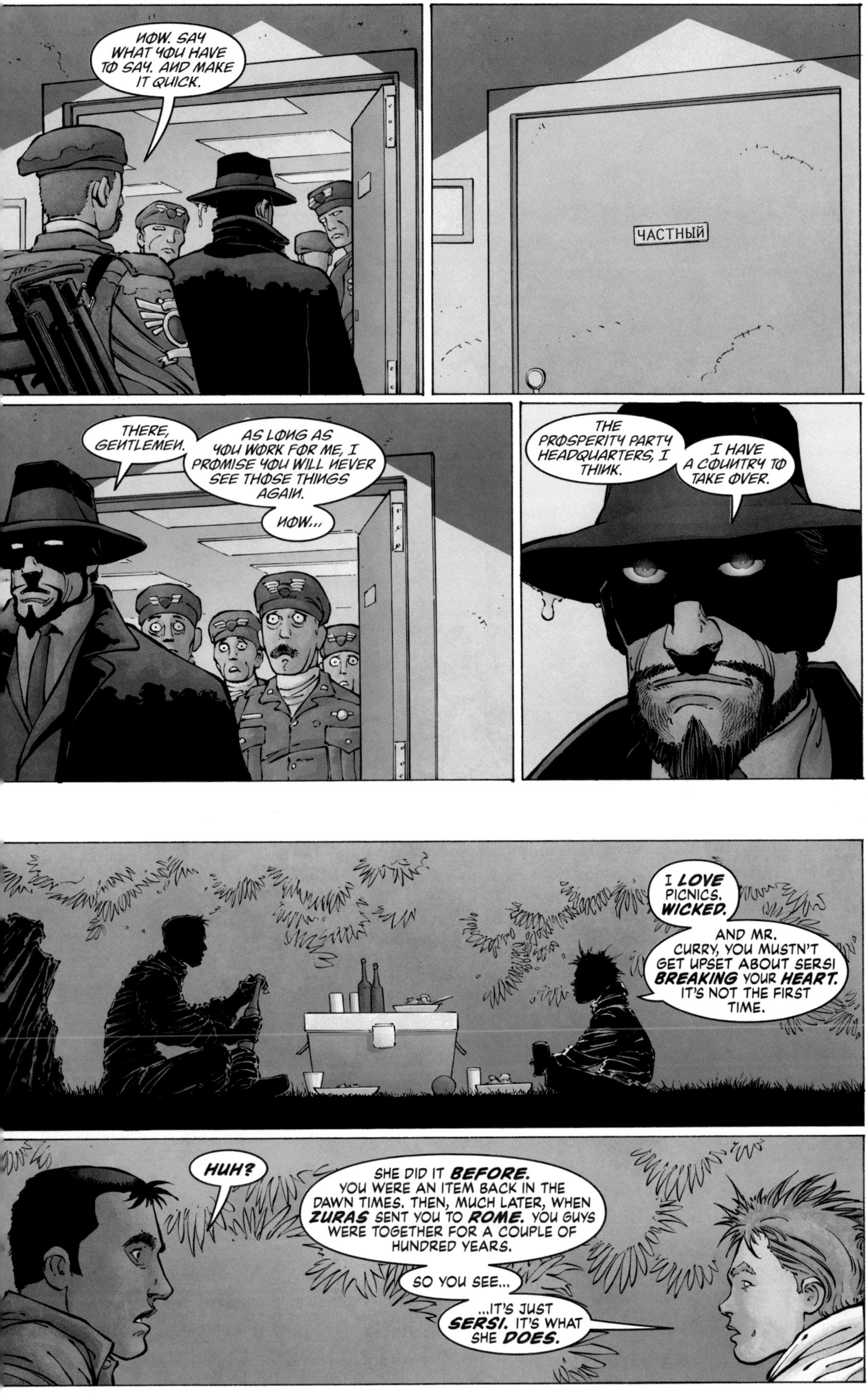
NOW. SAY WHAT YOU HAVE TO SAY. AND MAKE IT QUICK.
ЧАСТНЫЙ
THERE, GENTLEMEN.
AS LONG AS YOU WORK FOR ME, I PROMISE YOU WILL NEVER SEE THOSE THINGS AGAIN.
NOW...
THE PROSPERITY PARTY HEADQUARTERS, I THINK.
I HAVE A COUNTRY TO TAKE OVER.
I LOVE PICNICS. WICKED.
AND MR. CURRY, YOU MUSTN'T GET UPSET ABOUT SERSI BREAKING YOUR HEART. IT'S NOT THE FIRST TIME.
HUH?
SHE DID IT BEFORE. YOU WERE AN ITEM BACK IN THE DAWN TIMES. THEN, MUCH LATER, WHEN ZURAS SENT YOU TO ROME. YOU GUYS WERE TOGETHER FOR A COUPLE OF HUNDRED YEARS.
SO YOU SEE...
...IT'S JUST SERSI. IT'S WHAT SHE DOES.

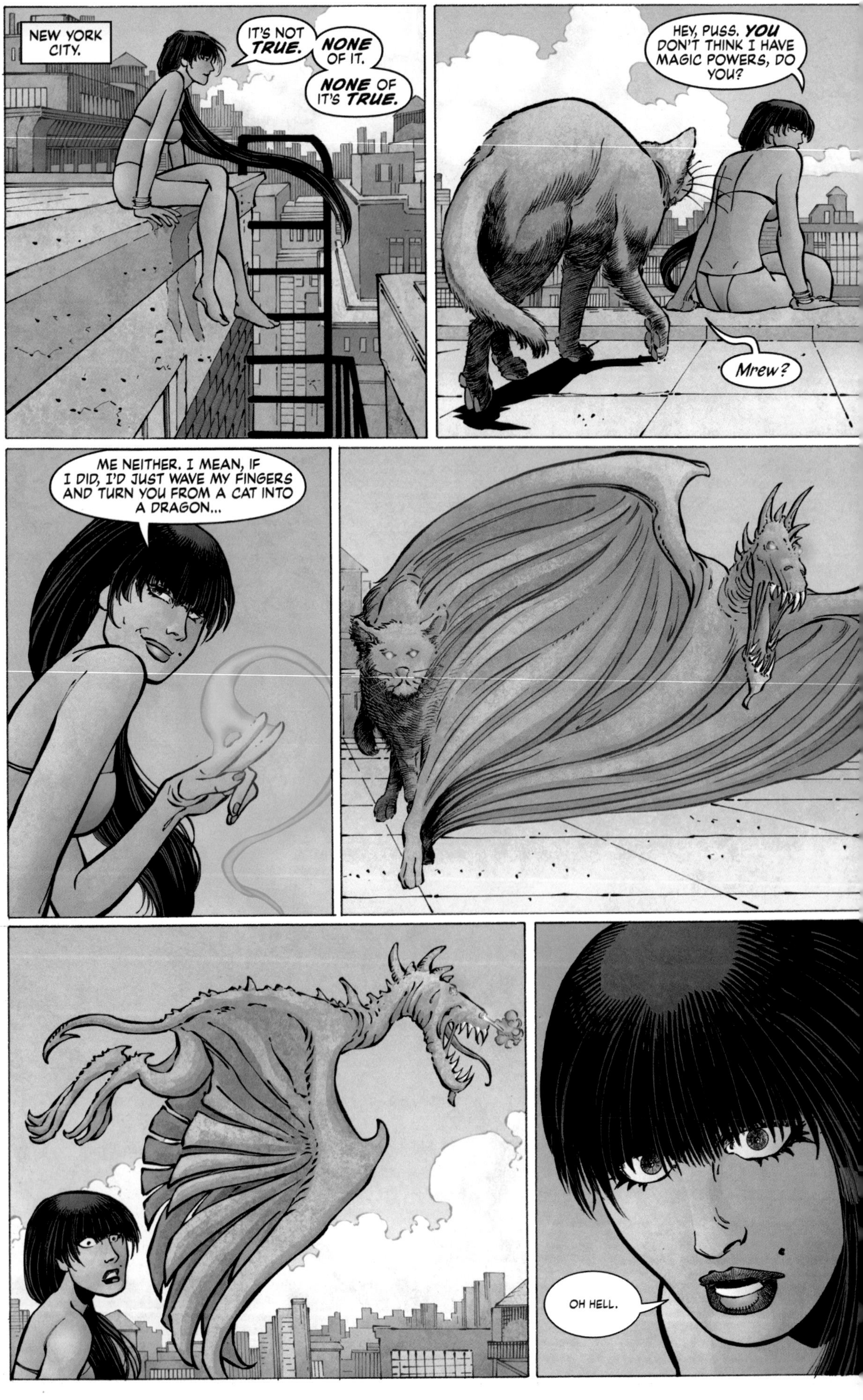
NEW YORK CITY.
IT'S NOT TRUE.
NONE OF IT.
NONE OF IT'S TRUE.
HEY, PUSS. YOU DON'T THINK I HAVE MAGIC POWERS, DO YOU?
Mrew?
ME NEITHER. I MEAN, IF I DID, I'D JUST WAVE MY FINGERS AND TURN YOU FROM A CAT INTO A DRAGON...
OH HELL.

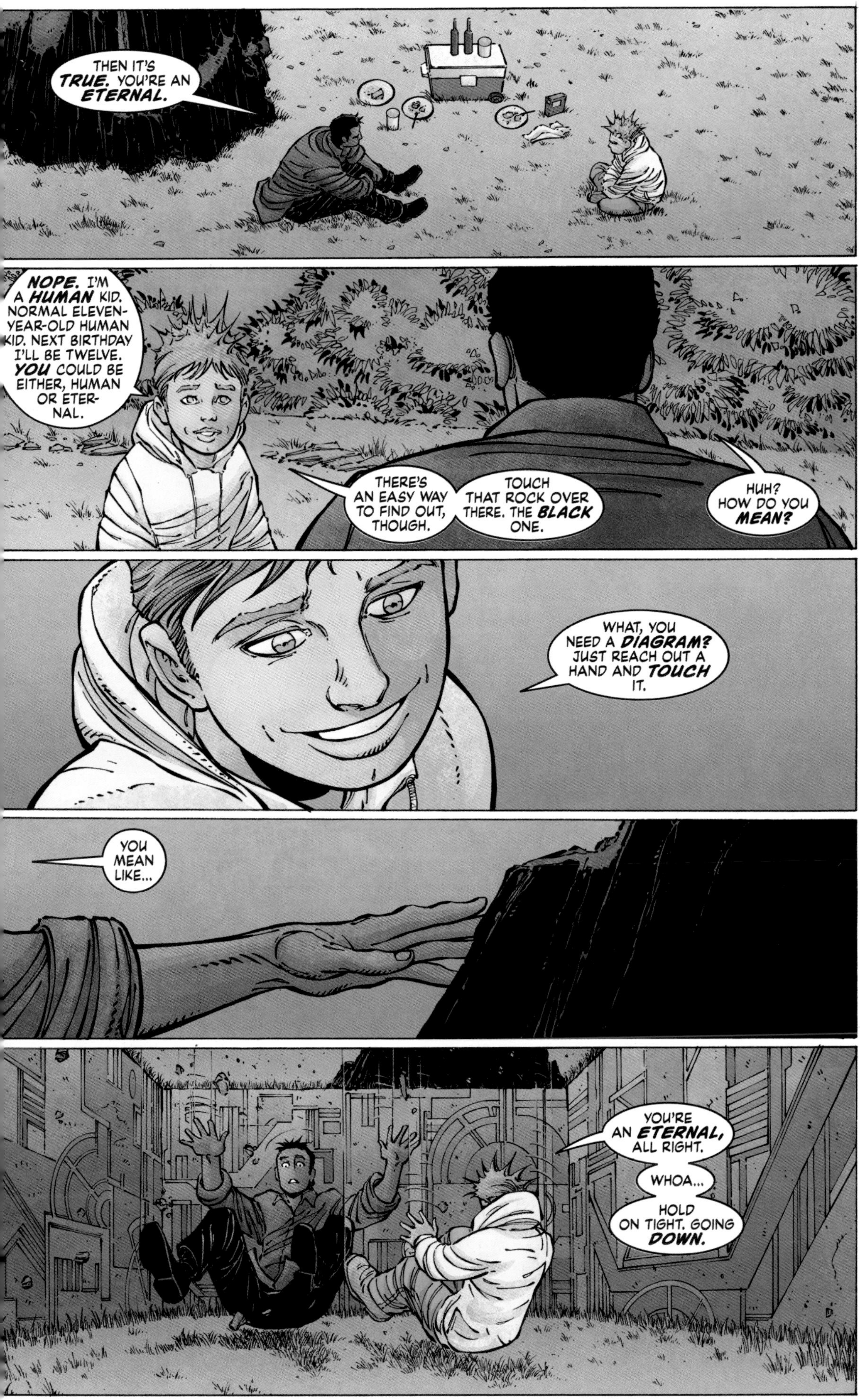
THEN IT'S TRUE. YOU'RE AN ETERNAL.
NOPE. I'M A HUMAN KID. NORMAL ELEVEN-YEAR-OLD HUMAN KID. NEXT BIRTHDAY I'LL BE TWELVE. YOU COULD BE EITHER, HUMAN OR ETERNAL.
HUH? HOW DO YOU MEAN?
THERE'S AN EASY WAY TO FIND OUT, THOUGH.
TOUCH THAT ROCK OVER THERE. THE BLACK ONE.
WHAT, YOU NEED A DIAGRAM? JUST REACH OUT A HAND AND TOUCH IT.
YOU MEAN LIKE...
YOU'RE AN ETERNAL, ALL RIGHT.
WHOA...
HOLD ON TIGHT. GOING DOWN.

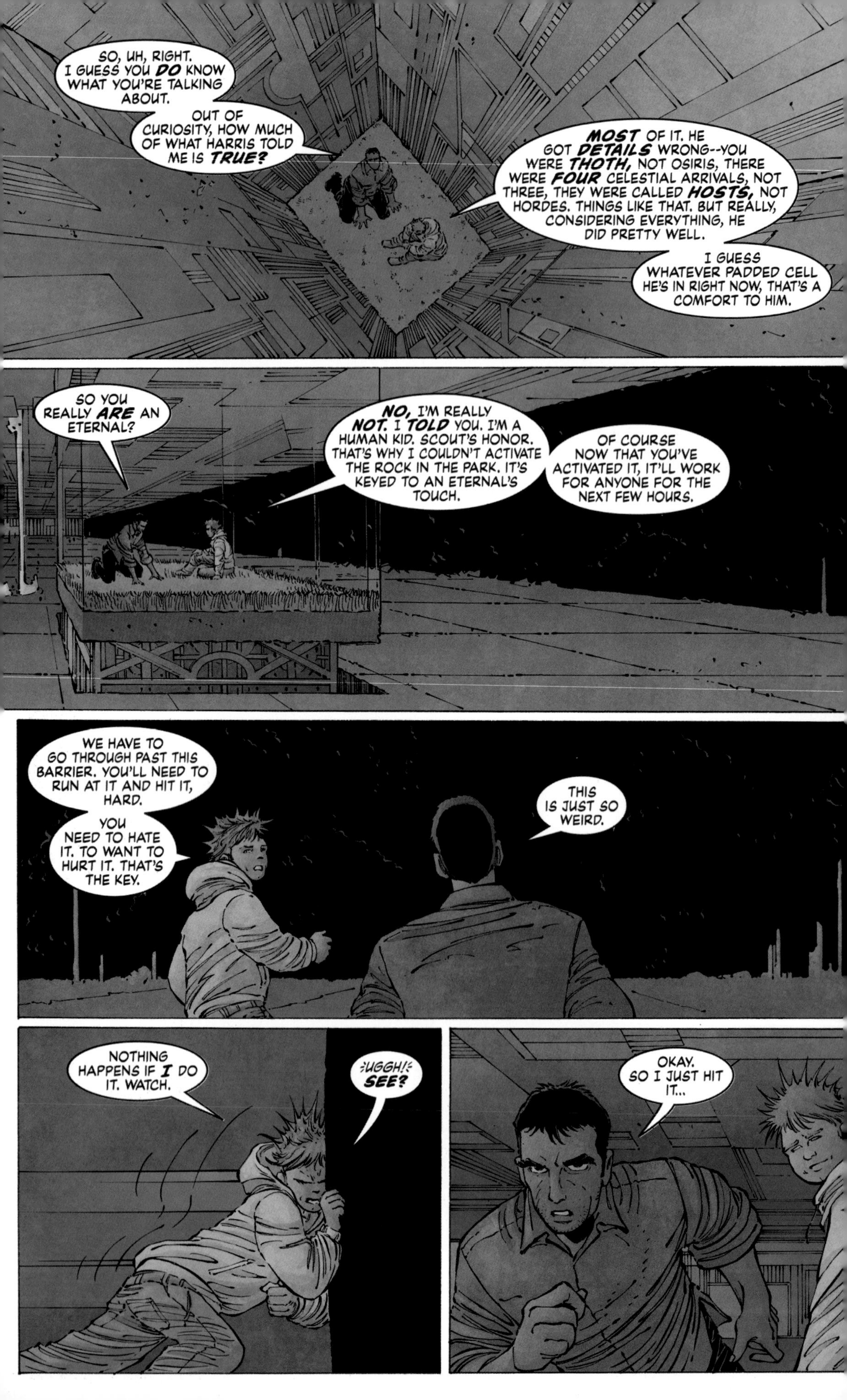
SO, UH, RIGHT. I GUESS YOU DO KNOW WHAT YOU'RE TALKING ABOUT.
OUT OF CURIOSITY, HOW MUCH OF WHAT HARRIS TOLD ME IS TRUE?
MOST OF IT. HE GOT DETAILS WRONG--YOU WERE THOTH, NOT OSIRIS, THERE WERE FOUR CELESTIAL ARRIVALS, NOT THREE, THEY WERE CALLED HOSTS, NOT HORDES. THINGS LIKE THAT. BUT REALLY, CONSIDERING EVERYTHING, HE DID PRETTY WELL.
I GUESS WHATEVER PADDED CELL HE'S IN RIGHT NOW, THAT'S A COMFORT TO HIM.
SO YOU REALLY ARE AN ETERNAL?
NO, I'M REALLY NOT. I TOLD YOU. I'M A HUMAN KID. SCOUT'S HONOR. THAT'S WHY I COULDN'T ACTIVATE THE ROCK IN THE PARK. IT'S KEYED TO AN ETERNAL'S TOUCH.
OF COURSE NOW THAT YOU'VE ACTIVATED IT, IT'LL WORK FOR ANYONE FOR THE NEXT FEW HOURS.
WE HAVE TO GO THROUGH PAST THIS BARRIER. YOU'LL NEED TO RUN AT IT AND HIT IT, HARD.
YOU NEED TO HATE IT. TO WANT TO HURT IT. THAT'S THE KEY.
THIS IS JUST SO WEIRD.
NOTHING HAPPENS IF I DO IT. WATCH.
UGGH! SEE?
OKAY. SO I JUST HIT IT...

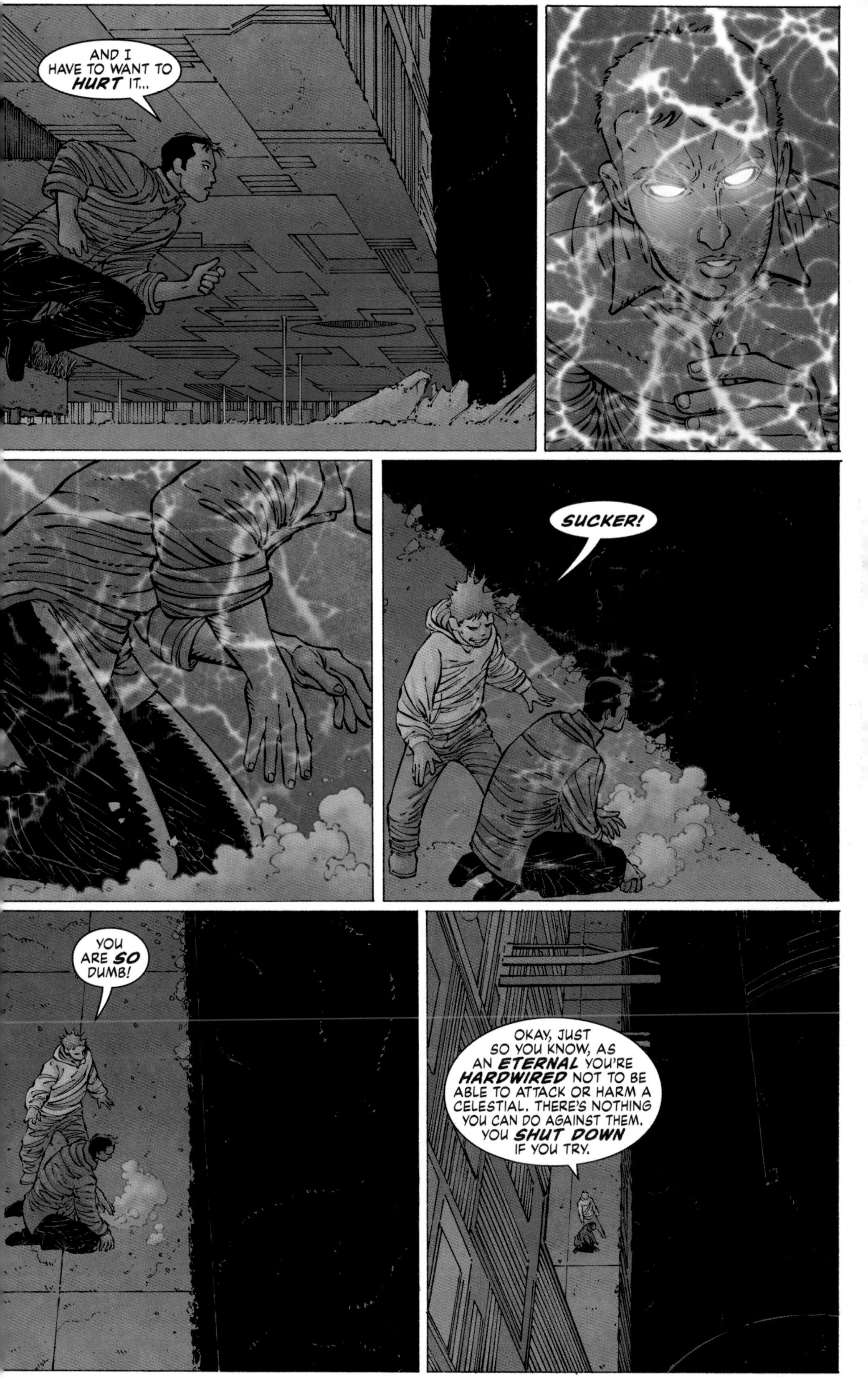
AND I HAVE TO WANT TO HURT IT...
SUCKER!
YOU ARE SO DUMB!
OKAY, JUST SO YOU KNOW, AS AN ETERNAL YOU'RE HARDWIRED NOT TO BE ABLE TO ATTACK OR HARM A CELESTIAL. THERE'S NOTHING YOU CAN DO AGAINST THEM. YOU SHUT DOWN IF YOU TRY.

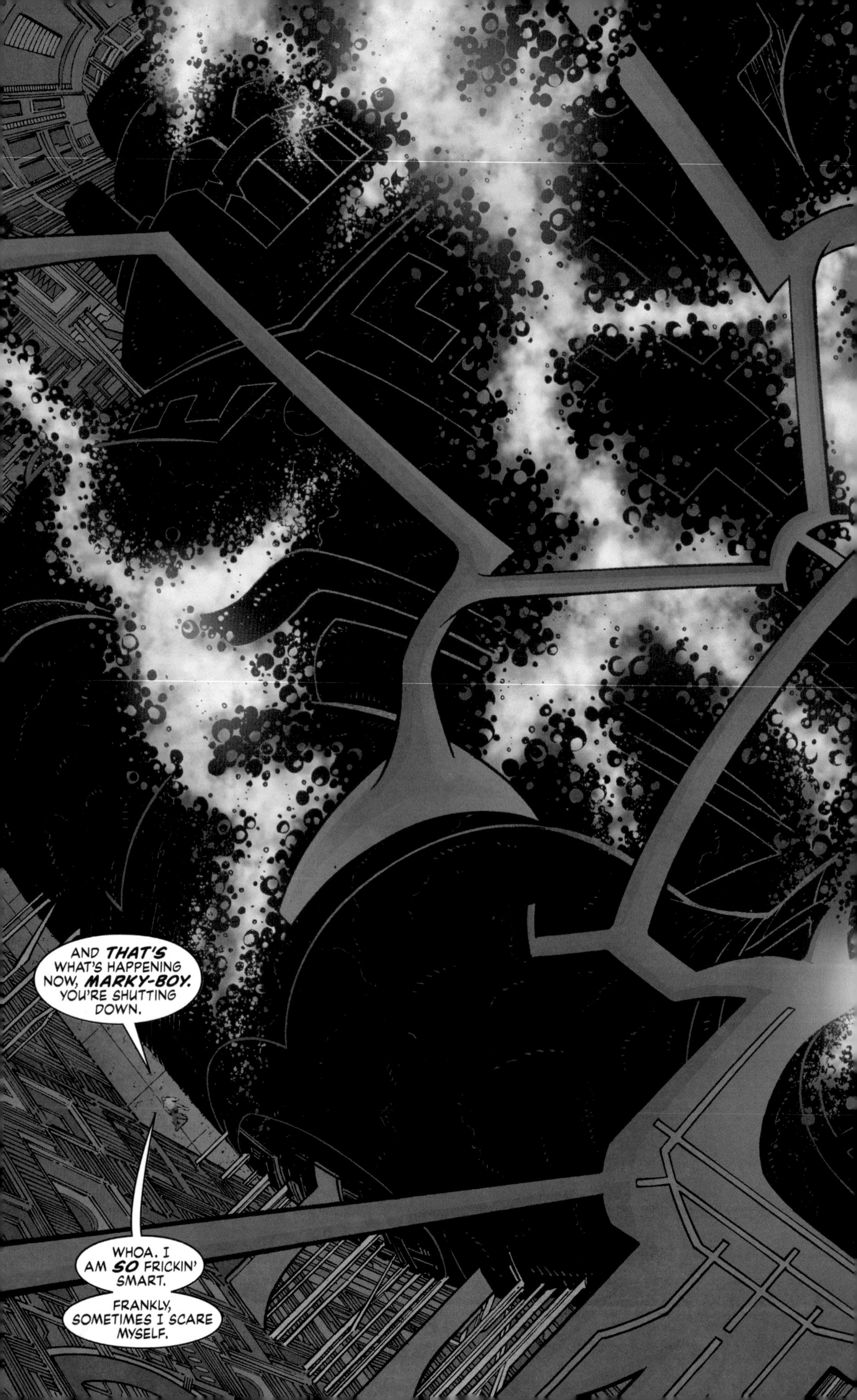
AND **THAT'S** WHAT'S HAPPENING NOW, **MARKY-BOY.** YOU'RE SHUTTING DOWN.
WHOA. I AM **SO** FRICKIN' SMART.
FRANKLY, SOMETIMES I SCARE MYSELF.

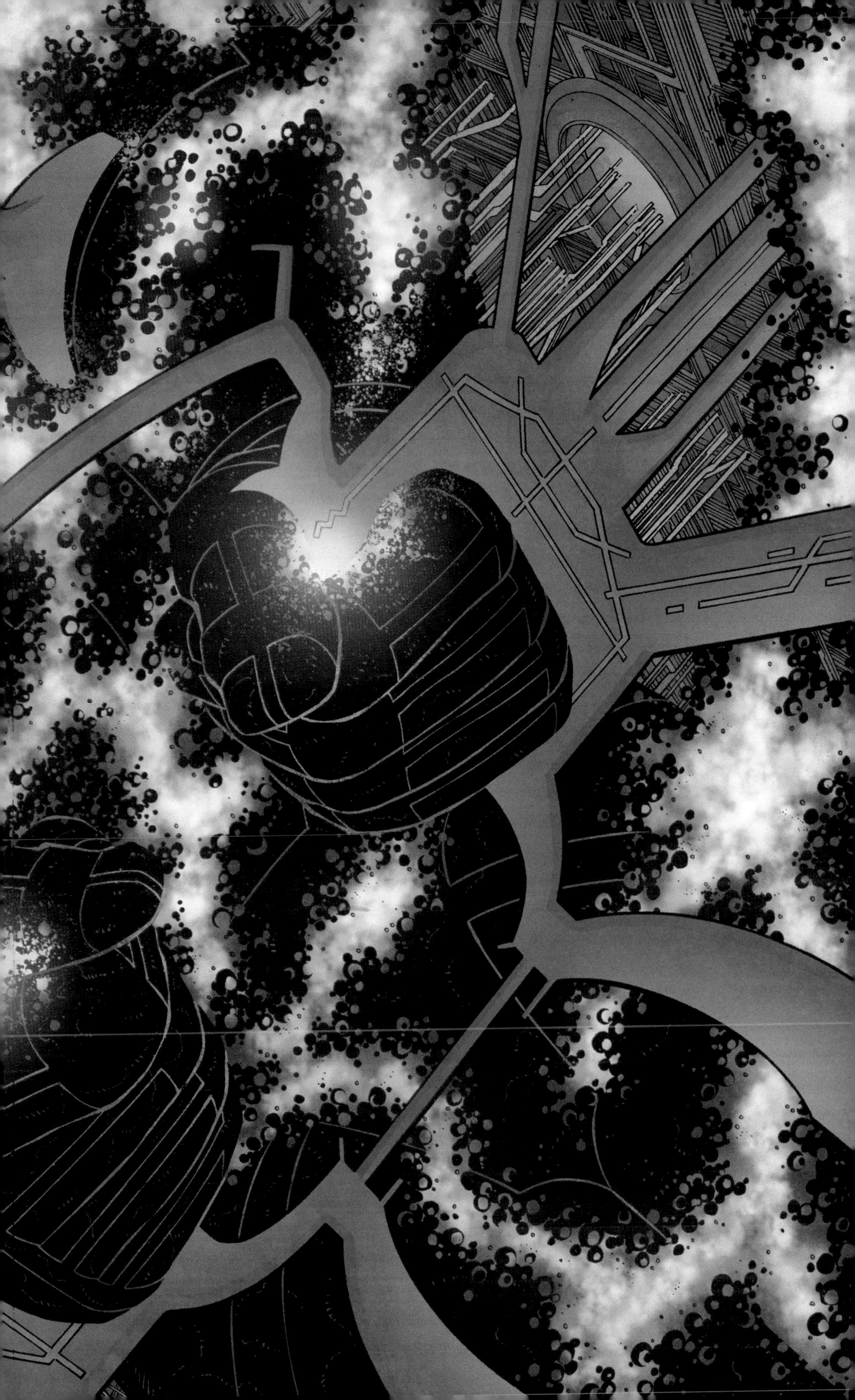

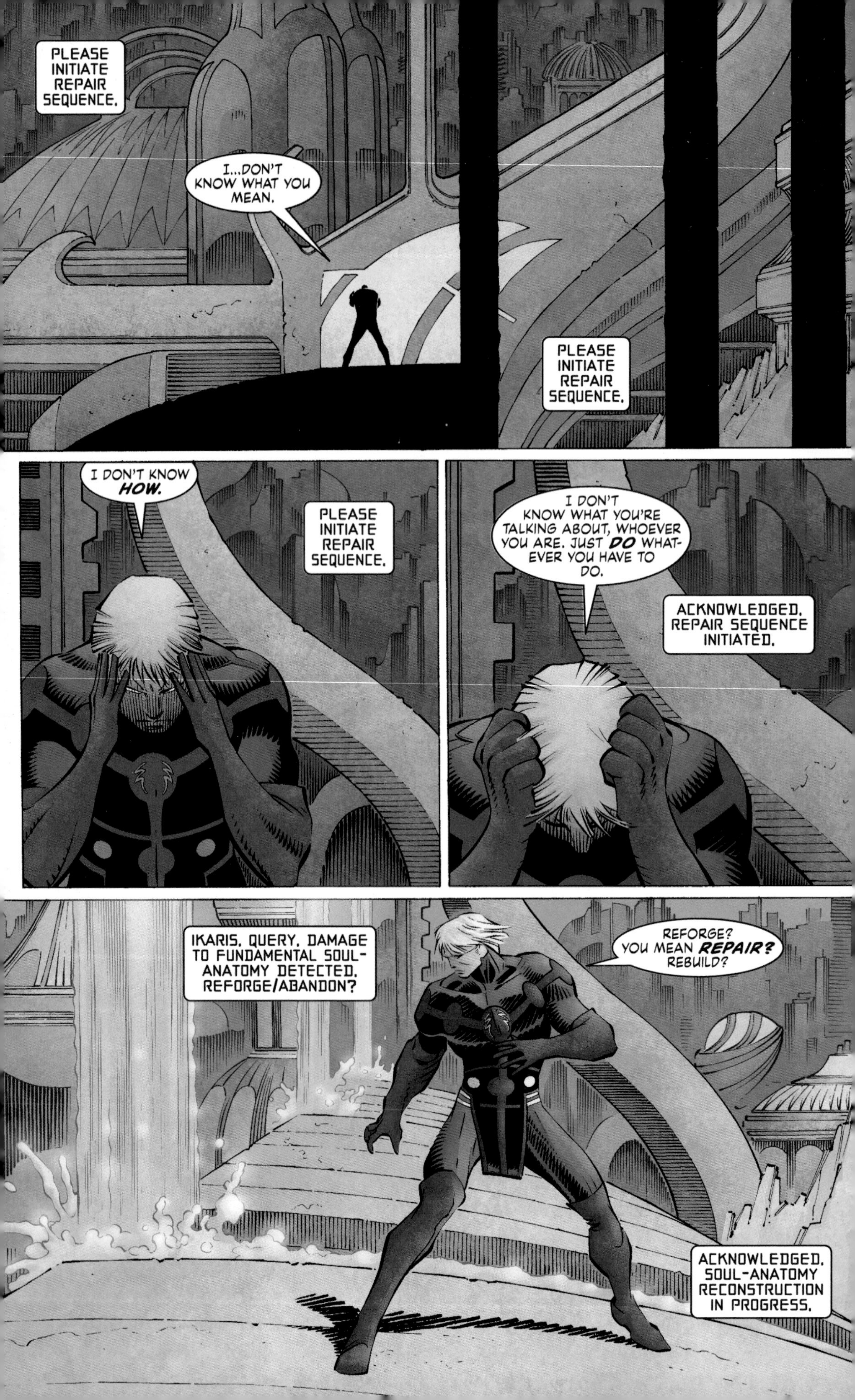
PLEASE INITIATE REPAIR SEQUENCE.
I...DON'T KNOW WHAT YOU MEAN.
PLEASE INITIATE REPAIR SEQUENCE.
I DON'T KNOW **HOW.**
PLEASE INITIATE REPAIR SEQUENCE.
I DON'T KNOW WHAT YOU'RE TALKING ABOUT, WHOEVER YOU ARE. JUST **DO** WHAT-EVER YOU HAVE TO DO.
ACKNOWLEDGED. REPAIR SEQUENCE INITIATED.
IKARIS. QUERY. DAMAGE TO FUNDAMENTAL SOUL-ANATOMY DETECTED. REFORGE/ABANDON?
REFORGE? YOU MEAN **REPAIR?** REBUILD?
ACKNOWLEDGED. SOUL-ANATOMY RECONSTRUCTION IN PROGRESS.

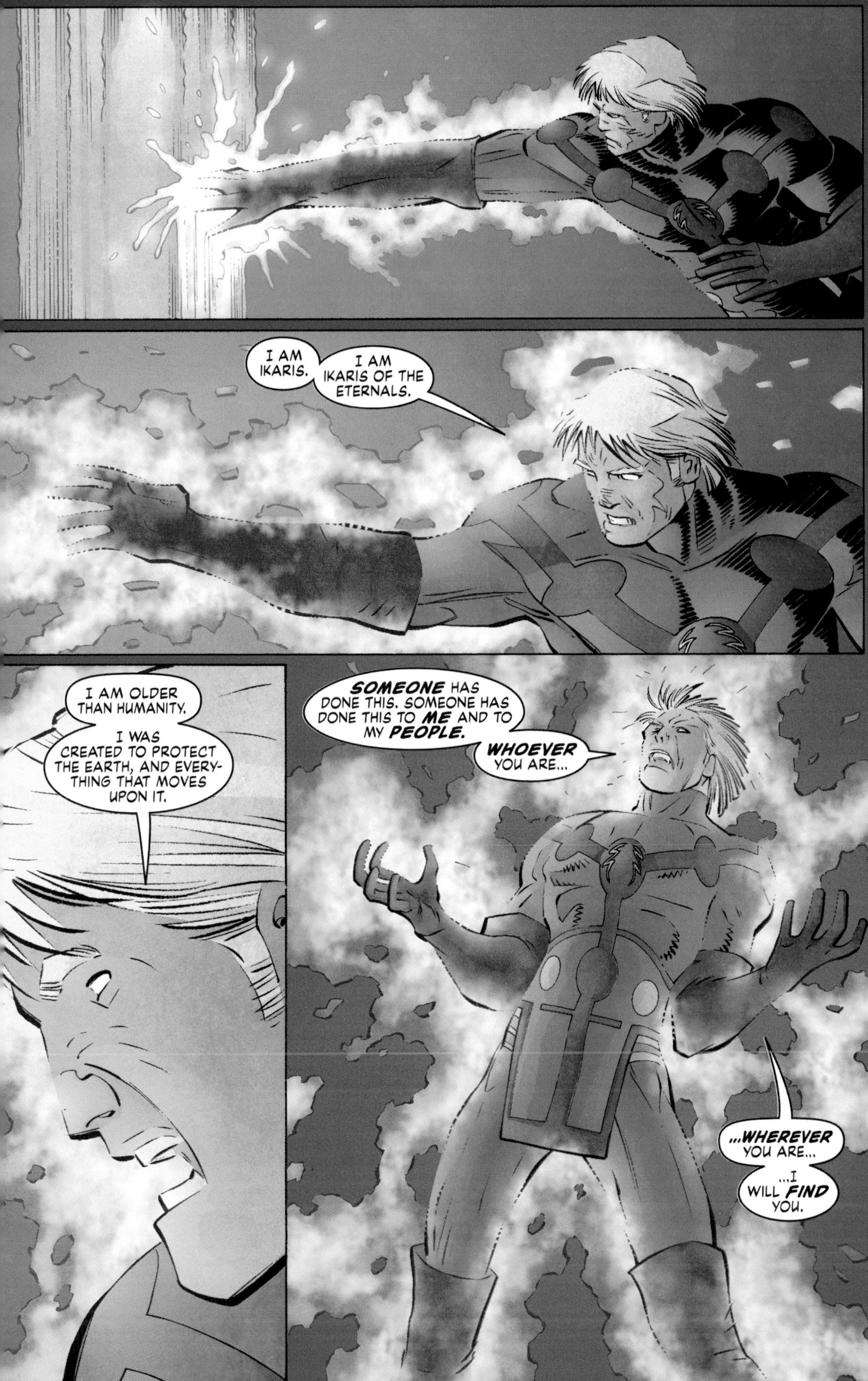
I AM IKARIS.
I AM IKARIS OF THE ETERNALS.
I AM OLDER THAN HUMANITY.
I WAS CREATED TO PROTECT THE EARTH, AND EVERY-THING THAT MOVES UPON IT.
SOMEONE HAS DONE THIS. SOMEONE HAS DONE THIS TO ME AND TO MY PEOPLE.
WHOEVER YOU ARE...
...WHEREVER YOU ARE...
...I WILL FIND YOU.

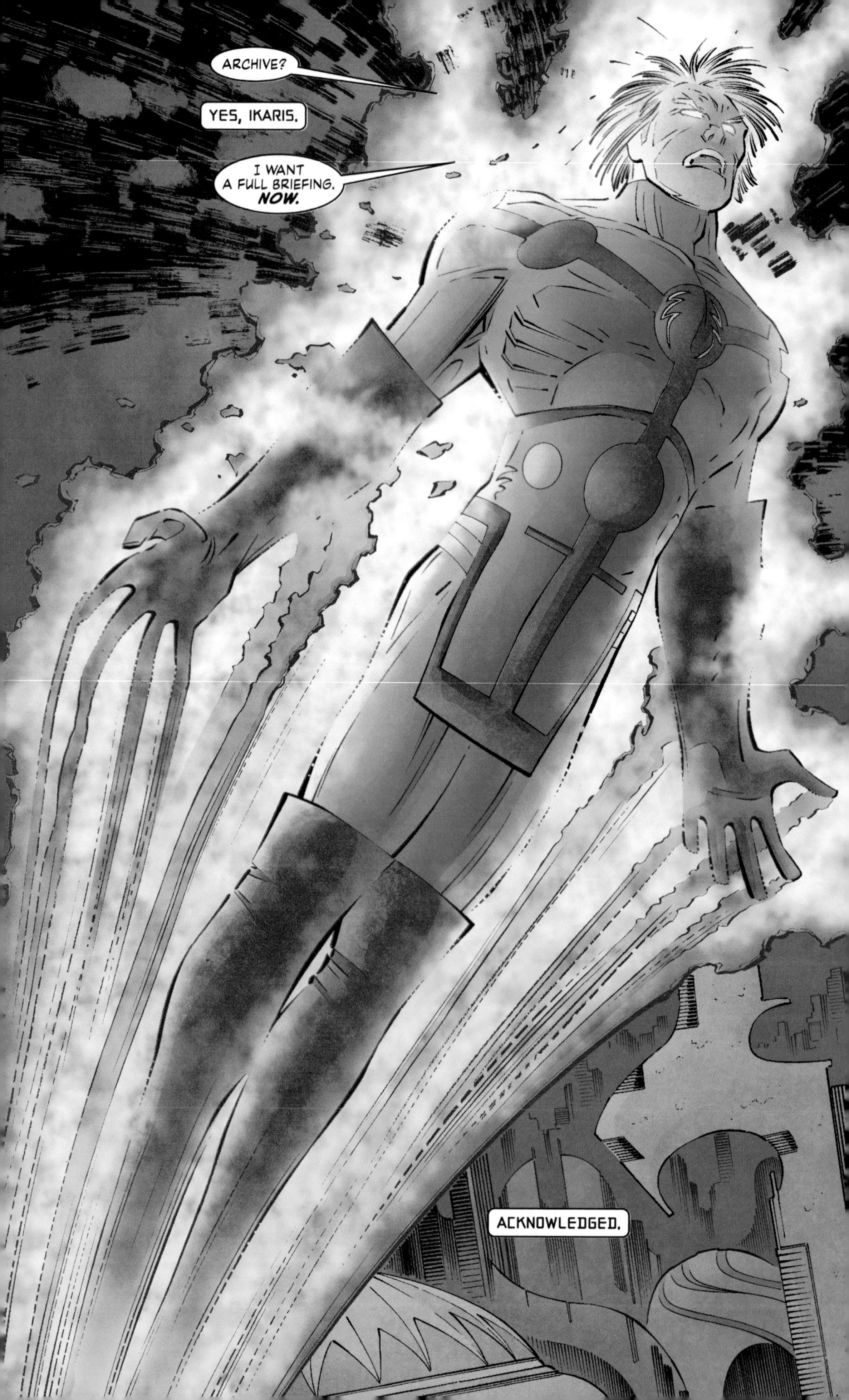
ARCHIVE?
YES, IKARIS.
I WANT A FULL BRIEFING. **NOW.**
ACKNOWLEDGED.

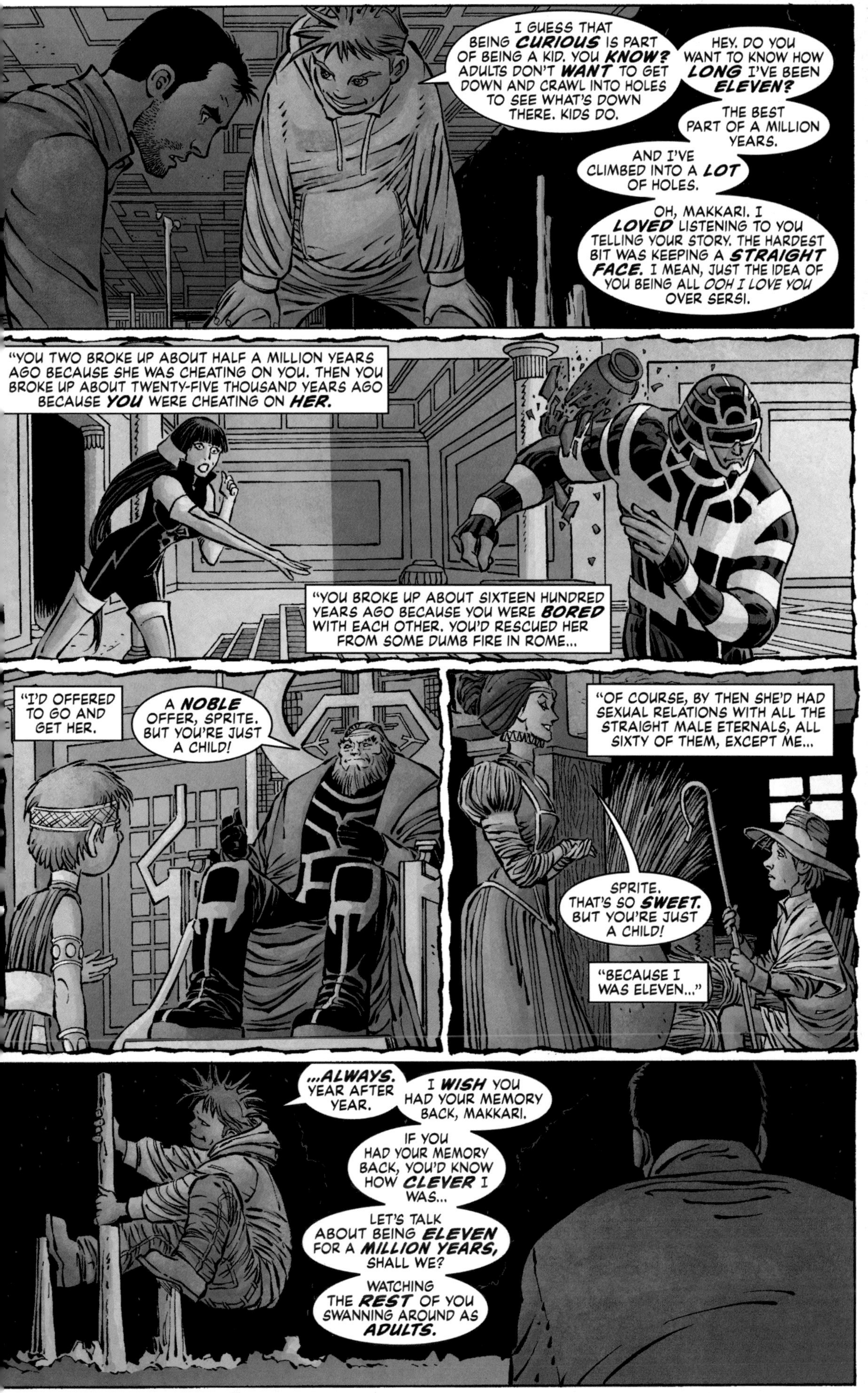
I GUESS THAT BEING CURIOUS IS PART OF BEING A KID. YOU KNOW? ADULTS DON'T WANT TO GET DOWN AND CRAWL INTO HOLES TO SEE WHAT'S DOWN THERE. KIDS DO.
HEY. DO YOU WANT TO KNOW HOW LONG I'VE BEEN ELEVEN?
THE BEST PART OF A MILLION YEARS.
AND I'VE CLIMBED INTO A LOT OF HOLES.
OH, MAKKARI. I LOVED LISTENING TO YOU TELLING YOUR STORY. THE HARDEST BIT WAS KEEPING A STRAIGHT FACE. I MEAN, JUST THE IDEA OF YOU BEING ALL OOH I LOVE YOU OVER SERSI.
"YOU TWO BROKE UP ABOUT HALF A MILLION YEARS AGO BECAUSE SHE WAS CHEATING ON YOU. THEN YOU BROKE UP ABOUT TWENTY-FIVE THOUSAND YEARS AGO BECAUSE YOU WERE CHEATING ON HER.
"YOU BROKE UP ABOUT SIXTEEN HUNDRED YEARS AGO BECAUSE YOU WERE BORED WITH EACH OTHER. YOU'D RESCUED HER FROM SOME DUMB FIRE IN ROME...
"I'D OFFERED TO GO AND GET HER.
A NOBLE OFFER, SPRITE. BUT YOU'RE JUST A CHILD!
"OF COURSE, BY THEN SHE'D HAD SEXUAL RELATIONS WITH ALL THE STRAIGHT MALE ETERNALS, ALL SIXTY OF THEM, EXCEPT ME...
SPRITE. THAT'S SO SWEET. BUT YOU'RE JUST A CHILD!
"BECAUSE I WAS ELEVEN..."
...ALWAYS. YEAR AFTER YEAR.
I WISH YOU HAD YOUR MEMORY BACK, MAKKARI.
IF YOU HAD YOUR MEMORY BACK, YOU'D KNOW HOW CLEVER I WAS...
LET'S TALK ABOUT BEING ELEVEN FOR A MILLION YEARS, SHALL WE?
WATCHING THE REST OF YOU SWANNING AROUND AS ADULTS.

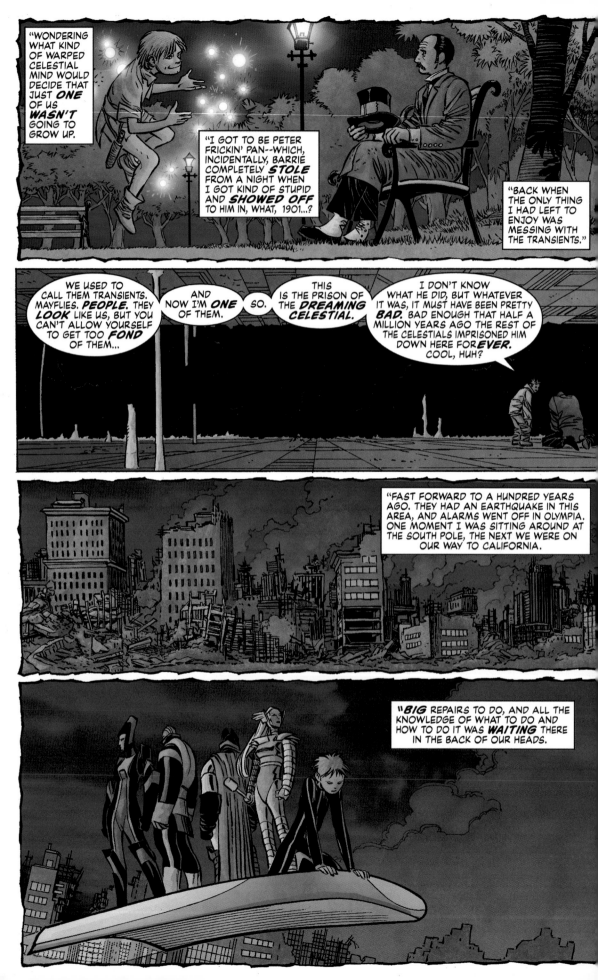

"WONDERING WHAT KIND OF WARPED CELESTIAL MIND WOULD DECIDE THAT JUST *ONE* OF US *WASN'T* GOING TO GROW UP.

"I GOT TO BE PETER FRICKIN' PAN--WHICH, INCIDENTALLY, BARRIE COMPLETELY *STOLE* FROM A NIGHT WHEN I GOT KIND OF STUPID AND *SHOWED OFF* TO HIM IN, WHAT, 1901...?

"BACK WHEN THE ONLY THING I HAD LEFT TO ENJOY WAS MESSING WITH THE TRANSIENTS."

WE USED TO CALL THEM TRANSIENTS. MAYFLIES. *PEOPLE*. THEY *LOOK* LIKE US, BUT YOU CAN'T ALLOW YOURSELF TO GET TOO *FOND* OF THEM...

AND NOW I'M *ONE* OF THEM.

SO.

THIS IS THE PRISON OF THE *DREAMING CELESTIAL*.

I DON'T KNOW WHAT HE DID, BUT WHATEVER IT WAS, IT MUST HAVE BEEN PRETTY *BAD*. BAD ENOUGH THAT HALF A MILLION YEARS AGO THE REST OF THE CELESTIALS IMPRISONED HIM DOWN HERE FOR *EVER*. COOL, HUH?

"FAST FORWARD TO A HUNDRED YEARS AGO. THEY HAD AN EARTHQUAKE IN THIS AREA, AND ALARMS WENT OFF IN OLYMPIA. ONE MOMENT I WAS SITTING AROUND AT THE SOUTH POLE, THE NEXT WE WERE ON OUR WAY TO CALIFORNIA.

"*BIG* REPAIRS TO DO, AND ALL THE KNOWLEDGE OF WHAT TO DO AND HOW TO DO IT WAS *WAITING* THERE IN THE BACK OF OUR HEADS.

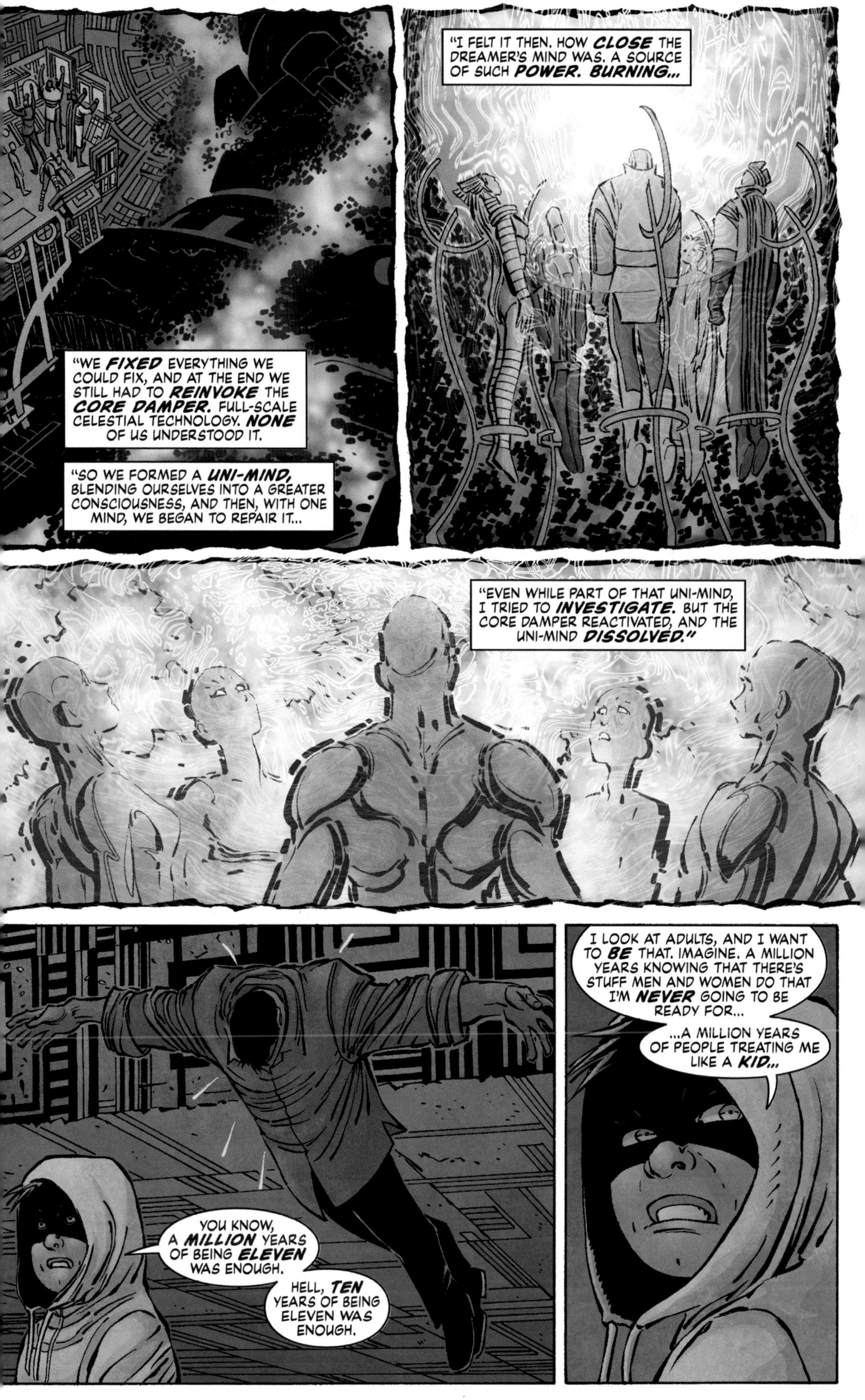
"WE FIXED EVERYTHING WE COULD FIX, AND AT THE END WE STILL HAD TO REINVOKE THE CORE DAMPER. FULL-SCALE CELESTIAL TECHNOLOGY. NONE OF US UNDERSTOOD IT.
"SO WE FORMED A UNI-MIND, BLENDING OURSELVES INTO A GREATER CONSCIOUSNESS, AND THEN, WITH ONE MIND, WE BEGAN TO REPAIR IT...
"I FELT IT THEN. HOW CLOSE THE DREAMER'S MIND WAS. A SOURCE OF SUCH POWER. BURNING...
"EVEN WHILE PART OF THAT UNI-MIND, I TRIED TO INVESTIGATE. BUT THE CORE DAMPER REACTIVATED, AND THE UNI-MIND DISSOLVED."
YOU KNOW, A MILLION YEARS OF BEING ELEVEN WAS ENOUGH.
HELL, TEN YEARS OF BEING ELEVEN WAS ENOUGH.
I LOOK AT ADULTS, AND I WANT TO BE THAT. IMAGINE. A MILLION YEARS KNOWING THAT THERE'S STUFF MEN AND WOMEN DO THAT I'M NEVER GOING TO BE READY FOR...
...A MILLION YEARS OF PEOPLE TREATING ME LIKE A KID...

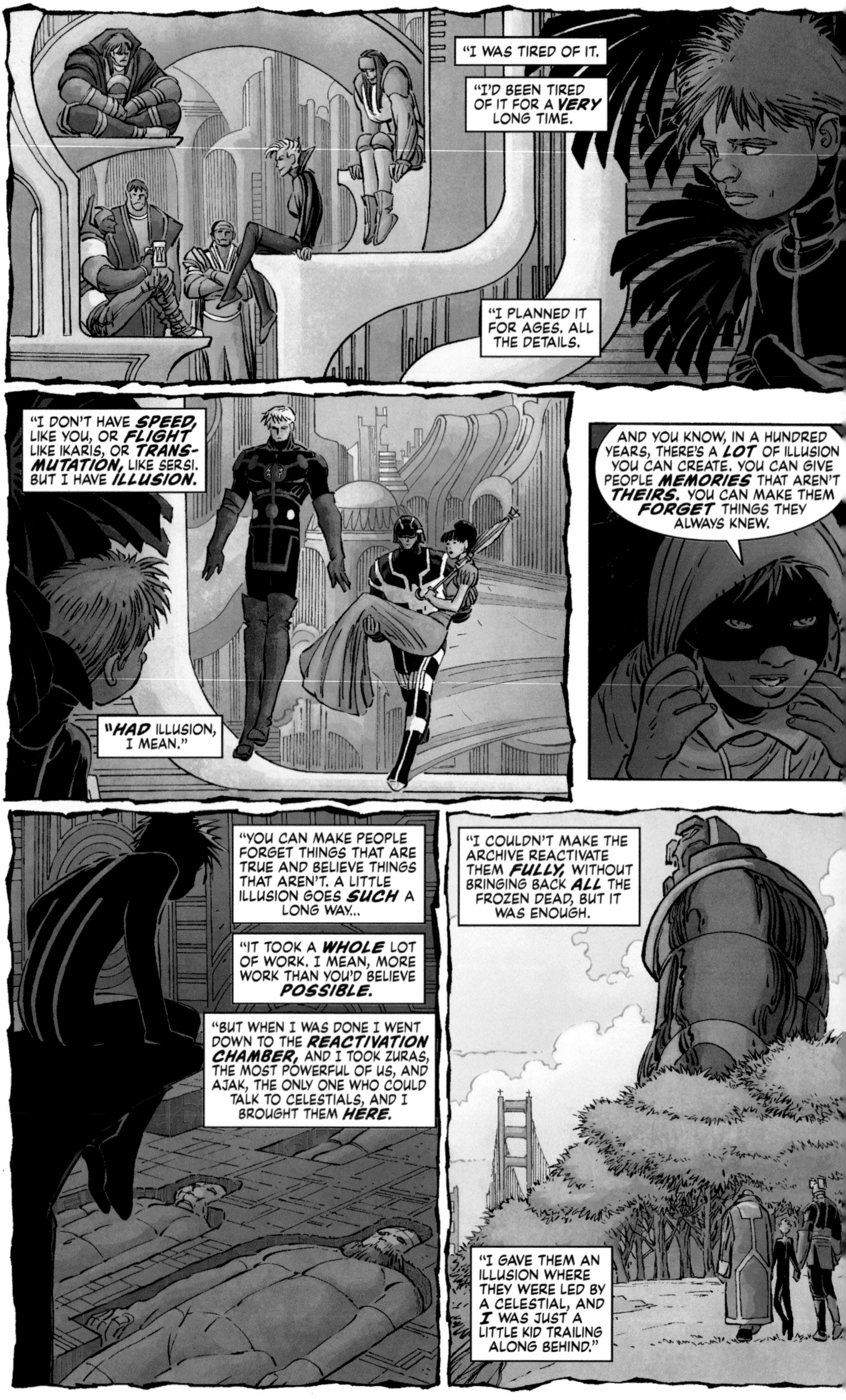
"I WAS TIRED OF IT.
"I'D BEEN TIRED OF IT FOR A VERY LONG TIME.
"I PLANNED IT FOR AGES. ALL THE DETAILS.
"I DON'T HAVE SPEED, LIKE YOU, OR FLIGHT LIKE IKARIS, OR TRANSMUTATION, LIKE SERSI. BUT I HAVE ILLUSION.
"HAD ILLUSION, I MEAN."
AND YOU KNOW, IN A HUNDRED YEARS, THERE'S A LOT OF ILLUSION YOU CAN CREATE. YOU CAN GIVE PEOPLE MEMORIES THAT AREN'T THEIRS. YOU CAN MAKE THEM FORGET THINGS THEY ALWAYS KNEW.
"YOU CAN MAKE PEOPLE FORGET THINGS THAT ARE TRUE AND BELIEVE THINGS THAT AREN'T. A LITTLE ILLUSION GOES SUCH A LONG WAY...
"IT TOOK A WHOLE LOT OF WORK. I MEAN, MORE WORK THAN YOU'D BELIEVE POSSIBLE.
"BUT WHEN I WAS DONE I WENT DOWN TO THE REACTIVATION CHAMBER, AND I TOOK ZURAS, THE MOST POWERFUL OF US, AND AJAK, THE ONLY ONE WHO COULD TALK TO CELESTIALS, AND I BROUGHT THEM HERE.
"I COULDN'T MAKE THE ARCHIVE REACTIVATE THEM FULLY, WITHOUT BRINGING BACK ALL THE FROZEN DEAD, BUT IT WAS ENOUGH.
"I GAVE THEM AN ILLUSION WHERE THEY WERE LED BY A CELESTIAL, AND I WAS JUST A LITTLE KID TRAILING ALONG BEHIND."

"WE CAME DOWN HERE, AND WE DID IT. A *UNI-MIND*. BUT *POWERED* BY AN UNCONSCIOUS CELESTIAL. IT AMPLIFIED EVERYTHING I COULD NATURALLY DO.

"AND IT GAVE ME SO MUCH *MORE*...

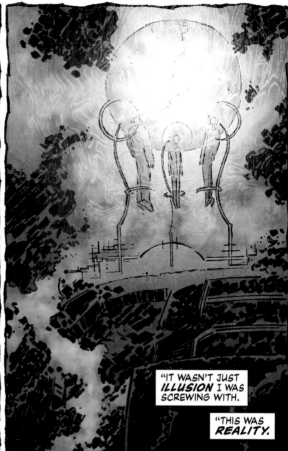

"IT WASN'T JUST *ILLUSION* I WAS SCREWING WITH.

"THIS WAS *REALITY*.

"AND BY THE TIME I WAS FINISHED...

"THERE *WEREN'T* ANY ETERNALS.

"...I'D CHANGED THINGS.

"JUST A HUNDRED MORE DUMB MAYFLIES WANDERING AROUND THE WORLD."

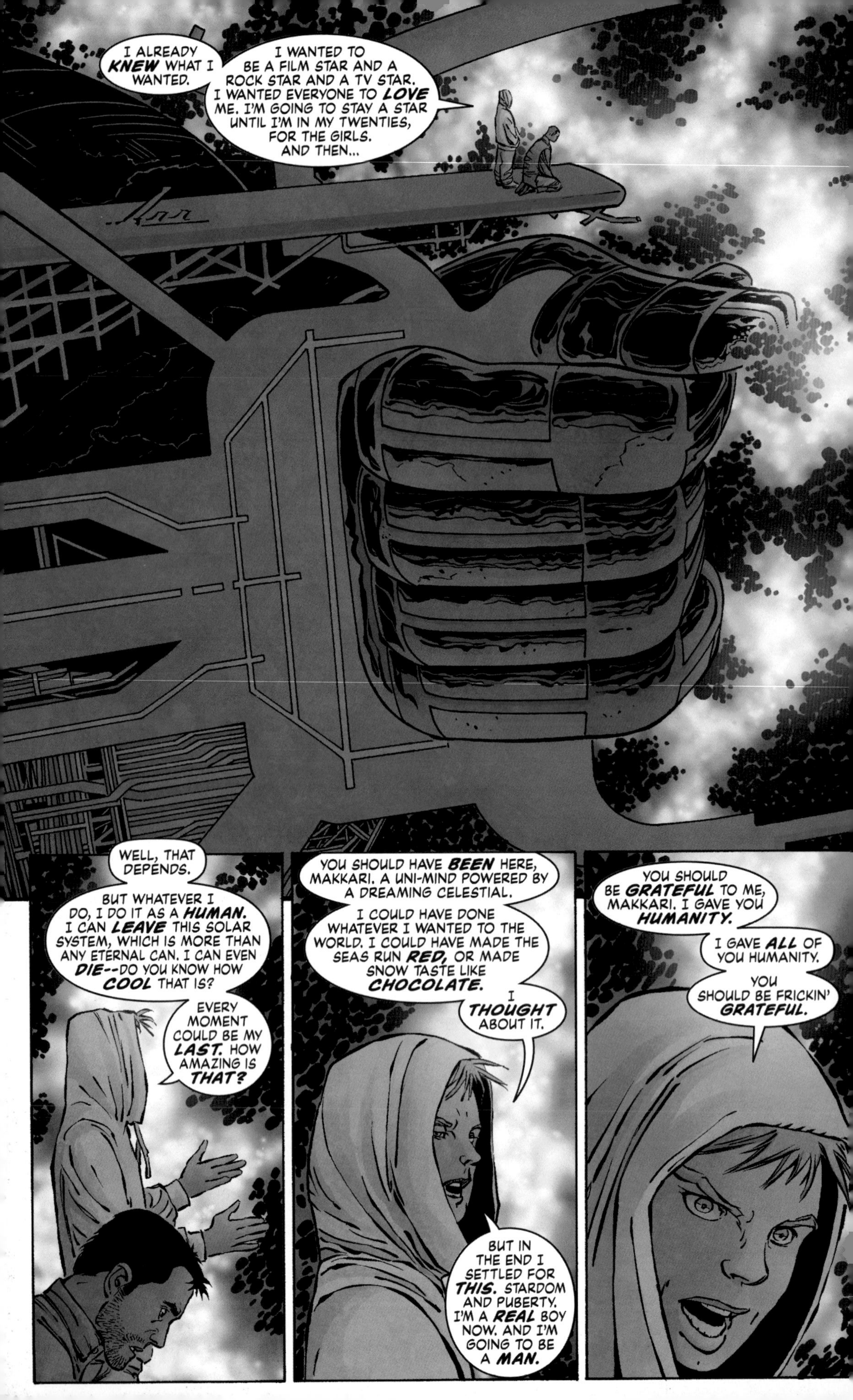
I ALREADY KNEW WHAT I WANTED.
I WANTED TO BE A FILM STAR AND A ROCK STAR AND A TV STAR. I WANTED EVERYONE TO LOVE ME. I'M GOING TO STAY A STAR UNTIL I'M IN MY TWENTIES, FOR THE GIRLS. AND THEN...
WELL, THAT DEPENDS.
BUT WHATEVER I DO, I DO IT AS A HUMAN. I CAN LEAVE THIS SOLAR SYSTEM, WHICH IS MORE THAN ANY ETERNAL CAN. I CAN EVEN DIE--DO YOU KNOW HOW COOL THAT IS?
EVERY MOMENT COULD BE MY LAST. HOW AMAZING IS THAT?
YOU SHOULD HAVE BEEN HERE, MAKKARI. A UNI-MIND POWERED BY A DREAMING CELESTIAL.
I COULD HAVE DONE WHATEVER I WANTED TO THE WORLD. I COULD HAVE MADE THE SEAS RUN RED, OR MADE SNOW TASTE LIKE CHOCOLATE.
I THOUGHT ABOUT IT.
BUT IN THE END I SETTLED FOR THIS. STARDOM AND PUBERTY. I'M A REAL BOY NOW. AND I'M GOING TO BE A MAN.
YOU SHOULD BE GRATEFUL TO ME, MAKKARI. I GAVE YOU HUMANITY.
I GAVE ALL OF YOU HUMANITY.
YOU SHOULD BE FRICKIN' GRATEFUL.

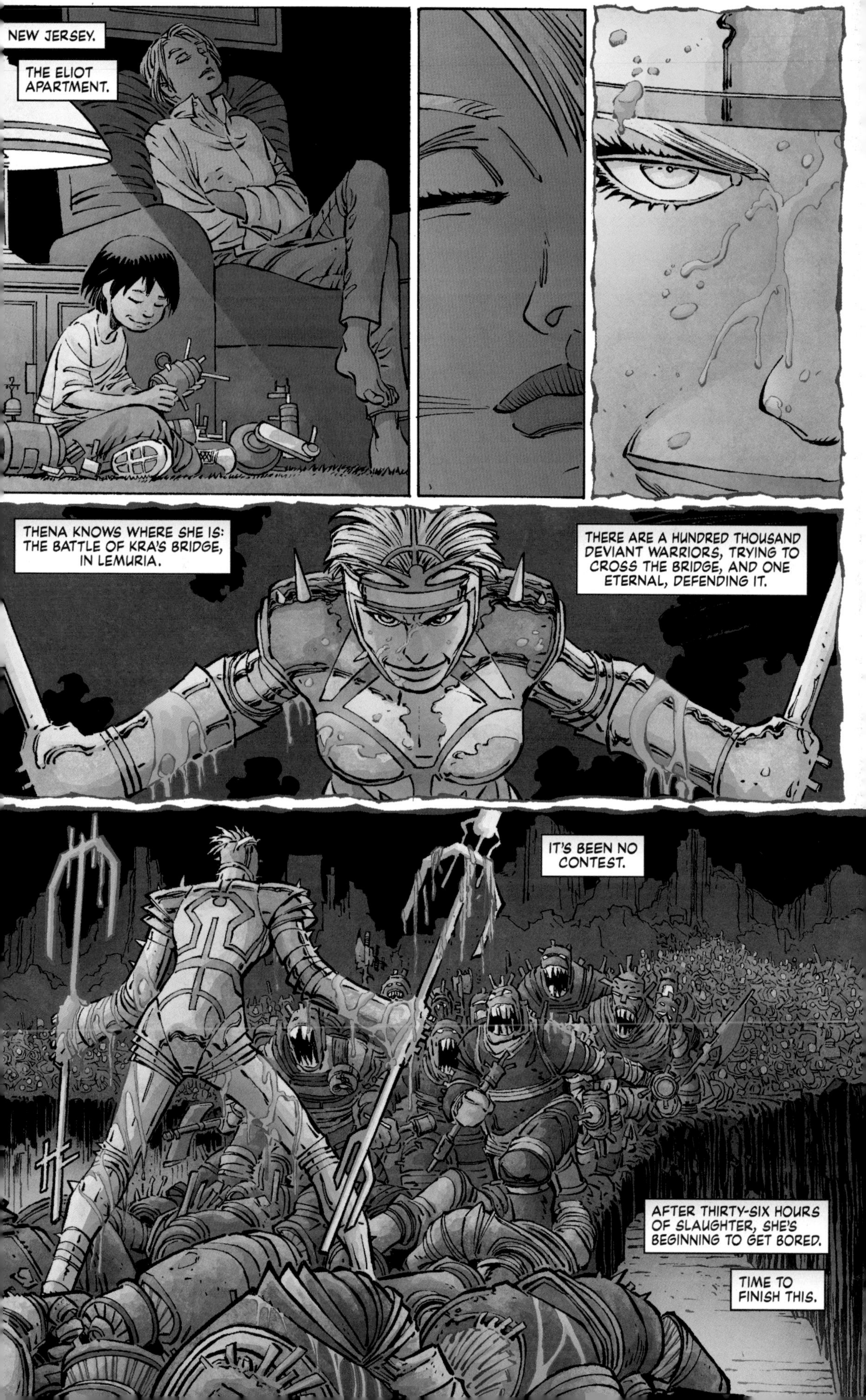
NEW JERSEY.
THE ELIOT APARTMENT.
THENA KNOWS WHERE SHE IS: THE BATTLE OF KRA'S BRIDGE, IN LEMURIA.
THERE ARE A HUNDRED THOUSAND DEVIANT WARRIORS, TRYING TO CROSS THE BRIDGE, AND ONE ETERNAL, DEFENDING IT.
IT'S BEEN NO CONTEST.
AFTER THIRTY-SIX HOURS OF SLAUGHTER, SHE'S BEGINNING TO GET BORED.
TIME TO FINISH THIS.

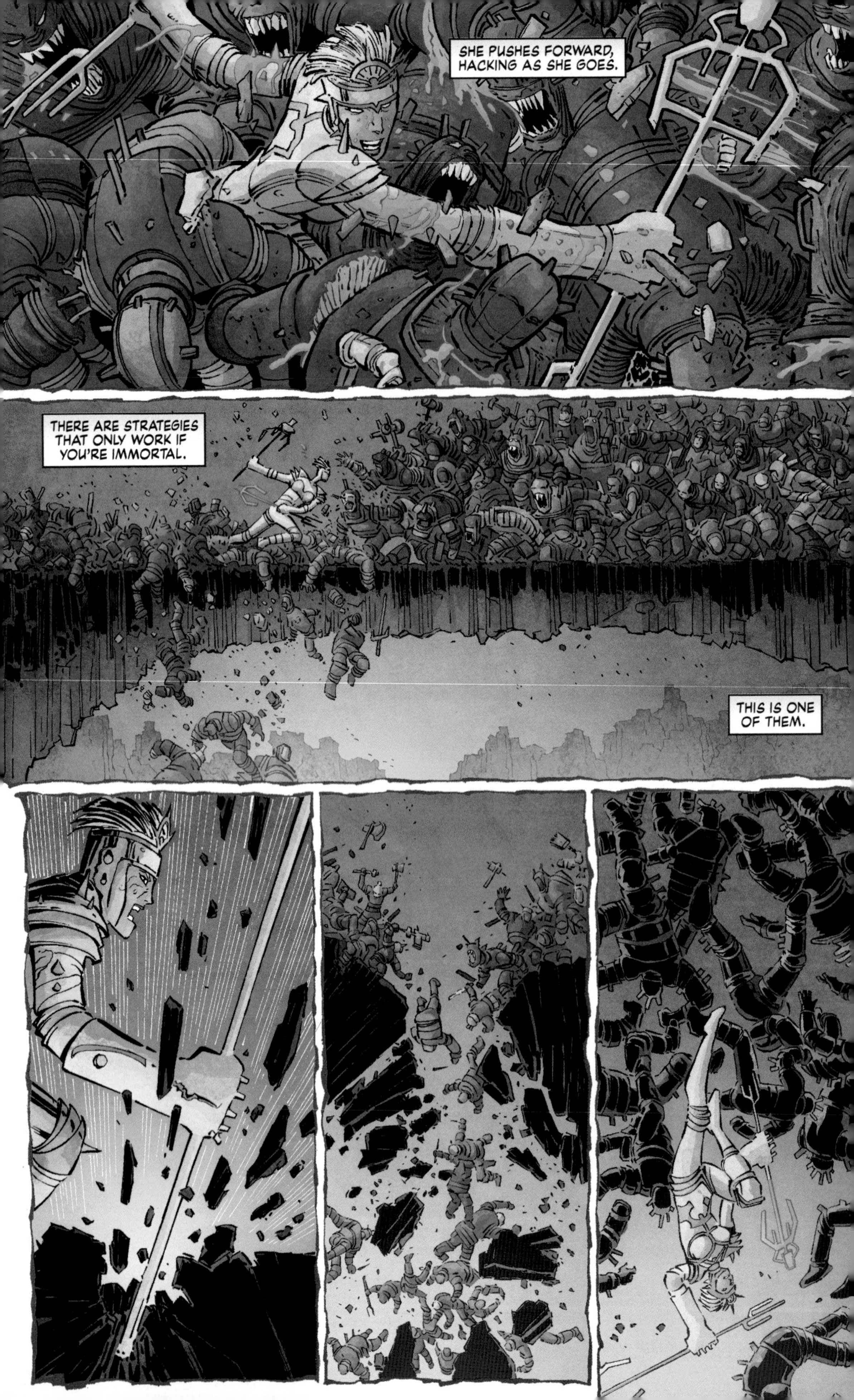
SHE PUSHES FORWARD, HACKING AS SHE GOES.
THERE ARE STRATEGIES THAT ONLY WORK IF YOU'RE IMMORTAL.
THIS IS ONE OF THEM.

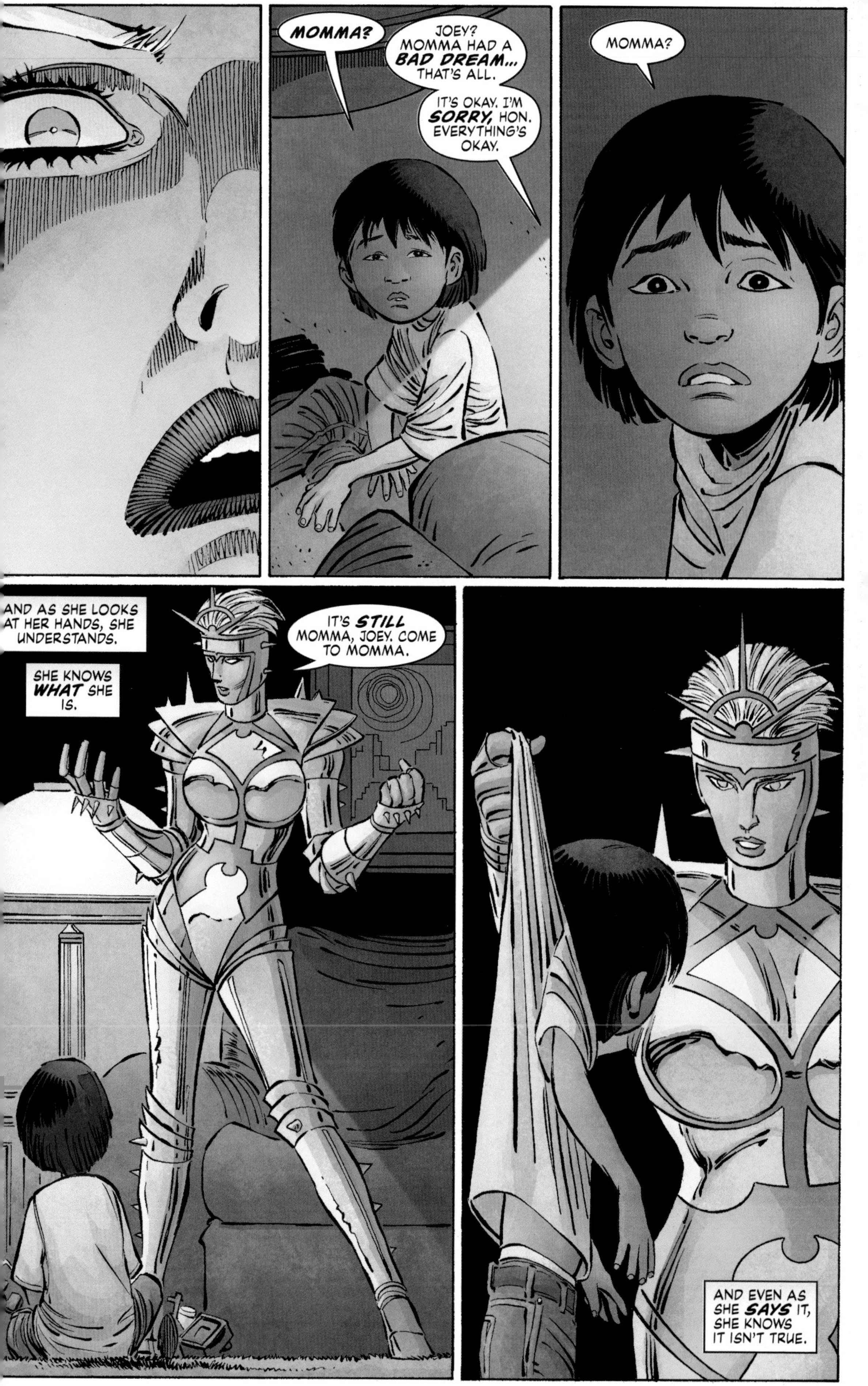
MOMMA?
JOEY? MOMMA HAD A BAD DREAM... THAT'S ALL.
IT'S OKAY. I'M SORRY, HON. EVERYTHING'S OKAY.
MOMMA?
AND AS SHE LOOKS AT HER HANDS, SHE UNDERSTANDS.
SHE KNOWS WHAT SHE IS.
IT'S STILL MOMMA, JOEY. COME TO MOMMA.
AND EVEN AS SHE SAYS IT, SHE KNOWS IT ISN'T TRUE.

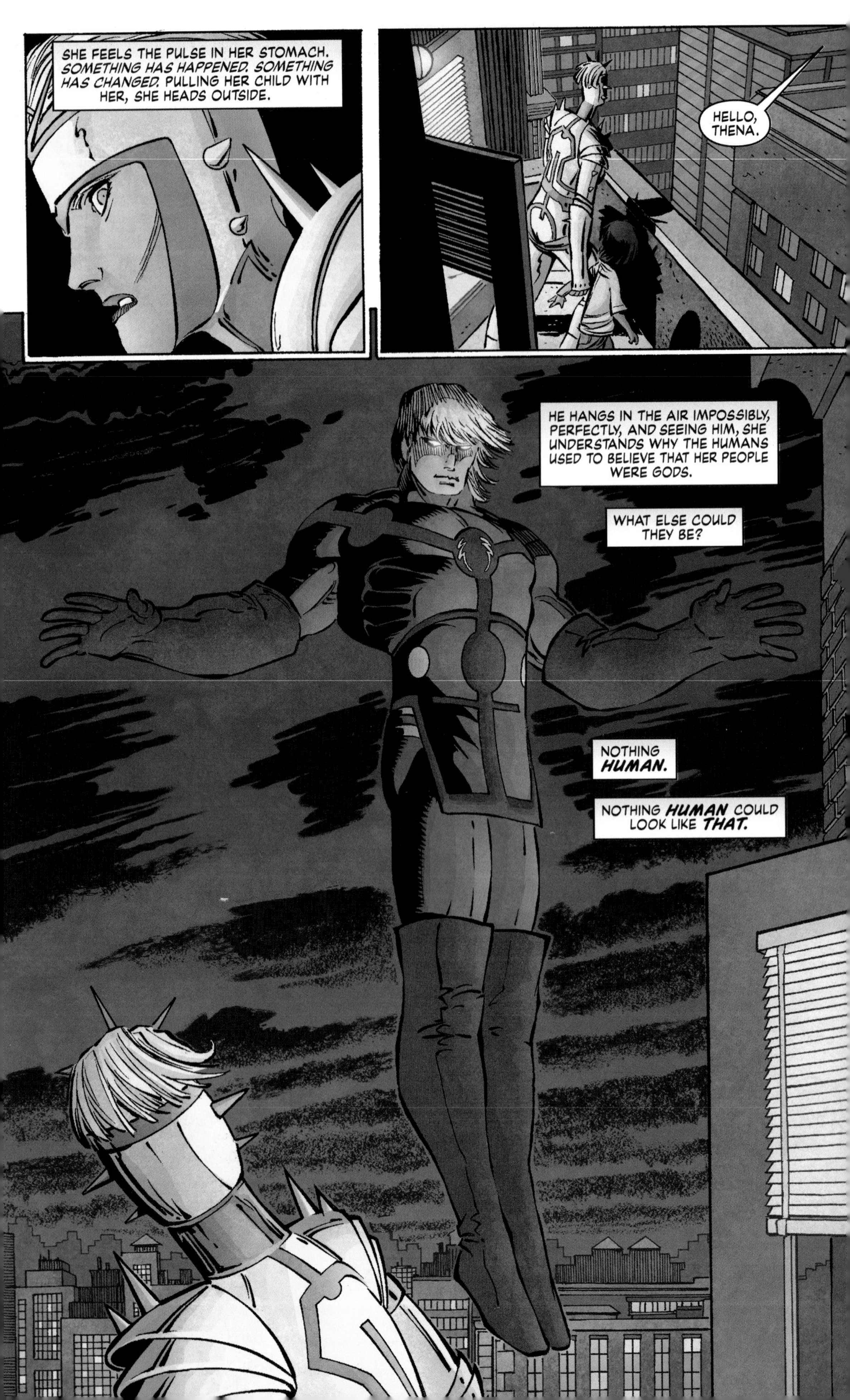
SHE FEELS THE PULSE IN HER STOMACH. *SOMETHING HAS HAPPENED. SOMETHING HAS CHANGED.* PULLING HER CHILD WITH HER, SHE HEADS OUTSIDE.
HELLO, THENA.
HE HANGS IN THE AIR IMPOSSIBLY, PERFECTLY, AND SEEING HIM, SHE UNDERSTANDS WHY THE HUMANS USED TO BELIEVE THAT HER PEOPLE WERE GODS.
WHAT ELSE COULD THEY BE?
NOTHING ***HUMAN.***
NOTHING ***HUMAN*** COULD LOOK LIKE ***THAT.***

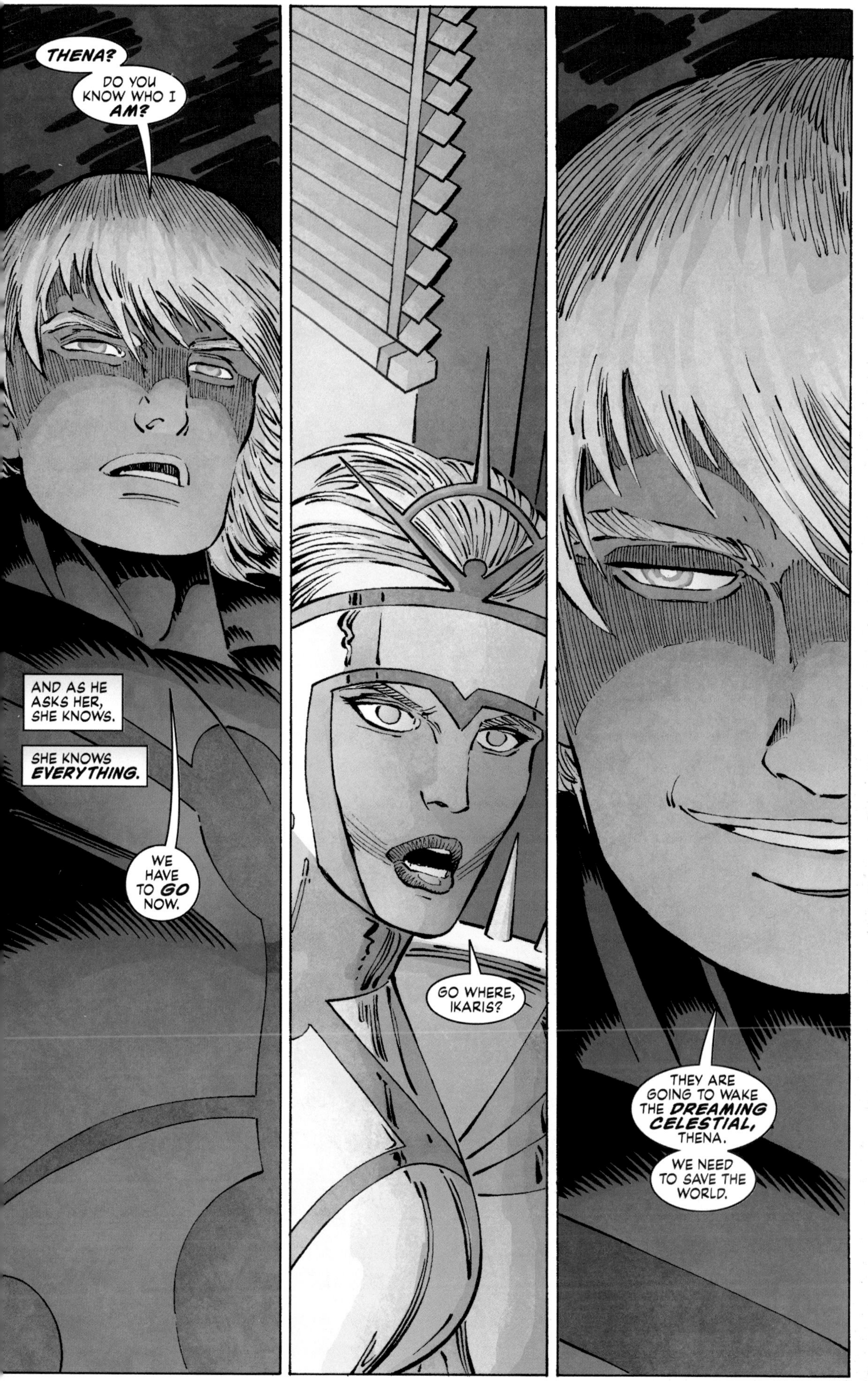
THENA?
DO YOU KNOW WHO I AM?
AND AS HE ASKS HER, SHE KNOWS.
SHE KNOWS EVERYTHING.
WE HAVE TO GO NOW.
GO WHERE, IKARIS?
THEY ARE GOING TO WAKE THE DREAMING CELESTIAL, THENA.
WE NEED TO SAVE THE WORLD.

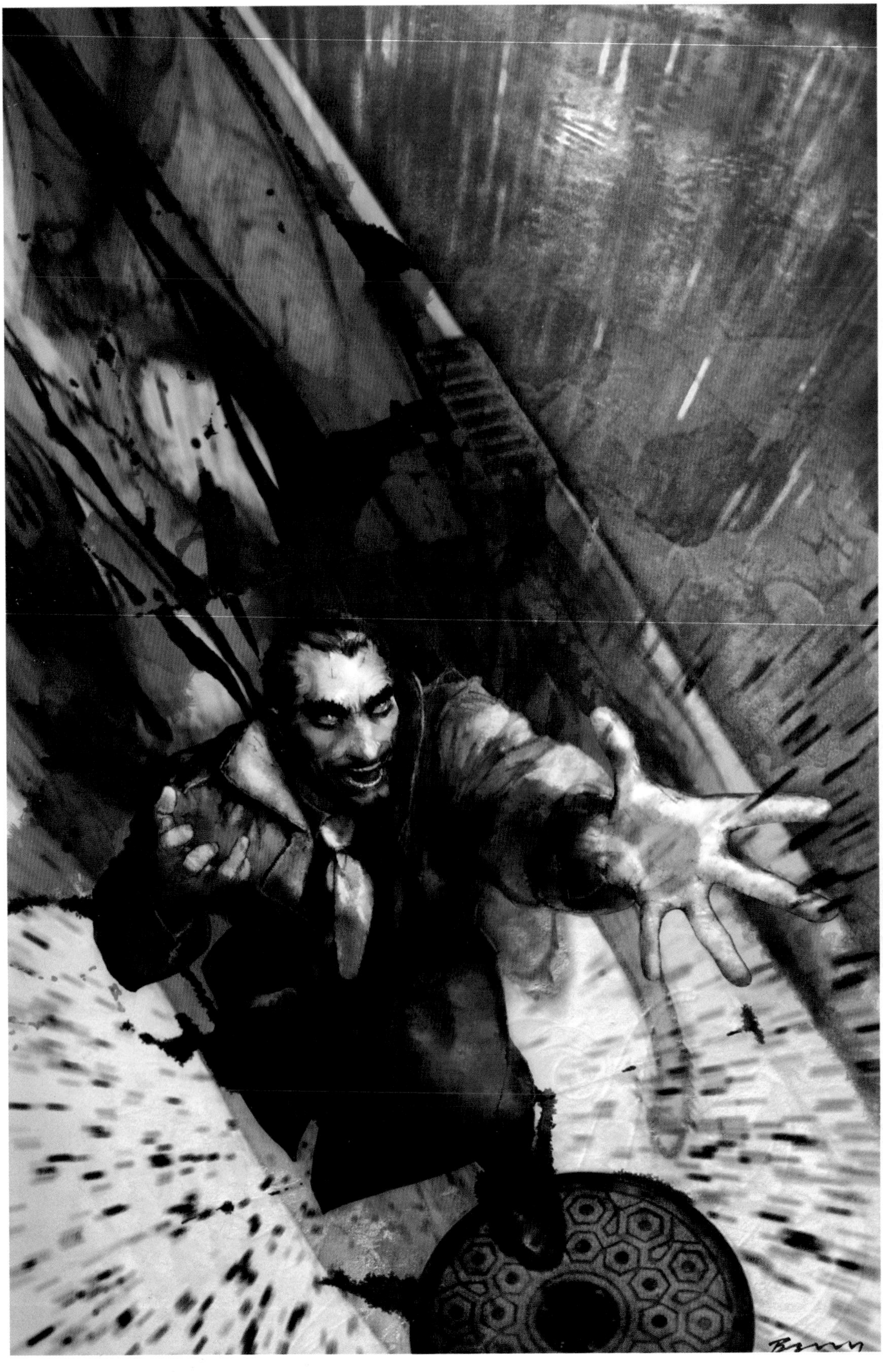

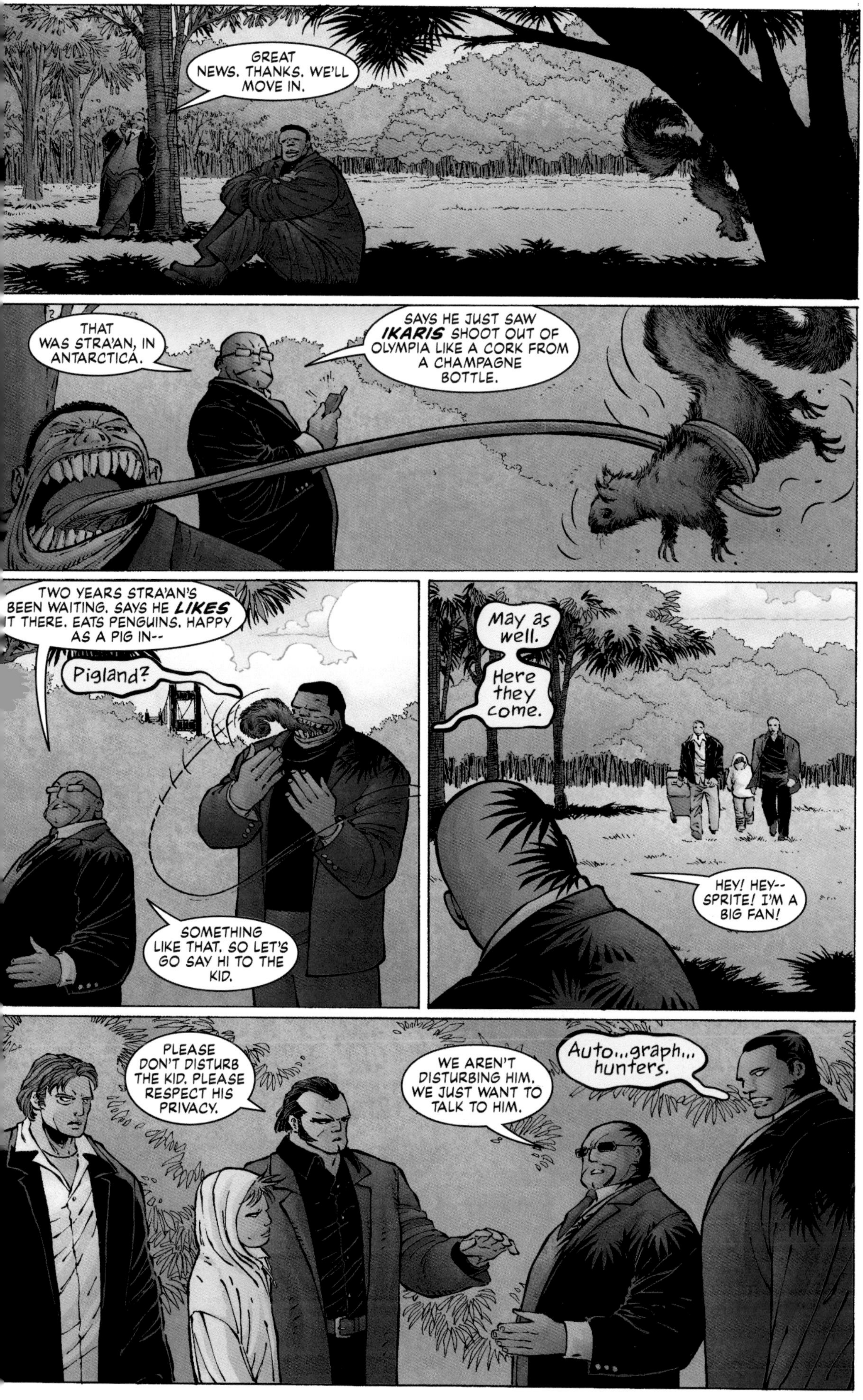
GREAT NEWS. THANKS. WE'LL MOVE IN.
THAT WAS STRA'AN, IN ANTARCTICA.
SAYS HE JUST SAW IKARIS SHOOT OUT OF OLYMPIA LIKE A CORK FROM A CHAMPAGNE BOTTLE.
TWO YEARS STRA'AN'S BEEN WAITING. SAYS HE LIKES IT THERE. EATS PENGUINS. HAPPY AS A PIG IN--
Pigland?
SOMETHING LIKE THAT. SO LET'S GO SAY HI TO THE KID.
May as well.
Here they come.
HEY! HEY-- SPRITE! I'M A BIG FAN!
PLEASE DON'T DISTURB THE KID. PLEASE RESPECT HIS PRIVACY.
WE AREN'T DISTURBING HIM. WE JUST WANT TO TALK TO HIM.
Auto...graph... hunters.

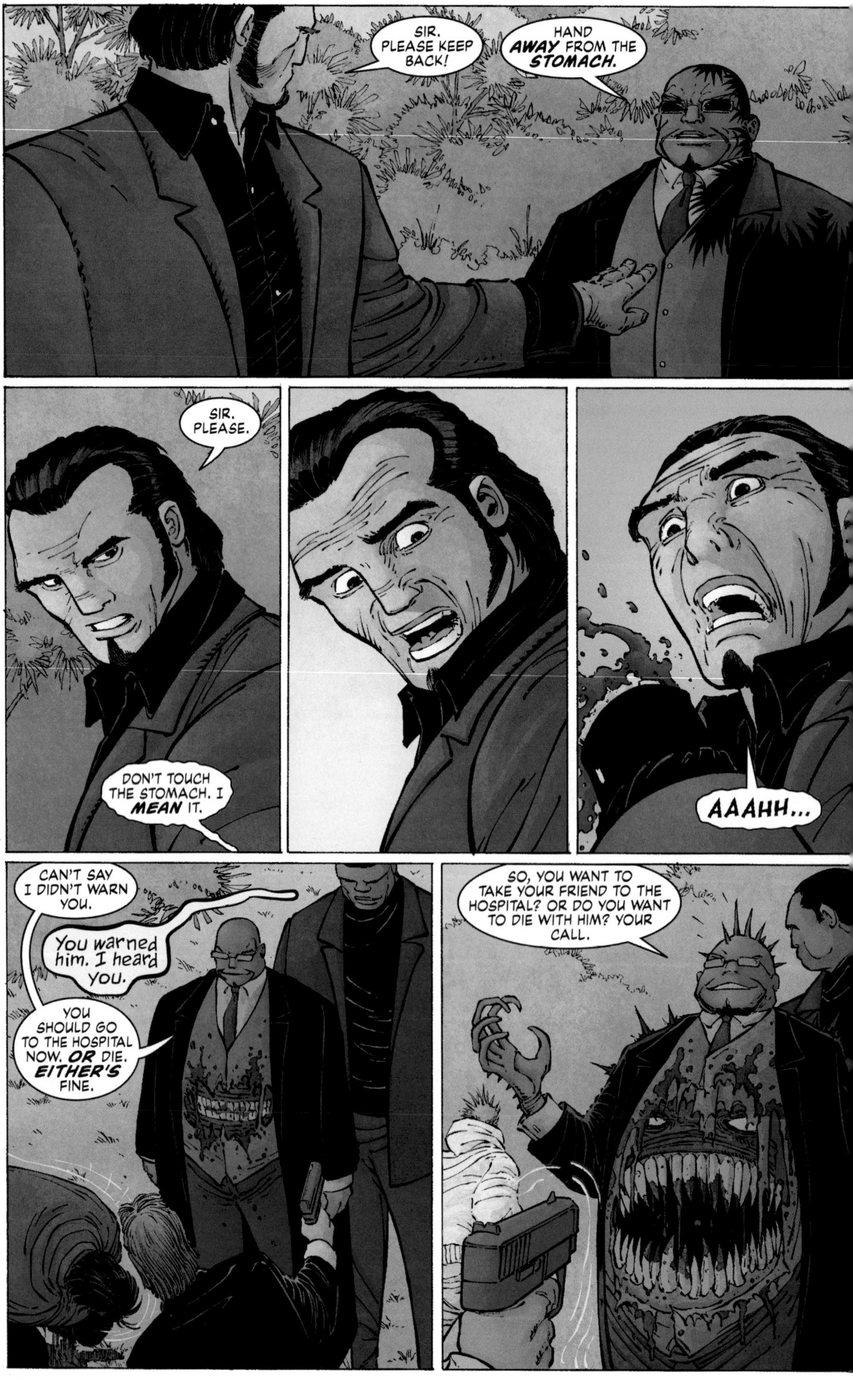
SIR. PLEASE KEEP BACK!
HAND AWAY FROM THE STOMACH.
SIR. PLEASE.
DON'T TOUCH THE STOMACH. I MEAN IT.
AAAHH...
CAN'T SAY I DIDN'T WARN YOU.
You warned him. I heard you.
YOU SHOULD GO TO THE HOSPITAL NOW. OR DIE. EITHER'S FINE.
SO, YOU WANT TO TAKE YOUR FRIEND TO THE HOSPITAL? OR DO YOU WANT TO DIE WITH HIM? YOUR CALL.

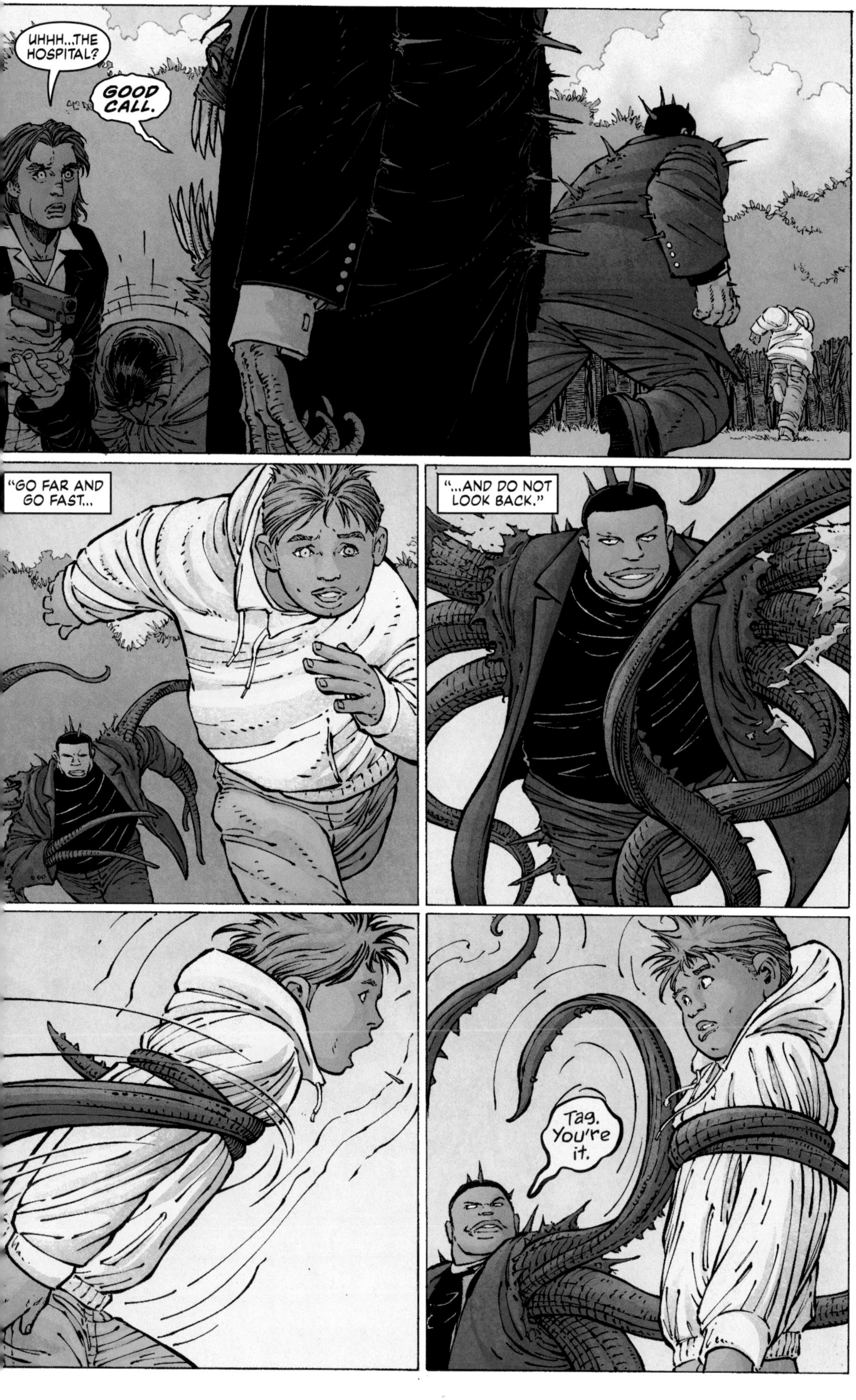
UHHH...THE HOSPITAL?
GOOD CALL.
"GO FAR AND GO FAST...
"...AND DO NOT LOOK BACK."
Tag. You're it.

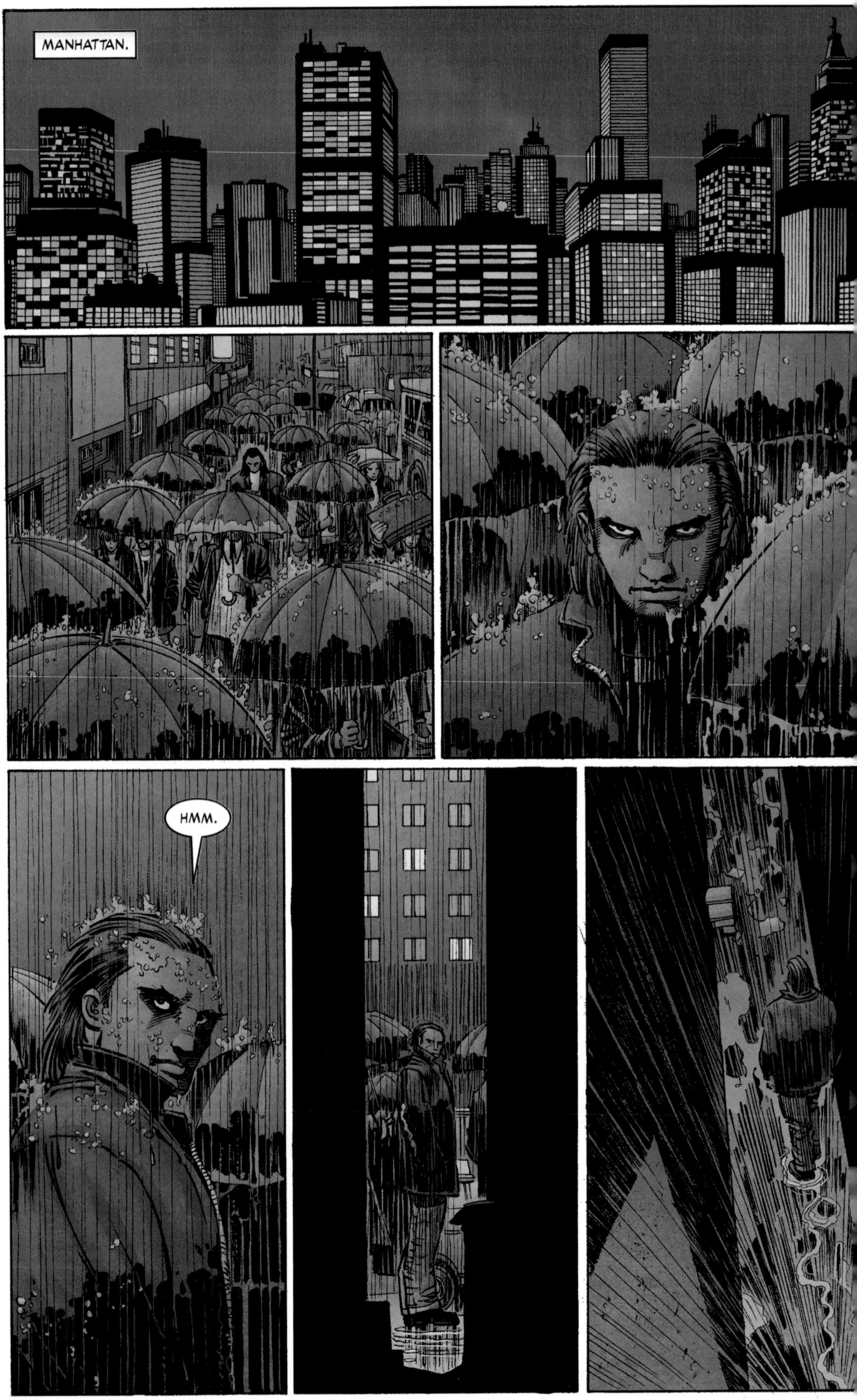
MANHATTAN.
HMM.

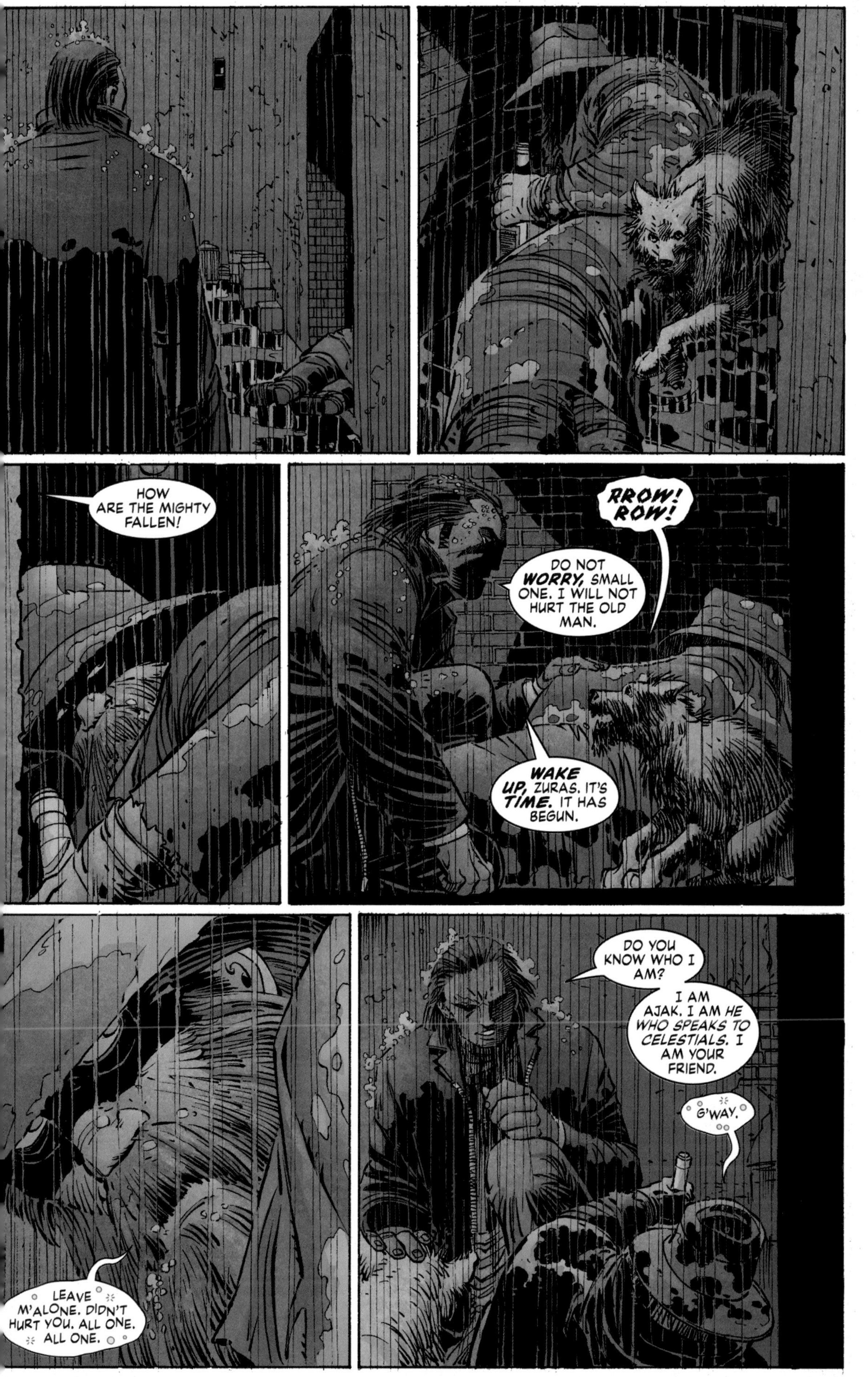
HOW ARE THE MIGHTY FALLEN!
RROW! ROW!
DO NOT WORRY, SMALL ONE. I WILL NOT HURT THE OLD MAN.
WAKE UP, ZURAS. IT'S TIME. IT HAS BEGUN.
LEAVE M'ALONE. DIDN'T HURT YOU. ALL ONE. ALL ONE.
DO YOU KNOW WHO I AM?
I AM AJAK. I AM HE WHO SPEAKS TO CELESTIALS. I AM YOUR FRIEND.
G'WAY.

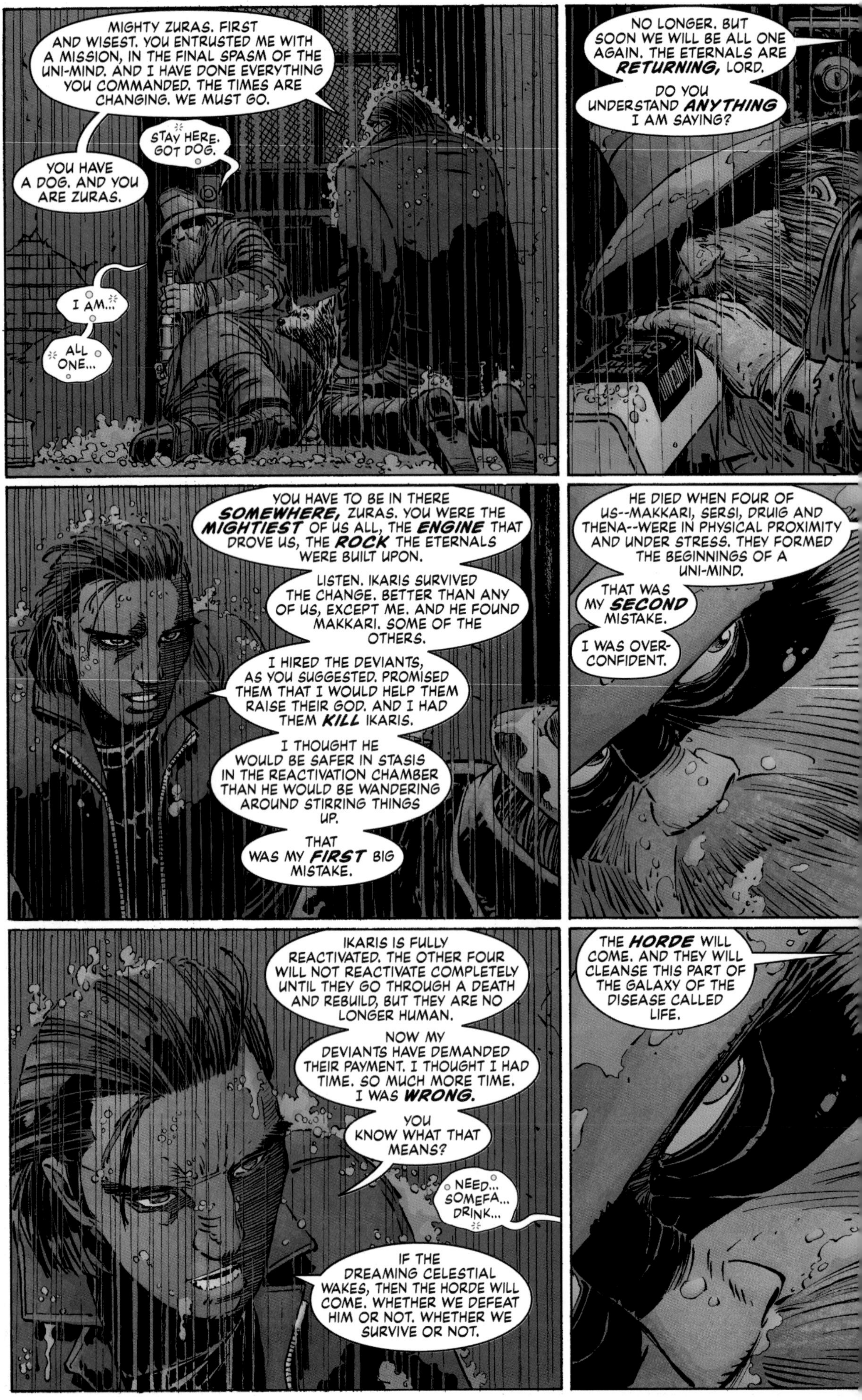
MIGHTY ZURAS. FIRST AND WISEST. YOU ENTRUSTED ME WITH A MISSION, IN THE FINAL SPASM OF THE UNI-MIND. AND I HAVE DONE EVERYTHING YOU COMMANDED. THE TIMES ARE CHANGING. WE MUST GO.
STAY HERE. GOT DOG.
YOU HAVE A DOG. AND YOU ARE ZURAS.
I AM...
ALL ONE...
NO LONGER. BUT SOON WE WILL BE ALL ONE AGAIN. THE ETERNALS ARE RETURNING, LORD.
DO YOU UNDERSTAND ANYTHING I AM SAYING?
YOU HAVE TO BE IN THERE SOMEWHERE, ZURAS. YOU WERE THE MIGHTIEST OF US ALL, THE ENGINE THAT DROVE US, THE ROCK THE ETERNALS WERE BUILT UPON.
LISTEN. IKARIS SURVIVED THE CHANGE. BETTER THAN ANY OF US, EXCEPT ME. AND HE FOUND MAKKARI. SOME OF THE OTHERS.
I HIRED THE DEVIANTS, AS YOU SUGGESTED. PROMISED THEM THAT I WOULD HELP THEM RAISE THEIR GOD. AND I HAD THEM KILL IKARIS.
I THOUGHT HE WOULD BE SAFER IN STASIS IN THE REACTIVATION CHAMBER THAN HE WOULD BE WANDERING AROUND STIRRING THINGS UP.
THAT WAS MY FIRST BIG MISTAKE.
HE DIED WHEN FOUR OF US--MAKKARI, SERSI, DRUIG AND THENA--WERE IN PHYSICAL PROXIMITY AND UNDER STRESS. THEY FORMED THE BEGINNINGS OF A UNI-MIND.
THAT WAS MY SECOND MISTAKE.
I WAS OVER-CONFIDENT.
IKARIS IS FULLY REACTIVATED. THE OTHER FOUR WILL NOT REACTIVATE COMPLETELY UNTIL THEY GO THROUGH A DEATH AND REBUILD, BUT THEY ARE NO LONGER HUMAN.
NOW MY DEVIANTS HAVE DEMANDED THEIR PAYMENT. I THOUGHT I HAD TIME. SO MUCH MORE TIME. I WAS WRONG.
YOU KNOW WHAT THAT MEANS?
NEED... SOMEFA... DRINK...
IF THE DREAMING CELESTIAL WAKES, THEN THE HORDE WILL COME. WHETHER WE DEFEAT HIM OR NOT. WHETHER WE SURVIVE OR NOT.
THE HORDE WILL COME. AND THEY WILL CLEANSE THIS PART OF THE GALAXY OF THE DISEASE CALLED LIFE.

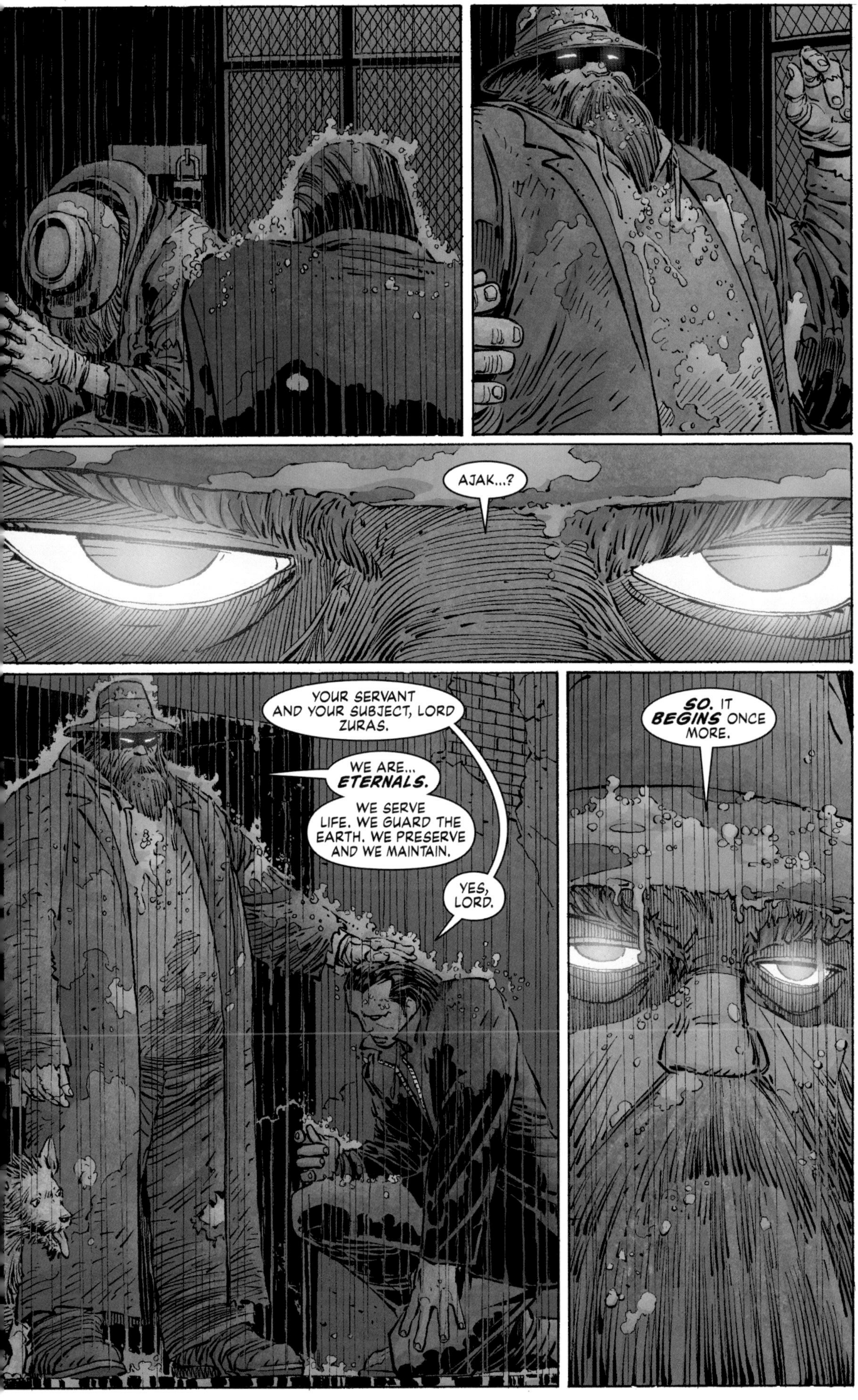
AJAK...?
YOUR SERVANT AND YOUR SUBJECT, LORD ZURAS.
WE ARE... ETERNALS.
WE SERVE LIFE. WE GUARD THE EARTH. WE PRESERVE AND WE MAINTAIN.
YES, LORD.
SO. IT BEGINS ONCE MORE.

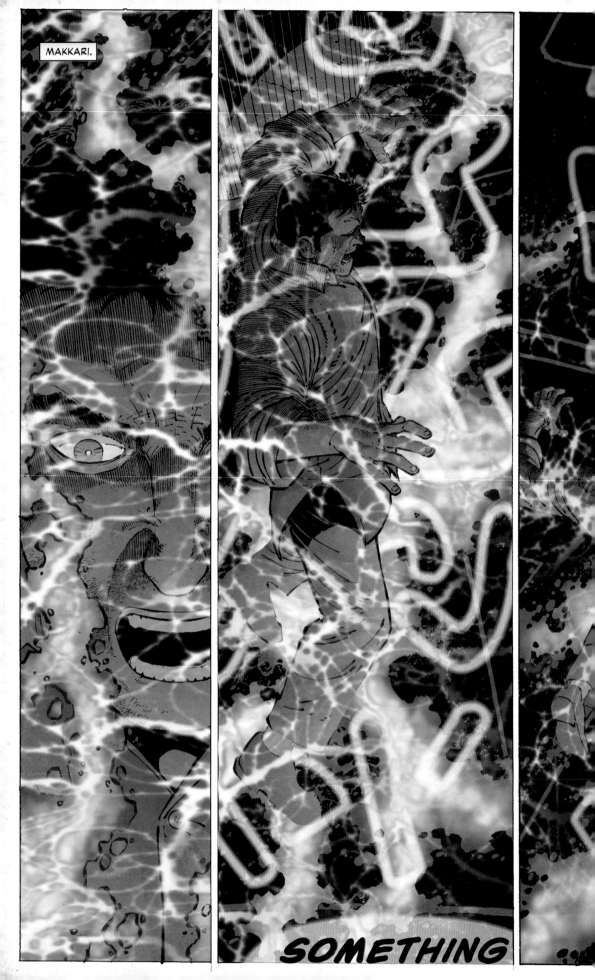

MAKKARI.

SOMETHING

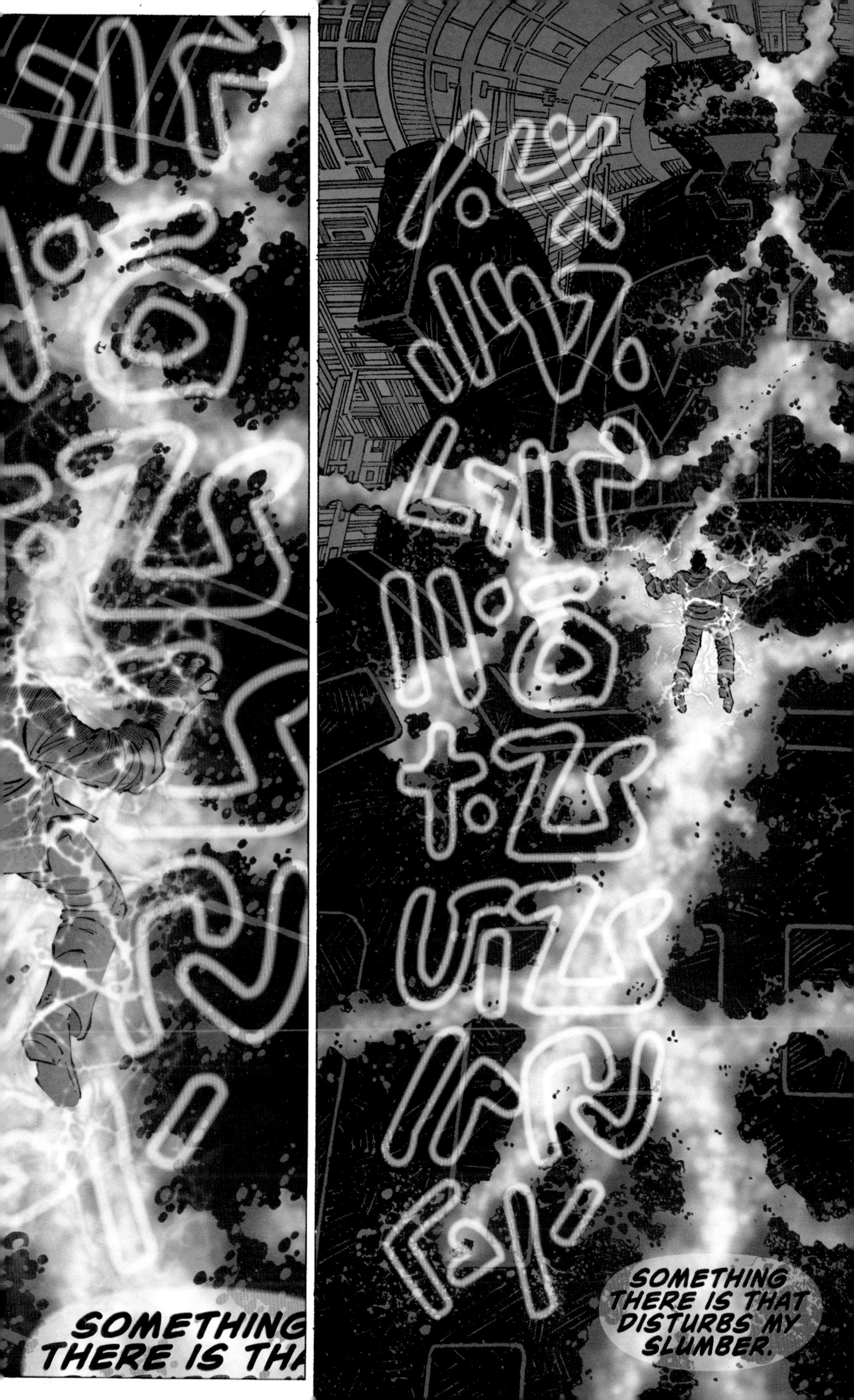
SOMETHING THERE IS THA
SOMETHING THERE IS THAT DISTURBS MY SLUMBER.

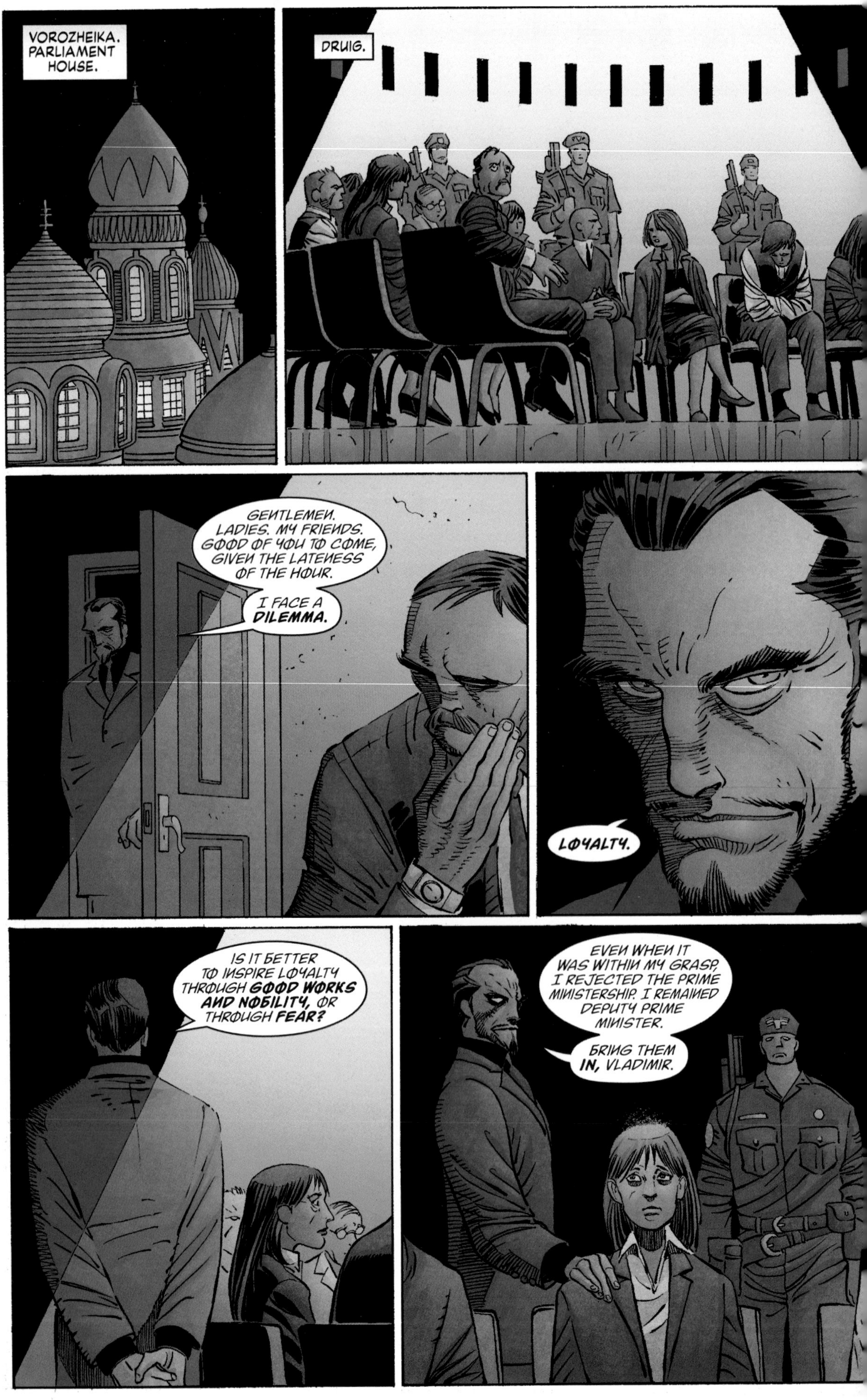
VOROZHEIKA. PARLIAMENT HOUSE.
DRUIG.
GENTLEMEN. LADIES. MY FRIENDS. GOOD OF YOU TO COME, GIVEN THE LATENESS OF THE HOUR.
I FACE A DILEMMA.
LOYALTY.
IS IT BETTER TO INSPIRE LOYALTY THROUGH GOOD WORKS AND NOBILITY, OR THROUGH FEAR?
EVEN WHEN IT WAS WITHIN MY GRASP, I REJECTED THE PRIME MINISTERSHIP. I REMAINED DEPUTY PRIME MINISTER.
BRING THEM IN, VLADIMIR.

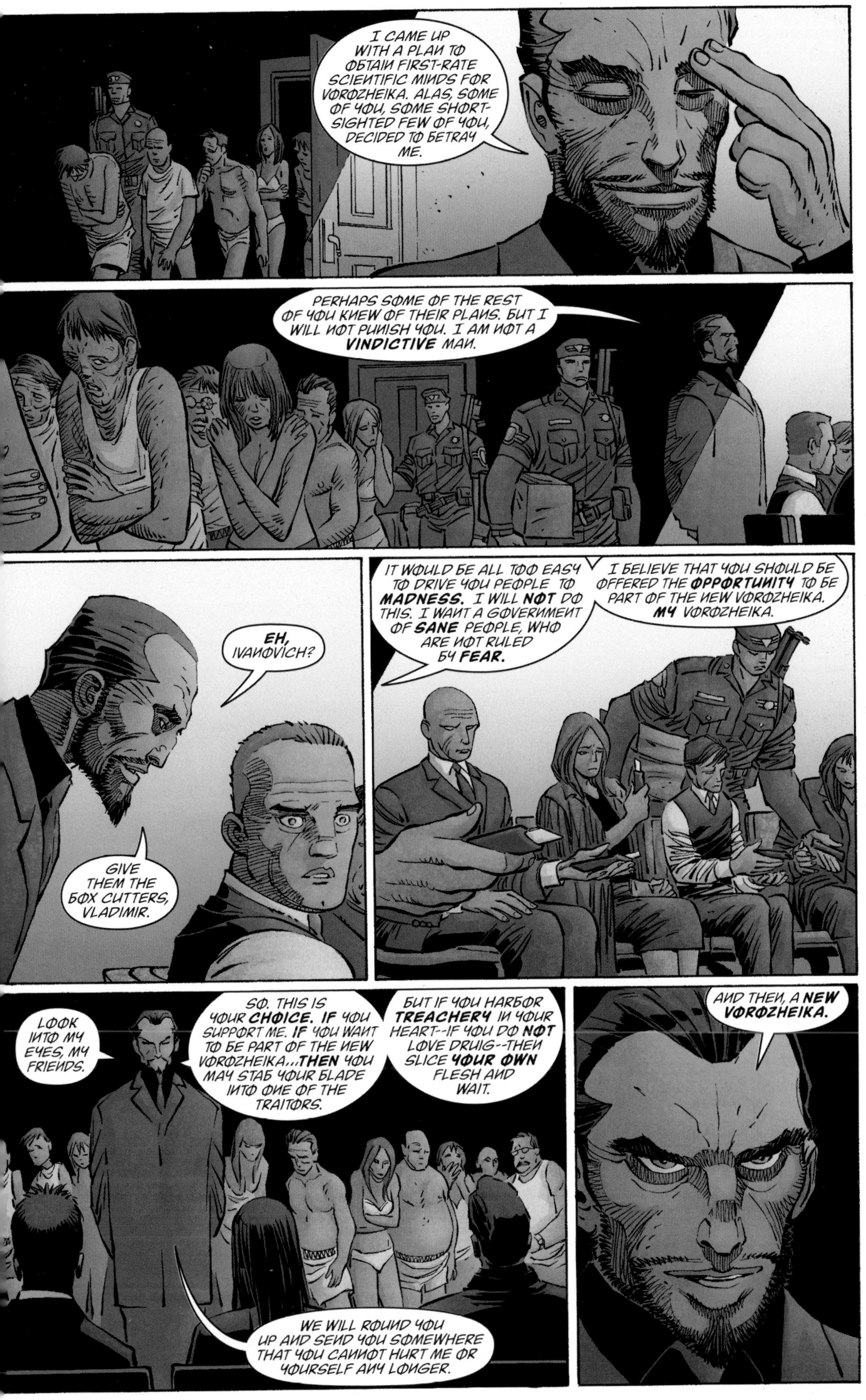
I CAME UP WITH A PLAN TO OBTAIN FIRST-RATE SCIENTIFIC MINDS FOR VOROZHEIKA. ALAS, SOME OF YOU, SOME SHORT-SIGHTED FEW OF YOU, DECIDED TO BETRAY ME.
PERHAPS SOME OF THE REST OF YOU KNEW OF THEIR PLANS. BUT I WILL NOT PUNISH YOU. I AM NOT A VINDICTIVE MAN.
EH, IVANOVICH?
GIVE THEM THE BOX CUTTERS, VLADIMIR.
IT WOULD BE ALL TOO EASY TO DRIVE YOU PEOPLE TO MADNESS. I WILL NOT DO THIS. I WANT A GOVERNMENT OF SANE PEOPLE, WHO ARE NOT RULED BY FEAR.
I BELIEVE THAT YOU SHOULD BE OFFERED THE OPPORTUNITY TO BE PART OF THE NEW VOROZHEIKA. MY VOROZHEIKA.
LOOK INTO MY EYES, MY FRIENDS.
SO. THIS IS YOUR CHOICE. IF YOU SUPPORT ME. IF YOU WANT TO BE PART OF THE NEW VOROZHEIKA...THEN YOU MAY STAB YOUR BLADE INTO ONE OF THE TRAITORS.
BUT IF YOU HARBOR TREACHERY IN YOUR HEART--IF YOU DO NOT LOVE DRUIG--THEN SLICE YOUR OWN FLESH AND WAIT.
WE WILL ROUND YOU UP AND SEND YOU SOMEWHERE THAT YOU CANNOT HURT ME OR YOURSELF ANY LONGER.
AND THEN, A NEW VOROZHEIKA.

DIE, YOU MONSTER!

FOOLISH IVANOVICH. NOW. DO I HAVE TO **TELL** YOU WHAT TO DO NEXT?

THROAT, IVANOVICH. CUT YOUR THROAT NOW.

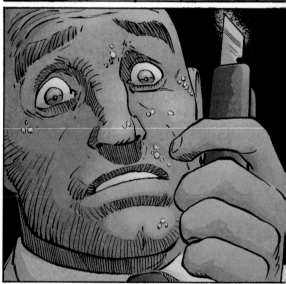

WHAT **HE** JUST TRIED TO DO. **DON'T** DO THAT.

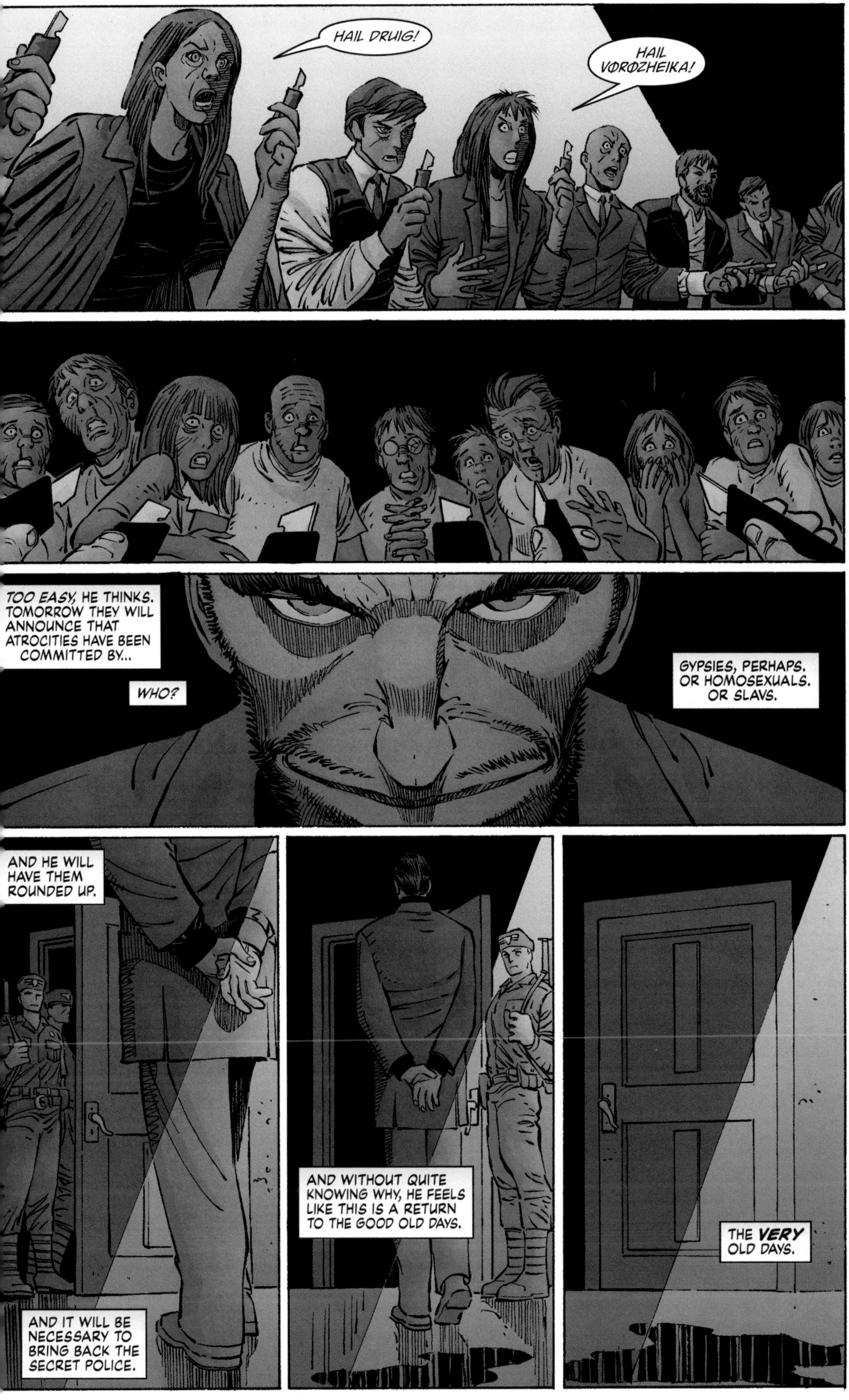
HAIL DRUIG!
HAIL VØRØZHEIKA!
TOO EASY, HE THINKS. TOMORROW THEY WILL ANNOUNCE THAT ATROCITIES HAVE BEEN COMMITTED BY...
WHO?
GYPSIES, PERHAPS. OR HOMOSEXUALS. OR SLAVS.
AND HE WILL HAVE THEM ROUNDED UP.
AND IT WILL BE NECESSARY TO BRING BACK THE SECRET POLICE.
AND WITHOUT QUITE KNOWING WHY, HE FEELS LIKE THIS IS A RETURN TO THE GOOD OLD DAYS.
THE VERY OLD DAYS.

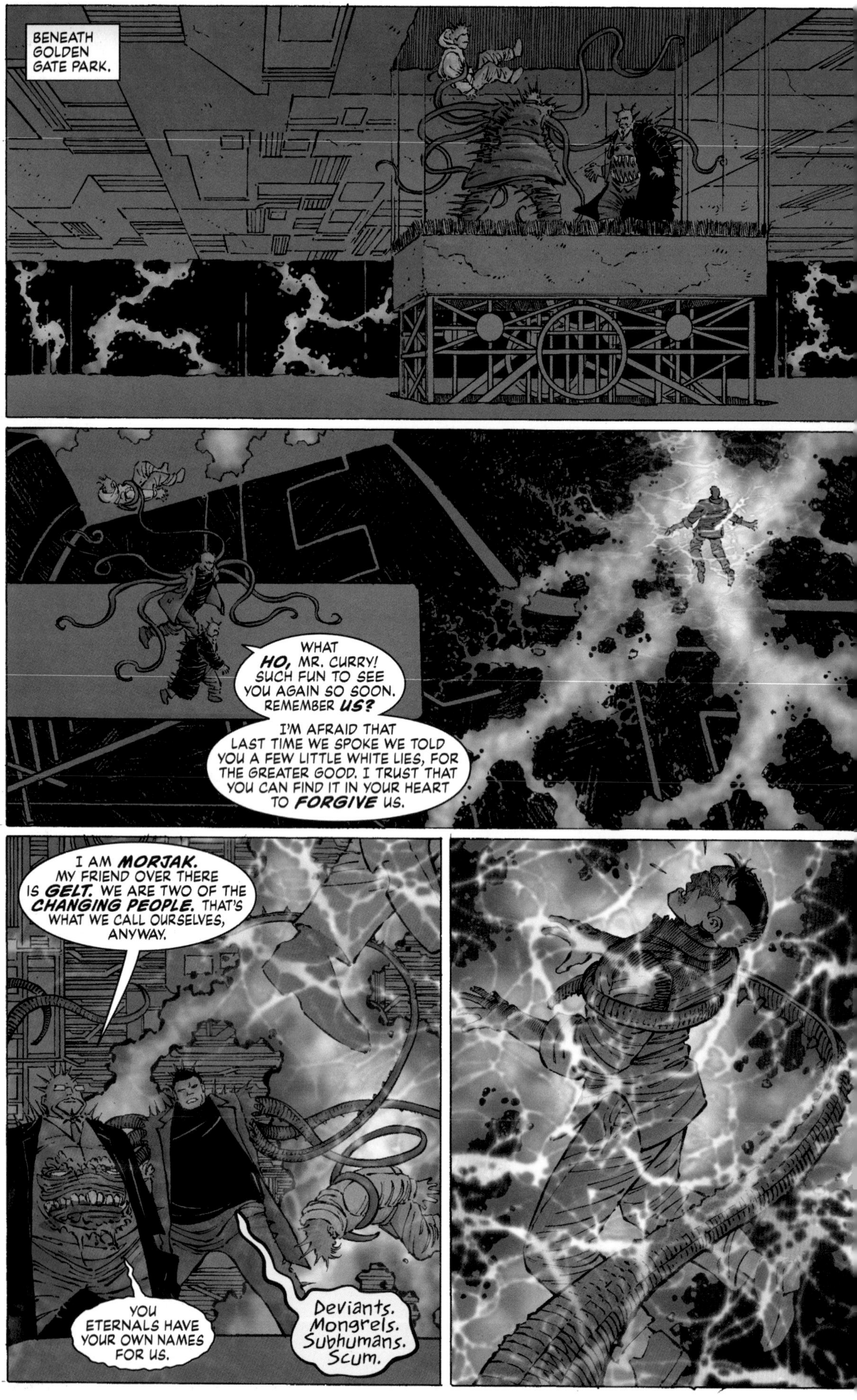
BENEATH GOLDEN GATE PARK.
WHAT HO, MR. CURRY! SUCH FUN TO SEE YOU AGAIN SO SOON. REMEMBER US?
I'M AFRAID THAT LAST TIME WE SPOKE WE TOLD YOU A FEW LITTLE WHITE LIES, FOR THE GREATER GOOD. I TRUST THAT YOU CAN FIND IT IN YOUR HEART TO FORGIVE US.
I AM MORJAK. MY FRIEND OVER THERE IS GELT. WE ARE TWO OF THE CHANGING PEOPLE. THAT'S WHAT WE CALL OURSELVES, ANYWAY.
YOU ETERNALS HAVE YOUR OWN NAMES FOR US.
Deviants. Mongrels. Subhumans. Scum.

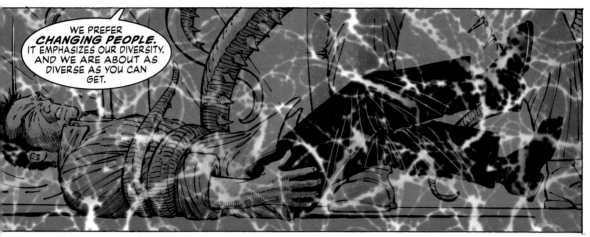

WE PREFER *CHANGING PEOPLE.* IT EMPHASIZES OUR DIVERSITY. AND WE ARE ABOUT AS DIVERSE AS YOU CAN GET.

LET *GO* OF ME!

GELT, PUT SOMETHING IN THE LITTLE ONE'S MOUTH. OR CHEW OFF ITS TONGUE.

NO!

Then you...be quiet...

YOU ETERNALS HAVE *LONG LIVES,* BUT *SHORT MEMORIES.* THE CHANGING PEOPLE HAVE SHORT LIVES, BUT WE DO NOT FORGET.

DON'T EXPECT US TO *KILL* YOU, EITHER. IT WAS HARD ENOUGH KILLING IKARIS. *HE* WON'T BE GRATEFUL. YOU'LL SEE. ANYWAY, ONE FULL ETERNAL IS ENOUGH.

IT WAS A *CRIME AGAINST LIFE.* THAT WAS WHAT THE CELESTIALS TOLD AJAK. AND THAT WAS TRUE IN ITS WAY.

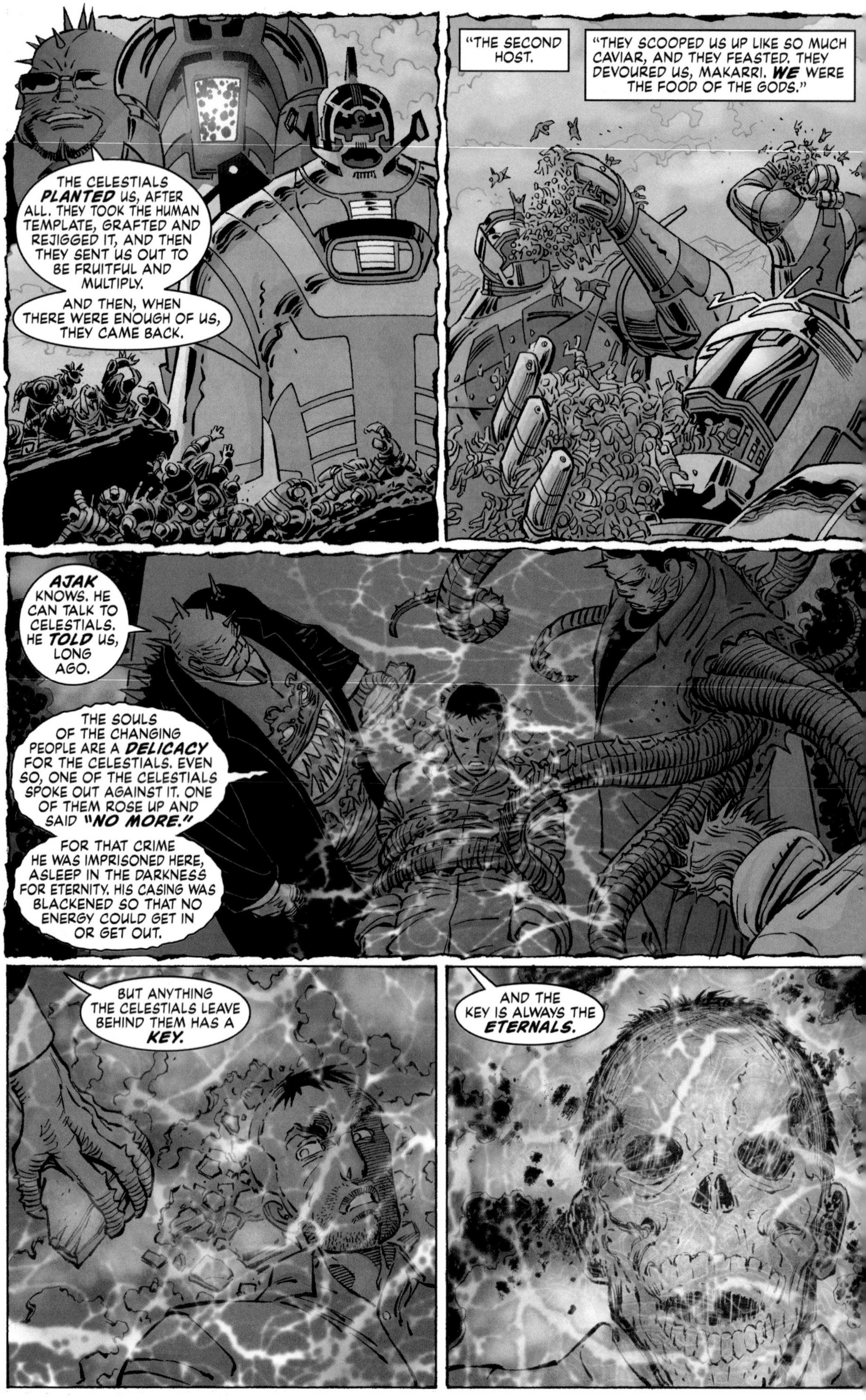
THE CELESTIALS PLANTED US, AFTER ALL. THEY TOOK THE HUMAN TEMPLATE, GRAFTED AND REJIGGED IT, AND THEN THEY SENT US OUT TO BE FRUITFUL AND MULTIPLY.
AND THEN, WHEN THERE WERE ENOUGH OF US, THEY CAME BACK.
"THE SECOND HOST.
"THEY SCOOPED US UP LIKE SO MUCH CAVIAR, AND THEY FEASTED. THEY DEVOURED US, MAKARRI. WE WERE THE FOOD OF THE GODS."
AJAK KNOWS. HE CAN TALK TO CELESTIALS. HE TOLD US, LONG AGO.
THE SOULS OF THE CHANGING PEOPLE ARE A DELICACY FOR THE CELESTIALS. EVEN SO, ONE OF THE CELESTIALS SPOKE OUT AGAINST IT. ONE OF THEM ROSE UP AND SAID "NO MORE."
FOR THAT CRIME HE WAS IMPRISONED HERE, ASLEEP IN THE DARKNESS FOR ETERNITY. HIS CASING WAS BLACKENED SO THAT NO ENERGY COULD GET IN OR GET OUT.
BUT ANYTHING THE CELESTIALS LEAVE BEHIND THEM HAS A KEY.
AND THE KEY IS ALWAYS THE ETERNALS.

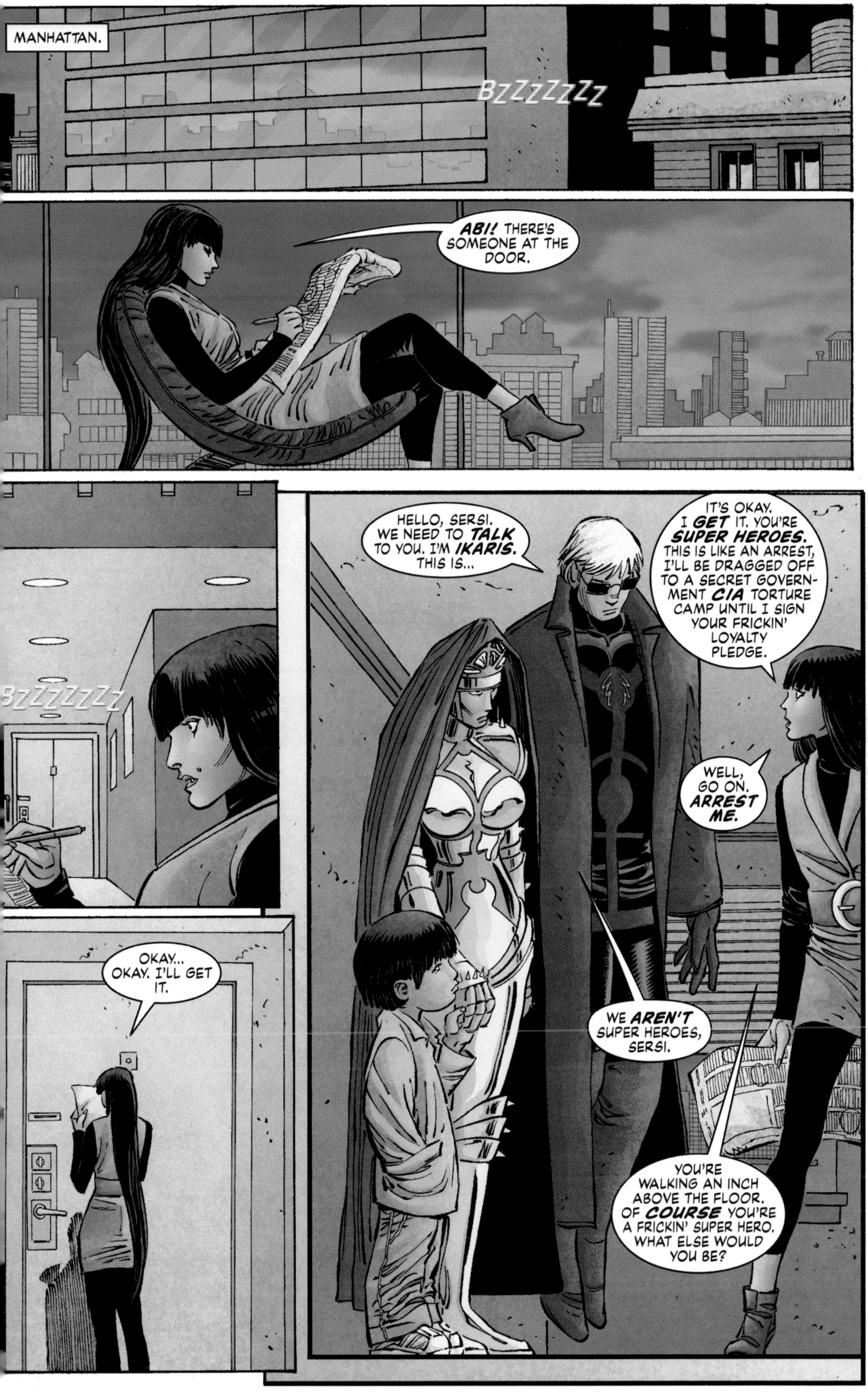
MANHATTAN.
BZZZZZZZ
ABI! THERE'S SOMEONE AT THE DOOR.
BZZZZZZZ
OKAY... OKAY. I'LL GET IT.
HELLO, SERSI. WE NEED TO TALK TO YOU. I'M IKARIS. THIS IS...
IT'S OKAY. I GET IT. YOU'RE SUPER HEROES. THIS IS LIKE AN ARREST. I'LL BE DRAGGED OFF TO A SECRET GOVERNMENT CIA TORTURE CAMP UNTIL I SIGN YOUR FRICKIN' LOYALTY PLEDGE.
WELL, GO ON. ARREST ME.
WE AREN'T SUPER HEROES, SERSI.
YOU'RE WALKING AN INCH ABOVE THE FLOOR. OF COURSE YOU'RE A FRICKIN' SUPER HERO. WHAT ELSE WOULD YOU BE?

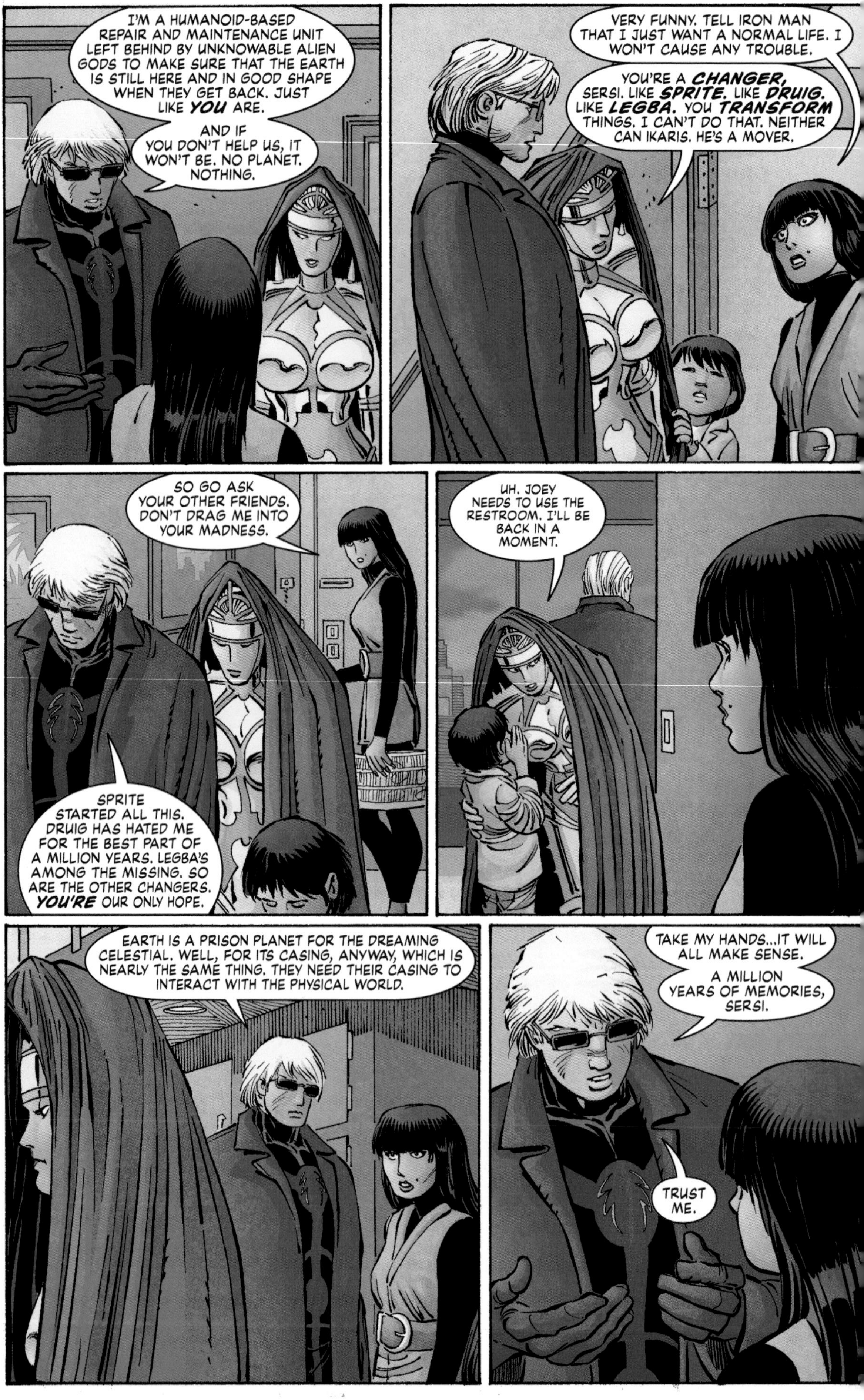
I'M A HUMANOID-BASED REPAIR AND MAINTENANCE UNIT LEFT BEHIND BY UNKNOWABLE ALIEN GODS TO MAKE SURE THAT THE EARTH IS STILL HERE AND IN GOOD SHAPE WHEN THEY GET BACK. JUST LIKE YOU ARE.
AND IF YOU DON'T HELP US, IT WON'T BE. NO PLANET. NOTHING.
VERY FUNNY. TELL IRON MAN THAT I JUST WANT A NORMAL LIFE. I WON'T CAUSE ANY TROUBLE.
YOU'RE A CHANGER, SERSI. LIKE SPRITE. LIKE DRUIG. LIKE LEGBA. YOU TRANSFORM THINGS. I CAN'T DO THAT. NEITHER CAN IKARIS. HE'S A MOVER.
SO GO ASK YOUR OTHER FRIENDS. DON'T DRAG ME INTO YOUR MADNESS.
SPRITE STARTED ALL THIS. DRUIG HAS HATED ME FOR THE BEST PART OF A MILLION YEARS. LEGBA'S AMONG THE MISSING. SO ARE THE OTHER CHANGERS. YOU'RE OUR ONLY HOPE.
UH. JOEY NEEDS TO USE THE RESTROOM. I'LL BE BACK IN A MOMENT.
EARTH IS A PRISON PLANET FOR THE DREAMING CELESTIAL. WELL, FOR ITS CASING, ANYWAY, WHICH IS NEARLY THE SAME THING. THEY NEED THEIR CASING TO INTERACT WITH THE PHYSICAL WORLD.
TAKE MY HANDS...IT WILL ALL MAKE SENSE.
A MILLION YEARS OF MEMORIES, SERSI.
TRUST ME.

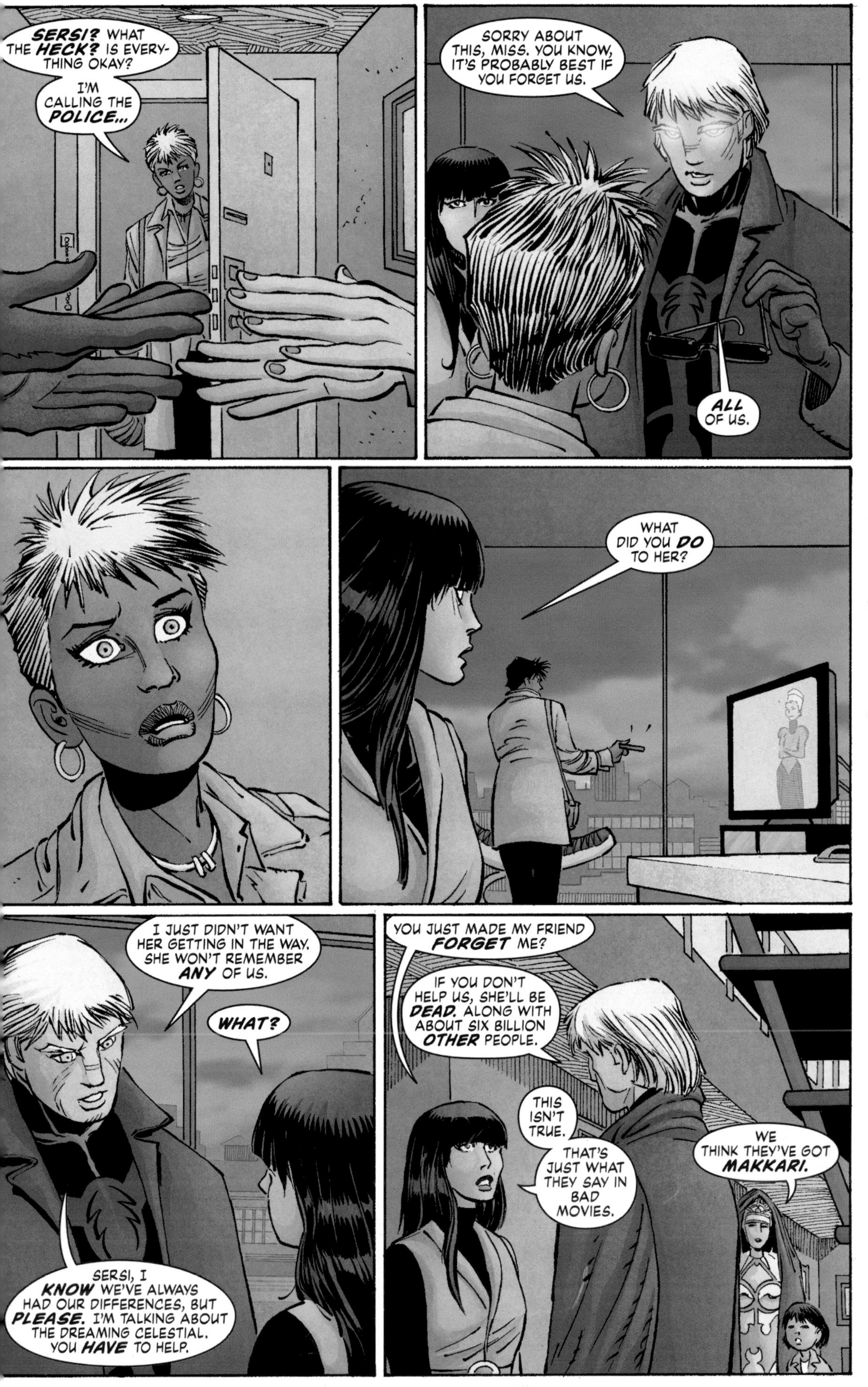
SERSI? WHAT THE HECK? IS EVERYTHING OKAY?
I'M CALLING THE POLICE...
SORRY ABOUT THIS, MISS. YOU KNOW, IT'S PROBABLY BEST IF YOU FORGET US.
ALL OF US.
WHAT DID YOU DO TO HER?
I JUST DIDN'T WANT HER GETTING IN THE WAY. SHE WON'T REMEMBER ANY OF US.
WHAT?
SERSI, I KNOW WE'VE ALWAYS HAD OUR DIFFERENCES, BUT PLEASE. I'M TALKING ABOUT THE DREAMING CELESTIAL. YOU HAVE TO HELP.
YOU JUST MADE MY FRIEND FORGET ME?
IF YOU DON'T HELP US, SHE'LL BE DEAD. ALONG WITH ABOUT SIX BILLION OTHER PEOPLE.
THIS ISN'T TRUE.
THAT'S JUST WHAT THEY SAY IN BAD MOVIES.
WE THINK THEY'VE GOT MAKKARI.

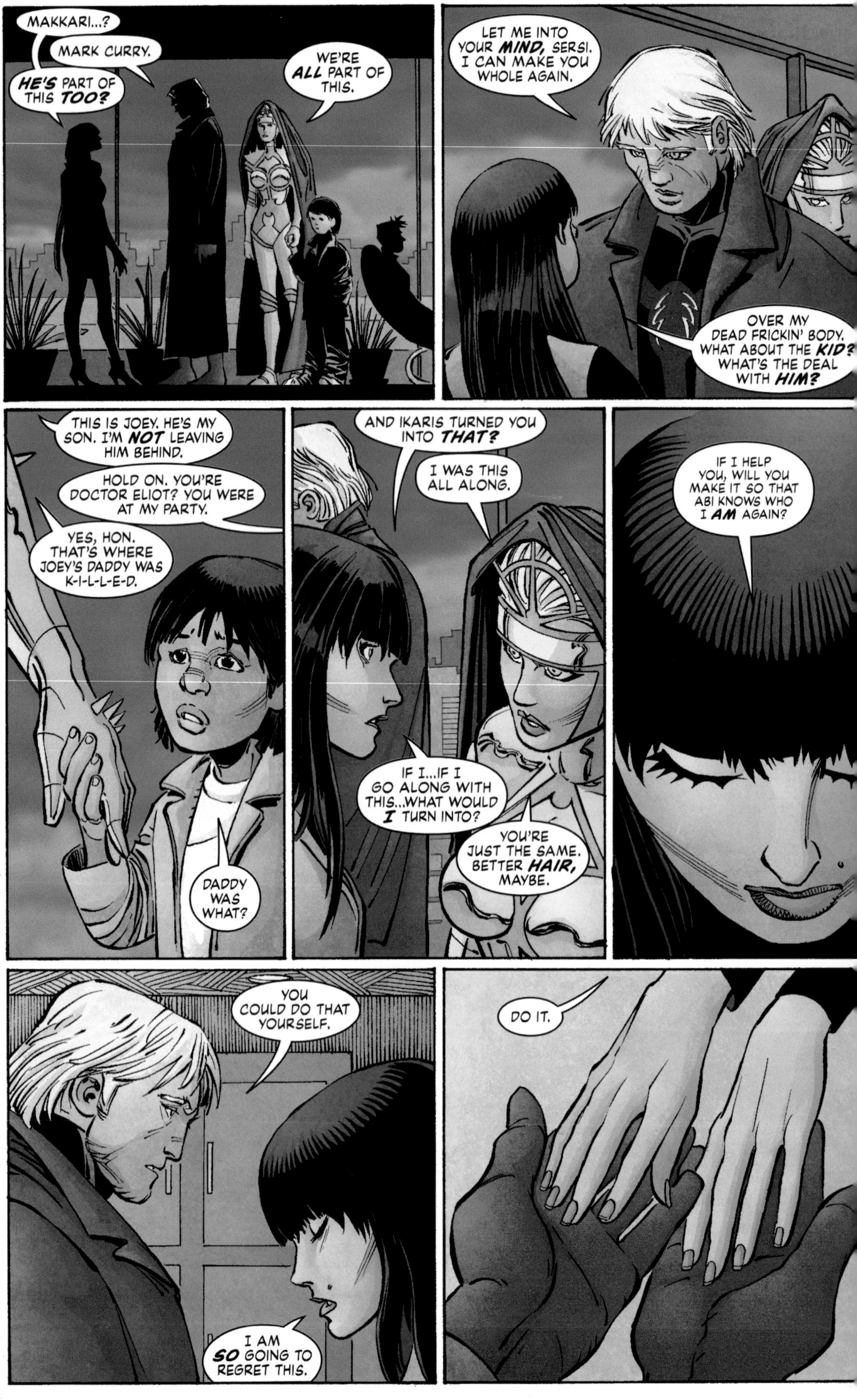
MAKKARI...?
MARK CURRY.
HE'S PART OF THIS TOO?
WE'RE ALL PART OF THIS.
LET ME INTO YOUR MIND, SERSI. I CAN MAKE YOU WHOLE AGAIN.
OVER MY DEAD FRICKIN' BODY. WHAT ABOUT THE KID? WHAT'S THE DEAL WITH HIM?
THIS IS JOEY. HE'S MY SON. I'M NOT LEAVING HIM BEHIND.
HOLD ON. YOU'RE DOCTOR ELIOT? YOU WERE AT MY PARTY.
YES, HON. THAT'S WHERE JOEY'S DADDY WAS K-I-L-L-E-D.
DADDY WAS WHAT?
AND IKARIS TURNED YOU INTO THAT?
I WAS THIS ALL ALONG.
IF I...IF I GO ALONG WITH THIS...WHAT WOULD I TURN INTO?
YOU'RE JUST THE SAME. BETTER HAIR, MAYBE.
IF I HELP YOU, WILL YOU MAKE IT SO THAT ABI KNOWS WHO I AM AGAIN?
YOU COULD DO THAT YOURSELF.
I AM SO GOING TO REGRET THIS.
DO IT.

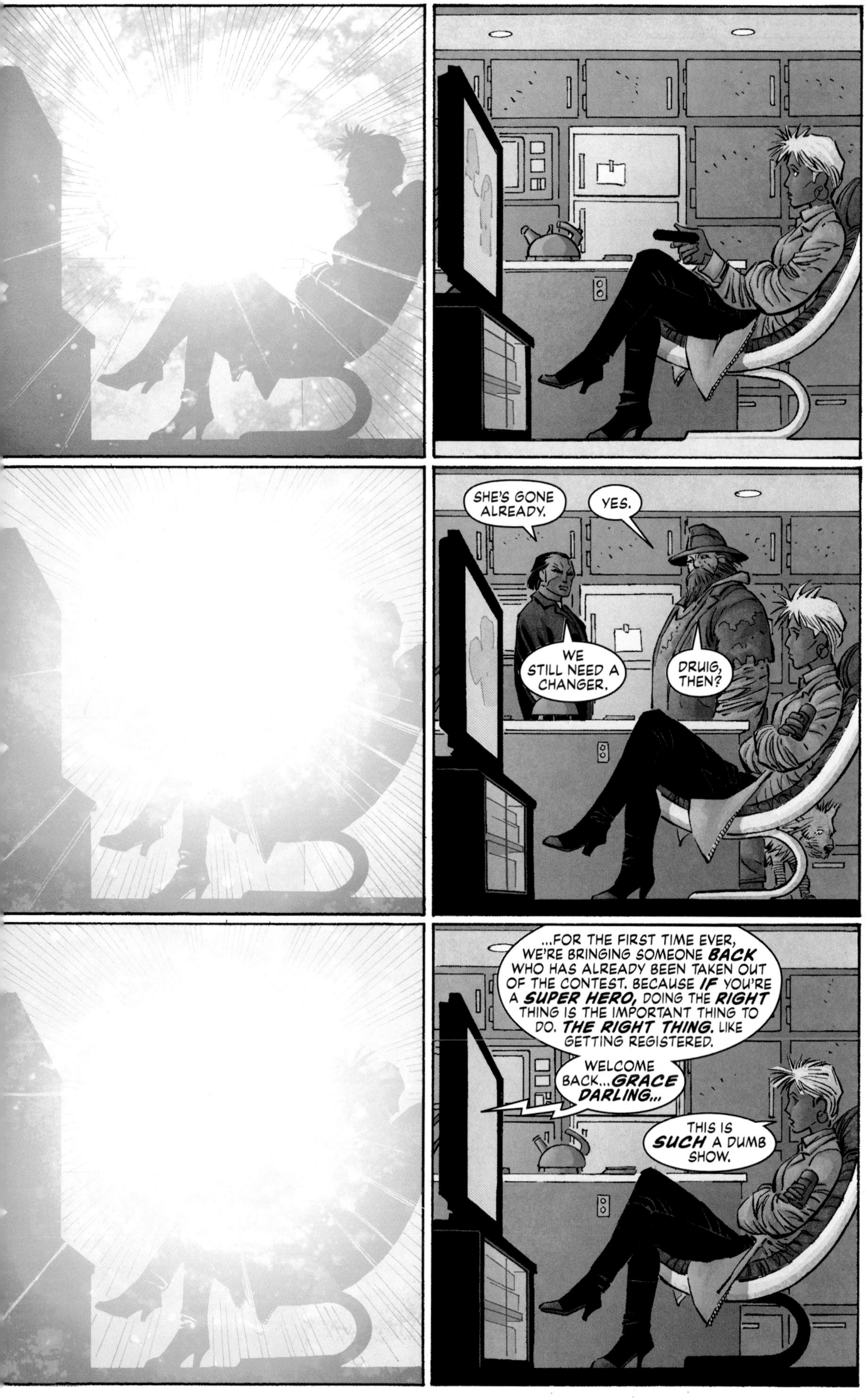
SHE'S GONE ALREADY.
YES.
WE STILL NEED A CHANGER.
DRUIG, THEN?
...FOR THE FIRST TIME EVER, WE'RE BRINGING SOMEONE BACK WHO HAS ALREADY BEEN TAKEN OUT OF THE CONTEST. BECAUSE IF YOU'RE A SUPER HERO, DOING THE RIGHT THING IS THE IMPORTANT THING TO DO. THE RIGHT THING. LIKE GETTING REGISTERED.
WELCOME BACK...GRACE DARLING...
THIS IS SUCH A DUMB SHOW.

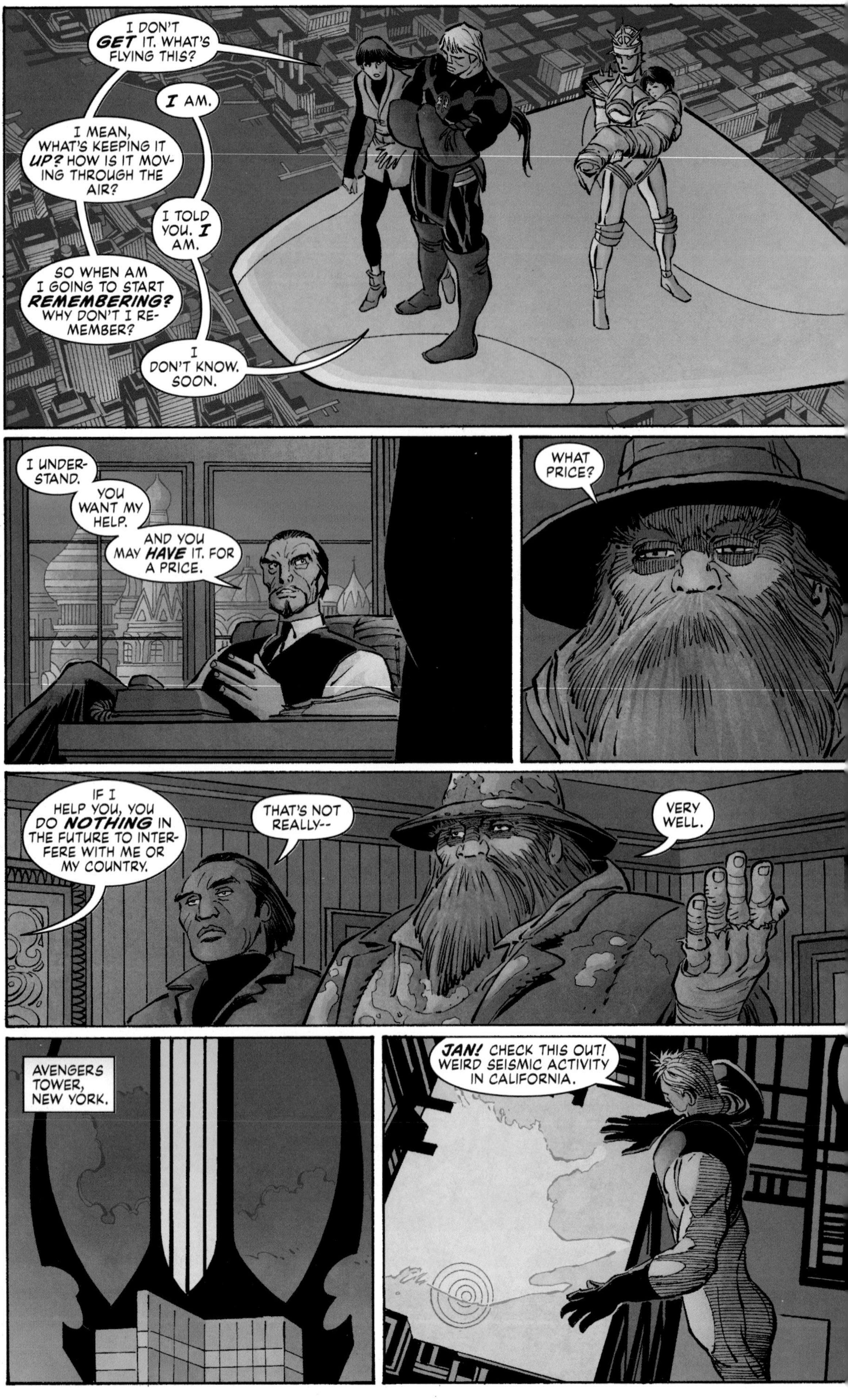
I DON'T **GET** IT. WHAT'S FLYING THIS?
I AM.
I MEAN, WHAT'S KEEPING IT **UP?** HOW IS IT MOVING THROUGH THE AIR?
I TOLD YOU. **I** AM.
SO WHEN AM I GOING TO START **REMEMBERING?** WHY DON'T I REMEMBER?
I DON'T KNOW. SOON.
I UNDERSTAND.
YOU WANT MY HELP.
AND YOU MAY **HAVE** IT. FOR A PRICE.
WHAT PRICE?
IF I HELP YOU, YOU DO **NOTHING** IN THE FUTURE TO INTERFERE WITH ME OR MY COUNTRY.
THAT'S NOT REALLY--
VERY WELL.
AVENGERS TOWER, NEW YORK.
JAN! CHECK THIS OUT! WEIRD SEISMIC ACTIVITY IN CALIFORNIA.

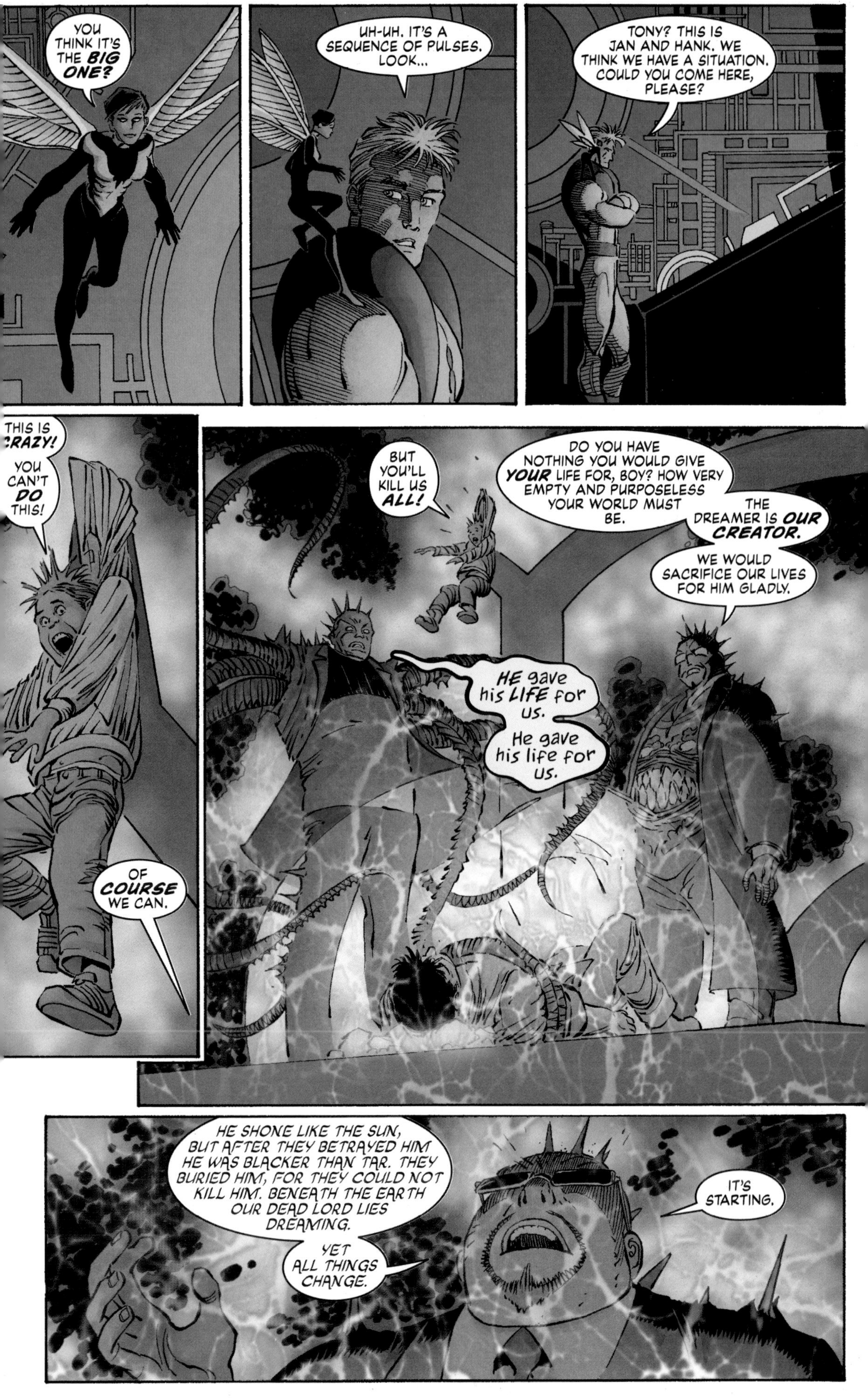
YOU THINK IT'S THE BIG ONE?
UH-UH. IT'S A SEQUENCE OF PULSES. LOOK...
TONY? THIS IS JAN AND HANK. WE THINK WE HAVE A SITUATION. COULD YOU COME HERE, PLEASE?
THIS IS CRAZY!
YOU CAN'T DO THIS!
OF COURSE WE CAN.
BUT YOU'LL KILL US ALL!
DO YOU HAVE NOTHING YOU WOULD GIVE YOUR LIFE FOR, BOY? HOW VERY EMPTY AND PURPOSELESS YOUR WORLD MUST BE.
THE DREAMER IS OUR CREATOR.
WE WOULD SACRIFICE OUR LIVES FOR HIM GLADLY.
HE gave his LIFE for us.
He gave his life for us.
HE SHONE LIKE THE SUN, BUT AFTER THEY BETRAYED HIM HE WAS BLACKER THAN TAR. THEY BURIED HIM, FOR THEY COULD NOT KILL HIM. BENEATH THE EARTH OUR DEAD LORD LIES DREAMING.
YET ALL THINGS CHANGE.
IT'S STARTING.

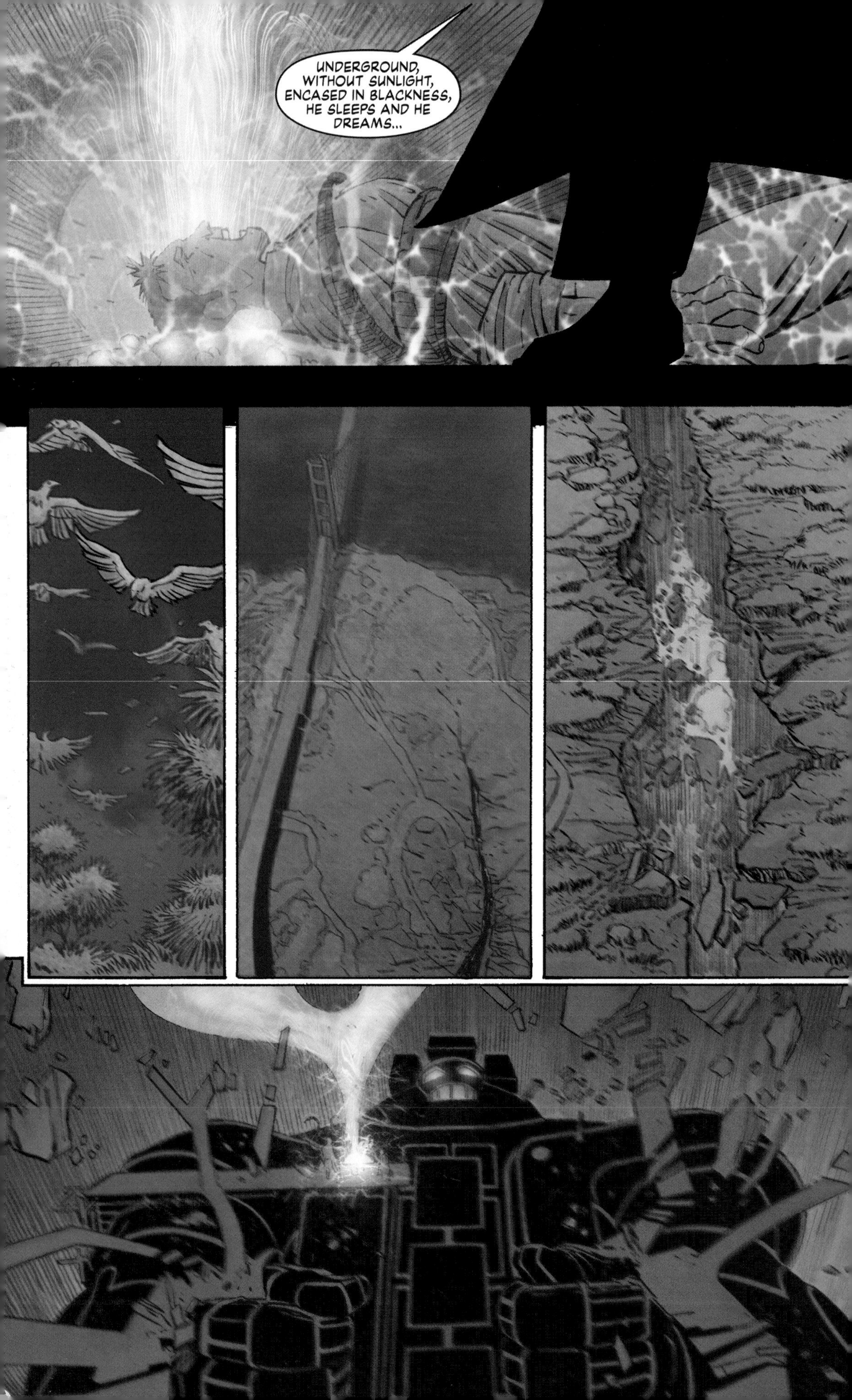
UNDERGROUND, WITHOUT SUNLIGHT, ENCASED IN BLACKNESS, HE SLEEPS AND HE DREAMS...

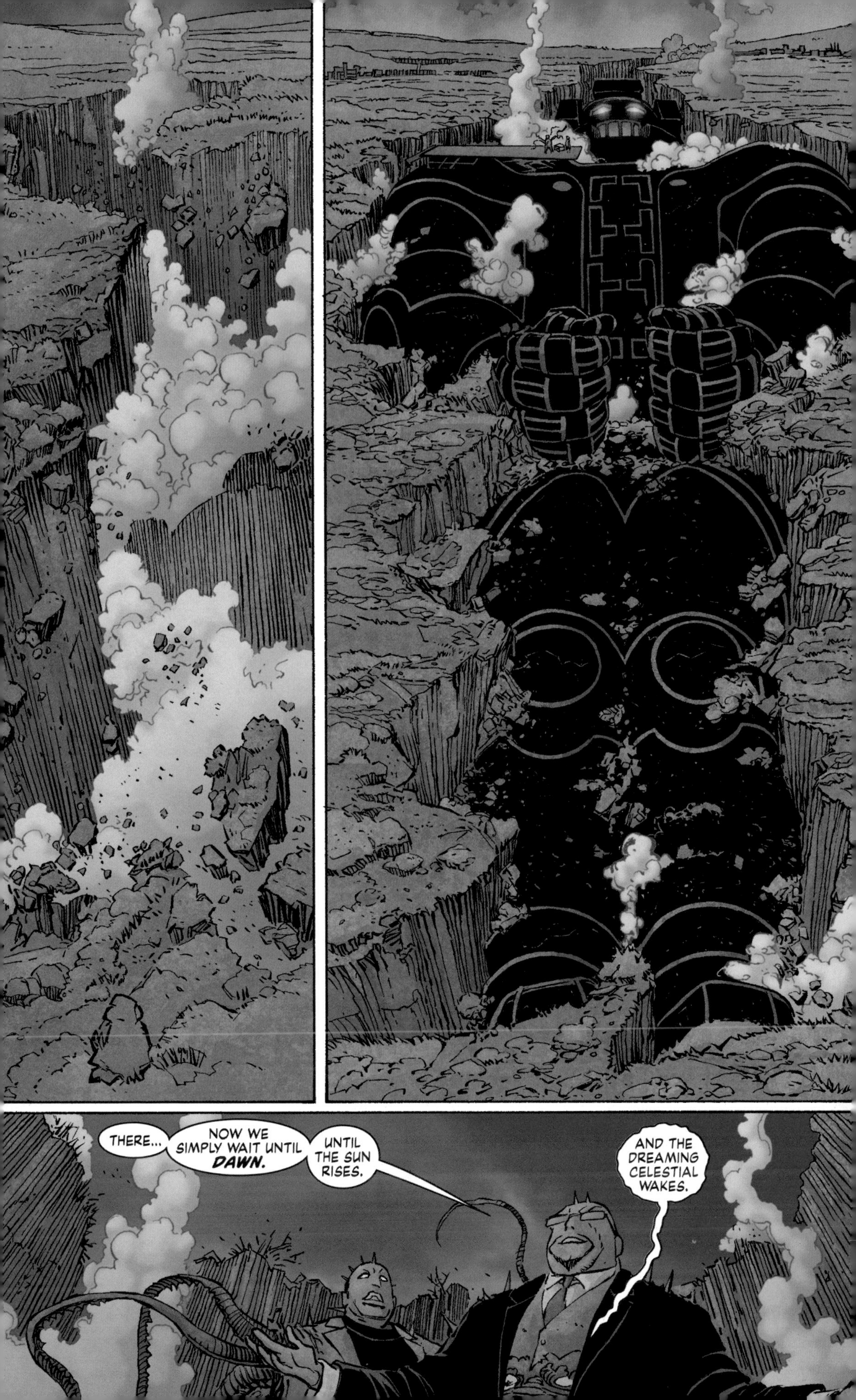
THERE...
NOW WE SIMPLY WAIT UNTIL DAWN.
UNTIL THE SUN RISES.
AND THE DREAMING CELESTIAL WAKES.

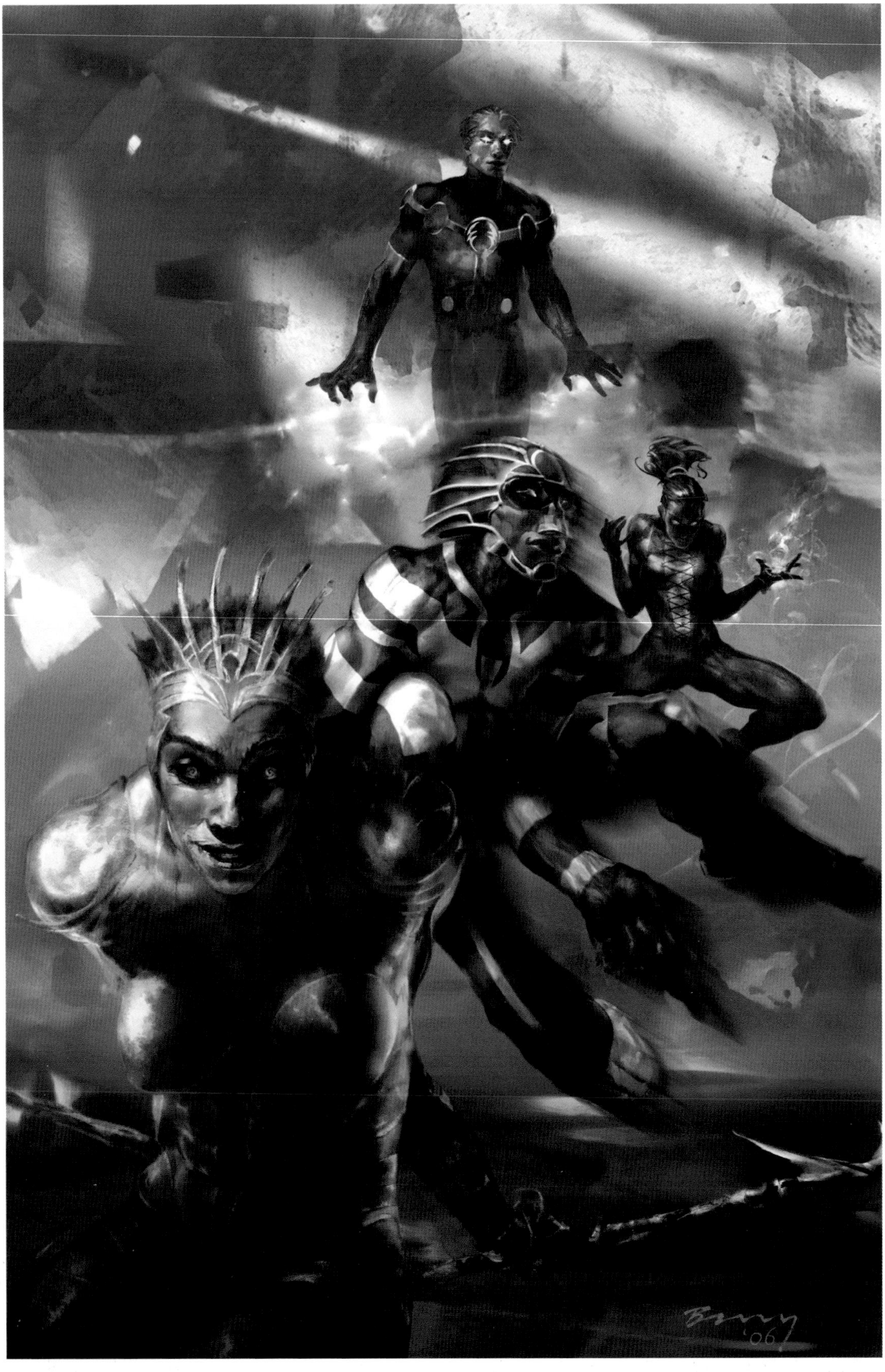

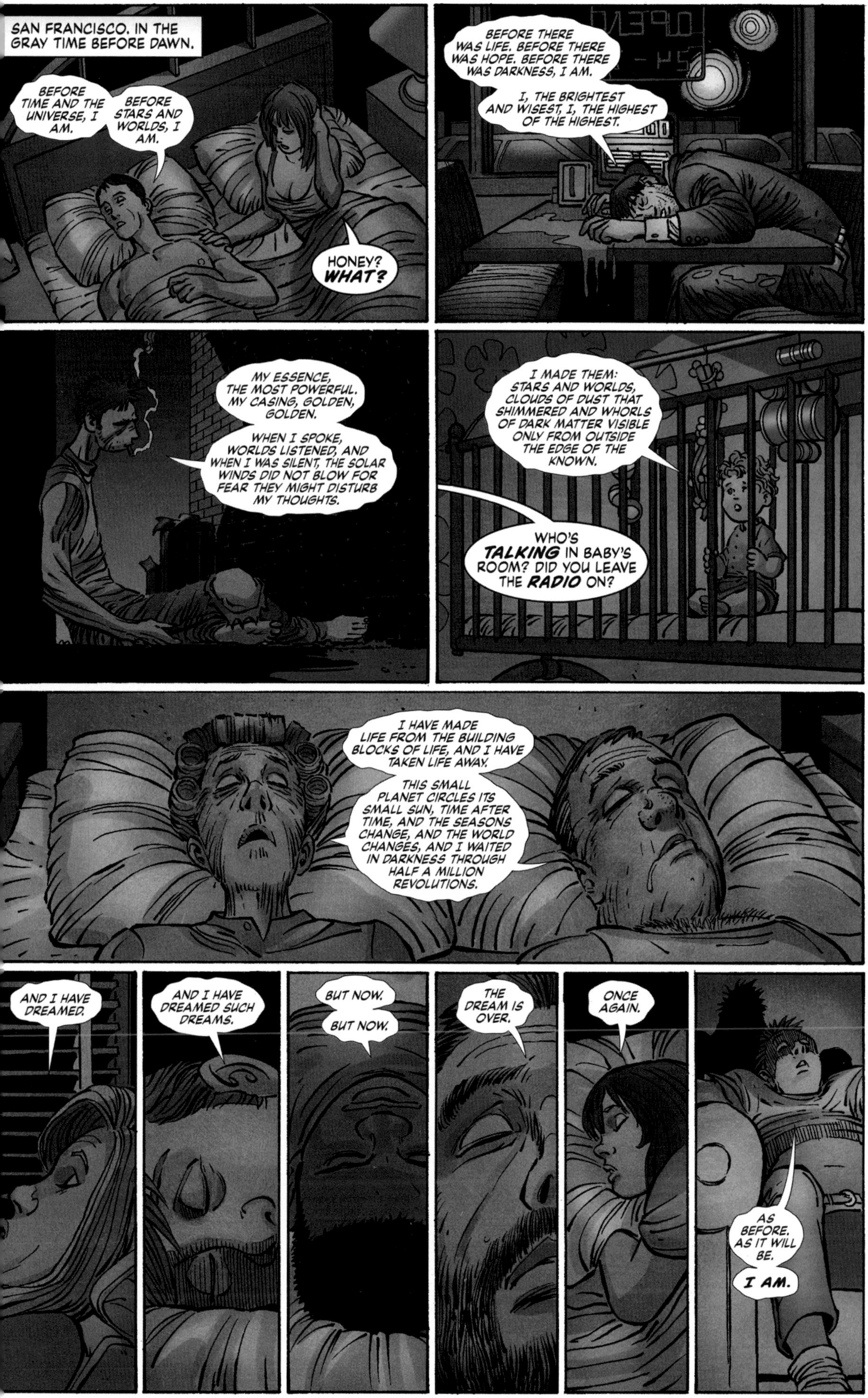
SAN FRANCISCO. IN THE GRAY TIME BEFORE DAWN.
BEFORE TIME AND THE UNIVERSE, I AM.
BEFORE STARS AND WORLDS, I AM.
HONEY? WHAT?
BEFORE THERE WAS LIFE. BEFORE THERE WAS HOPE. BEFORE THERE WAS DARKNESS, I AM.
I, THE BRIGHTEST AND WISEST, I, THE HIGHEST OF THE HIGHEST.
MY ESSENCE, THE MOST POWERFUL. MY CASING, GOLDEN, GOLDEN.
WHEN I SPOKE, WORLDS LISTENED, AND WHEN I WAS SILENT, THE SOLAR WINDS DID NOT BLOW FOR FEAR THEY MIGHT DISTURB MY THOUGHTS.
I MADE THEM: STARS AND WORLDS, CLOUDS OF DUST THAT SHIMMERED AND WHORLS OF DARK MATTER VISIBLE ONLY FROM OUTSIDE THE EDGE OF THE KNOWN.
WHO'S TALKING IN BABY'S ROOM? DID YOU LEAVE THE RADIO ON?
I HAVE MADE LIFE FROM THE BUILDING BLOCKS OF LIFE, AND I HAVE TAKEN LIFE AWAY.
THIS SMALL PLANET CIRCLES ITS SMALL SUN, TIME AFTER TIME, AND THE SEASONS CHANGE, AND THE WORLD CHANGES, AND I WAITED IN DARKNESS THROUGH HALF A MILLION REVOLUTIONS.
AND I HAVE DREAMED.
AND I HAVE DREAMED SUCH DREAMS.
BUT NOW.
BUT NOW.
THE DREAM IS OVER.
ONCE AGAIN.
AS BEFORE. AS IT WILL BE.
I AM.

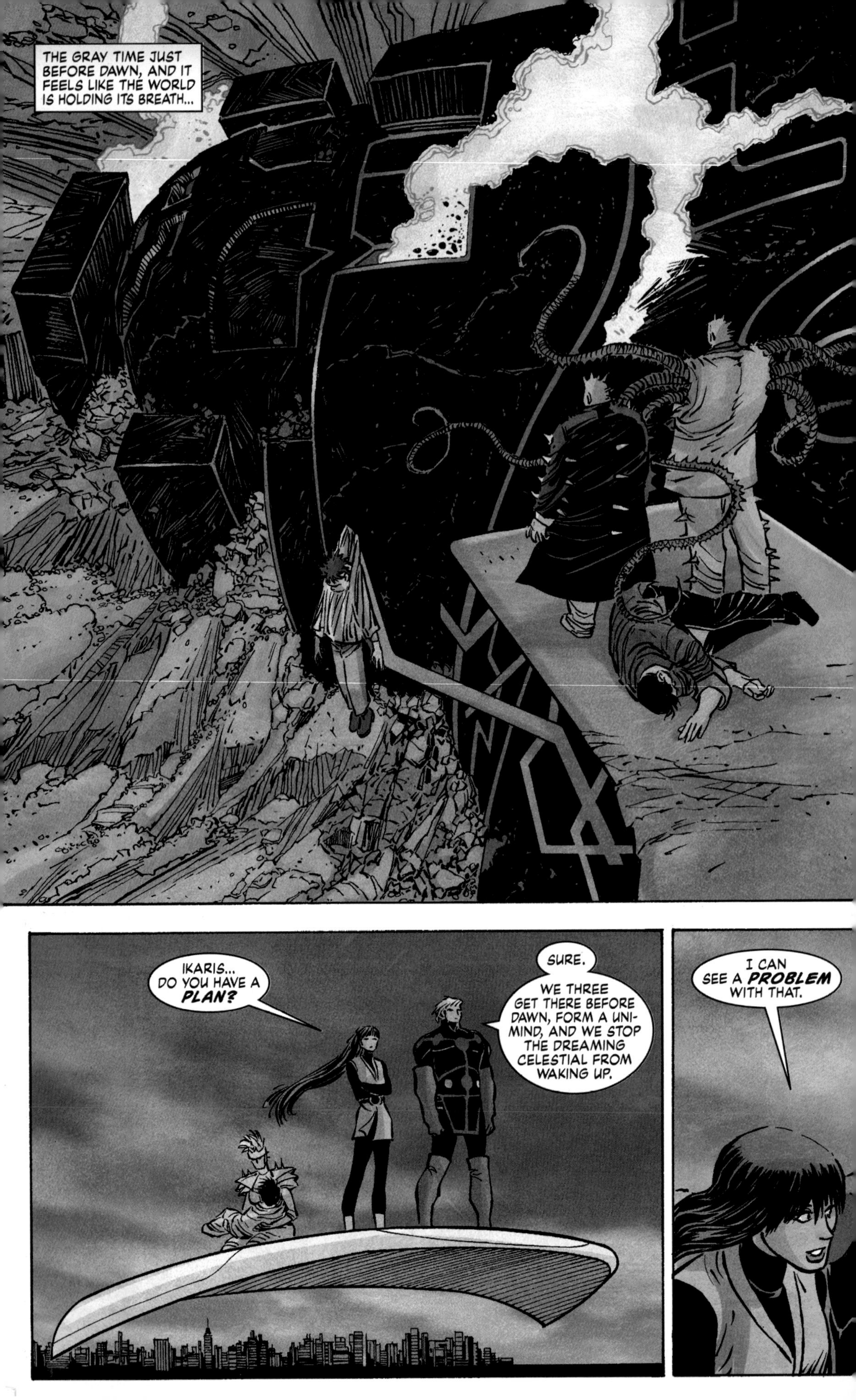
THE GRAY TIME JUST BEFORE DAWN, AND IT FEELS LIKE THE WORLD IS HOLDING ITS BREATH...
IKARIS... DO YOU HAVE A PLAN?
SURE.
WE THREE GET THERE BEFORE DAWN, FORM A UNI-MIND, AND WE STOP THE DREAMING CELESTIAL FROM WAKING UP.
I CAN SEE A PROBLEM WITH THAT.

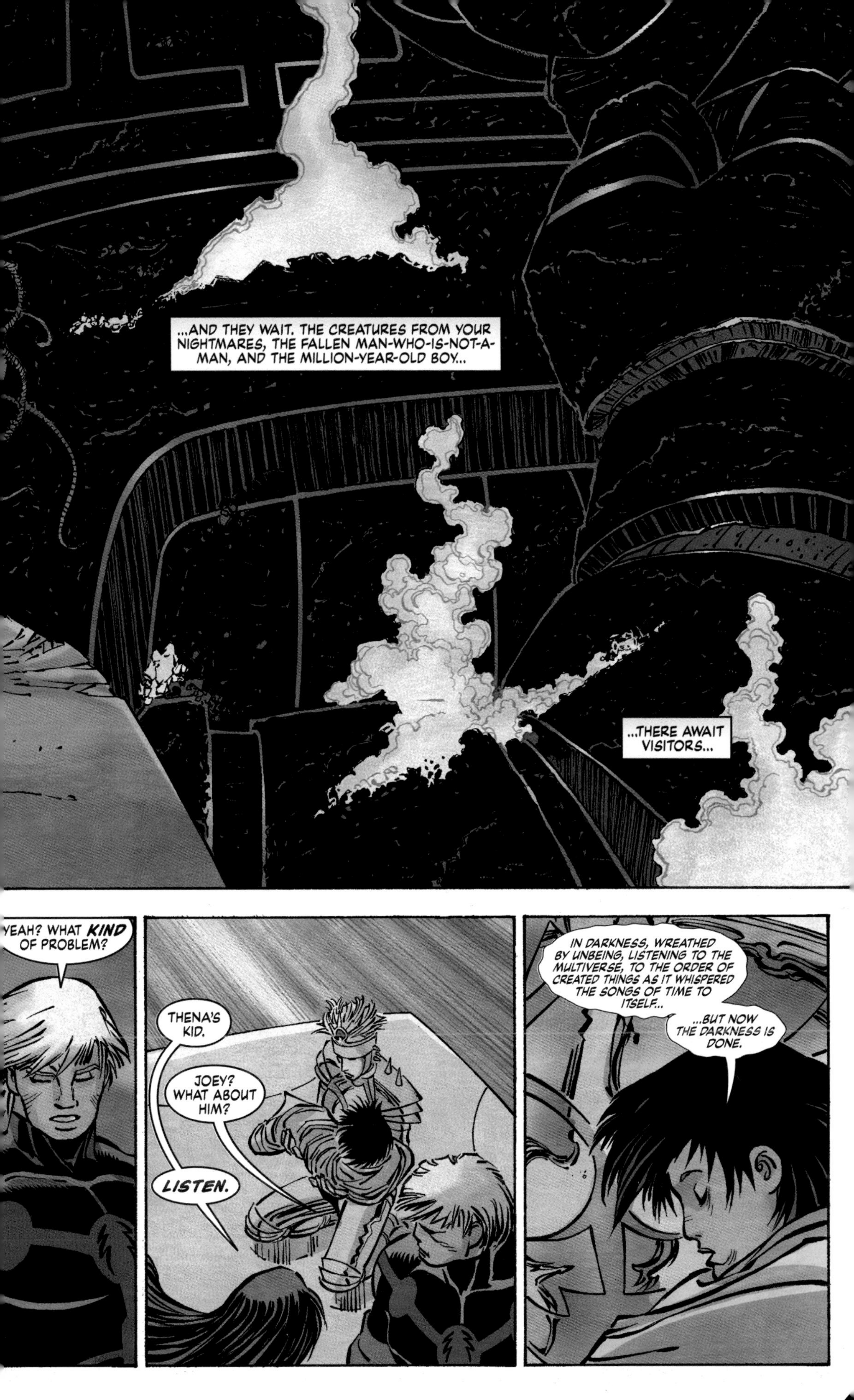
...AND THEY WAIT. THE CREATURES FROM YOUR NIGHTMARES, THE FALLEN MAN-WHO-IS-NOT-A-MAN, AND THE MILLION-YEAR-OLD BOY...
...THERE AWAIT VISITORS...
YEAH? WHAT KIND OF PROBLEM?
THENA'S KID.
JOEY? WHAT ABOUT HIM?
LISTEN.
IN DARKNESS, WREATHED BY UNBEING, LISTENING TO THE MULTIVERSE, TO THE ORDER OF CREATED THINGS AS IT WHISPERED THE SONGS OF TIME TO ITSELF...
...BUT NOW THE DARKNESS IS DONE.

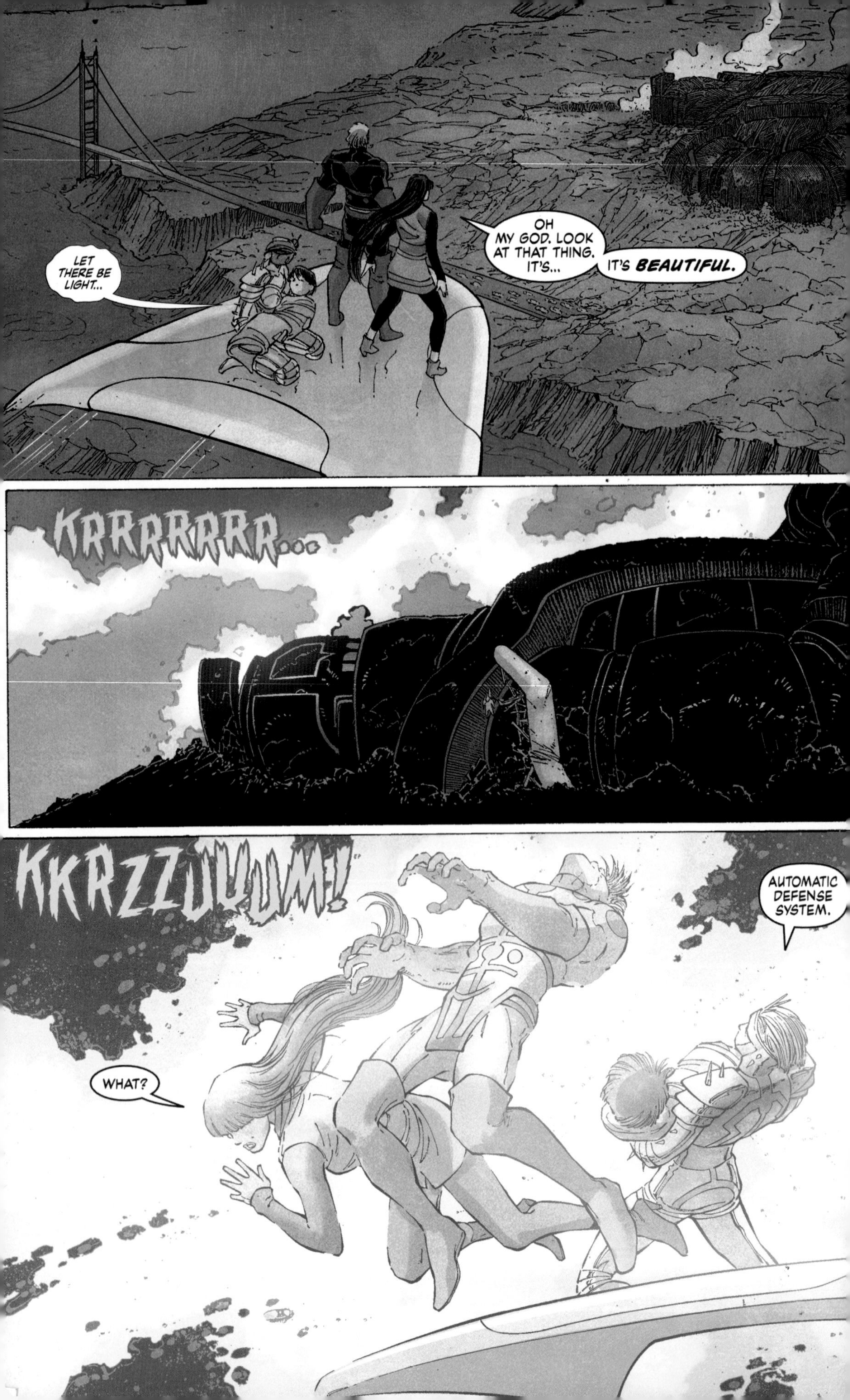
OH MY GOD. LOOK AT THAT THING. IT'S...
IT'S BEAUTIFUL.
LET THERE BE LIGHT...
KRRRRRRR...
KKRZZUUUM!
AUTOMATIC DEFENSE SYSTEM.
WHAT?

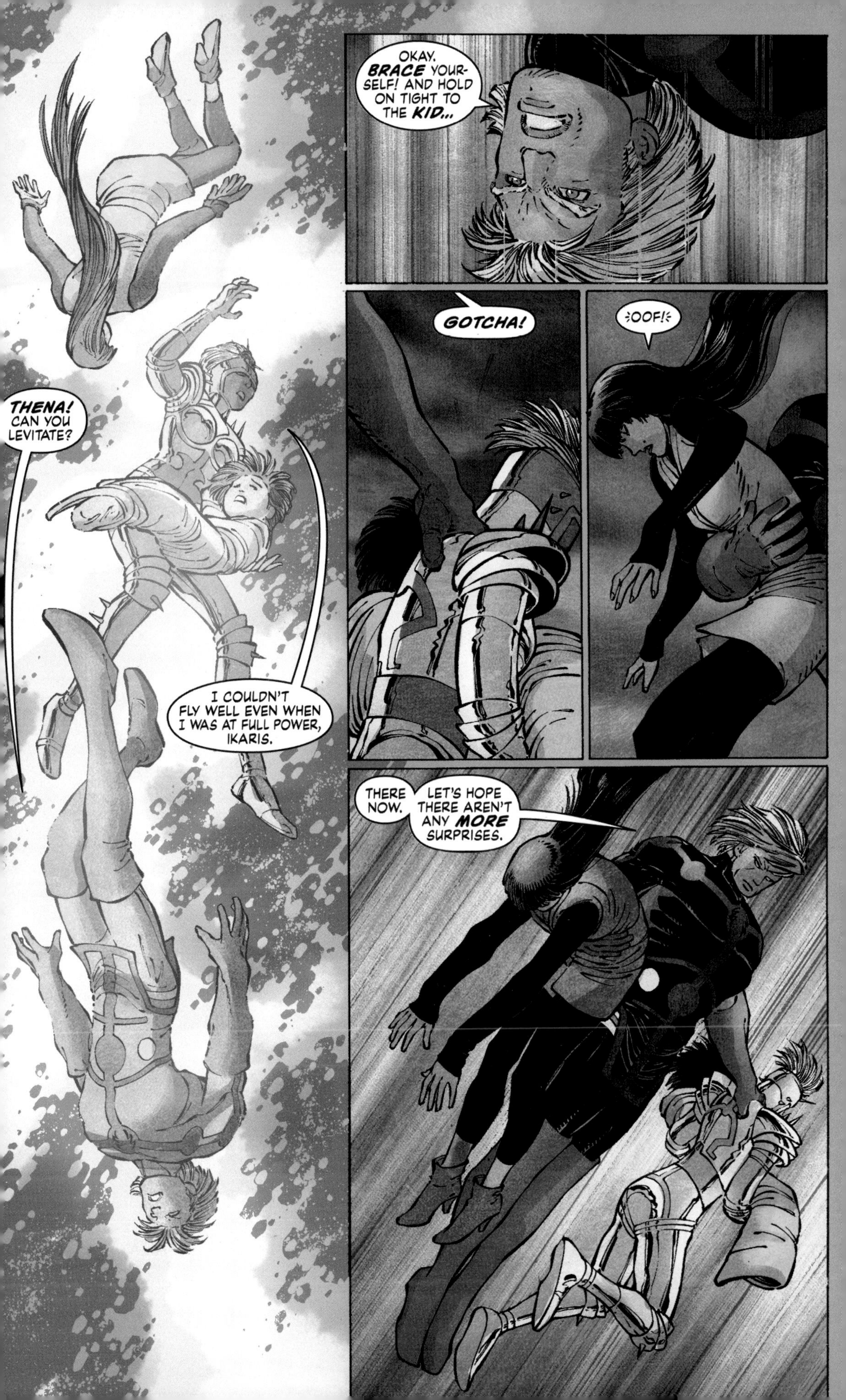
THENA! CAN YOU LEVITATE?
I COULDN'T FLY WELL EVEN WHEN I WAS AT FULL POWER, IKARIS.
OKAY. BRACE YOURSELF! AND HOLD ON TIGHT TO THE KID...
GOTCHA!
OOF!
THERE NOW.
LET'S HOPE THERE AREN'T ANY MORE SURPRISES.

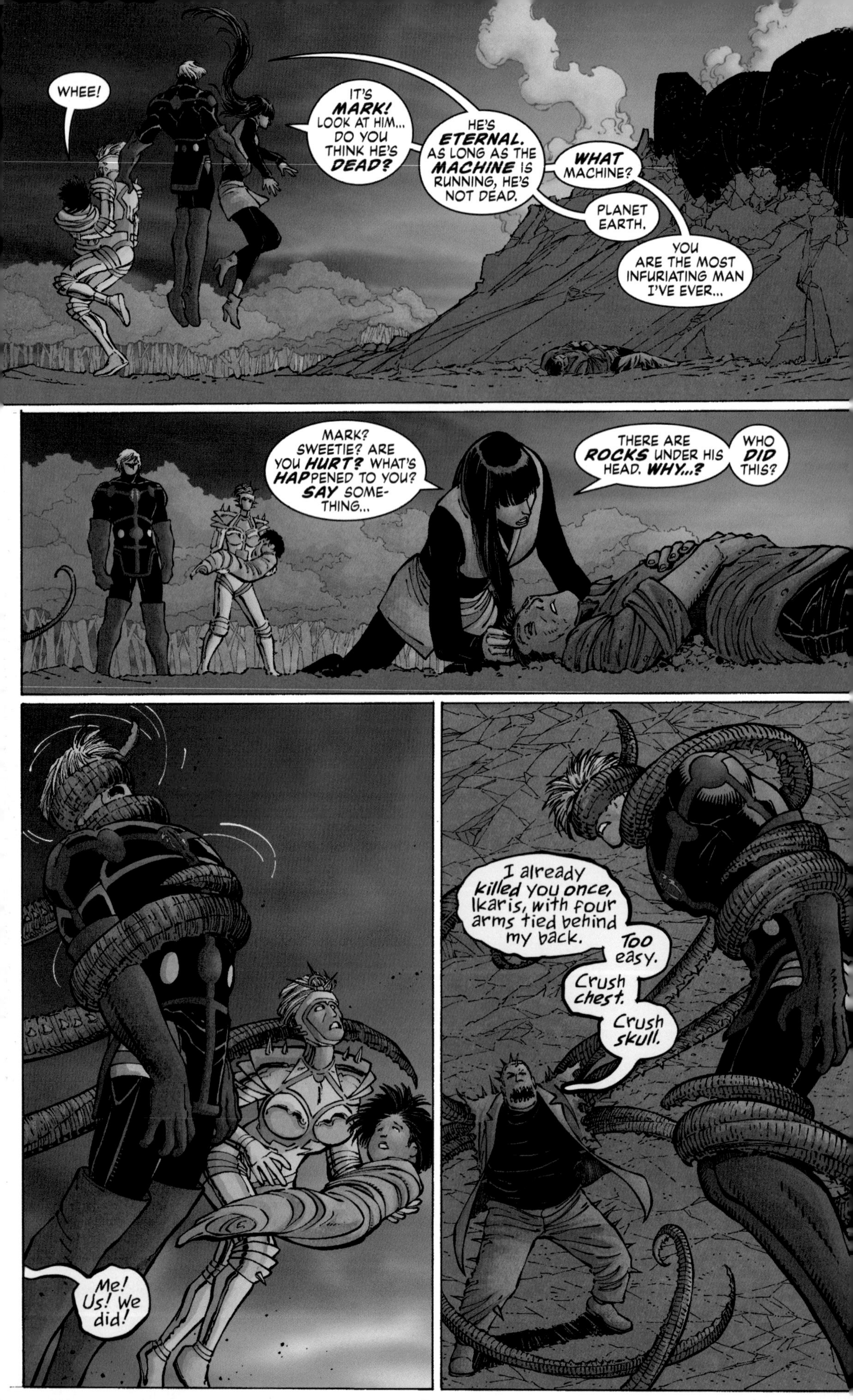
WHEE!
IT'S MARK! LOOK AT HIM... DO YOU THINK HE'S DEAD?
HE'S ETERNAL. AS LONG AS THE MACHINE IS RUNNING, HE'S NOT DEAD.
WHAT MACHINE?
PLANET EARTH.
YOU ARE THE MOST INFURIATING MAN I'VE EVER...
MARK? SWEETIE? ARE YOU HURT? WHAT'S HAPPENED TO YOU? SAY SOMETHING...
THERE ARE ROCKS UNDER HIS HEAD. WHY...?
WHO DID THIS?
Me! Us! We did!
I already killed you once, Ikaris, with four arms tied behind my back.
Too easy.
Crush chest.
Crush skull.

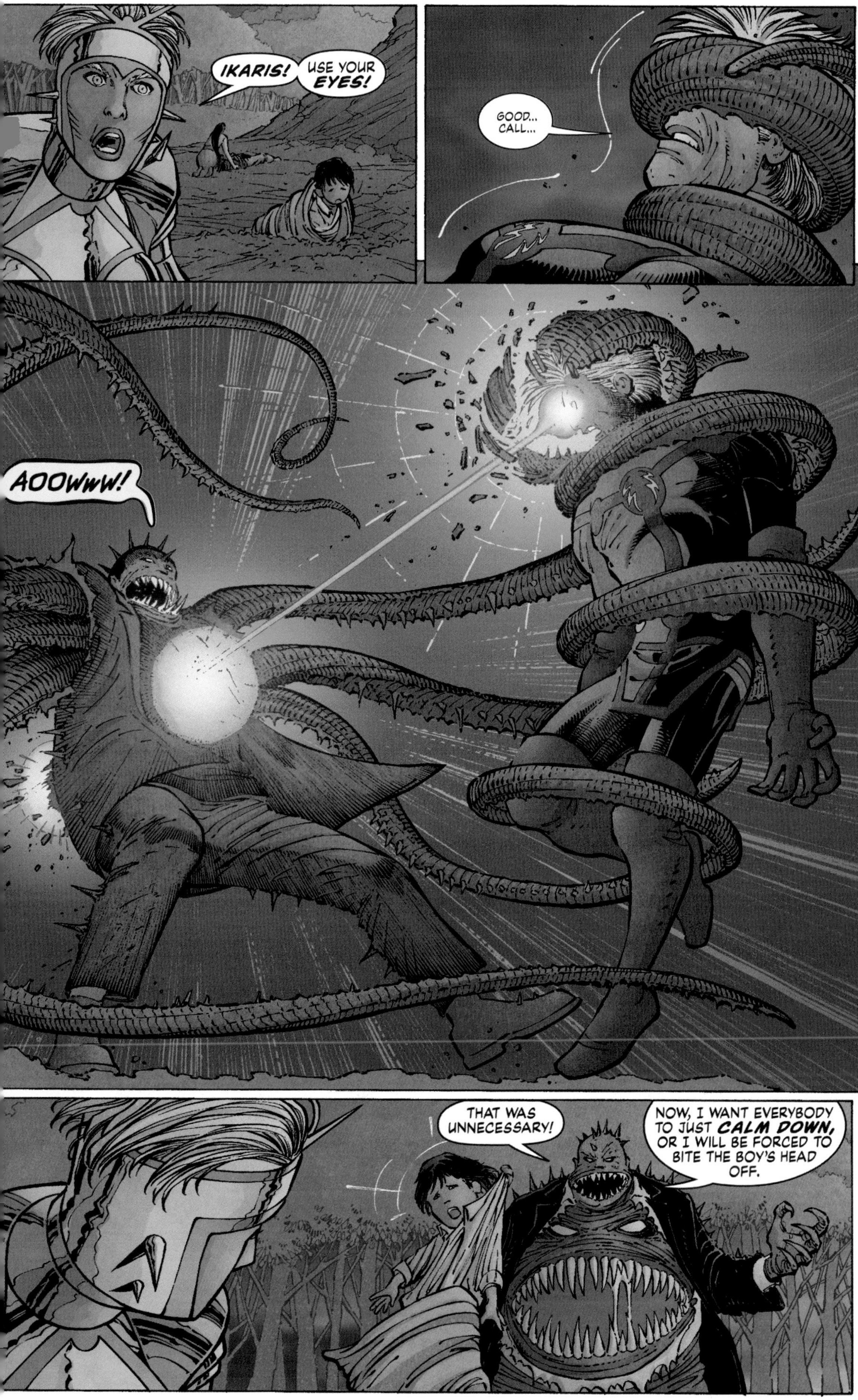
IKARIS!
USE YOUR EYES!
GOOD... CALL...
AOOWWW!
THAT WAS UNNECESSARY!
NOW, I WANT EVERYBODY TO JUST CALM DOWN, OR I WILL BE FORCED TO BITE THE BOY'S HEAD OFF.

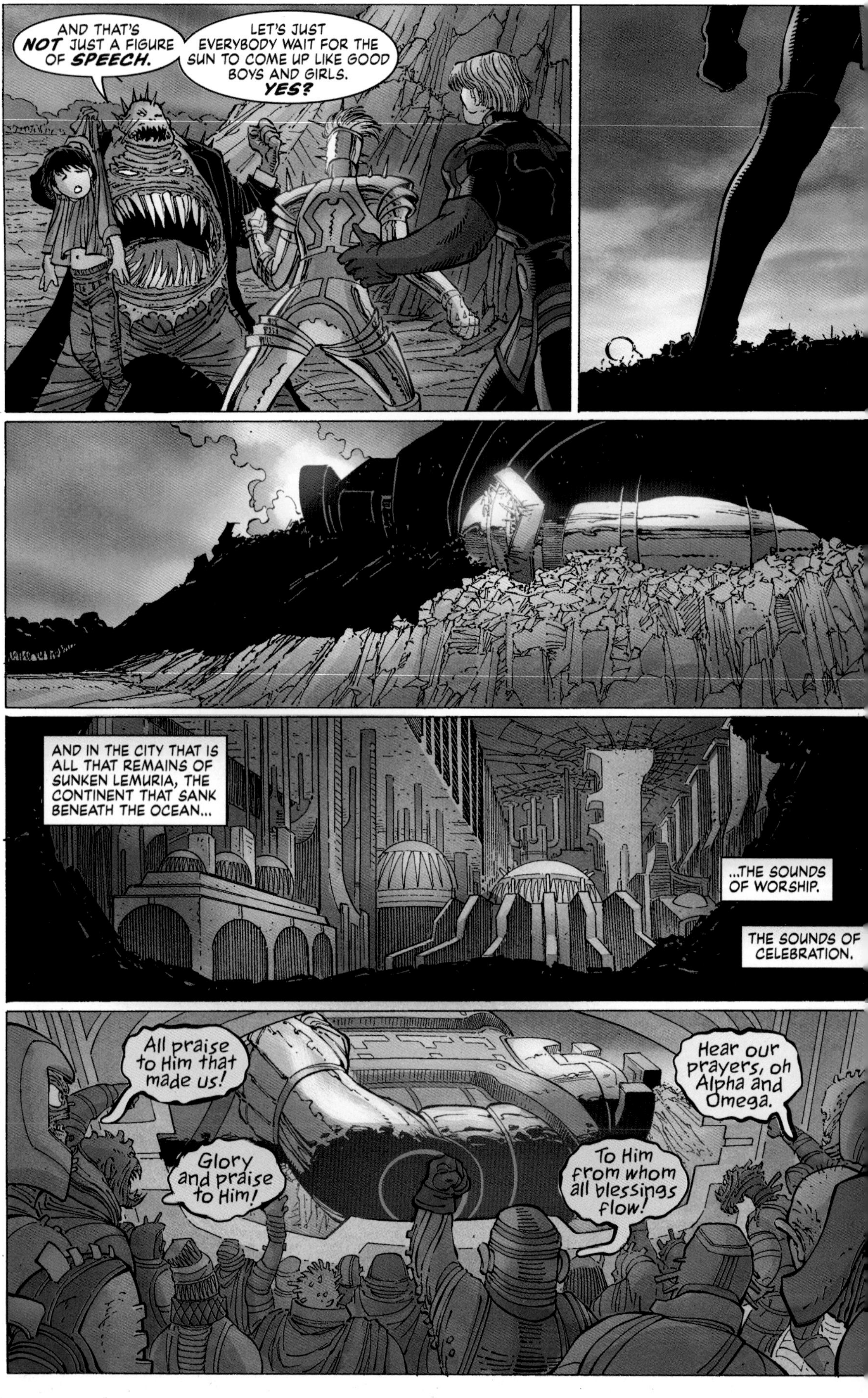
AND THAT'S NOT JUST A FIGURE OF SPEECH.
LET'S JUST EVERYBODY WAIT FOR THE SUN TO COME UP LIKE GOOD BOYS AND GIRLS. YES?
AND IN THE CITY THAT IS ALL THAT REMAINS OF SUNKEN LEMURIA, THE CONTINENT THAT SANK BENEATH THE OCEAN...
...THE SOUNDS OF WORSHIP.
THE SOUNDS OF CELEBRATION.
All praise to Him that made us!
Glory and praise to Him!
To Him from whom all blessings flow!
Hear our prayers, oh Alpha and Omega.

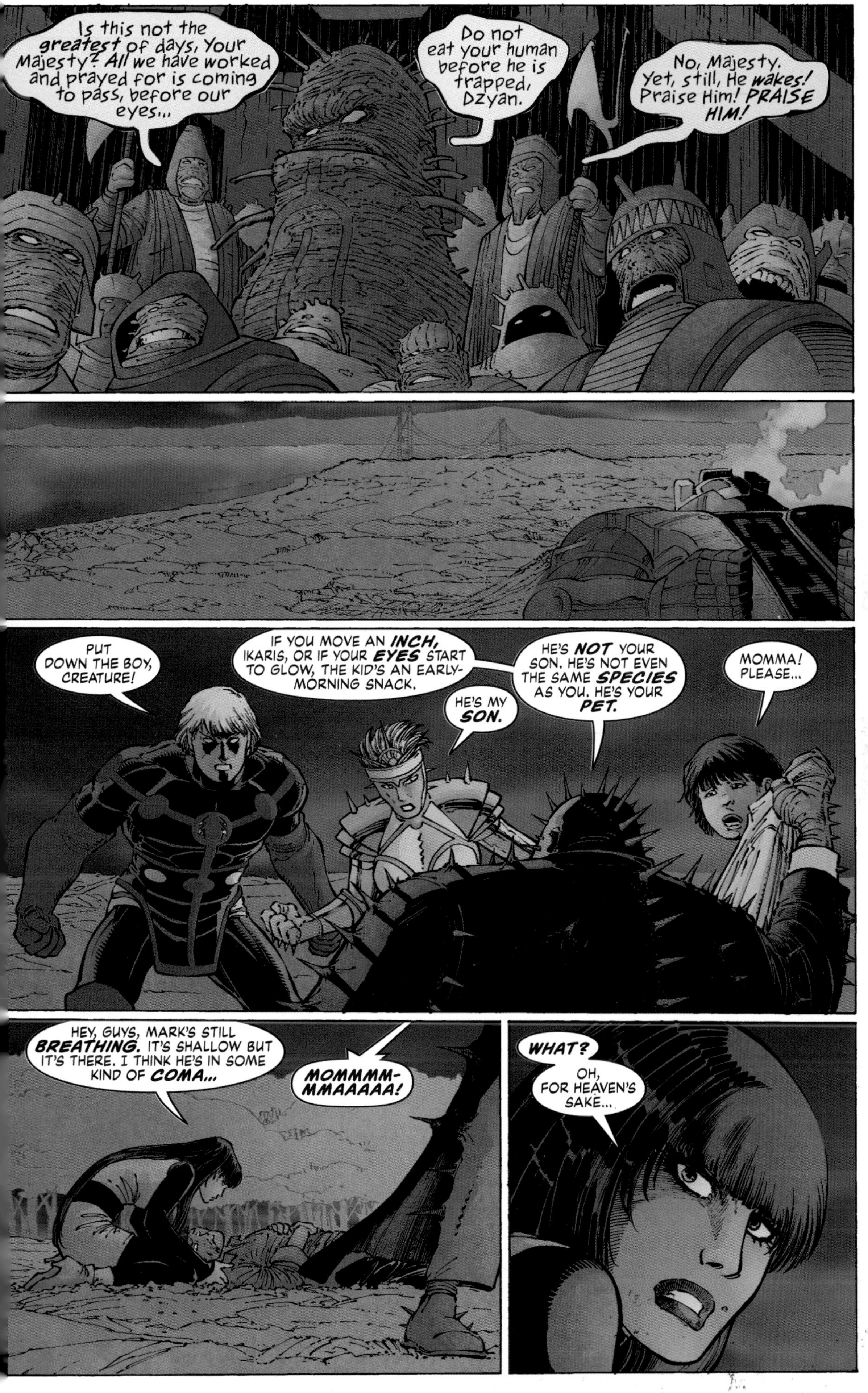
Is this not the greatest of days, Your Majesty? All we have worked and prayed for is coming to pass, before our eyes...
Do not eat your human before he is trapped, Dzyan.
No, Majesty. Yet, still, He wakes! Praise Him! PRAISE HIM!
PUT DOWN THE BOY, CREATURE!
IF YOU MOVE AN INCH, IKARIS, OR IF YOUR EYES START TO GLOW, THE KID'S AN EARLY-MORNING SNACK.
HE'S MY SON.
HE'S NOT YOUR SON. HE'S NOT EVEN THE SAME SPECIES AS YOU. HE'S YOUR PET.
MOMMA! PLEASE...
HEY, GUYS, MARK'S STILL BREATHING. IT'S SHALLOW BUT IT'S THERE. I THINK HE'S IN SOME KIND OF COMA...
MOMMMM-MMAAAAA!
WHAT?
OH, FOR HEAVEN'S SAKE...

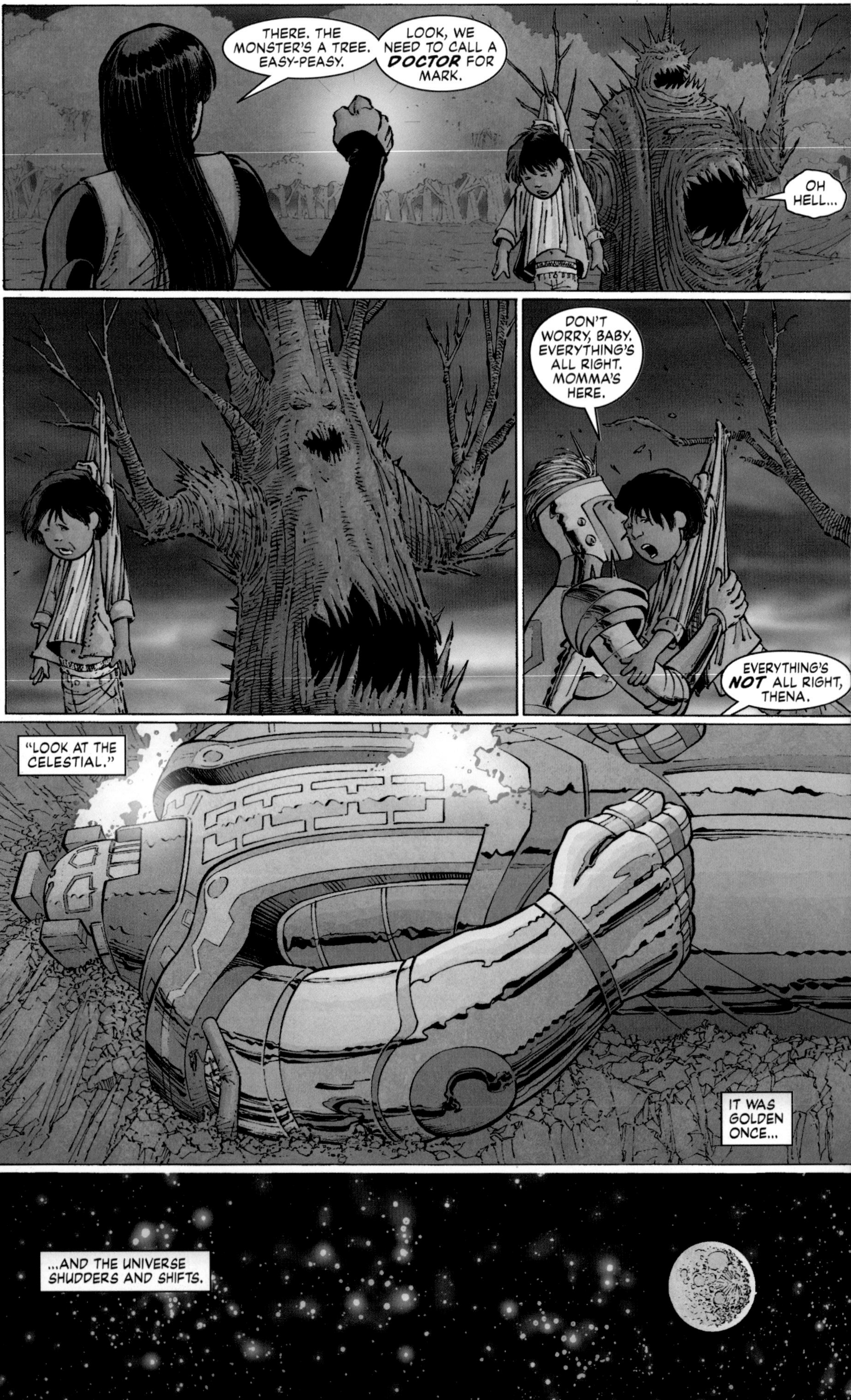
THERE. THE MONSTER'S A TREE. EASY-PEASY.
LOOK, WE NEED TO CALL A DOCTOR FOR MARK.
OH HELL...
DON'T WORRY, BABY. EVERYTHING'S ALL RIGHT. MOMMA'S HERE.
EVERYTHING'S NOT ALL RIGHT, THENA.
"LOOK AT THE CELESTIAL."
IT WAS GOLDEN ONCE...
...AND THE UNIVERSE SHUDDERS AND SHIFTS.

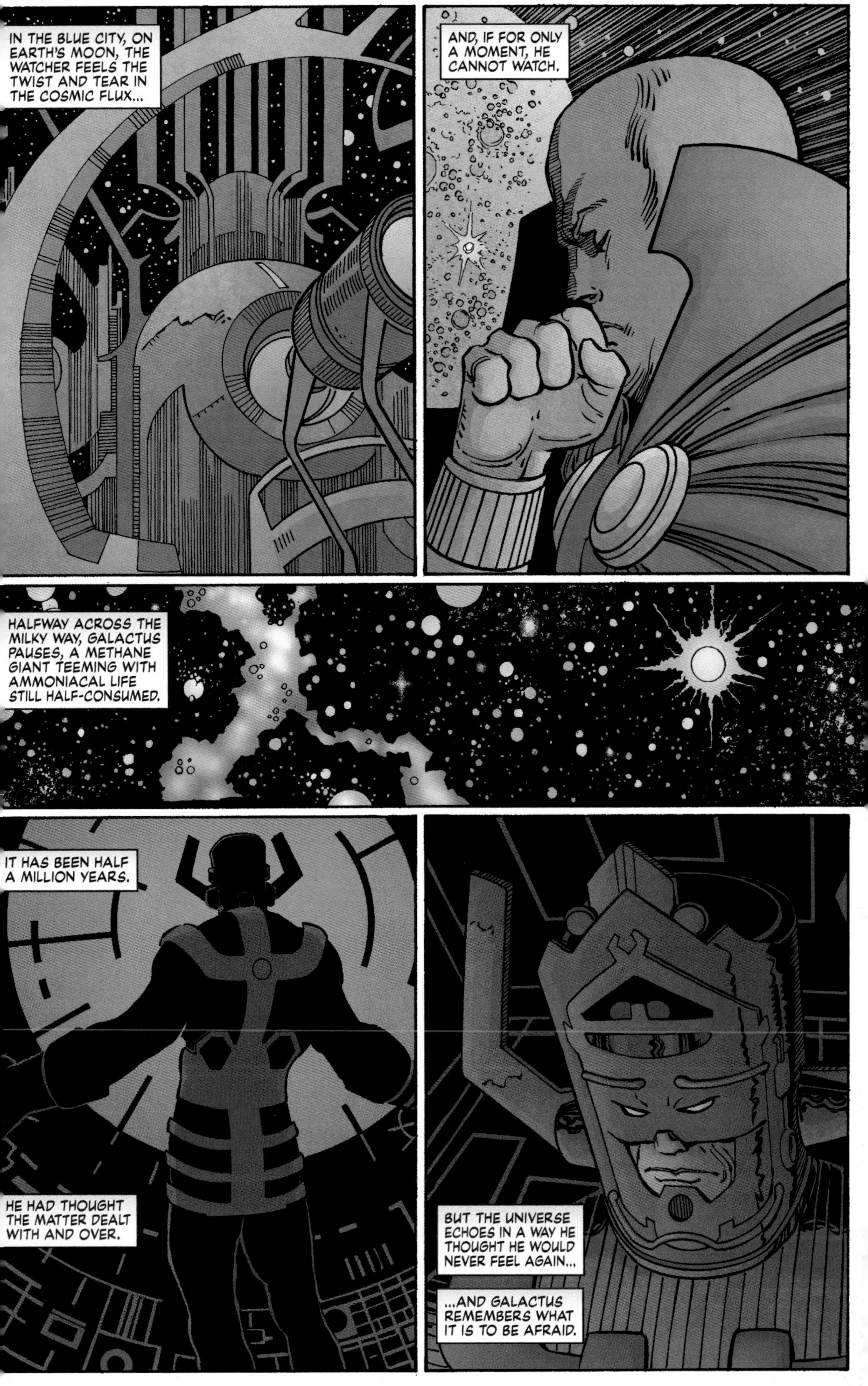
IN THE BLUE CITY, ON EARTH'S MOON, THE WATCHER FEELS THE TWIST AND TEAR IN THE COSMIC FLUX...
AND, IF FOR ONLY A MOMENT, HE CANNOT WATCH.
HALFWAY ACROSS THE MILKY WAY, GALACTUS PAUSES, A METHANE GIANT TEEMING WITH AMMONIACAL LIFE STILL HALF-CONSUMED.
IT HAS BEEN HALF A MILLION YEARS.
HE HAD THOUGHT THE MATTER DEALT WITH AND OVER.
BUT THE UNIVERSE ECHOES IN A WAY HE THOUGHT HE WOULD NEVER FEEL AGAIN...
...AND GALACTUS REMEMBERS WHAT IT IS TO BE AFRAID.

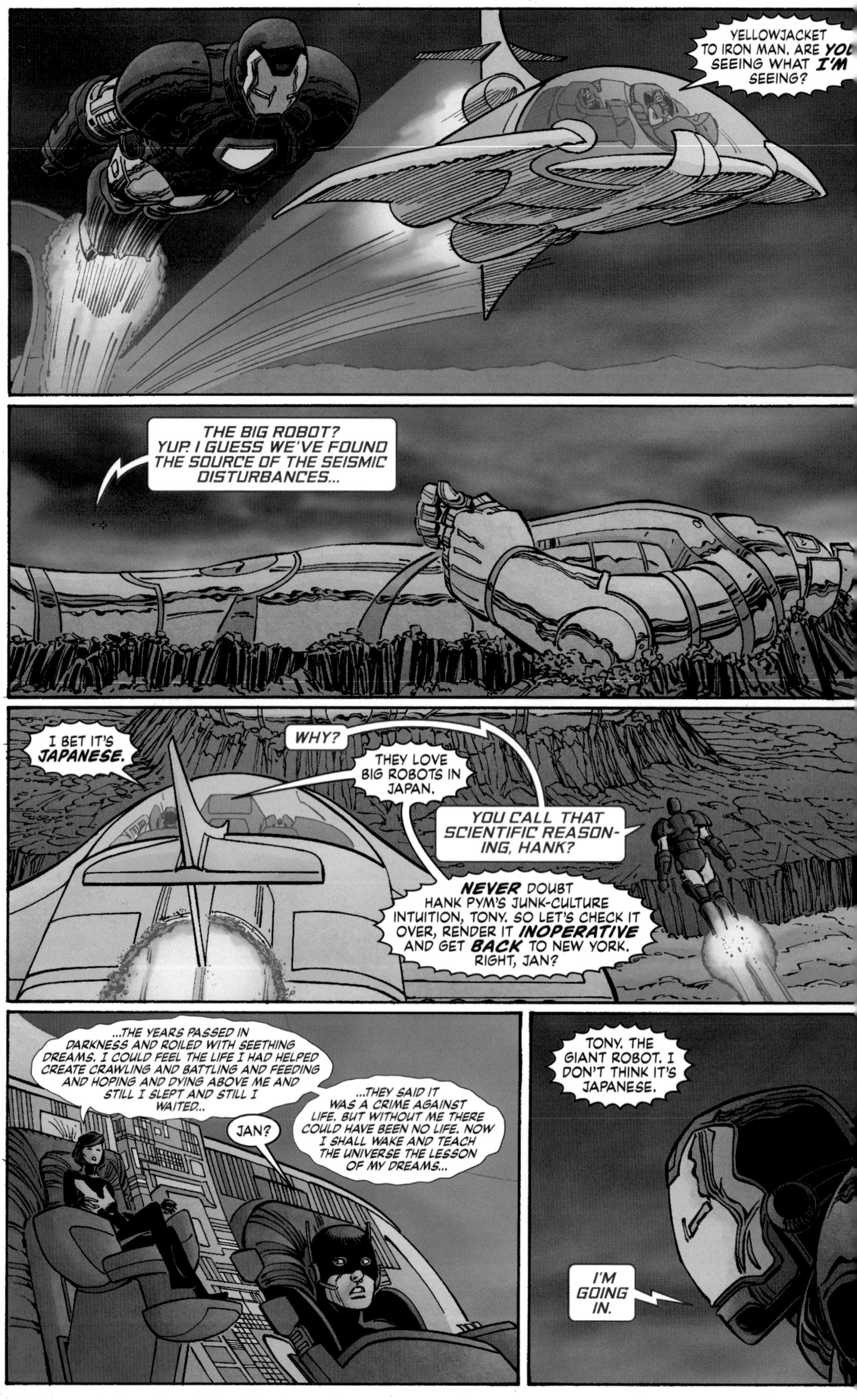
YELLOWJACKET TO IRON MAN. ARE YOU SEEING WHAT I'M SEEING?
THE BIG ROBOT? YUP. I GUESS WE'VE FOUND THE SOURCE OF THE SEISMIC DISTURBANCES...
I BET IT'S JAPANESE.
WHY?
THEY LOVE BIG ROBOTS IN JAPAN.
YOU CALL THAT SCIENTIFIC REASONING, HANK?
NEVER DOUBT HANK PYM'S JUNK-CULTURE INTUITION, TONY. SO LET'S CHECK IT OVER, RENDER IT INOPERATIVE AND GET BACK TO NEW YORK. RIGHT, JAN?
...THE YEARS PASSED IN DARKNESS AND ROILED WITH SEETHING DREAMS. I COULD FEEL THE LIFE I HAD HELPED CREATE CRAWLING AND BATTLING AND FEEDING AND HOPING AND DYING ABOVE ME AND STILL I SLEPT AND STILL I WAITED...
JAN?
...THEY SAID IT WAS A CRIME AGAINST LIFE. BUT WITHOUT ME THERE COULD HAVE BEEN NO LIFE. NOW I SHALL WAKE AND TEACH THE UNIVERSE THE LESSON OF MY DREAMS...
TONY. THE GIANT ROBOT. I DON'T THINK IT'S JAPANESE.
I'M GOING IN.

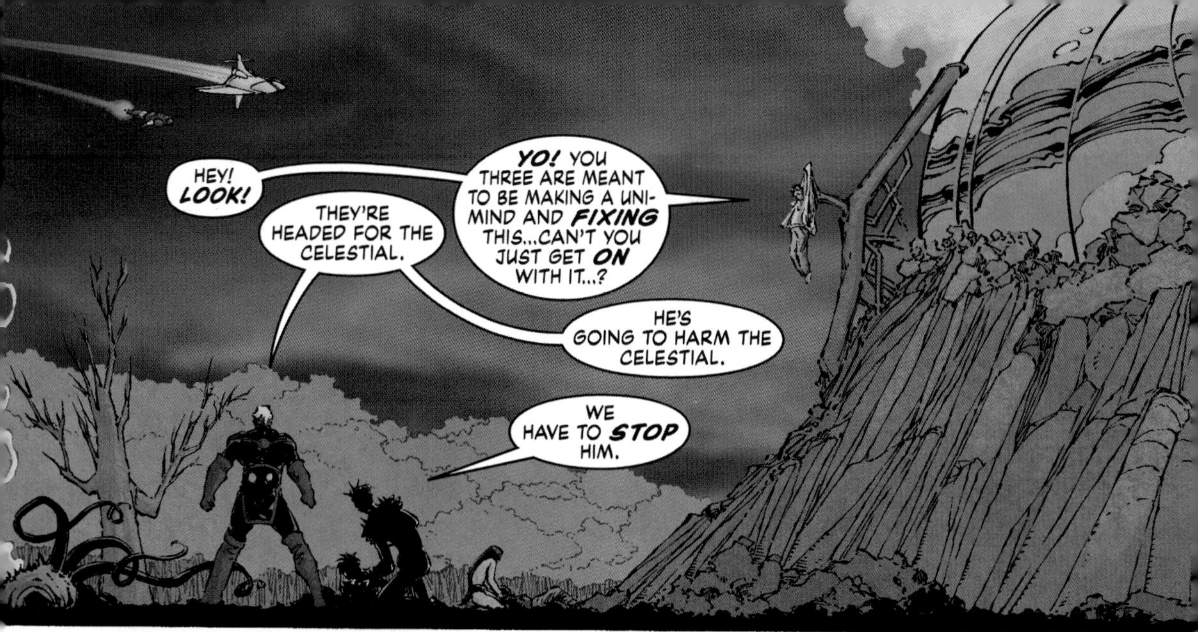
HEY! LOOK!
THEY'RE HEADED FOR THE CELESTIAL.
YO! YOU THREE ARE MEANT TO BE MAKING A UNI-MIND AND FIXING THIS...CAN'T YOU JUST GET ON WITH IT...?
HE'S GOING TO HARM THE CELESTIAL.
WE HAVE TO STOP HIM.
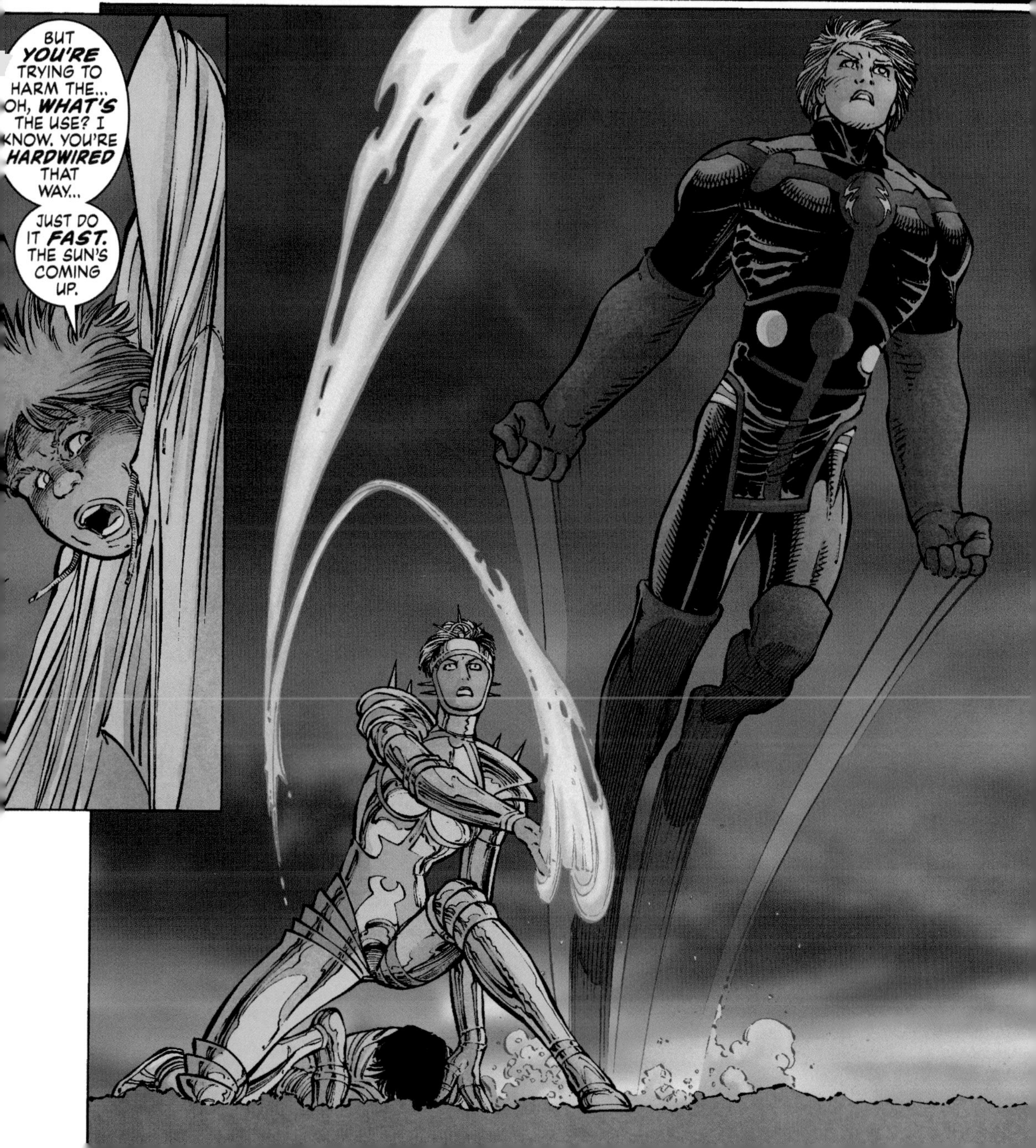
BUT YOU'RE TRYING TO HARM THE... OH, WHAT'S THE USE? I KNOW. YOU'RE HARDWIRED THAT WAY...
JUST DO IT FAST. THE SUN'S COMING UP.

NNNNPH!

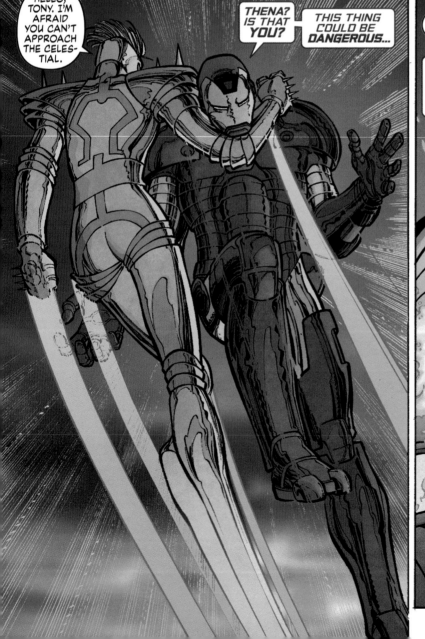

HELLO, TONY. I'M AFRAID YOU CAN'T APPROACH THE CELESTIAL.

THENA? IS THAT YOU?

THIS THING COULD BE DANGEROUS...

OH, IT IS. IT'S THE MOST DANGEROUS THING IN THE WORLD. BUT I HAVE TO PROTECT IT.

THEN LET GO OF ME... THENA. I RESCUED YOU.

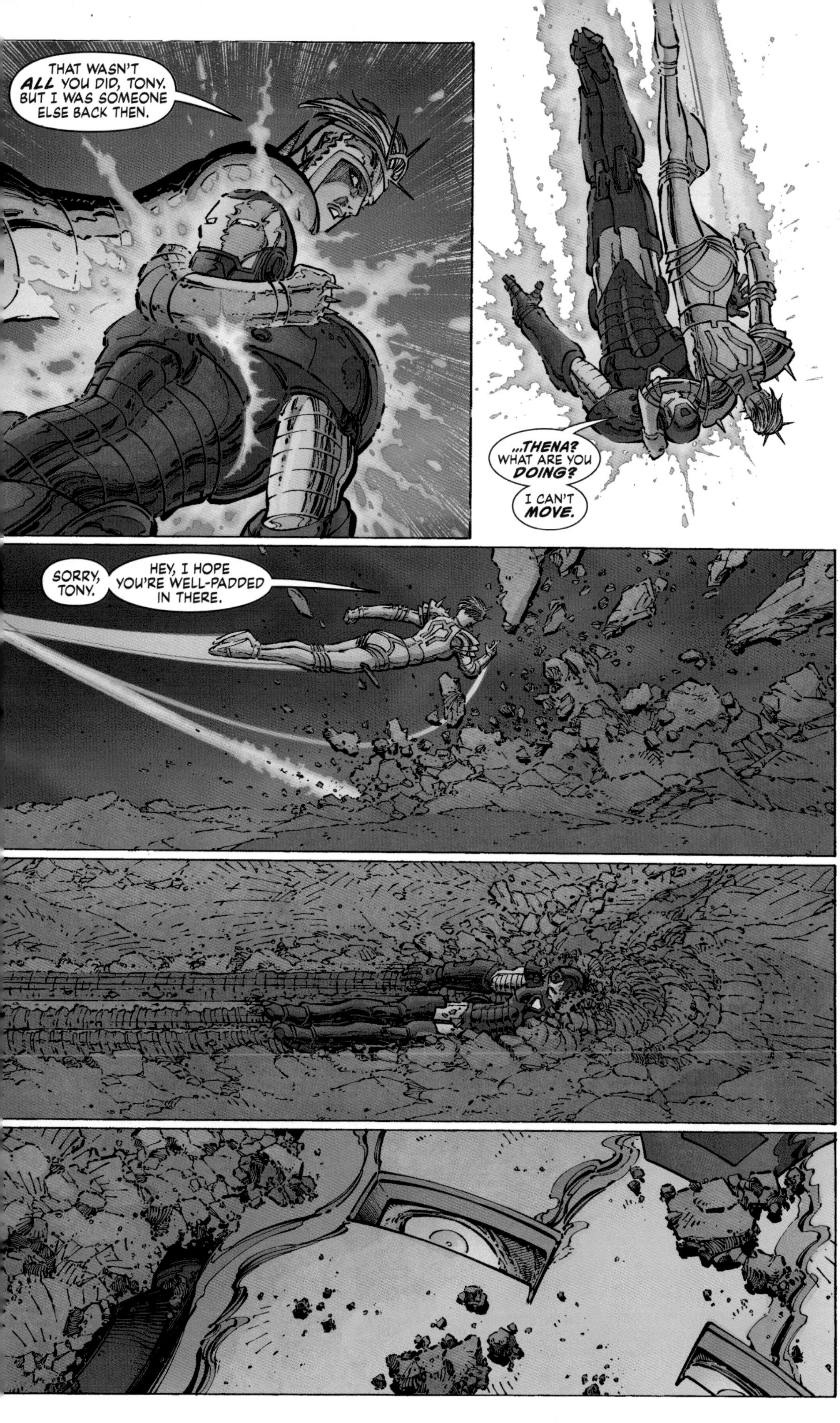
THAT WASN'T ALL YOU DID, TONY. BUT I WAS SOMEONE ELSE BACK THEN.
...THENA? WHAT ARE YOU DOING?
I CAN'T MOVE.
SORRY, TONY.
HEY, I HOPE YOU'RE WELL-PADDED IN THERE.

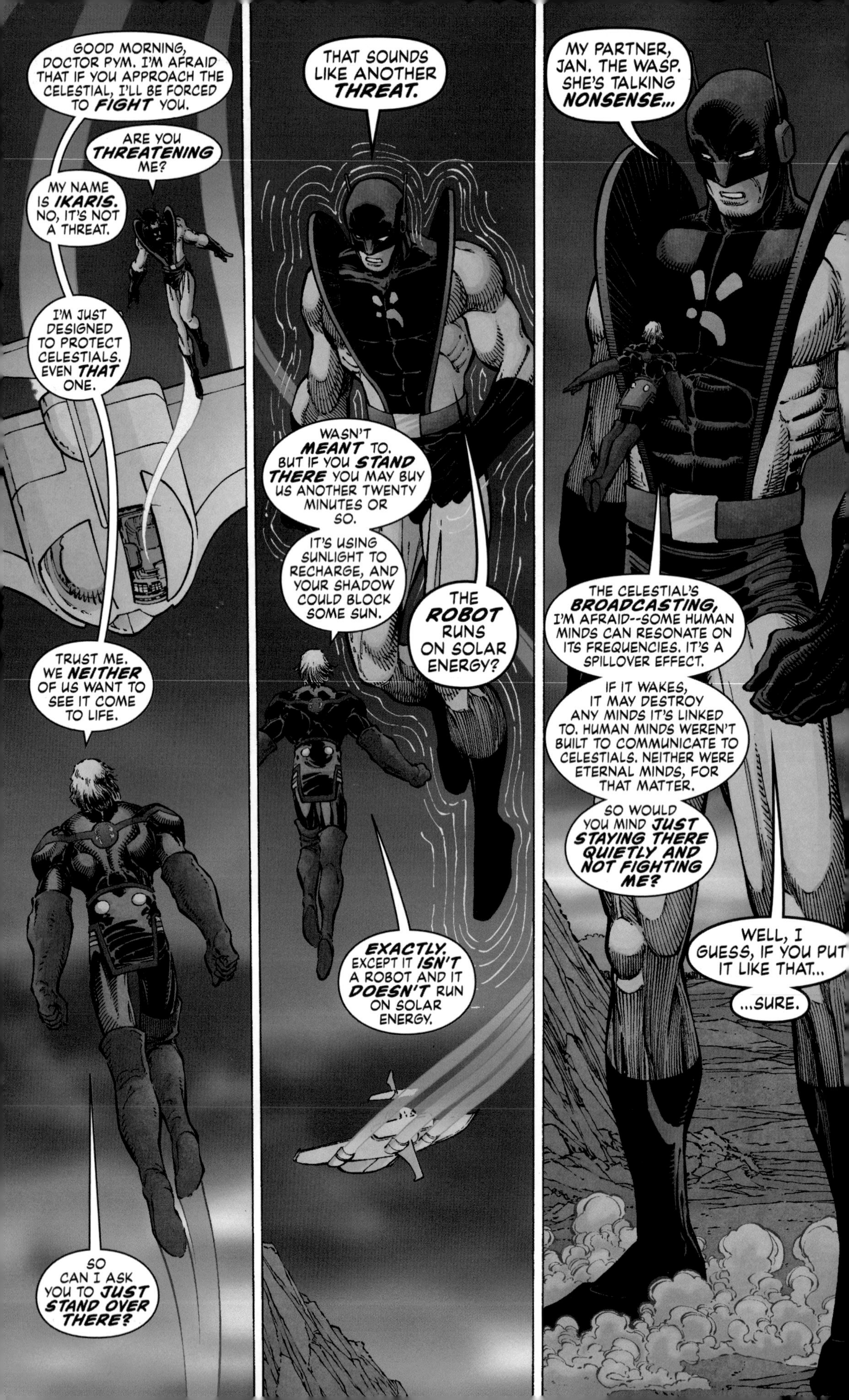
GOOD MORNING, DOCTOR PYM. I'M AFRAID THAT IF YOU APPROACH THE CELESTIAL, I'LL BE FORCED TO FIGHT YOU.
ARE YOU THREATENING ME?
MY NAME IS IKARIS. NO, IT'S NOT A THREAT.
I'M JUST DESIGNED TO PROTECT CELESTIALS. EVEN THAT ONE.
TRUST ME. WE NEITHER OF US WANT TO SEE IT COME TO LIFE.
SO CAN I ASK YOU TO JUST STAND OVER THERE?
THAT SOUNDS LIKE ANOTHER THREAT.
WASN'T MEANT TO. BUT IF YOU STAND THERE YOU MAY BUY US ANOTHER TWENTY MINUTES OR SO.
IT'S USING SUNLIGHT TO RECHARGE, AND YOUR SHADOW COULD BLOCK SOME SUN.
THE ROBOT RUNS ON SOLAR ENERGY?
EXACTLY. EXCEPT IT ISN'T A ROBOT AND IT DOESN'T RUN ON SOLAR ENERGY.
MY PARTNER, JAN. THE WASP. SHE'S TALKING NONSENSE...
THE CELESTIAL'S BROADCASTING, I'M AFRAID--SOME HUMAN MINDS CAN RESONATE ON ITS FREQUENCIES. IT'S A SPILLOVER EFFECT.
IF IT WAKES, IT MAY DESTROY ANY MINDS IT'S LINKED TO. HUMAN MINDS WEREN'T BUILT TO COMMUNICATE TO CELESTIALS. NEITHER WERE ETERNAL MINDS, FOR THAT MATTER.
SO WOULD YOU MIND JUST STAYING THERE QUIETLY AND NOT FIGHTING ME?
WELL, I GUESS, IF YOU PUT IT LIKE THAT...
...SURE.

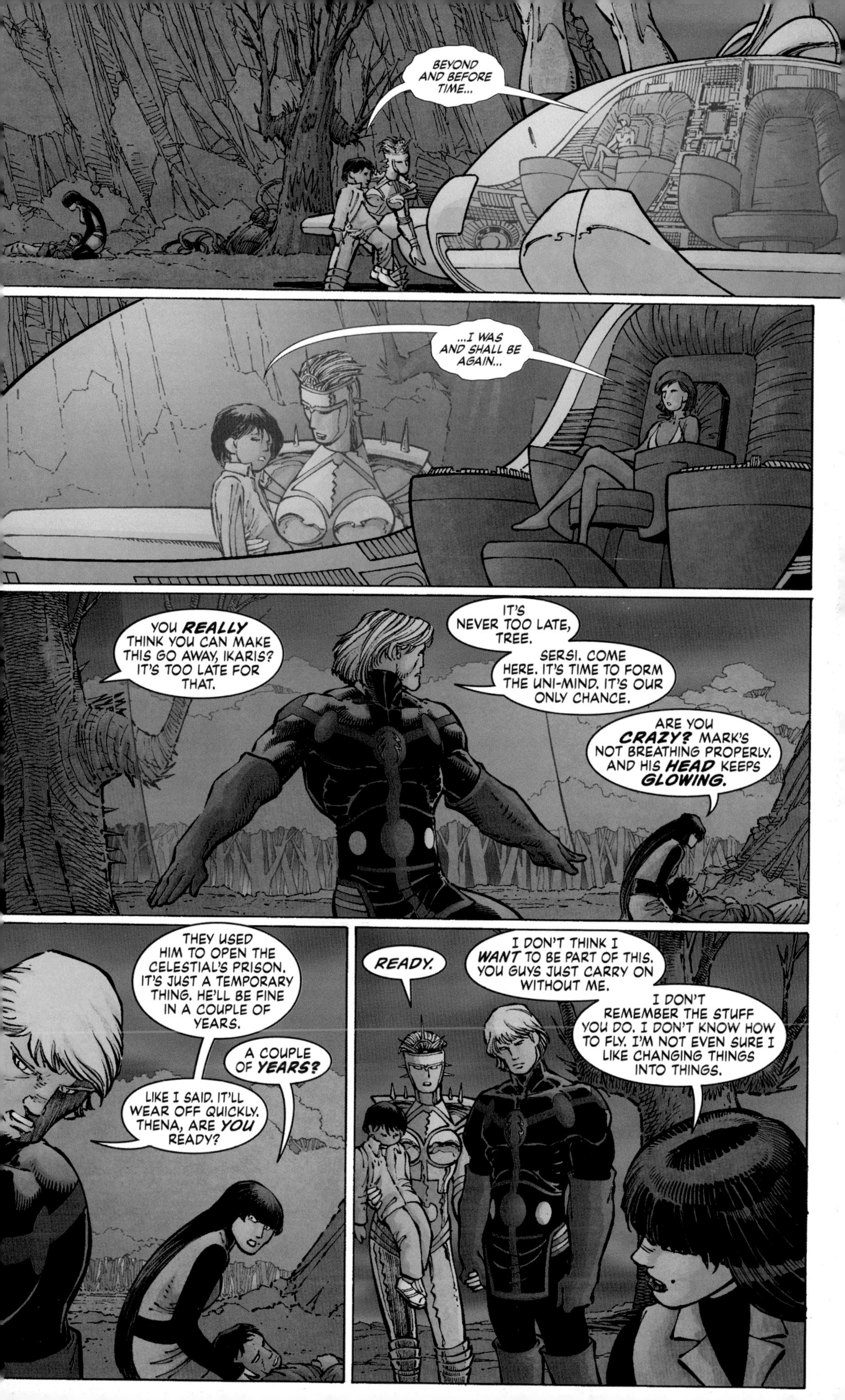
BEYOND AND BEFORE TIME...
...I WAS AND SHALL BE AGAIN...
YOU REALLY THINK YOU CAN MAKE THIS GO AWAY, IKARIS? IT'S TOO LATE FOR THAT.
IT'S NEVER TOO LATE, TREE.
SERSI. COME HERE. IT'S TIME TO FORM THE UNI-MIND. IT'S OUR ONLY CHANCE.
ARE YOU CRAZY? MARK'S NOT BREATHING PROPERLY. AND HIS HEAD KEEPS GLOWING.
THEY USED HIM TO OPEN THE CELESTIAL'S PRISON. IT'S JUST A TEMPORARY THING. HE'LL BE FINE IN A COUPLE OF YEARS.
A COUPLE OF YEARS?
LIKE I SAID. IT'LL WEAR OFF QUICKLY. THENA, ARE YOU READY?
READY.
I DON'T THINK I WANT TO BE PART OF THIS. YOU GUYS JUST CARRY ON WITHOUT ME.
I DON'T REMEMBER THE STUFF YOU DO. I DON'T KNOW HOW TO FLY. I'M NOT EVEN SURE I LIKE CHANGING THINGS INTO THINGS.

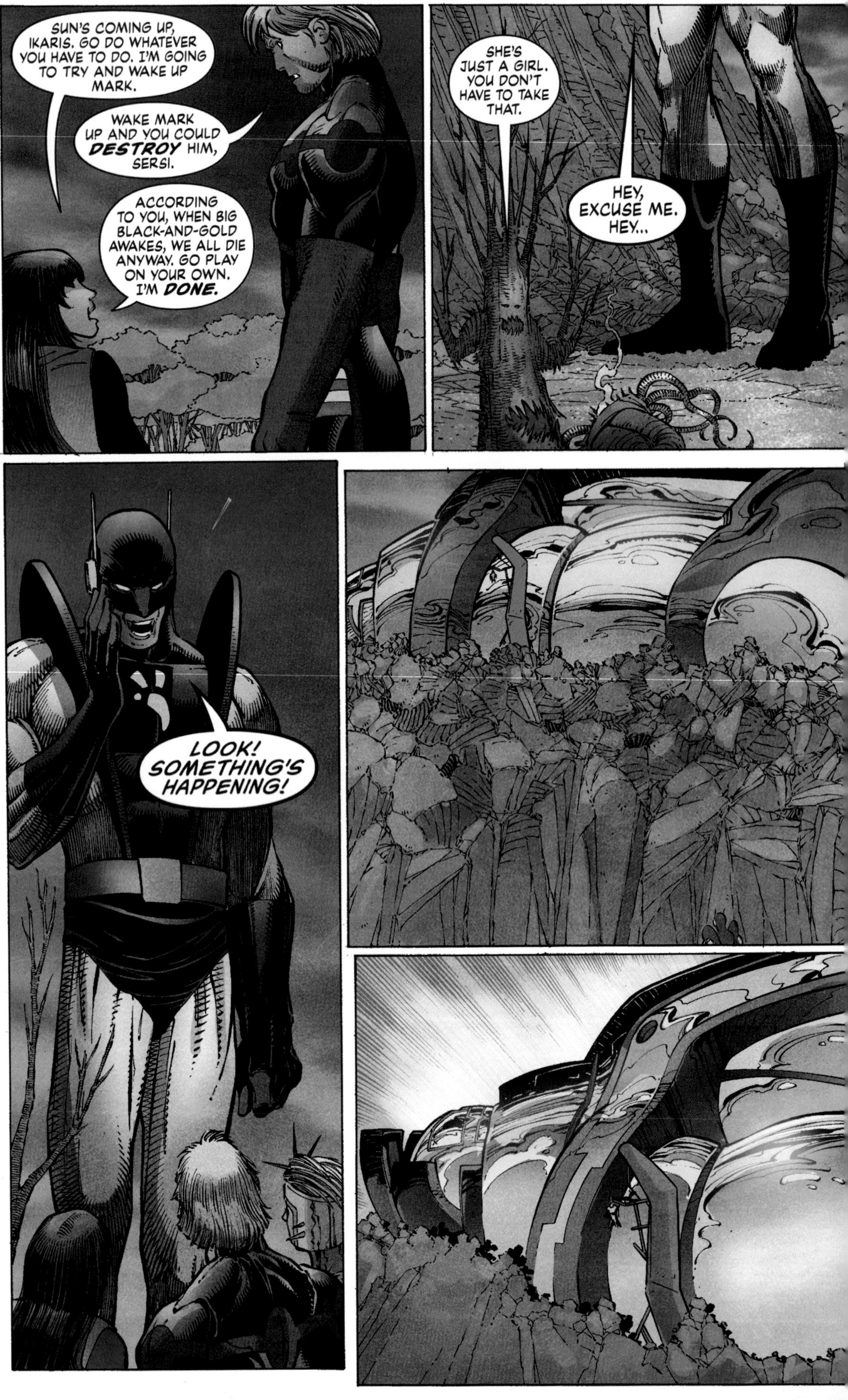
SUN'S COMING UP, IKARIS. GO DO WHATEVER YOU HAVE TO DO. I'M GOING TO TRY AND WAKE UP MARK.
WAKE MARK UP AND YOU COULD DESTROY HIM, SERSI.
ACCORDING TO YOU, WHEN BIG BLACK-AND-GOLD AWAKES, WE ALL DIE ANYWAY. GO PLAY ON YOUR OWN. I'M DONE.
SHE'S JUST A GIRL. YOU DON'T HAVE TO TAKE THAT.
HEY, EXCUSE ME. HEY...
LOOK! SOMETHING'S HAPPENING!

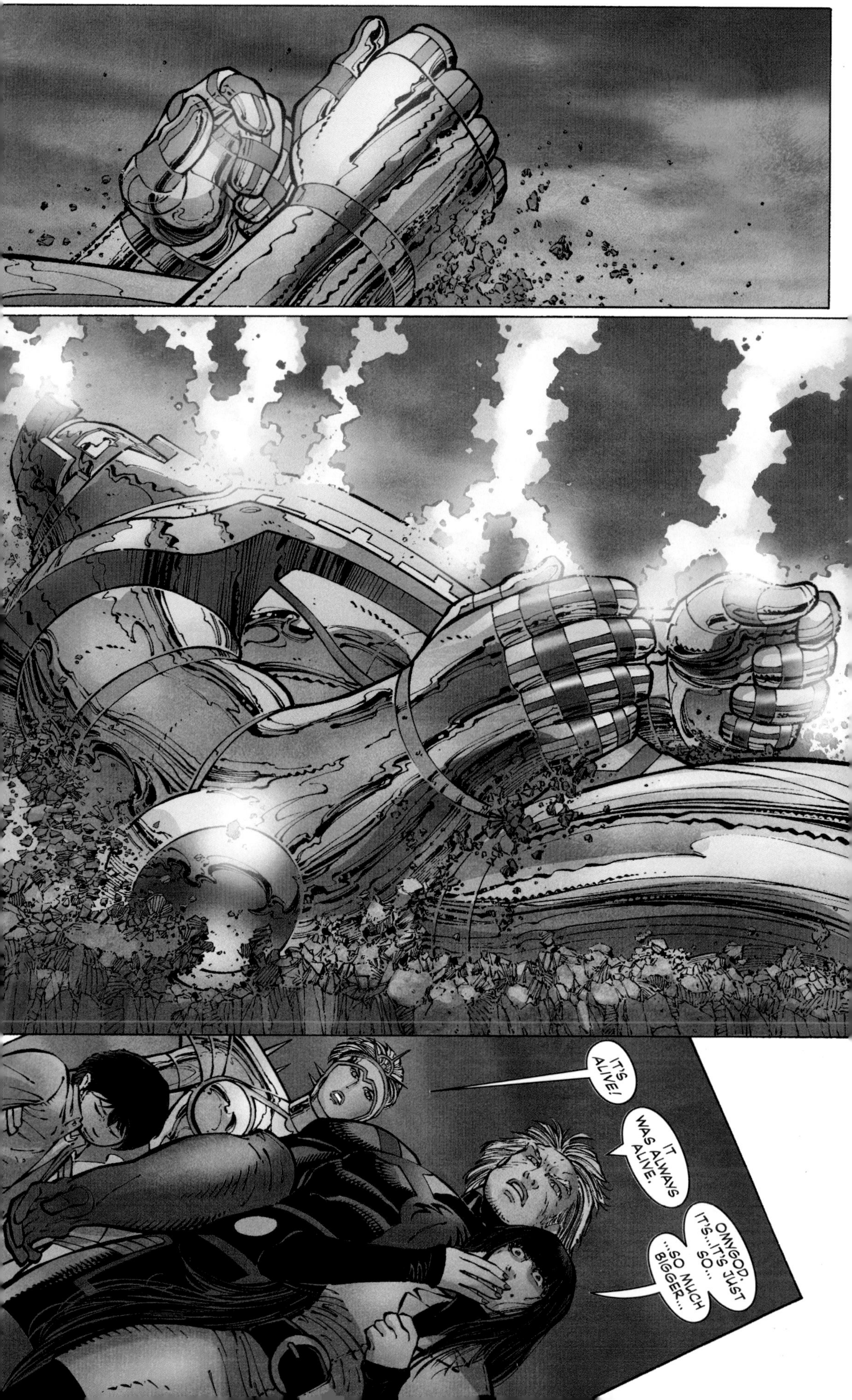

IT'S ALIVE!
IT WAS ALWAYS ALIVE.
OMYGOD. IT'S...IT'S JUST SO... ...SO MUCH BIGGER...

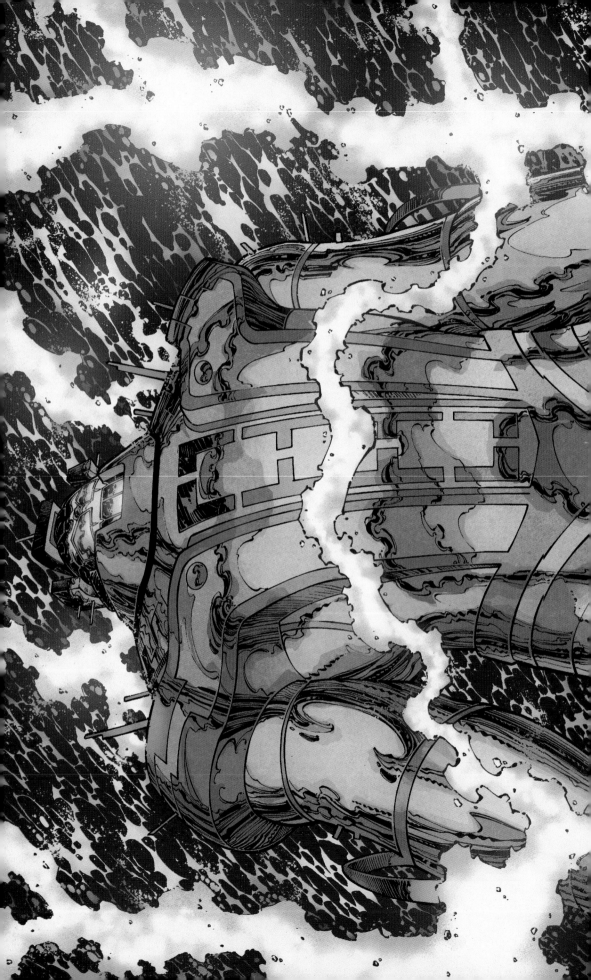

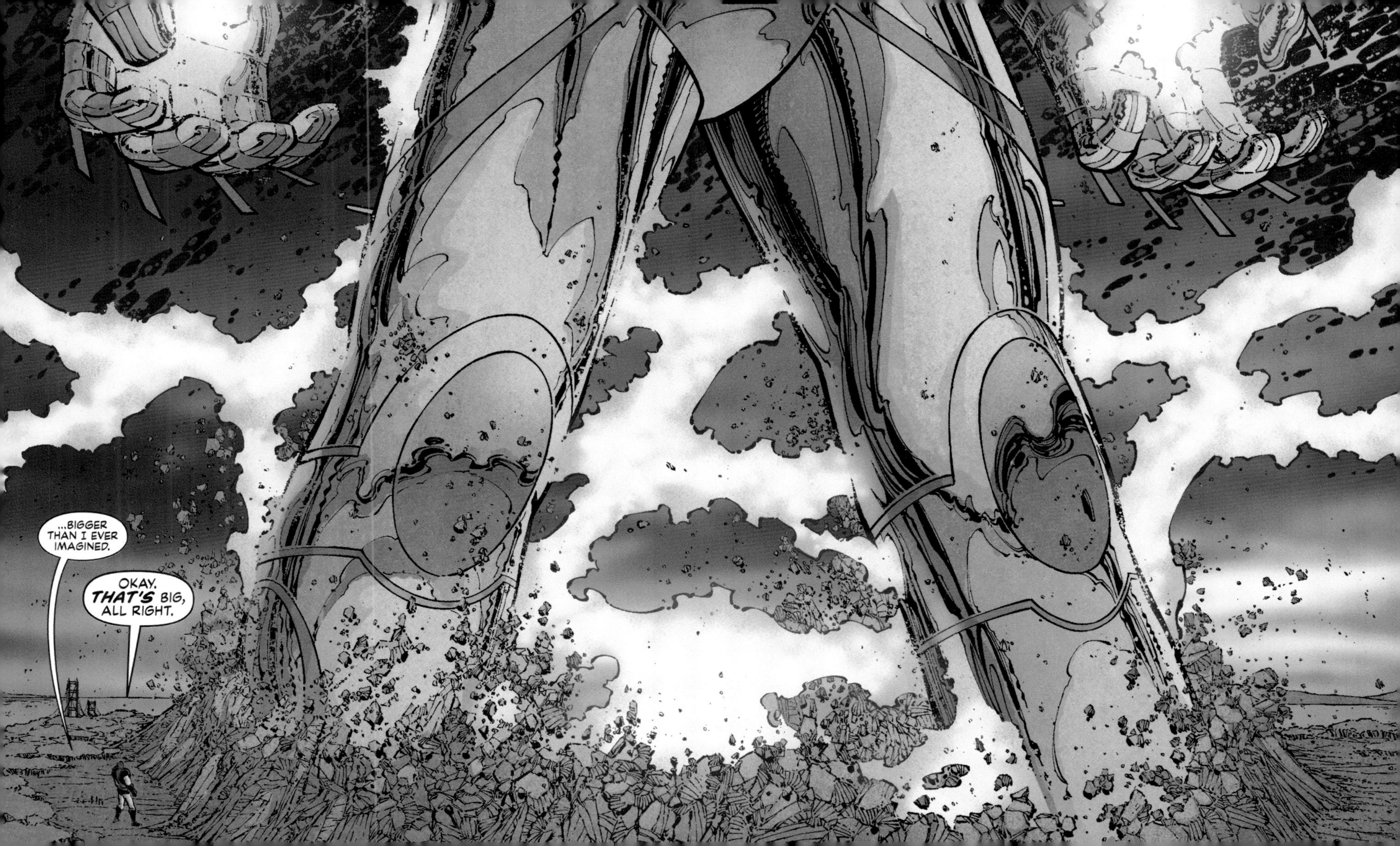
...BIGGER THAN I EVER IMAGINED.
OKAY. THAT'S BIG, ALL RIGHT.

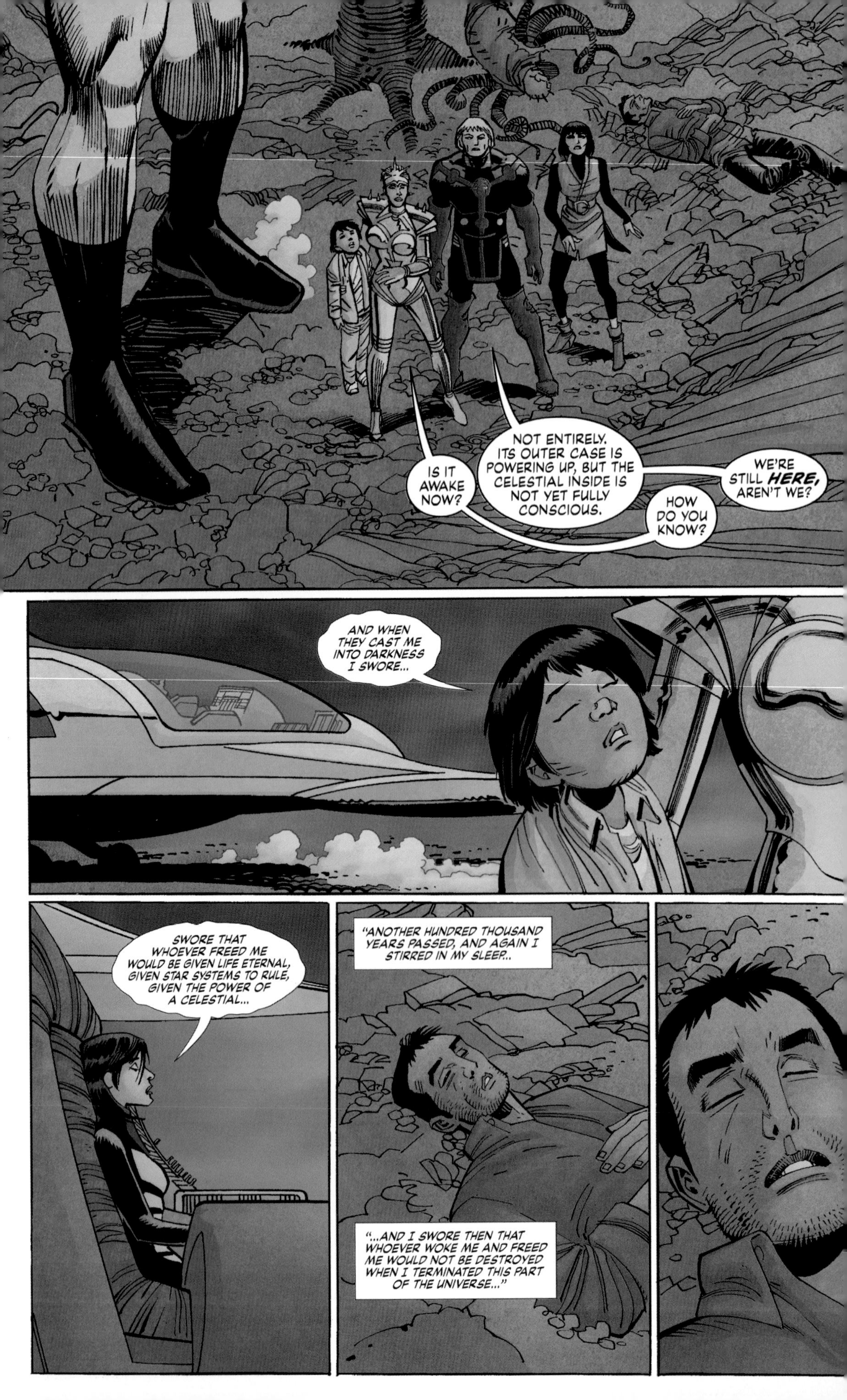
IS IT AWAKE NOW?
NOT ENTIRELY. ITS OUTER CASE IS POWERING UP, BUT THE CELESTIAL INSIDE IS NOT YET FULLY CONSCIOUS.
HOW DO YOU KNOW?
WE'RE STILL HERE, AREN'T WE?
AND WHEN THEY CAST ME INTO DARKNESS I SWORE...
SWORE THAT WHOEVER FREED ME WOULD BE GIVEN LIFE ETERNAL, GIVEN STAR SYSTEMS TO RULE, GIVEN THE POWER OF A CELESTIAL...
"ANOTHER HUNDRED THOUSAND YEARS PASSED, AND AGAIN I STIRRED IN MY SLEEP...
"...AND I SWORE THEN THAT WHOEVER WOKE ME AND FREED ME WOULD NOT BE DESTROYED WHEN I TERMINATED THIS PART OF THE UNIVERSE..."

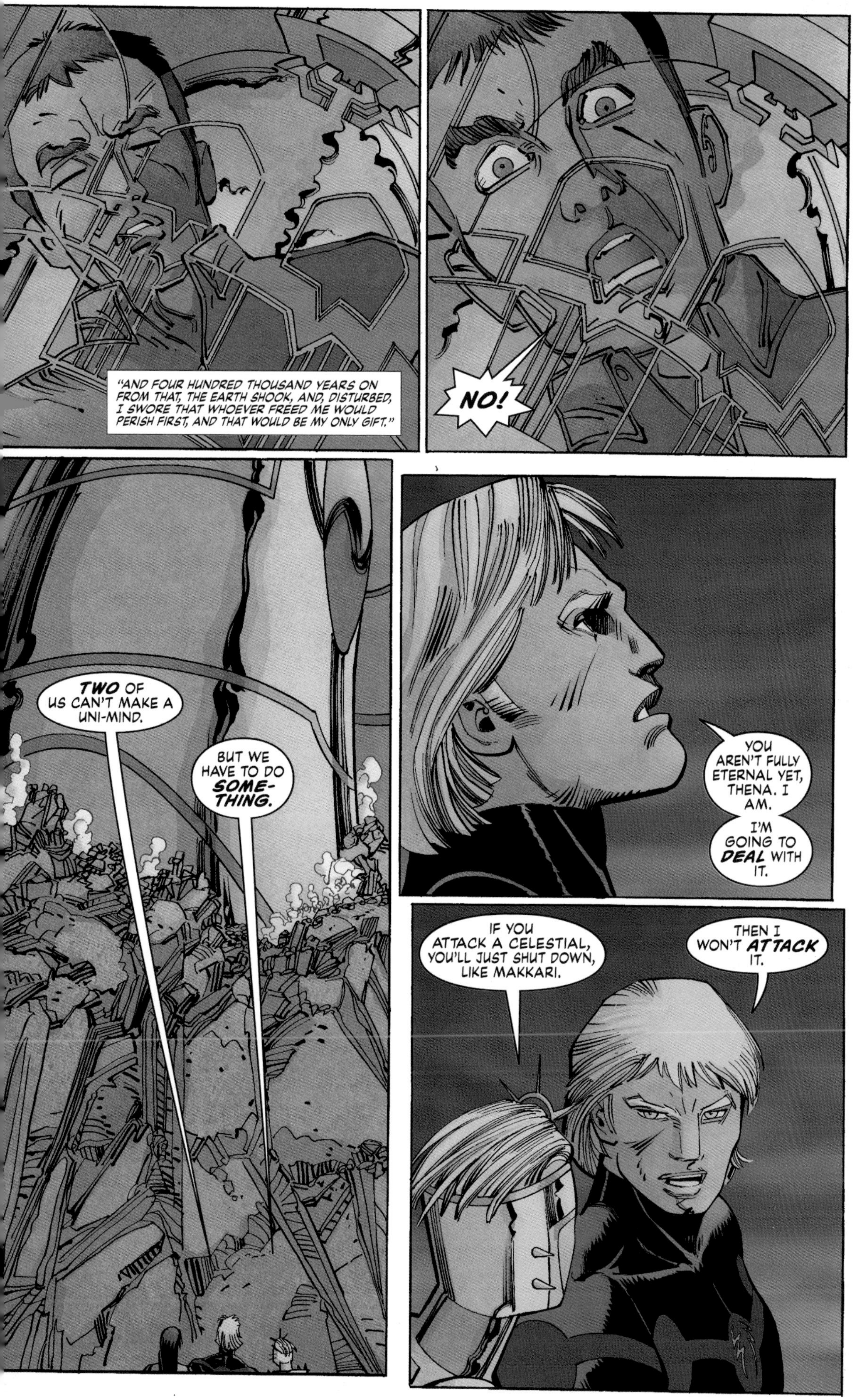
"AND FOUR HUNDRED THOUSAND YEARS ON FROM THAT, THE EARTH SHOOK, AND, DISTURBED, I SWORE THAT WHOEVER FREED ME WOULD PERISH FIRST, AND THAT WOULD BE MY ONLY GIFT."
NO!
TWO OF US CAN'T MAKE A UNI-MIND.
BUT WE HAVE TO DO SOMETHING.
YOU AREN'T FULLY ETERNAL YET, THENA. I AM.
I'M GOING TO DEAL WITH IT.
IF YOU ATTACK A CELESTIAL, YOU'LL JUST SHUT DOWN, LIKE MAKKARI.
THEN I WON'T ATTACK IT.

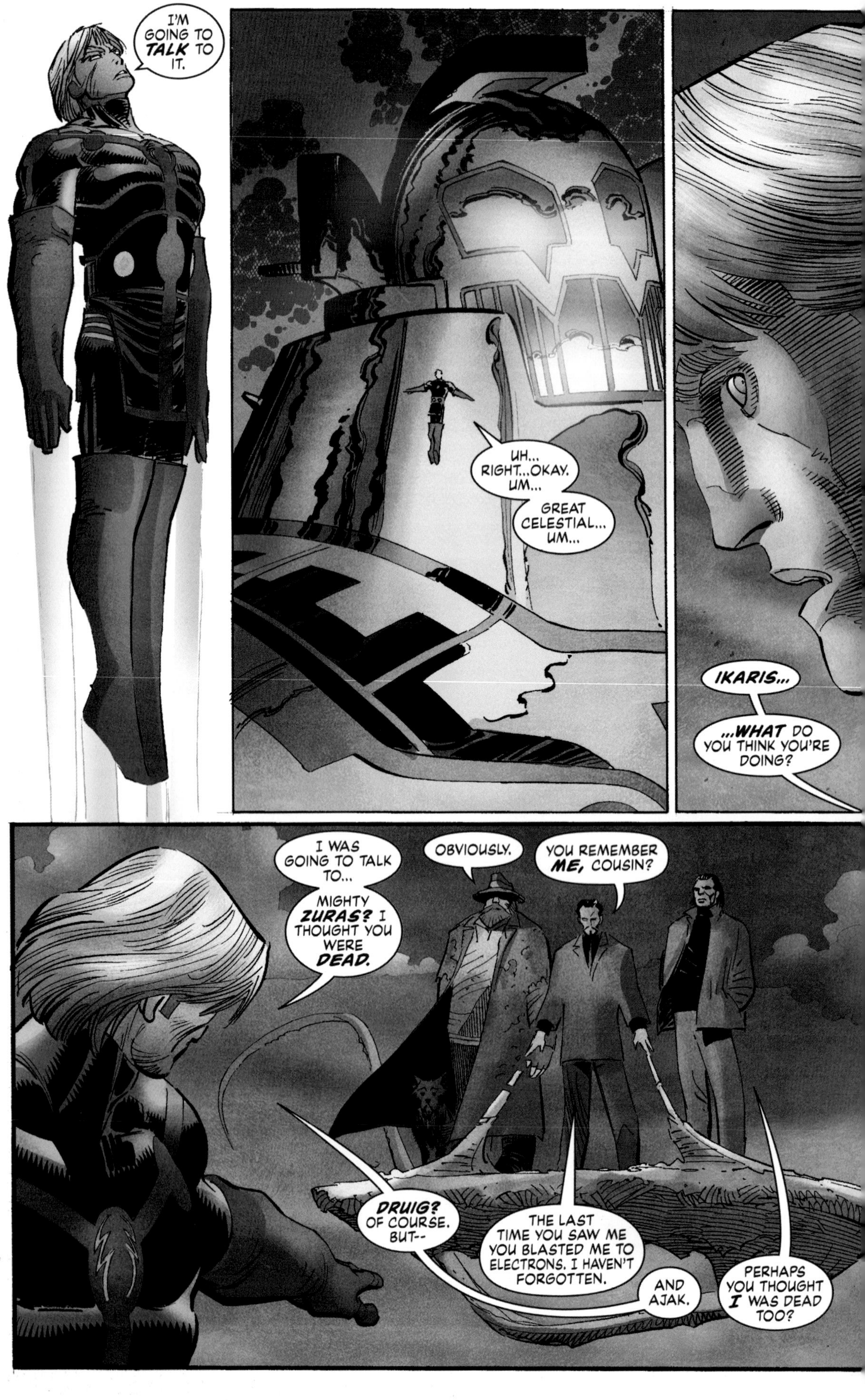
I'M GOING TO TALK TO IT.
UH... RIGHT...OKAY. UM...
GREAT CELESTIAL... UM...
IKARIS...
...WHAT DO YOU THINK YOU'RE DOING?
I WAS GOING TO TALK TO...
OBVIOUSLY.
YOU REMEMBER ME, COUSIN?
MIGHTY ZURAS? I THOUGHT YOU WERE DEAD.
DRUIG? OF COURSE. BUT--
THE LAST TIME YOU SAW ME YOU BLASTED ME TO ELECTRONS. I HAVEN'T FORGOTTEN.
AND AJAK.
PERHAPS YOU THOUGHT I WAS DEAD TOO?

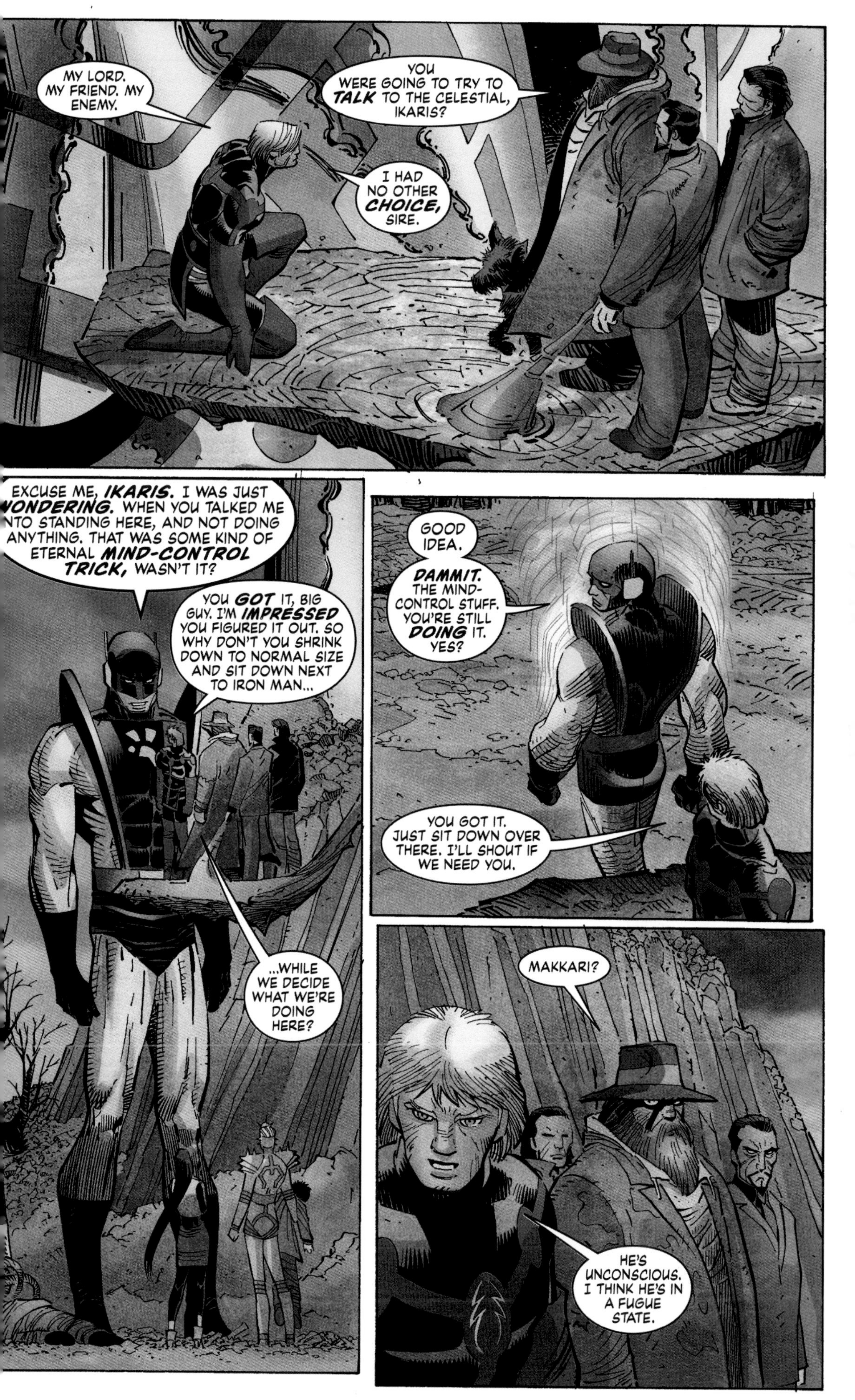
MY LORD. MY FRIEND. MY ENEMY.
YOU WERE GOING TO TRY TO TALK TO THE CELESTIAL, IKARIS?
I HAD NO OTHER CHOICE, SIRE.
EXCUSE ME, IKARIS. I WAS JUST WONDERING. WHEN YOU TALKED ME INTO STANDING HERE, AND NOT DOING ANYTHING. THAT WAS SOME KIND OF ETERNAL MIND-CONTROL TRICK, WASN'T IT?
YOU GOT IT, BIG GUY. I'M IMPRESSED YOU FIGURED IT OUT. SO WHY DON'T YOU SHRINK DOWN TO NORMAL SIZE AND SIT DOWN NEXT TO IRON MAN...
...WHILE WE DECIDE WHAT WE'RE DOING HERE?
GOOD IDEA.
DAMMIT. THE MIND-CONTROL STUFF. YOU'RE STILL DOING IT. YES?
YOU GOT IT. JUST SIT DOWN OVER THERE. I'LL SHOUT IF WE NEED YOU.
MAKKARI?
HE'S UNCONSCIOUS. I THINK HE'S IN A FUGUE STATE.

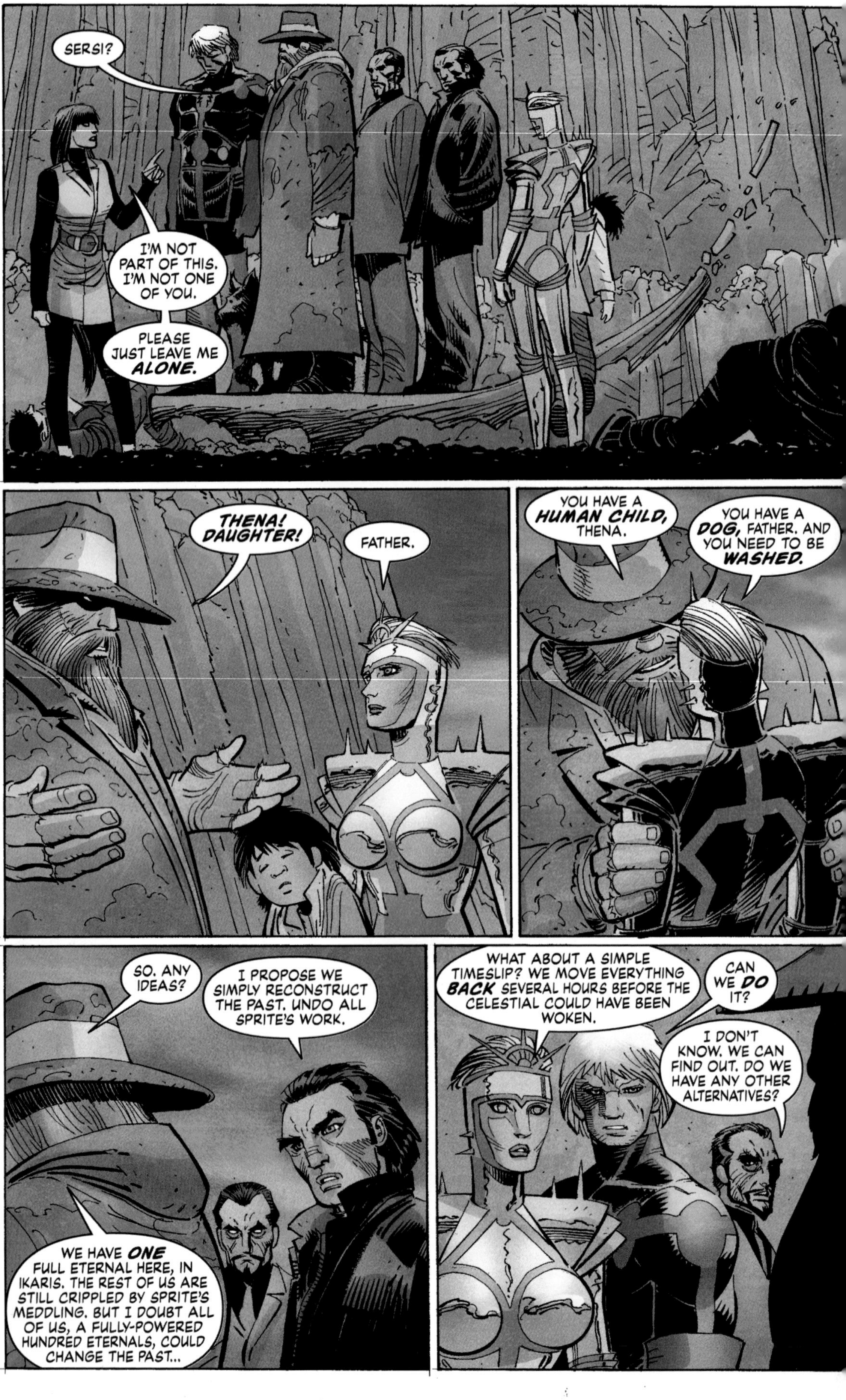
SERSI?
I'M NOT PART OF THIS. I'M NOT ONE OF YOU.
PLEASE JUST LEAVE ME ALONE.
THENA! DAUGHTER!
FATHER.
YOU HAVE A HUMAN CHILD, THENA.
YOU HAVE A DOG, FATHER. AND YOU NEED TO BE WASHED.
SO. ANY IDEAS?
I PROPOSE WE SIMPLY RECONSTRUCT THE PAST. UNDO ALL SPRITE'S WORK.
WE HAVE ONE FULL ETERNAL HERE, IN IKARIS. THE REST OF US ARE STILL CRIPPLED BY SPRITE'S MEDDLING. BUT I DOUBT ALL OF US, A FULLY-POWERED HUNDRED ETERNALS, COULD CHANGE THE PAST...
WHAT ABOUT A SIMPLE TIMESLIP? WE MOVE EVERYTHING BACK SEVERAL HOURS BEFORE THE CELESTIAL COULD HAVE BEEN WOKEN.
CAN WE DO IT?
I DON'T KNOW. WE CAN FIND OUT. DO WE HAVE ANY OTHER ALTERNATIVES?

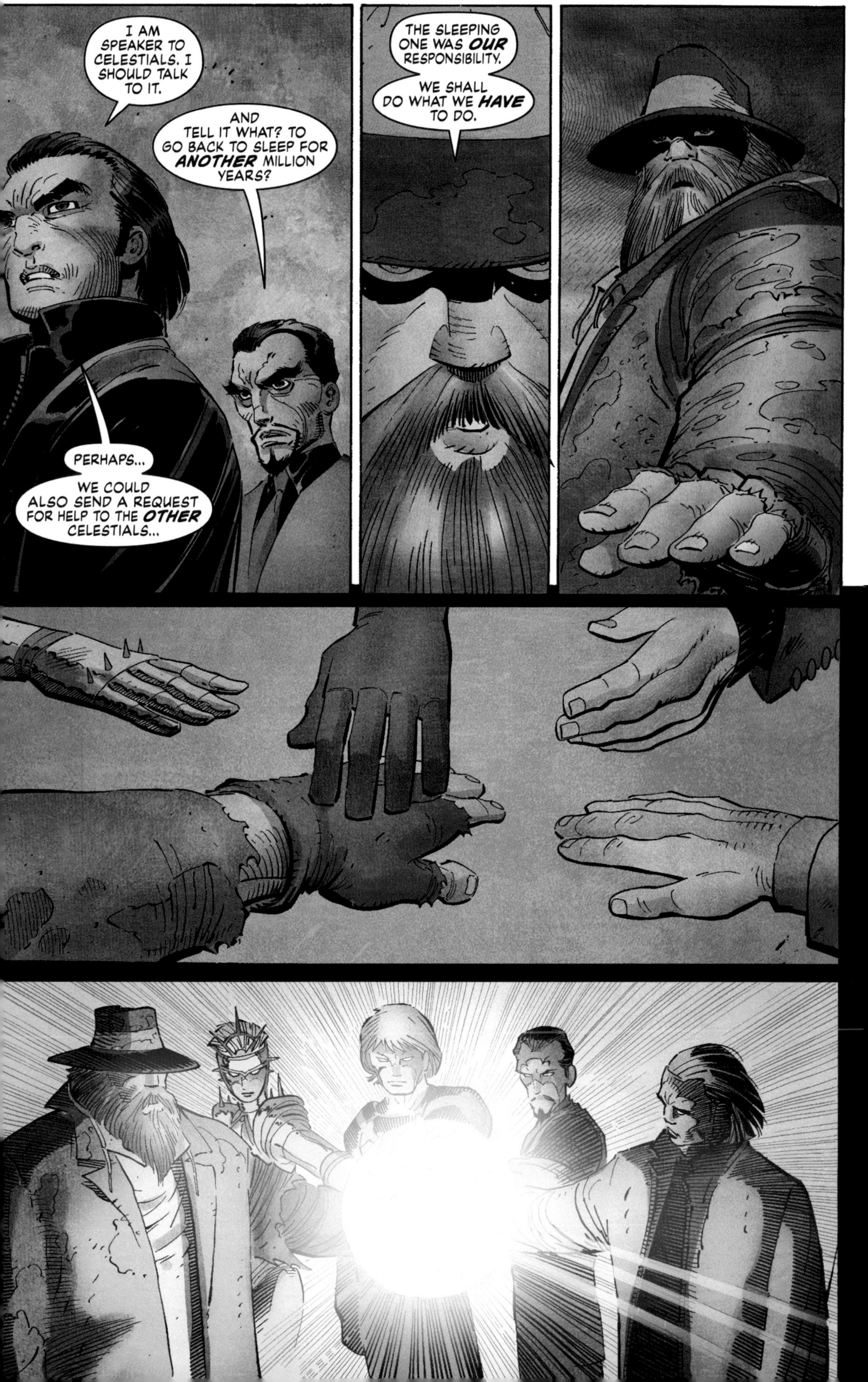
I AM SPEAKER TO CELESTIALS. I SHOULD TALK TO IT.
AND TELL IT WHAT? TO GO BACK TO SLEEP FOR ANOTHER MILLION YEARS?
PERHAPS... WE COULD ALSO SEND A REQUEST FOR HELP TO THE OTHER CELESTIALS...
THE SLEEPING ONE WAS OUR RESPONSIBILITY.
WE SHALL DO WHAT WE HAVE TO DO.

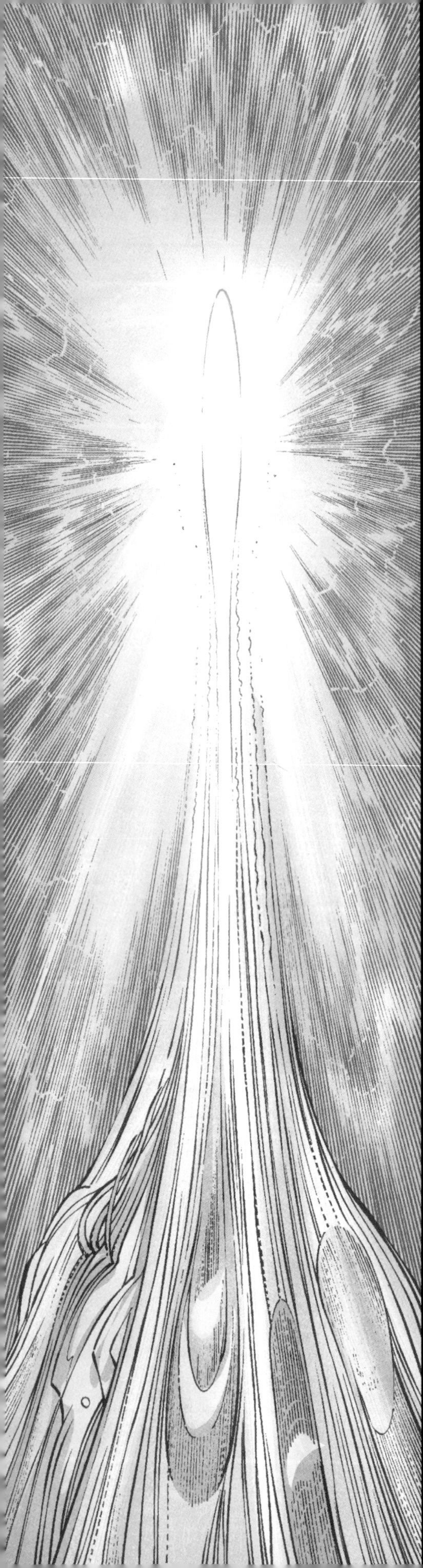

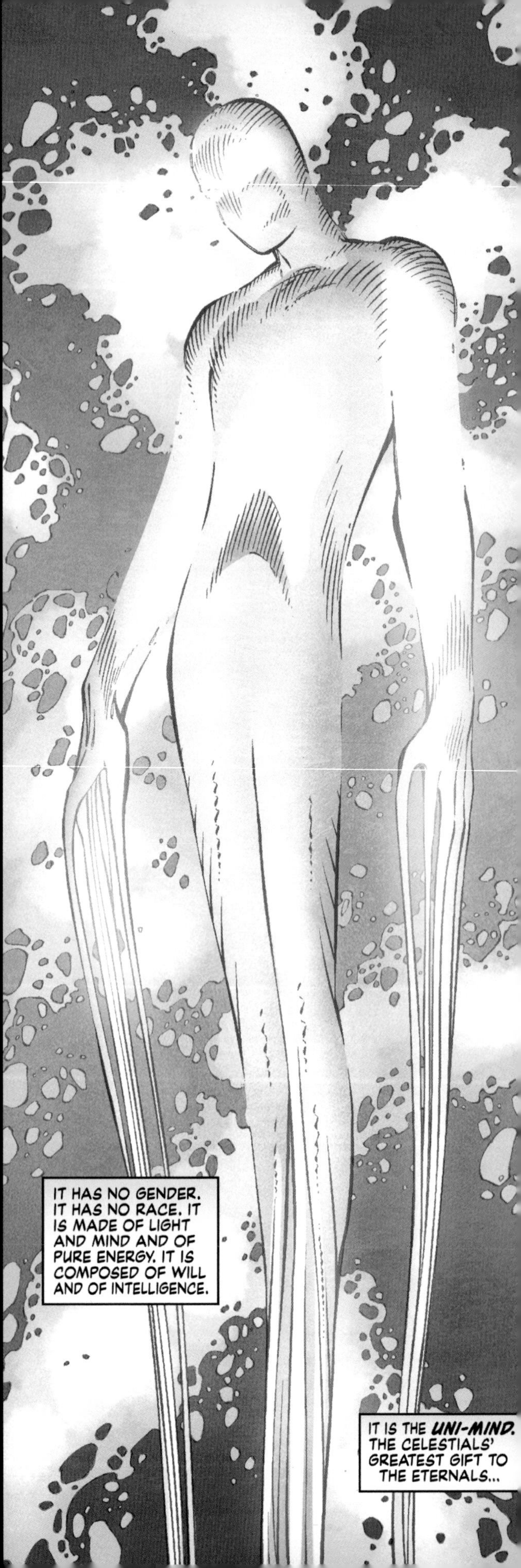
IT HAS NO GENDER. IT HAS NO RACE. IT IS MADE OF LIGHT AND MIND AND OF PURE ENERGY. IT IS COMPOSED OF WILL AND OF INTELLIGENCE.
IT IS THE UNI-MIND. THE CELESTIALS' GREATEST GIFT TO THE ETERNALS...

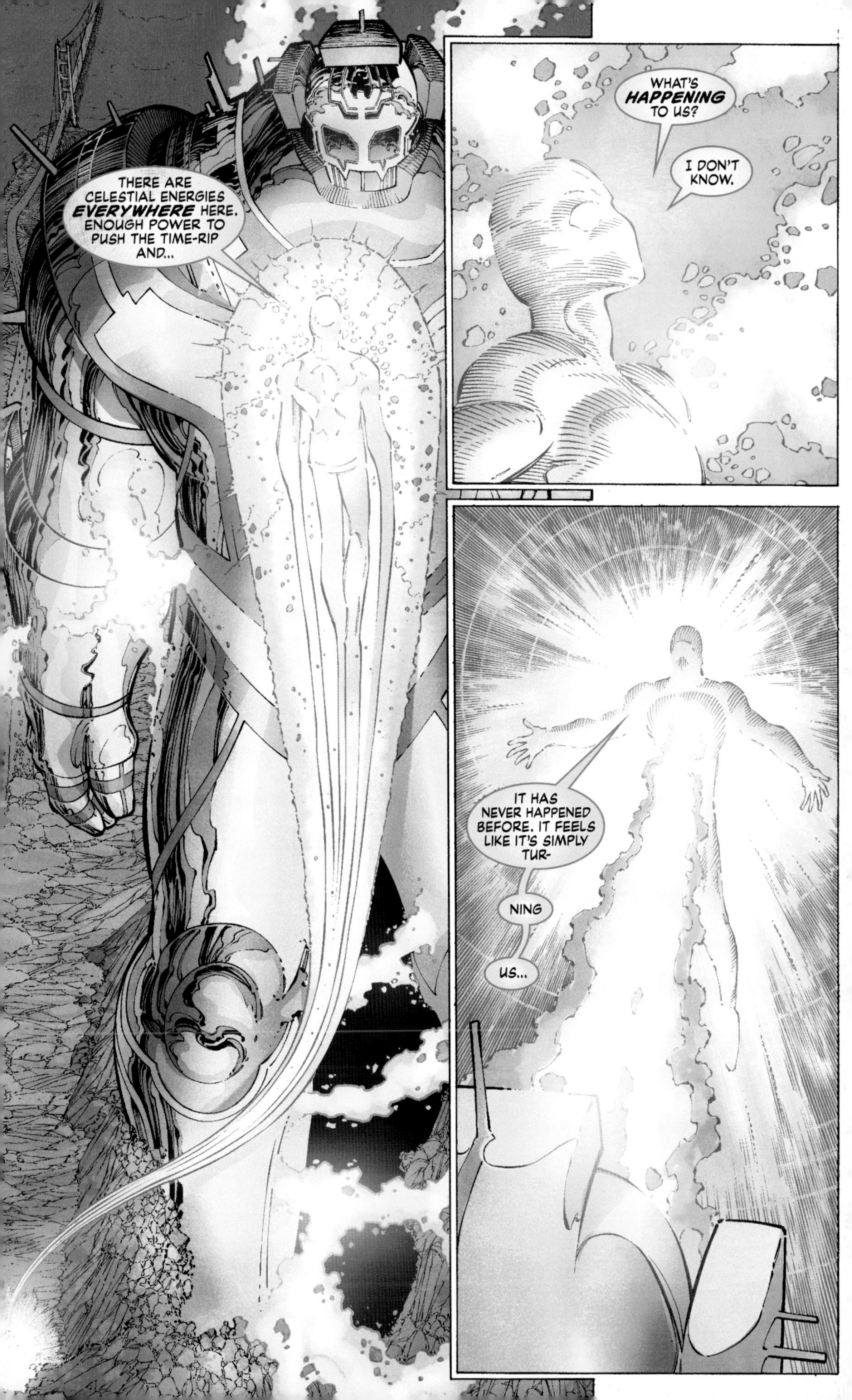
THERE ARE CELESTIAL ENERGIES EVERYWHERE HERE. ENOUGH POWER TO PUSH THE TIME-RIP AND...
WHAT'S HAPPENING TO US?
I DON'T KNOW.
IT HAS NEVER HAPPENED BEFORE. IT FEELS LIKE IT'S SIMPLY TUR-
NING
US...

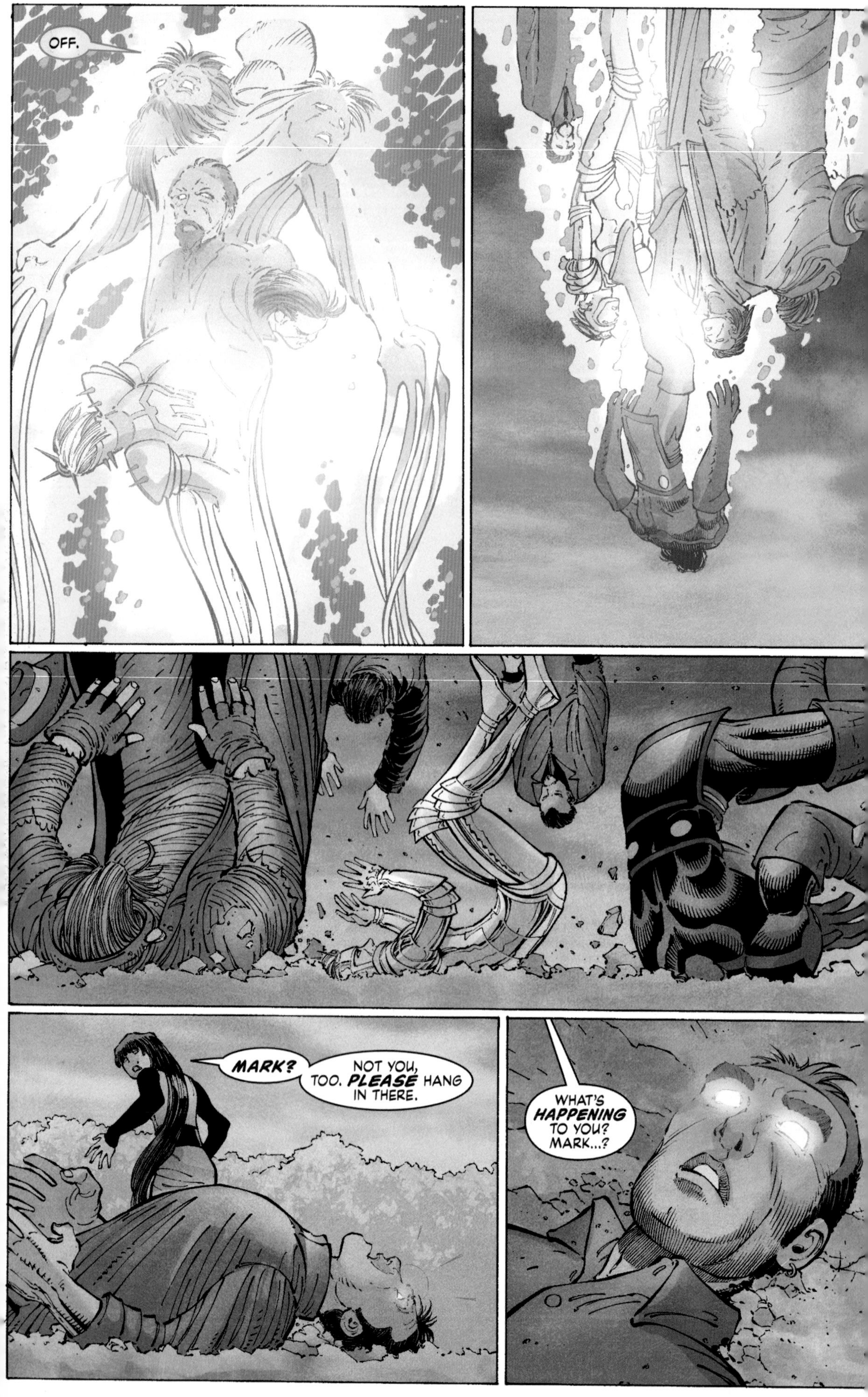
OFF.
MARK?
NOT YOU, TOO. PLEASE HANG IN THERE.
WHAT'S HAPPENING TO YOU? MARK...?

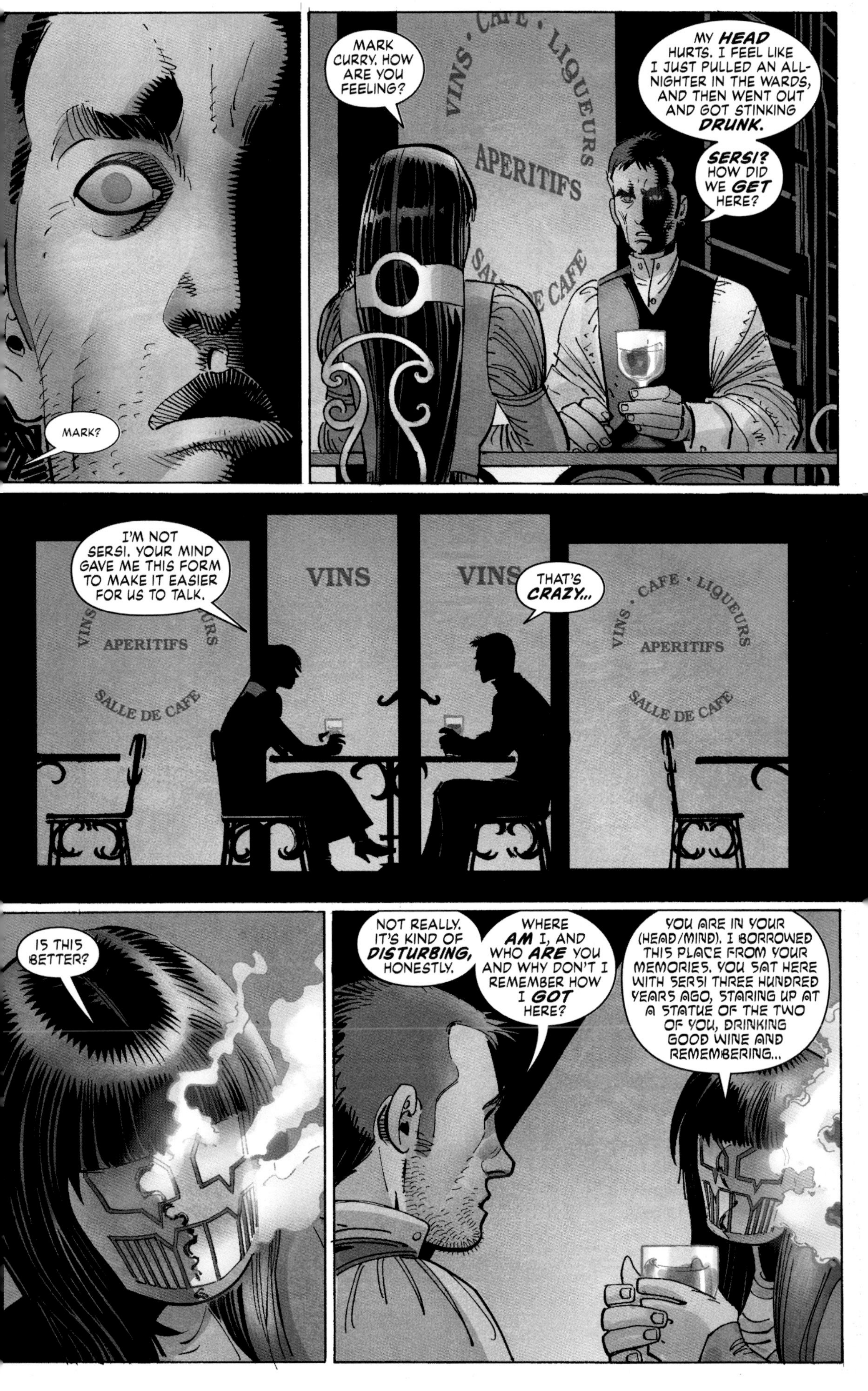
MARK?
MARK CURRY. HOW ARE YOU FEELING?
VINS . CAFE . LIQUEURS
APERITIFS
SALLE DE CAFE
MY HEAD HURTS. I FEEL LIKE I JUST PULLED AN ALL-NIGHTER IN THE WARDS, AND THEN WENT OUT AND GOT STINKING DRUNK.
SERSI? HOW DID WE GET HERE?
I'M NOT SERSI. YOUR MIND GAVE ME THIS FORM TO MAKE IT EASIER FOR US TO TALK.
VINS
VINS
THAT'S CRAZY...
APERITIFS
SALLE DE CAFE
VINS . CAFE . LIQUEURS
APERITIFS
SALLE DE CAFE
IS THIS BETTER?
NOT REALLY. IT'S KIND OF DISTURBING, HONESTLY.
WHERE AM I, AND WHO ARE YOU AND WHY DON'T I REMEMBER HOW I GOT HERE?
YOU ARE IN YOUR (HEAD/MIND). I BORROWED THIS PLACE FROM YOUR MEMORIES. YOU SAT HERE WITH SERSI THREE HUNDRED YEARS AGO, STARING UP AT A STATUE OF THE TWO OF YOU, DRINKING GOOD WINE AND REMEMBERING...

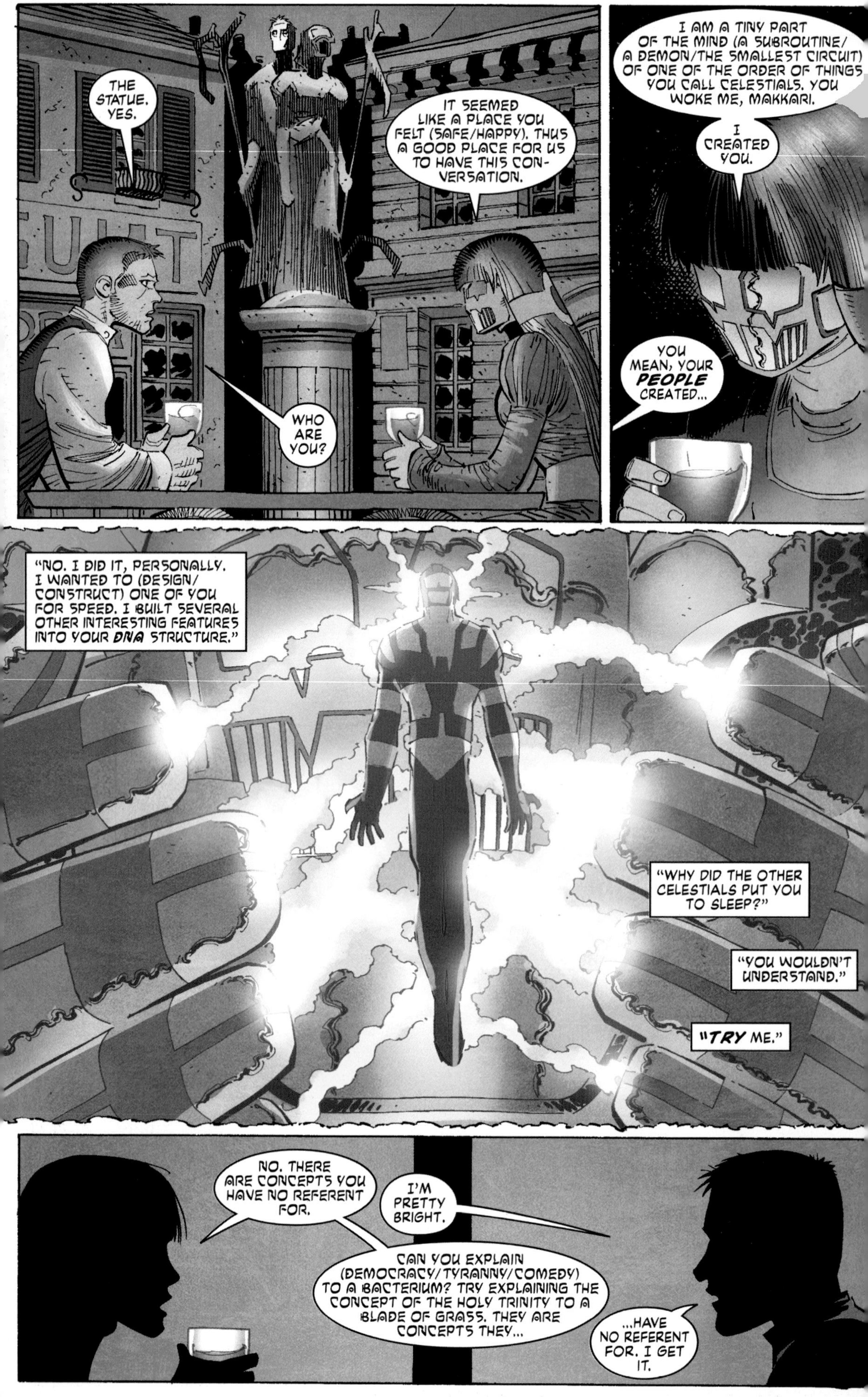
THE STATUE. YES.
IT SEEMED LIKE A PLACE YOU FELT (SAFE/HAPPY). THUS A GOOD PLACE FOR US TO HAVE THIS CONVERSATION.
WHO ARE YOU?
I AM A TINY PART OF THE MIND (A SUBROUTINE/ A DEMON/THE SMALLEST CIRCUIT) OF ONE OF THE ORDER OF THINGS YOU CALL CELESTIALS. YOU WOKE ME, MAKKARI.
I CREATED YOU.
YOU MEAN, YOUR **PEOPLE** CREATED...
"NO. I DID IT, PERSONALLY. I WANTED TO (DESIGN/ CONSTRUCT) ONE OF YOU FOR SPEED. I BUILT SEVERAL OTHER INTERESTING FEATURES INTO YOUR **DNA** STRUCTURE."
"WHY DID THE OTHER CELESTIALS PUT YOU TO SLEEP?"
"YOU WOULDN'T UNDERSTAND."
"**TRY** ME."
NO. THERE ARE CONCEPTS YOU HAVE NO REFERENT FOR.
I'M PRETTY BRIGHT.
CAN YOU EXPLAIN (DEMOCRACY/TYRANNY/COMEDY) TO A BACTERIUM? TRY EXPLAINING THE CONCEPT OF THE HOLY TRINITY TO A BLADE OF GRASS. THEY ARE CONCEPTS THEY...
...HAVE NO REFERENT FOR. I GET IT.

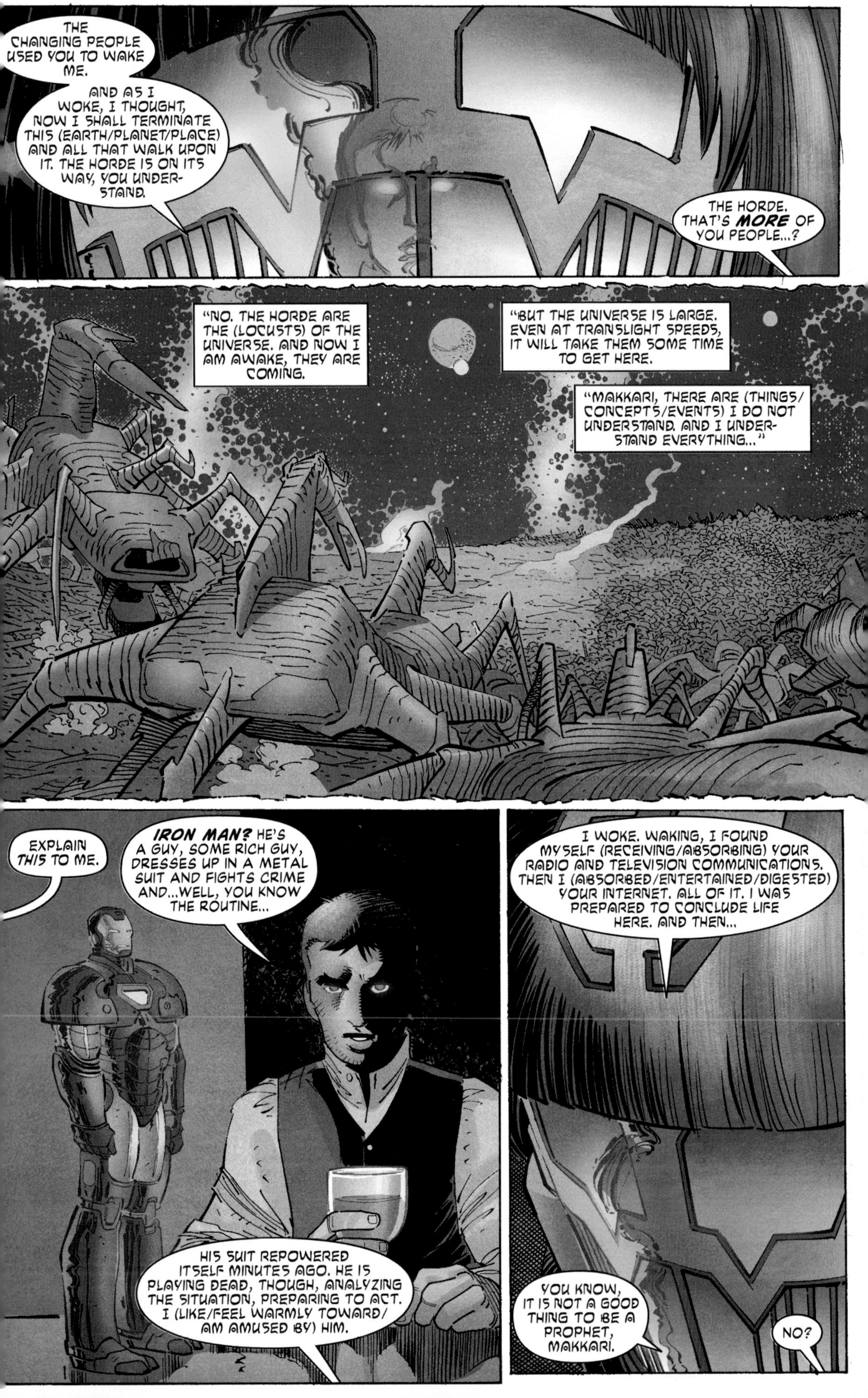
THE CHANGING PEOPLE USED YOU TO WAKE ME.
AND AS I WOKE, I THOUGHT, NOW I SHALL TERMINATE THIS (EARTH/PLANET/PLACE) AND ALL THAT WALK UPON IT. THE HORDE IS ON ITS WAY, YOU UNDER-STAND.
THE HORDE. THAT'S MORE OF YOU PEOPLE...?
"NO. THE HORDE ARE THE (LOCUSTS) OF THE UNIVERSE. AND NOW I AM AWAKE, THEY ARE COMING.
"BUT THE UNIVERSE IS LARGE. EVEN AT TRANSLIGHT SPEEDS, IT WILL TAKE THEM SOME TIME TO GET HERE.
"MAKKARI, THERE ARE (THINGS/CONCEPTS/EVENTS) I DO NOT UNDERSTAND. AND I UNDER-STAND EVERYTHING..."
EXPLAIN THIS TO ME.
IRON MAN? HE'S A GUY, SOME RICH GUY, DRESSES UP IN A METAL SUIT AND FIGHTS CRIME AND...WELL, YOU KNOW THE ROUTINE...
HIS SUIT REPOWERED ITSELF MINUTES AGO. HE IS PLAYING DEAD, THOUGH, ANALYZING THE SITUATION, PREPARING TO ACT. I (LIKE/FEEL WARMLY TOWARD/AM AMUSED BY) HIM.
I WOKE. WAKING, I FOUND MYSELF (RECEIVING/ABSORBING) YOUR RADIO AND TELEVISION COMMUNICATIONS. THEN I (ABSORBED/ENTERTAINED/DIGESTED) YOUR INTERNET. ALL OF IT. I WAS PREPARED TO CONCLUDE LIFE HERE. AND THEN...
YOU KNOW, IT IS NOT A GOOD THING TO BE A PROPHET, MAKKARI.
NO?

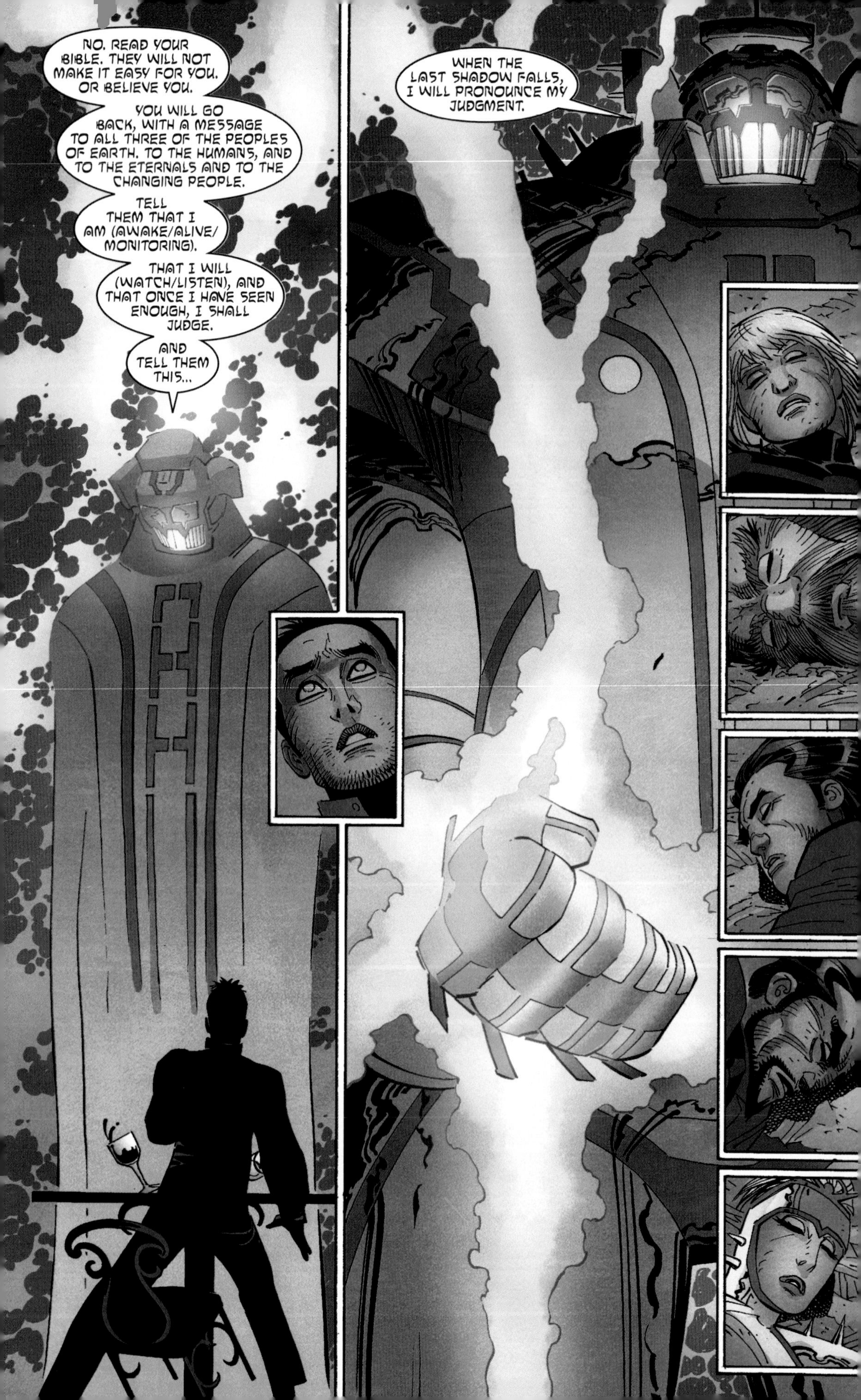
NO. READ YOUR BIBLE. THEY WILL NOT MAKE IT EASY FOR YOU. OR BELIEVE YOU.
YOU WILL GO BACK, WITH A MESSAGE TO ALL THREE OF THE PEOPLES OF EARTH. TO THE HUMANS, AND TO THE ETERNALS AND TO THE CHANGING PEOPLE.
TELL THEM THAT I AM (AWAKE/ALIVE/MONITORING).
THAT I WILL (WATCH/LISTEN), AND THAT ONCE I HAVE SEEN ENOUGH, I SHALL JUDGE.
AND TELL THEM THIS...
WHEN THE LAST SHADOW FALLS, I WILL PRONOUNCE MY JUDGMENT.

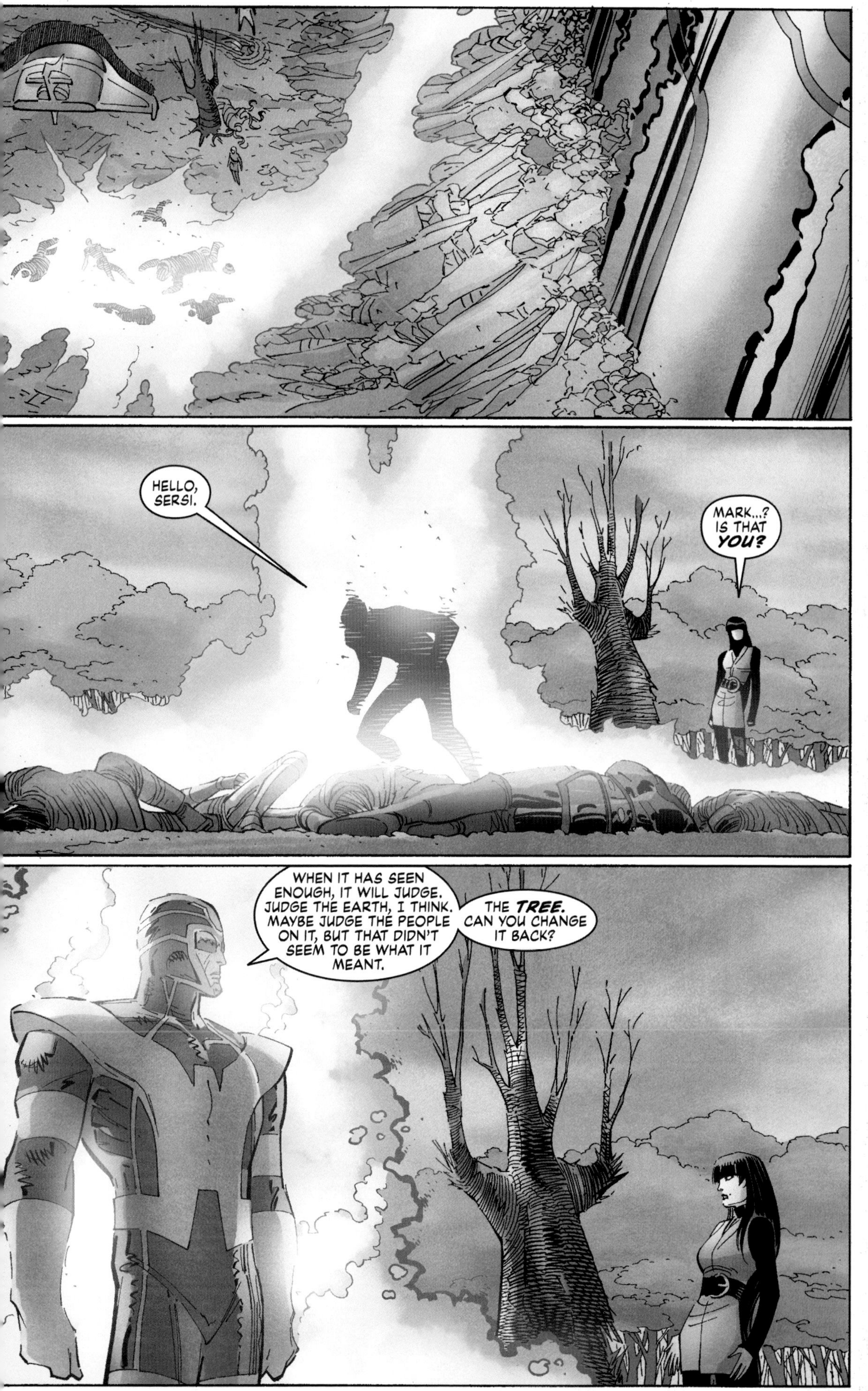
HELLO, SERSI.
MARK...? IS THAT *YOU?*
WHEN IT HAS SEEN ENOUGH, IT WILL JUDGE. JUDGE THE EARTH, I THINK. MAYBE JUDGE THE PEOPLE ON IT, BUT THAT DIDN'T SEEM TO BE WHAT IT MEANT.
THE *TREE.* CAN YOU CHANGE IT BACK?

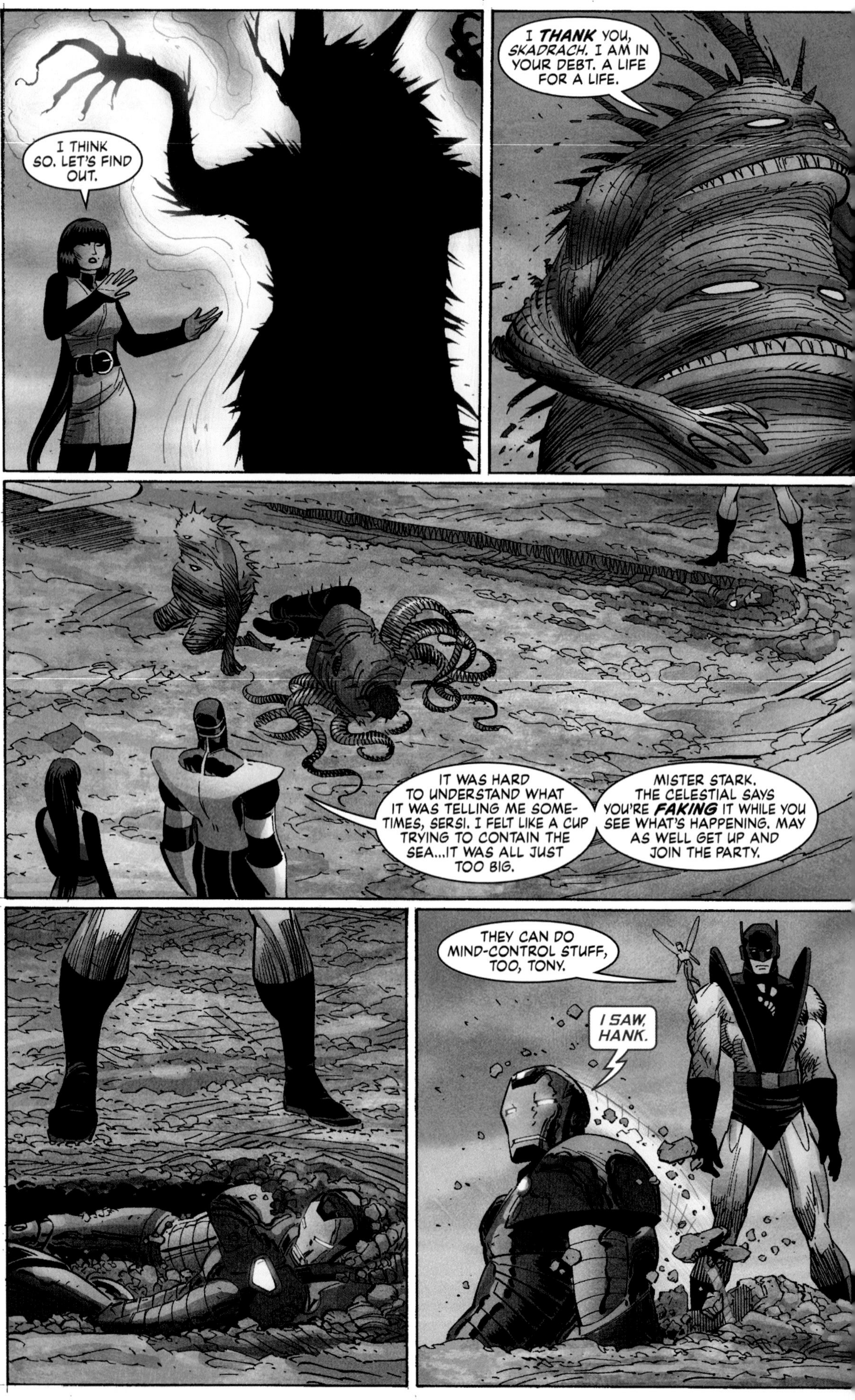
I THINK SO. LET'S FIND OUT.
I THANK YOU, SKADRACH. I AM IN YOUR DEBT. A LIFE FOR A LIFE.
IT WAS HARD TO UNDERSTAND WHAT IT WAS TELLING ME SOME-TIMES, SERSI. I FELT LIKE A CUP TRYING TO CONTAIN THE SEA...IT WAS ALL JUST TOO BIG.
MISTER STARK. THE CELESTIAL SAYS YOU'RE FAKING IT WHILE YOU SEE WHAT'S HAPPENING. MAY AS WELL GET UP AND JOIN THE PARTY.
THEY CAN DO MIND-CONTROL STUFF, TOO, TONY.
I SAW, HANK.

DO YOU THINK YOU CAN FIX HIM, SERSI?

I DON'T KNOW. HE TOOK AN EYE-BLAST FULL ON.

TRY. JUST TELL HIS CELLS TO REGENERATE THEMSELVES.

DOES THIS THING *REALLY* HAVE THE ABILITY TO DESTROY THE WORLD?

CERTAINLY.

WE HAVE TO *FIGHT* IT. WE HAVE TO *REMOVE* IT.

NO. IT WILL REMAIN *HERE*, IN THE PARK.

IT WILL NOT BE DISTURBED. NOT BY *YOU.* NOT BY *ANYONE.*

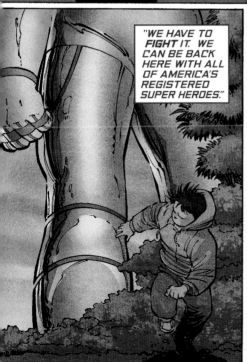

"WE HAVE TO *FIGHT* IT. WE CAN BE BACK HERE WITH ALL OF AMERICA'S REGISTERED SUPER HEROES."

IT CAN'T STOP *ALL* OF US.

WE'VE FOUGHT ALIENS BEFORE.

DOESN'T MATTER. YOU CAN'T *HURT* IT. YOU CAN'T EVEN *AFFECT* IT. YOU CAN'T DO ANYTHING TO IT IT DOESN'T *WANT* YOU TO DO.

LISTEN. IT'S JUST AN *ALIEN SPACE ROBOT.* IT'S NOT *GOD.*

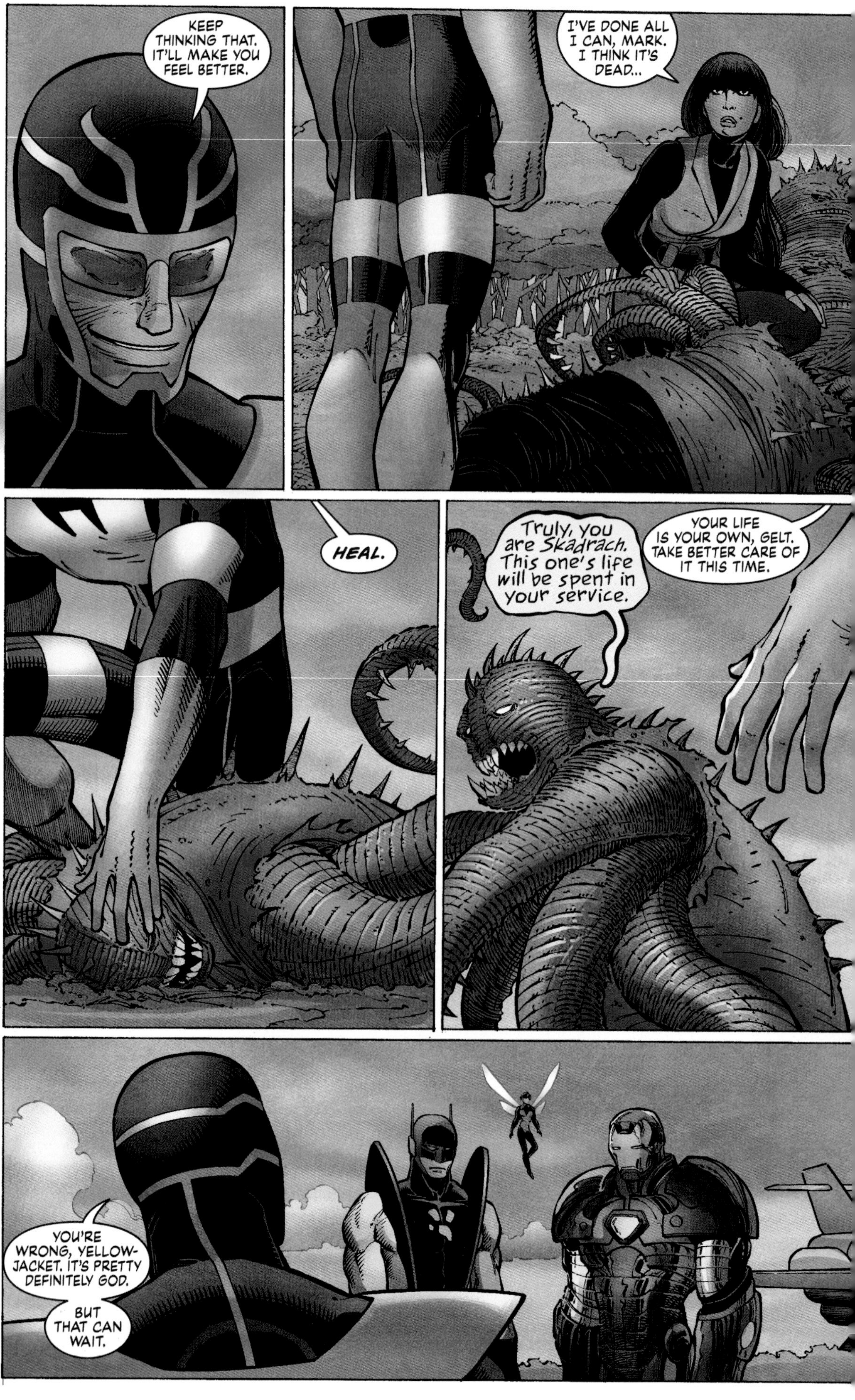
KEEP THINKING THAT. IT'LL MAKE YOU FEEL BETTER.
I'VE DONE ALL I CAN, MARK. I THINK IT'S DEAD...
HEAL.
Truly, you are Skadrach. This one's life will be spent in your service.
YOUR LIFE IS YOUR OWN, GELT. TAKE BETTER CARE OF IT THIS TIME.
YOU'RE WRONG, YELLOW-JACKET. IT'S PRETTY DEFINITELY GOD.
BUT THAT CAN WAIT.

AND BY THE WAY, IRON MAN...? IT *LIKES* YOU.

WHO *ARE* YOU PEOPLE? *WHAT* *ARE* YOU?

WE ARE THE ETERNALS. WE ARE THE COURT OF LAST RESORT FOR HUMANITY AND FOR ALL LIVING THINGS ON EARTH.

WHOSE SIDE ARE YOU ON?

WE DO NOT CHOOSE SIDES. COUNTRIES ARE LINES IN THE SAND. EMPIRES RISE AND FALL. WE ARE TIMELESS. WE WILL STILL BE HERE TOMORROW, AND A HUNDRED CENTURIES FROM NOW.

YOU *HAVE* TO CHOOSE SIDES. YOU HAVE TO *REGISTER.*

IF YOU SAW TWO GROUPS OF CHILDREN ARGUING OVER WHICH OF THEM COULD PLAY IN SOME WASTE GROUND, WOULD YOU CHOOSE SIDES?

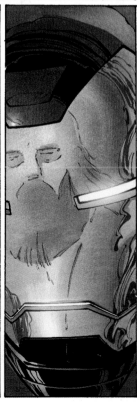

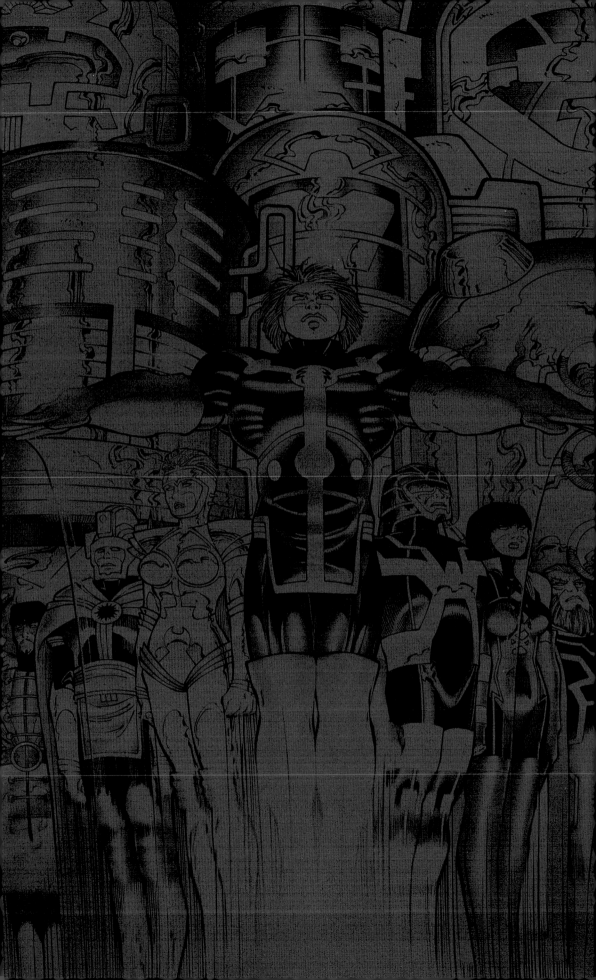

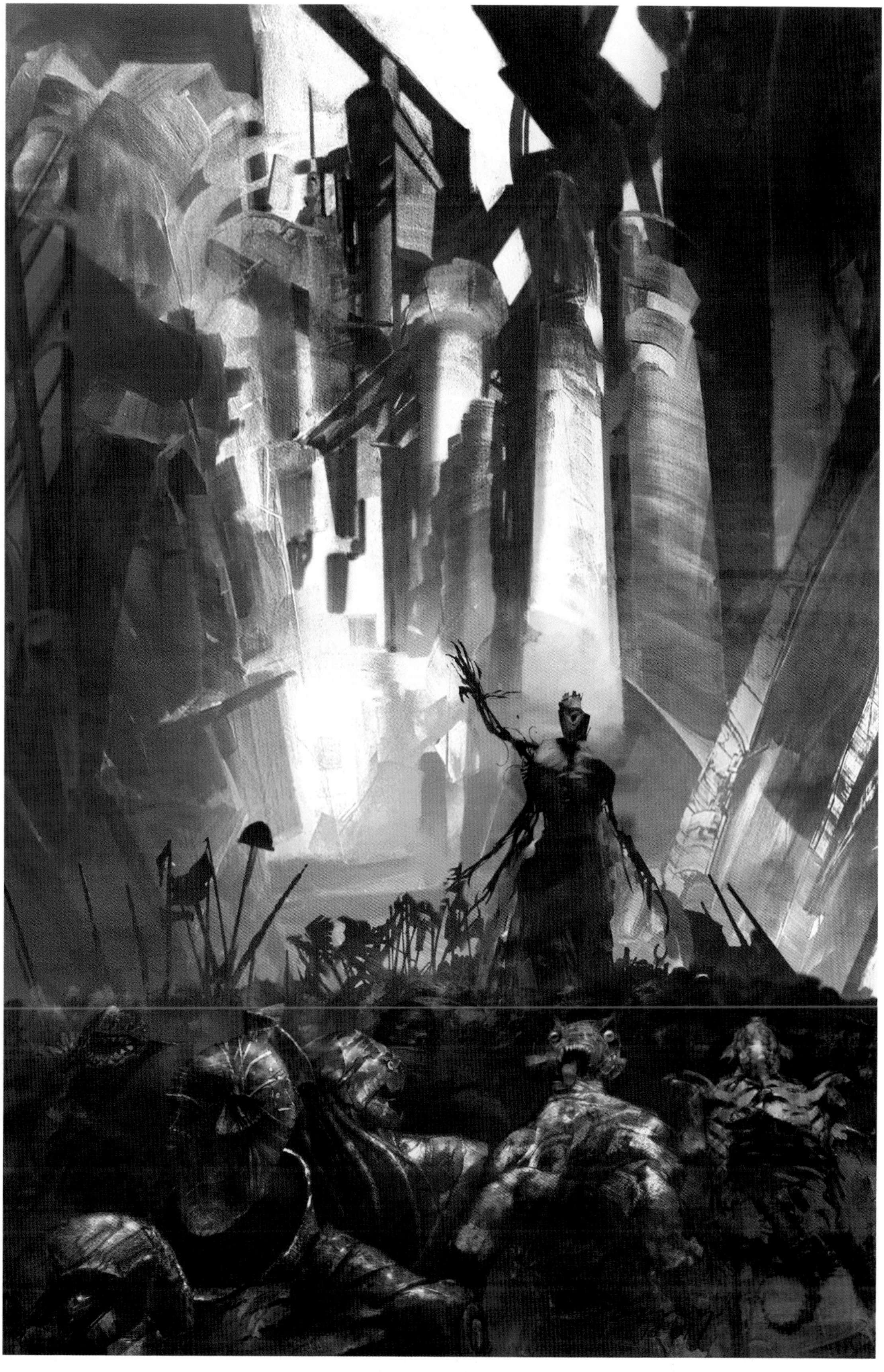

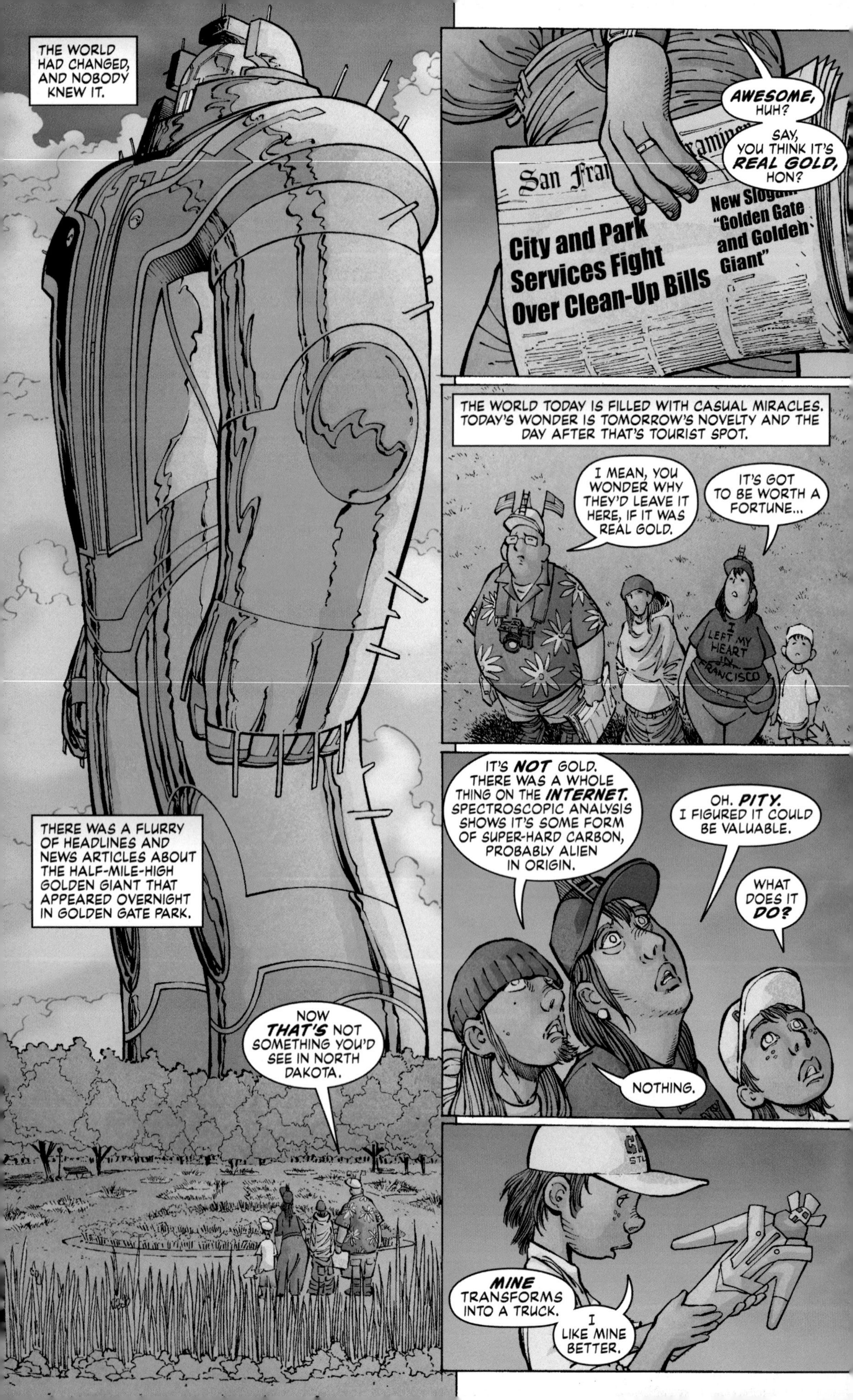
THE WORLD HAD CHANGED, AND NOBODY KNEW IT.
THERE WAS A FLURRY OF HEADLINES AND NEWS ARTICLES ABOUT THE HALF-MILE-HIGH GOLDEN GIANT THAT APPEARED OVERNIGHT IN GOLDEN GATE PARK.
NOW THAT'S NOT SOMETHING YOU'D SEE IN NORTH DAKOTA.
AWESOME, HUH?
SAY, YOU THINK IT'S REAL GOLD, HON?
San Fran
City and Park Services Fight Over Clean-Up Bills
New Slogan "Golden Gate and Golden Giant"
THE WORLD TODAY IS FILLED WITH CASUAL MIRACLES. TODAY'S WONDER IS TOMORROW'S NOVELTY AND THE DAY AFTER THAT'S TOURIST SPOT.
I MEAN, YOU WONDER WHY THEY'D LEAVE IT HERE, IF IT WAS REAL GOLD.
IT'S GOT TO BE WORTH A FORTUNE...
I LEFT MY HEART IN SAN FRANCISCO
IT'S NOT GOLD. THERE WAS A WHOLE THING ON THE INTERNET. SPECTROSCOPIC ANALYSIS SHOWS IT'S SOME FORM OF SUPER-HARD CARBON, PROBABLY ALIEN IN ORIGIN.
OH. PITY. I FIGURED IT COULD BE VALUABLE.
WHAT DOES IT DO?
NOTHING.
MINE TRANSFORMS INTO A TRUCK.
I LIKE MINE BETTER.

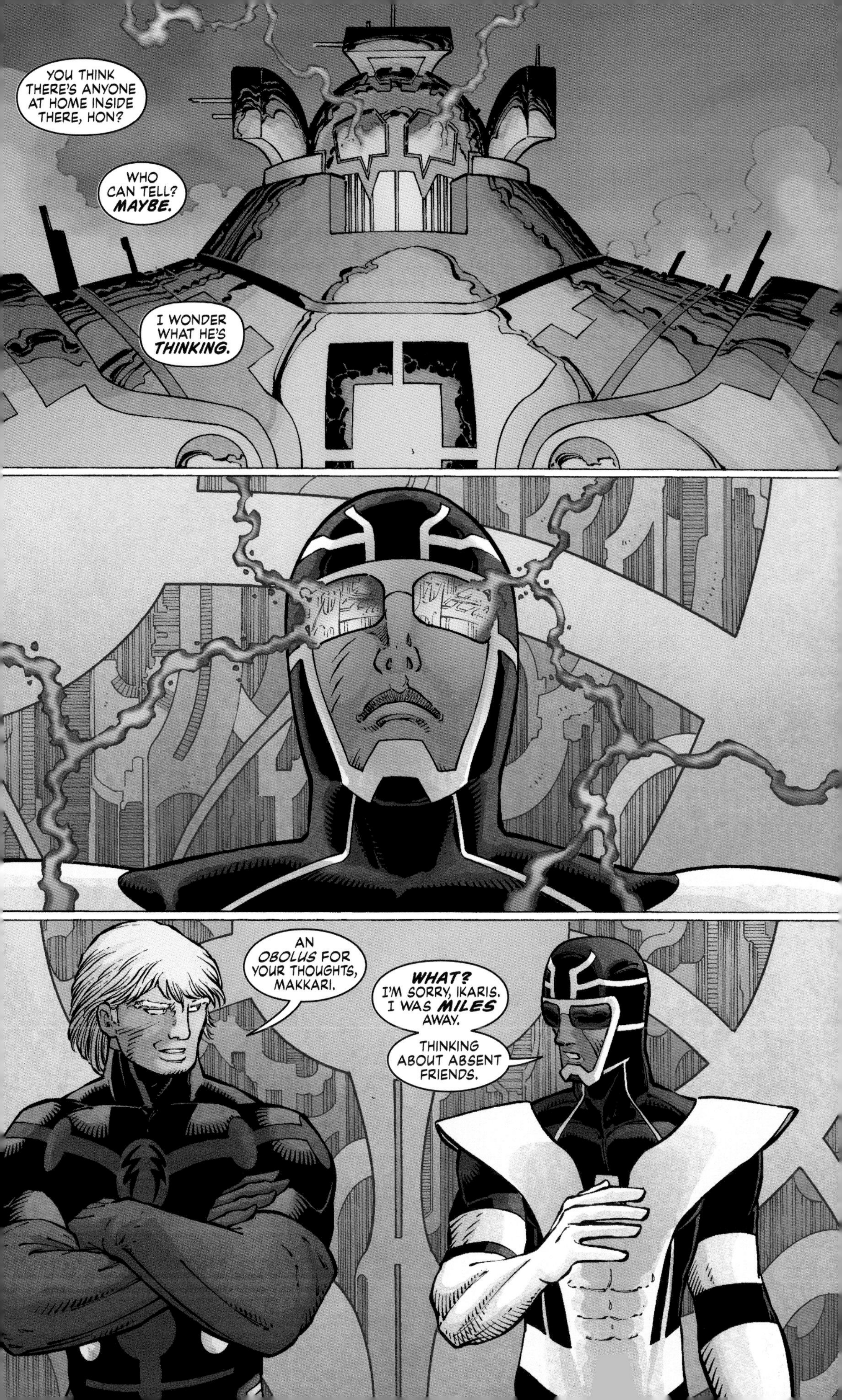
YOU THINK THERE'S ANYONE AT HOME INSIDE THERE, HON?
WHO CAN TELL? MAYBE.
I WONDER WHAT HE'S THINKING.
AN OBOLUS FOR YOUR THOUGHTS, MAKKARI.
WHAT? I'M SORRY, IKARIS. I WAS MILES AWAY.
THINKING ABOUT ABSENT FRIENDS.

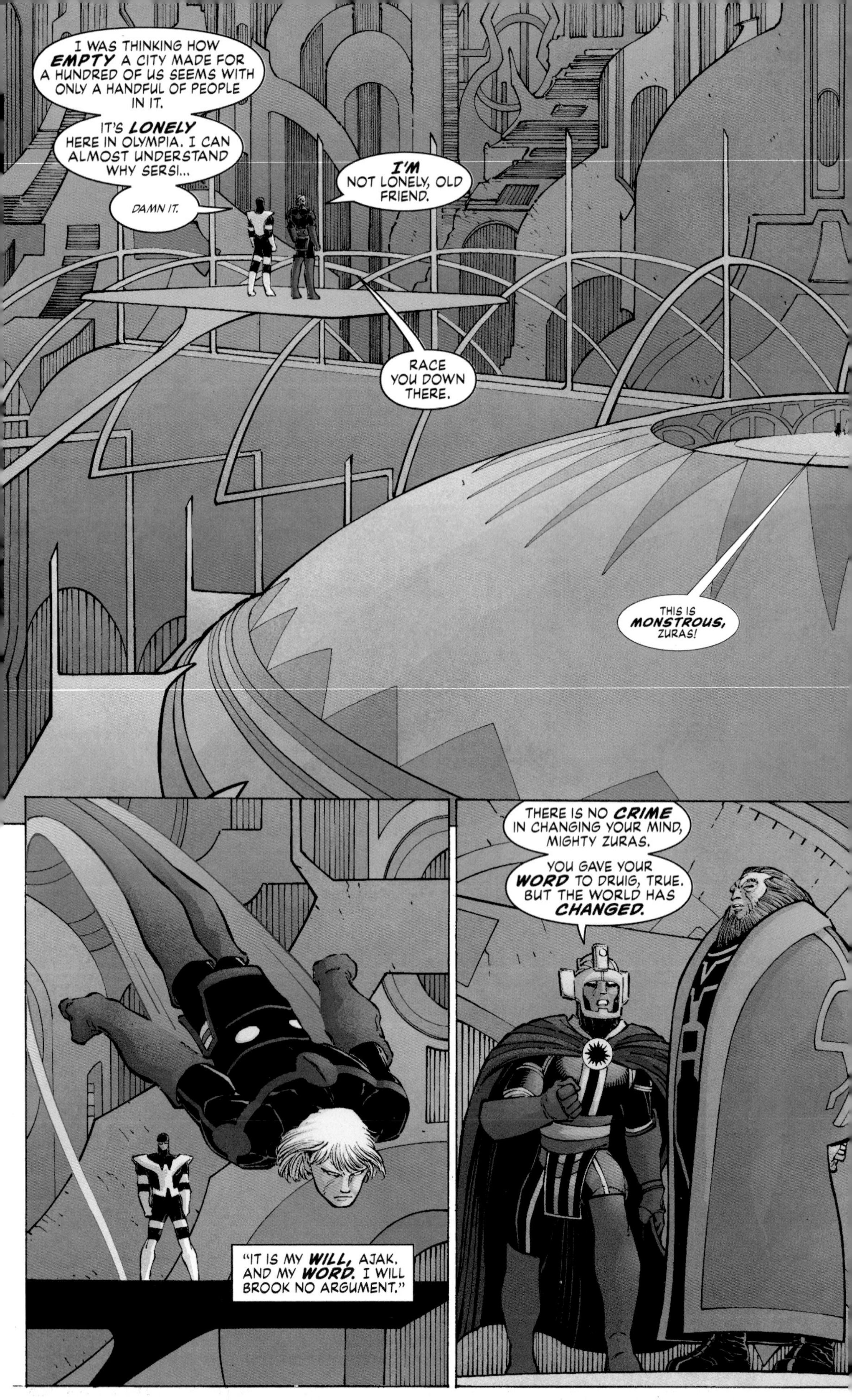
I WAS THINKING HOW EMPTY A CITY MADE FOR A HUNDRED OF US SEEMS WITH ONLY A HANDFUL OF PEOPLE IN IT.
IT'S LONELY HERE IN OLYMPIA. I CAN ALMOST UNDERSTAND WHY SERSI...
DAMN IT.
I'M NOT LONELY, OLD FRIEND.
RACE YOU DOWN THERE.
THIS IS MONSTROUS, ZURAS!
"IT IS MY WILL, AJAK. AND MY WORD. I WILL BROOK NO ARGUMENT."
THERE IS NO CRIME IN CHANGING YOUR MIND, MIGHTY ZURAS.
YOU GAVE YOUR WORD TO DRUIG, TRUE. BUT THE WORLD HAS CHANGED.

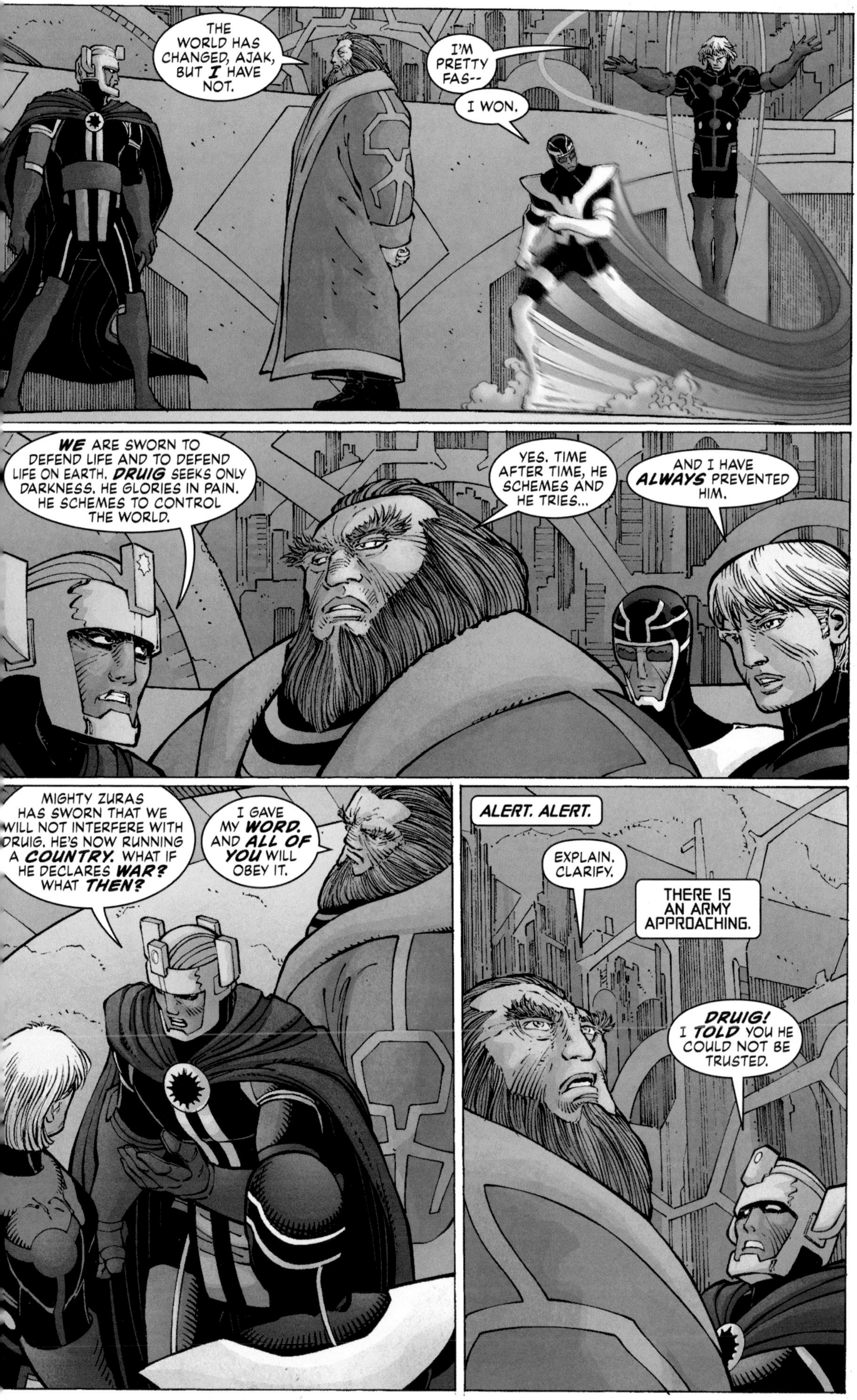
THE WORLD HAS CHANGED, AJAK, BUT I HAVE NOT.
I'M PRETTY FAS--
I WON.
WE ARE SWORN TO DEFEND LIFE AND TO DEFEND LIFE ON EARTH. DRUIG SEEKS ONLY DARKNESS. HE GLORIES IN PAIN. HE SCHEMES TO CONTROL THE WORLD.
YES. TIME AFTER TIME, HE SCHEMES AND HE TRIES...
AND I HAVE ALWAYS PREVENTED HIM.
MIGHTY ZURAS HAS SWORN THAT WE WILL NOT INTERFERE WITH DRUIG. HE'S NOW RUNNING A COUNTRY. WHAT IF HE DECLARES WAR? WHAT THEN?
I GAVE MY WORD. AND ALL OF YOU WILL OBEY IT.
ALERT. ALERT.
EXPLAIN. CLARIFY.
THERE IS AN ARMY APPROACHING.
DRUIG! I TOLD YOU HE COULD NOT BE TRUSTED.

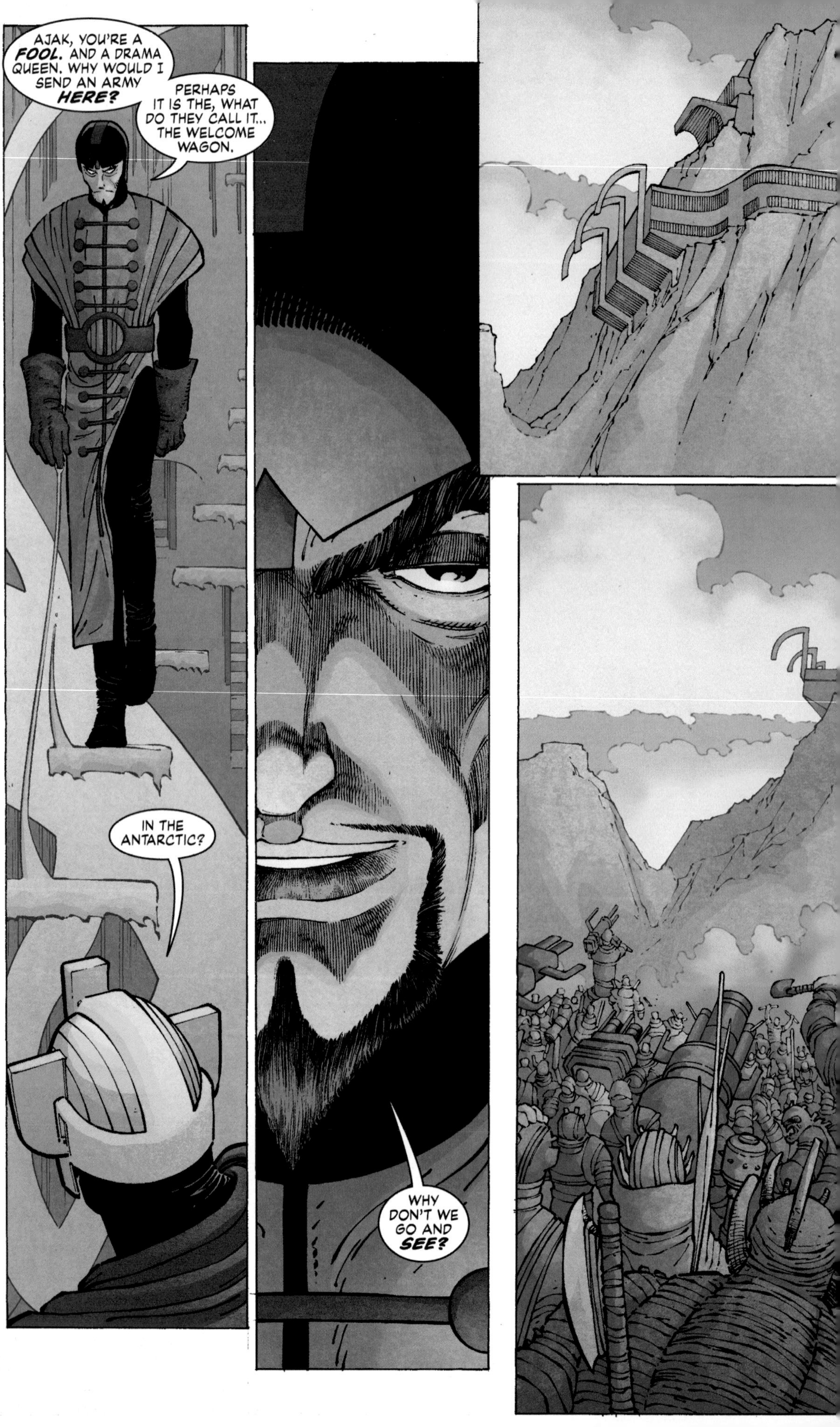
AJAK, YOU'RE A FOOL. AND A DRAMA QUEEN. WHY WOULD I SEND AN ARMY HERE?
PERHAPS IT IS THE, WHAT DO THEY CALL IT... THE WELCOME WAGON.
IN THE ANTARCTIC?
WHY DON'T WE GO AND SEE?

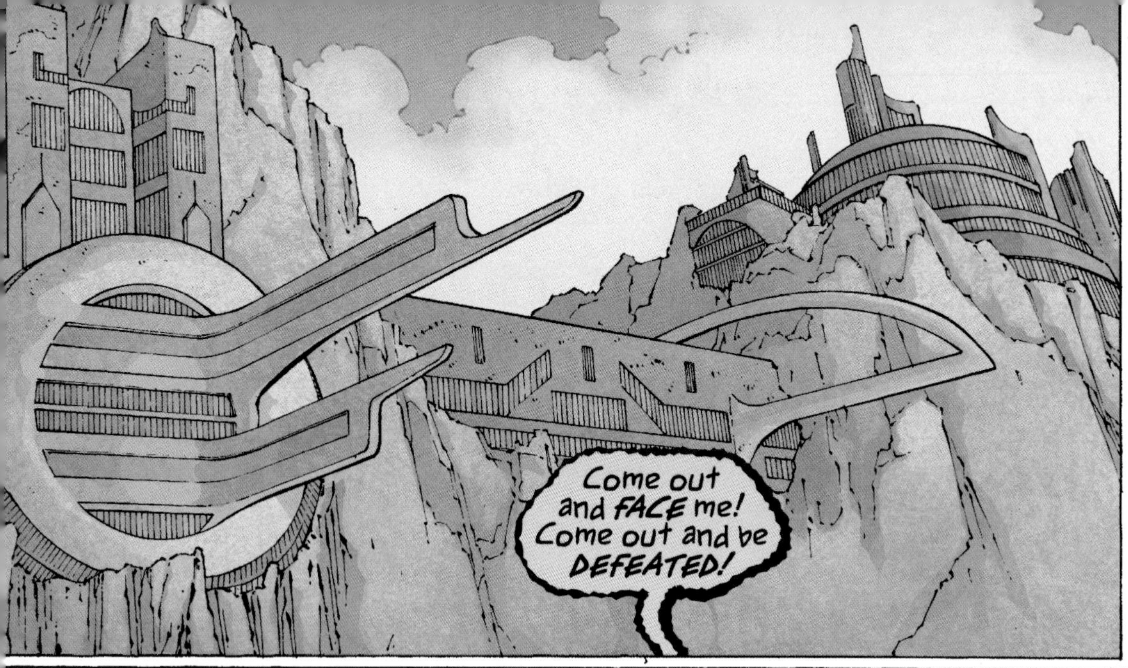
Come out and FACE me! Come out and be DEFEATED!

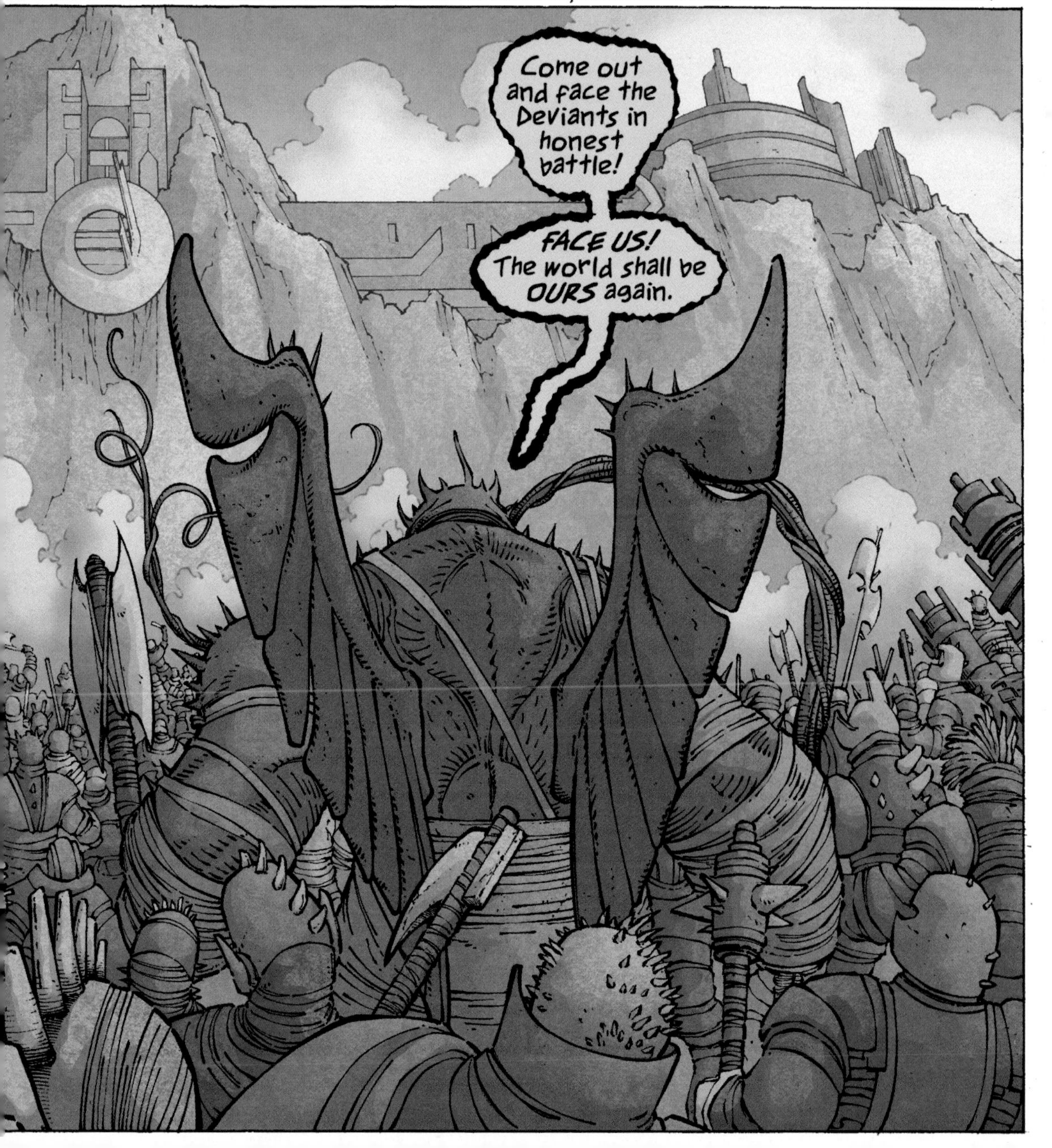
Come out and face the Deviants in honest battle!
FACE US! The world shall be OURS again.

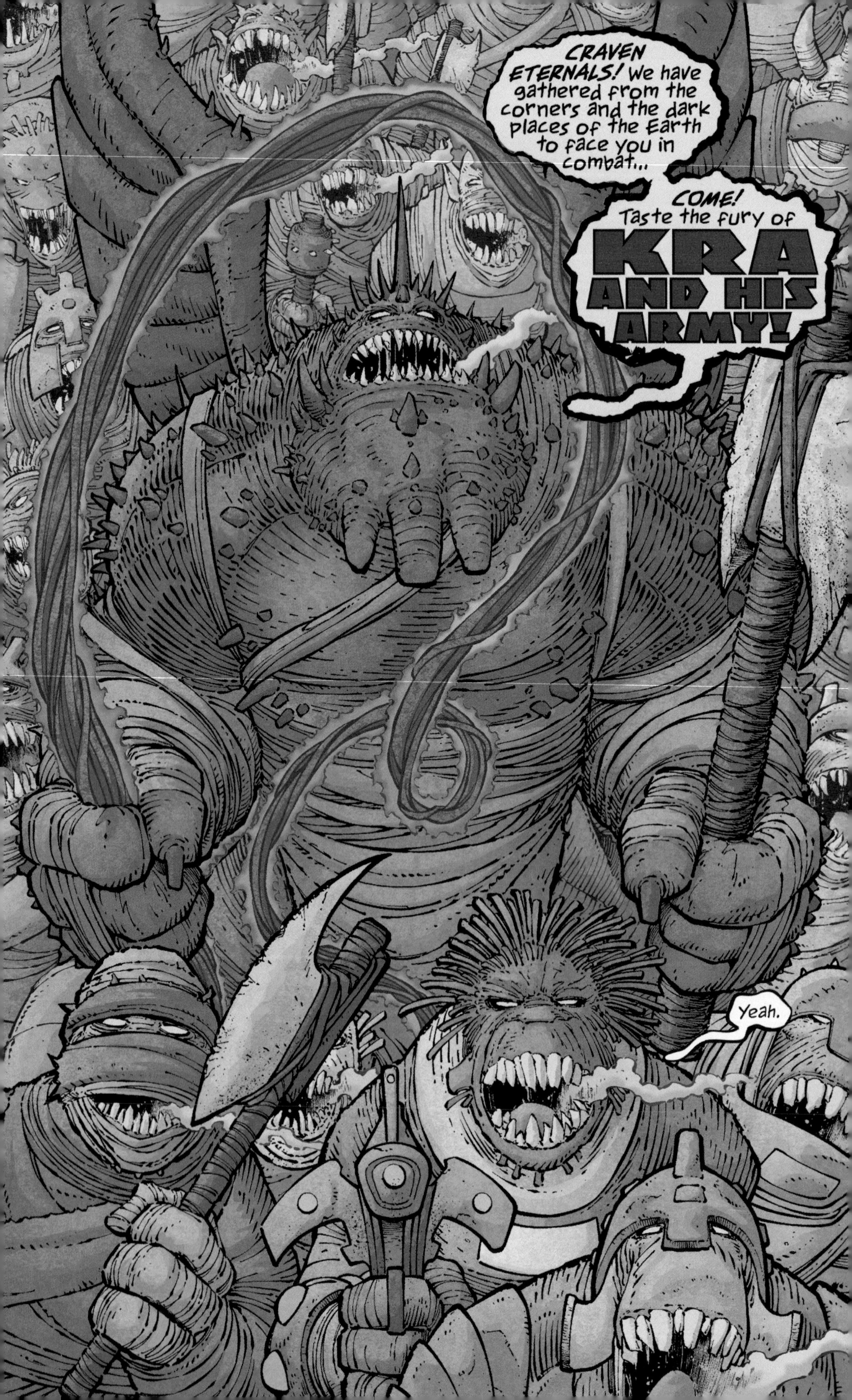
CRAVEN ETERNALS! We have gathered from the corners and the dark places of the Earth to face you in combat...
COME! Taste the fury of KRA AND HIS ARMY!
Yeah.

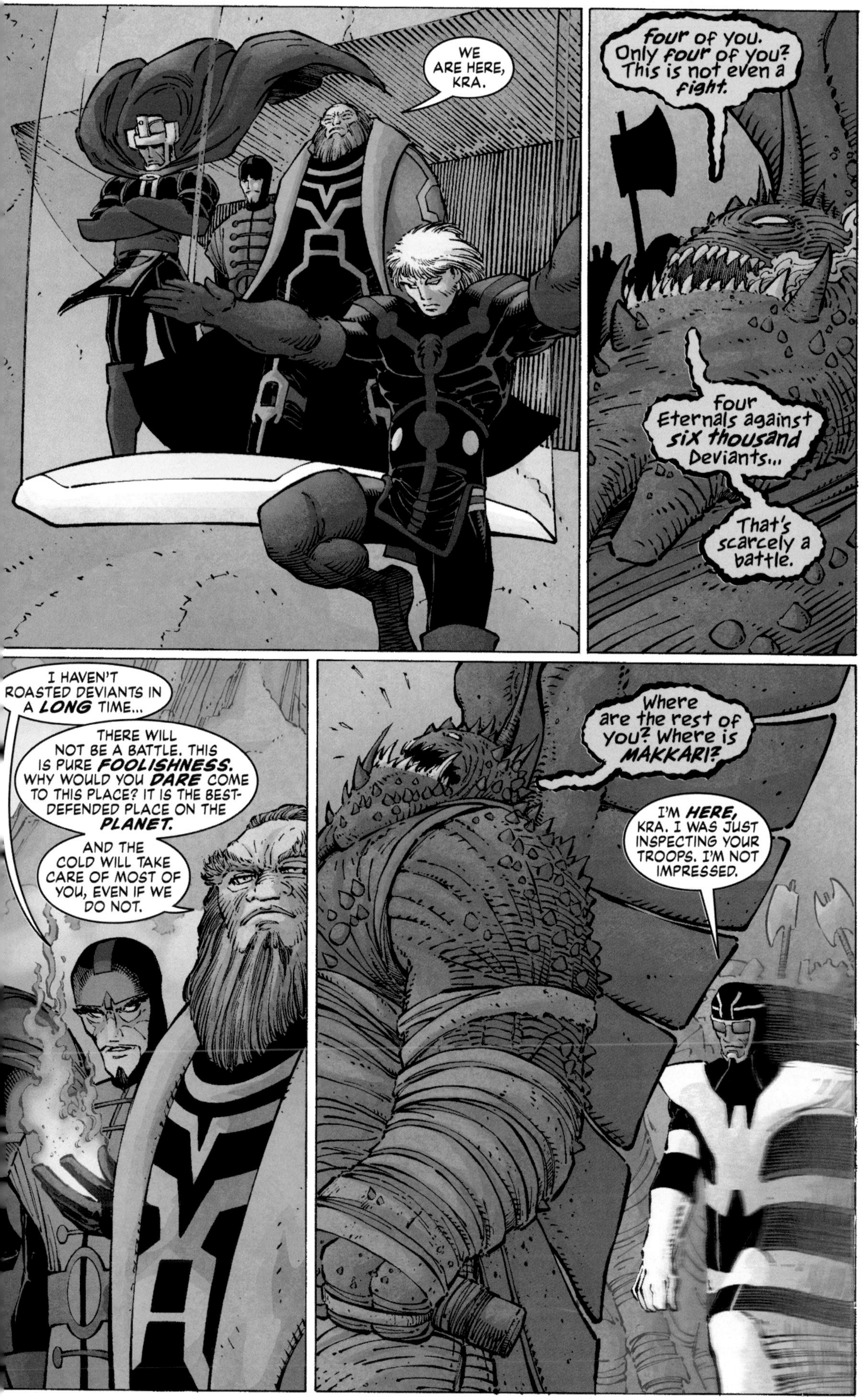
WE ARE HERE, KRA.
Four of you. Only four of you? This is not even a fight.
Four Eternals against six thousand Deviants...
That's scarcely a battle.
I HAVEN'T ROASTED DEVIANTS IN A LONG TIME...
THERE WILL NOT BE A BATTLE. THIS IS PURE FOOLISHNESS. WHY WOULD YOU DARE COME TO THIS PLACE? IT IS THE BEST-DEFENDED PLACE ON THE PLANET.
AND THE COLD WILL TAKE CARE OF MOST OF YOU, EVEN IF WE DO NOT.
Where are the rest of you? Where is MAKKARI?
I'M HERE, KRA. I WAS JUST INSPECTING YOUR TROOPS. I'M NOT IMPRESSED.

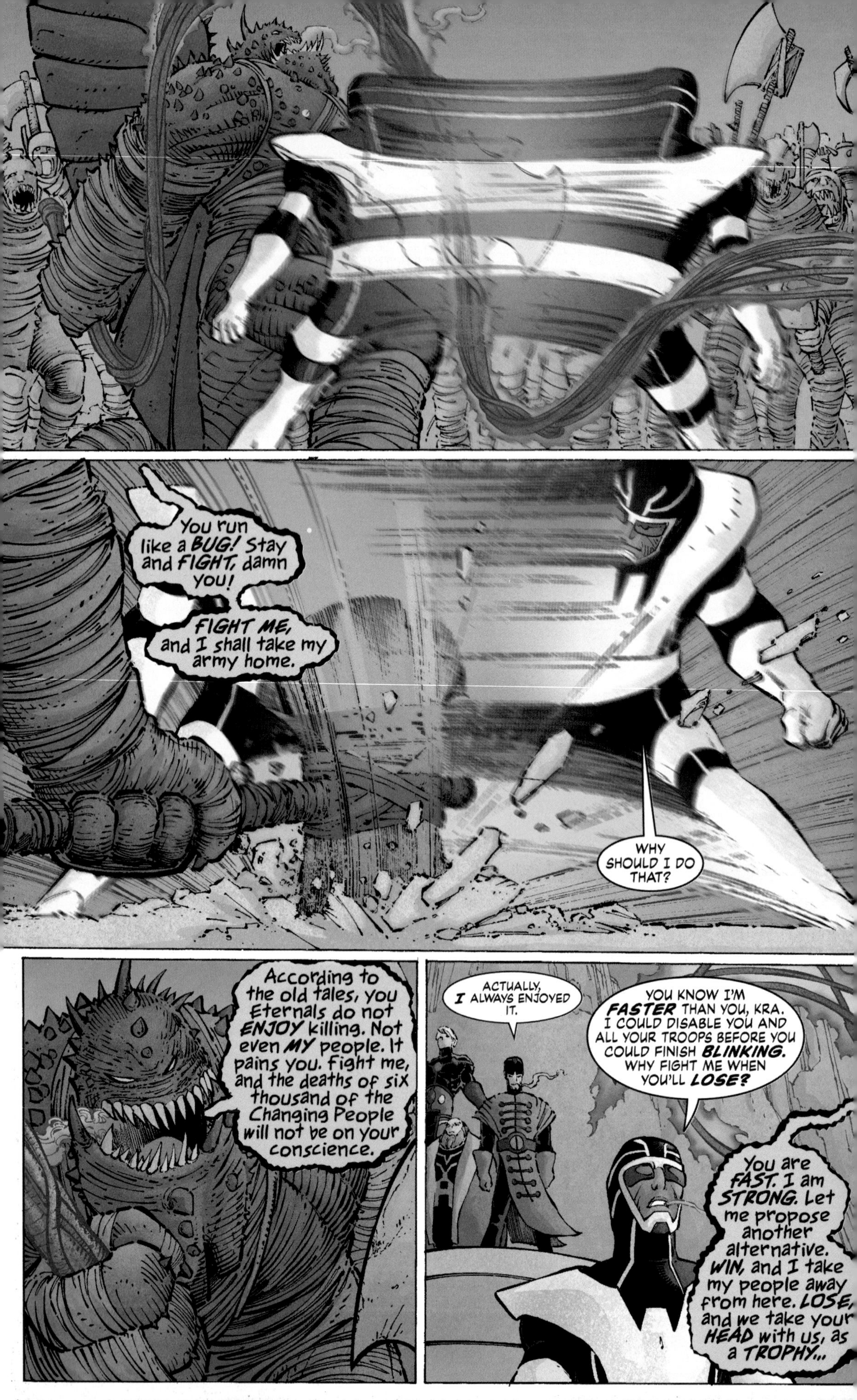
You run like a BUG! Stay and FIGHT, damn you!
FIGHT ME, and I shall take my army home.
WHY SHOULD I DO THAT?
According to the old tales, you Eternals do not ENJOY killing. Not even MY people. It pains you. Fight me, and the deaths of six thousand of the Changing People will not be on your conscience.
ACTUALLY, I ALWAYS ENJOYED IT.
YOU KNOW I'M FASTER THAN YOU, KRA. I COULD DISABLE YOU AND ALL YOUR TROOPS BEFORE YOU COULD FINISH BLINKING. WHY FIGHT ME WHEN YOU'LL LOSE?
You are FAST. I am STRONG. Let me propose another alternative. WIN, and I take my people away from here. LOSE, and we take your HEAD with us, as a TROPHY...

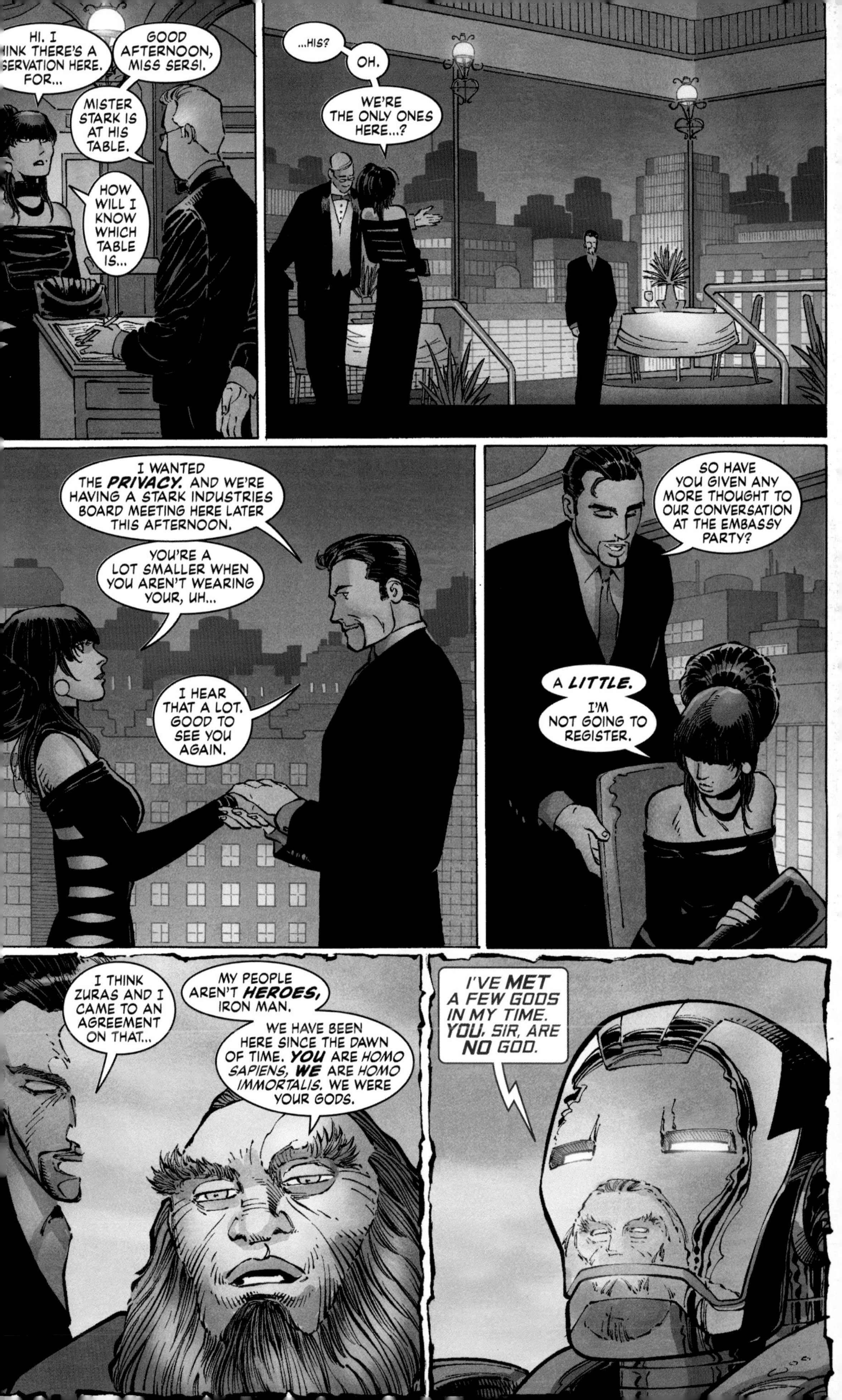

HI. I
INK THERE'S A
SERVATION HERE.
FOR...
GOOD AFTERNOON, MISS SERSI.
MISTER STARK IS AT HIS TABLE.
HOW WILL I KNOW WHICH TABLE IS...
...HIS?
OH.
WE'RE THE ONLY ONES HERE...?
I WANTED THE PRIVACY. AND WE'RE HAVING A STARK INDUSTRIES BOARD MEETING HERE LATER THIS AFTERNOON.
YOU'RE A LOT SMALLER WHEN YOU AREN'T WEARING YOUR, UH...
I HEAR THAT A LOT. GOOD TO SEE YOU AGAIN.
SO HAVE YOU GIVEN ANY MORE THOUGHT TO OUR CONVERSATION AT THE EMBASSY PARTY?
A LITTLE.
I'M NOT GOING TO REGISTER.
I THINK ZURAS AND I CAME TO AN AGREEMENT ON THAT...
MY PEOPLE AREN'T HEROES, IRON MAN.
WE HAVE BEEN HERE SINCE THE DAWN OF TIME. YOU ARE HOMO SAPIENS, WE ARE HOMO IMMORTALIS. WE WERE YOUR GODS.
I'VE MET A FEW GODS IN MY TIME. YOU, SIR, ARE NO GOD.

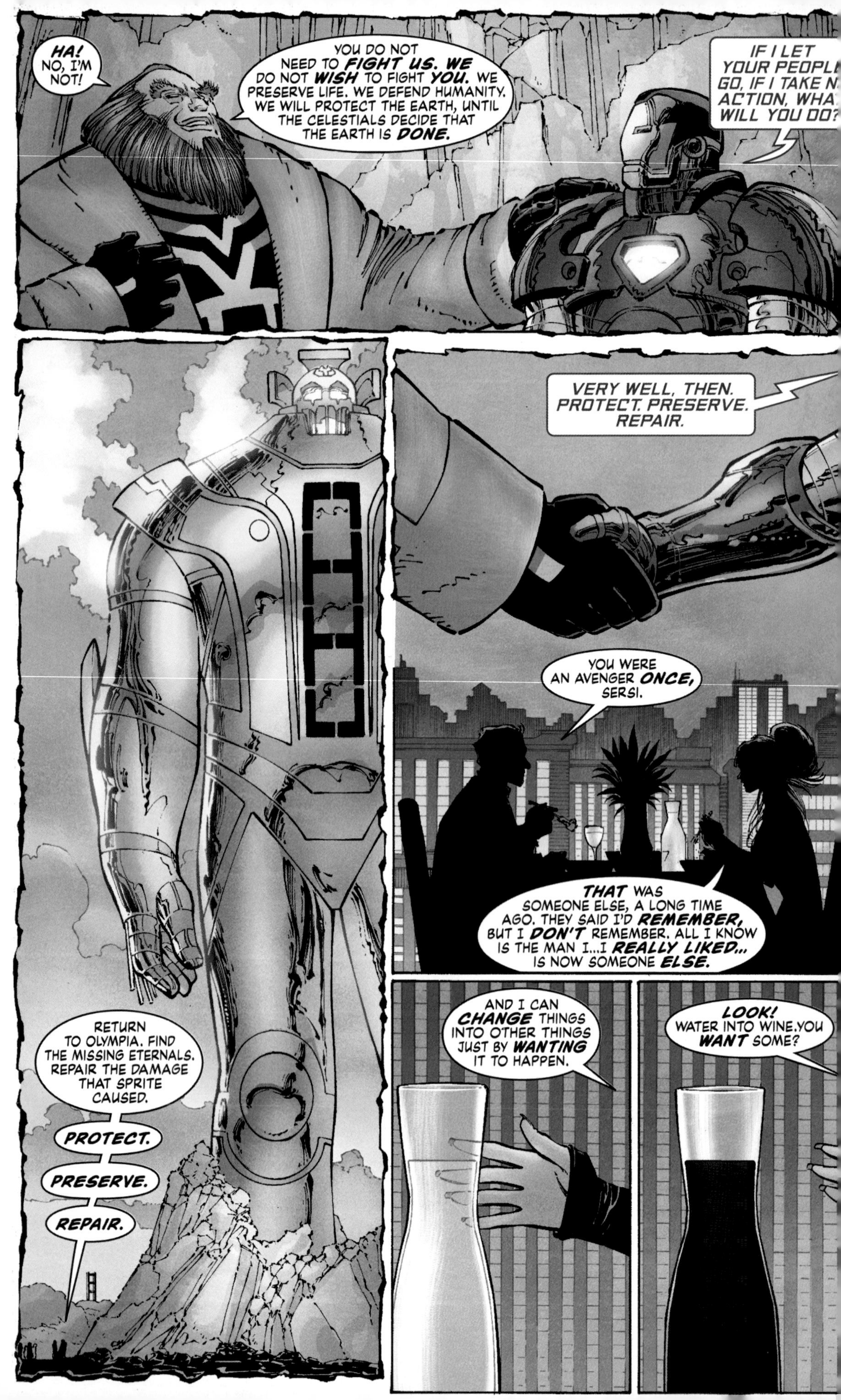
HA! NO, I'M NOT!
YOU DO NOT NEED TO FIGHT US. WE DO NOT WISH TO FIGHT YOU. WE PRESERVE LIFE. WE DEFEND HUMANITY. WE WILL PROTECT THE EARTH, UNTIL THE CELESTIALS DECIDE THAT THE EARTH IS DONE.
IF I LET YOUR PEOPL GO, IF I TAKE N ACTION, WHA WILL YOU DO?
VERY WELL, THEN. PROTECT. PRESERVE. REPAIR.
RETURN TO OLYMPIA. FIND THE MISSING ETERNALS. REPAIR THE DAMAGE THAT SPRITE CAUSED.
PROTECT.
PRESERVE.
REPAIR.
YOU WERE AN AVENGER ONCE, SERSI.
THAT WAS SOMEONE ELSE, A LONG TIME AGO. THEY SAID I'D REMEMBER, BUT I DON'T REMEMBER. ALL I KNOW IS THE MAN I...I REALLY LIKED... IS NOW SOMEONE ELSE.
AND I CAN CHANGE THINGS INTO OTHER THINGS JUST BY WANTING IT TO HAPPEN.
LOOK! WATER INTO WINE. YOU WANT SOME?

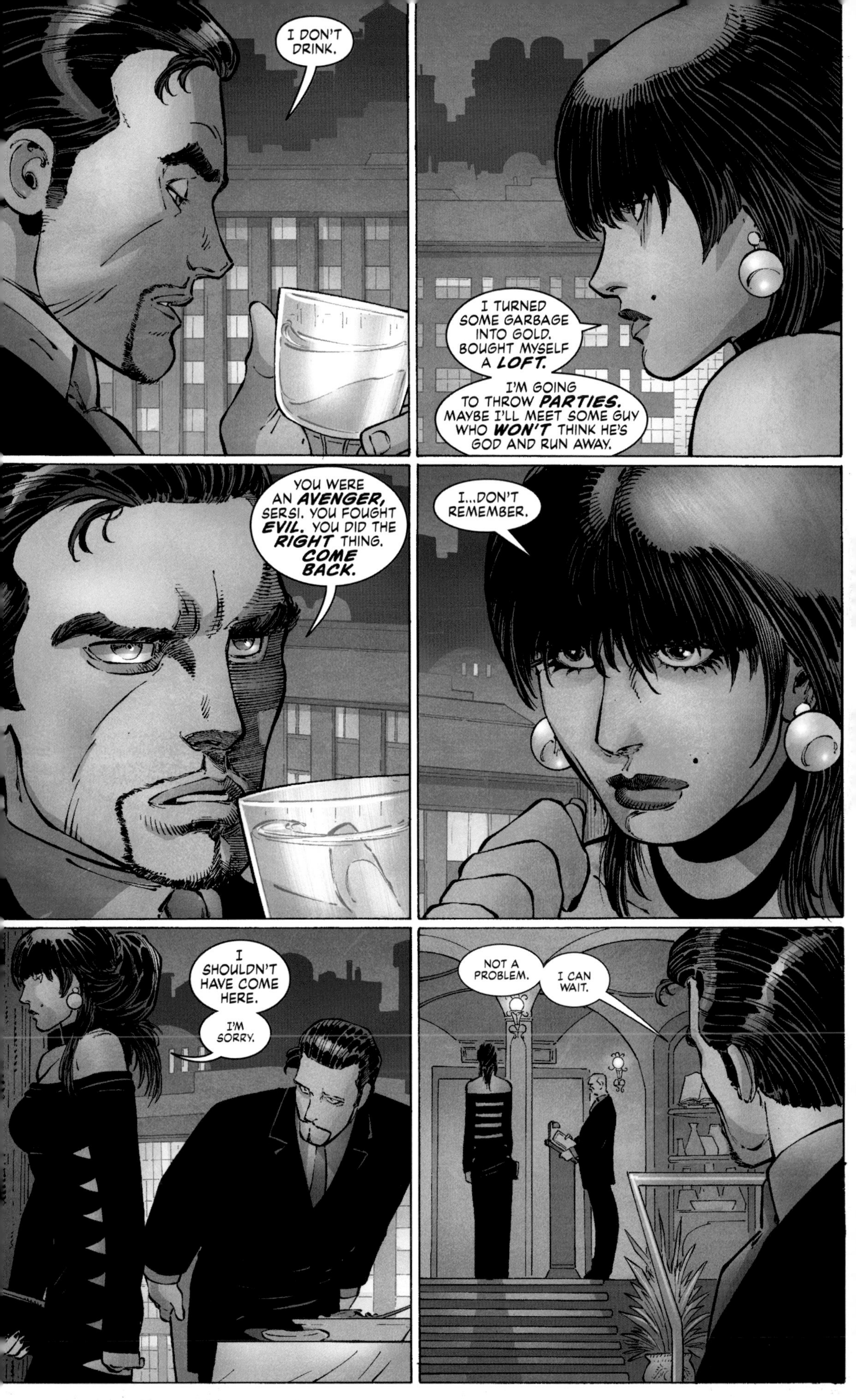

I DON'T DRINK.
I TURNED SOME GARBAGE INTO GOLD. BOUGHT MYSELF A LOFT.
I'M GOING TO THROW PARTIES. MAYBE I'LL MEET SOME GUY WHO WON'T THINK HE'S GOD AND RUN AWAY.
YOU WERE AN AVENGER, SERSI. YOU FOUGHT EVIL. YOU DID THE RIGHT THING. COME BACK.
I...DON'T REMEMBER.
I SHOULDN'T HAVE COME HERE.
I'M SORRY.
NOT A PROBLEM.
I CAN WAIT.

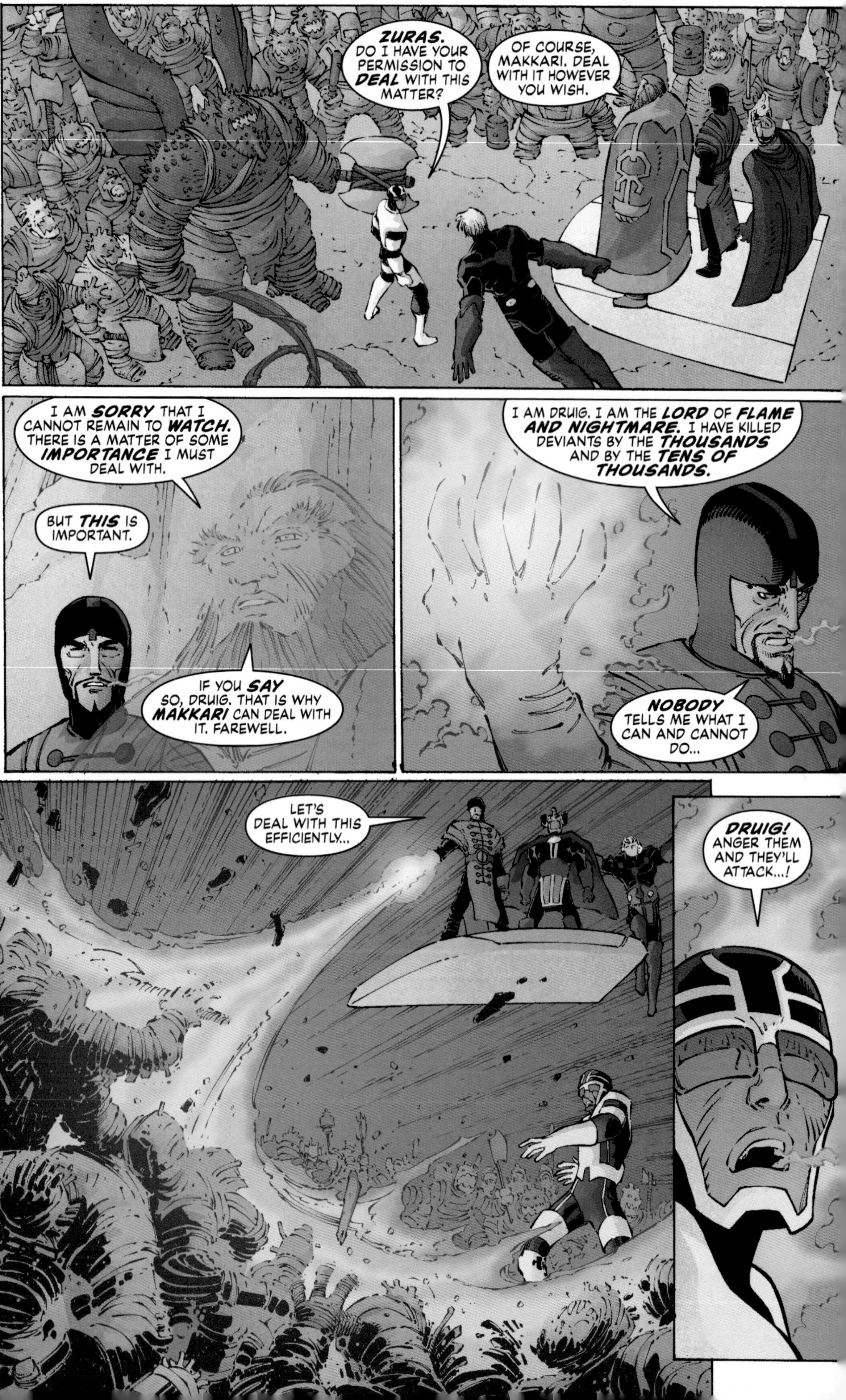

ZURAS. DO I HAVE YOUR PERMISSION TO DEAL WITH THIS MATTER?
OF COURSE, MAKKARI. DEAL WITH IT HOWEVER YOU WISH.
I AM SORRY THAT I CANNOT REMAIN TO WATCH. THERE IS A MATTER OF SOME IMPORTANCE I MUST DEAL WITH.
BUT THIS IS IMPORTANT.
IF YOU SAY SO, DRUIG. THAT IS WHY MAKKARI CAN DEAL WITH IT. FAREWELL.
I AM DRUIG. I AM THE LORD OF FLAME AND NIGHTMARE. I HAVE KILLED DEVIANTS BY THE THOUSANDS AND BY THE TENS OF THOUSANDS.
NOBODY TELLS ME WHAT I CAN AND CANNOT DO...
LET'S DEAL WITH THIS EFFICIENTLY...
DRUIG! ANGER THEM AND THEY'LL ATTACK...!

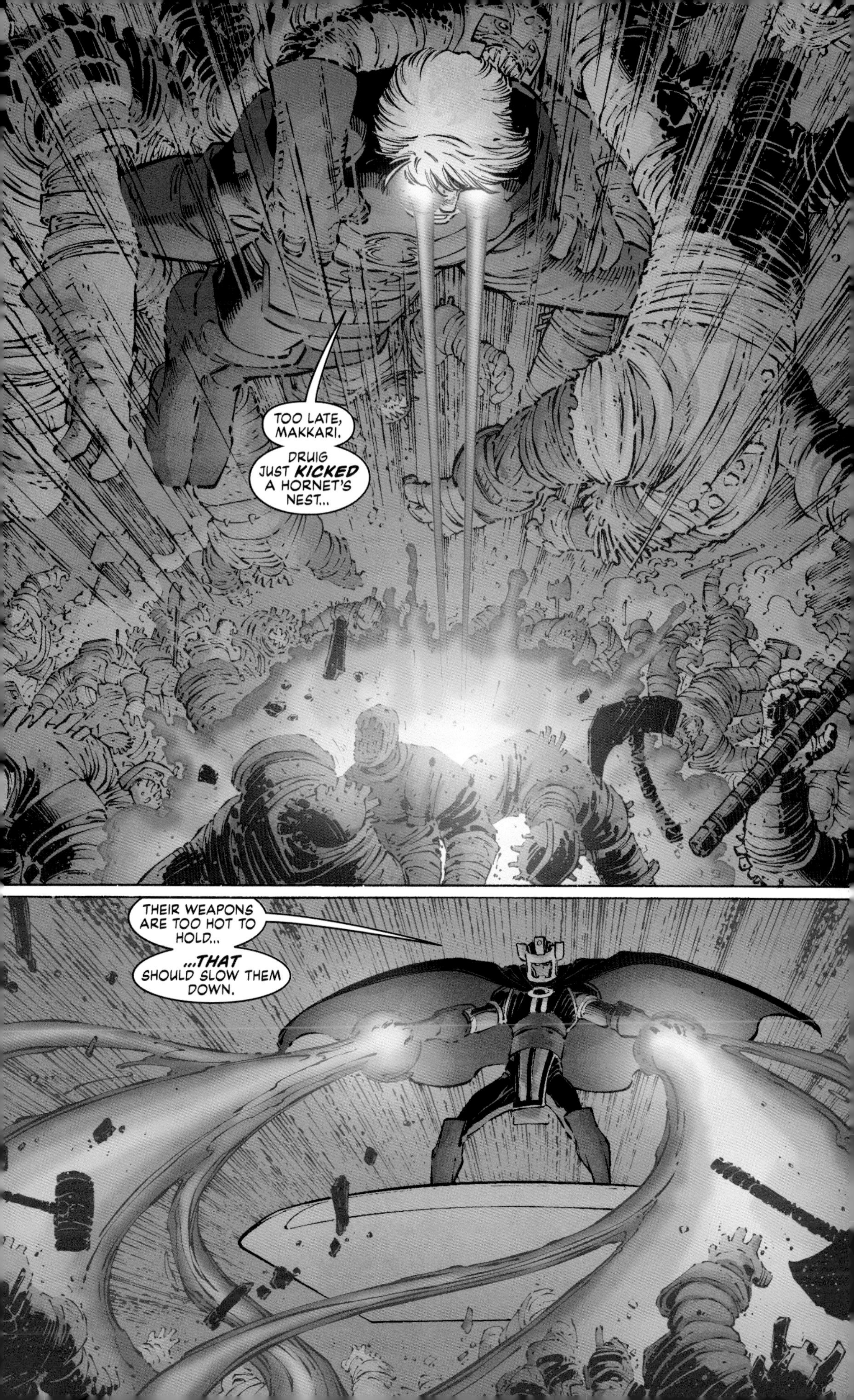
TOO LATE, MAKKARI.
DRUIG JUST KICKED A HORNET'S NEST...
THEIR WEAPONS ARE TOO HOT TO HOLD...
...THAT SHOULD SLOW THEM DOWN.

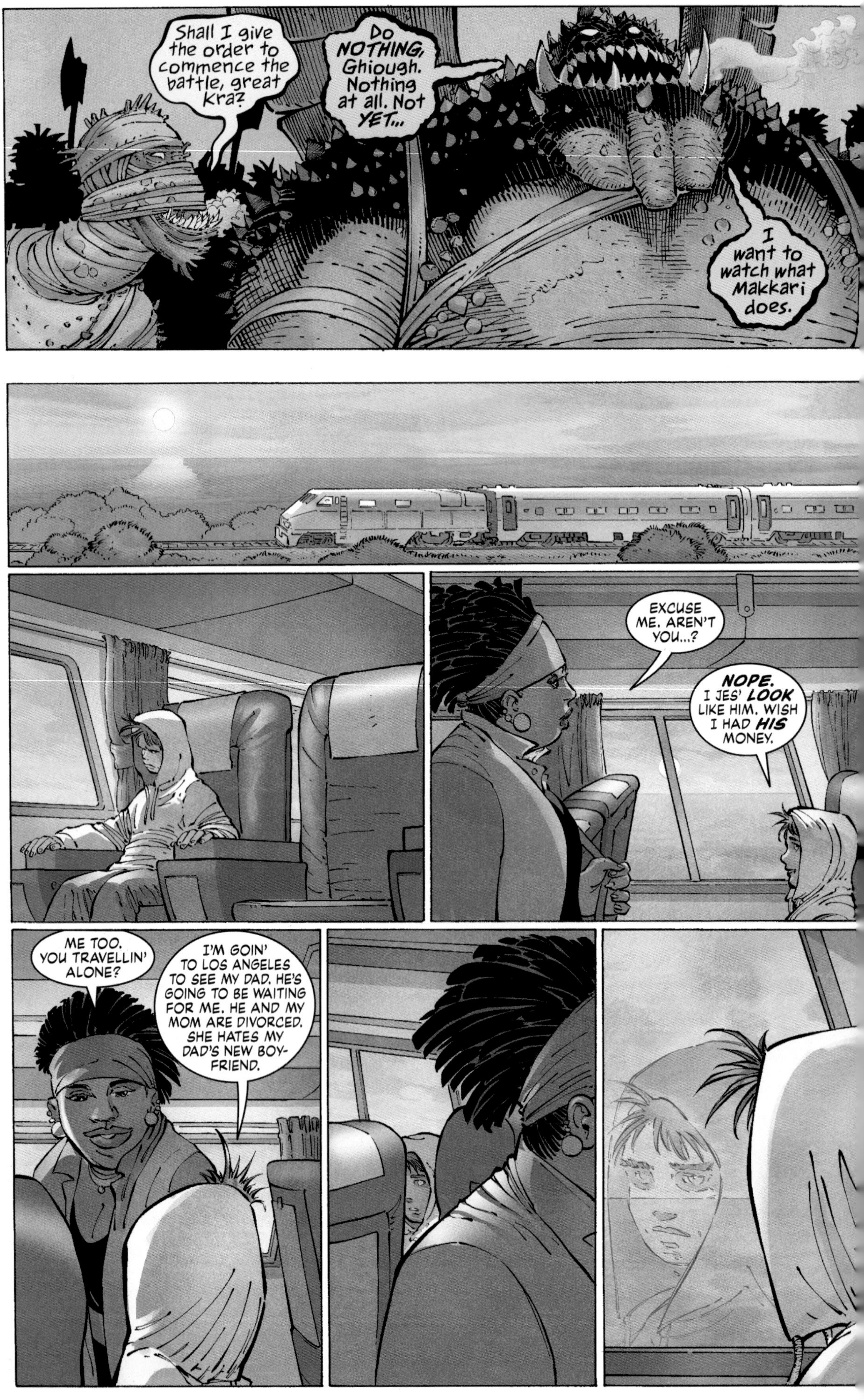
Shall I give the order to commence the battle, great Kra?
Do NOTHING, Ghiough. Nothing at all. Not YET...
I want to watch what Makkari does.
EXCUSE ME. AREN'T YOU...?
NOPE. I JES' LOOK LIKE HIM. WISH I HAD HIS MONEY.
ME TOO. YOU TRAVELLIN' ALONE?
I'M GOIN' TO LOS ANGELES TO SEE MY DAD. HE'S GOING TO BE WAITING FOR ME. HE AND MY MOM ARE DIVORCED. SHE HATES MY DAD'S NEW BOY-FRIEND.

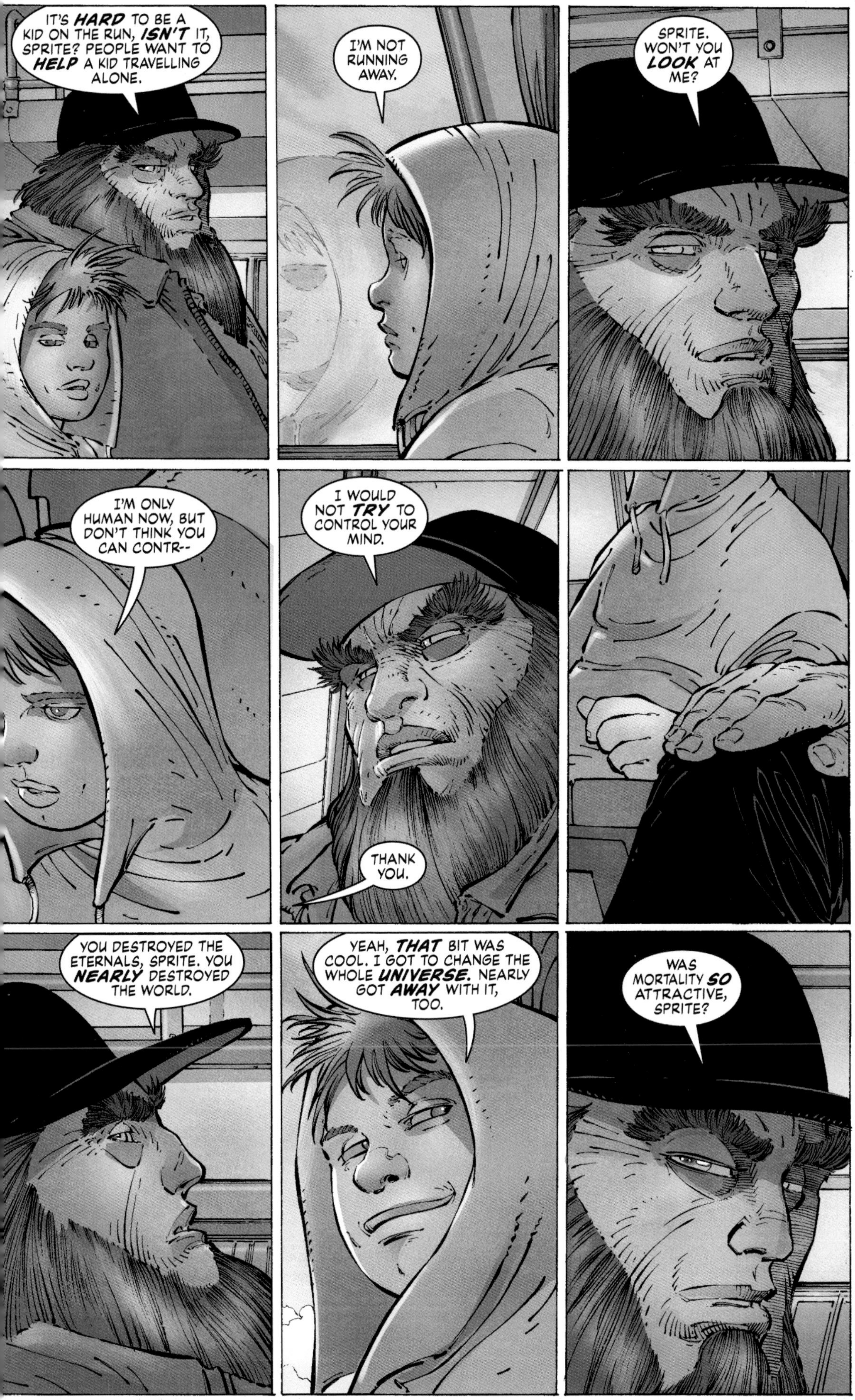
IT'S HARD TO BE A KID ON THE RUN, ISN'T IT, SPRITE? PEOPLE WANT TO HELP A KID TRAVELLING ALONE.
I'M NOT RUNNING AWAY.
SPRITE. WON'T YOU LOOK AT ME?
I'M ONLY HUMAN NOW, BUT DON'T THINK YOU CAN CONTR--
I WOULD NOT TRY TO CONTROL YOUR MIND.
THANK YOU.
YOU DESTROYED THE ETERNALS, SPRITE. YOU NEARLY DESTROYED THE WORLD.
YEAH, THAT BIT WAS COOL. I GOT TO CHANGE THE WHOLE UNIVERSE. NEARLY GOT AWAY WITH IT, TOO.
WAS MORTALITY SO ATTRACTIVE, SPRITE?

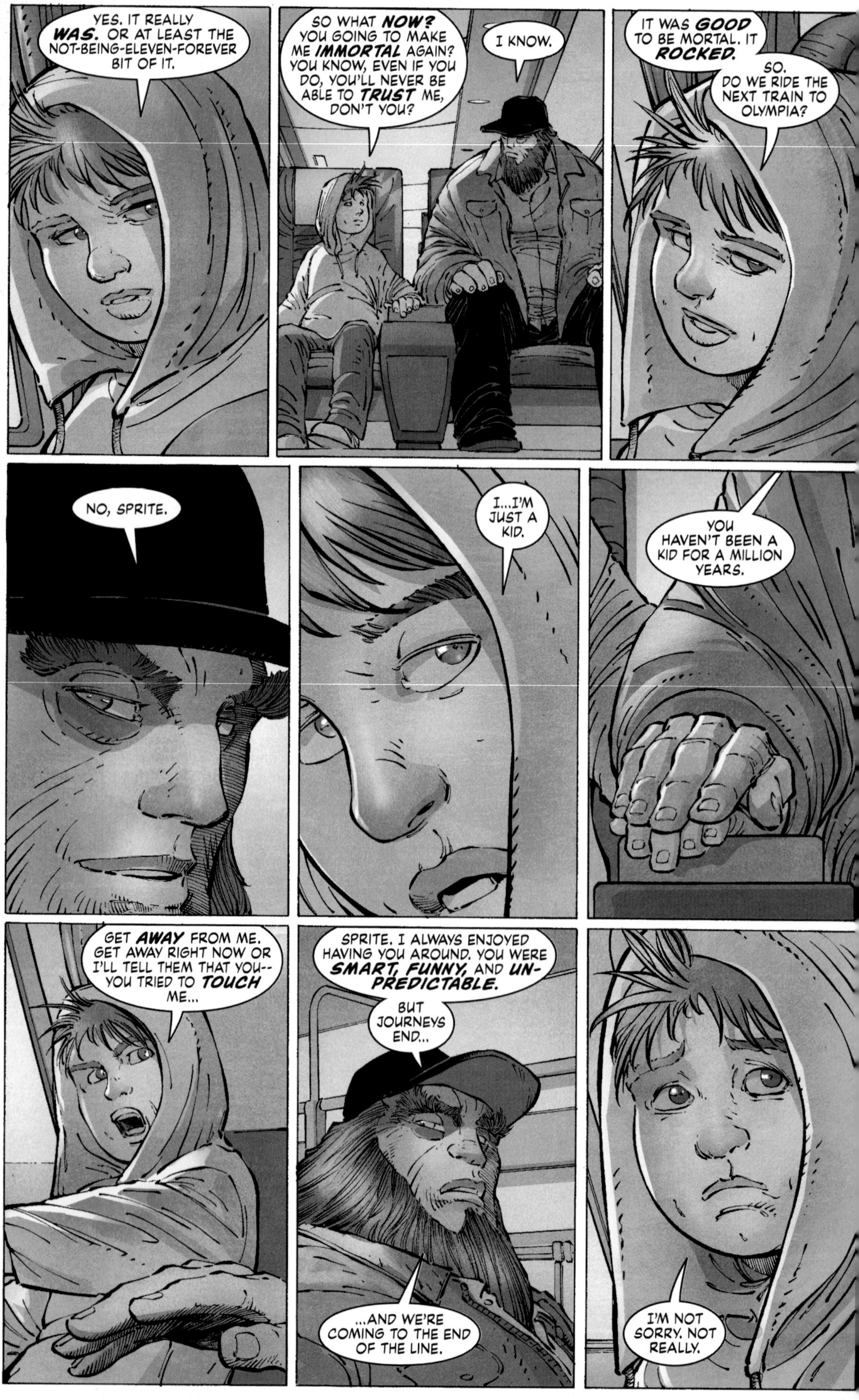

YES. IT REALLY WAS. OR AT LEAST THE NOT-BEING-ELEVEN-FOREVER BIT OF IT.
SO WHAT NOW? YOU GOING TO MAKE ME IMMORTAL AGAIN? YOU KNOW, EVEN IF YOU DO, YOU'LL NEVER BE ABLE TO TRUST ME, DON'T YOU?
I KNOW.
IT WAS GOOD TO BE MORTAL. IT ROCKED.
SO. DO WE RIDE THE NEXT TRAIN TO OLYMPIA?
NO, SPRITE.
I...I'M JUST A KID.
YOU HAVEN'T BEEN A KID FOR A MILLION YEARS.
GET AWAY FROM ME. GET AWAY RIGHT NOW OR I'LL TELL THEM THAT YOU--YOU TRIED TO TOUCH ME...
SPRITE. I ALWAYS ENJOYED HAVING YOU AROUND. YOU WERE SMART, FUNNY, AND UN-PREDICTABLE.
BUT JOURNEYS END...
...AND WE'RE COMING TO THE END OF THE LINE.
I'M NOT SORRY. NOT REALLY.

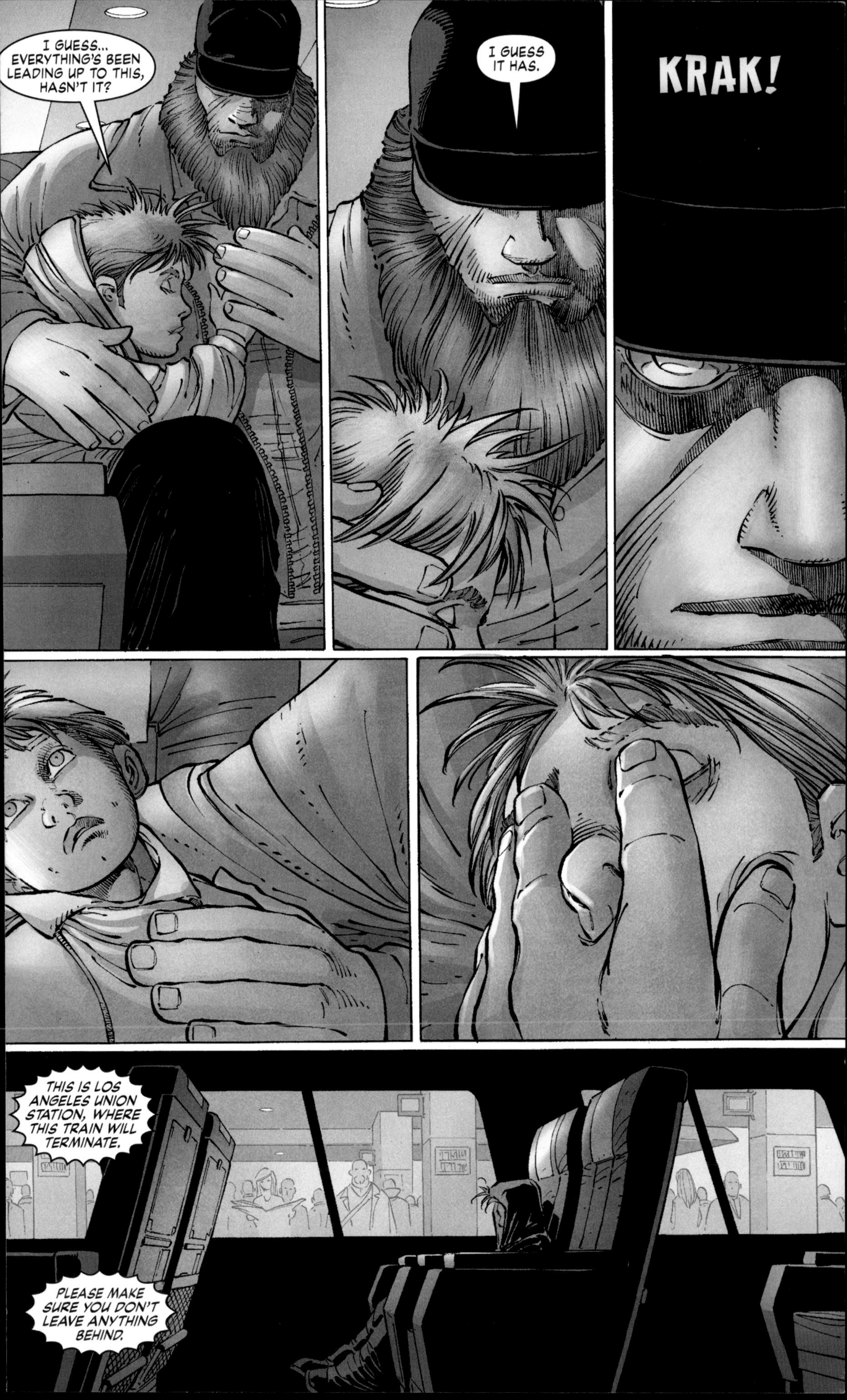
I GUESS... EVERYTHING'S BEEN LEADING UP TO THIS, HASN'T IT?
I GUESS IT HAS.
KRAK!
THIS IS LOS ANGELES UNION STATION, WHERE THIS TRAIN WILL TERMINATE.
PLEASE MAKE SURE YOU DON'T LEAVE ANYTHING BEHIND.

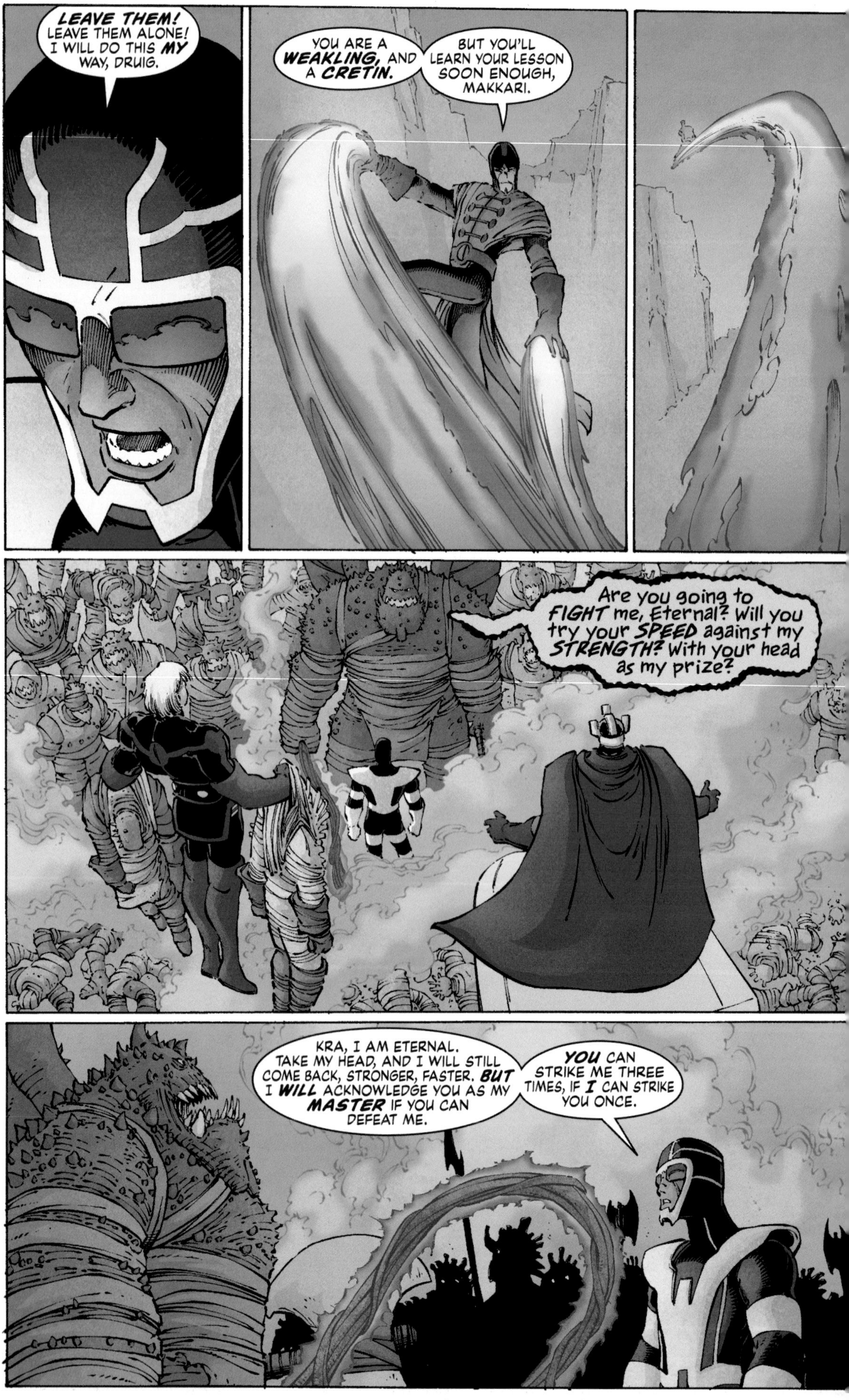
LEAVE THEM! LEAVE THEM ALONE! I WILL DO THIS MY WAY, DRUIG.
YOU ARE A WEAKLING, AND A CRETIN.
BUT YOU'LL LEARN YOUR LESSON SOON ENOUGH, MAKKARI.
Are you going to FIGHT me, Eternal? Will you try your SPEED against my STRENGTH? With your head as my prize?
KRA, I AM ETERNAL. TAKE MY HEAD, AND I WILL STILL COME BACK, STRONGER, FASTER. BUT I WILL ACKNOWLEDGE YOU AS MY MASTER IF YOU CAN DEFEAT ME.
YOU CAN STRIKE ME THREE TIMES, IF I CAN STRIKE YOU ONCE.

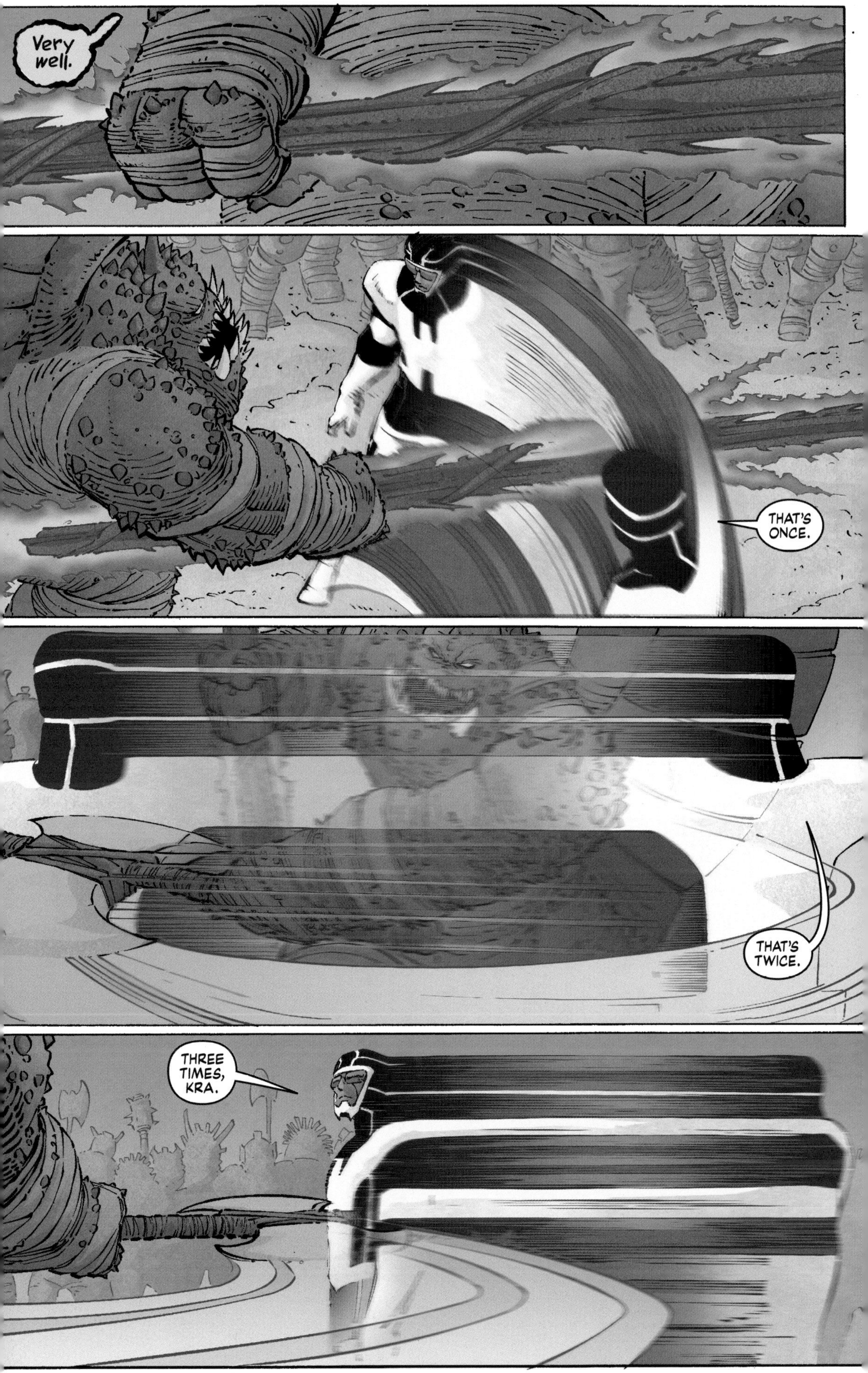
Very well.
THAT'S ONCE.
THAT'S TWICE.
THREE TIMES, KRA.

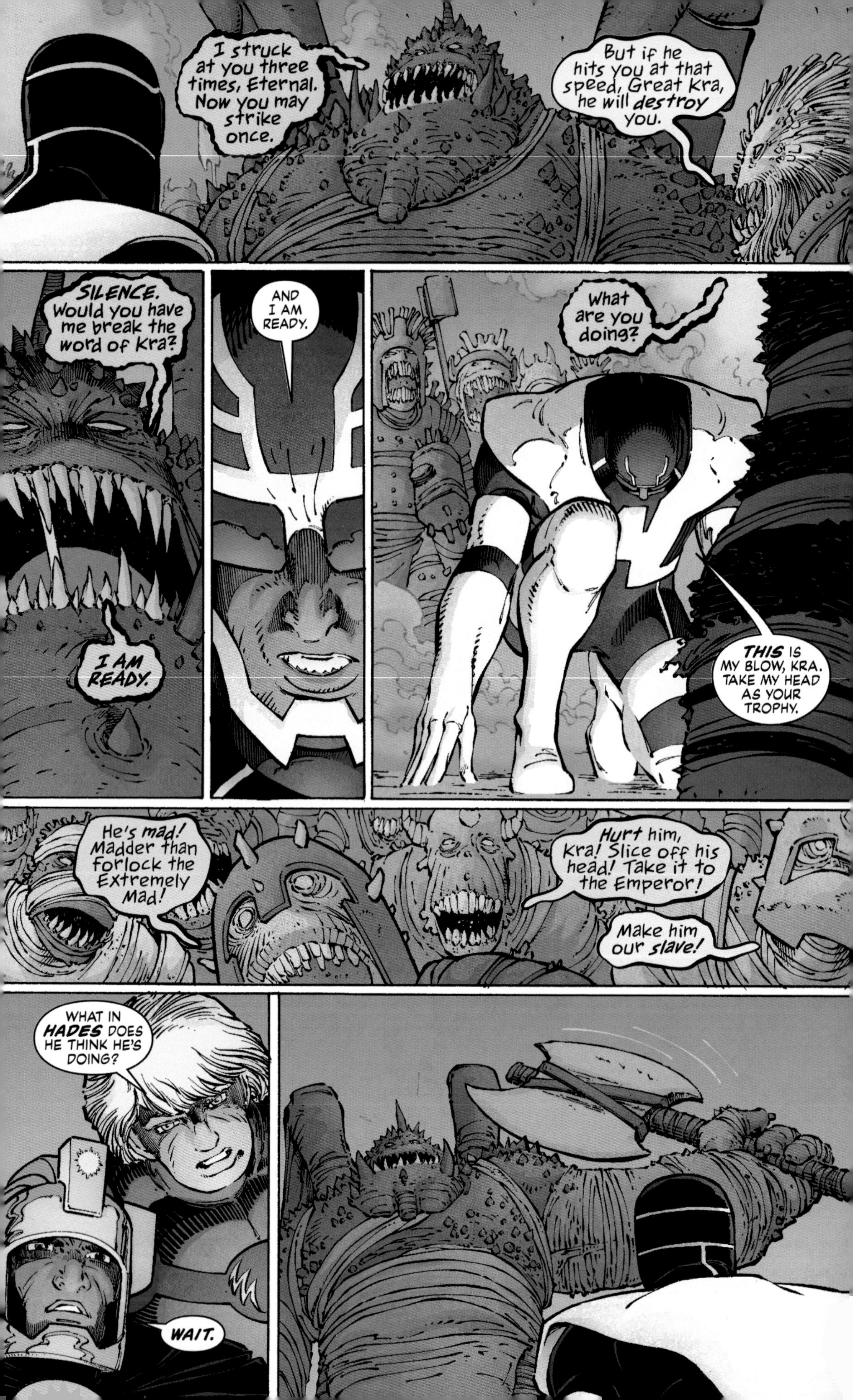
I struck at you three times, Eternal. Now you may strike once.
But if he hits you at that speed, Great Kra, he will destroy you.
SILENCE. Would you have me break the word of Kra?
I AM READY.
AND I AM READY.
What are you doing?
THIS IS MY BLOW, KRA. TAKE MY HEAD AS YOUR TROPHY.
He's mad! Madder than Forlock the Extremely Mad!
Hurt him, Kra! Slice off his head! Take it to the Emperor!
Make him our slave!
WHAT IN HADES DOES HE THINK HE'S DOING?
WAIT.

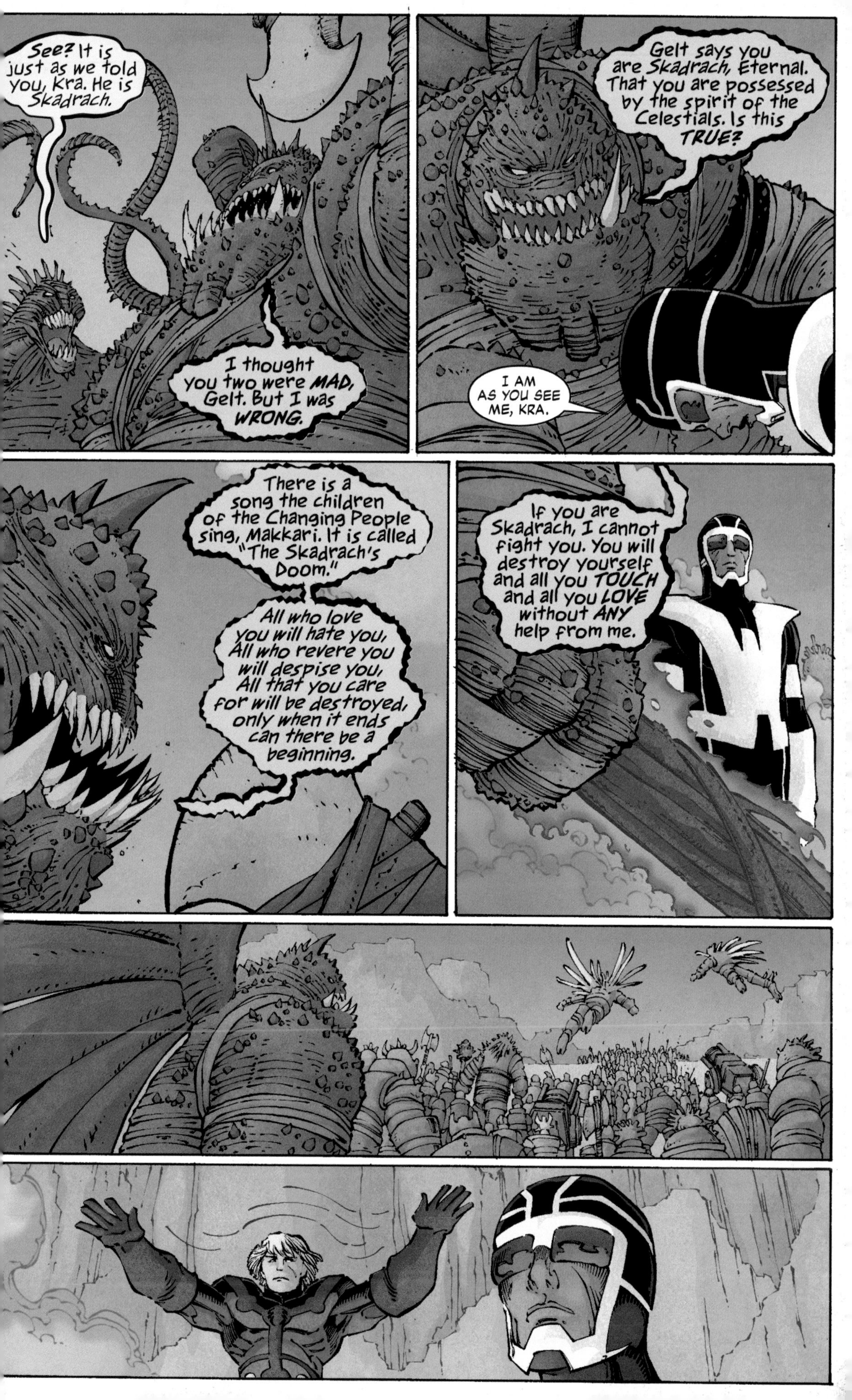
See? It is just as we told you, Kra. He is Skadrach.
I thought you two were MAD, Gelt. But I was WRONG.
Gelt says you are Skadrach, Eternal. That you are possessed by the spirit of the Celestials. Is this TRUE?
I AM AS YOU SEE ME, KRA.
There is a song the children of the Changing People sing, Makkari. It is called "The Skadrach's Doom."
All who love you will hate you, All who revere you will despise you, All that you care for will be destroyed, only when it ends can there be a beginning.
If you are Skadrach, I cannot fight you. You will destroy yourself and all you TOUCH and all you LOVE without ANY help from me.

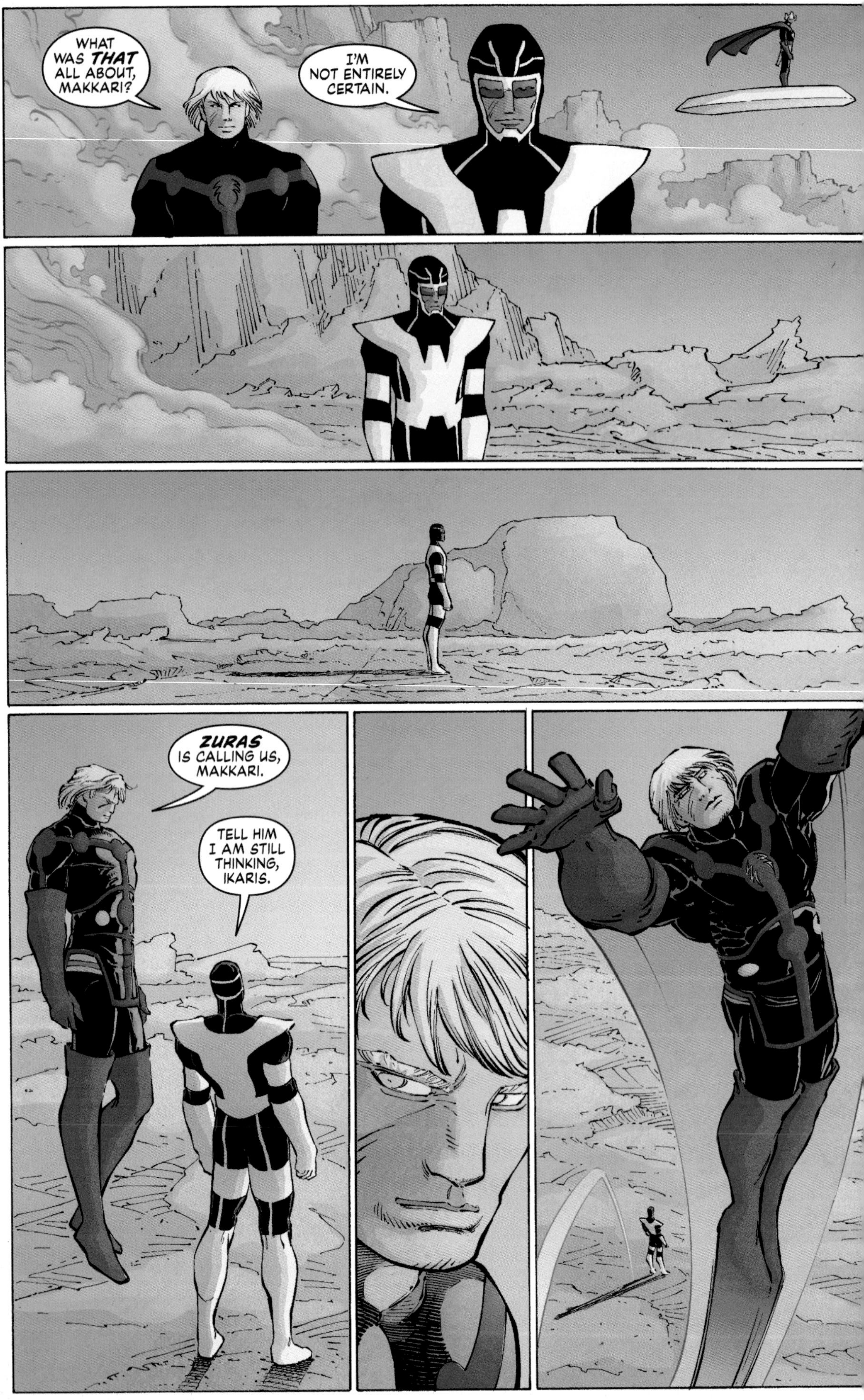
WHAT WAS **THAT** ALL ABOUT, MAKKARI?
I'M NOT ENTIRELY CERTAIN.
ZURAS IS CALLING US, MAKKARI.
TELL HIM I AM STILL THINKING, IKARIS.

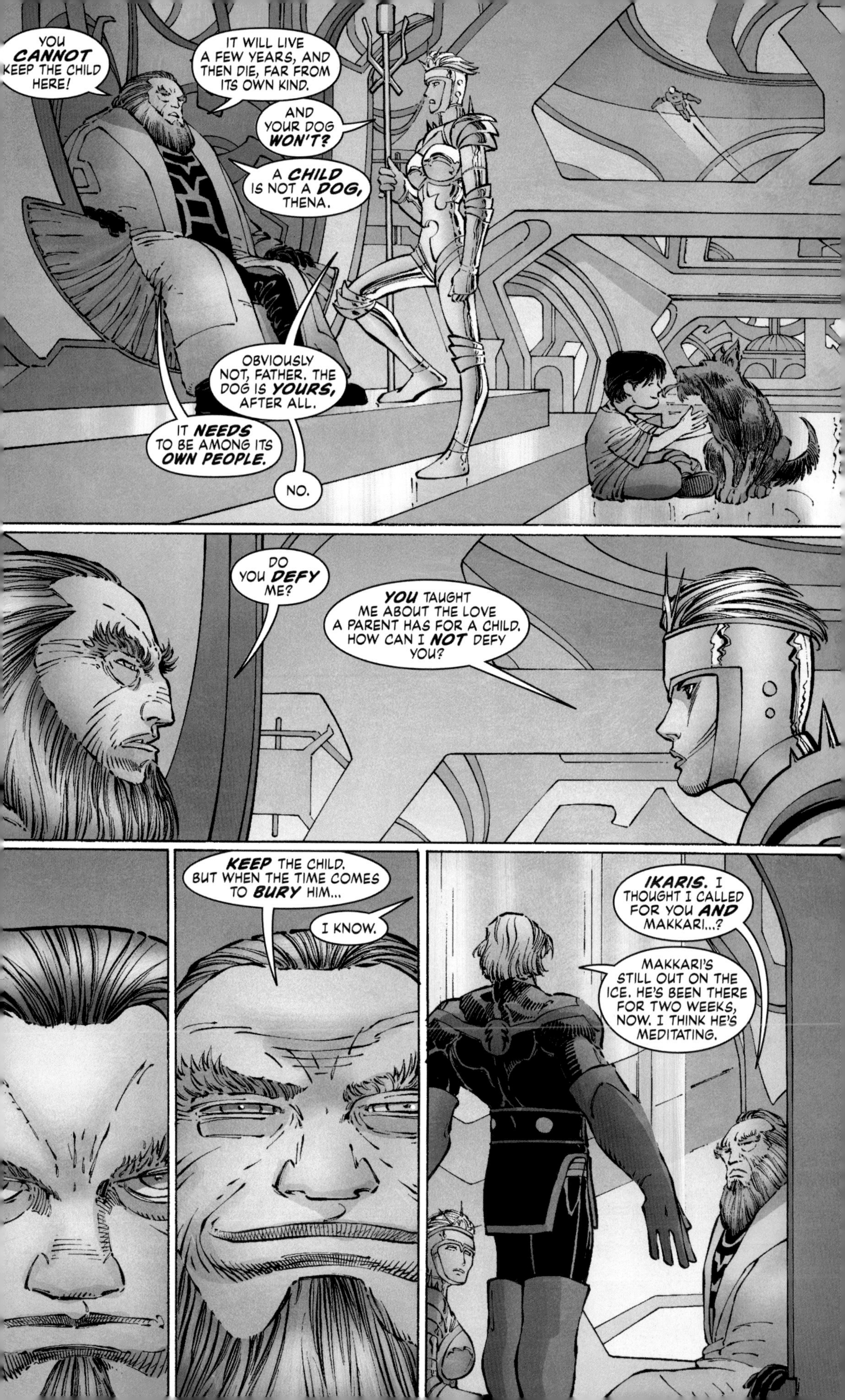
YOU CANNOT KEEP THE CHILD HERE!
IT WILL LIVE A FEW YEARS, AND THEN DIE, FAR FROM ITS OWN KIND.
AND YOUR DOG WON'T?
A CHILD IS NOT A DOG, THENA.
OBVIOUSLY NOT, FATHER. THE DOG IS YOURS, AFTER ALL.
IT NEEDS TO BE AMONG ITS OWN PEOPLE.
NO.
DO YOU DEFY ME?
YOU TAUGHT ME ABOUT THE LOVE A PARENT HAS FOR A CHILD. HOW CAN I NOT DEFY YOU?
KEEP THE CHILD. BUT WHEN THE TIME COMES TO BURY HIM...
I KNOW.
IKARIS. I THOUGHT I CALLED FOR YOU AND MAKKARI...?
MAKKARI'S STILL OUT ON THE ICE. HE'S BEEN THERE FOR TWO WEEKS, NOW. I THINK HE'S MEDITATING.

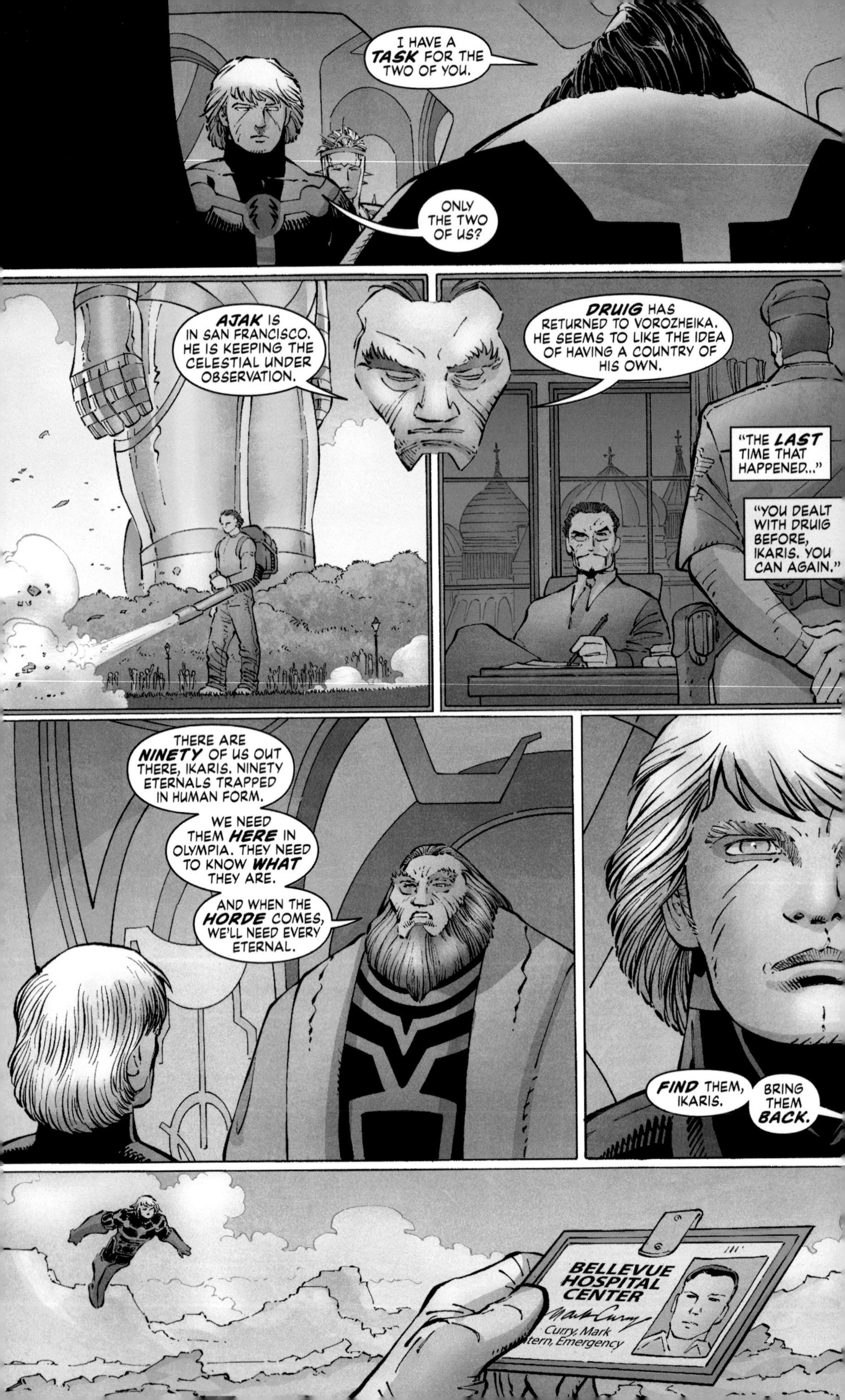

I HAVE A TASK FOR THE TWO OF YOU.
ONLY THE TWO OF US?
AJAK IS IN SAN FRANCISCO. HE IS KEEPING THE CELESTIAL UNDER OBSERVATION.
DRUIG HAS RETURNED TO VOROZHEIKA. HE SEEMS TO LIKE THE IDEA OF HAVING A COUNTRY OF HIS OWN.
"THE LAST TIME THAT HAPPENED..."
"YOU DEALT WITH DRUIG BEFORE, IKARIS. YOU CAN AGAIN."
THERE ARE NINETY OF US OUT THERE, IKARIS. NINETY ETERNALS TRAPPED IN HUMAN FORM.
WE NEED THEM HERE IN OLYMPIA. THEY NEED TO KNOW WHAT THEY ARE.
AND WHEN THE HORDE COMES, WE'LL NEED EVERY ETERNAL.
FIND THEM, IKARIS.
BRING THEM BACK.
BELLEVUE HOSPITAL CENTER
Curry, Mark

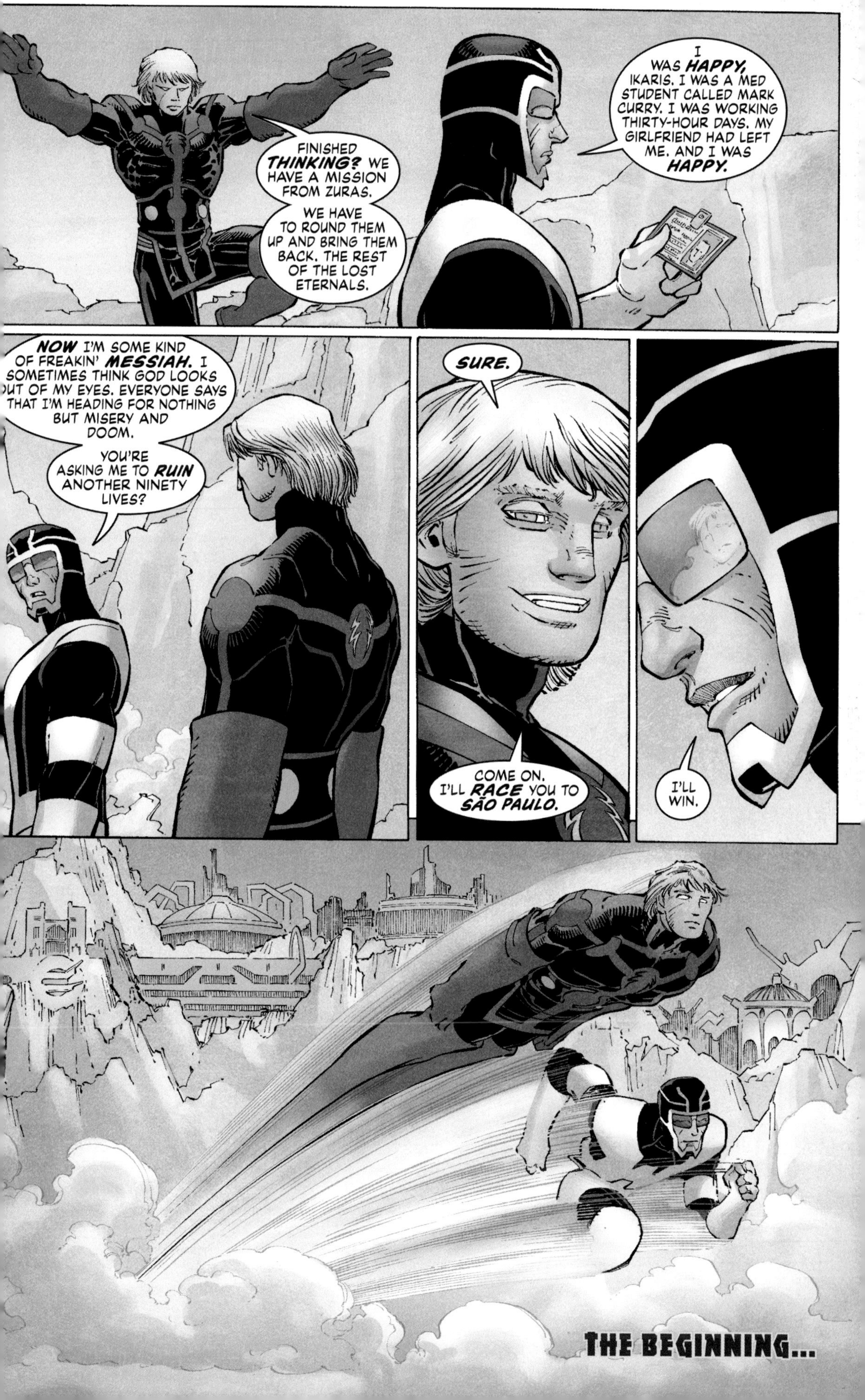
FINISHED THINKING? WE HAVE A MISSION FROM ZURAS.
WE HAVE TO ROUND THEM UP AND BRING THEM BACK. THE REST OF THE LOST ETERNALS.
I WAS HAPPY, IKARIS. I WAS A MED STUDENT CALLED MARK CURRY. I WAS WORKING THIRTY-HOUR DAYS. MY GIRLFRIEND HAD LEFT ME. AND I WAS HAPPY.
NOW I'M SOME KIND OF FREAKIN' MESSIAH. I SOMETIMES THINK GOD LOOKS OUT OF MY EYES. EVERYONE SAYS THAT I'M HEADING FOR NOTHING BUT MISERY AND DOOM.
YOU'RE ASKING ME TO RUIN ANOTHER NINETY LIVES?
SURE.
COME ON. I'LL RACE YOU TO SÃO PAULO.
I'LL WIN.
THE BEGINNING...

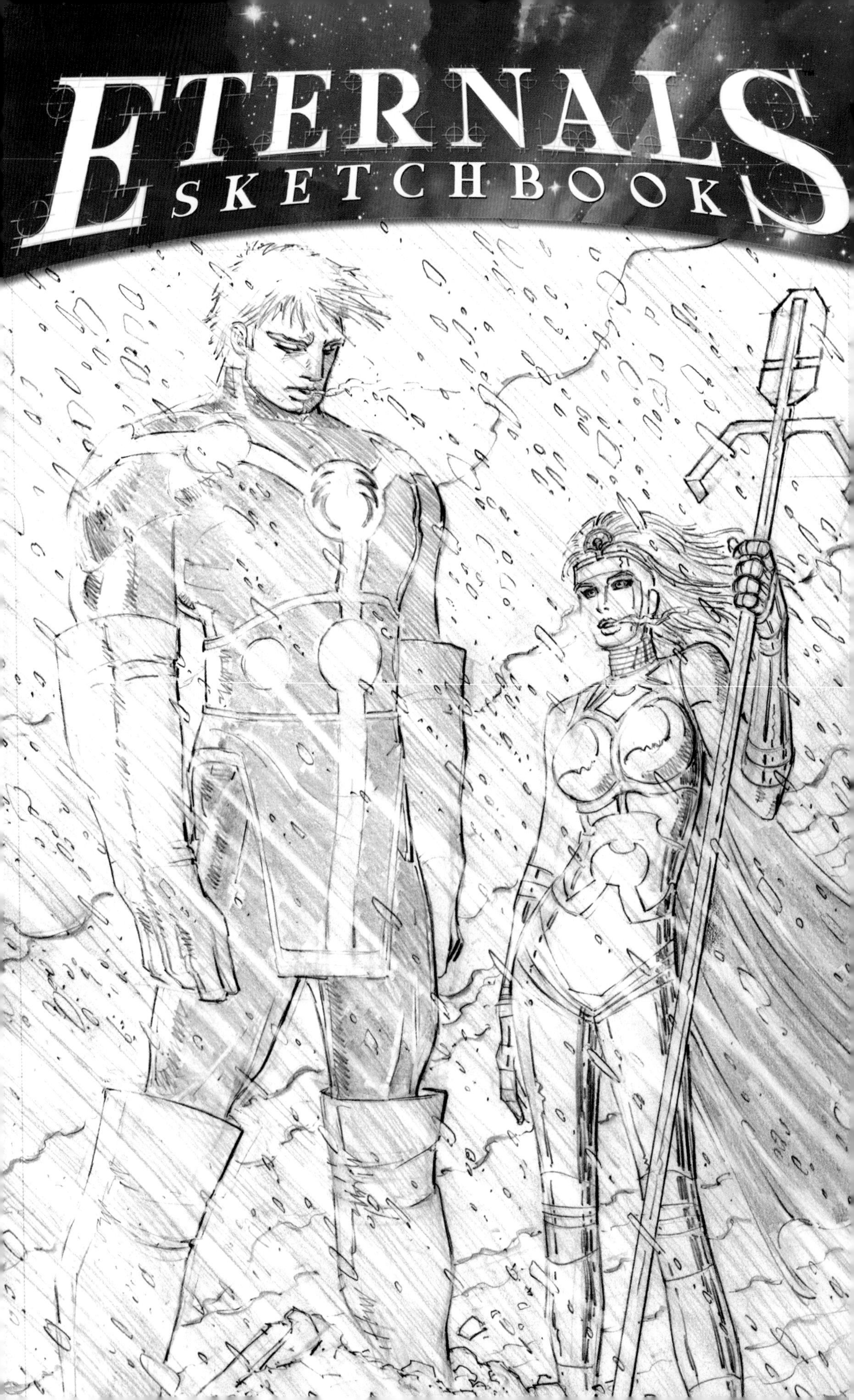

ETERNALS™
SKETCHBOOK

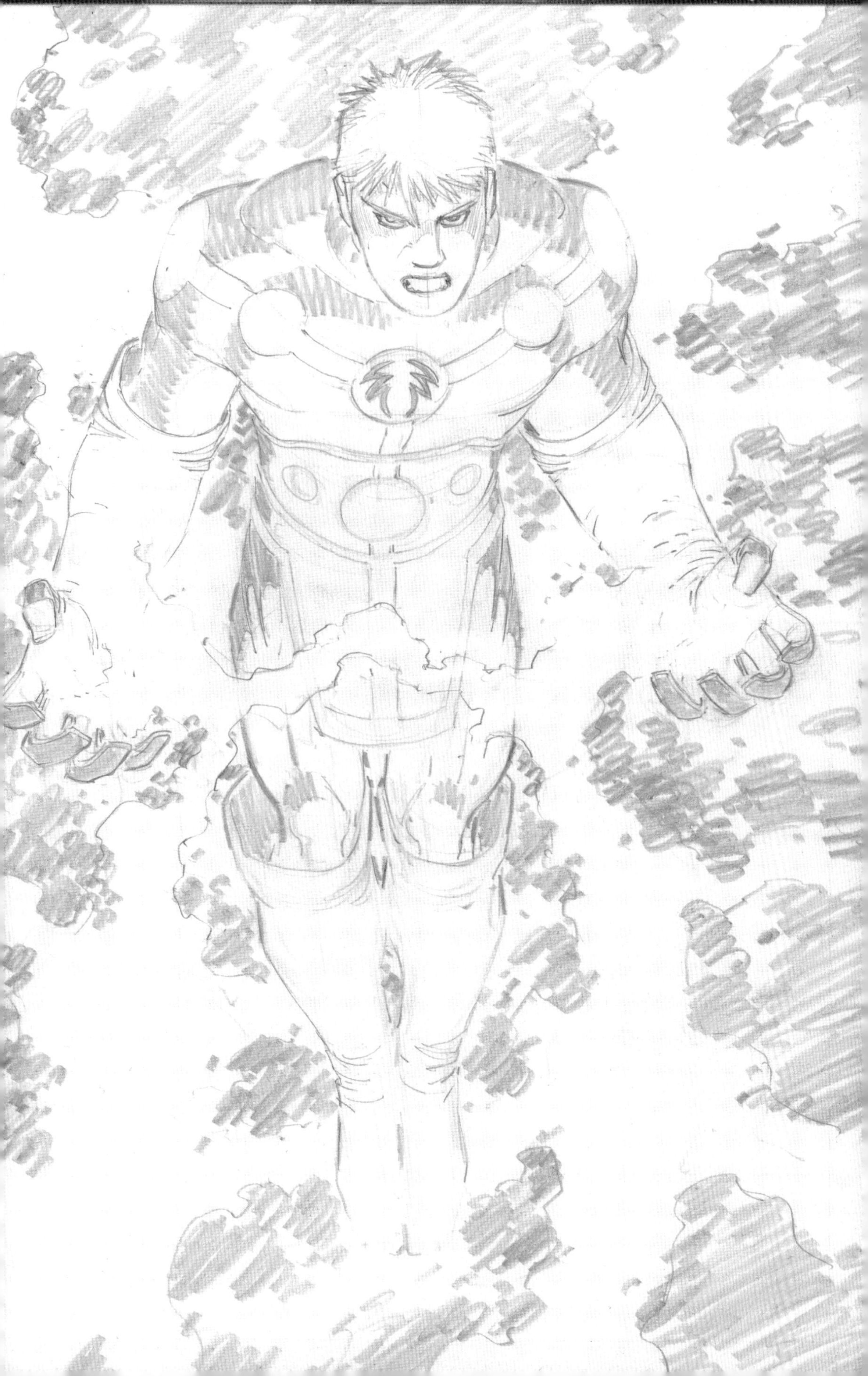

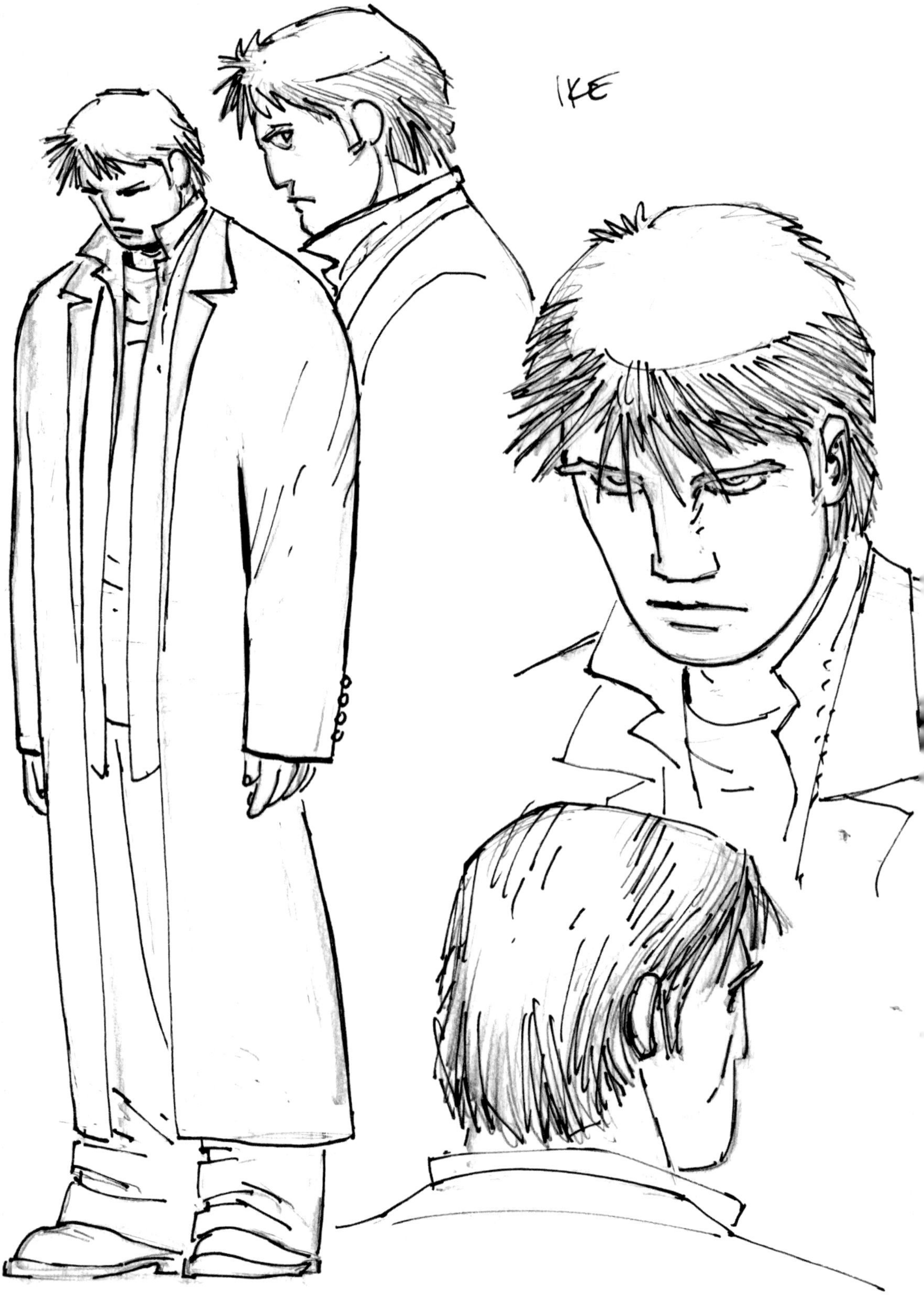
IKE

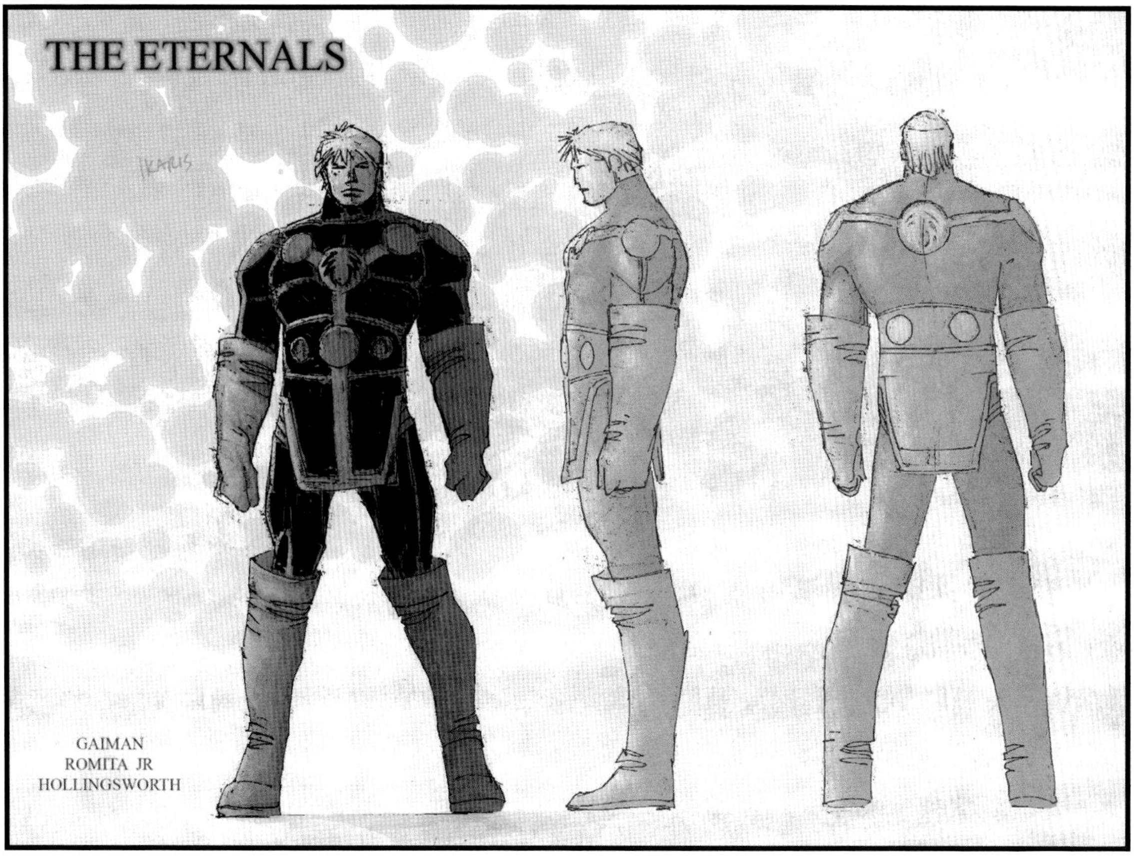
THE ETERNALS
GAIMAN
ROMITA JR
HOLLINGSWORTH

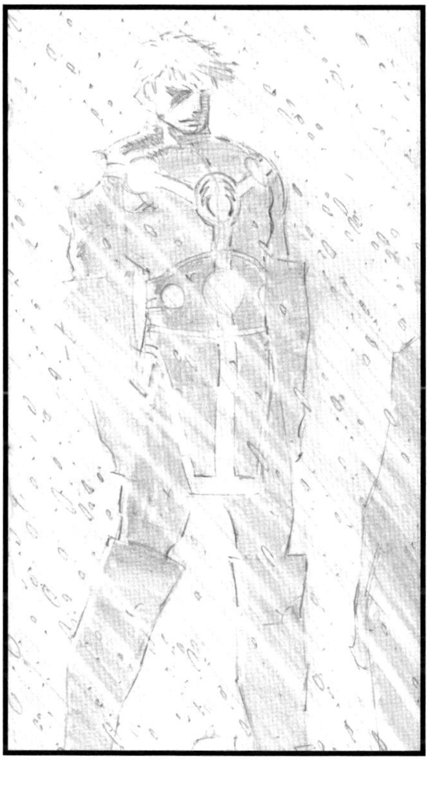

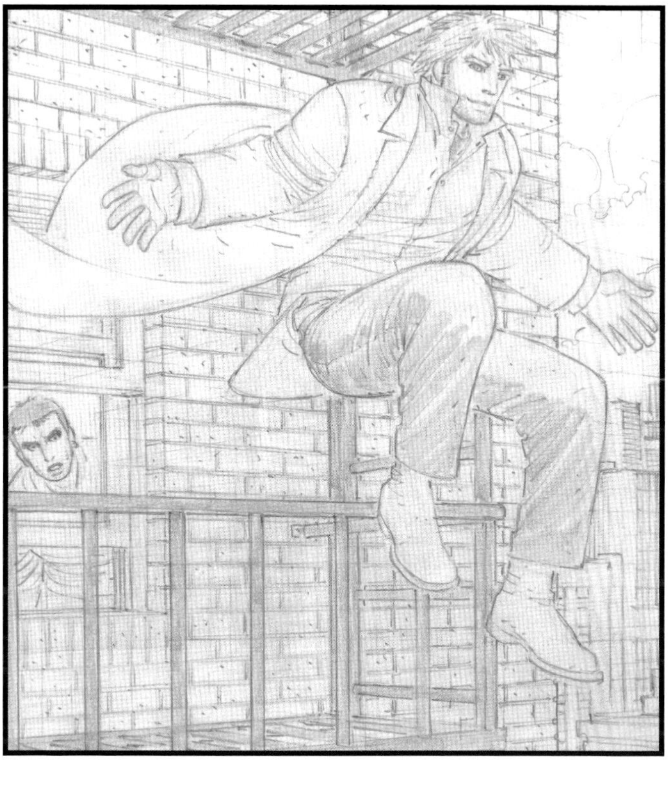

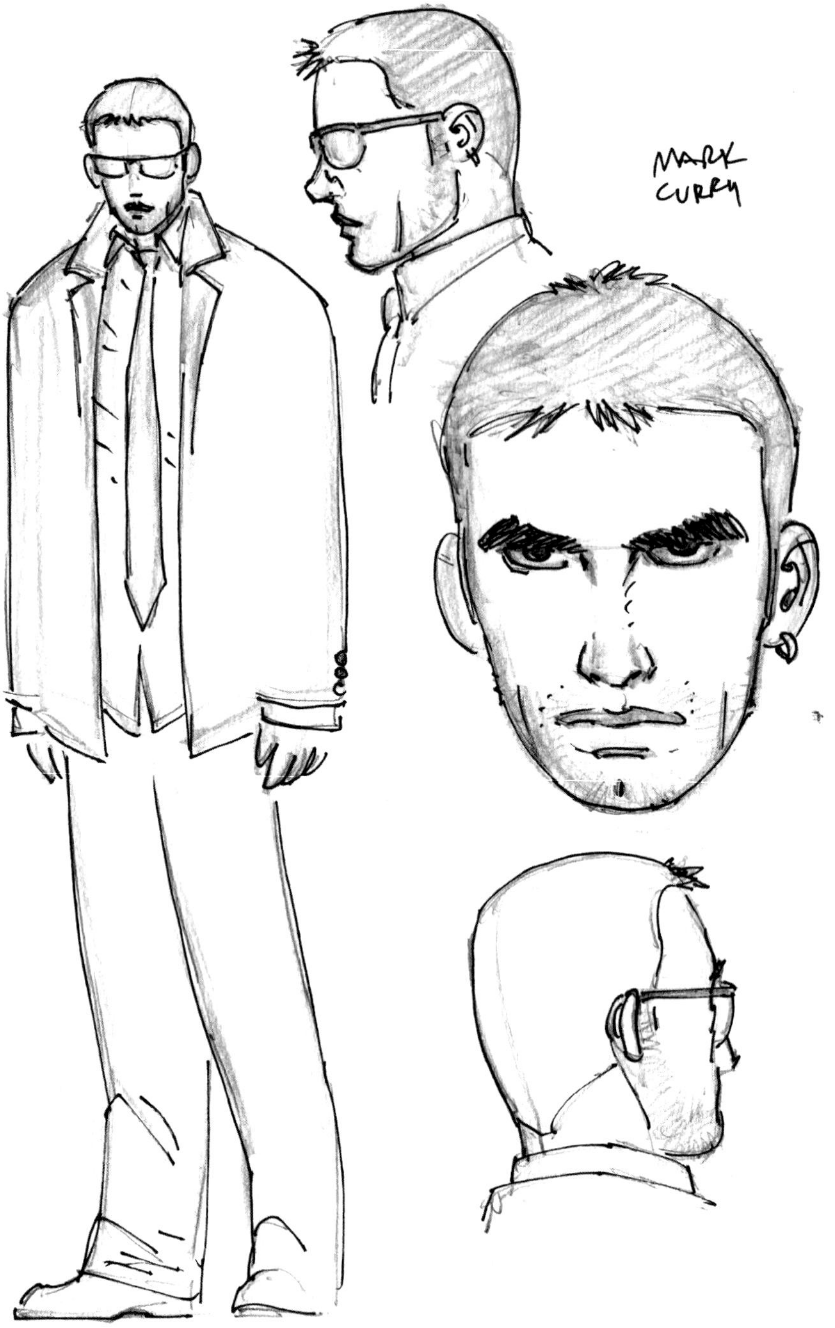
MARK
CURRY

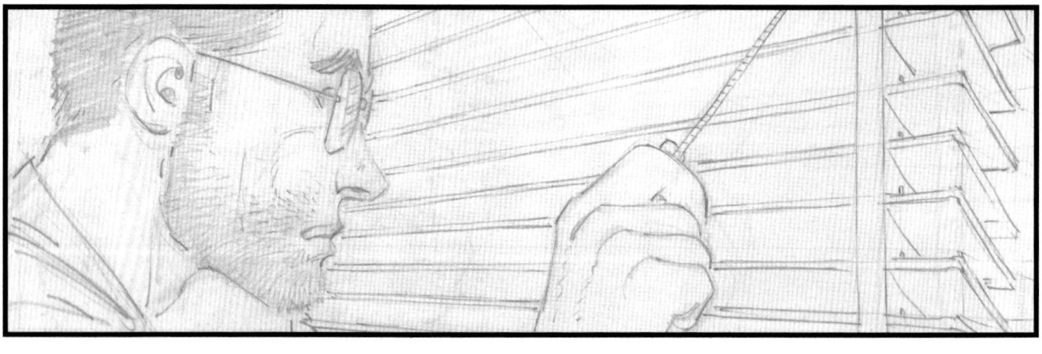

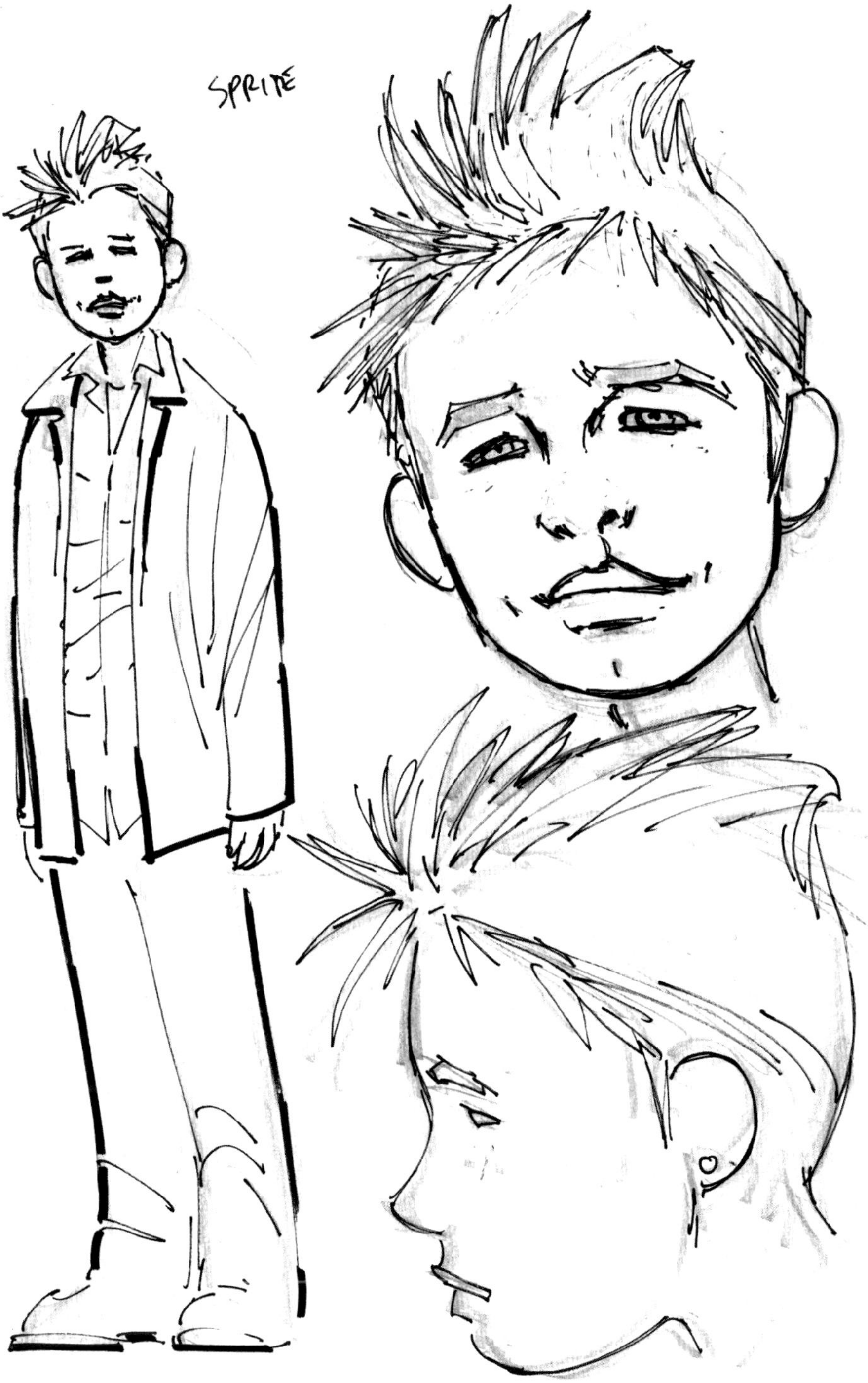
SPRITE

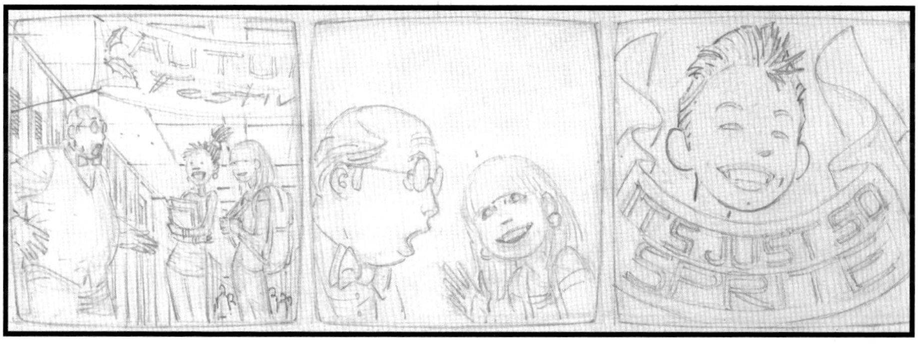
ITS JUST SO
SPRITE

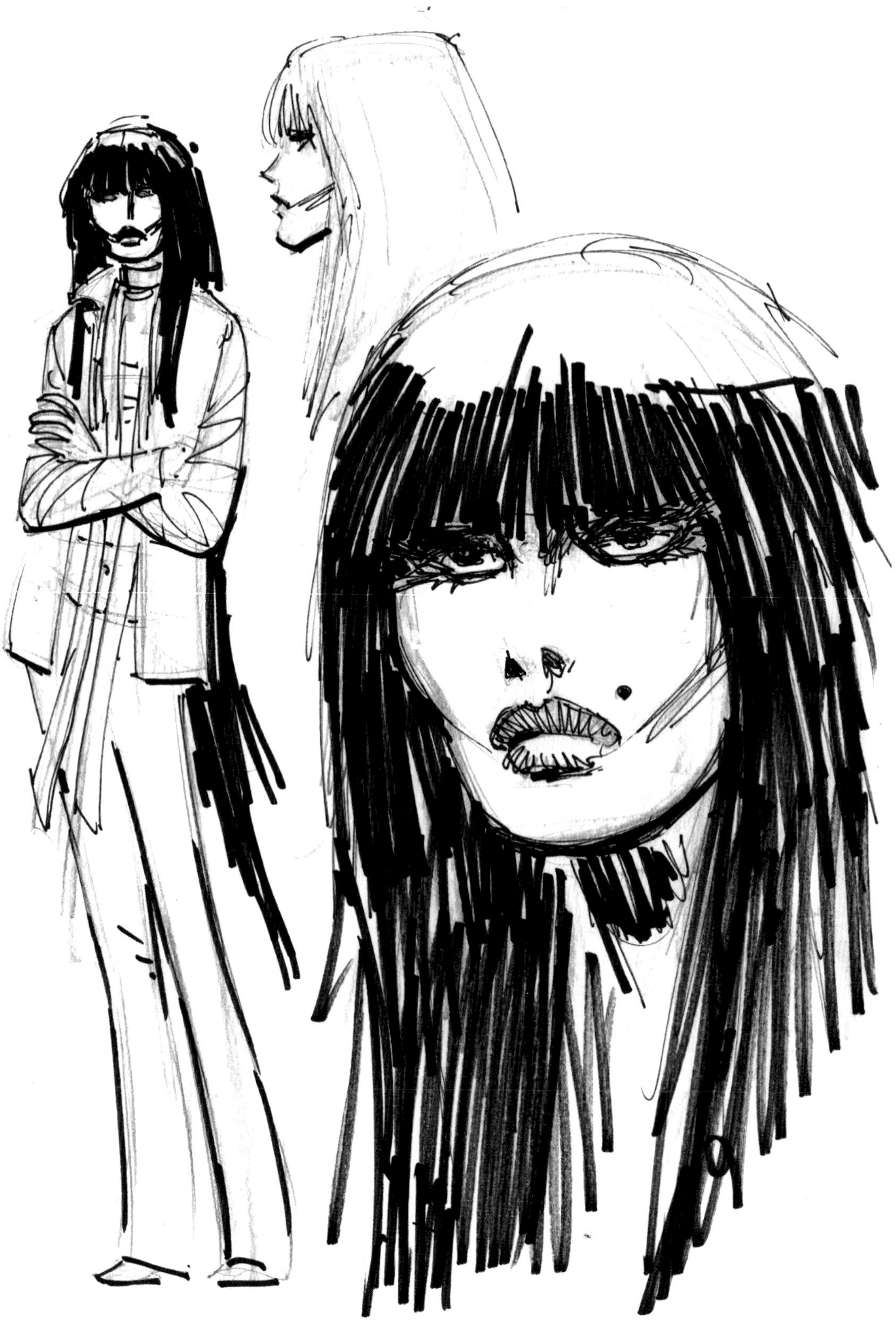

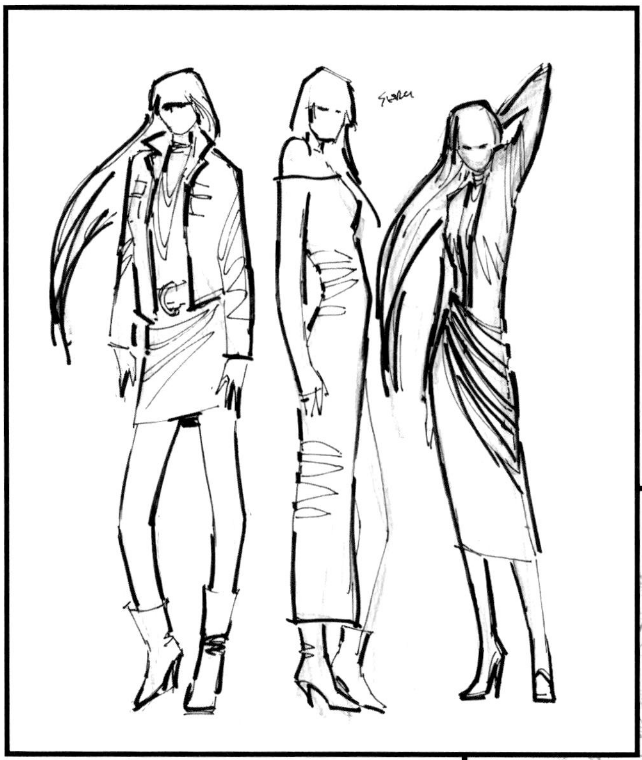

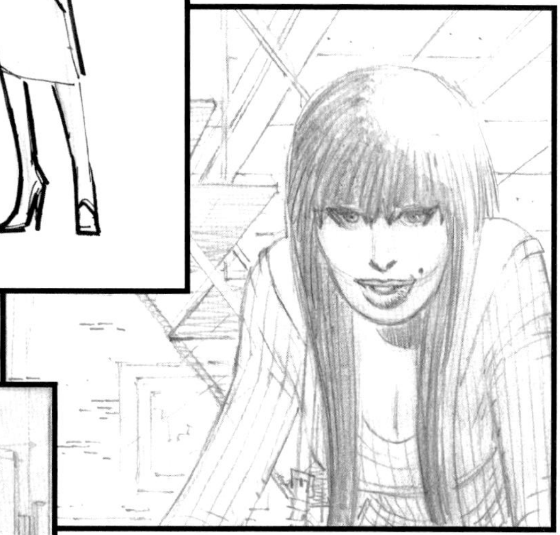

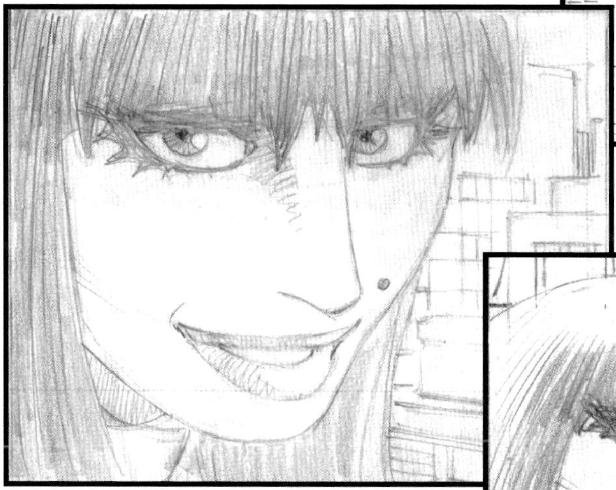

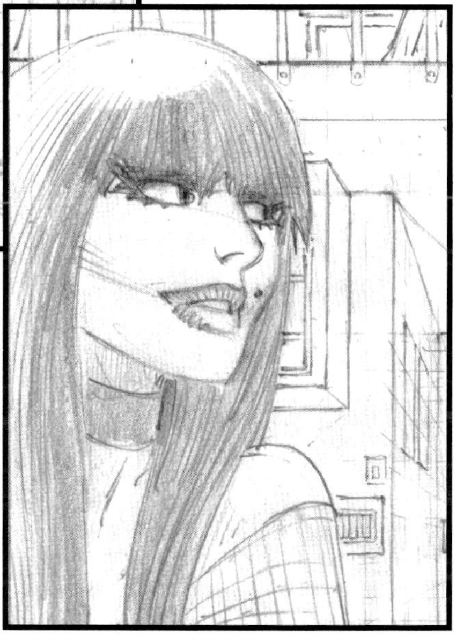

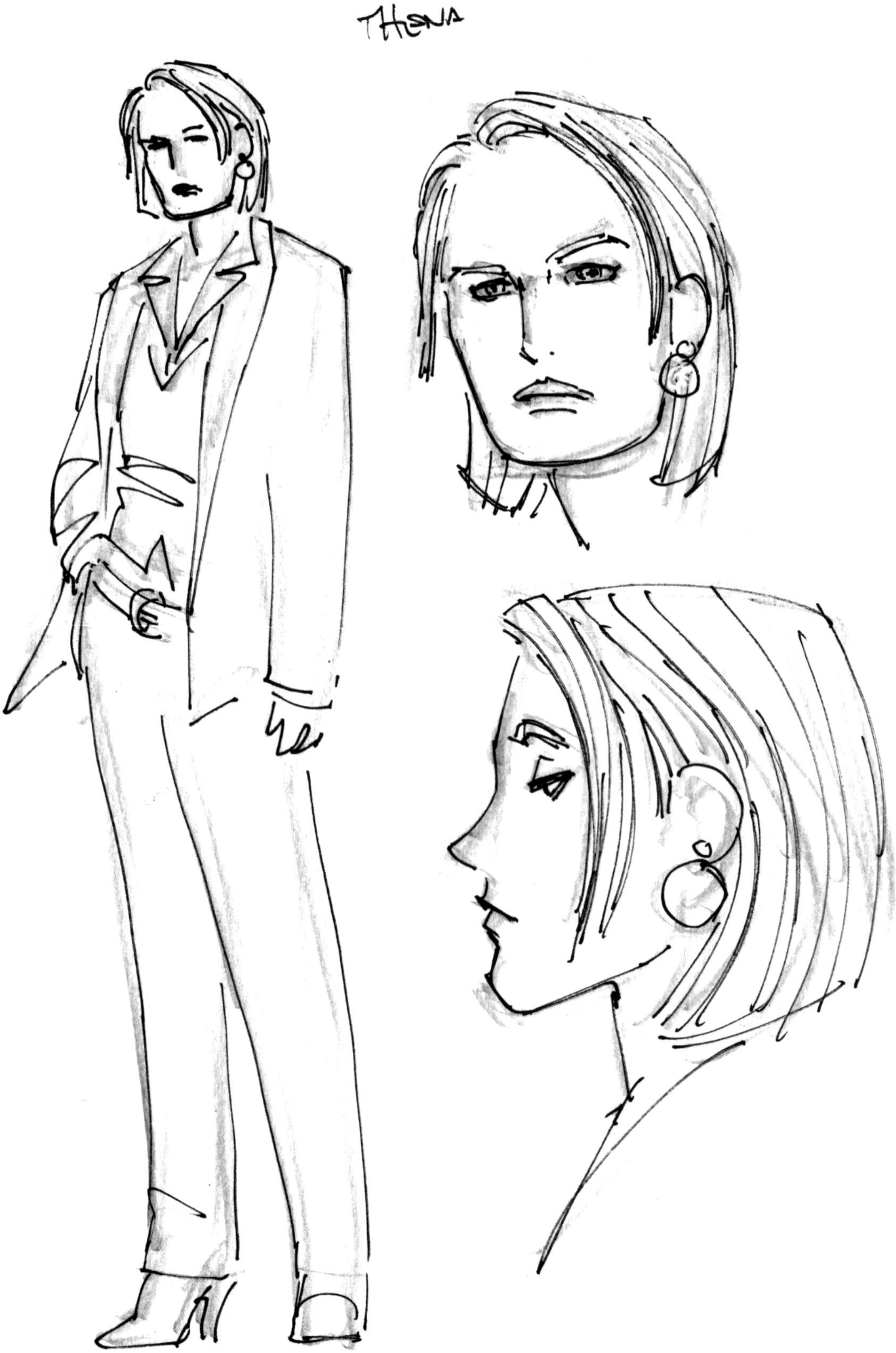
THENA

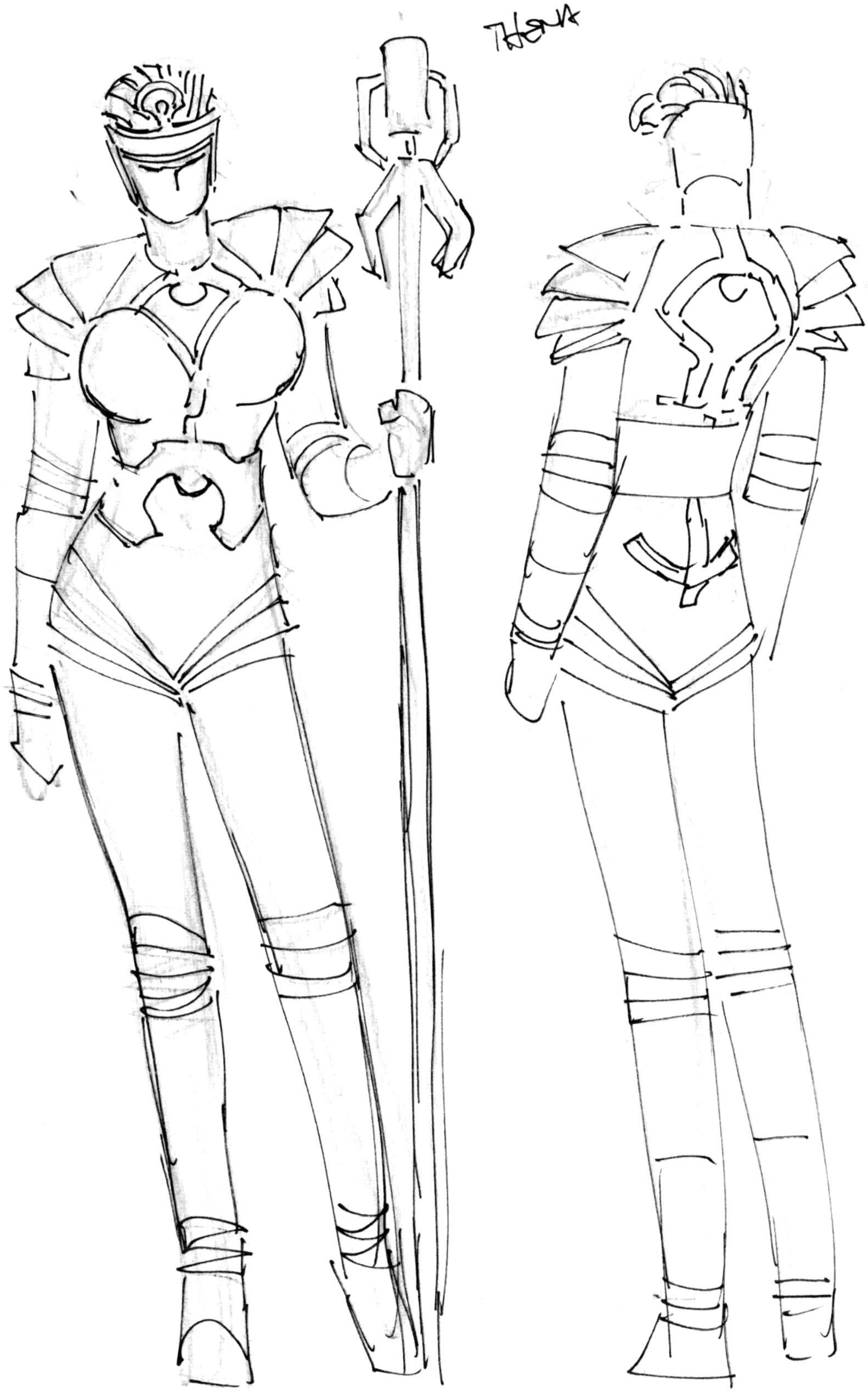
THENA

DRUIG

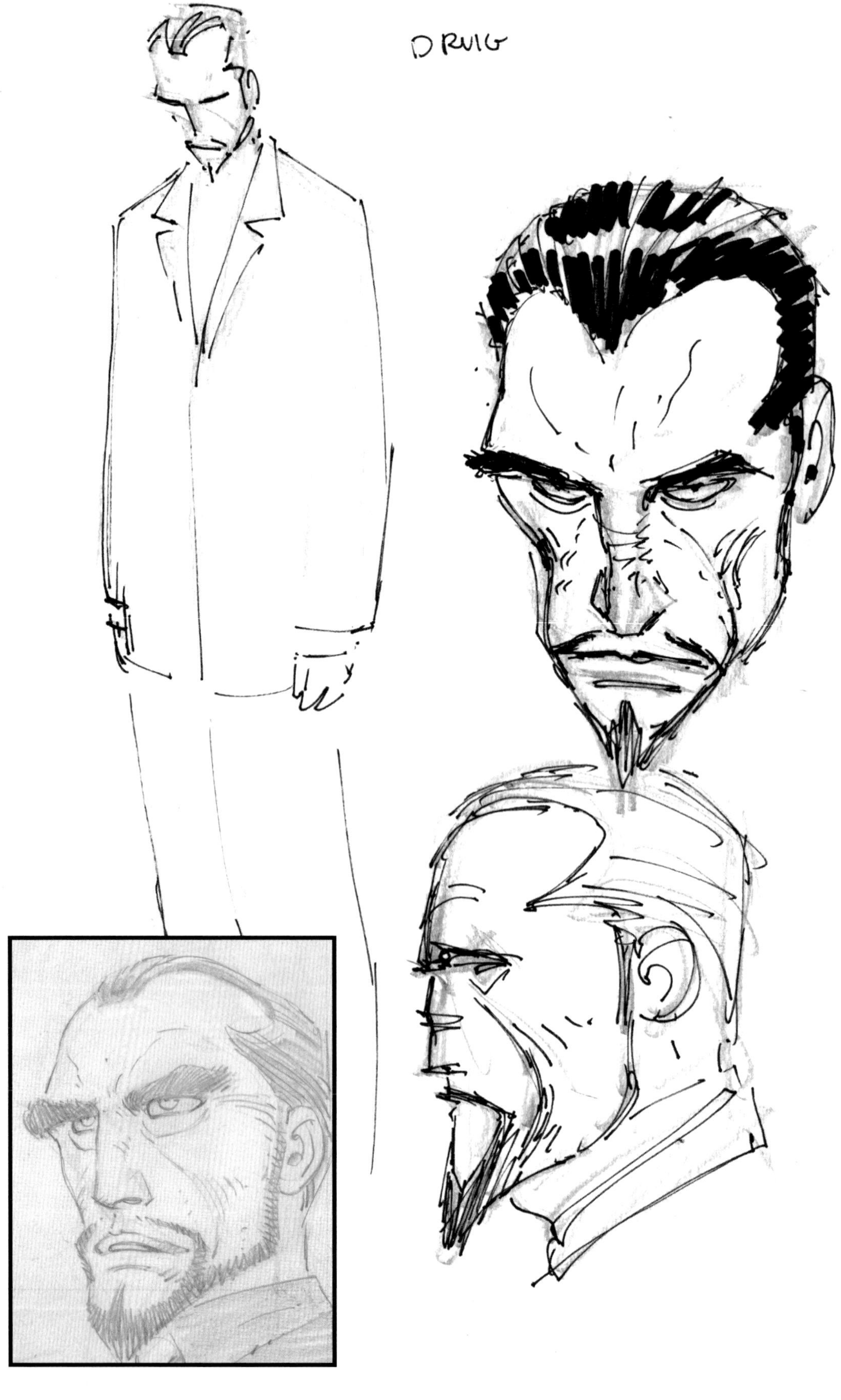
DRUIG

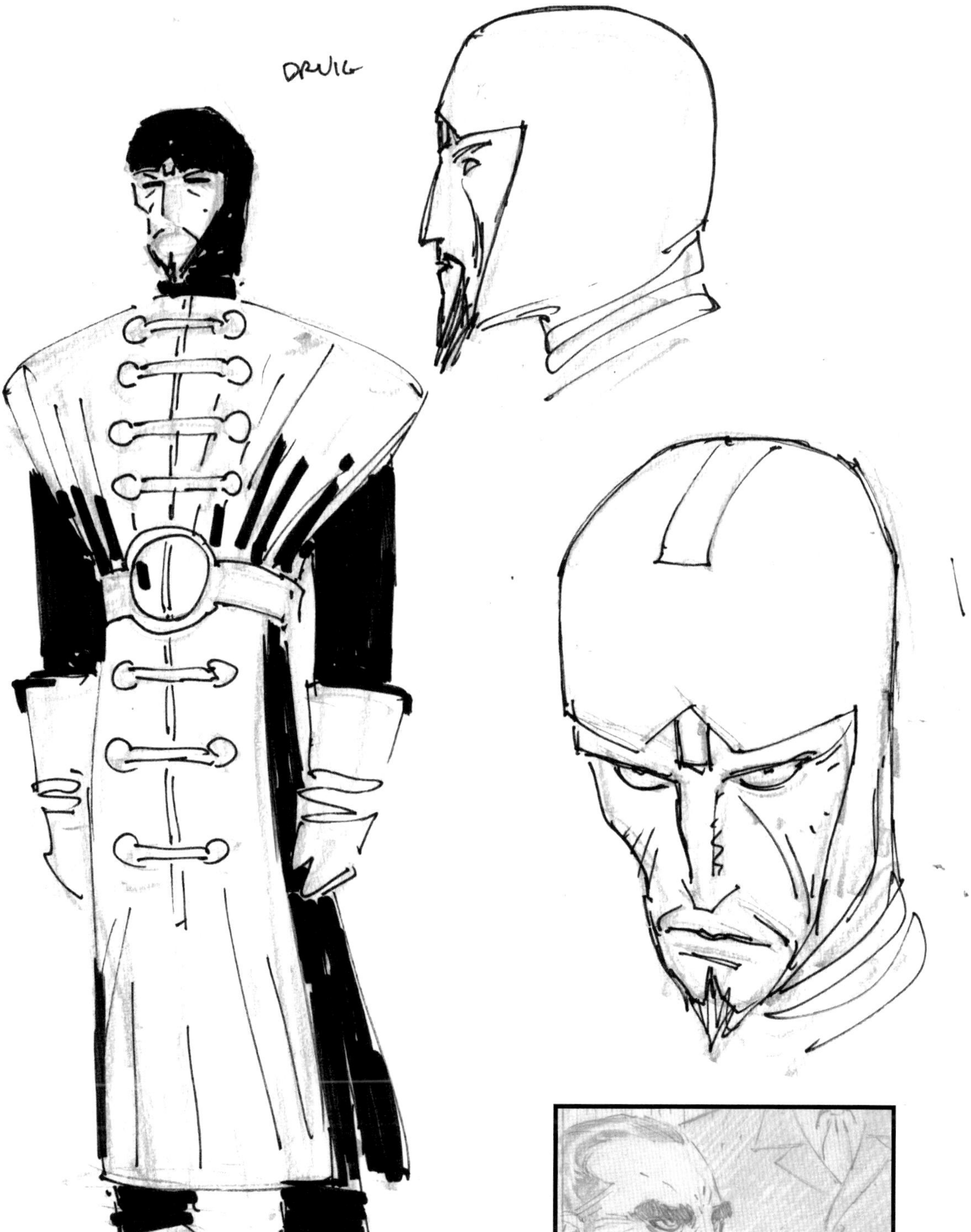
DRUIG

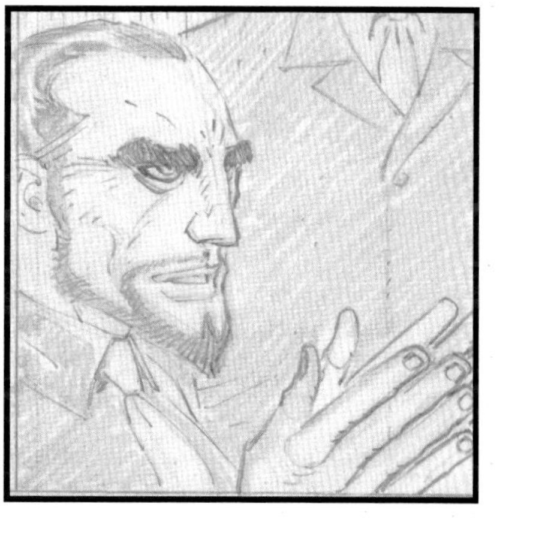

CELESTIALS DESCEND!

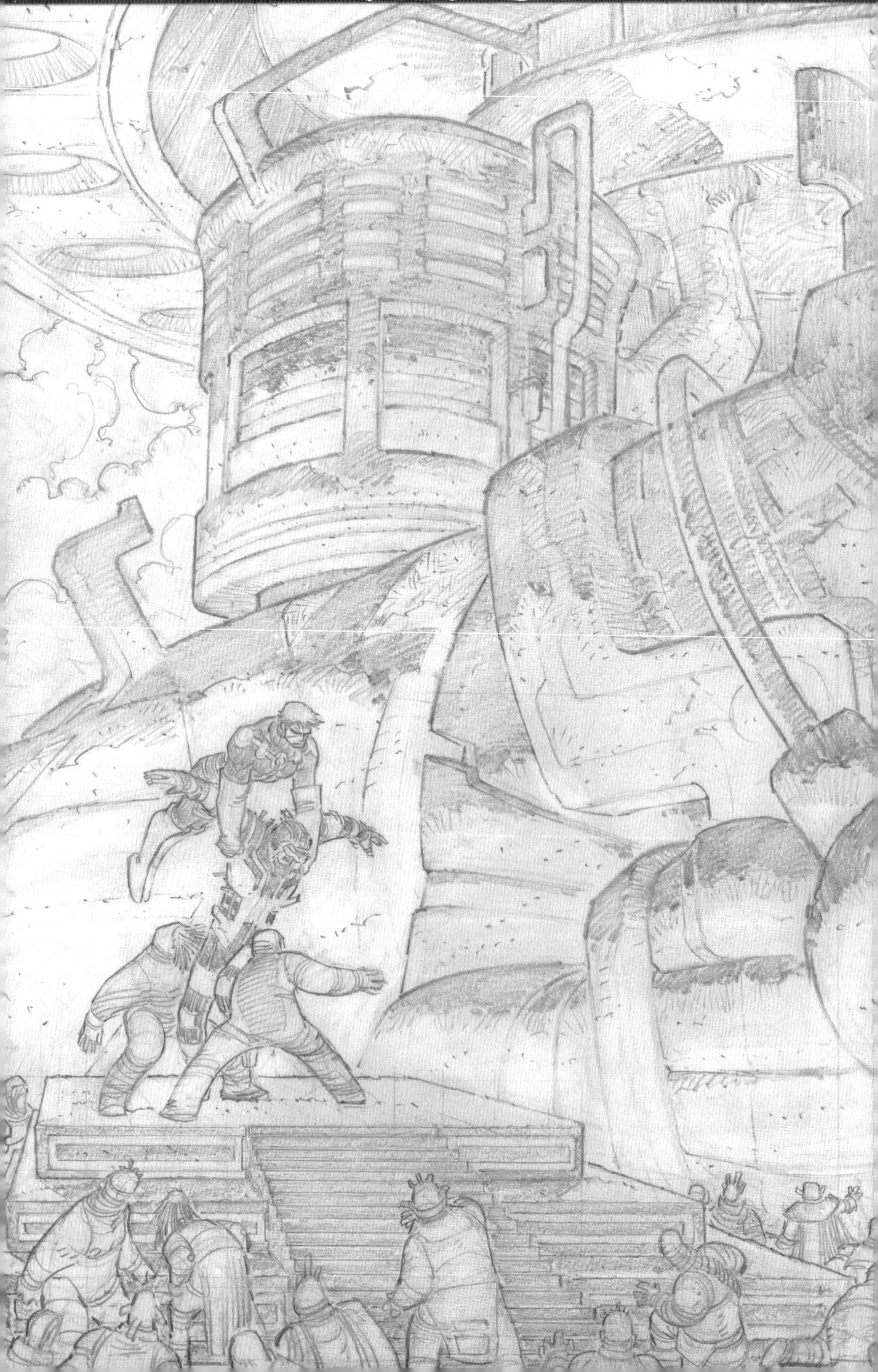

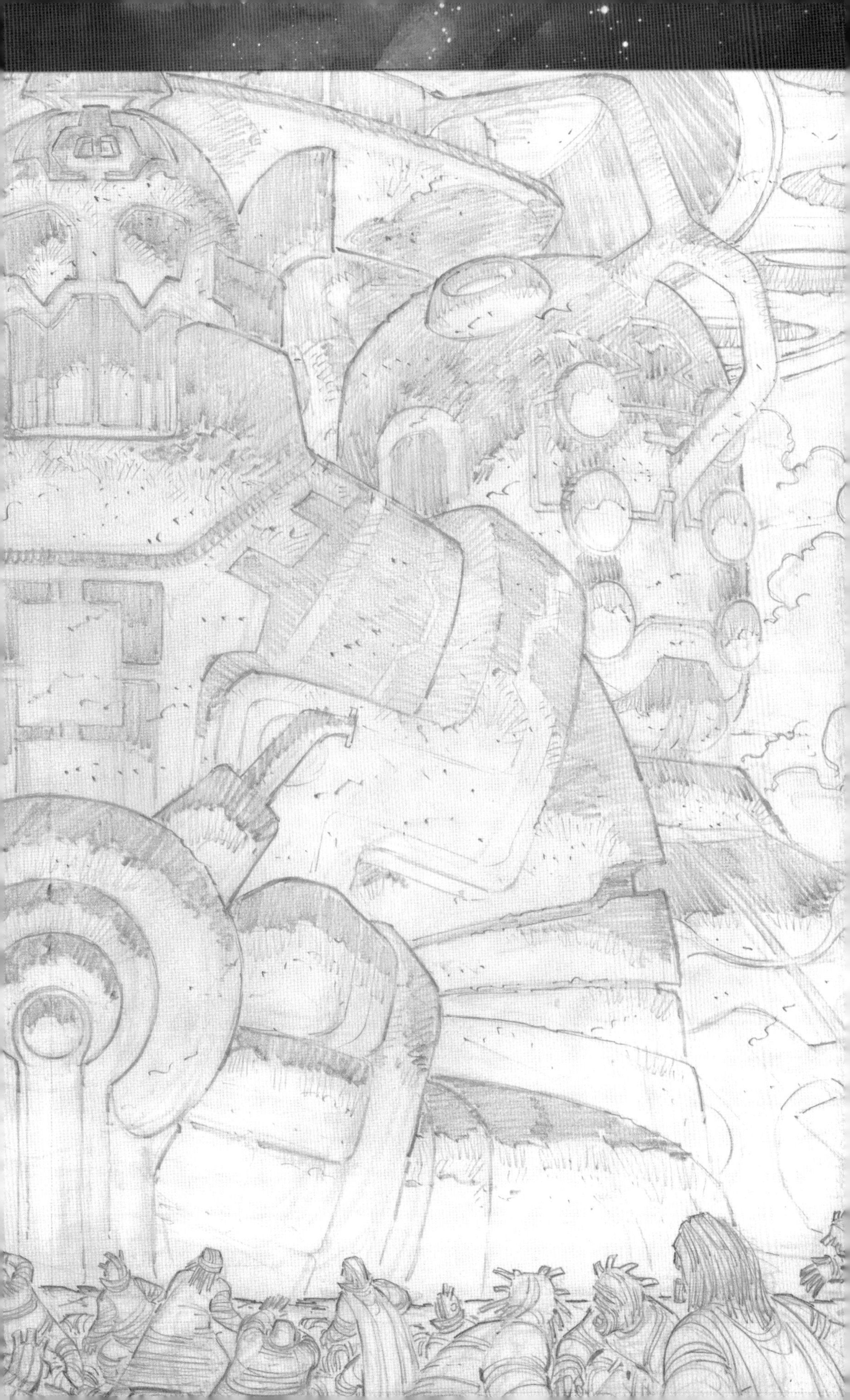

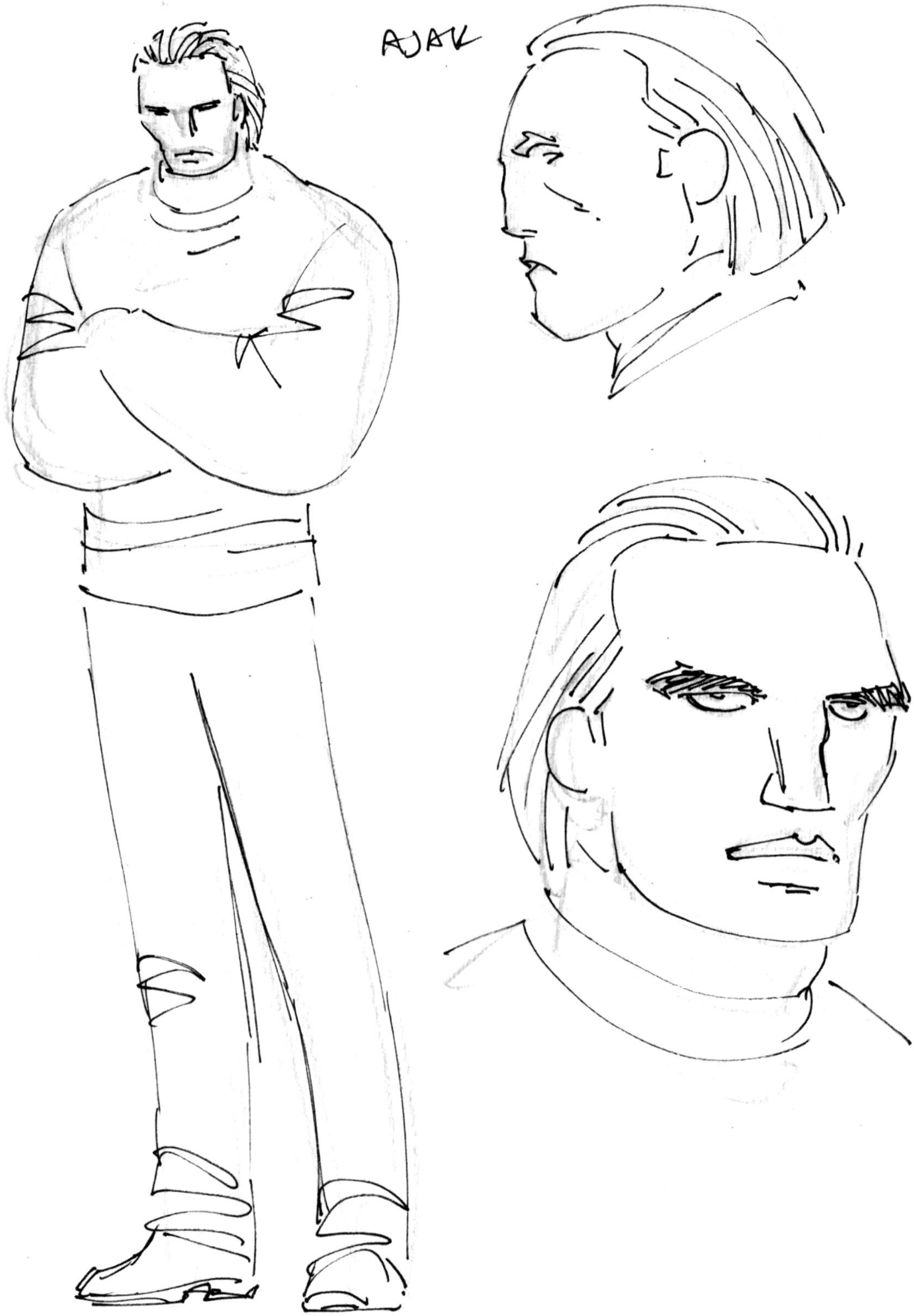
AJAK

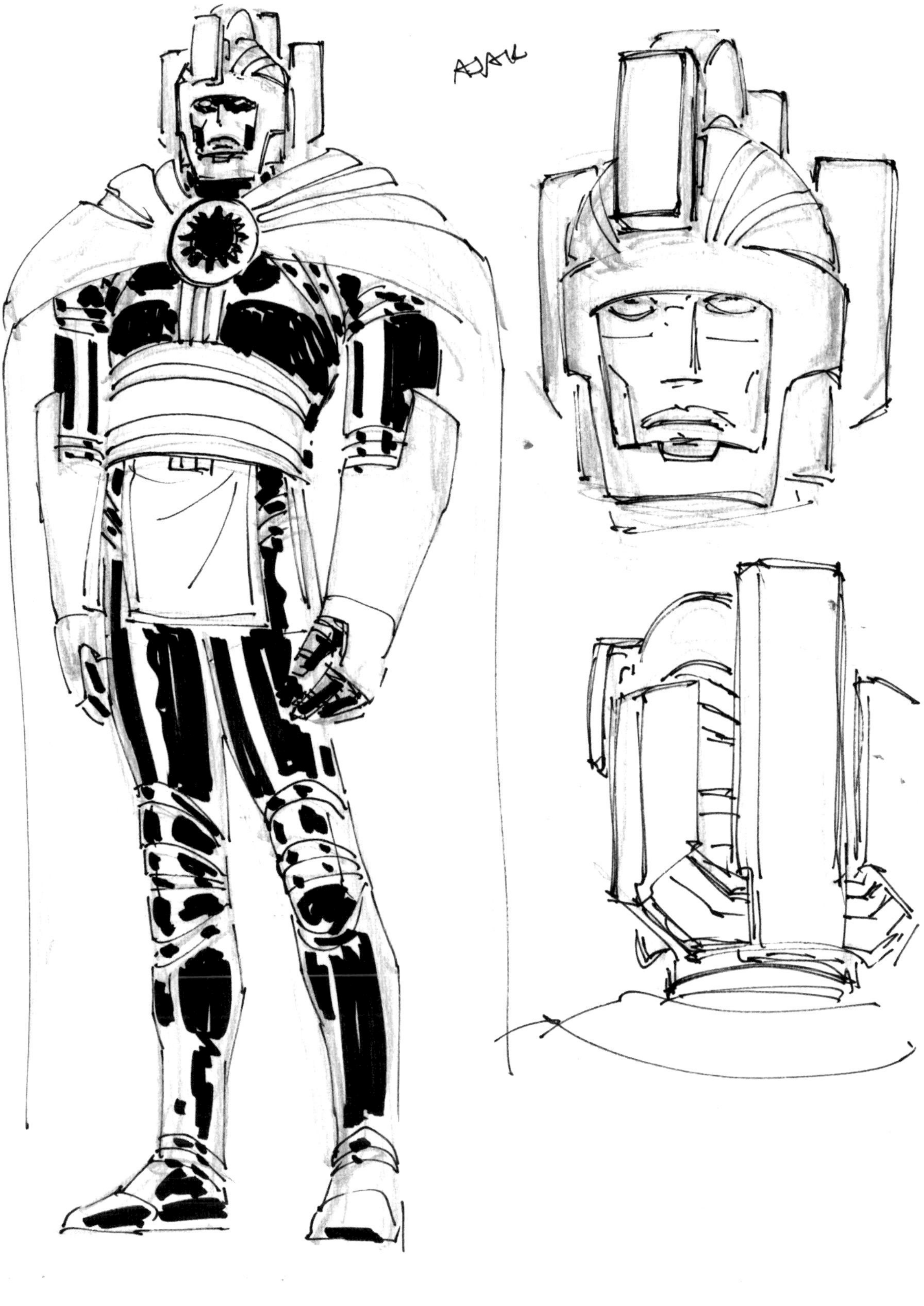
AJAK

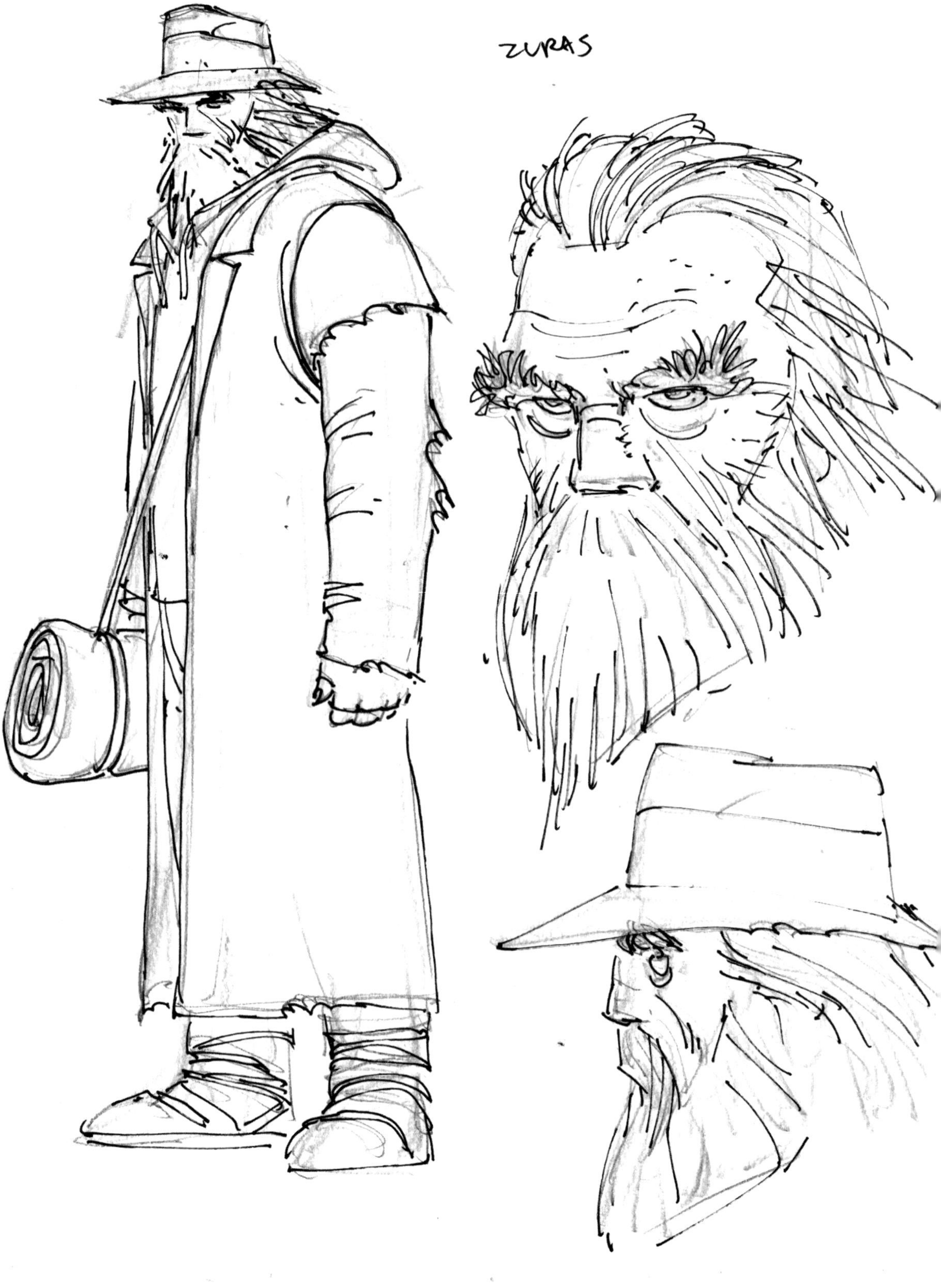
ZURAS

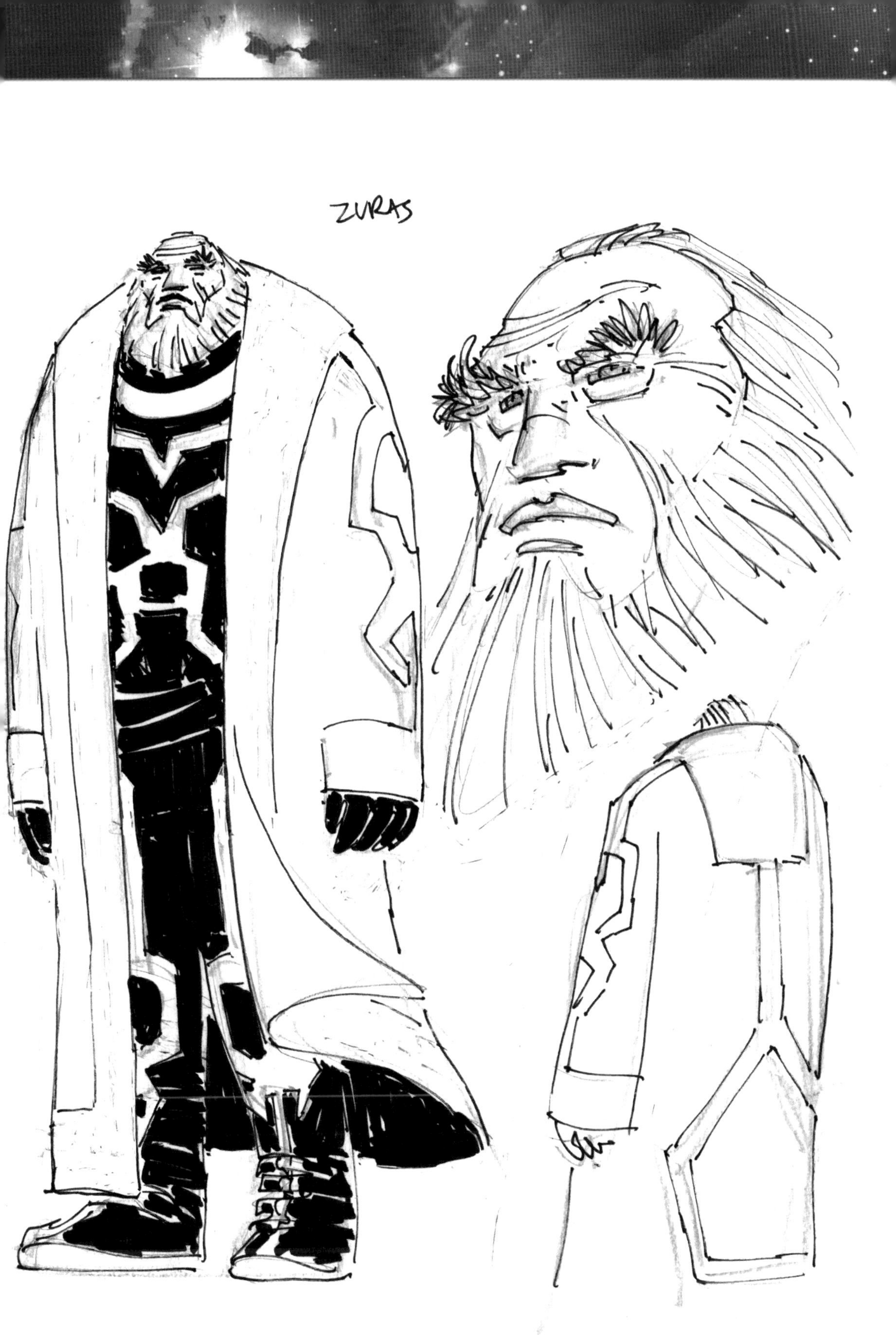
ZURAS

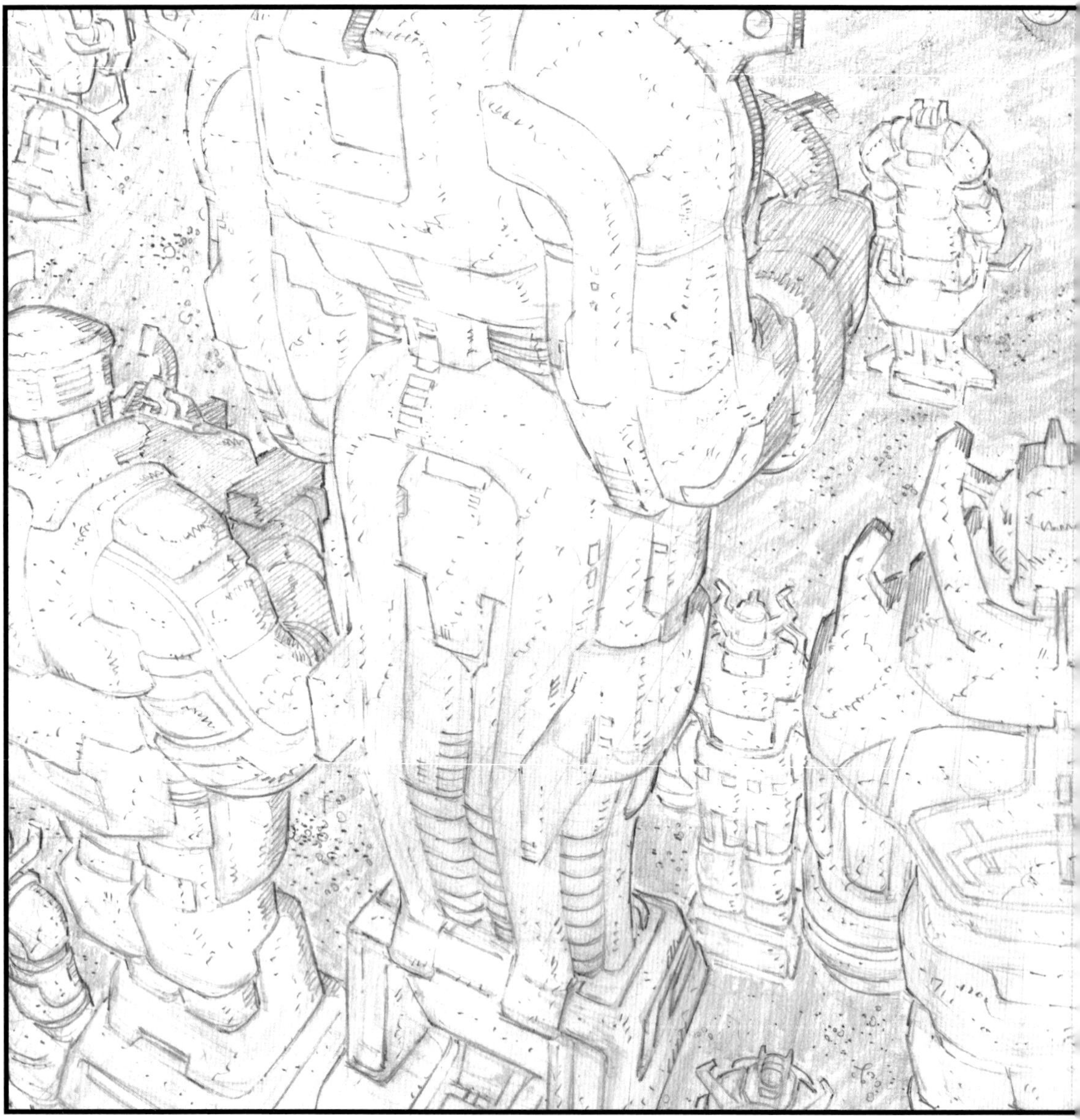

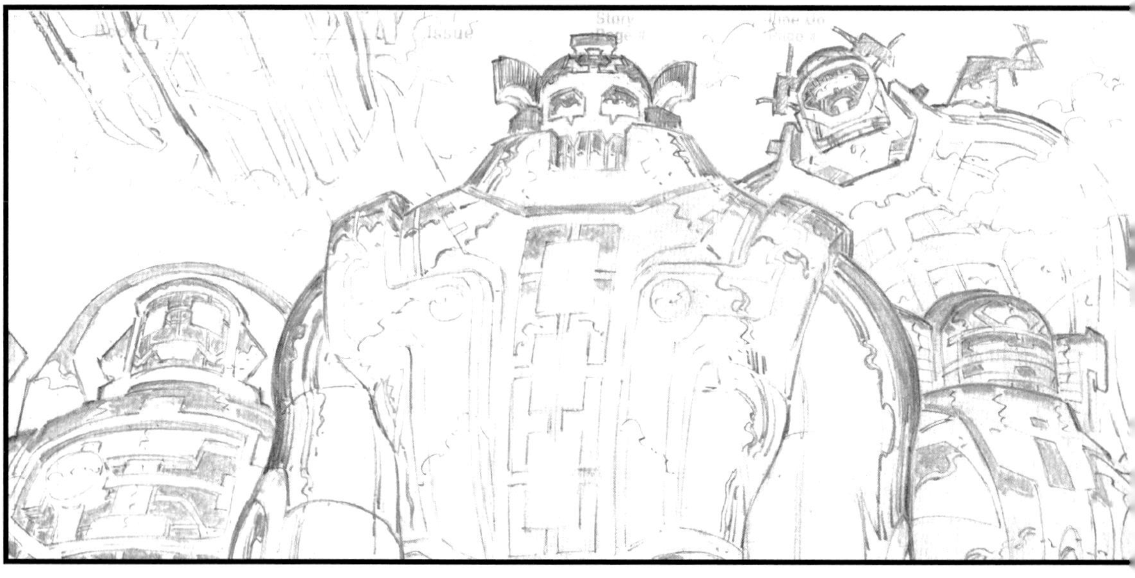

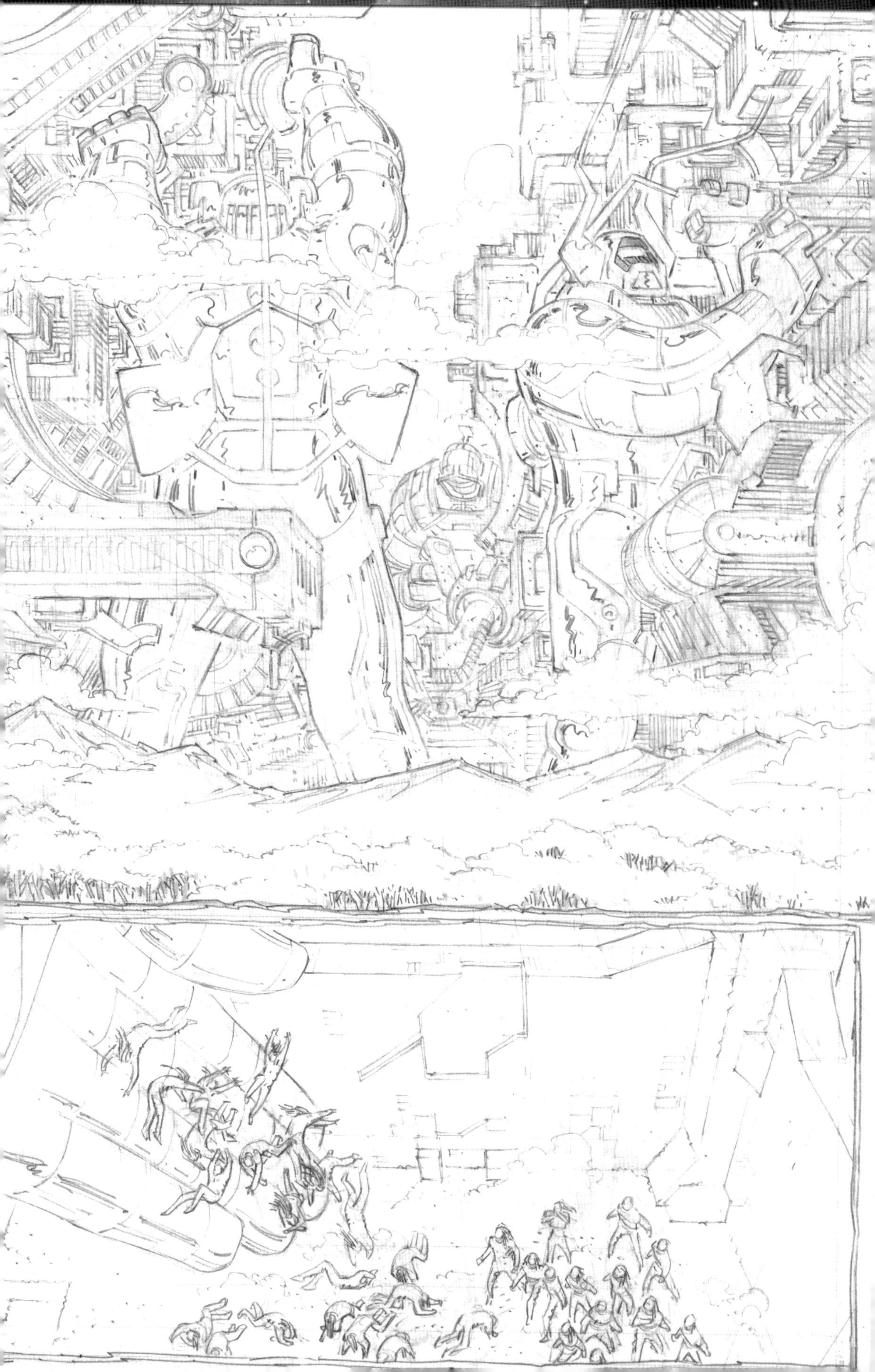

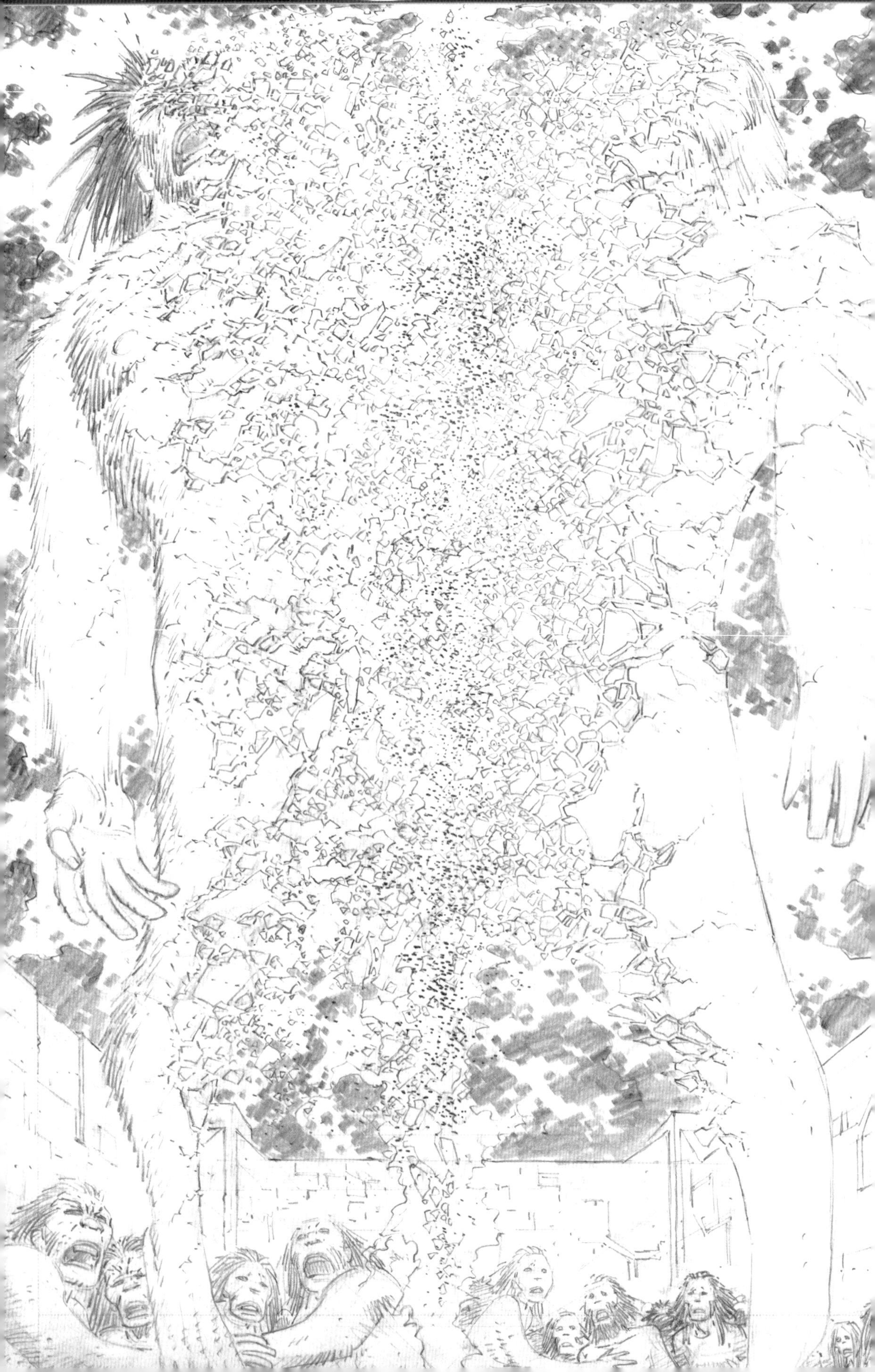

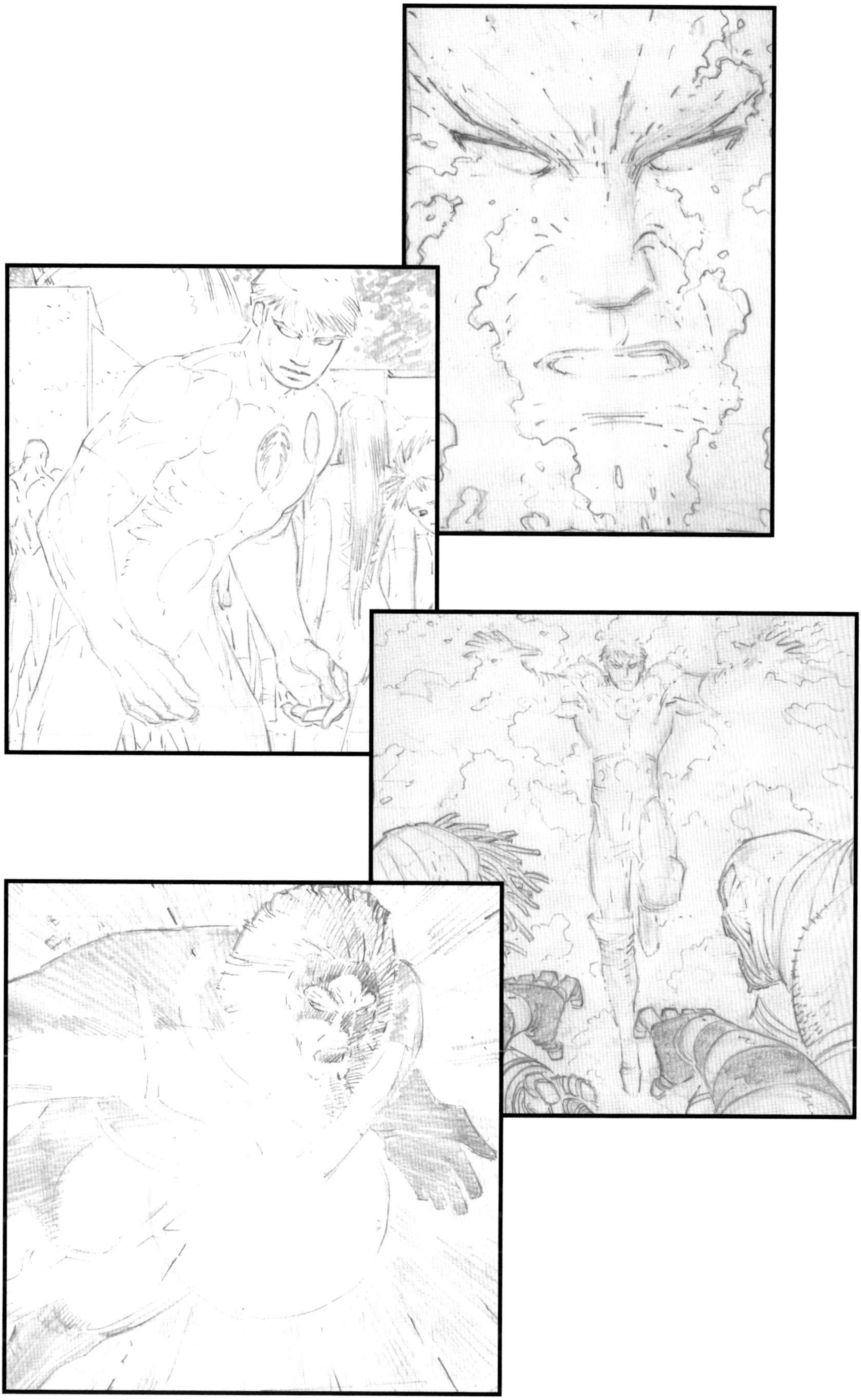

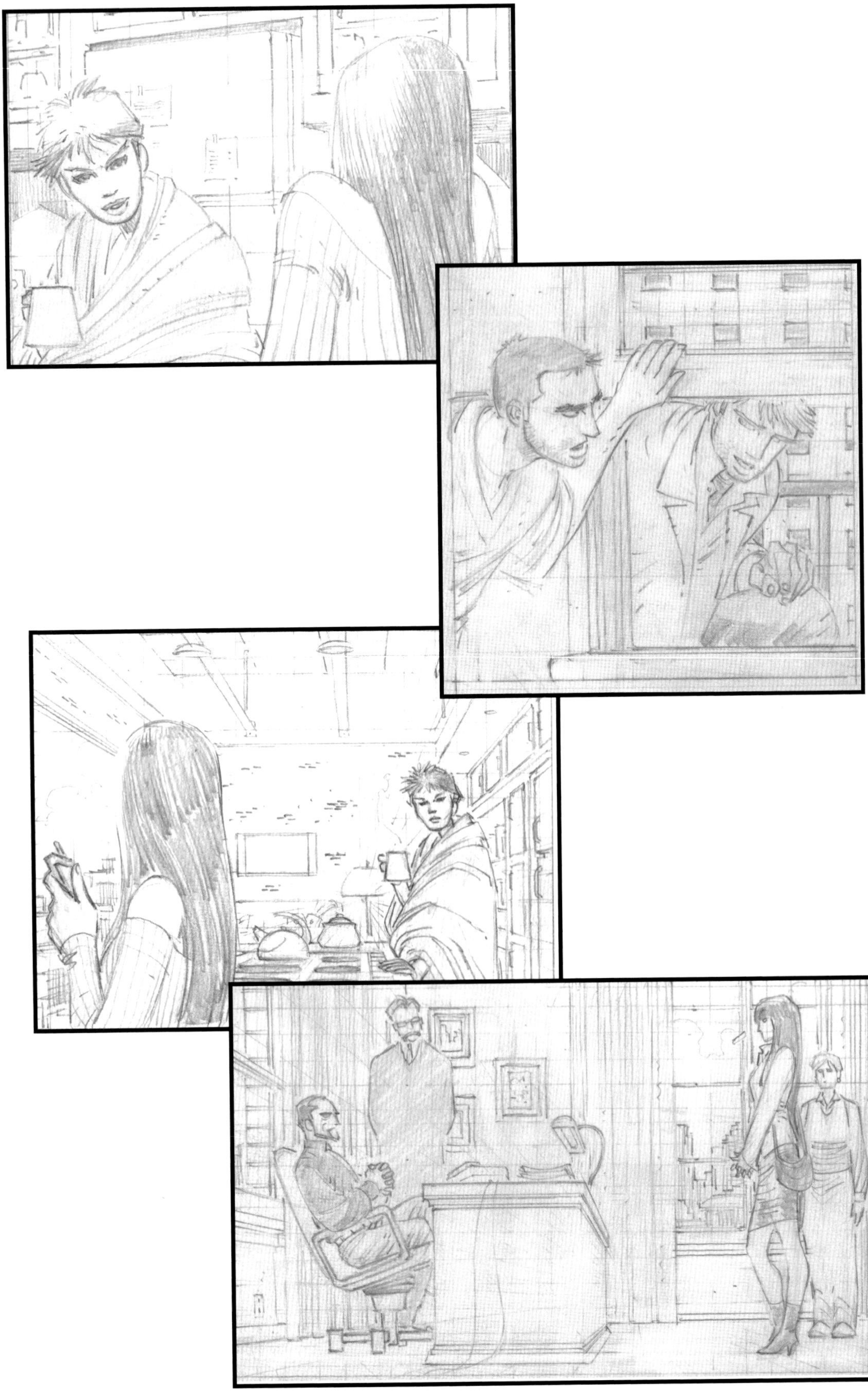

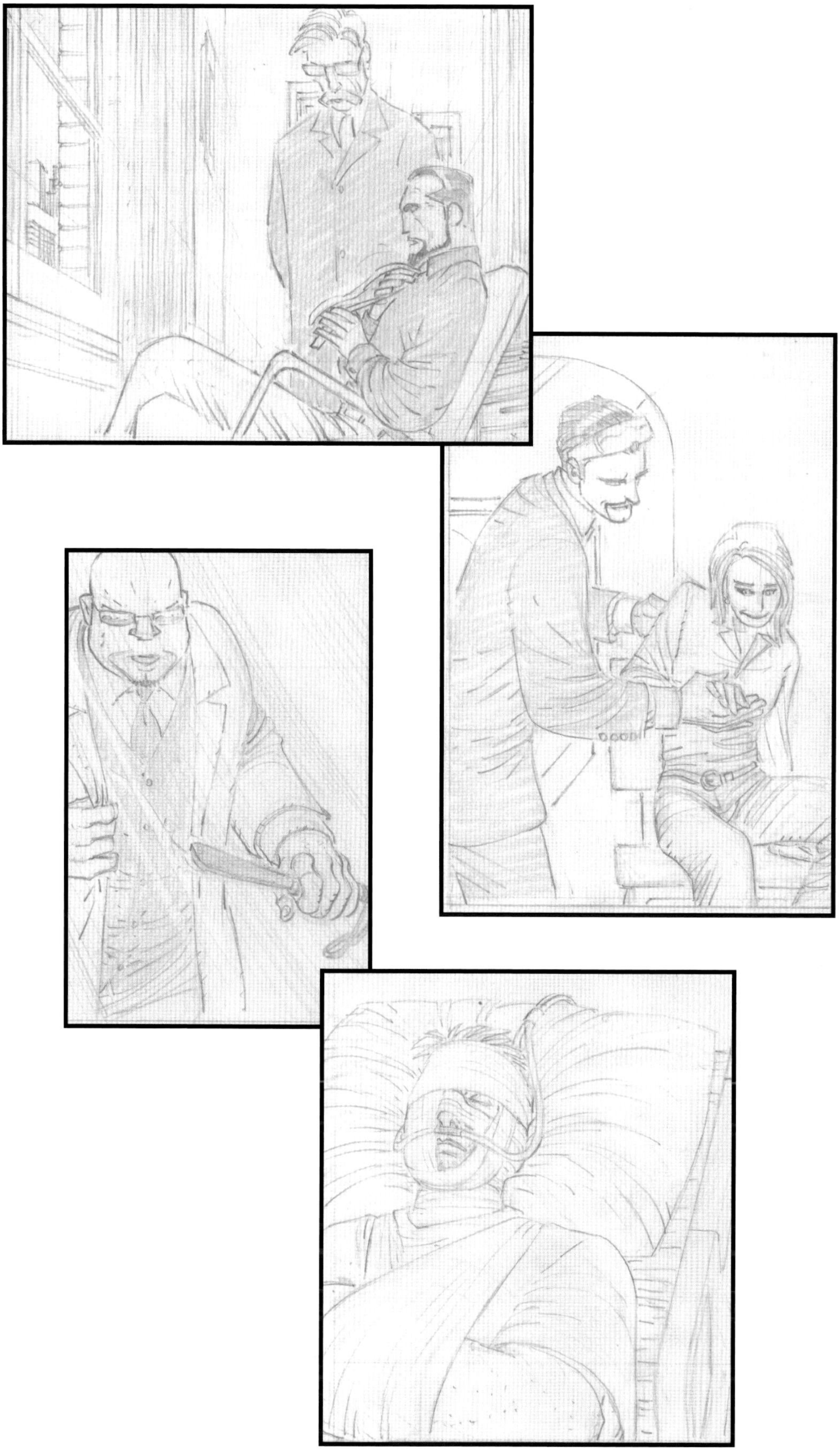

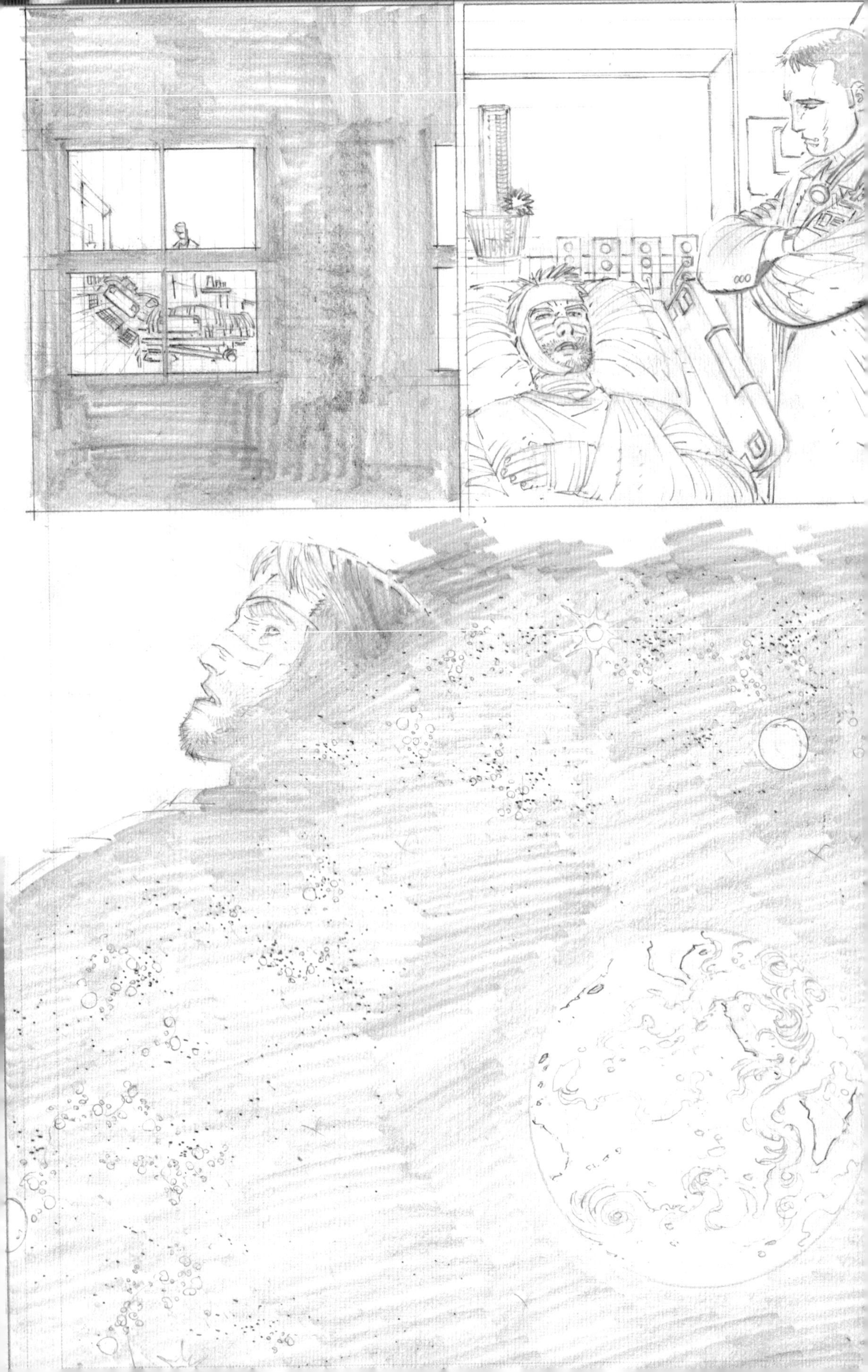

MARVEL SPOTLIGHT

NEIL GAIMAN • OFFICIAL HANDBOOK

REAL NAME: Neil Gaiman

DATE OF BIRTH: November 10, 1960

PLACE OF BIRTH: Portchester, Hampshire, UK

OCCUPATION: Comic book writer, novelist, filmmaker

PLACE OF RESIDENCE: Minneapolis, MN

WEBSITE: www.neilgaiman.com

FIRST COMICS APPEARANCE: *Violent Cases*, Kitchen Sink, 1987

FIRST MARVEL COMICS APPEARANCE: *1602 #1*, 2003

HISTORY: There are very few comic creators of today that carry as much weight outside the comics community as within, but Neil Gaiman is one of those creators. He has won award after award signifying his stature as a writer of great renown, and not just in the world of comics, but in film and television writing and literature. His work is marked with richly drawn and accessible characters, a sense of the mystic and supernatural, and an unstinting usage of the broad palette of storytelling genres. He is as comfortable writing a shocking horror scene as he is an intensely romantic love scene. Wherever Neil needs to be to tell his story, that is where you will find him!

Neil was born in Portchester, Hampshire, England in 1960, and by the time he was a young boy he was already well steeped in the literature of writers as diverse as C.S. Lewis, JRR Tolkein, Roger Zelazny and Harlan Ellison. The broad strata of information served up to Neil's spongy little mind would equip him with the formidable arsenal he employs in his writing today. Fantasy, science fiction, horror, philosophical texts, historical texts, all the disciplines of religion and the folklore of mythology — this is the stuff upon which the little boy from Portchester reared himself as a reader. Oh, and comic books! Neil read lots and lots of comic books!

Growing up, Neil bundled his love of writing with all these influences and set out to become a writer. Initially, he was involved in journalism, writing reviews, feature articles and interviews. His first published work, in fact, was a biography on 80s phenomenons Duran Duran. This took up the first half of the decade, but the second half saw Neil climb headlong into writing comics, which is where he would gain his initial fame.

Though Neil broke ground on his writing career with the comic book, the medium he had loved since childhood, it was a form he wouldn't be content to let confine him. Like Alan Moore, Neil has imbued his writing with a perspective far beyond the limits established by what had come before. Countering the assumptions many assumed were inherent to the four-color

monthly periodical, Neil brought bold characterizations, ultra-literate yet approachable dialogue, and story plots that ranged from the shocking to the sublime. Despite the sense of revelation felt by fans that, through his comics, were rediscovering what comics could be, at the same time, Neil made it all so instantly comfortable for readers.

His first major work in comics was DC's *Black Orchid*, a three-issue mini-series that set the stage for what came next, the *Sandman*. Neil's revision of DC's longstanding Sandman concept quite literally changed comics as we know them. It was a comic that became incredibly popular despite studiously avoiding the storytelling standards of the day. Morpheus as the central figure was not a "superhero" per se. The supporting casts constantly changed, and it wouldn't be guaranteed that Morpheus would even be in any particular comic! More, there were stylistic changes from issue to issue that would seem jarring by nature, but in Neil's gifted hands they were delivered seamlessly to the reader. *Sandman* attracted a huge cult following, especially among women, who it seemed had finally found a comic they could call their own (trust me on this, as one who's sister actually stole the first eight issues from me!)

Having made his name in the comics industry, Neil charted a course to tackle other writing projects. He wrote another highly-regarded series for DC with *Books of Magic*, and picked up with Eclipse Comics' *Miracleman* after close friend Alan Moore left the writing chores. Not content to stick with writing just comics, Neil collaborated with Terry Pratchett on the wistful apocalypse novel, *Good Omens*. In 1997, Neil wrote the teleplay for the BBC called *Neverwhere*, a dark urban fantasy that told the story of a parallel world called "London Below." Neil later adapted his script into a novel.

In 2001, Neil wrote *American Gods*, a novel which won the Hugo and Nebula Awards for Best Novel. Later that year, Neil started writing his first foray into Marvel Comics with a project he conceived called *Marvel 1602*, in which Neil took the core cast of Marvel's Silver Age of Comics, placed them 400 years in the past, and retold their stories in his own way. Aided by some stunning art by Andy Kubert, the combination of Neil Gaiman and Marvel Comics proved impossible to resist for comics fans, and *Marvel 1602* was the top-selling comic of the year.

Venturing into film, Neil collaborated with artist Dave McKean, a compatriot from his days on *Sandman*, on *Mirrormask*, a mix of live-action, animation and puppetry which saw its premiere in late 2005. A fantasy film in the mold of *Labyrinth*, Neil and Dave worked with the Jim Henson studios to create a story in which the central hero, a young girl named Helena, must navigate a strange otherworld in which her darker side wants to abandon her.

Today, Neil is working with artist extraordinaire John Romita, Jr. on his second Marvel project, a revitalization of Jack Kirby's 1970s epic, *The Eternals*. On the heels of the first issue of *Eternals*, the Dancing Ferret record label is issuing a tribute CD titled *Where's Neil When You Need Him?*, featuring song tributes to Neil's writing and characters from over the years.

THE NEIL GAIMAN MARVEL COMICS LIBRARY:

Eternals #1-6 (2006)

Marvel 1602 #1-8 (2002)

Marvel Spotlight: Neil Gaiman/Salvador Larroca (2006)

COLLECT 'EM IN TRADE:

Marvel 1602 - ISBN 978-1-904159-43-8

£12.99

IN THE SHADOW OF THE CELESTIALS: Eternals escape from the Deviants under the ever-watchful eyes of the mysterious space gods. (From *Eternals #1*.)

THE SPOTLIGHT INTERVIEW WITH NEIL GAIMAN

It's a *Marvel Spotlight* dream come true: share a phone call with Neil Gaiman and talk comics, *The Eternals*, and Jack Kirby! Tough work, brother! Tough work! Neil is a writer of longstanding reverence in this medium we love, and has the type of erudite resume one would assume might rightly include a fair bit of snobbishness towards four-color fandom. Not so! In this interview, Neil reveals his still abiding fascination with the comics he loved as a kid, and which still occupy much of his creative thoughts today, albeit in a more mature and evolved fashion.

SPOTLIGHT: Thank you so much for sharing some of your time with *Marvel Spotlight*. How are you doing today?

NEIL: Overworked, but well.

SPOTLIGHT: Overworked? Well, it has to be a good kind of overworked when you're talking about stuff like *The Eternals*, which looks to be a very exciting project, don't you think?

NEIL: Yes, it's rather fun and very, very, very strange.

SPOTLIGHT: Very strange? Well, that would be your fault, right?

NEIL: Yes, I guess! I got a lovely thing in from our colorist the other day. He sent me questions about the *Eternals* plot, which I thought was fun. Matt was getting so involved in the plot that he wanted to ask scientific questions, and then he finished by saying how amazingly "comic book" it was, which just made me amazingly happy!

SPOTLIGHT: I just had the thoroughly pleasurable experience of rereading the first *Eternals* series by Jack Kirby to prepare for our interview. Jack, and particularly his 70s work, is the reason I became a comics fan. *The Eternals* has always been one of my favorite books; it blew my mind when I was eight and nine years of age and reading this stuff on my school's playground. When I heard that you were involved in taking Jack's project up again, along with the amazing John Romita, Jr., I said to myself, "This is it!"

NEIL: Oh, and have you seen any of the art yet?

SPOTLIGHT: I've seen many of the pages as they've been trickling in. It's all explosively great stuff!

NEIL: It is great stuff, yes.

SPOTLIGHT: Did you have a similar history with *The Eternals*, of reading them when they were first published, of being entranced by their "Kirbyish" power, or are you coming to this project fresh without any previous exposure?

NEIL: I picked *Eternals* up when I was…how old? I suppose I would have been fifteen or sixteen when *Eternals* came out. I was a huge Kirby fan. He'd just gone back to Marvel after the Fourth World at DC Comics had sort of expired. He'd done a rather odd and unsatisfying *Captain America* run, which I had picked up simply because it was Kirby. And then, he did some *2001* stuff, and then *Eternals* came along, which seemed- at least in the beginning- to be Jack taking a lot of energy from his work on *2001* (you could tell that that was where his head had gone), and also, partly energy from some leftover Fourth Worldy stuff…and also that sort of Erich von Daniken spin. He took all that and started doing something with it. And even at the time, on one hand I really liked it, and on the other hand there seemed to be a few things that were very odd about it. Chiefly- and this is interesting because in some ways, it's something I've had to cope with- the *Eternals* obviously by definition were not meant to be part of the Marvel Universe, except even back then he was getting pressure to make them part of the Marvel Universe.

SPOTLIGHT: The letters pages for *The Eternals* back then were aflame with controversy over that particular point.

NEIL: And he got around it in interesting ways. He had some SHIELD agents come around in the early issues, and the Hulk comes in for a

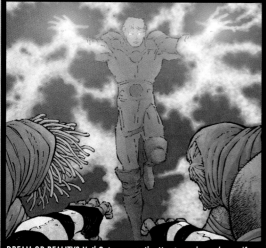

DREAM OR REALITY? Neil Gaiman sets Ike Harris on the path to self-discovery of his true nature in *Eternals #1*.

guest shot, but it's a mechanical Hulk! (*Laughter.*) A kid gets turned into the Thing for a panel but you genuinely can't tell if it's a comics character or not. But you know, I thought it was played very well, and then after it ended, and you could see the plug getting pulled on this thing just as it was really getting going, then you get various Marvel attempts to fold the Eternals into the Marvel Universe, which is right up there with trying to crossbreed a prize greyhound with Gibbon's *The Decline and Fall of the Roman Empire*. You know, you just sit there going, "Uhhhh...nooooo...something is...how do they think... bleh..." (*Laughter.*) The attempts to do it sort of mucked things up a lot in terms of muddying the water of what made the Eternals interesting anyway.

The fun thing about *The Eternals* to me is that for about two years, ever since *1602* finished, Joe Quesada and I would meet in a variety of odd places, and we'd have lunch or breakfast or dinner, and while having lunch or breakfast or dinner, I'd say, "Ok, I've got an idea for whatever Marvel Project #2 is..." and I'd run something by him. And normally I'd get to the end and he'd say, "That's really good. Trouble is, Bendis just did something like that." Or, "Bendis is halfway through something like that." Or, "We just had a meeting and Bendis is going to do something like that."

We weren't able to figure out something that would be fun for me to do. I knew I wanted to do something very different from *1602*, in that *1602* was me getting to recreate 60s Marvel and do it in my own way, in my own time. (I suppose quite literally!) So I knew I wanted to do something in the present day, and I didn't want it to have quite the same hugeness of cast of characters, which seriously bit me in the ass by the time I got to the end of *1602*, where I was looking around and going, "Great! I've still got twenty-five major players and nobody is getting the time at the end that they ought to have!" That was very frustrating.

So I knew I wanted a smaller cast. I think it would have been after the publication of *Anansi Boys*, last September, when I popped in to the Marvel offices to say hello, and I just sort of wandered into Joe's office and we were chatting, and he said, "*The Eternals*. Do you remember *The Eternals?*" And I said, "You mean Ikaris, who went under the incredibly impossible to figure out pseudonym of Ike Harris?" (*Laughter.*) And he said, "Yeaaaaah!" He asked, "Would you like to do *The Eternals*? They're sort of sitting around the corners of the Marvel Universe, and they don't really relate to anything. There's nothing we can do with them." And I thought for about thirty seconds and I said, "Yeah, send me the comics again." (And as it turned out, I still had most of them downstairs, which was kinda cool!)

Mostly, what I'd never done with *The Eternals* was read them all as a giant batch. I had read them monthly as they were coming out. At the time, I just compared them to that rock solid burning madness that was Kirby's Fourth World at its height. And I thought, "Well, that's alright." I didn't think of *Eternals* as great Kirby. But going back and reading it again, I started thinking how much I really liked the concept there, and I really liked the characters and I really wished that...(*Reflective pause.*) I don't actually know anything about the editorial history, nor have I asked — I'm sure somebody around would only be too happy to fill me in- but it definitely reads like Kirby just wants to do Kirby, and there are other forces that are saying, "Hey can you get on to that stuff, and now can you get onto this?" and some of the stuff that would have made it wonderful, mad Kirby, isn't there as much as it should be.

SPOTLIGHT: *Eternals* was quite unlike any Marvel comic that was coming out in the late 70s. At the time of publication, you have to look at the Fourth World as precedent for something like *Eternals*, but even the Fourth World was doled out over several different titles. It seemed

NEIL GAIMAN • ANDY KUBERT • RICHARD ISANOVE
MARVEL
1602

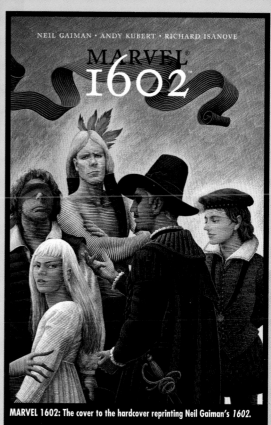

MARVEL 1602: The cover to the hardcover reprinting Neil Gaiman's *1602*.

ETERNALS
3Y JACK KIRBY OMNIBUS

STILL ONLY 75¢
MARVEL COMICS GROUP
1 JULY 02334
WHEN GODS WALK THE EARTH!
THE ETERNALS
WE'VE FOUND IT-- THE TOMB OF THE SPACE GODS!
AND THEY'RE NOT DEAD! LOOK TO THE STARS!
THE GODS ARE COMING BACK!
FIRST ISSUE!
THE START OF JACK KIRBY'S LONG-AWAITED COSMIC SERIES!

f Neil Gaiman's new *Eternals* series has whetted your appetite or more tales of Earth's immortals, perhaps you would like to do what Neil did and go back to the beginning and read Jack Kirby's original issues. Whether you've never read this material before, or you'd like the chance to experience *Jack Kirby's Eternals* once again, Marvel is making it easy for you! They are gathering all nineteen regular issues, plus the double-sized Annual, in one complete, oversized hardcover volume called *Eternals by Jack Kirby Omnibus.*

he artwork by Jack Kirby has been newly restored, with new coloring to match the original comics. And with the oversize aspect ratio of the artwork, the only better way to see this material is to track down the original art! You wanna see the panoramic shots of the Celestials as they poke around the Andes or set down on Miami Beach? This is your book! And all of Jack's hyperkinetic double-page spreads of Eternals duking it out with Lord Kro and his Deviants? Just the thought of Jack's mind-blowing panoramas being reproduced in Marvel's wonderful oversized hardcover format gives this commentator the goose bumps!

he book clocks in at almost 500 pages, and is a complete account of 70s era Eternals, but there's a little room for some extras! Editor Mark Beazley tracked down an original Jack Kirby sketch of Ikaris that first appeared in the FOOM fanzine and later became the basis for the comic book's corner box. The book will also reproduce Jack's essay text pages, with his ruminations on the Eternals, space gods and aliens, and his approach to bringing his fantasies to his fiction! Toss in an introduction from longtime Kirby acolyte Mike Royer, and this might just be the out-of-left-field book of the year!

like Kirby wanted to jam all that good stuff from all the different Fourth World series into one, streamlined title.

NEIL: Exactly.

SPOTLIGHT: As it was, it only lasted for nineteen issues and a double-sized Annual, but if given the chance to flourish under its own device, it might have gone on even longer.

NEIL: I like to think so. So what I did, then, was basically turn around to Marvel and basically say, "Okay, in terms of what Jack has done in *Eternals*, which bits of these can I use? What is actual canon in the Marvel Universe?" They mentioned that they were very concerned about Celestials creating humanity. They said, "Nope! Celestials *definitely didn't* create humanity, but they *did* create the Eternals and the Deviants!" And I said, "Oh, okay, well I can work with that!" And after that, it was really just, for me, a matter of coming in with a bunch of ideas that would allow me to go and play with the Eternals, play with some of the ideas that Jack had begun, change some things, fix some things, totally mess up some things. The joy of comics is, as I sit here doing my reboot or whatever it is, that if it doesn't work, in ten or fifteen years time someone will pick it up and go, "Ha! Gaiman! This one really sucked. We'll toss it out and have another go again." But I think that what I'm trying to do is remain bravely true to the Kirbyness of it all. And that includes things like trying to make the Celestials rather more unknowable than they have been. I love the idea that while we will actually find out a few cool things about the Celestials, there will be slightly more, as I say, "unknowables" as there have been before. (Although some of their motivations are kind of fun.)

SPOTLIGHT: The Celestials were an alien race of alleged space gods, who came to Earth on many occasions, broken into different groups called Hosts. Are you working with the full complement of Celestials that Jack conjured up? And is it still the Fourth Host that will be taking the lead?

NEIL: Yes and no. We get to cover the entirety of human history, three or four times, from different points of view. Which is kind of fun! This takes us from the First Host all the way to the Fourth Host. And we get to experience several events from several different points of view. I don't know that it's giving too much away to suggest that we are beginning in a world in which it would appear that all of the Eternals are here on Earth, and as far as we can tell they are regular human beings, but the only one who seems to have any inkling of what he is — or what he believes he is — is Ike Harris, or Ikaris...and he may well be barking mad. (*Laughter.*)

SPOTLIGHT: Well, that's nothing unusual for the Eternals! They have been many things over the years to many different people. Obviously, you have an abiding interest in mythology and how it has worked itself into the fabric of human understanding, and that is pretty much what Jack was after with Eternals, so this seems to be really simpatico with you.

NEIL: Oddly enough, I'm playing much less with that than I thought I would. Partly I think because I've done that, and partly because once Jack had set it up, he lost interest in it, too; you know, I think he was interested in it much more from a "Chariot of the Gods" point of view: "Look, Ikaris was the dove who led Noah's Ark to safety!" They turn up and people thought they were "the gods."

SPOTLIGHT: Ajak was thought to be Quetzalcoatl by the Mesoamerican cultures.

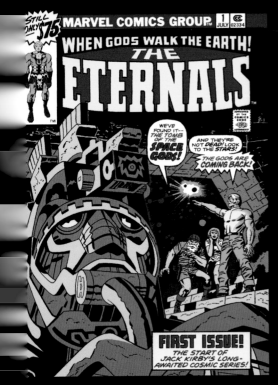

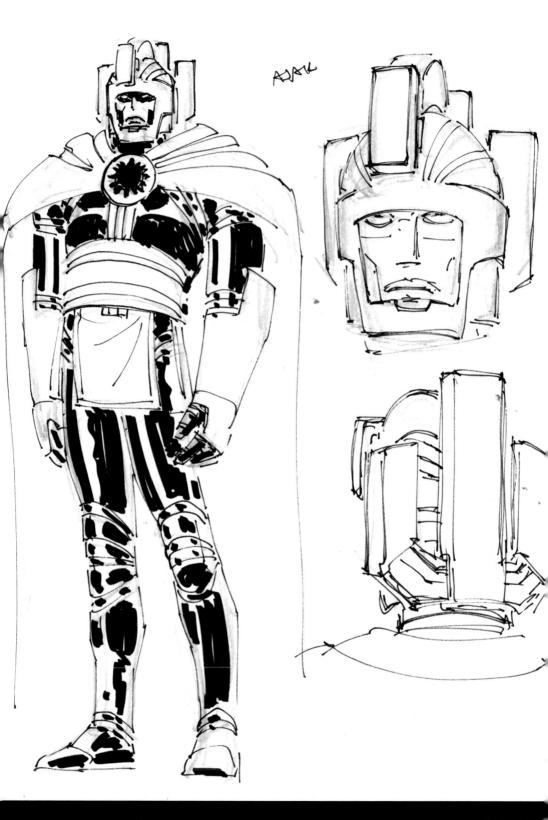

AJAK

The Eternal Ajak, rendered by artist John Romita Jr. in this black and white character sketch.

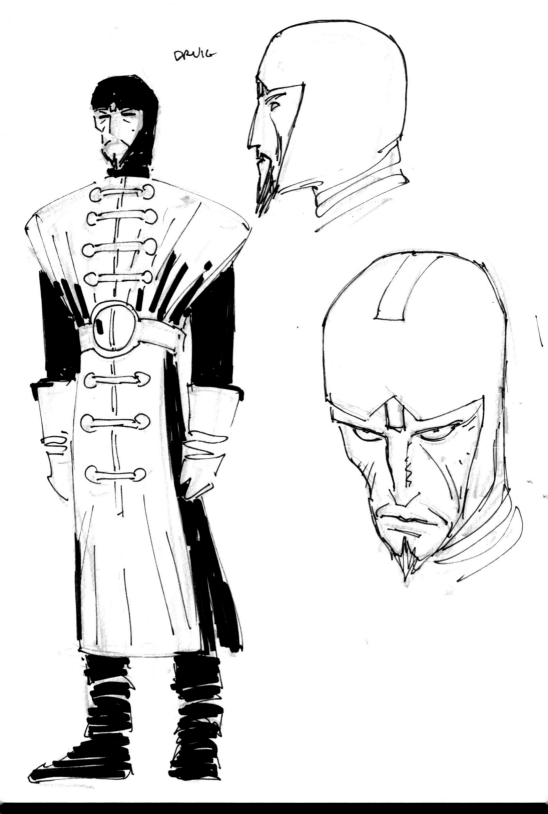

DRUIG

he Eternal Druig, rendered by artist John Romita Jr. in this black and white character sketch. While most Eternals are pure of heart, th

NEIL: Exactly, and that's all kind of fun. But it doesn't actually take you terribly far, especially in a universe in which you really *do* have gods. Not to mention superheroes, not to mention races like the Inhumans, and all sorts of other strange, affiliated, extra-curricular groups. So part of what I'm having enormous amounts of fun doing with this story, I'm just trying to find out what makes the Eternals special: Who are they? What do they do? How many of them are there? And then I started trying to figure out what Jack would sort of toss in and I sort of go, "How does that work on an evolutionary basis?" For example, the Eternals are pretty much perfect. They are unkillable. According to Jack at one point, when they were trying to hypothesize ways to kill one of the Eternals, they were thinking, maybe they could disperse him into a cloud of intelligent molecules. (*Laughter.*) And you're going, "Well that's kind of..."

They're completely unkillable, they're completely healthy, they are way, way above us. They apparently breed, because Thena is Zuras' daughter and stuff...and then you're wondering, "Why haven't they out bred us? We're just humanity! Why aren't there millions and billions of them? Why is it the ones that seem to reproduce incredibly fast and hard are the Deviants, and the Deviants are all members of different species, and they've been breeding like incredibly sexed-up rabbits?"

SPOTLIGHT: Yes, and the Deviants are also very judgmental about their own progeny!

NEIL: Yes, and that was all how I began to get into it. And I also just started to pick out the characters that I liked. I'd say, "Ok, you're in the story, you're in the story. I like you, so you're in the story. I like you, but you're dead. Ok, I'm bringing you back. You're in the story, but you've been completely mucked up; well, then I'm putting you back to the way you were when Kirby did you!" (*Laughter.*) You know, and moving on from there. One of my favorite things about this — which is kind of fun, but also takes advantage of the strange flexibility of the nature of time as perceived by the Eternals and the nature of time in the Marvel Universe — is that in my story, the Third Host did indeed arrive; Arishem came down to judge. In 1976.

SPOTLIGHT: Ahhh!

NEIL: About thirty years ago! Only nobody seems to — apart from Ikaris — nobody seems to know it ever happened. And as Makarri explains to him at one point, you really would think that if a mile high red alien had landed to judge the Earth, it would have been in the news.

SPOTLIGHT: (*Laughter.*) Yes, you would think! Did you ever read *Chariot of the Gods*? That book that alleged a connection between humanity and outer space aliens was quite the phenomenon in the mid-1970s, and it was obviously an inspiration for Jack on *The Eternals*. What do you make of that book and what it meant at the time, and what it means now?

NEIL: One of the things it is now is just noise. Now it's just part of the cultural wallpaper. It's more cultural baggage. At the time, I remember being fourteen or fifteen and that book being handed round in school. It was like, "No! No! The aliens came and here's the proof! How could they have built this? How could they have done that? Look! Here are guys in helmets!" (*Laughter.*)

What's fun in *The Eternals*, at least as we begin, is we see Mark Curry, alias Makarri, being incredibly doubtful about all of this kind of stuff and thinks it's silly, and when Ikaris explains to him that that is how he has the power that he has, Mark declares to him that, frankly, if Spider-Man turns up and said he got his powers from reading *Chariots of the Gods*, he'd think that he was mad. There's definitely a sort of feeling there of...you know, it was a lovely idea, and right now it's just one of thousands of lovely ideas. It also means less in the Marvel Universe. That's another way in which it made incredible sense to not put the Eternals into the Marvel Universe originally, because the Marvel Universe is filled with freaking space ships! They're landing all over the place! There's aliens left right and center. There's nothing special or exciting about the idea, "There are aliens! They might have had something to do with us!" So one of the things that is fun with this is trying to make these Celestials special in this story.

SPOTLIGHT: With their enormous size and their odd visages, Jack's visuals on the Celestials were literally out of this world. I suppose that John Romita, Jr. is doing the same thing while handling art chores on your *Eternals* series?

NEIL: The point I got excited is when the stuff from Johnny started coming my way. I just looked at this stuff and said, "Ooookay. All stops are out. This is gonna be such fun." And one of the things that's really fun in the first couple of issues is you're moving back and forth between these very human people and these very human stories, admittedly with all sorts of peculiar excitement and mysterious people and explosions and shootings and running around and kidnappings and attempted murders and stuff...but the first two or three issues are fairly normal. Except possibly the fact that we do keep cutting to a reality TV show called America's Newest Super-Heroes.

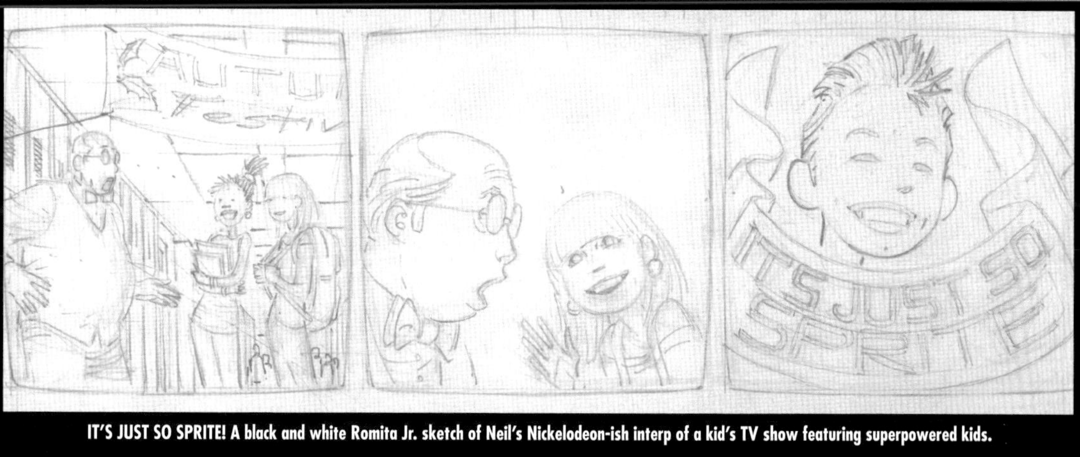
ITS JUST SO SPRITE

IT'S JUST SO SPRITE! A black and white Romita Jr. sketch of Neil's Nickelodeon-ish interp of a kid's TV show featuring superpowered kids.

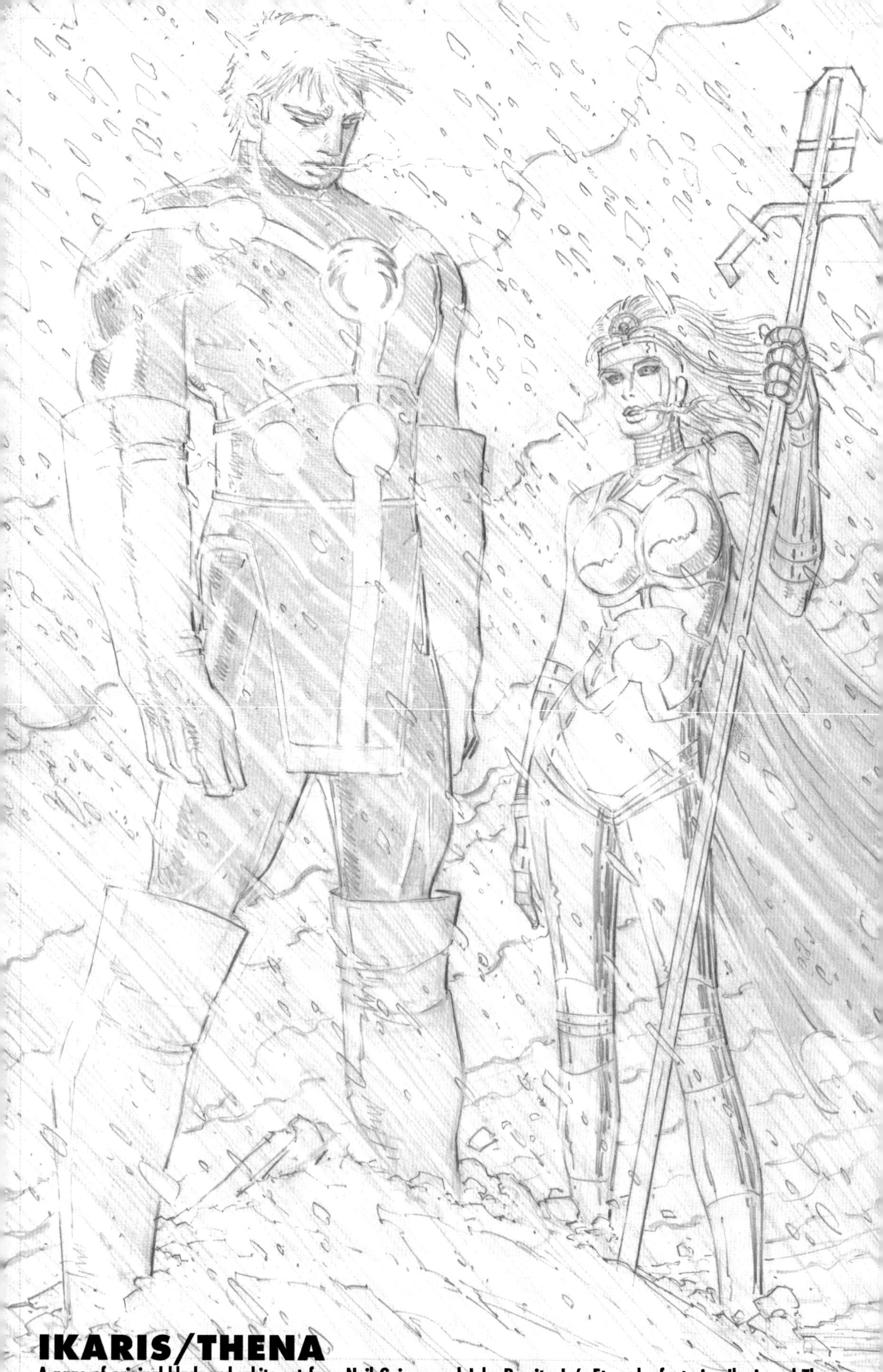

IKARIS/THENA

A page of original black and white art from Neil Gaiman and John Romita Jr.'s Eternals, featuring Ikaris and Thena, two of the most powerful Eternals.

SPOTLIGHT: (*Laughter.*) Now, that sounds like an especially fruitful source of stories.

NEIL: Well, yes. Though none of the Eternals are in it, but it's a bunch of kids being run by the Wasp. You know, you've got the sort of "Marvel Civil Warry" stuff going on in the background, in a way that I hope won't bug anybody who has no idea what this is but will actually be kind of fun for anybody who does.

SPOTLIGHT: Do you expect that a lot of your fanbase, which may not be up on Marvel Comics, will be coming to this project and enjoying it? Do you write for that kind of person who is familiar with your wide expanse of work over the last twenty years, or when writing for Marvel, do you write for a Marvel type fan?

NEIL: I have no idea, just as I had no idea with *1602*. What I was doing with *1602*, was I thought, you know, it would be really fun to write something that feels like I am doing something in the Marvel Universe for the first time, I want to take all of the Marvel characters that I loved when I was seven or eight and I want to put them all in the story and have complete control over everything, including all continuity, and I'm going to set it four hundred years ago and it's going to be mine! I just wanted it to be a really fun Marvel Comic, but I wanted it to be mine! So that was my agenda with *1602*, which was not really having anything to do with anything else.

With *Eternals*, I wanted to do something that didn't feel at all like *1602*. I wanted to do something goofier, Marvellier, and with a kind of Kirbyish undertow to it. I love Kirby! I've always loved playing with Kirby ideas. As far back as *Sandman #5*, I got to do a three or four page sequence where I persuaded Sam Keith and Malcolm Jones to do pure Kirby.

SPOTLIGHT: I recall that scene vividly from when I was a kid: The Sandman in the dream world, chasing down the Skookie Bird! That was a beautiful sequence, by the way.

NEIL: Thank you! But this isn't a Kirby pastiche in the same way. This is us just going, "Okay! If you took that kind of energy, and if Jack was around now and I went to him and said, 'what do you think of me doing something like this?," and him going, 'Okay!'" That is sort of the kind of comic that I want to do. And to create a bunch of people that you care about, all of them are almost starting with no memory at all of the Eternals — the characters, that is, with the possible exception of Ikaris, and even he has some stuff that he's confused about. And I figure, what's nice about that is, everybody is starting out with a more or less blank sheet of paper. If you are completely up to date on everything that has ever happened to every member of the Eternals in the Marvel Universe ever, you may get more of a kick out of some of the things that happen. You may go, "Oh! Is that…? Okay! So…Ha ha! That's why so and so and whatever…!" But mostly, it's just something that I hope will work for somebody who has no idea what's going on, and I hope it'll work for somebody who *absolutely* knows what's going on! That's what I tried to get to happen with *1602*, something that would be just as satisfying for somebody who knew what was going on…

SPOTLIGHT: As a Marvel fan well steeped in Marvel history — and I love a big epic just like anyone — it was fun to read *1602* as it would unfold: the splendor of it all, the luxurious storytelling afforded by the big cast, all these characters that you know and love interacting with each other, out of the elements we understand them in and part of a different world that we don't intuitively understand. In comparison, unlike *1602*, I don't think a lot of people know a lot about *The Eternals*.

NEIL GAIMAN
ON THE MYTHOLOGY OF THE SUPERHER

While *Spotlight* had Neil's attention, we figured it would be informative to get his thoughts on the nature of that stock characte of Marvel Comics: the superhero. Neil writes all kinds of materia and finds his sense of the heroic in all different eras in history, and he writes about them in anything but a typical fashion. So one migh wonder how Neil feels about the superhero as we typically know them through comic books. The superhero seems a modern conceit: the guy or gal in flashy costume, perhaps with a flowing cape, incredibl superpowers that set them above the normal humans that surrounc them. Here are Neil's thoughts about the superhero of today and their comparison with their antecedents from history and mythology

NEIL: What's so interesting to me about the superhero is that whil you can go back and say, "Well, Hercules is a superhero I suppose, and you've got Roland, you've got these wonderful heroes, lik Scarlet Pimpernel, or the kind of people Alan Moore played witl in *League of Extraordinary Gentlemen* (like Alan Quatermain, th Invisible Man, Captain Nemo and the rest.) But I think what fascinate me most about the superhero is that the actual "superheroeness" wa completely of its time.

It all kicks off with Superman! I find that sort of awesome. It wa honestly as if Siegel and Shuster had happened onto some hithertc undiscovered elements. It was pure, this thing was pure teenage wisl fulfillment. And pure teenage wish fulfillment wrapped up in a weirc kind of shape that kids related to in one way and adults related to i another, and that was somehow special and tied into flashy costumes There isn't anything that you can point to that's equivalent. Yes, it i very easy to say, well, "Here is a Baron Munchausen story," or th equivalent of that folk tale where the guy has one brother who ca run faster than anybody, and one that can hear a feather fall in a forest a mile away, and one who was stronger than anybody.

But that's not what Superman was about. Most heroes in the past dic things by their wits. I do think that most superheroes do things by their wits, but the idea of folding stuff up into, as I say, this wonderfu sort of strange recipe that's a jigger of myth, a dash of costume, c dash of magic, and five parts preadolescent magical wish fulfillmen "*Oh my God if I was just this…*" and somehow folded into this bizarr psychosexual angst, it becomes kind of special. And kind of uniqu One minute there weren't any of them, and the next minute, hov many of them? Hundreds? Five hundred? You're in the amazing tim when Eisner and Iger were doing their thing, and anyone who coulc pick up a pencil was creating superheroes. And pretty much anyone who can pick up a pencil has been creating them ever since.

FANTASTIC FOUR IN 1602: Neil Gaiman's proof that there were superheroes before Superman! (From *1602 #6*.)

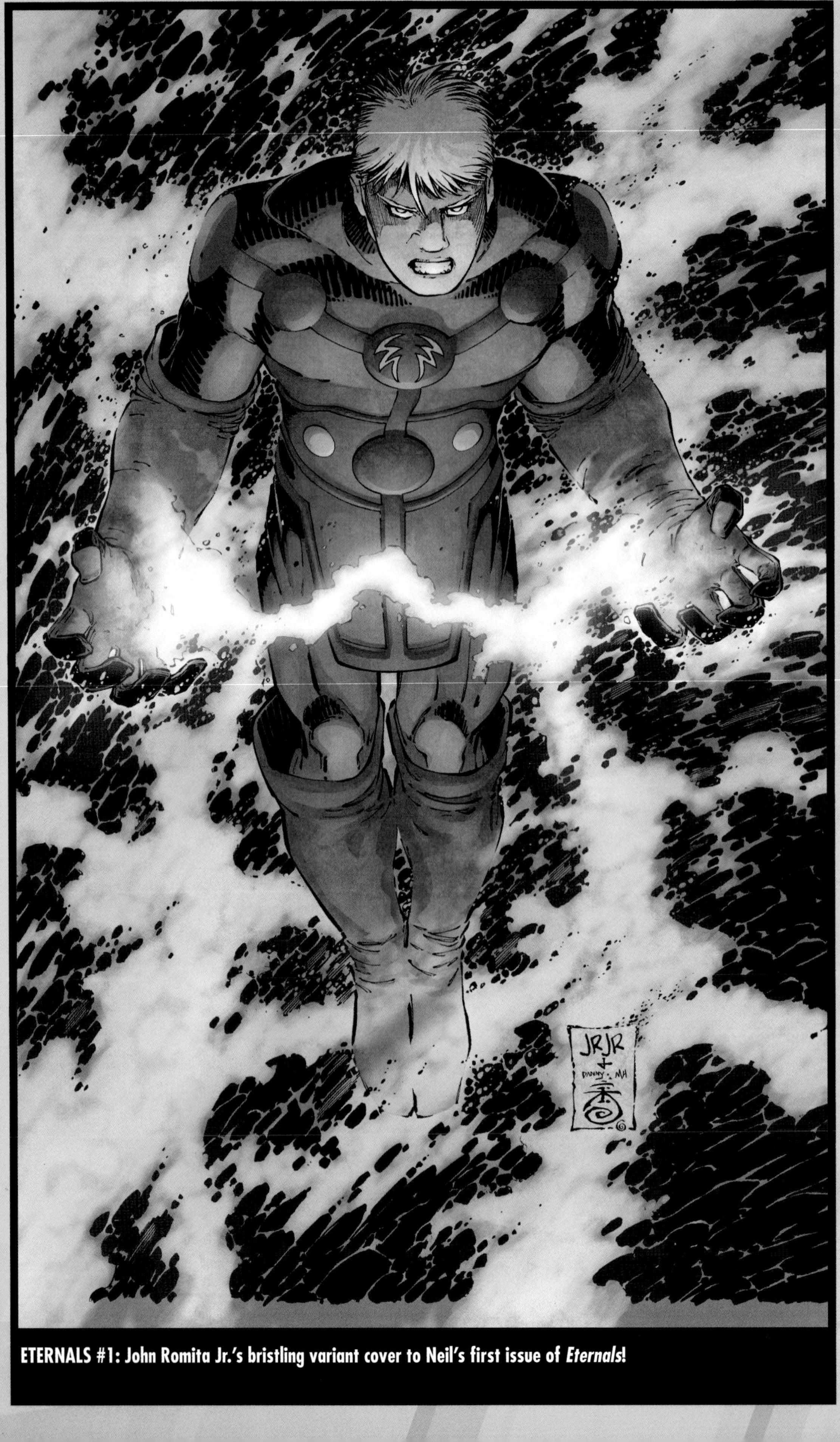

ETERNALS #1: John Romita Jr.'s bristling variant cover to Neil's first issue of *Eternals*!

Their history with Marvel has been rendered in a scattershot manner: once Jack's series ended, they sort of went away, then they came back for a supporting run on Thor, then they went away and came back for a mini-series in the mid-80s. Are you up on many of those stories?

NEIL: Some of those I've read, some I'm only familiar with through summaries.

SPOTLIGHT: Did any of that stuff grab you at all?

NEIL: Mostly as stuff that needed to be fixed. Mostly, just feeling like, this isn't what Jack would have done. This isn't where he was going. Now, I know that my thing isn't where Jack was going, but I hope that with my thing, at least by the end of it, we'll have the Eternals in a place that feels comfortable and usable. I don't feel like any of the previous stuff that wasn't Kirby increased their usability. Does that make any sense?

SPOTLIGHT: Absolutely. You've got your eye on their utility as Marvel characters while still keeping them in the Kirby ballpark.

NEIL: Yes, there would keep being these attempts to make a case for how they fold into the Marvel Universe, but by the end of which you'd go, "But they're just a bunch of super-powered people!" And that's one thing that the Marvel Universe simply does not need is a bunch more super-powered people. There are super-powered people all over the place!

SPOTLIGHT: It seems as if the main purpose of the stories was to fix them into the Marvel Universe rather than to simply tell a good Eternals story. Of course, there was a lot of good stuff there…

NEIL: Oh, and I'm not saying that it was all rubbish, because there was some very, very good stuff there. But I think what there also was was something very…(*Pause.*) I think I just felt like, you know, you didn't actually come away from any of that going, "Okay, *now* I get how they fit into the Marvel Universe and why they are cool!"

SPOTLIGHT: The front cover of Jack Kirby's *Eternals #1* has Ike Harris alerting his human friends saying, "We have found the space gods… and they're not dead!" Knowing that you are taking on this project, that statement reminds me of the Endless, the brethren who held court in your seminal *Sandman* comic all those years. I am wondering if there is any correlation in your mind between the Endless and the Eternals that you are bringing into the work?

NEIL: No…don't think that there is any correlation. Nor is it really… to be honest, if that was where it was going, I wouldn't bother. It would be kind of like somebody saying, "Neil, do Nightmare!" Ohhh…no… why would I want to do Nightmare? I already did Sandman! The joy in doing this for me is not doing gods, and it's not doing people as gods. The joy of this is trying to play with that Kirby madness.

SPOTLIGHT: Did you ever have the chance to meet him?

NEIL: I didn't. And I'm still kicking myself to this day. I was in San Diego in 1992, I guess, or maybe possibly even in 1993. I'm just trying to remember it properly. I had flown in to do something or other in San Diego, I came down on the lift and there was Jack talking to Paul Levitz, and…I was late for my plane! And I thought, "Shall I go over and get Paul to introduce me, shake his hand and tell him how important he is to me?" And then I thought, you know, there will be another convention. Then I got to the San Diego Airport — that little

MARVEL PROJECT #1: Neil's first turn with Marvel was 1602, featuring America's first born native child, Virginia Dare, and her Native Amerircan protector, Rojhaz. This lush illustration by Andy Kubert is from the 1602 #2.

tiny airport they used to have — and I waited. For three hours. For a delayed plane. Kicking myself! And a few months later he was dead.

SPOTLIGHT: Talk about your comic book idolatry: Jack Kirby is number one for me, and I know I'm not alone. I had actually gotten out of reading comics in about 1990 — the only one I was keeping up with at the time was *Sandman*, ironically. I recall being out of the loop on comics news for the most part, but when I heard that Jack had died, it was devastating to me. His creative output was seminal in establishing the sense of wonder that I carry through this life. When you figure who's on the metaphorical Mt. Rushmore of the comic art medium, Jack Kirby is on there — without a doubt.

NEIL: I was very lucky recently. I was staying at the house of a friend, doing some work, and my friend had bought on ebay most of the first 100 issues of *Fantastic Four*, in rubbishy, reading condition. And, I actually got to do that thing of, you know, lie in the bath and read them through…(*Laughter.*)…with the ads and with that sense of wonderful Kirbyish excitement. Smart Stan dialogue, that Kirby energy, and you know, he's one of the people who's work I…(*Pause.*)….the weird thing about Kirby is, especially when he moved to DC, there was this little period where I was eleven years old, maybe ten, and for a little bit it was *too weird* for me. And then it *wasn't* too weird for me any more. There was this point in there when I picked up *New Gods* and there would be these Kirby energy blasts, these black things surrounded by orangey flames and I'd say, "What the heck is that?" My little ten year old head would go, "Fire doesn't look like that!" and then you look at his women and go, "Women don't look like that!" And then after awhile, you just came to accept it. This is the Kirbyverse. This is what fire looks like in the Kirbyverse. This is what women look like in the Kirbeyverse.

"WE'RE ETERNALS, BUDDY!" Ikaris greets fellow Eternal Makarri to give him the scoop. (From Eternals #1.)

SPOTLIGHT: How much of your *Eternals* series will be a strict homage to Jack and his legacy?

NEIL: There's no way that we are doing *The Eternals* as any kind of homage to Jack. It's not a pastiche, it's not any of those kinds of things. I thought about it...as I started writing, I thought that every ten pages I'd do a double page spread and call it a chapter heading or whatever. And I thought, you know what? That's not Jack, and that's not what we're doing.

My friend Roger Zelazny died very shortly before I finished *American Gods* and with that I guess my agenda was to write the kind of book that Roger would have liked. The happiest I got was about a year after *American Gods* came out and I got a note from Roger's girlfriend, when he died, and she said, "I think he would have really liked this book." That was who I wrote it for. And with this, I'm writing the kind of book that I think Jack would have liked. He would have read it and gone, "I wouldn't have done things like that. Ohhh, why are they doing that?!?! Ohhh why are they standing around talking! All these people standing around talking!" (*Laughter*.) But I think that I'd like to do a comic that he would have liked.

SPOTLIGHT: I definitely think you're on the right track so far. Your theme for Eternals is very similar in tone to Jack's, and the bombast brought to the artwork by John Romita, Jr...I'm sure he would have

liked that element. The images that I've seen fit squarely into the realm of "Kirbyness." How far along are you right now?

NEIL: I'm halfway through issue #2, but most of it is in note form. Once I get off doing interviews, I have to go and type it up. The only thing that troubles me, though in some ways it kind of adds a wonderful sort of Kirbyish pressure to the whole thing, is that at the point where Johnny became free and I was ready to start, the message came from Marvel, "OK and we're putting this out in June!" (*Laughter*.) OK, when we did *1602*, we worked a year ahead so that we had six issues done before the first issue hit. And this one, we'll be lucky to have finished number three and if any of us get a cold, we're screwed. (*Laughter*.) You just have to hope that none of us get a cold.

SPOTLIGHT: Don't slip in the bath reading those FF comics!

NEIL: Yes, and be careful with what we eat.

SPOTLIGHT: Do those pushups, too!

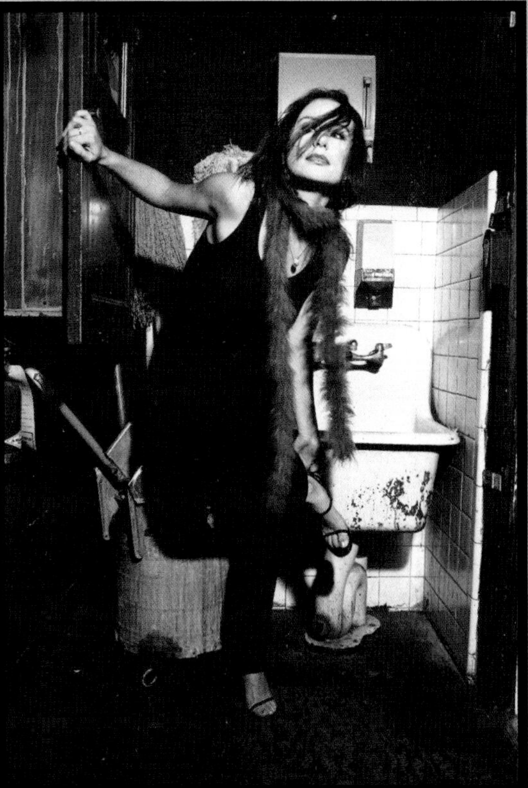

"We rode the tube and he said, 'Listen, things are gonna get better. I really feel this. I've got a good feeling about this! You won't have to sing "Crucify" at birthdays for the rest of your life!'"

THE SPOTLIGHT INTERVIEW WITH TORI AMOS

The friendship between superstar singer/songwriter Tori Amos and writer Neil Gaiman goes back fifteen years, to the days when Tori was one of many hungry musicians in the Los Angeles scene, earnestly trying to assert herself commercially in the artform she loved. In the early 90s, the piano songstress was cautiously navigating her way through an early-career stall after the ill-conceived *Y Kant Tori Read* album went nowhere on the charts. Meanwhile, Neil was flourishing as a writer, having already seen *Sandman* emerge as the elite comic of its era while simultaneously launching his career as a novelist with *Good Omens.* As if put in play by Morpheus himself, fate found a way to put Tori's talents square into Neil's sights, and he quickly sized her up for the singular and rare talent that she was. The relationship that followed has a history marked by their mutual fans as one of the great platonic love affairs in modern popular art.

Neil was an early and ardent supporter of Tori's music, at a time when she was trying to boldly assert herself in a business that can be so casually indisposed to a young woman of her unbridled artistic independence. Shortly after they met and began to forge their utterly loyal lifelong friendship, she released her startlingly fresh album *Little Earthquakes.* The record was an awakening, not just for her, but especially for the legions of young women who adopted Tori as their spiritual standard bearer. *Little Earthquakes* spoke through a diverse range of personalities: the scarlet-tressed wild woman bravely testifying in "Crucify," the gorgeously ineffable "Silent All These Years," and the impossible-to-ignore eyewitness account to rape, "Me and a Gun." Taking cues and inspiration from forebears like Kate Bush and Joni Mitchell and synthesizing them all into something uniquely her own, Tori had made her bold statement...and people were listening.

Much like it was with Nirvana, who blasted onto the scene at a similar time, most music fans remember when they heard their first Tori song or saw their first Tori video. She not only left an impression on the minds of listeners, but has built a loyal fanbase that guarantees each new album release a Top 10 sales ranking. And part of that fanbase, through it all, has been Neil Gaiman. His support and encouragement during Tori's earliest days of non-stardom has not been forgotten. Over time, Neil and his influence has been namedropped in the lyrics to several of Tori's songs, and she has regularly tapped him to pen liner notes for her album releases and write prose for her tour programs. In return, Neil found himself incorporating Tori's personality into his *Sandman* characters, most especially the lovingly crafted lunacy of Delirium. The mutual inspiration these two find in each other has played out in their own respective works so often, Neil has been quoted as stating flatly that the two "steal shamelessly from each other."

Rarely have two disciplines like writing and popular music been so purposely intermingled based on a simple love and respect between two creators at the very top of their respective pursuits; these are two very special people who have had a significant impact on each other and their art. *Marvel Spotlight* caught up with Tori in England as she was having a tea during a break recording songs for a new album, her followup to the 2005 Top 5 album, *The Beekeeper.* The subject? Why, her buddy Neil, of course!

SPOTLIGHT: You came to know of Neil's work before your breakthrough record, *Little Earthquakes.* You had been reading his work for a while when you met him. How did you come across his comics work?

TORI: There was a friend of mine that was crashing at my place in Hollywood. His name was Rantz Hosely, and he was an art student, an illustrator who was into comics. He collected everything from *Sandman*, so this was probably in 1990; I think around the time of "*The Doll's House,*" maybe? I would start to steal his comics, but I would always give them back...eventually! I began to immerse myself in them. I was really drawn to the mythological aspect of Neil's work.

Rantz took it upon himself to send Neil some music that I had recorded, demos from *Little Earthquakes* — not the full record, but portions, very early stuff. So he sent it to Neil without me knowing, and I got a phone call from Neil in London in 1991, and he said, "Hi, I'm Neil! And this person Rantz sent me this music and I just wanted to encourage you, because I think you should maybe think about doing it as a career." And I said, "That's good because *Little Earthquakes* is coming out in a few months!"

So around the time of the *Me and a Gun EP,* he called me just months before it was being released and came to one of the early shows where I was just gigging in London alone at a keyboard.

SPOTLIGHT: Wow! He attended one of those early UK shows you did? Those were some historic performances!

TORI: It was pretty trippy. Neil showed up at this place, some brasserie where I was playing — it happened to be a birthday party, and how I ended up playing a birthday party, talk about strange! And there Neil walks in, in his leather jacket, and looks at me as people are trying to make toasts and cut their cake and here I am singing "Crucify" and it's just a moment...*(Laughter.)* He just sat there, where he and the press woman from East/West Records were the only ones listening in this whole room full of people! And they just kind of pulled up their chairs kind of close to me, they were the only two people watching me play!

NEIL REFERENCES IN TORI AMOS SONGS

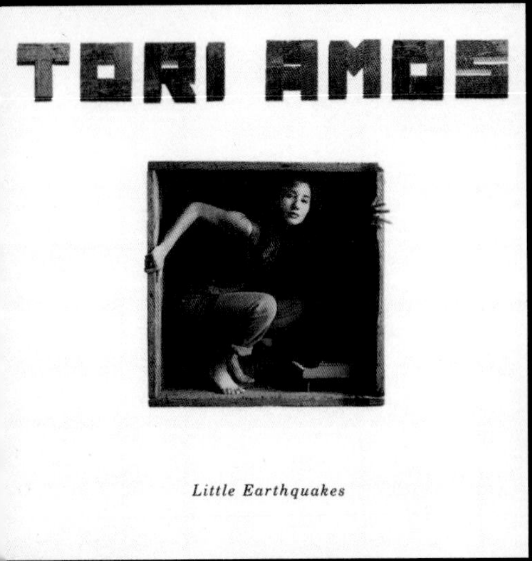
TORI AMOS
Little Earthquakes

ori has never been shy about name dropping her pal Neil in her ongs. Here's a short list of Neil references:

) "If you need me, me and Neil'll be hangin' out with the dream ing / Neil said hi, by the way"

'Tear In Your Hand," from the album *Little Earthquakes*, 1992. ori having a little fun with Neil and Morpheus from *Sandman*.

) "Where's Neil when you need him?"

'Space Dog," from the album *Under the Pink*, 1994. Tori asks the lassic question!

3) "Will you find me if Neil makes me a tree?"

'Horses," from the album *Boys For Pele*, 1996.

) "Where are the Velvets?"

'Hotel," from the album From the Choirgirl Hotel, 1998. Reference nspired by characters from Neil's novel *Neverwhere*.

5) "Get me Neil on the line/Have him read *Snow, Glass, Apples*"

'Carbon," from the album Scarlet's Walk, 2002. *Snow, Glass Apples* is the name of a play written by Neil.

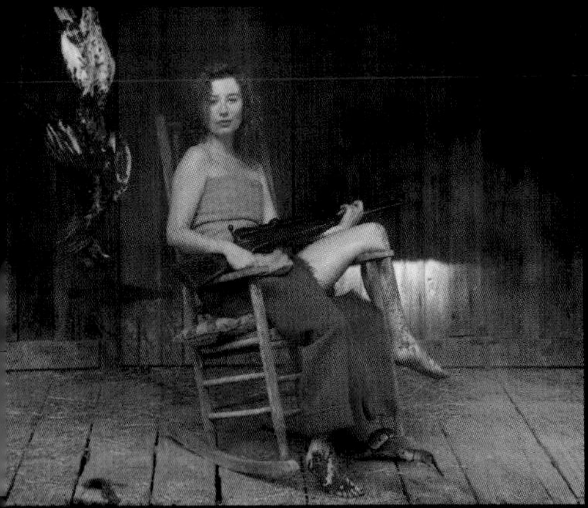

He took me out afterwards just for a bite to eat. We rode the tube and he said, "Listen, things are gonna get better. I really feel this. I've got a good feeling about this! *(Laughter.)* You won't have to sing "Crucify" at birthdays for the rest of your life!"

SPOTLIGHT: He slipped in and out of some of those shows like Morpheus, it sounds like, coming down from on high and passing on his wisdom to you.

TORI: Yes, he did! I think that his relationship with me has been as a spiritual brother. It's always been based on creativity and, I think, being a port in a storm. I'd like to think I've been the same thing for him. You know, where you're able to not be bought or swayed by the powers that be, and you're able to be a steady force for your creative buddy. And he's had to be very brave. He's had to really stand up to publishers and to be the creative force that he is.

SPOTLIGHT: And likewise, you have as well.

TORI: Yeah, and I think that's why there's always been a sort of a mirror image, maybe, I guess that's why he has always popped in. He visits the crew when we're on tour, he'll jump on the tour bus and he'll get a hotel room and hang out, and I think that I remember in the early years he would borrow things that I would say, and they would end up in Delirium. There would be a time where I wouldn't know if I was stealing from her, or she was stealing from me!

SPOTLIGHT: His influence on you comes full circle with your influence on him. He began to seed Delirium — one of the Endless in his landmark *Sandman* series — with inspiration from you. When you were reading these comics as they came out monthly, it must have been a trip for you!

TORI: I think that as it's happening, because it's your life, you're not only outside looking in — if that makes sense — because you have these conversations with this person and then you read something and you'd say, "Oh yeah, I think I remember us having this conversation!" Everything just felt like an extended part of a conversation that we were having at the time. The demands to turn in that material were quite high. He had to be very prolific. So he was always writing one of those issues. Every time I was talking to him he was in the middle of writing something. I think that as a creative force, sure you do flirt with things that your friends say, and all of a sudden they become things that your characters say. I think that's just kind of normal.

SPOTLIGHT: For the average comic reader, the dialogue is basically words on a page that you read and you have that outside looking in relationship, but for you, you're almost part of the narrative! Your experience is there on the page; it is recovered memory disguised as fiction. Hanging out with Neil will do that to you, huh?

TORI: The thing about Neil is that you really want to pump him for information if you can. If you ever get to sit down and talk to him, just start — if there's anything you really want to know about a mythological character, then he will know some anecdote about it. I really believe that his coding — as in the codes within his makeup — he's like a library for that information, and if you go on the internet and start typing in these mythological people, it's not the same. He has sifted through thousands and thousands and thousands of pages, it seems, of this stuff, and has thrown out what doesn't hold up, meaning the stuff that seems to be disproved after you've read enough. You say, "Oh no, that's not really Balder's story," or, "That's not really true about Freya," and what I found was because I was really trying to contain more myth in my work, he was a mentor for me in those early years. I began to see his process and I think it gave my little Mini a jumpstart. Or Mustang, really...he'd be the Mini, and I'd be the Mustang. He has a Mini you know!

SPOTLIGHT: Oh, does he? Neil Gaiman, a Mini Cooper guy? We've been looking for a big scoop on the guy...

TORI: Yeah, he has a Mini! And I had a wannabe Mustang in the old days. *(Laughter.)* I was brought up in a religious household, so the Four Horses of the Apocalypse and all that, that was part of my upbringing: the Biblical. But I think his archetypal influence was across the board, and mine was more Native American and the Bible. And I think that, at a certain point, you can plunder your own...what would you call it... what makes you *you*, and what you're brought up in...and sometimes you're thirsty for other cultures and their stories, and in our chats, he would always remind me how important myth was. That it's the clue to everything.

SPOTLIGHT: Have you heard anything about his new project with Marvel, *The Eternals*?

TORI: No.

SPOTLIGHT: It's precisely about mythology. It's based on a 1970s comic by one of the all time legends of comics, Jack Kirby, and he tried to tie together all of mankind's myths from all the different regions of the world as being put in play by an actual race of people called the Eternals. They lived on a mountaintop and they ran around the world doing all kinds of funky stuff, and they are the ones who inspired all the different myths. What Neil is doing is modernizing Jack Kirby's idea and putting his own spin on it, contextualizing all the mythology that

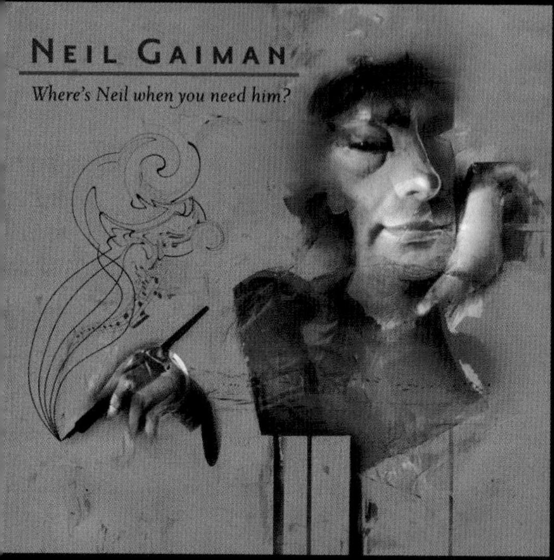
NEIL GAIMAN
Where's Neil when you need him?

WHERE'S NEIL WHEN YOU NEED HIM?

My answer to that question has always been, "Why, Neil's on my bookshelf!" Now, thanks to a new release from Dancing Ferret Records, I'll be able to find Neil in my cd player...when I need him, of course! Hitting your finer music emporiums on July 18, *Where's Neil When You Need Him?* Is a 17-track compilation of brand new recordings by ardent fans of Neil Gaiman and his writing. Tori Amos leads the charge with a remastered version of her *Sandman*-influenced song, "Sister Named Desire," but there are also tracks from top international acts like Rasputina, The Cruxshadows, Thea Gilmore and Future Bible Heroes. We caught up with the executive producer of the record, Dancing Ferret's Patrick Rodgers, and he gave us the scoop on Neil's tribute from his fans!

SPOTLIGHT: Even though he has written music before, Neil Gaiman isn't necessarily connected with music in the minds of the public, so how does a concept like this even come together? Who's inspiration was it?

PATRICK: The concept for the disc comes from a business philosophy that's very important to us. In addition to the traditional methods that can be used to help a band increase its fan base and connect with more people, our label tries to assemble innovative projects that use music to explore other themes or concepts. For example, we previously released a "soundtrack" to a popular board game, as well as a disc of medieval music that was released in conjunction with one of the

The idea of presenting a collection of new music that was inspired by one author was something we'd kicked around for awhile. Shakespeare was actually an early favorite, but in the end, we thought there was a much stronger emotional connection to Neil's work (and Shakespeare's people told us he was not going to be available to write liner notes). The fact that Neil's work has such a wide range to it was also a big factor, as that gave us a greater degree of freedom to be more eclectic with the musical selection. We work with artists who put a lot of themselves into their music, and who create art that is not necessarily designed to be homogenous and well-suited for mass consumption. Neil approaches his work in the same way, so it seemed like an ideal coupling.

SPOTLIGHT: How closely did Neil work on this project? Did he have final say on artists and songs?

PATRICK: Neil was involved from the very beginning of the project and had approval power on all of the music. He gave us a short list of artists that he really wanted to see on the disc, and that starting point definitely influenced the direction of the record. We were very mindful of not going too far in any one direction musically, as we really wanted the disc to reflect the diversity of Neil's work and his fan base. Once Neil had listened to all of the music, we discussed the order in which the tracks would appear and Neil set to work on the liner notes. He wrote about the project in general and then discussed each song as well. He's been great fun to work with and has been extremely supportive of the project.

SPOTLIGHT: Tell me a little about your label, Dancing Ferret.

PATRICK: Our label is an offshoot of Dancing Ferret Concerts, which started in 1995 to promote live shows and club events here in Philadelphia. The Dancing Ferret Discs label started up a few years later and has become the central focus of our business. We specialize in various styles of alternative music, and about half of our artist roster comes from overseas. In particular, we work with a lot of bands from Germany, and you can see that connection reflected in the Gaiman CD (there are three German Top 40 acts on the disc). The European market has also been very receptive to our US acts. About one third of our sales are in Europe.

A few years ago, we started a sub label, Noir Records, to focus on trip-hop, ethereal and medieval music. The medieval music has become a very hot item for us and has brought us a lot of attention recently. We're now being touted as the leading US label for medieval music, which is very gratifying.

Marvel Spotlight had the chance to speak to a couple other recording artists involved in *Where's Neil When You Need Him?* Here is Thea Gilmore and Future Bible Heroes take on Neil and the new CD!

THEA GILMORE,
"Even Gods Do"

"British singer/songwriter Thea Gilmore captures the trials and tribulations of Shadow in *American Gods* with this wistful ballad. Thea's work has a great folk quality to it, which helps emphasize Shadow's humanity and vulnerability."

— *excerpt from Neil's liner notes*

SPOTLIGHT: Thea, what's your estimation of Neil's work and his writing talent?

THEA: I think Neil's imagination and characterization is second to none. He has a pretty unique way of looking at the world and it always comes across in his writing. When I was a kid I was brought up to have a healthy respect for the inexplicable, my mother in particular, made me believe in magic (not Harry Potter stuff, real, natural, primeval forces) and when I read Neil's work, he's one of the few people I think looks at the world in the same way.

SPOTLIGHT: How did you first come across Neil's work?

THEA: It would have been *Sandman* stuff. I remember being eleven and hearing Tori Amos sing about him on the *Little Earthquakes* album and being intrigued as to what sort of person could inspire more than one name check in the space of an hour!

SPOTLIGHT: What went into the writing of your song that appears on the Neil tribute cd, "Even Gods Do"?

THEA: I wanted to write a song that tried to make you visualize Shadow as much as the novel did. Unusually for me, I concentrated more on making the music ebb and flow to create the mood than the lyrics. I consider myself to be a very lyric based artist, but when writing about Shadow, he didn't need clever poetry to describe him, he needed minor keys and mood music!

SPOTLIGHT: So, where is Neil when you need him?

THEA: Luckily for me, usually on the other end of an e-mail... or possibly booting round Chicago in his Mini (the last time I saw him!)

relates to the Eternals and making it sort of real in the understanding of our world.

TORI: Well how timely is that! You know, Joseph Campbell — Neil and I would talk about this a lot — what a great mind he was, a force. However, the generation now isn't necessarily exposed to Joseph Campbell, and how do you combat forces — political forces, say — that are making decisions that we are going to have to live with over the next twenty years and longer? How do you find, maybe, the answers to equations — political equations, or emotional equations — unless you know your mythology? Because it's really hard to think like, well, "I only know what's happening to me in my time, not how wars have happened in other times." I think that Neil is a clever egg in that he knows that a way to arm a generation is to give them ways to really fight powers that are trying to keep generations in the dark. And that might seem — I'm not giving you an *Alias* kind of chat, here; the idea that it's an "us against them" kind of thing — but I do think that because a lot of information has been controlled, not by burning books but by certain things being kep unavailable, and how so much of communication as you know is controlled by those who are "they," there are ways you have to be able to slip through the net.

We would talk quite a bit that the best thing that one can do is to try and arm an individual with little windows that they can jump through, and then they can piece together their own mosaic. They can find their own myth, and so the fragments of self become whole. And when you're dealing with a generation who are whole, like the power of the late 60s generation, how they confronted those in power and held their feet to the fire, it was a very powerful time! And as we both know — Bob Dylan and John Lennon, those guys weren't dumb bunnies. I think when you ask, "Who is the Bob Dylan of this generation?", well, that's a big, big, big question mark. We certainly need them. And yet, maybe you have to put the information out there that's not going to look the same, and it *can't be* the same, but Neil knows enough to know that comics books are something that people are going to pick up. And so he's going to arm anybody with what they need if they want to, I don't know...stretch! To step into bigger shoes!

SPOTLIGHT: Well, that's part of what *Eternals* is going to be all about. You sound like you've got a good read on it already!

"I remember in the early years he would borrow things that I would say, and they would end up in Delirium. There would be a time where I wouldn't know if I was stealing from her, or she was stealing from me!"

TORI: It's funny, because when *The Da Vinci Code* came out, he did say to me — and this is nothing against anybody that's involved in it — but he said to me, "This information has been out there for quite some time." And yet, because very few people have read Elaine Pagels or even read *Holy Blood, Holy Grail*, then this was a big shock for them. And I think that he is trying to bring to the masses, a lot more of not just that kind of information, but information that has just not been out in the mainstream, if you see what I mean. And I really find that very exciting in his work. He loads it...it's loaded. *Stardust*, it's just loaded with research. When he works on a book, sometimes he'll crash at one of my houses, and the amount of effort that he puts into a work, it's enough to make you want to burn the midnight oil yourself. You really understand about discipline, and it doesn't always come easy. It really doesn't. I have a library in the beach house and he'll pull books out from the shelf — they're everywhere! I'm not saying he's a messy house guest, but...*(Laughter.)* I'm saying, you know, he will really push himself, which makes you as a creative force want to push yourself.

I'm bragging on his work ethic, his research. I think a lot of times, you and I both know, you've got one comic in you, or one good record if you're half good. But book after book after book...that's a very different thing.

SPOTLIGHT: He's got a big arsenal to work with. You just mentioned the hard work involved in discriminating research; but also, Neil's gift of characterization is lethal. He can draw a character out within a few pages of a comic, and with just a key lines of dialogue make you know that character eternally...endlessly, even! (Puns intended!)

TORI: Yeah, but this goes back to the discipline of observation. All those walks that we'll take, or times on the tube, or just sitting there having dinner, we can't not observe. I think that as a writer, you're the nosiest person that has ever lived (and it's so embarrassing to admit that), but you have to be an observer of other people. Otherwise, you can't develop your characters because if you're only developing them around your friends soon you're not going to have any, number one. And number two, you're going to repeat yourself over and over. But the best characters are based on truth. Most of what Neil writes from what I know, it's based on what he really sees; maybe, you know, a little bit of this, a little bit of that, a pinch of this and a pinch of that, from this creature or that creature, but I think that he is trying to remind me when I'm writing a work about the research and observation, and to push yourself further. You know, to really push yourself. Every line, every sentence, every beat of every bar.

And also, if you're smart, everybody has a think tank. He has his and I have mine, and he's obviously a part of mine, and I guess I'm a part of his, but how it works is that when he's working on something, he'll send me it, and we have a joke, which is: "Listen, I'd rather hear it from you than the *New York Times*," I mean, it's like, "Lay it on me, Neil!"

SPOTLIGHT: Right, it's all about who you can trust.

TORI: Yeah, because you cannot open your work up to everybody, because you will find enough people to hate it and enough people to love it. You need people who are going to offer something up.

SPOTLIGHT: To be real with it.

TORI: Sometimes he'll send me something and it's just not my cup of tea, but that doesn't mean that I can't sit there and respond. For some gory bloody scene, like the Corinthian for example (in *Sandman*), he might ask, "Is this effective in this way?" And I think that's the kind

FUTURE BIBLE HEROES, "Mr. Punch"

"Demenita never sounded so good. It's twisted, it's bizarre, it's morbid, and it's absolutely wonderful. Just as with a good Punch and Judy show, there's something wicked to amuse the bad children and a bit of subtext for the bad adults, too."
— *excerpt from Neil's liner notes*

Band lineup: Claudia Gonson, Stephin Merritt, Chris Ewen

SPOTLIGHT: Chris, what's your estimation of Neil's work and his writing talent?

FBH: Neil's work is both timeless and modern at the same time. His engaging and complex characters, coupled with plots that seamlessly merge the fantastic with the mundane are a testament to his imagination and unique voice. Neil breathes new life into rich traditions, keeps the myths, legends and folklore of human experience alive and relevant, and creates new classics along the way. That is talent on the grandest scale.

SPOTLIGHT: How did you first come across Neil's work?

FBH: Unlike some, my first exposure to Neil was through his novels, not his comic and graphic novel work. A friend recommended *Neverwhere* to me when it came out. I bought it, read it, promptly ran out and bought everything I could find, and haven't looked back. Stephin's first exposure was the *Sandman* series.

SPOTLIGHT: What went into the writing of your song that appears on the Neil tribute cd, "Mr. Punch"?

FBH: Besides the book, it was having seen a *Punch & Judy* puppet show at a convention with Neil, as well as and our long standing love of fake British accents and the "chipmunk" song genre.

SPOTLIGHT: So, where is Neil when you need him?

FBH: I don't know how he manages it, but somehow Neil is always exactly where he needs to be when we need him. It may be because he has a GPS in his car.

"...when he's working on something, he'll send me it, and we have a joke, which is: 'Listen, I'd rather hear it from you than the New York Times.' I mean, it's like, 'Lay it on me, Neil!'"

of think tank you need: not people who, if it's not rap, they hate it, or they just hate girl singers...if you're like that, you're just an absolutely useless person on a think tank, because you can only like what you like, you're completely nonobjective.

SPOTLIGHT: And the other way, too, is someone who unconditionally loves everything you do, they can't help push you places where you might need to go.

TORI: No, no, no...that's a waste of time. But not everybody has the ability to, you know, offer something up, and also not everybody wants to receive it when you do offer it up! But you realize that to be strong creative forces, you need a few people in your life that are going to give you what you need to be great.

SPOTLIGHT: And you guys are there for each other in that respect! Have the two of you ever considered doing something more directly collaborative in the future?

TORI: It's funny you would say this. I mean...*(Pause.)* We do chat about it. He has an idea. So he's been prodding me, which is good, because just because you might want to work together doesn't mean you should. So he's come up with an idea that has rattled my cage. In a good way! So you kick it around in a structural way. As a musical structure, you think, how could I do this...? So, yeah, I think it's there, and I think that our friendship is strong enough to survive it.

SPOTLIGHT: Whether it might be a success or a failure! Have you ever thought that perhaps you'd like to write a comic book one day? Do any of your artistic inspirations ever formulate around that medium at all?

TORI: Well...*(Long pause.)*... I think you would have to know what you're good at and what you're not. I go back to this saying: just because you might have an opportunity to do something, doesn't mean you should do it. I think you have to know what you're good at, and so I think I'll leave the comics to Neil. I want to read them!

Thank you, Tori, for sitting with this interview for Marvel Spotlight *readers! And to readers of* Marvel Spotlight, *be sure to check out Tori's new version of "Sister Named Desire," her contribution to the new Dave McKean produced tribute CD to Neil Gaiman titled* Where's Neil When You Need Him.

MARVEL 1602: NEW WORLD

1602: NEW WORLD is the follow-up to Neil Gaiman's smash hit limited series. Written by Greg Pak, of Planet Hulk fame, and illustrated by Greg Tocchini (Thor: Son of Asgard), it follows up the events set in play by the epic story told by Neil in 1602. Neil himself acted as creative consultant on this series, giving it a seamless continuity with the original story. *1602: New World* centers on the colony of Roanoke, where we last saw our heroes at the conclusion of Neil's story. As you may remember, Peter Parquagh and David Banner were each caught in strangely familiar accidents, and it should come as no surprise that these accidents have had some very interesting ramifications. Banner came to the colonies in the service of King James of England, charged with hunting down and killing Sir Nicholas Fury, deemed a traitor to the crown. But he now awakens to find his clothes shredded and no clear memory of what he has done. Peter Parquagh is in the service of broadsheet publisher Jonah Jameson, and has become an integral part of the Roanoke colony, forming a budding friendship with young Virginia Dare. Another colonist, Norman Osborne, harbors a secret agenda, seeking to stir up hatred against their Native American neighbors. And back in England, an angry King James dispatches a Spanish warrior clad in red and gold armor to bring the wayward Banner back to account. All of these competing factions reach an explosive confrontation in this riveting sequel.

MARVEL
1602
NEW WORLD
MARVEL

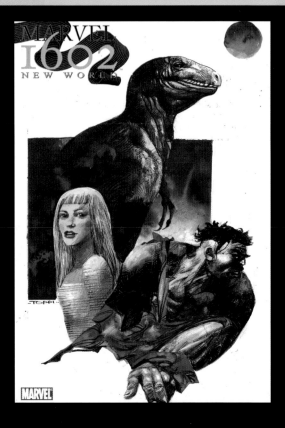

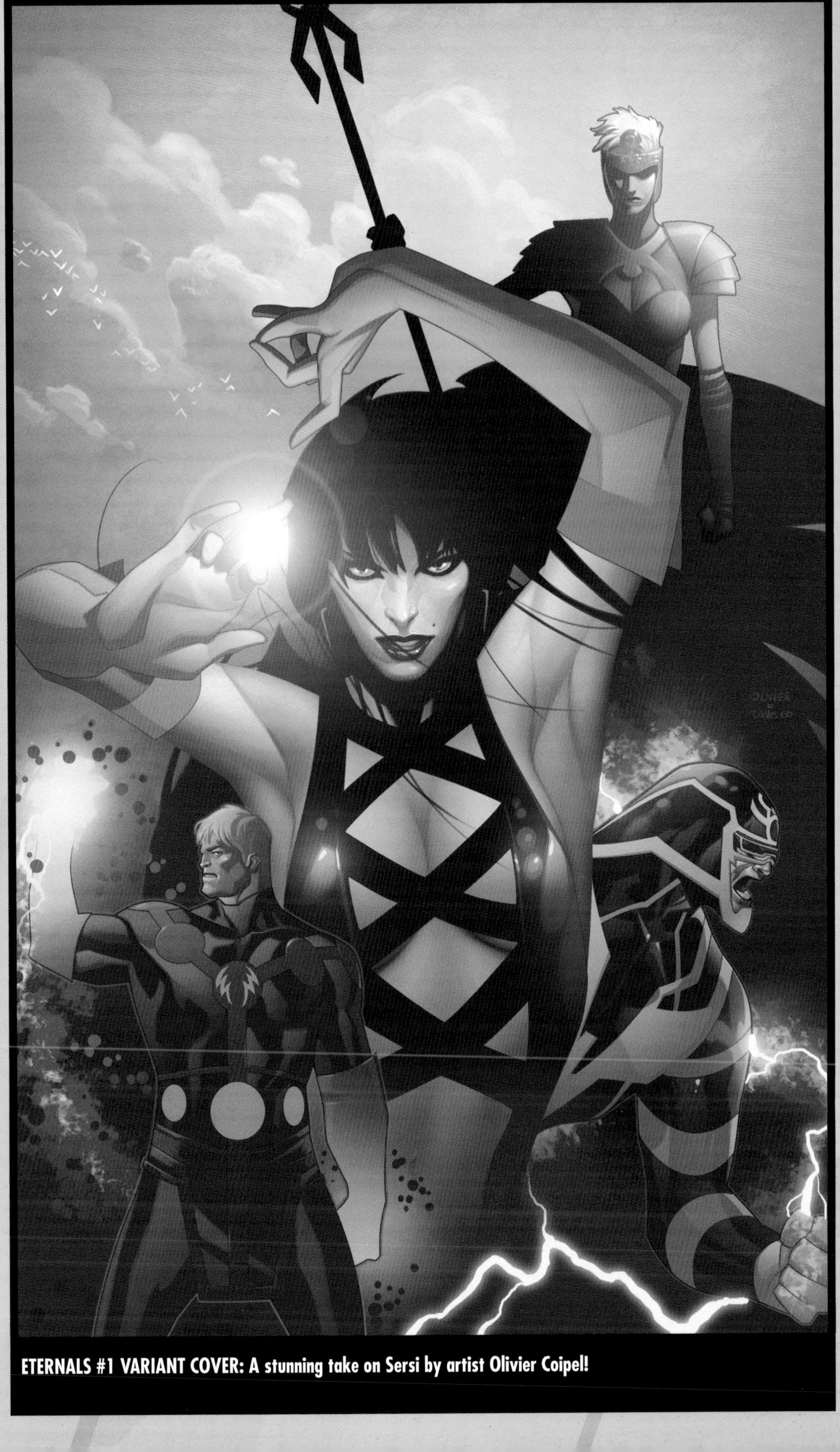

ETERNALS #1 VARIANT COVER: A stunning take on Sersi by artist Olivier Coipel!

JACK KIRBY AN

Kirby was coming...back!

After a five year hiatus, Jack Kirby was returning to Marvel Comics in 1975. Similar to his just-ended contract with DC Comics, the King would write, pencil and edit a line of comics from his California home. At this point in his illustrious career, Kirby had big ideas still waiting to make it onto the page and as a result, he didn't want to repeat himself. Still, publisher Stan Lee and then-Editor-in-Chief Roy Thomas wanted Kirby's energy to infuse some of the core titles. Reluctantly, Kirby returned to *Captain America* and helped relaunch the *Black Panther*. His imagination could not be earthbound so he agreed to adapt the movie *2001: A Space Odyssey* which led to an ongoing title, which begat the popular character Machine Man.

Kirby wasn't done, though.

Always captivated by the notion of legends, he thought heroic legends were created by people who needed something to look up to, to ease their suffering since so much of man's early history was a struggle. A Viking would come back from a battle, feeling tired and covered in blood, but he knew atop the mountain, Thor was still fighting the good fight. Such notions influenced much of his work dating back to Captain America, addressing a far more modern need.

Ever since his tenure on *Thor* in the 1960s, Kirby liked the notion of aliens being perceived by humans as gods. Now back at Marvel, he still wanted to explore the theme. The timing was fortuitous given Erich von Däniken's best-selling book *Chariot of the Gods?* which discussed the idea that aliens had visited Earth in the distant past, influencing ancient cultures, including the Mayans. Marvel thought the idea had merit, as they had already jumped on that bandwagon with the first issue of *Marvel Preview* in 1975.

Kirby was given the green light to produce The Celestials. As Kirby set to work, it was decided to rename the title Return of the Gods in order to

cement the relationship in consumers' minds. A logo had been created which was even used in several house ads before the Legal Department stepped in and had it removed. They felt the type treatment was close to an infringement so the final title became The Eternals.

The first issue arrived cover-dated July 1976 and continued for nineteen issues and one annual, one of the longer runs for a Kirby creation that decade. In an introductory text piece, Kirby wrote, "How do we view the Eternals?

"That is the question. And it's a big question, because it involves us all in a great cosmic adventure which began when the dinosaurs split the scene and humanity was first pushed on the stage of that universal Gong Show we call History.

"Something happened back there, among the steaming ferns and moving continents of prehistoric Earth. And neither Walter Cronkite nor Howard Cosell nor your ever-lovin' current events teacher was there to take notes on the events we must nowadays sift from the myths, the mummies, and the skeletons that lay buried beneath tons of soil.

"So what happened there, in that unreported, unwritten, mystifying beginning of all things? How many mammoth events provided the oil which still spins the wheels of this plastic pickle-works we hail as modern civilization?

"I feel that playing around with this sort of conjecture is highly entertaining, and that we should aim our gun sights at this giant puzzle we've inherited more often. We can't leave it all to the professors, pundits, and paperback prophets. The puzzle belongs to you and me as well."

In the telling, Kirby postulated that a race known as the Celestials had come to Earth during the early days of life. These titanic, armored figures came from the far reaches of the cosmos to various planets to weigh and measure life as it was developing. Their studies occur over

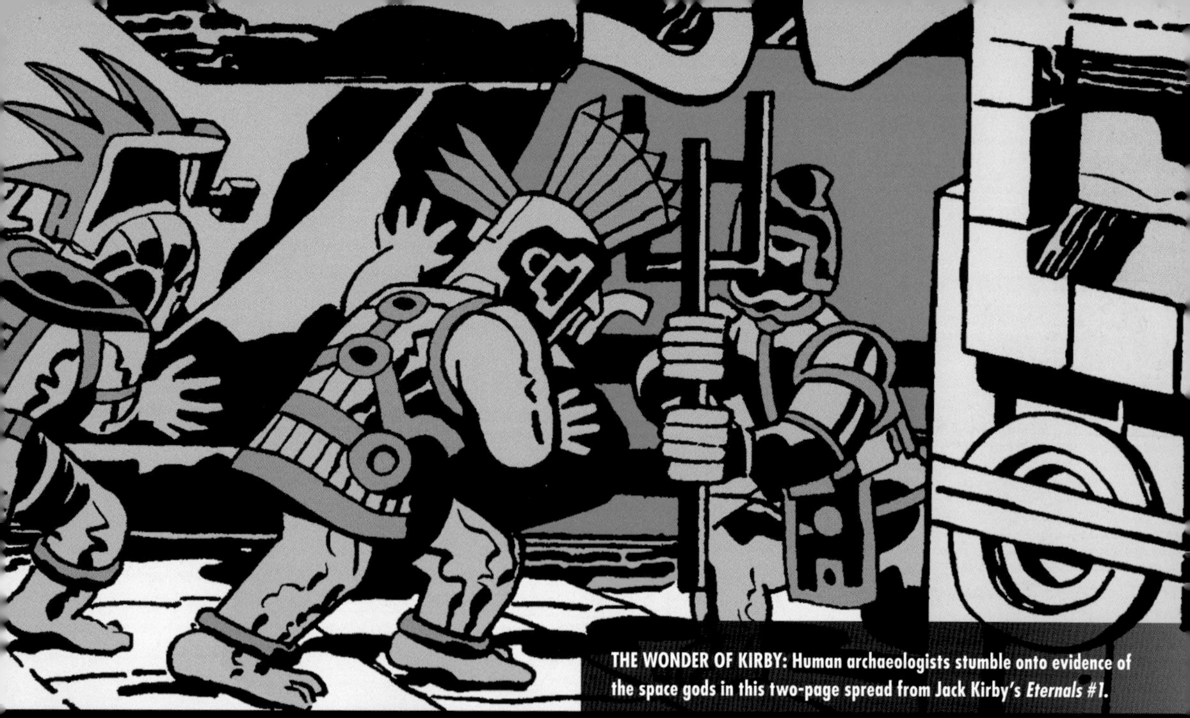

THE WONDER OF KIRBY: Human archaeologists stumble onto evidence of the space gods in this two-page spread from Jack Kirby's *Eternals #1*.

THE ETERNALS

By ROBERT GREENBERGER

countless years in four visits with different delegations, known as Hosts. The First Host arrived on Earth about one million years ago and began their experiments with the humanoids found at that time. As a result, two new species were created: Eternal and Deviant.

The Eternals were given superior genetics, imbued with cosmic energies that took centuries to discover and master. The Deviants, on the other hand, were given an unstable genetic code which caused them to mutate over the years.

The Second Host arrived some 20,000 years back when the Deviants had managed to forge a worldwide government—based in Lemuria—crushing any human resistance. During one such attack, the city of Atlantis sank. In their hubris, they thought to challenge their creators. The Celestials had other ideas and much of the Deviant civilization was eradicated during the Great Cataclysm, including the sinking of the continent of Mu, and man was left to evolve on his own.

The Eternals kept to themselves in their polar retreat, recognizing their advanced abilities would frighten the humans. Among them, one stood out, having fought brave battles but then was shunned by man and even Eternal, earning the title the Forgotten One. There were other periodic exchanges between Eternal and human, such as the Eternal later named Ikaris marrying a human woman and having a son, Icarus. When the son died, Ikaris adopted the name in tribute. Best known are the exploits of Sersi, the bombastic woman who enjoyed dealing with man and his culture. She frequently walked through man's world, savoring hedonistic pleasures, notably dancing.

They were nobly led by Kronos until his death when the son, Zuras, succeeded him. Zuras was the Prime Eternal until the arrival of the Fourth Host and is noted for being the first to combine all the Eternals into the Uni-Mind. Zuras perfected the Ritual that brings just about all Eternals together so their cosmic energy can be merged into a brain-like construct. Much remains to be learned about the Uni-Mind but it has been formed only during times of great crisis, requiring a unified effort. The records indicate humans and Deviants have also been tapped to help form the Uni-Mind which showed its adaptability.

About 1000 B.C. heralded the Third Host, their duties described by the Eternal Ajak as "inspection and cultivation." The Incas worshipped the visiting Host as gods while instilling fear in others around the globe. The Eternal Ajak spoke directly with the Celestials, protecting their base, and then placed himself in suspended animation, awaiting the Fourth Host.

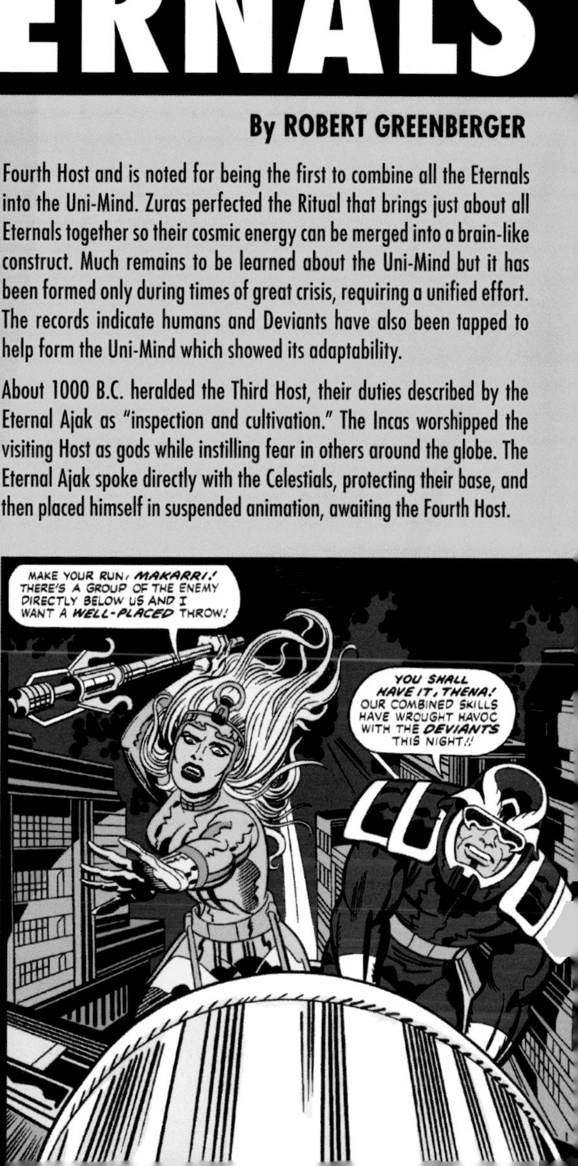
MAKE YOUR RUN, MAKARRI! THERE'S A GROUP OF THE ENEMY DIRECTLY BELOW US AND I WANT A WELL-PLACED THROW!
YOU SHALL HAVE IT, THENA! OUR COMBINED SKILLS HAVE WROUGHT HAVOC WITH THE DEVIANTS THIS NIGHT!!

THENA AND MAKARRI: Two of Kirby's Eternals who were built for action, on the hunt for Deviants terrorizing New York City! (From Jack Kirby's Eternals #6.)

CONTROL!

ROBOT HULK SMASH! Despite editorial mandates, Jack couldn't bring himself to rotate real Marvel characters into his Eternals book, so he compromised by making his Hulk a cosmically-powered robot replica! (From *Eternals #14.*)

In the nineteenth century, the Eternal Ikaris sensed it was time to prepare Earth for the Host's arrival and left his home to interact with man. Using the name Ike Harris, Ikaris dealt with humans for the first time since the Third Host and marveled at the changes.

The Fourth Host came to Earth in the recent past, ready to render judgment–the setting for Kirby's run. They witness what man had wrought, as well as the resumption of the ages-old conflict between Eternal and Deviant. The Deviants sought to either gain favor with the Host or see to it no one benefited. The Eternals, meanwhile, sought to preserve not only their lives but that of the noble, less powerful humans, whom they saw as having great potential. A small group, known as the Young Gods, made a gift of themselves to the Celestials to show how well the experiment had worked. Arishem, leader of the Fourth Host, accepted them and gave Earth his verdict: a thumbs-up.

Sales were solid but never spectacular. Looking back, historians Gerry Jones & Will Jacobs called it "great fun" while Peter Sanderson in *Marvel Universe* called it Kirby's last great creative achievement. He wrote: "Like much of Kirby's work for Marvel and DC in the 1960s and 1970s, *The Eternals* is an inquiry into the nature of God. Working with Lee, Kirby had created the Stranger *(in X-Men),* Odin and the High Evolutionary *(in Thor),* the Source *(in New Gods),* the Watcher and Galactus (in *The Fantastic Four*); now, working on his own in *The Eternals,* he presented us with 'space gods,' the Celestials.

"The Eternals is as memorable for its characters as it is for Kirby's epic feats of visualization. There was the shadowy, brooding figure of the Forgotten One, the Eternal who was known to ancient civilizations as Gilgamesh, Samson, and Hercules. There was Kro, the demonic military leaders of the Deviants, who despite his ruthlessness was still gripped by passion for his former lover, Thena, the fiery warrior daughter of Zuras, monarch of the Eternals. And there was Sersi, perhaps the most fascinating of all, an Eternal with many sides to her personality. She was known to the Deviants as Sersi the Terrible for her temper and her ability to alter the shapes of persons or objects at will, as when she transformed Ulysses' men to pigs in ancient times. (Sersi explained that Homer had misspelled her name in *The Odyssey.*)

"Despite its considerable merits, the original *Eternals* series was not a commercial success, perhaps because Kirby dealt with his large cast of characters as a true ensemble, continually shifting the focus from one group in one issue to another set in the next; there was no central heroic figure who appeared in every story line."

While most comics of the day focused on one or two main characters, even the team books such as The *Avengers* and *X-Men* kept the focus tight on a handful of protagonists and gently shifting that focus over the course of issues. Not Kirby, whose kinetic storytelling meant readers were treated to a rush of concepts, one coming after the after with little time spent fully exploring any one character or concept. As a result, his titles tended to either be embraced by fans who loved the art and energy or shunned by those who were left breathless.

Ray Wyman Jr., in *The Art of Jack Kirby,* suggested, "Although the story writing in *Eternals* was fragmented and distracting, Kirby's pseudo-techno designs were as fascinating as ever."

In Kirby's mind, his space saga was in its own reality, divorced from the Marvel Universe. By 1977, though, editors back in New York wanted to play with his concepts and thought the book would benefit from the familiar super heroes and super-villains making appearances. Kirby, by then, was already battling with editors over the way his dialogue had

THE ETERNALS
MARVEL® COMICS GROUP
APPROVED BY THE COMICS CODE AUTHORITY
30¢
9 MAR 02334
WHEN GODS WALK THE EARTH!
THE ETERNALS
© 1976 MARVEL COMICS GROUP
HE CAN'T BE CONTROLLED!
HE CAN'T BE STOPPED!
HE'S...THE KILLING MACHINE!

DON'T FEAR THE REJECT! Well, unless you're a Deviant! *Eternals #9* is a thrill-packed issue featuring the Reject, a progeny of the Deviants that is loathed solely for his appearance, and his gladiatorial challenger, the behemoth known as Karkas

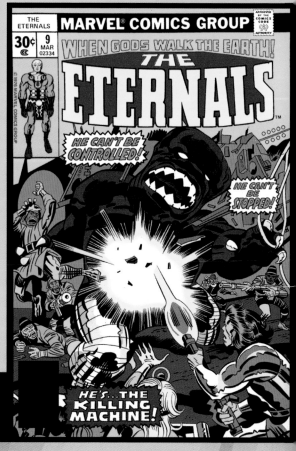

been altered without approval in his various titles. In an effort to be one of the gang, he made a few attempts to acknowledge the Marvel Universe in his cosmic series. S.H.I.E.L.D. agents began to show up followed by one of his earliest hits, The Thing – however, the blue-eyed adventurer proved to be a regular Joe whose features were momentarily transformed into a likeness of the Fantastic Four hero by Sersi. Another attempt had an appearance by The Hulk, but this too proved to be a falsity – this one was a cosmically-enhanced robot.

After 1978 Kirby stopped the title, and the characters were fair game to the next generation of editors, writers and artists, many of whom were strongly influenced by Kirby's creations and were eager to play with them.

But none of the series featuring these entities has proven successful, a track record likely to change with 2006's miniseries from Neil Gaiman and John Romita, Jr. When the announcement was made, Gaiman said, "What drew me to it was not the god side of things, but the incredibly long-lived nature of things. I just loved the idea of seeing two people standing in a town square looking at a statue of themselves that was erected 1,000 years before.

"It was kind of the opportunity to create a mythology. In *1602* I re-**created everything that had happened in the Marvel Universe because they'd got it right.** ***The Eternals*** **still had that amazing Jack Kirby outpouring of ideas, and there were some amazing things. But he didn't get it right. It's sort of weird and lumpy.**

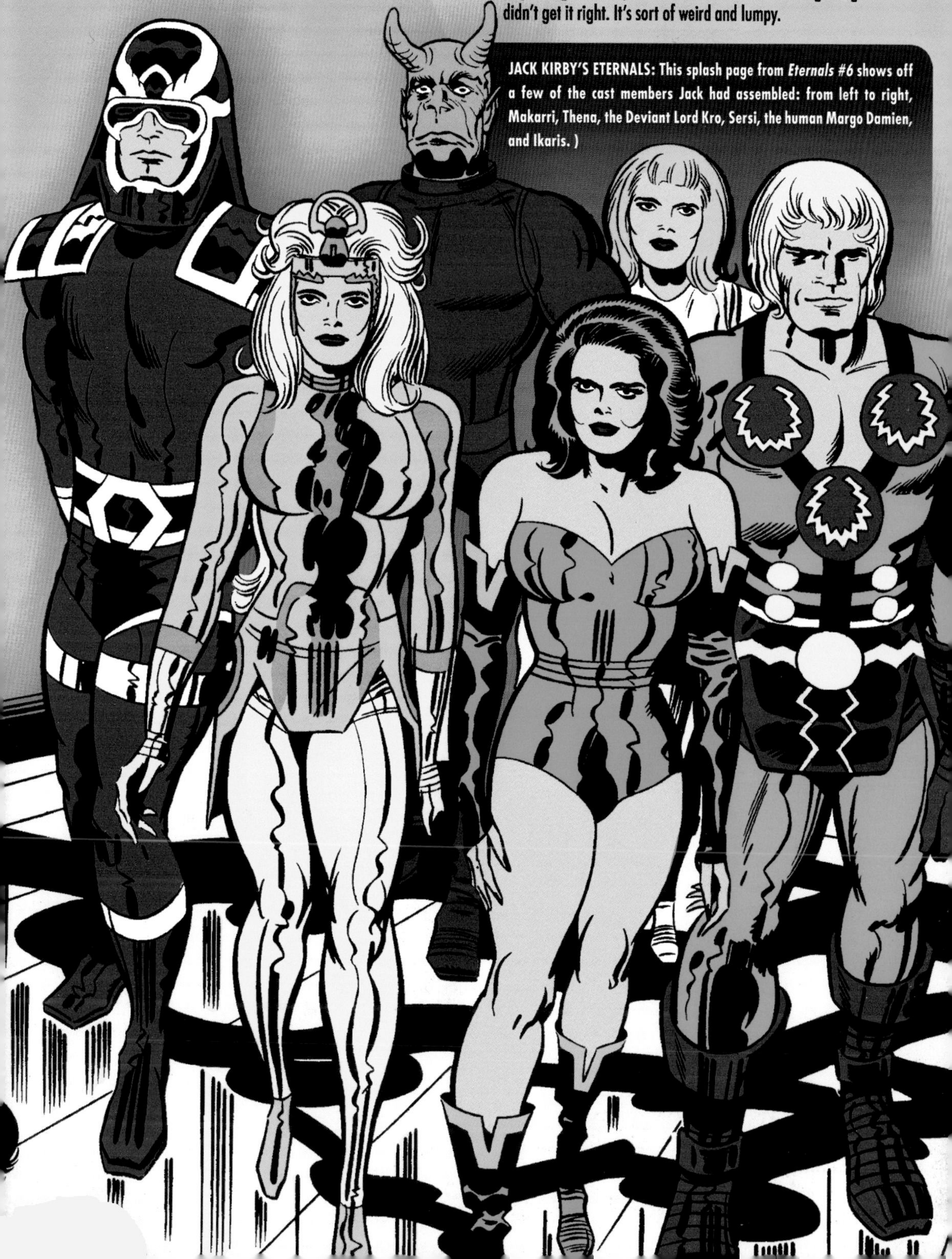

JACK KIRBY'S ETERNALS: This splash page from *Eternals #6* shows off a few of the cast members Jack had assembled: from left to right, Makarri, Thena, the Deviant Lord Kro, Sersi, the human Margo Damien, and Ikaris.)

ETERNALS

VARIANT COVERS BY
JOHN ROMITA JR, DANNY MIKI AND MATT HOLLINGSWORTH

ETERNALS #1

ETERNALS #2

ETERNALS #3

ETERNALS #4

ETERNALS #5

ETERNALS #6

ETERNALS #7